Lecture Notes in Computer Science 5944

Commenced Publication in 1973
Founding and Former Series Editors:
Gerhard Goos, Juris Hartmanis, and Jan van Leeuwen

Gilles Barthe Manuel Hermenegildo (Eds.)

Verification, Model Checking, and Abstract Interpretation

11th International Conference, VMCAI 2010
Madrid, Spain, January 17-19, 2010
Proceedings

Springer

Volume Editors

Gilles Barthe
IMDEA Software
Facultad de Informatica (UPM)
Campus Montegancedo, 28660 Boadilla del Monte, Madrid, Spain
E-mail: gilles.barthe@imdea.org

Manuel Hermenegildo
IMDEA Software and Technical University of Madrid
Facultad de Informatica (UPM)
Campus Montegancedo, 28660 Boadilla del Monte, Madrid, Spain
E-mail: manuel.hermenegildo@imdea.org

Library of Congress Control Number: 2009942234

CR Subject Classification (1998): D.2, D.3, F.3.1, F.3.2, D.2.4, D.2.5, D.3.4

LNCS Sublibrary: SL 1 – Theoretical Computer Science and General Issues

ISSN 0302-9743
ISBN-10 3-642-11318-4 Springer Berlin Heidelberg New York
ISBN-13 978-3-642-11318-5 Springer Berlin Heidelberg New York

springer.com

Printed in Germany

Typesetting: Camera-ready by author, data conversion by Scientific Publishing Services, Chennai, India
Printed on acid-free paper SPIN: 12829729 06/3180 5 4 3 2 1 0

Preface

This volume contains the proceedings of the 11th International Conference on Verification, Model Checking, and Abstract Interpretation (VMCAI 2010), held in Madrid, Spain, January 17–19, 2010.

VMCAI 2010 was the 11th in a series of meetings. Previous meetings were held in Port Jefferson (1997), Pisa (1998), Venice (2002), New York (2003), Venice (2004), Paris (2005), Charleston (2006), Nice (2007), San Francisco (2008), and Savannah (2009).

VMCAI centers on state-of-the-art research relevant to analysis of programs and systems and drawn from three research communities: verification, model checking, and abstract interpretation. A goal is to facilitate interaction, cross-fertilization, and the advance of hybrid methods that combine two or all three areas. Topics covered by VMCAI include program verification, program certification, model checking, debugging techniques, abstract interpretation, abstract domains, static analysis, type systems, deductive methods, and optimization.

The Program Committee selected 21 papers out of 57 submissions based on anonymous reviews and discussions in an electronic Program Committee meeting. The principal selection criteria were relevance and quality.

VMCAI has a tradition of inviting distinguished speakers to give talks and tutorials. This time the program included three invited talks by:

- Javier Esparza (Technical University of Munich)
- Rustan Leino (Microsoft Research)
- Reinhard Wilhelm (Saarland University)

There were also three invited tutorials by:

- Roberto Giacobazzi (University of Verona)
- Joost Pieter Katoen (Aachen University)
- Viktor Kuncak (EPFL Lausanne)

We would like to thank the members of the Program Committee and the subreviewers for their dedicated effort in the paper selection process. This was crucial for the quality of the conference. Our thanks also go to the Steering Committee members for helpful advice, in particular to Dave Schmidt and Lenore Zuck for their invaluable experience with VMCAI organization-related aspects. VMCAI 2010 was co-located with POPL 2010 (the ACM SIGACT/SIGPLAN Symposium on Principles of Programming Languages) and we thank Manuel Clavel for his non-ending support as local arrangements chair. Finally, we are also grateful to Andrei Voronkov for creating (and helping us with) the EasyChair system.

VMCAI 2010 was sponsored by EAPLS (European Association for Programming Languages and Systems), ACM (the Association for Computing Machinery), and IMDEA Software (the Madrid Institute for Advanced Studies in Software Development Technology).

January 2010

Gilles Barthe
Manuel Hermenegildo

Conference Organization

Program Chairs

Gilles Barthe	IMDEA Software, Spain
Manuel Hermenegildo	IMDEA Software and Technical University of Madrid, Spain

Program Committee

Christel Baier	Technische Universität Dresden, Germany
Patrick Cousot	École Normale Supérieure, France
Javier Esparza	Technische Universität München, Germany
Patrice Godefroid	Microsoft Research, USA
Orna Grumberg	Technion, Israel
Sumit Gulwani	Microsoft Research, USA
Joxan Jaffar	National University of Singapore
Rustan Leino	Microsoft Research, USA
Ken McMillan	Cadence, USA
Markus Müller-Olm	Universität Münster, Germany
Hanne Riis Nielson	Technical University of Denmark
Xavier Rival	École Normale Supérieure and INRIA, France
David Sands	Chalmers University of Technology, Sweden
David Schmidt	Kansas State University, USA
Hongseok Yang	Queen Mary University of London, UK
Kwangkeun Yi	Seoul National University, Korea
Greta Yorsh	IBM TJ Watson Research Center, NY, USA

Local Organization

Manuel Clavel	IMDEA and Complutense University of Madrid, Spain

Steering Committee

Agostino Cortesi	Universita' Ca' Foscari, Venice, Italy
Patrick Cousot	École Normale Supérieure, France
E. Allen Emerson	University of Texas at Austin, USA
Giorgio Levi	University of Pisa, Italy
Andreas Podelski	Universität Freiburg, Germany

Thomas W. Reps   University of Wisconsin at Madison, USA
David Schmidt   Kansas State University, USA
Lenore Zuck   University of Illinois at Chicago, USA

External Reviewers

Ahrendt, Wolfgang	Mauborgne, Laurent
Amtoft, Torben	Meller, Yael
Berdine, Josh	Meyer, Roland
Brazdil, Tomas	Miné, Antoine
Bubel, Richard	Molnar, David
Burckhardt, Sebastian	Monniaux, David
Chen, Liqian	Navas, Jorge
Dax, Christian	Nielson, Flemming
Doser, Jürgen	Oh, Hakjoo
Feret, Jérôme	Ostrovsky, Karol
Fisman, Dana	Peled, Doron
Ganty, Pierre	Pilegaard, Henrik
Gao, Han	Piterman, Nir
Gawlitza, Thomas	Platzer, Andre
Griggio, Alberto	Probst, Christian W.
Hedin, Daniel	Ranzato, Francesco
Hernandez, Alejandro	Santosa, Andrew
Hobor, Aquinas	Schwoon, Stefan
Jain, Himanshu	Simon, Axel
Jung, Yungbum	Skrypnyuk, Nataliya
Kinder, Johannes	Smith, Michael
Kong, Soonho	Strecker, Martin
Kreiker, Joerg	Stuckey, Peter
Kunz, César	Sun, Jun
Lahiri, Shuvendu	Suwimonteerabuth, Dejvuth
Lal, Akash	Urbain, Xavier
Laviron, Vincent	Voicu, Razvan
Lee, Oukseh	Wang, Bow-Yaw
Lev-Ami, Tal	Weber, Michael
Logozzo, Francesco	Yadgar, Avi
Lustig, Yoad	Yahav, Eran
Luttenberger, Michael	Yap, Roland
Magill, Stephen	Yuksel, Ender
Martel, Matthieu	Zuleger, Florian
Massé, Damien	Smith, Michael

Table of Contents

Invited Talks

Invited Tutorials

Regular Papers

Analysis of Systems with Stochastic Process Creation

Javier Esparza

Institut für Informatik, Technische Universität München
Boltzmannstr. 3, 85748 Garching, Germany

In many computer science systems entities can "reproduce", "replicate", or "create new instances". Paramount examples are threads in multithreaded programs, processes in operating systems, and computer viruses, but many others exist: procedure calls create new incarnations of the callees, web crawlers discover new pages to be explored (and so "create" new tasks), divide-and-conquer procedures split a problem into subproblems, and leaves of tree-based data structures become internal nodes with children. I use the generic term *systems with process creation* to refer to all these entities.

In the last year, Tomáš Brázdil, Stefan Kiefer, Michael Luttenberger and myself have started to investigate the behaviour of systems with *stochastic* process creation [2,3]. We assume that the probabilities with which entities create new ones is known or has been estimated. We study random variables modelling the computational resources needed to completely execute the system, i.e., to execute the initial process and all of its descendants.

Stochastic process creation has been studied by mathematicians for decades under the name *branching (stochastic) processes* [4,1]. However, this work has been motivated by applications to biology (study of animal populations), physics (study of particle cascades) or chemistry (study of chemical reactions). From a computer scientist's point of view, in these scenarios no process ever waits to be executed, because there is no separation between processes (software) and processor (hardware); for instance, in biology scenarios each individual animal is both a process and the processor executing it. So, in computer science terms, probability theorists have studied systems with an *unbounded* number of processors. The model in which one single or a fixed number of processors execute a possibly much larger number of processes, seems to have received little attention.

In my talk I interpret some results of the theory of branching processes for a computer science audience, and present the results of [2,3] on the single processor case.

References

1. Athreya, K.B., Ney, P.E.: Branching Processes. Springer, Heidelberg (1972)
2. Brázdil, T., Esparza, J., Kiefer, S.: On the memory consumption of probabilistic pushdown automata. In: Proceedings of FSTTCS 2009 (2009)
3. Brázdil, T., Esparza, J., Kiefer, S., Luttenberger, M.: Space-efficient scheduling of stochastically generated tasks. Technical report, TU München (2009)
4. Harris, T.E.: The Theory of Branching Processes. Springer, Heidelberg (1963)

G. Barthe and M. Hermenegildo (Eds.): VMCAI 2010, LNCS 5944, p. 1, 2010.

Verifying Concurrent Programs with Chalice

K. Rustan M. Leino

Microsoft Research, Redmond, WA, USA
leino@microsoft.com

Abstract. One of the problems in verifying concurrent programs is keeping track of which threads have access to which data at which times. The experimental language Chalice makes this explicit by requiring every data access to be justified with a sufficient set of permissions. Permissions can be transferred between threads and can be stored in the heap. The programming language includes specification constructs for describing data invariants and permission transfers. Chalice supports synchronization via shared memory and locks as well as via channels. The Chalice program verifier checks the correctness of programs with respect to their specifications and the rules for data access. Programs that have been proved correct compile to executable code for the .NET platform.

In this talk, I will give an overview and demo of the Chalice language and its permission model. I will describe the semantic model used to reason about programs and how this model is encoded in the Boogie intermediate verification language, from which first-order verification conditions are generated and fed to an SMT solver. I will also outline some remaining challenges in making the language and its specifications easy to use, in making the encoding efficient for SMT solvers, and in presenting verification errors to the user.

Joint work with Peter Müller and Jan Smans.

References

1. Chalice web site, `http://research.microsoft.com/chalice`
2. Leino, K.R.M., Müller, P.: A basis for verifying multi-threaded programs. In: Castagna, G. (ed.) ESOP 2009. LNCS, vol. 5502, pp. 378–393. Springer, Heidelberg (2009)
3. Leino, K.R.M., Müller, P., Smans, J.: Verification of concurrent programs with Chalice. In: FOSAD 2009. LNCS, vol. 5705, pp. 195–222. Springer, Heidelberg (2009)

G. Barthe and M. Hermenegildo (Eds.): VMCAI 2010, LNCS 5944, p. 2, 2010.

Static Timing Analysis for Hard Real-Time Systems*

Reinhard Wilhelm, Sebastian Altmeyer, Claire Burguière, Daniel Grund, Jörg Herter, Jan Reineke, Björn Wachter, and Stephan Wilhelm

Saarland University, Saarbrücken, Germany

Abstract. Hard real-time systems have to satisfy strict timing constraints. To prove that these constraints are met, timing analyses aim to derive safe upper bounds on tasks' execution times. Processor components such as caches, out-of-order pipelines, and speculation cause a large variation of the execution time of instructions, which may induce a large variability of a task's execution time. The architectural platform also determines the precision and the complexity of timing analysis.

This paper provides an overview of our timing-analysis technique and in particular the methodological aspects of interest to the verification community.

1 Introduction

Hard real-time systems have to satisfy strict timing constraints. Traditionally, measurement has been used to show their satisfaction. However, the use of modern high-performance processors has created a severe problem. Processor components such as caches, out-of-order pipelines, and all kinds of speculation cause a large variability of the execution times of instructions, which induces a potentially high variability of whole programs' execution times. For individual instructions, the execution time may vary by a factor of 100 and more. The actual execution time depends on the architectural state in which the instruction is executed, i.e. the contents of the caches, the occupancy of the pipeline units, contention on the busses etc.

Different kinds of timing analyses are being used today [1]; measurement-based/hybrid [2,3,4] and static analysis [5] being the most prominent. Both methods compute estimates of the worst-case execution times for program fragments like basic blocks. If these estimates are correct, i.e. they are upper bounds on the worst-case execution time of the program fragment, they can be combined to obtain an upper bound on the worst-case execution time of the task.

* The research leading to these results has received funding from the following projects (in alphabetical order): the Deutsche Forschungsgemeinschaft in SFB/TR 14 *AVACS*, the German-Israeli Foundation (GIF) in the *Encasa* project, and the European Community's Seventh Framework Programme FP7/2007-2013 under grant agreement number 216008 (*Predator*).

G. Barthe and M. Hermenegildo (Eds.): VMCAI 2010, LNCS 5944, pp. 3–22, 2010.

While using similar methods in the combination of execution times of program fragments, the two methods take fundamentally different approaches to compute these estimates:

- Static analyses based on abstract models of the underlying hardware compute invariants about the set of all execution states at each program point under *all* possible initial states and inputs and derive upper bounds on the execution time of program fragments based on these invariants.
- Measurement executes each program fragment with a subset of the possible initial states and inputs. The maximum of the measured execution times is in general an underestimation of the worst-case execution time.

If the abstract hardware models are correct, static analysis computes safe upper bounds on the WCETs of program fragments and thus also of tasks. However, creating abstract hardware models is an error-prone and laborious process, especially if no precise specification of the hardware is available.

The advantage of measurement over static analysis is that it is more easily portable to new architectures, as it does not rely on such abstract models of the architecture. On the other hand, soundness of measurement-based approaches is hard to guarantee. Measurement would trivially be sound if all initial states and inputs would be covered. Due to their huge number this is usually not feasible. Instead, only a subset of the initial states and inputs can be considered in the measurements.

This paper provides an overview of our state-of-the-art timing-analysis approach. In Section 2, we describe the architecture and the component functionalities of our framework for static timing analysis.

Section 3 is devoted to several aspects of the memory hierarchy, in particular caches. Memory-system performance often dominates overall system performance. This makes cache analysis so important for timing analysis. The most relevant property is *predictability* [6,7]. This notion—a hot topic of current research—is fully clarified for caches [8,9]. A second notion, exemplified for caches, is the *relative competitiveness* of different cache architectures. They allow one to use the cache-analysis results of one cache architecture to predict cache performance for another one. A third property of cache architectures is their *sensitivity to the initial state*. Results show that some frequently used cache replacement-strategies are highly sensitive. This has severe consequences for measurement-based approaches to timing analysis. Missing one initial cache state in a non-exhaustive set of measurements may lead to dramatically wrong results.

Data-cache analysis would fail for programs allocating data in the heap since the addresses and therefore the mapping to cache sets would be statically unknown. We approach this problem in two different ways, firstly, by converting dynamic to static allocation and using a parametric timing analysis, and secondly, by allocating in a cache-aware way.

Pipelines are much more complex than caches and therefore more difficult to model. The analysis of their behavior needs much more effort than cache analysis since a huge search space has to be explored and no abstract domain with a compact representation of sets of pipeline states has been found so far. Symbolic data structures as used in model checking offer some potential to increase the efficiency. A novel symbolic approach to timing analysis has shown promising results [10]. We give a short overview in Section 4.

This article centers around static timing analysis. An extended description of our approach can be found in [11]. A comprehensive survey of timing-analysis approaches is given in [1].

1.1 The Architectural Challenge—and How to Cope with It

Hard real-time systems need guarantees expressed in terms of worst-case performance. However, the architectures on which the real-time programs are executed are optimized for average-case performance. Caches, pipelines, and all kinds of speculation are key features for improving average-case performance. Caches are used to bridge the gap between processor speed and the access time of main memory. Pipelines enable acceleration by overlapping the executions of different instructions. The consequence is that the execution time of individual instructions, and thus the contribution to the program's execution time can vary widely. The interval of execution times for one instruction is bounded by the execution times of the following two cases:

- The instruction goes "smoothly" through the pipeline; all loads hit the cache, no pipeline hazard happens, i.e. all operands are ready, no resource conflicts with other currently executing instructions exist.
- "Everything goes wrong", i.e. instruction and/or operand fetches miss the cache, resources needed by the instruction are occupied, etc.

We will call any increase in execution time during an instruction's execution a *timing accident* and the number of cycles by which it increases the *timing penalty* of this accident. Timing penalties for an instruction can add up to several hundred processor cycles. Whether the execution of an instruction encounters

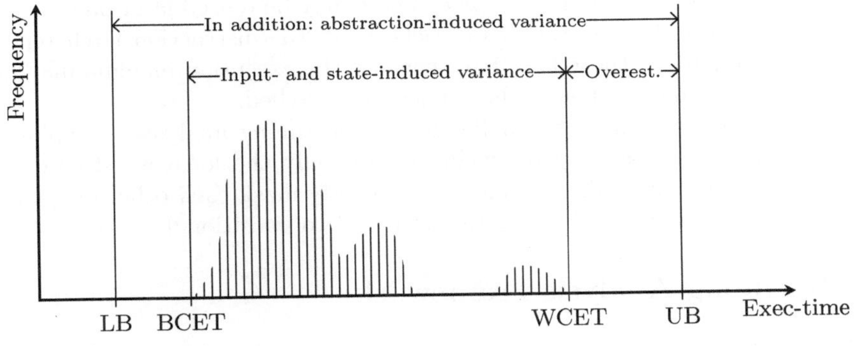

Fig. 1. Notions in Timing Analysis. Best-cast and worst-case execution time (BCET and WCET), and computed lower and upper bounds.

a timing accident depends on the architectural state, e.g. the contents of the cache(s), the occupancy of other resources, and thus on the execution history. It is therefore obvious that the attempt to predict or exclude timing accidents needs information about the execution history.

We use static analysis to compute invariants about the set of all possible architectural states at all program points. Indeed, due to abstraction, over-approximations of these sets are computed. They are used to derive safety properties of the kind: "A certain timing accident will not happen at this program point.". Such a safety property allows the timing-analysis tool to prove a tighter worst-case bound.

Some abstraction of the execution platform is necessary to make a timing analysis of the system feasible. These abstractions lose information, and thus are in part responsible for the gap between WCETs and upper bounds and between BCETs and lower bounds. How much is lost depends both on the methods used for timing analysis and on system properties, such as the hardware architecture and the analyzability of the software.

1.2 Timing Anomalies

Most powerful microprocessors have so-called *timing anomalies* [12]. Timing anomalies are contra-intuitive influences of the (local) execution time of one instruction on the (global) execution time of the whole program. Several processor features can interact in such a way that a locally faster execution of an instruction can lead to a globally longer execution time of the whole program. Hence, resolving uncertainty in the analysis by only assuming local worst-cases might be unsound.

One would assume that a cache miss is always the worst-case possibility for a memory access. However, the cache miss may prevent an expensive branch misprediction and, thus, globally be the better case. This was observed for the MCF 5307 [13,5]. Since the MCF 5307 has a unified cache and the fetch and execute pipelines are independent, the following can happen: A data access hitting in the cache is served directly from the cache. At the same time, the pipeline fetches another instruction block from main memory, performing branch prediction and replacing two lines of *data* in the cache. These may be reused later on and cause two misses. If the data access was a cache miss, the instruction fetch pipeline may not have fetched those two lines, because the execution pipeline may have resolved a misprediction before those lines were fetched.

The existence of timing anomalies forces the timing analysis to explore *all* successor states that cannot be excluded, not only the local worst-case ones. Besides the fact that timing penalties may partly mask each other out, timing anomalies are another reason why timing is *not* compositional.

2 A Timing Analysis Framework

Over roughly the last decade, a more or less standard architecture for timing-analysis tools has emerged. Figure 2 gives a general view of this architecture. First, one can distinguish four major building blocks:

– control-flow reconstruction
– static analyses for control and data flow
– micro-architectural analysis computing upper and lower bounds on the execution times of basic blocks
– global bounds analysis computing upper and lower bounds for the whole program

The following list presents the individual phases and describes their objectives and main challenges.

1. *Control-flow reconstruction* [14] takes a binary executable to be analyzed, reconstructs the program's control flow and transforms the program into a suitable intermediate representation. Problems encountered are dynamically computed control-flow successors, e.g. those stemming from switch statements, function pointers, etc.
2. *Value analysis* [15] computes an over-approximation of the set of possible values in registers and memory locations by an interval analysis and/or congruence analysis. The computed information is used for a precise data-cache analysis and in the subsequent control-flow analysis. Value analysis is the only one to use an abstraction of the processor's arithmetic. A subsequent pipeline analysis can therefore work with a simplified pipeline where the arithmetic units are removed. One is not interested in what is computed, but only in how long it will take.

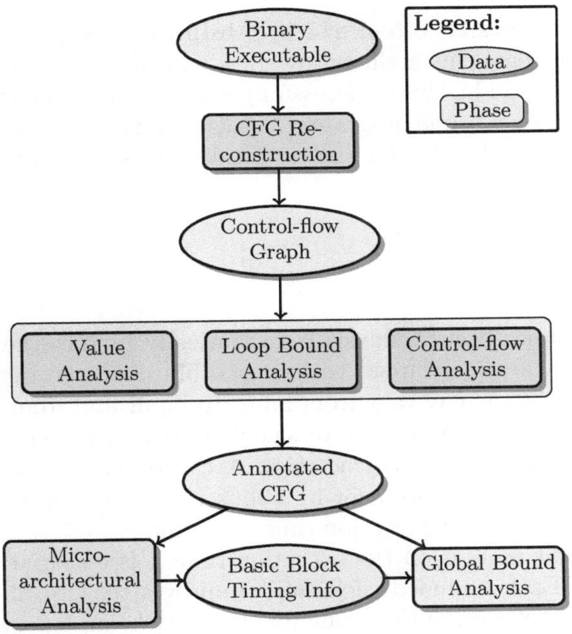

Fig. 2. Main components of a timing-analysis framework and their interaction

3. *Loop bound analysis* [16,17] identifies loops in the program and tries to determine bounds on the number of loop iterations; information indispensable to bound the execution time. Problems are the analysis of arithmetic on loop counters and loop exit conditions, as well as dependencies in nested loops.
4. *Control-flow analysis* [16,18] narrows down the set of possible paths through the program by eliminating infeasible paths or by determining correlations between the number of executions of different blocks using the results of value analysis. These constraints will tighten the obtained timing bounds.
5. *Micro-architectural analysis* [19,20,21] determines bounds on the execution time of basic blocks by performing an abstract interpretation of the program, combining analyses of the processor's pipeline, caches, and speculation. Static cache analyses determine safe approximations to the contents of caches at each program point. Pipeline analysis analyzes how instructions pass through the pipeline accounting for occupancy of shared resources like queues, functional units, etc.
6. *Global bounds analysis* [22,23] finally determines bounds on the execution times for the whole program by implicit path enumeration using an integer linear program (ILP). Bounds of the execution times of basic blocks are combined to compute longest paths through the program. The control flow is modeled by Kirchhoff's law. Loop bounds and infeasible paths are modeled by additional constraints. The target function weights each basic block with its time bound. A solution of the ILP maximizes the sum of those weights and corresponds to an upper bound on the execution times.

The commercially available tool `aiT` by AbsInt, cf. `http://www.absint.de/wcet.htm` implements this architecture. It is used in the aeronautics and automotive industries and has been successfully used to determine precise bounds on execution times of real-time programs [21,5,24,13]. The European Airworthiness Authorities have validated it for the certification of several avionics subsystems of the Airbus A380.

3 Cache Analysis

The goal of a static cache analysis is to statically predict the cache behavior of a program on a set of inputs with a possibly unknown initial cache state. As the cache behavior may vary from input to input and from one initial state to another, it may not be possible to safely classify each memory access in the program as a cache hit or a cache miss. A cache analysis is therefore forced to approximate the cache behavior in a conservative way if it shall be used to provide guarantees on the execution time of a task.

To obtain tight bounds on the execution time it is essential to use a precise cache analysis. Each excluded cache miss improves the provable upper bound on the worst-case execution time roughly by the cache miss penalty. Conversely, each guaranteed cache miss improves the provable lower bound on the best-case execution time.

WCET and BCET analyses need a classification of individual memory accesses in the program as cache hits or misses. For most architectures, it is not sufficient to determine upper and lower bounds on the number of misses for the execution of the entire program because caches interact with other architectural components such as pipelines. For instance, a cache reload may overlap with a pipeline stall. To precisely take such effects into account, a timing analysis needs to know where and when the cache misses happen.

One may compute *may* and *must* cache information in static cache analysis: *may* and *must* caches at a program point are upper and lower approximations, respectively, to the contents of all concrete caches that will occur whenever program execution reaches this program point. The *must* cache at a program point is a set of memory blocks that are definitely in each concrete cache at that point. The *may* cache is a set of memory blocks that may be in a concrete cache whenever program execution reaches that program point. We call the two analyses *may* and *must* cache analyses.

Must cache information is used to derive safe information about cache hits; in other words it is used to exclude the timing accident "cache miss". The complement of the *may* cache information is used to safely predict cache misses.

3.1 Influence of the Cache Replacement Policy

Caches have a particularly strong influence on both the variation of execution times due to the initial hardware state and on the precision of static WCET analyses. A cache's behavior is controlled by its replacement policy. In [9], we investigate the influence of the cache replacement policy on

- the amount of *inherent uncertainty in static cache analysis*, i.e. cache misses that cannot be excluded statically but never happen during execution
- the *maximal variation in cache performance* due to the initial cache state
- the *construction of static cache analyses*, analyses that statically classify memory references as cache hits or misses

The following subsections explain the three problems in more detail and sketch our approaches and contributions.

Predictability Metrics—Limits on the Precision of Cache Analyses. Usually there is some uncertainty about the cache contents, i.e. the *may* and *must* caches do not coincide; there are memory blocks which can neither be guaranteed to be in the cache nor not to be in it. The greater the uncertainty in the *must* cache, the worse the upper bound on the WCET. Similarly, greater uncertainty in the *may* cache entails a less precise lower bound on the BCET.

There are several reasons for uncertainty about cache contents:

- Static cache analyses usually cannot make any assumptions about the initial cache contents. Cache contents on entry depend on previously executed tasks. Even assuming an empty cache may not be conservative [25].

- At control-flow joins, analysis information about different paths needs to be safely combined. Intuitively, one must take the intersection of the incoming *must* information and the union of the incoming *may* information. A memory block can only be in the *must* cache if it is in the *must* caches of all predecessor control-flow nodes, correspondingly for *may* caches.
- In data-cache analysis, the *value analysis* may not be able to exactly determine the address of a memory reference. Then the *cache analysis* must conservatively account for all possible addresses.
- Preempting tasks may change the cache state in an unpredictable way at preemption points [26].

Since information about the cache state may thus be unknown or lost, it is important to recover information quickly to be able to classify memory references safely as cache hits or misses. This is possible for most caches. However, the *speed* of this recovery greatly depends on the cache replacement policy. It influences how much uncertainty about cache hits and misses remains. Thus, the *speed of recovery* is an indicator of timing predictability.

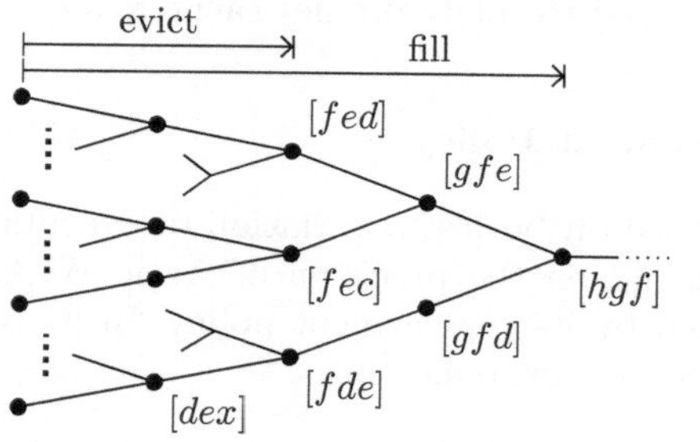

Fig. 3. Initially different cache sets converge when accessing a sequence $\langle a, b, c, d, e, f, g, h, \ldots \rangle$ of pairwise different memory blocks

The two metrics, *evict* and $fill$, indicate how quickly knowledge about cache hits and misses can be (re-)obtained under a particular replacement policy [8]. They mark a limit on the precision that *any* cache analysis can achieve, be it by abstract interpretation or any other sound method. Figure 3 illustrates the two metrics. *evict* tells us at which point we can safely predict that some memory blocks are no more in the cache, i.e. they are in the complement of may information. Any memory block not contained in the last *evict* accesses cannot be in the cache set. The greater *evict*, the longer it takes to gain may information. $fill$ accesses are required to converge to one completely determined cache set. At this point, complete may and must information is obtained, which allows to precisely classify each memory access as a hit or a miss. The two metrics mark a limit on *any* cache analysis: no analysis can infer any may information (complete must information) given an unknown cache-set state and less than *evict* ($fill$) memory accesses.

Under the two metrics, LRU is optimal, i.e. *may*- and *must*-information can be obtained in the least possible number of memory accesses. PLRU, MRU, and FIFO, perform considerably worse. Compared to an 8-way LRU, it takes more than twice as many accesses to regain complete *must*-information for equally-sized PLRU, MRU, and FIFO caches. As a consequence, it is *impossible* to construct cache analyses for PLRU, MRU, and FIFO that are as precise as known LRU analyses.

Relative Competitiveness of Replacement Policies. Developing cache analyses—analyses that statically determine whether a memory access associated with an instruction will always be a hit or a miss—is a difficult problem. Precise and efficient analyses have been developed for set-associative caches that employ the least-recently-used (LRU) replacement policy [21,27,28,29]. Other commonly used policies, like first-in-first-out (FIFO) or Pseudo-LRU(PLRU) are more difficult to analyze [8].

Relative competitive analyses yield upper (lower) bounds on the number of misses (hits) of a policy P relative to the number of misses (hits) of another policy Q. For example, a competitive analysis may find out that policy P will incur at most 30% more misses than policy Q and at most 20% less hits in the execution of any task.

The following approach determines safe bounds on the number of cache hits and misses by a task T under FIFO(k), PLRU(l)[1], or any another replacement policy [9]:

1. Determine competitiveness of the desired policy P relative to a policy Q for which a cache analysis exists, like LRU.
2. Perform cache analysis of task T for policy Q to obtain a cache-performance prediction, i.e. upper (lower) bounds on the number of misses (hits) by Q.
3. Calculate upper (lower) bounds on the number of misses (hits) for P using the cache analysis results for Q and the competitiveness results of P relative to Q.

Step 1 has to be performed only once for each pair of replacement policies.

A limitation of this approach is that it only produces upper (lower) bounds on the number of misses (hits) for the whole program execution. It does not reveal at which program points the misses (hits) will happen, something many timing analyses need. Relative competitiveness results can also be used to obtain sound *may* and *must* cache analyses, i.e. analyses that can classify individual accesses as hits or misses. Relative competitive ratios can be computed automatically for a pair of policies [30][2].

One of our results is that for any associativity k and any workload, FIFO(k) generates at least half the number of hits that LRU(k) generates. Another result is that *may* cache analyses for LRU can be safely used as *may* cache analyses for MRU and FIFO of other associativities.

Sensitivity of Replacement Policies. The sensitivity of a cache replacement policy expresses to what extent the initial state of the cache may influence the number of cache hits and misses during program execution [9]. Analysis results demonstrate that the initial state of the cache can have a strong impact on the number of cache hits and misses during program execution if FIFO, MRU, or PLRU replacement is used. A simple model of execution time demonstrates the impact of cache sensitivity on measured execution times. It shows that underestimating the number of misses as strongly as possible for FIFO, MRU,

[1] k and l denote the respective associativities of FIFO(k) and PLRU(l).

[2] See `http://rw4.cs.uni-sb.de/~reineke/relacs` for a corresponding applet.

$$q_1 = [\bot,\bot,\bot,\bot] \xrightarrow[\text{M}]{a} [a,\bot,\bot,\bot] \xrightarrow[\text{H}]{a} [a,\bot,\bot,\bot] \xrightarrow[\text{M}]{b} [b,a,\bot,\bot] \xrightarrow[\text{M}]{c} [c,b,a,\bot] = q_1'$$
$$q_2 = [a,x,b,c] \xrightarrow[\text{H}]{a} [a,x,b,c] \xrightarrow[\text{H}]{a} [a,x,b,c] \xrightarrow[\text{H}]{b} [a,x,b,c] \xrightarrow[\text{H}]{c} [a,x,b,c] = q_2'$$
$$q_3 = [x,y,z,a] \xrightarrow[\text{H}]{a} [x,y,z,a] \xrightarrow[\text{H}]{a} [x,y,z,a] \xrightarrow[\text{M}]{b} [b,x,y,z] \xrightarrow[\text{M}]{c} [c,b,x,y] = q_3'$$
$$q_4 = [x,y,b,z] \xrightarrow[\text{M}]{a} [a,x,y,b] \xrightarrow[\text{H}]{a} [a,x,y,b] \xrightarrow[\text{H}]{b} [a,x,y,b] \xrightarrow[\text{M}]{c} [c,a,x,y] = q_4'$$

Fig. 4. Dependency of FIFO cache set contents on the initial state

and PLRU may yield worst-case-execution-time estimates that are dramatically wrong. Further analysis revealed that the "empty cache is worst-case initial state" assumption [2] is wrong for FIFO, MRU, and PLRU.

3.2 FIFO Cache Analysis

Precise and efficient analyses have been developed for the least-recently-used (LRU) replacement policy [21,27,28,29]. Generally, research in the field of embedded real-time systems assumes LRU replacement. In practice however, other policies like first-in first-out (FIFO) or pseudo-LRU (PLRU) are also commonly used. In [31], we discuss challenges in FIFO cache analysis. We identify a generic policy-independent framework for cache analysis that couples may- and must-analyses by means of domain cooperation. The main contribution is a more precise may-analysis for FIFO. It not only increases the number of predicted misses, but also—due to the domain cooperation—the number of predicted hits. We instantiate the framework with a canonical must-analysis and three different may-analyses, including the new one, and compare the resulting three analyses to the collecting semantics.

To see the difficulty inherent in FIFO, consider the examples in Figure 4. The access sequence $s = \langle a, a, b, c\rangle$ is carried out on different cache sets q_i of associativity 4. Although only 3 different memory blocks $\{a, b, c\}$ are accessed, some of the resulting cache sets q_i' do not contain all of the accessed blocks. In contrast, a k-way cache set with LRU replacement always consists of the k most-recently-used memory blocks, e.g. $\{a, b, c\}$ would be cached after carrying out s, independently of the initial state. This makes analysis of FIFO considerably more difficult than analysis of LRU.

To generalize, consider a FIFO cache set with unknown contents. After observing a memory access to a block a, trivial must-information is available: One knows that a must be cached, but the position of a within the cache set is unknown. For example the access to a could be a hit to the second position:

$$[?,?,?,?] \xrightarrow[hit]{a} [?,a,?,?] \xrightarrow[hit]{b} [?,a,?,b]$$
$$[?,?,?,?] \xrightarrow[hit]{a} [?,?,?,a] \xrightarrow[miss]{b} [b,?,?,?]$$

However, as in the second case, the access to a could also be a hit on the first-in (i.e., rightmost) position. Hence, a second access to a different block b may already evict the first accessed block a. Thus, without additional information about the accesses it is not possible to infer that two or more blocks are cached, i.e. one can only derive must information of poor quality.

However, there are means to gain more precise information: If one can classify the access to a as a miss for example, then the second access to a different block b cannot evict a because one knows that a was inserted at the last-in position.

$$[?,?,?,?] \xrightarrow[miss]{a} [a,?,?,?] \xrightarrow[miss]{b} [b,a,?,?]$$

On a more abstract level, what this actually means is that may-information can be used to obtain precise must-information. To do so however, one needs to realize information flow between may- and must-analyses. This gives rise to the policy-independent cache-analysis framework explained below that can couple different analyses to improve analysis precision.

Must- and May-analyses for FIFO. Here, we only describe the ideas behind the abstract domains and kindly refer the interested reader to [31] for details. The must-analysis borrows basic ideas from LRU-analysis [21]. For each memory block b, it infers an upper bound on the number of cache misses since the last insertion of b into the cache set. If the bound for b is smaller than the associativity, cache hits can be soundly predicted for b. Analogously, to predict cache misses, the may-analysis infers lower bounds on the number of cache misses to prove eviction. By distinguishing between hits and misses and taking into account the order in which they happen, we improve the may-analysis, thereby increasing the number of predicted cache misses. Through the cooperation of the two analyses in the generic framework, this also improves the precision of the must-analysis.

Cache Analysis Framework. As motivated above, for FIFO there needs to be some information flow between may- and must-analyses to obtain precise information. Indeed, this is not restricted to FIFO and can be generalized: This section presents a *policy-independent* cache analysis framework, in which any number of *independent* cache analyses can *cooperate*. The goal is to obtain information that is more precise than the best information obtained by any of the individual analyses. The only prerequisite is that the individual analyses implement a very small interface. Given correct analyses, the framework realizes the cooperation between these and guarantees correctness of the resulting analysis.

The framework constructs a cache analysis (A, C_A, U_A, J_A), with abstract domain A, classification function C_A, abstract transformer U_A, and join function J_A, given any number of cache analyses $(A_i, C_{A_i}, U_{A_i}, J_{A_i})$ for the same concrete cache set type $\mathcal{Q}_{P_k}$. The domain of the constructed analysis is the cartesian product

$$A := A_1 \times \ldots \times A_n$$

To classify a cache access to some memory block $b \in \mathcal{B}$, the classification function, $C_A : A \times \mathcal{B} \rightarrow \{\text{hit}, \text{miss}\}^\top$, combines the classifications of all individual analyses:

$$C_A((a_1, \ldots, a_n), b) := \bigsqcap_i C_{A_i}(a_i, b) \quad (1)$$

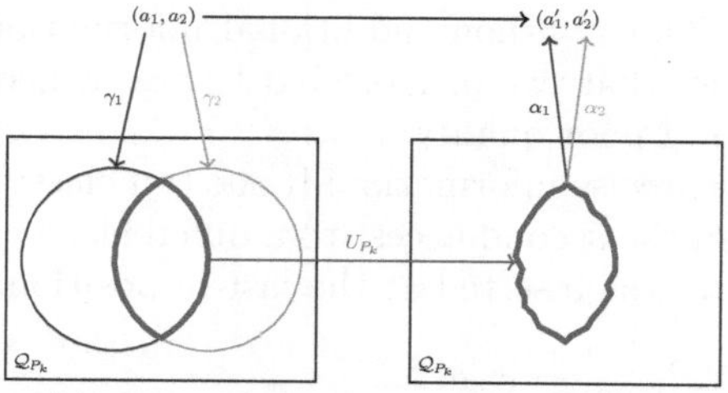

(a) Best abstract transformer would correspond to $\alpha_j(U_{P_k}(\bigcap_i \gamma_i(a_i), b))$ for all j.

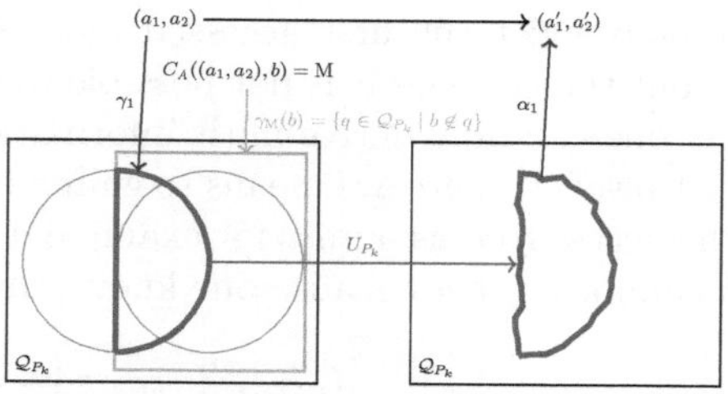

(b) Abstract transformer using reduction by classification corresponds to $\alpha_i(U_{P_k}(\gamma_i(a_i) \cap \gamma_{C_A(a,b)}(b), b))$ for all i.

Fig. 5. Information flow between analyses by update reduction

Since each individual analysis is sound, these classifications cannot contradict each other, i.e. their meet ($\sqcap$) is always defined.

In abstract interpretation, the term *reduction* refers to the process of refining information encoded in a domain by other, external, information. For an example, consider value analysis using the *Interval*- and *Parity*-domain: Assume the interval domain infers $n \in [2, 4]$ and the parity domain provides isOdd(n). Then, using the latter, one can *reduce* the interval to $n \in [3, 3]$.

However, in abstract domains for cache analysis, information expressible in one domain is not necessarily expressible in another one: The syntactical structure of constraints in domain A_1 does not allow to encode information provided by constraints of domain A_2. For example, a must-analysis maintains *upper* bounds on the number of cache misses while a may-analysis maintains *lower* bounds on that number. In such a case, a reduction on the abstract states would be ineffective.

Nonetheless, it is possible to use the information provided by other abstract domains to reduce the abstract transformers. First, consider the two extremes: On the one hand, the *independent* update of all A_i, and on the other hand a *best* abstract transformer. In an independent update of an A_i *no* information of the other domains is used. In a best abstract transformer, which is depicted in Figure 5(a), *all* information of the other domains is used: It would correspond to taking the intersection of all concretizations (sets of cache sets), updating them in the concrete, and then abstracting to the domains again. However, best abstract transformers counteract the wish to implement and prove correct individual domains *independently* and mostly are computationally expensive, anyway.

The update reduction of our framework lies in between these two extremes: The reduced abstract transformers are more precise than independent updates. And the information exchange is abstract enough such that it can be realized without knowledge about the participating domains, i.e. domains can be plugged in without changing the update functions of other domains. The update reduction of the framework uses the classification of the current access. Figure 5 shows this at hand of the domain A_1. Assume that some domain A_i can classify the access to block b as a miss, e.g. $C_{A_2}(a_2, b) = \mathrm{M}$. Then the overall classification, which depends on all individual classifications, will be $C_A((a_1, a_2), b) = \mathrm{M}$, too. With this information, one can further restrict the concretization $\gamma_{A_1}(a_1)$ to cache sets that additionally do not contain the accessed block $\{q \in \mathcal{Q}_{P_k} \mid b \notin q\}$. Using this additional information, one can define abstract transformers that are more precise than independent ones.

In an implementation, the update reduction amounts to refine the update functions of each domain by an additional parameter to pass the classification of the current access. Hence, the update function $U_A : A \times \mathcal{B} \rightarrow A$ is defined as:

$$U_A((a_1, \ldots, a_n), b) := \left(U_{A_1}(a_1, b, cl), \ldots, U_{A_n}(a_n, b, cl)\right), \tag{2}$$

where $cl := C_A((a_1, \ldots, a_n), b)$.

Finally, the join function J_A is simply defined component-wise.

3.3 Context Switch Costs

Previous timing analyses assume tasks running to completion, i.e. assuming non-preemptive execution. Some task sets, however, are only schedulable preemptively. For such systems, we also need to bound the context-switch costs in addition to the WCET. In case of preemption, cache memories may suffer interferences between memory accesses of the preempted and of the preempting task. These interferences lead to some additional reloads, which are referred to as cache-related preemption delay (CRPD). This CRPD constitutes the major part of the context switch costs.

Upper bounds on the CRPD are usually computed using the concept of useful cache blocks (UCB). Memory blocks are considered useful at a program point if they may be in cache before the program point and may be reused after it. When a preemption occurs at that point the number of additional cache-misses is bounded by the number of useful cache blocks. However, some cache accesses are taken into account as misses as part of the WCET bound anyway. These accesses do not have to be accounted for a second time as part of the CRPD bound [26].

A memory block m is called a definitely-cached UCB (DC-UCB) at program point P if (a) m must be cached before the preemption point and (b) m may be reused at program point Q, which may be reached from P, and must be cached along the path to its reuse. Using the notion of definitely-cached UCB, one computes the number of additional cache misses due to preemption that are not already taken into account as a miss by the timing analysis. This number does not bound the CRPD, but the part of the CRPD that is not already included in the WCET bound. Hence, the global bound on WCET+CRPD can be significantly improved.

The DC-UCB analysis uses information computed by a preceding cache analysis. In the following, we denote instruction j of basic block i as B_i^j and use $Access(B_i^j)$ to denote the memory block accessed by instruction B_i^j.

To determine the set of definitely-cached UCBs, we use a backward program analysis over the control flow graph. A memory block m is added to the set of

DC-UCBs of instruction B_i^j, if m is element of the must cache at B_i^j (computed by a preceding cache analysis) and if instruction B_i^j accesses m. The domain of our analysis is the powerset domain of the set of memory blocks M: $\mathbb{D} = 2^M$ The following two equations determine the data-flow value before (DC-UCB$_{in}$) and after (DC-UCB$_{out}$) instruction B_i^j:

$$\text{DC-UCB}_{in}(B_i^j) = gen(B_i^j) \cup (\text{DC-UCB}_{out}(B_i^j) \setminus kill(B_i^j)) \tag{3}$$

$$\text{DC-UCB}_{out}(B_i^j) = \bigcup_{successor B_k^l} \text{DC-UCB}_{in}(B_k^l) \tag{4}$$

where the gen/kill sets are defined as follows:

$$gen(B_i^j) = \begin{cases} \{Access(B_i^j)\} & \text{if } Access(B_i^j) \in Must\_Cache(B_i^j) \\ \emptyset & \text{otherwise} \end{cases} \tag{5}$$

$$kill(B_i^j) = M \setminus Must\_Cache(B_i^j) \tag{6}$$

Equation (4) combines the flow information of all successors of instruction B_i^j. Equation (3) represents the update of the flow information due to the execution of the instruction. First, all memory blocks not contained in the must cache at B_i^j are removed from the set of DC-UCBs (6)—only a memory block that is element of the must cache all along the way to its reuse is considered useful by our definition. Then, the accessed memory block of instruction B_i^j is added in case it is contained in the must cache at the instruction (5).

Using these equations, the set of UCBs can be computed via fixed-point iteration (see [15]). The initial values at instruction B_i^j are defined by DC-UCB$_{in}(B_i^j)$ $= gen(B_i^j)$ and DC-UCB$_{out}(B_i^j) = \emptyset$.

The analysis obtains a set of memory blocks at each program point P access that might cause an additional miss upon access in case of preemption at P. The program point P with the largest DC-UCB set determines an upper-bound on the number of additional misses for the whole task. In contrast to the former UCB analysis, the DC-UCB analysis only takes those misses into account that are not part of the WCET bound. Evaluation shows that up to 80% of the accesses to a UCB were also considered to be misses in the WCET analysis. The DC-UCB analysis omits these UCBs. Hence, the analysis derives much better bounds on the CRPD when used in the context of timing analysis.

3.4 Heap-Allocating Programs

Static timing analyses rely on high cache predictability in order to achieve precise bounds on a program's execution time. Such analyses, however, fail to cope with programs using dynamic memory allocation. This is due to the unpredictability of the cache behavior introduced by the dynamic memory allocators. Using standard allocators, the cache sets to which a newly allocated memory block is mapped to are statically unknown. This does not only prohibit a cache analysis to derive hits or misses for accesses to dynamically allocated objects. It also forces such analyses to conservatively treat an access to a dynamically allocated block as an access to all cache sets. In turn, information about the cache derived from an access sequence to statically allocated objects may easily be lost. Allocators normally traverse some internal structure of free memory blocks in order to find a suitable block to satisfy an allocation request or reinsert newly deallocated memory blocks. These statically unpredictable traversals have the same negative effect on static cache analyses. Additionally, the response times of allocators can in general not be tightly bounded.

We investigate two approaches to enable precise worst-case execution time analysis for programs that use dynamic memory allocation.

The first approach automatically transforms the dynamic memory allocation into a static allocation with comparable memory consumption [32]. Hence, we try to preserve the main advantage of dynamic memory allocation, namely the reduction of memory consumption achieved by reusing deallocated memory blocks for subsequent allocation requests. Ending up with a static allocation allows for using existing techniques for timing analyses. However, the techniques for transforming dynamic to static allocation as presented in [32] have limitations. In particular, the number and sizes of dynamically allocated blocks need to be statically known. Although this might be reasonable in the hard real-time setting, ongoing research addresses this problem by investigating a parametric approach to automatically precompute memory addresses for otherwise dynamically allocated memory.

The second approach replaces the unpredictable dynamic memory allocator by a predictable dynamic memory allocator [33]. Our predictable memory allocator takes an additional—possibly automatically generated—argument specifying the cache set newly allocated memory shall be mapped to. It further gives guarantees on the number of cache lines per cache set that may be *touched* during (de)allocation. It also features constant response times by managing free blocks in multi-layered segregated lists.

Both approaches rely on precise information about the dynamically allocated heap objects and data structures arising during program execution. This information could be obtained by shape analysis [34] or data structure analysis. However, these analyses are not allocation-site aware, i.e. they only know about the shape of a data structure and are ignorant of the allocation requests that created the nodes of that structure. If we want to modify allocation requests, either by adding an additional cache set argument to a call to malloc or by replacing malloc by some function returning a sequence of static addresses, we rely on this missing information. Our current approach extends the shape analysis framework via three-valued logic by adding information about allocation sites to the logical representatives of heap-allocated objects.

4 Symbolic Representation of Pipeline Domains

Microarchitectural analysis explores execution traces of the program with respect to a pipeline model. In the pipeline model, information about register values is needed to determine addresses of memory accesses and information about cache content is needed to predict cache hits and misses. To make the analysis computationally feasible, abstractions of register and cache content of the processor are used. These abstractions may lose information.

Value analysis is invoked prior to microarchitectural analysis. It computes information about register content, which is later on used in microarchitectural analysis. For example, for a specific load instruction, value analysis computes a range of the possible memory addresses that contains the possible values for *all* executions that reach the load instruction. Microarchitectural analysis may, on the other hand, distinguish different traces ending at the load instruction. However, it uses the less specific approximation of register content from value analysis and may thus be unable to classify the address.

Further, instead of a more precise and expensive set representation of values, abstract domains like intervals and congruences are used in value analysis. This incurs additional loss of information. Similarly, cache analysis employs abstract domains which also sacrifice precision for efficiency.

Thus, at the level of the pipeline model, the inevitable use of abstraction incurs uncertainty about memory accesses and cache content. Furthermore, program inputs are not statically known. The (abstract) pipeline model has to cope with this lack of information by offering non-deterministic choices. Existence of timing anomalies forces the pipeline analysis to exhaustively explore all of them. In certain cases, state explosion can make explicit enumeration of states infeasible due to memory and computation time constraints [20].

We address the state explosion problem in static timing analysis by storing and manipulating pipeline states in a more efficient data structure based on Ordered Binary Decision Diagrams (OBDDs) [35]. Our work is inspired by BDD-based symbolic model checking [36]. Symbolic model checking has been successfully applied to components of processors. Its success sparked a general interest in symbolic representations.

4.1 Symbolic Domain and Analysis

A pipeline model can be regarded as a large, non-deterministic finite state machine (FSM). Pipeline analysis determines sets of reachable pipeline states by a fixed-point iteration over the control-flow graph, which involves the computation of abstract execution traces on the basic block level. WCET bounds for basic blocks are derived from the lengths of their execution traces.

Sets of pipeline states as well as the transition relation of the model can be represented implicitly using BDDs. Execution traces are computed by repeated application of a symbolic image operator to an incoming set of pipeline states.

We account for required program information by translating them into symbolic relations that restrict the non-deterministic choices of the pipeline model.

The resulting symbolic state traversal proceeds in breadth-first search order where one traversal step corresponds to a particular execution cycle of the processor. Savings in memory consumption and running time, compared to explicit-state analysis, result from the more efficient representation, in particular for large sets of states with many redundancies, and from completely avoiding the explicit enumeration of states.

4.2 Optimizations and Performance

To arrive at an efficient symbolic analysis that scales to pipeline models of real-life processors and industrial-size programs, we incorporate well-known optimizations from symbolic model checking, e.g. the image computation methods of [37], and novel domain-specific optimizations that leverage properties of the processor and the program. The processor-specific optimizations follow the general pattern of

- reducing representation size of components by omitting information that is not timing-relevant and
- statically precomputing information.

For example, the prefetch buffer of the Infineon TriCore processor uses 16 bytes in hardware, while the timing-relevant information can be stored in only 16 bits. For the same processor, conditions for pipeline stalls in case of unresolved data dependencies can be precomputed by a data flow analysis. The symbolic representation then requires only one state bit per pipeline to encode such stalls.

Properties of the analyzed program are exploited to achieve an efficient handling of the many 32 bit instruction and data addresses used by pipeline models. The optimizations are based on two observations:

- Each program typically uses only a small fraction of the address space.
- The computation of execution traces for a single basic block requires only a bounded amount of information about neighbouring blocks.

Based on the first observation, we compactly enumerate all addresses used in the program and then encode these addresses using a number of state bits logarithmic in the size of the set of used addresses. This significantly reduces the required number of state bits.

However, the size of the symbolic representation still depends on the size of the analyzed program. This dependence can be eliminated using the second observation. For the symbolic computation of abstract execution traces we enumerate only the addresses within range of the current basic block. The resulting incompatible address encoding in pipeline states of different basic blocks can be translated during the fixed-point iteration using symbolic image computation.

We enhance the existing framework for static timing analysis with a symbolic representation of abstract pipeline models. Our prototype implementation is integrated into the commercial WCET analysis tool `aiT` and employs the model of a real-life processor, the Infineon TriCore. The model was developed and tested within `aiT`. This enables a meaningful performance comparison between the two implementations, which produce the same analysis results. Experiments with a set of industrial benchmarks show that the symbolic domain significantly improves the scalability of the analysis [10].

5 Conclusion and Ongoing Work

Computer architects have, for a long time, optimized processor architectures for average-case performance. This article has given an overview of the problems created by ignoring the needs of embedded systems, which often need guarantees for their worst-case performance. Formal methods have been described for the derivation of timing guarantees. Two architectural components have received a detailed treatment, caches and pipelines. Caches have nice abstractions, i.e. compact abstract domains and efficient abstract update functions. Static analysis of the cache behavior by abstract interpretation is therefore quite fast. Pipelines seem to require powerset domains with a huge state space. It has been described how to use symbolic representations popular in model checking to compactly represent sets of pipeline states. What is still missing is the interaction between the abstract-interpretation-based cache analysis and the BDD-based pipeline analysis. The tools (and the communities behind them) don't talk to each other.

Several important notions, e.g. predictability, sensitivity, and relative competitiveness have been clarified. Similar notions have to be found for non-cache like architecture components. Future architectures for use in safety-critical and time-critical applications should be designed under the design goals, high predictability of the timing behavior and low sensitivity against small changes of the execution state.

References

1. Wilhelm, R., et al.: The worst-case execution-time problem—overview of methods and survey of tools. Trans. on Embedded Computing Sys. 7(3), 1–53 (2008)
2. Petters, S.M.: Worst-Case Execution-Time Estimation for Advanced Processor Architectures. PhD thesis, Technische Universität München, Munich, Germany (2002)
3. Bernat, G., Colin, A., Petters, S.M.: WCET analysis of probabilistic hard real-time systems. In: Proceedings of the 23rd IEEE Real-Time Systems Symposium, Washington, DC, USA, p. 279. IEEE Computer Society, Los Alamitos (2002)
4. Wenzel, I.: Measurement-Based Timing Analysis of Superscalar Processors. PhD thesis, Technische Universität Wien, Vienna, Austria (2006)
5. Ferdinand, C., Heckmann, R., Langenbach, M., Martin, F., Schmidt, M., Theiling, H., Thesing, S., Wilhelm, R.: Reliable and precise WCET determination for a real-life processor. In: Henzinger, T.A., Kirsch, C.M. (eds.) EMSOFT 2001. LNCS, vol. 2211, pp. 469–485. Springer, Heidelberg (2001)
6. Thiele, L., Wilhelm, R.: Design for timing predictability. Real-Time Sys. 28, 157–177 (2004)
7. Wilhelm, R., Grund, D., Reineke, J., Schlickling, M., Pister, M., Ferdinand, C.: Memory hierarchies, pipelines, and buses for future architectures in time-critical embedded systems. IEEE Transactions on CAD of Integrated Circuits and Systems 28(7), 966–978 (2009)
8. Reineke, J., Grund, D., Berg, C., Wilhelm, R.: Timing predictability of cache replacement policies. Real-Time Sys. 37(2), 99–122 (2007)
9. Reineke, J.: Caches in WCET Analysis. PhD thesis, Saarland University, Saarbrücken, Germany (2008)

10. Wilhelm, S., Wachter, B.: Symbolic state traversal for WCET analysis. In: International Conference on Embedded Software, pp. 137–146 (2009)
11. Wilhelm, R.: Determining bounds on execution times. In: Zurawski, R. (ed.) Handbook on Embedded Systems, pp. 14–23. CRC Press, Boca Raton (2005)
12. Reineke, J., Wachter, B., Thesing, S., Wilhelm, R., Polian, I., Eisinger, J., Becker, B.: A definition and classification of timing anomalies. In: Proceedings of 6th Intl. Workshop on Worst-Case Execution Time (WCET) Analysis (2006)
13. Heckmann, R., Langenbach, M., Thesing, S., Wilhelm, R.: The influence of processor architecture on the design and the results of WCET tools. Real-Time Sys. 91(7), 1038–1054 (2003)
14. Theiling, H.: Control-Flow Graphs For Real-Time Systems Analysis. PhD thesis, Saarland University, Saarbrücken, Germany (2002)
15. Cousot, P., Cousot, R.: Abstract interpretation: A unified lattice model for static analysis of programs by construction or approximation of fixpoints. In: Proceedings of the 4th ACM SIGACT-SIGPLAN Symposium on Principles of Programming Languages, pp. 238–252. ACM Press, New York (1977)
16. Ermedahl, A., Gustafsson, J.: Deriving annotations for tight calculation of execution time. In: Lengauer, C., Griebl, M., Gorlatch, S. (eds.) Euro-Par 1997. LNCS, vol. 1300, pp. 1298–1307. Springer, Heidelberg (1997)
17. Healy, C., Sjödin, M., Rustagi, V., Whalley, D., van Engelen, R.: Supporting timing analysis by automatic bounding of loop iterations. Real-Time Sys., 129–156 (2000)
18. Stein, I., Martin, F.: Analysis of path exclusion at the machine code level. In: Proceedings of the 7th Intl. Workshop on Worst-Case Execution-Time Analysis (2007)
19. Engblom, J.: Processor Pipelines and Static Worst-Case Execution Time Analysis. PhD thesis, Dept. of Information Technology, Uppsala University (2002)
20. Thesing, S.: Safe and Precise WCET Determinations by Abstract Interpretation of Pipeline Models. PhD thesis, Saarland University, Saarbrücken, Germany (2004)
21. Ferdinand, C., Wilhelm, R.: Efficient and precise cache behavior prediction for real-time systems. Real-Time Sys. 17(2-3), 131–181 (1999)
22. Li, Y.T.S., Malik, S.: Performance analysis of embedded software using implicit path enumeration. In: Proceedings of the 32nd ACM/IEEE Design Automation Conference, pp. 456–461 (1995)
23. Theiling, H.: ILP-based interprocedural path analysis. In: Sangiovanni-Vincentelli, A.L., Sifakis, J. (eds.) EMSOFT 2002. LNCS, vol. 2491, pp. 349–363. Springer, Heidelberg (2002)
24. Thesing, S., Souyris, J., Heckmann, R., Randimbivololona, F., Langenbach, M., Wilhelm, R., Ferdinand, C.: An abstract interpretation-based timing validation of hard real-time avionics software systems. In: Proceedings of the 2003 Intl. Conference on Dependable Systems and Networks, pp. 625–632. IEEE Computer Society, Los Alamitos (2003)
25. Berg, C.: PLRU cache domino effects. In: Mueller, F. (ed.) 6th Intl. Workshop on Worst-Case Execution Time (WCET) Analysis, Internationales Begegnungs- und Forschungszentrum für Informatik (IBFI), Schloss Dagstuhl, Germany (2006)
26. Altmeyer, S., Burguière, C.: A new notion of useful cache block to improve the bounds of cache-related preemption delay. In: Proceedings of the 21st Euromicro Conference on Real-Time Systems, pp. 109–118. IEEE Computer Society Press, Los Alamitos (2009)

27. White, R.T., Healy, C.A., Whalley, D.B., Mueller, F., Harmon, M.G.: Timing analysis for data caches and set-associative caches. In: Proceedings of the 3rd IEEE Real-Time Technology and Applications Symposium, Washington, DC, USA, p. 192. IEEE Computer Society, Los Alamitos (1997)
28. Ghosh, S., Martonosi, M., Malik, S.: Precise miss analysis for program transformations with caches of arbitrary associativity. In: Proceedings of the 8th International Conference on Architectural Support for Programming Languages and Operating Systems, pp. 228–239 (1998)
29. Chatterjee, S., Parker, E., Hanlon, P.J., Lebeck, A.R.: Exact analysis of the cache behavior of nested loops. In: Proceedings of the ACM SIGPLAN 2001 Conference on Programming Language Design and Implementation, pp. 286–297. ACM Press, New York (2001)
30. Reineke, J., Grund, D.: Relative competitive analysis of cache replacement policies. In: Proceedings of the 2008 ACM SIGPLAN-SIGBED Conference on Languages, Compilers, and Tools for Embedded Systems, pp. 51–60. ACM, New York (2008)
31. Grund, D., Reineke, J.: Abstract interpretation of FIFO replacement. In: Palsberg, J., Su, Z. (eds.) SAS 2009. LNCS, vol. 5673, pp. 120–136. Springer, Heidelberg (2009)
32. Herter, J., Reineke, J.: Making dynamic memory allocation static to support WCET analyses. In: Proceedings of 9th Intl. Workshop on Worst-Case Execution Time (WCET) Analysis (2009)
33. Herter, J., Reineke, J., Wilhelm, R.: CAMA: Cache-aware memory allocation for WCET analysis. In: Caccamo, M. (ed.) Proceedings Work-In-Progress Session of the 20th Euromicro Conference on Real-Time Systems, pp. 24–27 (2008)
34. Sagiv, M., Reps, T., Wilhelm, R.: Parametric shape analysis via 3-valued logic. Trans. on Programming Languages and Sys. 24(3), 217–298 (2002)
35. Bryant, R.: Graph based algorithms for boolean function manipulation. IEEE Transactions on Computers (1986)
36. Burch, J., Clarke, E., McMillan, K., Dill, D., Hwang, J.: Symbolic model checking: 10^{20} states and beyond. In: Proceedings of the 5th Annual Symposium on Logic in Computer Science. IEEE Comp. Soc. Press, Los Alamitos (1990)
37. Ranjan, R., Aziz, A., Brayton, R., Plessier, B., Pixley, C.: Efficient BDD Algorithms for FSM Synthesis and Verification. In: Proceedings of IEEE/ACM International Workshop on Logic Synthesis, Lake Tahoe, USA (1995)

Abstract Interpretation-Based Protection

Roberto Giacobazzi

Università di Verona, Italy
roberto.giacobazzi@univr.it

Hiding information means both hiding as making it imperceptible and obscuring as making it incomprehensible [9]. In programming, perception and comprehension of code's structure and behaviour are deep semantic concepts, which depend on the relative degree of abstraction of the observer, which corresponds precisely to program semantics. In this tutorial we show that abstract interpretation can be used as an adequate model for developing a unifying theory for information hiding in software, by modeling observers (i.e., malicious host attackers) $\mathcal{O}$ as suitable abstract interpreters. An observation can be any static or dynamic interpretation of programs intended to extract properties from its semantics and abstract interpretation [2] provides the best framework to understand semantics at different levels of abstraction. The long standing experience in digital media protection by obscurity is inspiring here. It is known that practical steganography is an issue where compression methods are inefficient: *"Where efficient compression is available, information hiding becomes vacuous."* [1]. This means that the gain provided by compression can be used for hiding information. This, in contrast to cryptography, strongly relies upon the understanding of the supporting media: if we have a source which is completely understandable, i.e., it can be perfectly compressed, then steganography becomes trivial. In programming languages, a complete understanding of semantics means that no loss of precision is introduced by approximating data and control components while analysing computations. Complete abstractions [3,8] model precisely the complete understanding of program semantics by an approximate observer, which corresponds to the possibility of replacing, with no loss of precision, concrete computations with abstract ones —some sort of perfect semantic compressibility around a given property. This includes, for instance, both static and dynamic, via monitoring, approaches to information disclosure and reverse engineering [4]. The lack of completeness of the observer is therefore the corresponding of its poor understanding of program semantics, and provides the key aspect for understanding and designing a new family of methods and tools for software steganography and obfuscation. Consider the simple statement, $C : \mathtt{x} = \mathtt{a} * \mathtt{b}$, multiplying a and b, and storing the result in x. An automated program sign analysis replacing concrete computations with approximated ones (i.e., the rule of signs) is able to catch, with no loss of precision, the intended sign behaviour of C because the sign abstraction $\mathcal{O} = \{+, 0, -\}$, is complete for integer multiplication. If we replace C with $\mathfrak{O}(C)$: $\mathtt{x} = 0$; $\mathtt{if}\ \mathtt{b} \leq 0\ \mathtt{then}\ \{\mathtt{a} = -\mathtt{a}; \mathtt{b} = -\mathtt{b}\}$; $\mathtt{while}\ \mathtt{b} \neq 0\ \{\mathtt{x} = \mathtt{a} + \mathtt{x}; \mathtt{b} = \mathtt{b} - 1\}$ we obfuscate the observer $\mathcal{O}$ because the rule of signs is incomplete for integer addition. Intervals, i.e., a far more concrete observer, are required in order to automatically understand the sign

G. Barthe and M. Hermenegildo (Eds.): VMCAI 2010, LNCS 5944, pp. 23–24, 2010.

computed in $\mathfrak{O}(C)$. We show how this idea can be extended to arbitrary obfuscation methods and exploited for code steganography, providing the basis for a unifying theory for these technologies in terms of abstract interpretation. We show how obfuscation can be viewed as a program transformation making abstractions incomplete and at the same time we show how watermark extraction can be viewed as a complete abstract interpretation against a secret program property, extending abstract watermarking [5] to any watermarking method. Both obfuscation and watermarking can be specified as transformers to achieve completeness/incompleteness in abstract interpretation [7], provided that the transformed code does not interfere with the expected input/output behaviour of programs. This latter correctness criteria can be again specified as a completeness problem by considering abstract non-interference [6] as the method for controlling information leakage in obfuscation and steganography. Our approach is language independent and can be applied to most known obfuscation and watermarking methods, providing a common ground for their understanding and comparison.

References

1. Anderson, R.J., Petitcolas, F.: On the limits of steganography. IEEE J. of Selected Areas in Communications 16(4), 474–481 (1998)
2. Cousot, P., Cousot, R.: Abstract interpretation: A unified lattice model for static analysis of programs by construction or approximation of fixpoints. In: Proc. of POPL 1977, pp. 238–252. ACM Press, New York (1977)
3. Cousot, P., Cousot, R.: Systematic design of program analysis frameworks. In: Proc. of POPL 1979, pp. 269–282. ACM Press, New York (1979)
4. Cousot, P., Cousot, R.: Systematic design of program transformation frameworks by abstract interpretation. In: Proc. of POPL 2002, pp. 178–190. ACM Press, New York (2002)
5. Cousot, P., Cousot, R.: An abstract interpretation-based framework for software watermarking. In: Proc. of POPL 2004, pp. 173–185. ACM Press, New York (2004)
6. Giacobazzi, R., Mastroeni, I.: Abstract non-interference: Parameterizing non-interference by abstract interpretation. In: Proc. of POPL 2004, pp. 186–197. ACM-Press, New York (2004)
7. Giacobazzi, R., Mastroeni, I.: Transforming abstract interpretations by abstract interpretation. In: Alpuente, M., Vidal, G. (eds.) SAS 2008. LNCS, vol. 5079, pp. 1–17. Springer, Heidelberg (2008)
8. Giacobazzi, R., Ranzato, F., Scozzari, F.: Making abstract interpretations complete. J. of the ACM. 47(2), 361–416 (2000)
9. Petitcolas, F.A.P., Anderson, R.J., Kuhn, M.G.: Information hiding – A survey. Proc. of the IEEE 87(7), 1062–1078 (1999)

Advances in Probabilistic Model Checking

Joost-Pieter Katoen[1,2]

[1] RWTH Aachen University, Software Modeling and Verification Group, Germany
[2] University of Twente, Formal Methods and Tools, The Netherlands

Abstract. Random phenomena occur in many applications: security, communication protocols, distributed algorithms, and performance and dependability analysis, to mention a few. In the last two decades, efficient model-checking algorithms and tools have been developed to support the automated verification of models that incorporate randomness. Popular models are Markov decision processes and (continuous-time) Markov chains. Recent advances such as compositional abstraction-refinement and counterexample generation have significantly improved the applicability of these techniques. First promising steps have been made to cover more powerful models, real-time linear specifications, and parametric model checking. In this tutorial I will describe the state of the art, and will detail some of the major recent advancements in probabilistic model checking.

G. Barthe and M. Hermenegildo (Eds.): VMCAI 2010, LNCS 5944, p. 25, 2010.

Building a Calculus of Data Structures

Viktor Kuncak[1,*], Ruzica Piskac[1], Philippe Suter[1], and Thomas Wies[2]

[1] EPFL School of Computer and Communication Sciences, Lausanne, Switzerland
firstname.lastname@epfl.ch
[2] Institute of Science and Technology Austria, Klosterneuburg, Austria
wies@ist.ac.at

Abstract. Techniques such as verification condition generation, predicate abstraction, and expressive type systems reduce software verification to proving formulas in expressive logics. Programs and their specifications often make use of data structures such as sets, multisets, algebraic data types, or graphs. Consequently, formulas generated from verification also involve such data structures. To automate the proofs of such formulas we propose a logic (a "calculus") of such data structures. We build the calculus by starting from decidable logics of individual data structures, and connecting them through functions and sets, in ways that go beyond the frameworks such as Nelson-Oppen. The result are new decidable logics that can simultaneously specify properties of different kinds of data structures and overcome the limitations of the individual logics.

Several of our decidable logics include abstraction functions that map a data structure into its more abstract view (a tree into a multiset, a multiset into a set), into a numerical quantity (the size or the height), or into the truth value of a candidate data structure invariant (sortedness, or the heap property). For algebraic data types, we identify an asymptotic many-to-one condition on the abstraction function that guarantees the existence of a decision procedure.

In addition to the combination based on abstraction functions, we can combine multiple data structure theories if they all reduce to the same data structure logic. As an instance of this approach, we describe a decidable logic whose formulas are propositional combinations of formulas in: weak monadic second-order logic of two successors, two-variable logic with counting, multiset algebra with Presburger arithmetic, the Bernays-Schönfinkel-Ramsey class of first-order logic, and the logic of algebraic data types with the set content function. The subformulas in this combination can share common variables that refer to sets of objects along with the common set algebra operations. Such sound and complete combination is possible because the relations on sets definable in the component logics are all expressible in Boolean Algebra with Presburger Arithmetic. Presburger arithmetic and its new extensions play an important role in our decidability results. In several cases, when we combine logics that belong to NP, we can prove the satisfiability for the combined logic is still in NP.

* This research is supported in part by the Swiss National Science Foundation Grant "Precise and Scalable Analyses for Reliable Software".

G. Barthe and M. Hermenegildo (Eds.): VMCAI 2010, LNCS 5944, pp. 26–44, 2010.

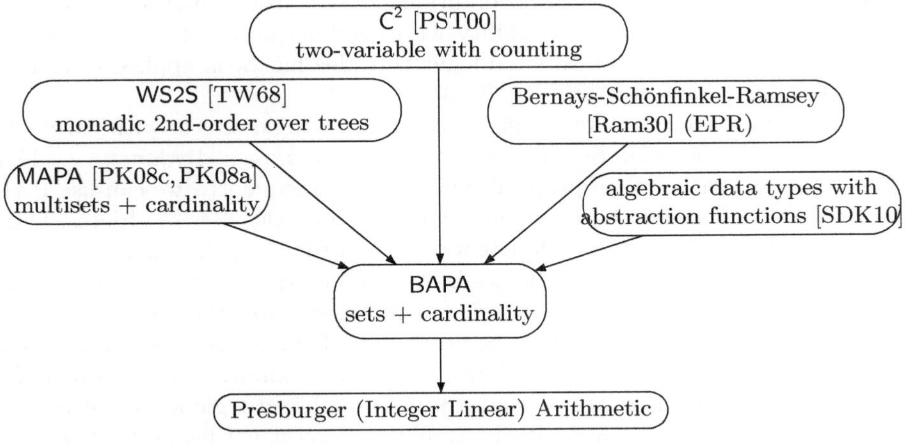

Fig. 1. Components of our decidable logic and reductions used to show its decidability

1 Introduction

A cornerstone of software verification is the problem of proving the validity of logical formulas that describe software correctness properties. Among the most effective tools for this task are the systems (e.g. [dMB08]) that incorporate decision procedures for data types that commonly occur in software (e.g. numbers, sets, arrays, algebraic data types). Such decision procedures leverage insights into the structure of these data types to reduce the amount of uninformed search they need to perform. Prominent examples of decision procedures are concerned with numbers, including (the quantifier-free fragment of) Presburger arithmetic (PA) [Pre29]. For the verification of modern software, data structures are at least as important as numerical constraints. Among the best behaved data structures are sets, with Boolean algebra of sets [Sko19] among the basic decidable examples, others include algebraic data types [Opp78,BST07] and arrays [SBDL01,BM07,dMB09]. Reasoning about imperative data structures can be described using formulas interpreted over graphs; decidable fragments of first-order logic present a good starting point for such reasoning [BGG97].

In this paper we give an overview of some recent decision procedures for reasoning about data structures, including sets and multisets with cardinality bounds, algebraic data types with abstraction functions, and combinations of expressive logics over trees and graphs. Our results illustrate the rich structure of connections between logics of different data structures and numerical constraints. Figure 1 illustrates some of these connections; they present combinations that go beyond the disjoint combination framework of Nelson-Oppen [NO79].

Given logics A and B we often consider a combined logic $c(A, B)$ that subsumes A and B and has additional operators that make the combined logic more useful (e.g. abstraction functions from A to B, or numerical measures of the data structure). In such situation, we have found it effective to reduce the combination $c(A, B)$ to one of the logic, say B. Under certain conditions, if we consider another combination $c'(A', B)$ we can obtain the decidability of the combination $c''(A, A', B)$ of all three logics. When B is the propositional logic, this idea has been applied to combine logics that share only equality (e.g. [LS04]).

In our approach, we take as the base logic B a logic of sets with cardinality operator, which we call *Boolean Algebra with Presburger Arithmetic (BAPA)*. BAPA is much richer than propositional logic. Consequently, we can use BAPA to combine logics that share not only equalities but also sets of objects. Different logics define the sets in different ways: first-order logic fragments use unary predicates to define sets, other logics have variables denoting sets (this includes monadic second-order logic, the logics of multisets, and the logic of algebraic data types with abstractions). A key technical challenge is establishing reductions from new logics to existing ones, and casting known decision procedures as reductions to BAPA. The formulas in our combined logic are quantifier-free combinations of possibly quantified formulas of component logics. Our approach leads to the decidability of classes of complex verification conditions for which we previously had only heuristic, incomplete, approaches.

The results we present follow [KR07, PK08a, PK08c, PK08b, SDK10, WPK09].

2 Boolean Algebra with Presburger Arithmetic

We start by considering a logic that combines two well-known decidable logics: 1) the algebra of sets (with operations such as union, intersection, complement, and relations such as extensional set equality and subset), and 2) Presburger arithmetic [Pre29] (with linear arithmetic expressions over integer variables). We establish a connection between these two logics by introducing the cardinality operator that computes the number of elements in the set expression. We call this logic BAPA (Boolean Algebra with Presburger Arithmetic) [KNR06], and focus on its quantifier-free fragment (QFBAPA). Figure 2 shows the syntax of QFBAPA. Figure 3 shows example verification conditions that it can express.

Methods to decide QFBAPA. Like Presburger arithmetic [Pre29], BAPA admits quantifier elimination [KNR06], which gives NEXPTIME decision procedure for quantifier-free formulas. The logic also admits small model property, but, due to formulas such as $|A_0| = 1 \wedge \bigwedge_i |A_i| = 2|A_{i-1}|$, the number of assignments to set variables can be doubly exponential, which would again give NEXPTIME

$$
\begin{aligned}
F &::= A \mid F_1 \wedge F_2 \mid F_1 \vee F_2 \mid \neg F \\
A &::= B_1 = B_2 \mid B_1 \subseteq B_2 \mid T_1 = T_2 \mid T_1 < T_2 \mid (K|T) \\
B &::= x \mid \emptyset \mid \mathcal{U} \mid B_1 \cup B_2 \mid B_1 \cap B_2 \mid B^c \\
T &::= k \mid K \mid T_1 + T_2 \mid K \cdot T \mid \; |B| \\
K &::= \ldots -2 \mid -1 \mid 0 \mid 1 \mid 2 \ldots
\end{aligned}
$$

Fig. 2. Quantifier-Free Boolean Algebra with Presburger Arithmetic (QFBAPA)

verification condition	property being checked
$x \notin \mathtt{content} \wedge \mathtt{size} = \mathtt{card\ content} \longrightarrow (\mathtt{size} = 0 \leftrightarrow \mathtt{content} = \emptyset)$	using invariant on size to prove correctness of an efficient emptiness check
$x \notin \mathtt{content} \wedge \mathtt{size} = \mathtt{card\ content} \longrightarrow \mathtt{size} + 1 = \mathtt{card}(\{x\} \cup \mathtt{content})$	maintaining correct size when inserting fresh element
$\mathtt{size} = \mathtt{card\ content} \wedge \mathtt{size1} = \mathtt{card}(\{x\} \cup \mathtt{content}) \longrightarrow \mathtt{size1} \leq \mathtt{size} + 1$	maintaining size after inserting any element
$\mathtt{content} \subseteq \mathtt{alloc} \wedge x_1 \notin \mathtt{alloc} \wedge x_2 \notin \mathtt{alloc} \cup \{x_1\} \wedge x_3 \notin \mathtt{alloc} \cup \{x_1\} \cup \{x_2\} \longrightarrow \mathtt{card}\,(\mathtt{content} \cup \{x_1\} \cup \{x_2\} \cup \{x_3\}) = \mathtt{card\,content} + 3$	allocating and inserting three objects into a container data structure
$x \in C \wedge C_1 = (C \setminus \{x\}) \wedge \mathtt{card}(\mathtt{alloc1} \setminus \mathtt{alloc0}) \leq 1 \wedge \mathtt{card}(\mathtt{alloc2} \setminus \mathtt{alloc1}) \leq \mathtt{card}\,C_1 \longrightarrow \mathtt{card}\,(\mathtt{alloc2} \setminus \mathtt{alloc0}) \leq \mathtt{card}\,C$	bound on the number of allocated objects in a recursive function that incorporates container C into another container

Fig. 3. Example verification conditions that belong to QFBAPA

procedure. We can obtain an optimal worst-case time decision procedure for QFBAPA using two insights. The first insight follows the quantifier elimination algorithm and introduces an integer variable for each Venn region (an intersection of set variables and their complements), reducing the formula to Presburger arithmetic. The second insight shows that the generated Presburger arithmetic formulas enjoy a *sparse model* property: if they are satisfiable, they are satisfiable in a model where most variables (denoting sizes of Venn regions) are zero. Using an appropriate encoding it is possible to generate a polynomial-sized instead of exponential-sized Presburger arithmetic formula. This can be used to show that the satisfiability problem for QFBAPA remains within NP [KR07].

3 Multisets Algebra with Presburger Arithmetic

The decidability and NP completeness of QFBAPA also extends to Multiset Algebra with Presburger Arithmetic, in which variables can denote both sets and multisets (and where one can test whether a set is a multiset, or convert a multiset into a set). The motivation for multisets comes from verification of data structures with possibly repeated elements, where, in addition to knowing whether an element occurs in the data structure, we are also interested how many times it occurs. A detailed description of decision procedures for satisfiability of multisets with cardinality constraints is in [PK08a, PK08c, PK08b].

A multiset is a function m from a fixed finite set E to $\mathbb{N}$, where $m(e)$ denotes the number of times an element e occurs in the multiset (multiplicity of e). In addition to multiset operations such as multiplicity-preserving union and the intersection, every PA formula defining a relation leads to an operation on multisets in our logic, defined point-wise using this relation. For example, $(m_1 \cap m_2)(e) = \min(m_1(e), m_2(e))$ and $m_1 \subseteq m_2$ means $\forall e. m_1(e) \leq m_2(e)$. The logic also supports the cardinality operator that returns the number of elements in a multiset. The cardinality operator is a useful in applications, yet it prevents the use of previous decision procedures for arrays [BM07] to decide our logic. Figure 4 summarizes the language of multisets with cardinality constraints. There are two levels at which integer linear arithmetic constraints occur: to define point-wise operations on multisets (inner formulas) and to define constraints on cardinalities of multisets (outer formulas). Integer variables from outer formulas cannot occur within inner formulas.

First, we sketch the decision procedure from [PK08a]. Given a formula F_M, we convert it to the following sum normal form:

$$P \wedge (u_1, \ldots, u_n) = \sum_{e \in E} (t_1, \ldots, t_n) \wedge \forall e. F$$

where

- P is a quantifier-free PA formula without any multiset variables
- the variables in $t_1, \ldots, t_n$ and F occur only as expressions of the form $m(e)$ for m a multiset variable and e the fixed index variable
- formula P can only share variables with terms $u_1, \ldots, u_n$.

The algorithm that reduces a formula to its sum normal form runs in polynomial time. The goal of our decision procedure is to express the subformula $(u_1, \ldots, u_n) = \sum_{e \in E} (t_1, \ldots, t_n) \wedge \forall e. F$ as a quantifier-free PA formula and thus

Top-level formulas:

$F ::= A \mid F \wedge F \mid \neg F$

$A ::= M{=}M \mid M \subseteq M \mid \forall e.\mathsf{F}^{\mathsf{in}} \mid \mathsf{A}^{\mathsf{out}}$

Outer linear arithmetic formulas:

$\mathsf{F}^{\mathsf{out}} ::= \mathsf{A}^{\mathsf{out}} \mid \mathsf{F}^{\mathsf{out}} \wedge \mathsf{F}^{\mathsf{out}} \mid \neg \mathsf{F}^{\mathsf{out}}$

$\mathsf{A}^{\mathsf{out}} ::= \mathsf{t}^{\mathsf{out}} \leq \mathsf{t}^{\mathsf{out}} \mid \mathsf{t}^{\mathsf{out}}{=}\mathsf{t}^{\mathsf{out}} \mid (\mathsf{t}^{\mathsf{out}}, \ldots, \mathsf{t}^{\mathsf{out}}){=}\sum_{\mathsf{F}^{\mathsf{in}}}(\mathsf{t}^{\mathsf{in}}, \ldots, \mathsf{t}^{\mathsf{in}})$

$\mathsf{t}^{\mathsf{out}} ::= k \mid |M| \mid C \mid \mathsf{t}^{\mathsf{out}} + \mathsf{t}^{\mathsf{out}} \mid C \cdot \mathsf{t}^{\mathsf{out}} \mid \text{if } \mathsf{F}^{\mathsf{out}} \text{ then } \mathsf{t}^{\mathsf{out}} \text{ else } \mathsf{t}^{\mathsf{out}}$

Inner linear arithmetic formulas:

$\mathsf{F}^{\mathsf{in}} ::= \mathsf{A}^{\mathsf{in}} \mid \mathsf{F}^{\mathsf{in}} \wedge \mathsf{F}^{\mathsf{in}} \mid \neg \mathsf{F}^{\mathsf{in}}$

$\mathsf{A}^{\mathsf{in}} ::= \mathsf{t}^{\mathsf{in}} \leq \mathsf{t}^{\mathsf{in}} \mid \mathsf{t}^{\mathsf{in}}{=}\mathsf{t}^{\mathsf{in}}$

$\mathsf{t}^{\mathsf{in}} ::= m(e) \mid C \mid \mathsf{t}^{\mathsf{in}} + \mathsf{t}^{\mathsf{in}} \mid C \cdot \mathsf{t}^{\mathsf{in}} \mid \text{if } \mathsf{F}^{\mathsf{in}} \text{ then } \mathsf{t}^{\mathsf{in}} \text{ else } \mathsf{t}^{\mathsf{in}}$

Multiset expressions:

$M ::= m \mid \emptyset \mid M \cap M \mid M \cup M \mid M \uplus M \mid M \setminus M \mid M \setminus\setminus M \mid \mathsf{set}(M)$

Terminals:

m - multiset variables; e - index variable (fixed)

k - integer variable; C - integer constant

Fig. 4. Quantifier-Free Multiset Constraints with Cardinality Operator

reduce the satisfiability of a formula belonging to the language of Figure 4 to satisfiability of quantifier-free PA formulas. As a first step, we use the fact that a formula in the sum normal form

$$P \ \wedge \ (u_1, \ldots, u_n) = \sum_{e \in E} (t_1, \ldots, t_n) \ \wedge \ \forall e.F$$

is equisatisfiable with the formula

$$P \ \wedge \ (u_1, \ldots, u_n) \in \{(t'_1, \ldots, t'_n) \mid F'\}^*$$

where the terms t'_i and the formula F' are formed from the terms t_i and the formula F in the following way: for each multiset expression $m_i(e)$ we introduce a fresh new integer variable x_i and then we substitute each occurrence of $m_j(e)$ in the terms terms t_i and the formula F with the corresponding variable x_j. The star-closure of a set C is defined as $C^* = \{\boldsymbol{v}_1 + \ldots + \boldsymbol{v}_n \mid \boldsymbol{v}_1, \ldots \boldsymbol{v}_n \in C \wedge n \geq 0\}$. We are left with the problem of deciding the satisfiability of quantifier-free PA formulas extended with the star operator [PK08c]. For this we need representations of solutions of PA formulas using semilinear sets.

3.1 Semilinear Sets

Let $S \subseteq \mathbb{N}^n$ be a set of vectors of non-negative integers and let $a \in \mathbb{N}^n$ be a vector of non-negative integers. A linear set $LS(a; S)$ is defined as $LS(a; S) = \{a + x_1 + \ldots + x_n \mid x_i \in S \wedge n \geq 0\}$. A vector a is called the *base* vector, while elements of S are called the *step* vectors. A semilinear set Z is defined as a finite union of linear sets: $Z = \cup_{i=1}^{n} LS(a_i; S_i)$.

By definition, a semilinear set can be described as a solution set of a PA formula. [GS66] showed that the converse also holds: the solution of a PA formula is a semilinear set.

Consider the set $\{(t'_1, \ldots, t'_n) \mid F'\}^*$. The set of all vectors which are solution of formula F' is a semilinear set. Moreover, it is not difficult to see that applying the star operator on a semiliner set results with the set which can be described with the Presburger arithmetic formula. Consequently, applying the star operator on a semiliner set results in a new semilinear set. Because $\{(t'_1, \ldots, t'_n) \mid F'\}^*$ is a semilinear set, checking whether $(u_1, \ldots, u_n) \in \{(t'_1, \ldots, t'_n) \mid F'\}^*$ is effectively expressible as a Presburger arithmetic formula. Consequently, satisfiability of an initial multiset constraints problem reduces to satisfiability of quantifier-free Presburger arithmetic formulas. Following the constructions behind these closure properties gives the decidability, but, unfortunately, not the optimal NP complexity.

3.2 NP Complexity of Multisets with Cardinality Constraints

To show NP membership of the language in Figure 4, we prove the linear arithmetic with positively occurring stars is in NP [PK08c]. We use theorems bounding the sizes of semilinear sets and again apply a sparse model theorem.

Bounds on Size of the Vectors Defining Semilinear Set. In [Pot91] Pottier investigates algorithms and bounds for solving a system of integer constraints. The algorithm presented there runs in singly exponential time and returns a semilinear set Z which is a solution of the given system. This paper also establishes the bounds on the size of base and step vectors which occurs in the definition of Z. Let $x = (x_1, \ldots, x_n)$ be an integer vector. We use two standard norms of the vector x:

- $||x||_1 = \sum_{i=1}^{n} |x_i|$
- $||x||_\infty = \max_{i=1}^{n} |x_i|$

For matrices we use the norm $||A||_{1,\infty} = sup_i\{\sum_j |a_{ij}|\}$.

Fact 1 ([Pot91], Corollary 1). *Given a system $Ax \leq b$, a semilinear set describing the solution can be computed in singly exponential time. Moreover, if v is a base or a step vector that occurs in the semilinear set, then*

$$||v||_1 \leq (2 + ||A||_{1,\infty} + ||b||_\infty)^m$$

Let F be a Presburger arithmetic formula and let Z be a semilinear set describing a set of solutions of F. Let S be a set of all base and step vectors of Z. Theorem 1 implies that there exists polynomial $p(s)$, where s is a size of the input formula, such that for each $v \in S$, $||v||_1 \leq 2^{p(s)}$.

Sparse Solutions of Integer Cones. Let S be a set of integer vectors. For a vector $v \in S^*$ we are interested in the minimal number of vectors from S such that v is their linear combination. Eisenbrand and Shmonin [ES06] proved that this minimal number depends only on the dimension of vectors and on the size of the coefficients of those vectors, as follows.

Fact 2 ([ES06], Theorem 1(ii)). *Let S be a finite set of integer vectors of the dimension n and let $v \in S^*$. Then there exists $S_1 \subseteq S$ such that $b \in S_1{}^*$ and $|S_1| \leq 2n \log(4nM)$, where $M = \max_{x \in S} ||x||_\infty$.*

Small Model Property for Integer Linear Programming. [Pap81] proves the small model property for systems of integer linear constrains $A\boldsymbol{x} = \boldsymbol{b}$.

Fact 3 ([Pap81]). *Given an $m \times n$ integer matrix A, an m-dimensional integer vector $\boldsymbol{b}$ and an integer M such that $||A||_{1,\infty} \leq M$ and $||\boldsymbol{b}||_\infty \leq M$, if the system $A\boldsymbol{x} = \boldsymbol{b}$ has a solution, then it also has a non-negative solution vector $\boldsymbol{v}$ such that $||\boldsymbol{v}||_\infty \leq n(mM)^{2m+1}$.*

Membership in NP. Back to our formula F', consider a semilinear set $Z = \cup_{i=1}^{k} LS(a_i; \{b_{i1}, \ldots, b_{ik_i}\})$ which corresponds to the set $\{\boldsymbol{t} \mid F'(\boldsymbol{t})\}$. Elimination of the star operator from the expression $\boldsymbol{u} \in \{\boldsymbol{t} \mid F'(\boldsymbol{t})\}^*$ results in the formula $\boldsymbol{u} = F_N(a_i, b_{ij})$, where F_N is a new Presburger arithmetic formula which has base vectors and step vectors of Z as variables. Using Theorem 2 we can show that there exists equisatisfiable formula $\boldsymbol{u} = F'_N(a_i, b_{ij})$ which uses only polynomially many ($O(n^2 \log n)$) vectors a_i and b_{ij}. The next problem is to verify in polynomial time whether a vector belongs to a set of vectors defining the semilinear set. We showed in [PK08c] that instead of guessing a_i and b_{ij}, it is enough to guess vectors v_c which are solutions of F'.

Using this we proved that $\boldsymbol{u} \in \{\boldsymbol{t} \mid F'(\boldsymbol{t})\}^*$ is equisatisfiable with the formula

$$\boldsymbol{u} = \sum_{i=1}^{Q} \lambda_i \boldsymbol{v}_i \wedge \bigwedge_{i=1}^{Q} F(\boldsymbol{v}_i)$$

where Q is a number (not a variable!) which can be computed from the proofs of the above theorems, and depends on

- dimension of a problem
- $||\cdot||_\infty$ of generating vectors of the semilinear sets

The important is that we do not actually need to compute vectors generating the semilinear set. We only require their norm $||\cdot||_\infty$ and it can be easily calculated by applying Theorem 1.

The last hurdle is that the derived formula does not seem to be linear as it contains multiplication of variables: $\lambda_i \boldsymbol{v}_i$. This problem is solved by applying Theorem 3. Because we know that there exists a bounded solution, we can calculate the concrete bound on the size of the solution and obtain the number r. Using this number we can rewrite v_i as a binary number and expand multiplication this way:

$$\lambda_i v_i = (\sum_{j=0}^{r} v_{ij} 2^j)\lambda_i = \sum_{j=0}^{r} 2^j (v_{ij}\lambda_i) = \sum_{j=0}^{r} 2^j \mathsf{ite}(v_{ij}, \lambda_i, 0) =$$
$$\mathsf{ite}(v_{i0}, \lambda_i, 0) + 2(\mathsf{ite}(v_{i1}, \lambda_i, 0) + 2(\mathsf{ite}(v_{i2}, \lambda_i, 0) + \cdots)))$$

This way we derive the linear arithmetic formula which polynomial in the size of the initial problem and obtain NP-completeness.

4 Algebraic Data Types with Abstraction Functions

In this section, we give an overview of a decision procedure for a logic which combines algebraic data types with an abstraction function mapping these types to elements of a collection theory. The full account of our results is available in [SDK10]. To simplify the presentation, we restrict ourselves to the data type of binary trees storing elements of a countably infinite type, which in Scala [OSV08] syntax would be written as

```
abstract class Tree case class Node(left: Tree, value: ℰ,
right: Tree) extends Tree case class Leaf() extends Tree
```

for an element type $\mathcal{E}$. We consider abstraction functions which are given as a catamorphism (generalized fold) over the trees, given as

```
def α(t: Tree): C = t match {
  case Leaf() ⇒ empty
  case Node(l,e,r) ⇒ combine(α(l), e, α(r))
}
```

for some functions empty : $\mathcal{C}$ and combine : $(\mathcal{C}, \mathcal{E}, \mathcal{C})$. Formally, our logic is parametrized by a collection theory $\mathcal{L}_\mathcal{C}$ and an abstraction function α given in terms of empty and combine as above. We denote the logic by $\mathcal{T}_\alpha$ (note that $\mathcal{L}_\mathcal{C}$ is implicit in α). Fig. 5 shows the syntax of $\mathcal{T}_\alpha$, and Fig. 6 its semantics. The description refers to the catamorphism α, as well as the semantics of the theory $\mathcal{L}_\mathcal{C}$, denoted $[\![\ ]\!]_\mathcal{C}$.

$T ::= t \mid \mathsf{Leaf} \mid \mathsf{Node}(T, E, T) \mid \mathsf{left}(T) \mid \mathsf{right}(T)$	Tree terms
$C ::= c \mid \alpha(t) \mid \mathfrak{T}_\mathcal{C}$	$\mathcal{C}$-terms
$F_T ::= T = T \mid T \neq T$	Equations over trees
$F_C ::= C = C \mid \mathfrak{F}_\mathcal{C}$	Formulas of $\mathcal{L}_\mathcal{C}$
$E ::= e$	Variables of type $\mathcal{E}$
$\phi ::= \bigwedge F_T \wedge \bigwedge F_C$	Conjunctions
$\psi ::= \phi \mid \neg\phi \mid \phi \vee \phi \mid \phi \wedge \phi \mid \phi \Rightarrow \phi \mid \phi \Leftrightarrow \phi$	Formulas

$\mathfrak{T}_\mathcal{C}$ and $\mathfrak{F}_\mathcal{C}$ represent terms and formulas of $\mathcal{L}_\mathcal{C}$ respectively. Formulas are assumed to be closed under negation.

Fig. 5. Syntax of $\mathcal{T}_\alpha$

$$
\begin{aligned}
[\![\mathsf{Node}(T_1, e, T_2)]\!] &= \mathsf{Node}([\![T_1]\!], [\![e]\!]_\mathcal{C}, [\![T_2]\!]) \\
[\![\mathsf{Leaf}]\!] &= \mathsf{Leaf} \\
[\![\mathsf{left}(\mathsf{Node}(T_1, e, T_2))]\!] &= [\![T_1]\!] \\
[\![\mathsf{right}(\mathsf{Node}(T_1, e, T_2))]\!] &= [\![T_2]\!] \\
[\![T_1 = T_2]\!] &= [\![T_1]\!] = [\![T_2]\!] \\
[\![T_1 \neq T_2]\!] &= [\![T_1]\!] \neq [\![T_2]\!] \\
[\![\alpha(\mathsf{Leaf})]\!] &= [\![\mathsf{empty}]\!]_\mathcal{C} \\
[\![\alpha(\mathsf{Node}([\![T_1]\!], [\![e]\!], [\![T_2]\!])]\!] &= [\![\mathsf{combine}([\![T_1]\!], [\![e]\!], [\![T_2]\!])]\!]_\mathcal{C} \\
[\![C_1 = C_2]\!] &= [\![C_1]\!]_\mathcal{C} = [\![C_2]\!]_\mathcal{C} \\
[\![\mathfrak{F}_\mathcal{C}]\!] &= [\![\mathfrak{F}_\mathcal{C}]\!]_\mathcal{C} \\
[\![\neg\phi]\!] &= \neg[\![\phi]\!] \\
[\![\phi_1 \star \phi_2]\!] &= [\![\phi_1]\!] \star [\![\phi_2]\!] \text{ where } \star \in \{\vee, \wedge, \Rightarrow, \Leftrightarrow\}
\end{aligned}
$$

Fig. 6. Semantics of $\mathcal{T}_\alpha$

4.1 Examples of Applications

A typical target application for our decision procedure is the verification of functional code. Fig. 7 presents an annotated code fragment of an implementation of a set data structure using a binary search tree.[1] Note that the abstraction function content is the catamorphism α defined by empty $= \emptyset$ and combine$(t_1, e, t_2) = \alpha(t_1) \cup \{e\} \cup \alpha(t_2)$, and that it is used within the postcondition of the function add.

[1] Set.empty, ++ and Set(e) are Scala notations for $\emptyset$, $\cup$ and $\{e\}$ respectively.

```
object BSTSet {
  type E = Int
  type C = Set[E]
  abstract class Tree
  case class Leaf() extends Tree
  case class Node(left: Tree, value: E, right: Tree) extends Tree

  // abstraction function α
  def content(t: Tree): C = t match {
    case Leaf() ⇒ Set.empty
    case Node(l,e,r) ⇒ content(l) ++ Set(e) ++ content(r)
  }

  // adds an element to a set
  def add(e: E, t: Tree): Tree = (t match {
    case Leaf() ⇒ Node(Leaf(), e, Leaf())
    case t @ Node(l,v,r) ⇒
      if (e < v) Node(add(e, l), v, r) else if (e == v) t else Node(l, v, add(e, r))
  }) ensuring (res ⇒ content(res) == content(t) ++ Set(e))
}
```

Fig. 7. A binary search tree implementation of a set

```
def sorted(t: Tree): (Option[Int],Option[Int],Boolean) = t match {
  case Leaf() ⇒ (None, None, true)
  case Node(l, v, r) ⇒ {
    (sorted(l),sorted(r)) match {
      case ((_,_,false),_) ⇒ (None, None, false)
      case (_,(_,_,false)) ⇒ (None, None, false)
      case ((None,None,_),(None,None,_)) ⇒ (Some(v), Some(v), true)
      case ((Some(minL),Some(maxL),_),(None,None,_))
        if (maxL < v) ⇒ (Some(minL),Some(v),true)
      case ((None,None,_),(Some(minR),Some(maxR),_))
        if (minR > v) ⇒ (Some(v), Some(maxR), true)
      case ((Some(minL),Some(maxL),_), (Some(minR),Some(maxR),_))
        if (maxL < v && minR > v) ⇒ (Some(minL),Some(maxR),true)
      case _ ⇒ (None,None,false)
}}}
```

Fig. 8. A catamorphism which computes a triple where the first and second elements are the minimal and maximal values of the tree, respectively, and the third is a boolean value indicating whether the tree is sorted

Such specifications in term of the abstraction function are natural because they concisely express the algebraic laws one expects to hold for the data structure.

By applying standard techniques to replace the recursive call in add by the function contract, we obtain (among others) the following verification condition:

$$\forall t_1, t_2, t_3, t_4 : \mathsf{Tree},\ e_1, e_2 : \mathsf{Int}\ .\ t_1 = \mathsf{Node}(t_2, e_1, t_3) \Rightarrow \\ \alpha(t_4) = \alpha(t_2) \cup \{e_2\} \Rightarrow \alpha(\mathsf{Node}(t_4, e_1, t_3)) = \alpha(t_1) \cup \{e_2\}$$

This formula combines constraints over tree terms and over terms in the collection theory (in this case, over sets), as well as a non-trivial connection given by α (the content function in the code).

Other abstraction functions of interest include the computation of a multiset preserving multiplicities instead of a set, the computation of a list of the elements read in, for instance, in-order traversal, the computation of minimal or maximal elements, etc. In fact, even invariants like sortedness of a tree can be expressed as a catamorphism, as shown in Fig 8.

4.2 The Decision Procedure

We give an overview of our decision procedure for conjunctions of literals of $\mathcal{T}_\alpha$. To lift it to formulas of arbitrary boolean structure, one can follow the DPLL(T) approach [GHN+04].

The general idea of the decision procedure is to first use unification to solve the constraints on the trees, then to derive and propagate all consequences relevant to the type $\mathcal{C}$ of collections that abstracts the trees. In such manner it reduces a problem over trees and their abstract values in $\mathcal{L}_\mathcal{C}$ to a problem in $\mathcal{L}_\mathcal{C}$. We assume a decision procedure is available for $\mathcal{L}_\mathcal{C}$. Instances of such procedures for sets and multisets were presented in sections 2 and 3, for example.

Rewriting into Normal Form. The first steps of the decision procedure consist in rewriting the problem in a normal form more suitable for the final reduction. To this end we:

- separate the equations and disequations between tree terms from the literals of $\mathcal{L}_\mathcal{C}$ by introducing fresh variables and new equalities of the form $c = \alpha(t)$, where c and t are variables representing a collection and a tree respectively (purification)
- flatten the tree terms by introducing fresh variables to represent the subtrees
- eliminate the selector functions (left and right in Fig. 5)

We then guess an arrangement over all tree variables, as well as over the variables denoting elements stored in the nodes of the trees. (Note that this is a non-deterministic polynomial process.) We add to the formula all the equalities and disequalities that represent this arrangement. We then apply unification on the equalities over tree variables and terms. At this point, we either detect unsatisfiability, or we obtain a solved form for the unified equalities. In this solved form, some tree variables are expressed as being terms built using the Node constructor, the Leaf constant and some other tree variables. We call all variables appearing in such a construction *parameter variables.* A property of unification is that parameter variables are never themselves defined as a term constructed over other variables.

As a final transformation step, we rewrite all terms of the form $\alpha(t)$ where t is a non-parameter tree variable as follows: we replace t by its definition in terms of parameter tree variables from the solved form, and partially evaluate α over this term, using the combine and empty functions which define α. After applying this rewriting everywhere, α is only applied to parameter tree variables, and we can write our formula in the following normal form:

$$N(\boldsymbol{T}(\boldsymbol{t}), \boldsymbol{t}) \wedge M(\boldsymbol{t}, \boldsymbol{c}) \wedge F_E \wedge F_C$$

where:

- $\boldsymbol{t}$ denotes all parameter tree variables
- $\boldsymbol{T}(\boldsymbol{t})$ denotes the terms mapped to the non-parameter variables in the solved form
- $N(\boldsymbol{T}(\boldsymbol{t}))$ is a formula expressing that all parameter variables are distinct, that none of them is equal to Leaf, and that they are all distinct from the terms $\boldsymbol{T}(\boldsymbol{t})$
- $M(\boldsymbol{t}, \boldsymbol{c})$ is a conjunction containing for each parameter variable t_i the conjunct $c_i = \alpha(t_i)$ (c_i is introduced if needed)
- F_E is a conjunction of literals of the form $e_i = e_j$ or $e_i \neq e_j$ expressing the arrangement we guessed over the element variables
- F_C is a formula of $\mathcal{L}_C$

The formulas F^E and F^C are already expressed in the collection theory. We call D the conjunction $N(\boldsymbol{T}(\boldsymbol{t}), \boldsymbol{t}) \wedge M(\boldsymbol{t}, \boldsymbol{c})$. To ensure the completeness of our decision procedure, we need to find a formula D_M entirely expressed in $\mathcal{L}_C$ which is equisatisfiable with D. We can then reduce the problem to the satisfiability of $D_M \wedge F_E \wedge F_C$, which we can solve with a decision procedure for $\mathcal{L}_C$. Note that if we choose a formula D_M which is weaker than D, our decision procedure is still sound, but the equisatisfiability is required for completeness. We now give a sufficient criterion for the existence of such an equisatisfiable formula D_M.

4.3 A Completeness Criterion

In [SDK10], we present two sufficient criteria for obtaining a complete decision procedure. Since the first one is strictly subsumed by the second, we omit it here.

Definition 1 (Tree Shape). *Let* SLeaf *be a new constant symbol and* $\mathsf{SNode}(t_1, t_2)$ *a new constructor symbol. The* shape *of a tree t, denoted $\check{s}(t)$, is a ground term built from* SLeaf *and* $\mathsf{SNode}(\_, \_)$ *as follows:*

$$\check{s}(\mathsf{Leaf}) = \mathsf{SLeaf}$$
$$\check{s}(\mathsf{Node}(T_1, e, T_2)) = \mathsf{SNode}(\check{s}(T_1), \check{s}(T_2))$$

Definition 2 (Sufficient Surjectivity). *We call an abstraction function* sufficiently surjective *if and only if, for each natural number $p > 0$ there exist, computable as a function of p*

- *a finite set of shapes S_p*
- *a closed formula M_p in the collection theory such that $M_p(c)$ implies $|\alpha^{-1}(c)| > p$*

such that, for every term t, $M_p(\alpha(t))$ or $\check{s}(t) \in S_p$.

In practice, the formula M_p can introduce new variables as long as it is existentially closed and the decision procedure for the collection theory can handle positive occurrences of existential quantifiers.

We give in [SDK10] a construction for D_M for any sufficiently surjective abstraction. The intuition behind it is that we can proceed by case analysis on the shapes of the parameter tree variables. Since there are finitely many shapes in S_p, we can encode in our formula D_M all possible assignments of these shapes to the tree variables. The situation where the assigned tree is not of a known shape is handled by adding the condition $M_p(\alpha(t))$, which is then guaranteed to hold by hypotheses on S_p and M_p using a strengthened version of the "independence of disequations lemma" [CD94, Page 178]. We omit the technical details, but the sufficient surjectivity condition implies that for n trees such that $M_p(t_1) \wedge \ldots \wedge M_p(t_n)$ and $\alpha(t_1) = \ldots = \alpha(t_n)$, we can always find assignments to $t_1,\ldots,t_n$ such that p disequalities between them are satisfied (see [SDK10, Section 5.3]). By setting p in our formula to the number of disequalities in $N(\boldsymbol{T}(\boldsymbol{t}), \boldsymbol{t})$ we obtain a formula equisatisfiable with D: since D_M encodes all possible assignments of trees to the variables, D_M is satisfiable if D is. In the other direction, if D_M is satisfiable, then we have an assignment for the elements of the trees of known shape, and by the sufficient surjectivity criterion we know that we can find a satisfying assignment for the other ones which will satisfy all disequalities of D.

We conclude by pointing out that the set abstraction, the multiset abstraction, the in-order traversal list abstraction and the sortedness abstraction are all infinitely surjective [SDK10].

5 Combining Theories with Shared Set Operations

We have seen several expressive decidable logics that are useful for specifying correctness properties of software and thus enable automated software verification. The correctness properties that are of practical interest often cannot be expressed in any single one of these logics, but only in their combination. This raises the question whether there exist decidable combinations of these logics and whether the decision procedure for such a combination can reuse the decision procedures for the component logics, e.g., in the style of the approach pioneered by Nelson and Oppen [NO79]. The Nelson-Oppen approach is one of the pillars of modern constraint solvers based on satisfiability modulo theories (SMT) [dMB08,BT07,GBT07]. It enables the combination of quantifier-free stably infinite theories with disjoint signatures. However, the theories that we considered in the previous sections do not fit into this framework because they all involve sets of objects and are therefore not disjoint.

To support a broader class of theories than the traditional Nelson-Oppen combination, we consider decision procedures for the combination of *possibly quantified* formulas in *non-disjoint* theories. In [WPK09] we explored the case of the combination of non-disjoint theories sharing operations on *sets of uninterpreted elements*, a case that was not considered before. The theories that we consider have the property that the tuples of cardinalities of Venn regions over shared set variables in the models of a formula are a semilinear set (i.e., expressible in Presburger arithmetic).

Reduction-based decision procedure. The idea of deciding a combination of logics is to check the satisfiability of a conjunction of formulas $A \wedge B$ by using one decision procedure, D_A, for A, and another decision procedure, D_B, for B. To obtain a complete decision procedure, D_A and D_B must communicate to ensure that a model found by D_A and a model found by D_B can be merged into a model for $A \wedge B$.

We follow a reduction approach to decision procedures. The first decision procedure, D_A, computes a *projection*, S_A, of A onto *shared* set variables, which are free in both A and B. This projection is semantically equivalent to existentially quantifying over predicates and variables that are free in A but not in B; it is the strongest consequence of A expressible only using the shared set variables. D_B similarly computes the projection S_B of B. This reduces the satisfiability of $A \wedge B$ to satisfiability of the formula $S_A \wedge S_B$, which contains only set variables.

A logic for shared constraints on sets. A key parameter of our combination approach is the logic of sets used to express the projections S_A and S_B. A suitable logic depends on the logics of formulas A and B. We consider as the logics for A, B the logics we have discussed in the previous sections and other expressive logics we found useful based on our experience with the Jahob verification system [ZKR08, Wie09]. Remarkably, the smallest logic needed to express the projection formulas in these logics has the expressive power of BAPA, described in Section 2. We showed that the decision procedures for these logics can be naturally extended to a reduction to BAPA that captures precisely the constraints on set variables. The existence of these reductions, along with quantifier elimination [KNR06] and NP membership of the quantifier-free fragment [KR07], make BAPA an appealing reduction target for expressive logics.

We proved that 1) (quantified) Boolean Algebra with Presburger Arithmetic (Section 2), 2) quantifier-free multisets with cardinality constraints (Section 3), 3) weak monadic second-order logic of trees [TW68], 4) two-variable logic with counting C^2 [PH05], 5) the Bernays-Schönfinkel-Ramsey-class of first-order logic [Ram30], and 6) certain algebraic data types with abstraction functions (Section 4), all meet the conditions of our combination technique. Consequently, we obtain the decidability of quantifier-free combination of formulas in these logics. In the following we give an overview of our combination technique.

5.1 Example: Proving a Verification Condition

Our example shows a verification condition formula generated when verifying an unbounded linked data structure. The formula belongs to our new decidable class obtained by combining several decidable logics.

Decidability of the verification condition. Fig. 9 shows the verification condition formula for a method (`insertAt`) that inserts a node into a linked list. The validity of this formula implies that invoking a method in a state satisfying

```
tree [left , right ] ∧ left p = null ∧ p ∈ nodes ∧
nodes={x. (root,x) ∈ {(x,y). left x = y|right x = y}^*} ∧
content={x. ∃ n. n ≠ null ∧ n ∈ nodes ∧ data n = x} ∧
e ∉ content ∧ nodes ⊆ alloc ∧
tmp ∉ alloc ∧ left tmp = null ∧ right tmp = null ∧
data tmp = null ∧ (∀ y. data y ≠ tmp) ∧
nodes1={x. (root,x) ∈ {(x,y). (left (p:=tmp)) x = y) | right x = y} ∧
content1={x. ∃ n. n ≠ null ∧ n ∈ nodes1 ∧ (data(tmp:=e)) n = x} →
        card content1 = card content + 1
```

Fig. 9. Verification condition

```
SHARED SETS: nodes, nodes1, content, content1, {e}, {tmp}
WS2S FRAGMENT: tree[left,right] ∧ left p = null ∧ p ∈ nodes ∧ left tmp = null ∧
  right tmp = null ∧ nodes={x. (root,x) ∈ {(x,y). left x = y|right x = y}^*} ∧
  nodes1={x. (root,x) ∈ {(x,y). (left (p:=tmp)) x = y) | right x = y}
CONSEQUENCE: nodes1=nodes ∪ {tmp}
C2 FRAGMENT: data tmp = null ∧ (∀ y. data y ≠ tmp) ∧ tmp ∉ alloc ∧ nodes ⊆ alloc ∧
   content={x. ∃ n. n ≠ null ∧ n ∈ nodes ∧ data n = x} ∧
   content1={x. ∃ n. n ≠ null ∧ n ∈ nodes1 ∧ (data(tmp:=e)) n = x}
CONSEQUENCE: nodes1 ≠ nodes ∪ {tmp} ∨ content1 = content ∪ {e}
BAPA FRAGMENT: e ∉ content ∧ card content1 ≠ card content + 1
CONSEQUENCE: e ∉ content ∧ card content1 ≠ card content + 1
```

Fig. 10. Negation of Fig. 9, and consequences on shared sets

the precondition results in a state that satisfies the postcondition of `insertAt`. The formula contains the transitive closure operator, quantifiers, set comprehensions, and the cardinality operator. Nevertheless, there is a (syntactically defined) decidable class of formulas that contains the verification condition in Fig. 9. This decidable class is a set-sharing combination of three decidable logics, and can be decided using the method we present in this paper.

To understand the method for proving the formula in Fig. 9, consider the problem of showing the unsatisfiability of the negation of the formula. Fig. 10 shows the conjuncts of the negation, grouped according to three decidable logics to which the conjuncts belong: 1) weak monadic second-order logic of two successors (WS2S) 2) two-variable logic with counting C^2 3) Boolean Algebra with Presburger Arithmetic (BAPA). For the formula in each of the fragments, Fig. 10 also shows a consequence formula that contains only shared sets and statements about their cardinalities. (We represent elements as singleton sets, so we admit formulas sharing elements as well.)

A decision procedure. Note that the conjunction of the consequences of three formula fragments is an unsatisfiable formula. This shows that the original formula is unsatisfiable as well (the verification condition is valid). In general, our decidability result shows that the decision procedures of logics such as WS2S and C^2 can be naturally extended to compute "precise" consequences of formulas involving given shared sets. When a precise consequence is satisfiable in some assignment to set variables, it means that the original formula is also satisfiable with the same values of set variables. The consequences are all expressed in BAPA, which is decidable. In summary, the following is a decision procedure for satisfiability of combined formulas:

1. split the formula into fragments (belonging to, e.g. WS2S, C^2, or BAPA);
2. for each fragment compute its strongest BAPA consequence;
3. check the satisfiability of the conjunction of consequences.

5.2 Combination by Reduction to BAPA

The Satisfiability Problem. We are interested in an algorithm to determine whether there exists a structure $\alpha \in \mathcal{M}$ in which the following formula is true

$$B(F_1, \dots, F_n) \tag{1}$$

where

1. $F_1, \dots, F_n$ are formulas with $\mathsf{FV}(F_i) \subseteq \{A_1, \dots, A_p, x_1, \dots, x_q\}$.
2. $V_S = \{A_1, \dots, A_p\}$ are variables of sort set, whereas $x_1, \dots, x_q$ are the remaining variables.[2]
3. Each formula F_i belongs to a given class of formulas, $\mathcal{F}_i$. For each $\mathcal{F}_i$ we assume that there is a corresponding theory $\mathcal{T}_i \subseteq \mathcal{F}_i$.
4. $B(F_1, \dots, F_n)$ denotes a formula built from $F_1, \dots, F_n$ using the propositional operations $\wedge, \vee$. [3]
5. As the set of structures $\mathcal{M}$ we consider all structures α of interest (with finite $[\![\mathsf{obj}]\!]$, interpreting BAPA symbols in the standard way) for which $\alpha(\cup_{i=1}^{n} \mathcal{T}_i)$.
6. (Set Sharing Condition) If $i \neq j$, then $\mathsf{FV}(\{F_i\} \cup \mathcal{T}_i) \cap \mathsf{FV}(\{F_j\} \cup \mathcal{T}_j) \subseteq V_S$.

Note that, as a special case, if we embed a class of first-order formulas into our framework, we obtain a framework that supports sharing unary predicates, but not e.g. binary predicates.

Combination Theorem. The formula B in (1) is satisfiable iff one of the disjuncts in its disjunctive normal form is satisfiable. Consider any of the disjuncts $F_1 \wedge \dots \wedge F_m$ for $m \leq n$. By definition of the satisfiability problem (1), $F_1 \wedge \dots \wedge F_m$ is satisfiable iff there exists a structure α such that for each $1 \leq i \leq m$, for each $G \in \{F_i\} \cup \mathcal{T}_i$, we have $\alpha(G) = \mathsf{true}$. Let each variable x_i have some sort s_i (such as $\mathsf{obj}^2 \to \mathsf{bool}$). Then the satisfiability of $F_1 \wedge \dots \wedge F_m$ is equivalent to the following condition:

$$\begin{array}{l}\exists \text{ finite set } u.\ \exists a_1, \dots, a_p \subseteq u.\ \exists v_1 \in [\![s_1]\!]^u. \dots\ \exists v_q \in [\![s_q]\!]^u.\ \bigwedge_{i=1}^{m} \\ \{\mathsf{obj} \to u, A_1 \mapsto a_1, \dots, A_p \mapsto a_p, x_1 \mapsto v_1, \dots, x_q \mapsto v_q\}(\{F_i\} \cup \mathcal{T}_i)\end{array} \tag{2}$$

---

[2] For notational simplicity we do not consider variables of sort obj because they can be represented as singleton sets, of sort set.

[3] The absence of negation is usually not a loss of generality because most $\mathcal{F}_i$ are closed under negation so B is the negation-normal form of a quantifier-free combination.

By the set sharing condition, each of the variables $x_1, \ldots, x_q$ appears only in one conjunct and can be moved inwards from the top level to this conjunct. Using x_{ij} to denote the j-th variable in the i-th conjunct we obtain the condition

$$\exists \text{ finite set } u.\ \exists a_1, \ldots, a_p \subseteq u.\ \bigwedge_{i=1}^{m} C_i(u, a_1, \ldots, a_p) \tag{3}$$

where $C_i(u, a_1, \ldots, a_p)$ is

$$\exists v_{i1} \ldots \exists v_{iw_i}.$$
$$\{\mathsf{obj} \to u, A_1 \mapsto a_1, \ldots, A_p \mapsto a_p, x_{i1} \mapsto v_{i1}, \ldots, x_{iw_i} \mapsto v_{iw_i}\}(\{F_i\} \cup \mathcal{T}_i)$$

The idea of our combination method is to simplify each condition $C_i(u, a_1, \ldots, a_p)$ into the truth value of a BAPA formula. If this is possible, we say that there exists a BAPA reduction.

Definition 3 (BAPA Reduction). *If $\mathcal{F}_i$ is a set of formulas and $\mathcal{T}_i \subseteq \mathcal{F}_i$ a theory, we call a function $\rho : \mathcal{F}_i \to \mathcal{F}_{\mathsf{BAPA}}$ a BAPA reduction for $(\mathcal{F}_i, \mathcal{T}_i)$ iff for every formula $F_i \in \mathcal{F}_i$ and for all finite u and $a_1, \ldots, a_p \subseteq u$, the condition*

$$\exists v_{i1} \ldots \exists v_{iw_i}.$$
$$\{\mathsf{obj} \to u, A_1 \mapsto a_1, \ldots, A_p \mapsto a_p, x_{i1} \mapsto v_{i1}, \ldots, x_{iw_i} \mapsto v_{iw_i}\}(\{F_i\} \cup \mathcal{T}_i)$$

is equivalent to the condition $\{\mathsf{obj} \to u, A_1 \mapsto a_1, \ldots, A_p \mapsto a_p\}(\rho(F_i))$.

A computable BAPA reduction is a BAPA reduction which is computable as a function on formula syntax trees.

Theorem 4. *Suppose that for every $1 \leq i \leq n$ for $(\mathcal{F}_i, \mathcal{T}_i)$ there exists a computable BAPA reduction ρ_i. Then the satisfiability problem (1) is decidable.*

Specifically, to check satisfiability of the formula $B(F_1, \ldots, F_n)$, compute $B(\rho_1(F_1), \ldots, \rho_n(F_n))$ and then check its satisfiability using a BAPA decision procedure [KNR06, KR07].

5.3 BAPA Reductions

The proof that a particular decidable logic exhibits a BAPA reduction follows a generic recipe. Given such a logic $\mathcal{L} = (\mathcal{F}, \mathcal{T})$ and a formula $F \in \mathcal{F}$, let $V_1, \ldots, V_n$ be the Venn regions over the free set variables in F. To prove that $\mathcal{L}$ is BAPA-reducible, one needs to characterize the cardinality vectors of the V_i in all the models of F: $\mathcal{V}(F) = \{\, (|\, \alpha(V_1)\, |, \ldots, |\, \alpha(V_n)\, |) \mid \alpha(\mathcal{T} \cup \{F\}) = 1 \,\}$ and show that this set is semilinear. Moreover, a finite representation of the set $\mathcal{V}(F)$ in terms of base and set vectors must be effectively computable from F, by extending the decision procedure for $\mathcal{L}$ appropriately. We have shown [WPK09, Theorems 5, 11, 12, 13], [SDK10] that the decision procedures for a number of expressive decidable logics can indeed be extended in this way to BAPA reductions.

Theorem 5. *There exist BAPA reductions for the following logics (see Figure 1)*

1. *weak monadic second-order logic of trees [TW68]*
2. *two-variable logic with counting* C^2 *[PH05]*
3. *the Bernays-Schönfinkel-Ramsey class of first-order logic [Ram30]*
4. *quantifier-free multisets with cardinality constraints (Figure 4)*
5. *logic of algebraic data types with the* content *function (in Figure 7)*

Thus, the set-sharing combination of all these logics is decidable.

References

[BGG97] Börger, E., Grädel, E., Gurevich, Y.: The Classical Decision Problem. Springer, Heidelberg (1997)

[BM07] Bradley, A.R., Manna, Z.: The Calculus of Computation. Springer, Heidelberg (2007)

[BST07] Barrett, C., Shikanian, I., Tinelli, C.: An abstract decision procedure for satisfiability in the theory of recursive data types. Electronic Notes in Theoretical Computer Science 174(8), 23–37 (2007)

[BT07] Barrett, C., Tinelli, C.: CVC3. In: Damm, W., Hermanns, H. (eds.) CAV 2007. LNCS, vol. 4590, pp. 298–302. Springer, Heidelberg (2007)

[CD94] Comon, H., Delor, C.: Equational formulae with membership constraints. Information and Computation 112(2), 167–216 (1994)

[dMB08] de Moura, L., Bjørner, N.S.: Z3: An efficient SMT solver. In: Ramakrishnan, C.R., Rehof, J. (eds.) TACAS 2008. LNCS, vol. 4963, pp. 337–340. Springer, Heidelberg (2008)

[dMB09] de Moura, L., Bjørner, N.: Generalized, efficient array decision procedures. In: FMCAD (2009)

[ES06] Eisenbrand, F., Shmonin, G.: Carathéodory bounds for integer cones. Operations Research Letters 34(5), 564–568 (2006)

[GBT07] Ge, Y., Barrett, C., Tinelli, C.: Solving quantified verification conditions using satisfiability modulo theories. In: Pfenning, F. (ed.) CADE 2007. LNCS (LNAI), vol. 4603, pp. 167–182. Springer, Heidelberg (2007)

[GHN+04] Ganzinger, H., Hagen, G., Nieuwenhuis, R., Oliveras, A., Tinelli, C.: DPLL(T): Fast decision procedures. In: Alur, R., Peled, D.A. (eds.) CAV 2004. LNCS, vol. 3114, pp. 175–188. Springer, Heidelberg (2004)

[GS66] Ginsburg, S., Spanier, E.: Semigroups, Presburger formulas and languages. Pacific Journal of Mathematics 16(2), 285–296 (1966)

[KNR06] Kuncak, V., Nguyen, H.H., Rinard, M.: Deciding Boolean Algebra with Presburger Arithmetic. J. of Automated Reasoning (2006)

[KR07] Kuncak, V., Rinard, M.: Towards efficient satisfiability checking for Boolean Algebra with Presburger Arithmetic. In: Pfenning, F. (ed.) CADE 2007. LNCS (LNAI), vol. 4603, pp. 215–230. Springer, Heidelberg (2007)

[LS04] Lahiri, S.K., Seshia, S.A.: The UCLID decision procedure. In: Alur, R., Peled, D.A. (eds.) CAV 2004. LNCS, vol. 3114, pp. 475–478. Springer, Heidelberg (2004)

[NO79] Nelson, G., Oppen, D.C.: Simplification by cooperating decision procedures. ACM TOPLAS 1(2), 245–257 (1979)

[Opp78] Oppen, D.C.: Reasoning about recursively defined data structures. In: POPL, pp. 151–157 (1978)

[OSV08] Odersky, M., Spoon, L., Venners, B.: Programming in Scala: a comprehensive step-by-step guide. Artima Press (2008)

[Pap81] Papadimitriou, C.H.: On the complexity of integer programming. J. ACM 28(4), 765–768 (1981)

[PH05] Pratt-Hartmann, I.: Complexity of the two-variable fragment with counting quantifiers. Journal of Logic, Language and Information 14(3), 369–395 (2005)

[PK08a] Piskac, R., Kuncak, V.: Decision procedures for multisets with cardinality constraints. In: Logozzo, F., Peled, D.A., Zuck, L.D. (eds.) VMCAI 2008. LNCS, vol. 4905, pp. 218–232. Springer, Heidelberg (2008)

[PK08b] Piskac, R., Kuncak, V.: Fractional collections with cardinality bounds. In: Kaminski, M., Martini, S. (eds.) CSL 2008. LNCS, vol. 5213, pp. 124–138. Springer, Heidelberg (2008)

[PK08c] Piskac, R., Kuncak, V.: Linear arithmetic with stars. In: Gupta, A., Malik, S. (eds.) CAV 2008. LNCS, vol. 5123, pp. 268–280. Springer, Heidelberg (2008)

[Pot91] Pottier, L.: Minimal solutions of linear diophantine systems: Bounds and algorithms. In: Book, R.V. (ed.) RTA 1991. LNCS, vol. 488. Springer, Heidelberg (1991)

[Pre29] Presburger, M.: Über die Vollständigkeit eines gewissen Systems der Aritmethik ganzer Zahlen, in welchem die Addition als einzige Operation hervortritt. In: Comptes Rendus du premier Congrès des Mathématiciens des Pays slaves, Warsawa, pp. 92–101 (1929)

[PST00] Pacholski, L., Szwast, W., Tendera, L.: Complexity results for first-order two-variable logic with counting. SIAM J. on Computing 29(4), 1083–1117 (2000)

[Ram30] Ramsey, F.P.: On a problem of formal logic. Proc. London Math. Soc., s2-30, 264–286 (1930)

[SBDL01] Stump, A., Barrett, C.W., Dill, D.L., Levitt, J.R.: A decision procedure for an extensional theory of arrays. In: LICS, pp. 29–37 (2001)

[SDK10] Suter, P., Dotta, M., Kuncak, V.: Decision procedures for algebraic data types with abstractions. In: POPL (2010)

[Sko19] Skolem, T.: Untersuchungen über die Axiome des Klassenkalküls und über Produktations- und Summationsprobleme, welche gewisse Klassen von Aussagen betreffen. Skrifter utgit av Vidnskapsselskapet i Kristiania, I. klasse, no. 3, Oslo (1919)

[TW68] Thatcher, J.W., Wright, J.B.: Generalized finite automata theory with an application to a decision problem of second-order logic. Mathematical Systems Theory 2(1), 57–81 (1968)

[Wie09] Wies, T.: Symbolic Shape Analysis. PhD thesis, University of Freiburg (2009)

[WPK09] Wies, T., Piskac, R., Kuncak, V.: Combining theories with shared set operations. In: FroCoS: Frontiers in Combining Systems (2009)

[ZKR08] Zee, K., Kuncak, V., Rinard, M.: Full functional verification of linked data structures. In: PLDI (2008)

Temporal Reasoning for Procedural Programs*

Rajeev Alur[1] and Swarat Chaudhuri[2]

[1] University of Pennsylvania, USA
[2] Pennsylvania State University, USA

Abstract. While temporal verification of programs is a topic with a long history, its traditional basis—semantics based on word languages—is ill-suited for modular reasoning about procedural programs. We address this issue by defining the semantics of procedural (potentially recursive) programs using *languages of nested words* and developing a framework for temporal reasoning around it. This generalization has two benefits. First, this style of reasoning naturally unifies Manna-Pnueli-style temporal reasoning with Hoare-style reasoning about structured programs. Second, it allows verification of "non-regular" properties of specific procedural contexts—e.g., "If a lock is acquired in a context, then it is released in the same context." We present proof rules for a variety of properties such as *local safety*, *local response*, and *staircase reactivity*; our rules are sufficient to prove all temporal properties over nested words. We show that our rules are sound and relatively complete.

1 Introduction

A prominent approach to program verification relies on identifying pre and post-conditions for every block. For example, the Hoare triple $\{\varphi\}P\{\psi\}$ for partial correctness means that if we execute the program P starting from a state satisfying the state predicate φ, then if the program terminates, the final state satisfies ψ [12,4,7]. The corresponding proof system contains a rule for each of the syntactic constructs for building complex programs, allowing modular proofs of structured programs. The last few years have seen renewed interest in such proofs, largely due to the coming-of-age of powerful decision procedures.

While Hoare-style reasoning can establish functional correctness of programs, it is not well-suited for reasoning about reactive programs. The most widely accepted formalism for verification of reactive programs is temporal logic [17]. In temporal reasoning, the semantics of a program P is defined to be a set of executions, where each execution is a sequence of program states; the specification is a formula φ of linear temporal logic (LTL); and P satisfies φ if all its executions are satisfying models of φ. Manna-Pnueli-style proof systems for temporal logics show how to establish temporal properties of programs by reasoning about state formulas [15,16]. A limitation of these rules, however, is that they do not exploit the modularity offered by the procedural structure of programs. Also, the temporal properties that they prove cannot refer to specific procedural contexts.

* This research was partially supported by NSF award CCF-0905464.

G. Barthe and M. Hermenegildo (Eds.): VMCAI 2010, LNCS 5944, pp. 45–60, 2010.

For example, the property "If a lock is acquired in a procedural context, then it is released before the context ends," which refers to the non-regular nesting of procedural contexts, is inexpressible in temporal logic.

There has been, of late, a resurgence of interest in program verification due to the success of model checking tools like SLAM [6]. In most of these settings, even though the analyzed program is sequential, the requirements are temporal (e.g., "Lock A must be acquired *after* lock B"); thus, temporal reasoning is needed. Yet, any verification method that does not exploit the modularity afforded by procedures will not scale to large programs. As a result, a form of *procedure-modular* temporal reasoning seems important to develop. Also, as properties of specific procedural contexts arise naturally in procedural programs, it seems natural to ask for proofs for these. This paper offers a framework for temporal reasoning that satisfies both these criteria.

Here, the execution of a program is modeled as a *nested word* [3]. Nested words are a model of data with both a linear ordering and a hierarchically nested matching of items. In nested-word modeling of program executions, we augment the linear sequencing of program states with *markup tags* matching procedure calls with returns. The benefits of this modeling have already been shown for software model checking: when all variables are boolean, viewing the program as a finite-state nested-word-automaton generating a regular language of nested words allows model checking of non-regular temporal properties [2,1,5].

In this paper, we first define a simple procedural language, then define its intensional semantics using nested words. Here, each state has information only about the variables currently in scope, and the procedure stack is not made explicit. Then we use it to develop a framework of modular reasoning for procedural programs. State formulas here can refer to the values of variables in scope as well as to their values when the procedure was invoked. We use them to capture *local invariants* (properties that hold at each reachable state of a procedure) and *summaries* (properties that hold when the procedure returns). The classical notion of inductive invariants is now extended to local invariants. Establishing such invariants requires mutually inductive reasoning using summaries—e.g., to establish a local invariant of a procedure $\mathtt{p}$ that calls a procedure $\mathtt{q}$, we use a summary of $\mathtt{q}$, establishing which may require the use of a summary of $\mathtt{p}$.

Based on these ideas, we develop proof rules for several safety and liveness properties of procedural programs. In a nested word, there are many notions of paths such as *global*, *local*, and *staircase* [2,1,13]—temporal logics for nested words contain modalities such as "always" and "eventually" parameterized by the path type. This makes these logics more expressive than LTL—e.g., we can now express *local safety properties* such as "At all points in the top-level procedural context, φ holds" and *local liveness properties* such as "φ holds eventually in the top-level context."

We show that the classical rules proving safety and liveness using inductive invariants and ranking functions can be generalized to these properties. For example, to prove the local safety property above, we use a local invariant for the top-level procedure $\mathtt{p}$ that implies φ. Proving local liveness requires us to combine reasoning using local invariants and summaries with ranking-function-based techniques. Along with known expressiveness results for nested words [13,5], they ensure that we have a proof system for all temporal logic properties of nested words.

We address soundness and completeness of our proof rules. For example, for *local safety*, we show that our rule is sound; that it is complete provided the set of locally reachable states is definable within the underlying assertion language for writing state properties; and that this set is definable provided the assertion language is first-order and can specify a tree data structure. This establishes *relative completeness* of this rule in the style of Manna and Pnueli [14]. Similar results hold for local liveness, as well as for safety and liveness properties interpreted on the global and staircase paths.

The paper is organized as follows. Section 2 reviews nested words. Sec. 3 fixes a procedural language, and Section 4 defines local invariants and summaries. Section 5, our main technical section, uses these in temporal verification.

Related Work. Hoare-style assertional reasoning [12,4] for sequential programs is inherently procedure-modular; local invariants and summaries also show up in this setting [7]. Analysis using summaries is also key to interprocedural program analysis [22,20,21,9] and software model checking [6,11]. The standard references for temporal logic are by Manna and Pnueli [15,16]; see [14] for completeness proofs. The theory of nested words is due to Alur and Madhusudan [3]. There have been many papers on nested words and associated logics recently [13,2,1,5]—while most of these focus on model checking (of pushdown models) and expressiveness, a recent paper uses the theory of nested words in Craig-interpolant-based verification of general recursive programs [10].

The paper most relevant to this work is by Podelski et al [19]; it uses summaries to compositionally verify termination and liveness of recursive programs. Also, an algorithmic termination analysis of recursive programs, also based on summaries, appears in [8]. In contrast, this paper uses a nested word semantics of programs, and handles all properties specifiable in temporal logics over nested words, including those explicitly referring to procedural contexts.

2 Nested Words

Let Σ be an alphabet and $\texttt{<}, \texttt{>} \notin \Sigma$ be two symbols respectively known as the *call and return tags*. For a word w and $i \in \mathbb{N}$, let $w(i)$ denote the symbol at the i-th position of w; and for $i, j \in \mathbb{N}$ and $j < i$, let w_{ji} denote the word $w_j w_{j+1} \dots w_i$. Let a word w_{ji} as above be *matched* if it is of the form $w ::= ww \mid \sigma \mid \texttt{<}w\texttt{>}$, where σ ranges over Σ. A *nested word* over Σ is now defined to be a finite or infinite word w over $(\Sigma \cup \{\texttt{<}, \texttt{>}\})$ such that for each i with $w(i) = \texttt{>}$, there is a $j < i$ such that $w(j) = \texttt{<}$ and w_{ji} is matched.

A position i in w (positions are numbered $0, 1, \dots$) is a *call* if $w(i+1) = \texttt{<}$, and a *return* if $w(i-1) = \texttt{>}$. If i is a call, j is a return, and $w_{(i+1)\ (j-1)}$ is matched, then j is the *matching return* of i. Calls without matching returns are *pending*. For example, consider a nested word $w' = s_0 s_1 \texttt{<} s_3 \texttt{<} s_5 \texttt{<} s_7 \texttt{>} s_9 \texttt{>} s_{11}$. Here, position

1 is a call (as $w(2) = <$), 9 is a return, 1 is a pending call, and 9 is the matching return of 5. A *language of nested words* is a set L of nested words.

Intuitively, we use nested words to model executions of procedural programs, and languages of nested words to define a program's intensional semantics. We interpret Σ as the set of program states, and the call and return tags as respectively marking the beginning and end of procedural contexts. Call and return positions respectively model the points right before and after control enters/exits a context, while a pending call is a call that does not terminate.

Notably, nested words can also be defined as a logical structure that enriches a word with a matching relation [5,1]. The present definition may be seen as defining a *linear encoding* of such structures.

Local, global, and staircase paths. The markup provided by the call/return tags in a nested word allows us to distinguish between the parts of the word corresponding to different procedural contexts. These "parts" are naturally viewed as subsequences. Of them, three are of particular interest.

The *global path* in w is the word obtained by removing all call and return tags from w. The *local path* in w is the word w' obtained by erasing from w: (1) every sub-word w_{jk} such that $w(j) = <$, $w(k) = >$, and w_{jk} is matched; and (2) the suffix of w starting at the position $(i+1)$, for the least i such that $w(i)$ is a pending call. For example, the local path in our example nested word w' is $s_0 s_1$.

The *staircase path* in w is the word w' obtained by first erasing from w every sub-word w_{jk} such that $w(j) = <$, $w(k) = >$, and w_{jk} is matched, and then erasing all call tags from the word that results. For example, the staircase path in our example nested word w' is $s_0 s_1 s_3 s_{11}$.

Intuitively, if w models a program execution, then the values of its global variables flow along its global path. The local path of captures the flow of local data in the "top-level" procedural context. If a local path reaches a call that eventually returns, it "jumps" to its matching return; if it reaches a pending call, it terminates. Staircase paths also skip across terminating procedure calls. Unlike local paths, they continue into the new context on seeing a pending call. Thus, staircase paths capture local data flow, as well flow of global data into nonterminating calls.

3 A Simple Procedural Language

Now we fix a simple, sequential language (called SPL from now on) whose programs we analyze. The language allows local and global variables and recursion. For brevity, we assume that procedures do not take parameters or return values; these features are encoded using global variables.

The syntax of programs *Prog* and commands *Com* of SPL is as in Fig. 1. Here, p is a procedure name, x is a variable, l is a label, and *Aexp*, *Bexp* and *AConst* respectively stand for arithmetic and boolean expressions, and arithmetic constants. We restrict ourselves to *well-formed* programs where each label appears at most once. From now on, we assume an arbitrary but fixed program P.

The set of global variables in P is denoted by GV, and the set of local variables in a procedure p is denoted by $LV(\mathtt{p})$. The set of procedures is denoted by $Proc(P)$ or simply $Proc$. For each procedure p, we denote by $Labels(\mathtt{p})$ the set of labels appearing in p; this set contains a special label $\perp_{\mathtt{p}}$ that is reached when p terminates. The *first* label executed when p is run is denoted by $First(\mathtt{p})$.

$Prog$ ::= [**global** $Gdec$] $Pdec$

$Gdec$ ::= x | $Gdec$, $Gdec$

$Ldec$ ::= x := $AConst$ | $Ldec$, $Ldec$

$Pdec$ ::= **proc** p() = $Pbody$ | $Pdec$ $Pdec$

$Pbody$ ::= [**local** $Ldec$] Com

Com ::= l: **skip** | l: x := $Aexp$ | l: p()
  | Com; Com | l: **while** $Bexp$ **do** Com
  | l: **if** $Bexp$ **then** Com **else** Com

Fig. 1. Syntax of SPL (terms in square brackets are optional)

We use a standard definition of the interprocedural control-flow graph (CFG) of P. Nodes here are labels of P. The edges are of three types: *call edges*, *local edges*, and *summary edges*. To define these, we construct a relation $Flow(\mathtt{p})$ between the labels of p. Suppose the label l in p does not label a procedure call, and suppose an execution proceeds from l to a label l' if the guard b is true. In this case, $(l, b, l') \in Flow(\mathtt{p})$. If l is the "last" label in p, then $(l, tt, \perp_{\mathtt{p}}) \in Flow(\mathtt{p})$. If l labels a call and l' is the label to which the called procedure returns control on termination, then $(l, tt, l') \in Flow(\mathtt{p})$.

```
global flag, n
proc inc_n (): void = ...
proc bar() = local cond:=true
L1: while (cond) do
L2:   flag:=true;
L3:   if (*) then (L4: inc_n()) else
  (L5: flag:=false; L6: cond:=false)

proc main() =
L7: flag:=false; L8: n:=0;
L9: while (true) do
          (L10: bar(); L11: inc_n())
```

Fig. 2. Flagging and unflagging

A *call edge* from procedure p to procedure q is now defined as a directed edge $e = (l, m)$, where $m = First(\mathtt{q})$ and l is the label of a command calling q. A *local edge* $e = (l, b, m)$ in the procedure p goes from l to m (both l and m are labels in p), and exists only if l does not label a procedure call and $(l, b, m) \in Flow(\mathtt{p})$. A *summary edge* $e = (l, \mathtt{q}, m)$ in p goes from l to m, and exists only if l labels a call to a procedure q, and $(l, tt, m) \in Flow(\mathtt{p})$.

The sets of call, local, and summary edges in the CFG of P are respectively denoted by E_{call}, E_{loc}, and E_{sum}. Finally, we define the *restriction* $P_{\mathtt{p}}$ of a program P with respect to a procedure p as the program obtained by removing from P all procedures unreachable from p in the CFG of P.

Figure 2 shows a program with procedures `main` and `bar`. The procedure `bar` need not terminate, but if it does, it sets the flag to `false` before doing so.

Nested execution semantics. Now we give a semantics for SPL programs using nested words. Let us fix a set Val from which the values of our variables are drawn, and a special variable pc that captures the program counter and does not appear in the text of any of our programs. Now we define a *state* of a procedure p to be a map σ such that $\sigma(pc)$ is a label in p, and for each

$x \in GV \cup LV(p)$, $\sigma(x) \in Val$. An *entry state* of a procedure p is a state σ such that $\sigma(pc) = First(p)$, and for each local variable u of p, we have $\sigma(u) = n$ if u is initialized to n in p. We denote the set of states of p by *States*(p), and the set of states in P by *States*.

Note that a state as defined above does not contain a procedure stack. Let a *nested execution* now be a finite or infinite nested word over *States*. Our semantics assigns, to each procedure p in P, a set of nested executions.

Let a state σ of p be a *call state*, calling a procedure q, if $\sigma(pc)$ is the label of a call to q. For a call state σ of p calling q, $Entry(\sigma, q)$ denotes the state $\sigma_{en} \in States(q)$ such that: (1) $\sigma_{en}(pc) = First(q)$; (2) for each $g \in GVar(P)$, we have $\sigma_{en}(g) = \sigma(g)$; (3) for each local variable u of q initialized to n, we have $\sigma_{en}(u) = n$. Intuitively, this is the entry state of q that is reached when q is called from the state σ. Likewise, for each call state σ_{call} of p that calls q, and state $\sigma_{ex} \in States(q)$ such that $\sigma_{ex}(pc) = \perp_q$, we define a *return state* $Retn(\sigma_{call}, \sigma_{ex})$ of p where control returns from the call.

Also, we define the *sequential composition* $w_1; w_2$ of two nested executions w_1 and w_2. Intuitively, this is the execution obtained by running w_1 till termination, then continuing with w_2. Formally, $w_1; w_2$ equals:
- w_1 if w_1 is infinite;
- $w_1'.\sigma_1.w_2'$, if $w_1 = w_1'.\sigma_1$ and $w_2 = \sigma_2.w_2'$ for σ_1 and σ_2 such that: (1) $\sigma_1(pc) = \perp_p$ for some p, and (2) σ_1 and σ_2 agree on the values of all variables; and
- undefined otherwise.

For languages L_1 and L_2 of nested executions, we define $L_1; L_2 = \{w; w' : w \in L_1, w' \in L_2\}$.

The semantics of a procedure p is now defined using sets $[\![p]\!]^*$ and $[\![p]\!]^\omega$ respectively comprising its finite and infinite executions. The semantics of p is the union of these sets. We define these using sets $[\![c]\!]_p^*$ and $[\![c]\!]_p^\omega$, respectively comprising the finite and infinite executions of each command c in p.

As $[\![p]\!]^*$ and $[\![c]\!]_p^*$ only contain terminating executions, they can be obtained by finite unrolling of loops and recursion. Accordingly, we define them as the *least fixpoint* of equations following the syntax of p and c. We only show a few cases:

1. $[\![c_1; c_2]\!]_p^* = [\![c_1]\!]_p^*; [\![c_2]\!]_p^*$.
2. $[\![l\colon x := Aexp]\!]_p^*$ comprises all nested executions of the form $\sigma.\sigma'$, where $\sigma(pc) = l$, and σ' is obtained by taking σ and setting pc to $\perp_p$ and x to the value of the expression *Aexp* in σ.
3. If c is a procedure call of the form $l\colon q()$, then $[\![c]\!]_p^* = L$, where L is the set of words $w' = \sigma.\langle.\sigma_{en}.w.\sigma_{ex}.\rangle.\sigma'$ such that: (1) $\sigma, \sigma' \in States(p)$ and $\sigma(pc) = l$; (2) $\sigma_{en} = Entry(\sigma, q)$; (3) $\sigma_{en}.w.\sigma_{ex} \in [\![q]\!]^*$; and (4) $\sigma' = Retn(\sigma_{ex}, \sigma)$.
4. If the procedure p has the command c as its body, then $[\![p]\!]^* = [\![c]\!]_p^* \cap L_{En}(p)$ where $L_{En}(p)$ is the set of nested words over *States* starting with an entry state of p.

Infinite nested executions of procedures and commands are defined similarly, except: (1) for commands that terminate—e.g., assignments—the set of infinite executions is empty; and (2) we have to take greatest fixpoints to define the semantics of loops and procedure calls. The semantics of the procedure p, denoted by $[\![\mathtt{p}]\!]$, is now given by $[\![\mathtt{p}]\!] = [\![\mathtt{p}]\!]^* \cup [\![\mathtt{p}]\!]^\omega$.

Finally, we define the notion of *local reachability* between states. For $\sigma, \sigma' \in States(\mathtt{p})$, σ' is *locally reachable* from σ if for some nested execution $w \in [\![\mathtt{p}]\!]$ and positions i and $j \geq i$, we have $w(i) = \sigma$, $w(j) = \sigma'$, and the word w_{ij} is matched.

4 Local Invariants and Summaries

Now we develop a class of invariants, called *local invariants*, that apply only to execution fragments within a single procedural context. To derive them, we use *procedure summaries* and reason with respect to environment assumptions.

We start by fixing an assertion language $\mathcal{A}$ and defining an *extended state* of a procedure p to be a pair (σ_{en}, σ) of states of p. Intuitively, in an extended state (σ_{en}, σ), σ is the current state, and σ_{en} is the state at the beginning of the current procedural context. An *extended state formula* φ over p is an assertion in $\mathcal{A}$ such that φ may use two free variables x_{en} and x for each variable (including the control variable *pc*) x in scope in p. [1] Such a formula is interpreted over extended states (σ_{en}, σ), with x_{en} and x capturing the values of x at σ_{en} and σ; every formula thus encodes a set of extended states. Therefore, an extended state formula $(x \leq 5x_{en})$ says the value of the program variable x at the point where the assertion is made is at most five times the value of x at the beginning of the present procedural context.

We write $(\sigma_{en}, \sigma) \models \varphi$ if (σ_{en}, σ) satisfies φ. If all extended states satisfy φ, then we write $\models \varphi$. Also, we denote the set of extended state formulas over p by $Assn(\mathtt{p})$.

A *local invariant* of $\mathtt{p} \in Proc$ is a formula $\pi \in Assn(\mathtt{p})$ such that for any nested execution $w \in [\![\mathtt{p}]\!]$, the local path w_l of w satisfies the following property: for all positions i in w_l, $(w_l(0), w_l(i)) \models \pi$. A *summary* of a procedure p is a formula $\psi \in Assn(\mathtt{p})$ such that for each finite nested execution $w \in [\![\mathtt{p}]\!]$ ending at a position n, $(w(0), w(n)) \models \psi$. Intuitively, local invariants assert conditions that hold on the path through the "top-level" context of a nested execution. Note that if the formula π is a local invariant of p, then the formula $(\pi \wedge (pc = \perp_{\mathtt{p}}))$ is a summary of the procedure p—i.e., a summary can be obtained by asserting the local invariant at the terminal label of the procedure.

Inductive local invariants and summaries. Our goal here is to obtain, for each procedure p, an *inductive local invariant.* This is done with respect to a summary of each procedure called from p. Due to recursion, these invariants and summaries may be interdependent, and need to be defined via mutual induction.

These notions are developed via a simple generalization of the non-procedural case. First we define a *predicate transformer* for each edge e in the CFG of P. Consider, first, a local edge $e = (l, b, m)$ in the procedure p. The transformer for

[1] As a convention, we use typewriter font to refer to program variables, and italics to refer to logical variables.

e takes a formula $\varphi \in Assn(\mathtt{p})$, and returns a formula $\varphi' = Post_e(\varphi) \in Assn(\mathtt{p})$. The latter formula encodes the least set S of extended states such that for each (σ_{en}, σ) that satisfies φ and is such that $\sigma(pc) = l$, if σ' is the state reached by executing from σ the command to which e corresponds, then $(\sigma_{en}, \sigma') \in S$. We write $\{\varphi\}\ e\ \{\varphi'\}$ if $Post_e(\varphi) \Rightarrow \varphi'$.

Predicate transformers for call edges e are similar, except for $\varphi \in Assn(\mathtt{p})$, $Post_e(\varphi) \in Assn(\mathtt{q})$, where $\mathtt{q}$ is a procedure called from $\mathtt{p}$. If e is a summary edge capturing execution within a called procedure $\mathtt{q}$, then its predicate transformer takes in a *summary* ψ of $\mathtt{q}$ as an extra parameter, and is of the form $Post_e(\varphi, \psi)$. Here, for given φ and ψ, $\varphi'' = Post_e(\varphi, \psi)$ represents the least set of extended states S such that if (σ_{en}, σ) satisfies φ and σ is a call to procedure $\mathtt{q}$, then assuming the summary ψ for $\mathtt{q}$ and the return state σ_{ret}, we have $(\sigma_{en}, \sigma_{ret}) \in S$. We write $\{\varphi\}\ (e, \psi)\ \{\varphi''\}$ if $Post_e(\varphi, \psi) \Rightarrow \varphi''$.

Finally, let us define a formula $\mathcal{I}_{\mathtt{p}}$ capturing the *initial condition* of a procedure p—i.e., the initialization of its local variables. Inductive local invariants and summaries are now defined as follows:

Definition 1. *Let P have procedures $\mathtt{p_1}, \dots, \mathtt{p_k}$ and initial procedure $\mathtt{p_{in}}$. The* inductive local invariant *and* summary *for each procedure $\mathtt{p_i}$ are respectively given by $I(\mathtt{p_i})$ and $\Psi(\mathtt{p_i})$, where I and Ψ are maps that assign an extended state formula to each procedure in P, and satisfy the following:*

1. $\models \mathcal{I}_{\mathtt{p_{in}}} \Rightarrow I(\mathtt{p_{in}}) \wedge (pc = pc_{en} = First(\mathtt{p_{in}}))$
2. *for each local edge* $e = (l, b, m)$ *in* $\mathtt{p}$, $\models \{I(\mathtt{p}) \wedge (pc = l)\}\ e\ \{I(\mathtt{p}) \wedge (pc = m)\}$
3. *for each summary edge* $e = (l, \mathtt{q}, m)$ *in* $\mathtt{p}$,
   $\models \{I(\mathtt{p}) \wedge (pc = l)\}\ (e, \Psi(\mathtt{q}))\ \{I(\mathtt{p}) \wedge (pc = m)\}$
4. *for each call edge* $e = (l, m)$ *from* $\mathtt{p}$ *to* $\mathtt{q}$,
   $\models \{I(\mathtt{p}) \wedge (pc = l) \wedge \mathcal{I}_{\mathtt{q}}\}\ e\ \{I(\mathtt{q}) \wedge (pc = First(\mathtt{q}))\}$
5. *for all* $\mathtt{p}$, *we have* $\models I(\mathtt{p}) \wedge (pc = \perp_{\mathtt{p}}) \Rightarrow \Psi(\mathtt{p})$.

A pair (I, Ψ) of maps as above is called an inductive pair.

Intuitively, condition (1) requires that the inductive local invariant, when asserted at the label where the program starts execution, satisfies the initial conditions of $\mathtt{p_{in}}$. Conditions (2) and (3) require that invariants are preserved under transitions along local and summary edges. Condition (4) asserts the initial conditions of a procedure at its entry states reached via calls. Condition (5) relates summaries given by Ψ to invariants given by I.

It is not hard to show that Definition 1 is sound:

Lemma 1. *If (I, Ψ) is an inductive pair, then for each $\mathtt{p} \in Proc$, $I(\mathtt{p})$ is a local invariant and $\Psi(\mathtt{p})$ a summary of* p.

For example, consider the program in Figure 2. Suppose, assuming `inc_n` only increments `n`, we want to derive the local invariant ($flag = ff$) for `main`. The required reasoning is performed in a procedure-modular way. First we just consider the body of `main`, while making the necessary *assumptions* about the procedures it calls (in this case, `bar`). We note that the invariant holds if ($flag = ff$) is a summary for `bar`. Now we must validate this summary by reasoning about `bar`. Here we assume the invariant $(cond \vee (flag = ff))$ for the label *L2* and show that this is a loop invariant. Verifying the summary is now easy.

5 Temporal Verification

Local invariants may be directly applied in proving temporal safety and liveness properties interpreted on nested program executions. We explore three classes of temporal properties—*safety*, *response*, and *reactivity*—each of which has three subclasses corresponding to interpretations on local, global, and staircase paths in nested executions. Of these, staircase reactivity properties can capture all properties expressible in temporal logic over nested words [13,5].

In the following, we write $P, \mathtt{p} \models f$ if the procedure p in the program P satisfies a temporal property f (we will define what this means for each property we consider). We write $P, \mathtt{p} \vdash_{\mathsf{R}} f$, often omitting P and/or R, if we can prove using a rule R that p satisfies f. Finally, we write $\vdash \varphi$ if we can prove the extended state formula φ.

A rule R proving a property f of a procedure p in a program P is called *sound* if $P, \mathtt{p} \vdash_{\mathsf{R}} f$ only when $P, \mathtt{p} \models f$. As for completeness, consider sets $S_1, \ldots, S_k$ of extended states. We call R *complete relative to these sets* if, assuming that each S_i can be encoded by an extended state formula and that all assertions in $\mathcal{A}$ can be proved or disproved, we have $P, \mathtt{p} \models f$ only if $P, \mathtt{p} \vdash_{\mathsf{R}} f$. We call R *relatively complete* if it is complete relative to a collection of sets of extended states, each of which can be captured using $\mathcal{A}$.

Local safety. A local safety property says: "In any nested execution of a procedure p, a certain assertion is never violated in the top-level procedural context." We define:

Definition 2. *Let $\varphi \in Assn(\mathtt{p})$ for a procedure* p. *The procedure* p *satisfies the* local safety property $\Box^l \varphi$ *(read as "Always locally φ") if for each $w \in [\![\mathtt{p}]\!]$ and for each position i in the local path $\sigma_0 \sigma_1 \ldots$ in w, (σ_0, σ_i) satisfies φ. This fact is written as $P, \mathtt{p} \models \Box^l \varphi$)*

Fig. 3 shows our rule L-SAFE for local safety. The rule is a generalization of the classic proof rule for temporal safety [15]. Unlike in the classical case, the inductive invariant we need here is a *local* invariant. To prove local safety for p, we only need to consider the program $P_{\mathtt{p}}$.

Input: (1) Procedure p in program P; (2) $\varphi \in Assn(\mathtt{p})$

Rule: Find an inductive pair (I, Ψ) for the program $P_{\mathtt{p}}$ such that $\vdash I(\mathtt{p}) \Rightarrow \varphi$

$$P, \mathtt{p} \vdash \Box^l \varphi$$

Fig. 3. Rule L-SAFE for local safety

Example 1. Recall the program in Fig. 2, and consider the safety property: "`flag` is always false." While this property is violated by global program executions, it holds locally in `main`. A proof follows from the inductive pair for this program derived earlier. In fact, this example represents a class of applications of local safety properties: those where an invariant may be legitimately broken by a called procedure, so long as it is restored before control returns.

Soundness of L-SAFE follows from Lemma 1:

Theorem 1. *The rule* L-SAFE *is sound.*

As for completeness, let $Proc(P_{\mathtt{p}})$ be the set of procedures in $P_{\mathtt{p}}$, and let $S^R_{\mathtt{q}}$ be, for each $\mathtt{q} \in Proc(P_{\mathtt{p}})$, the set of extended states (σ_{en}, σ) such that σ_{en} is an entry state of q and σ is locally reachable from σ_{en}. Thus, the set $S^R_{\mathtt{q}}$ captures local reachability from an entry state of q. We have:

Theorem 2. L-SAFE *is complete relative to the sets* $S^R_{\mathtt{q}}$*, where* $\mathtt{q} \in Proc(P_{\mathtt{p}})$.

Proof: Let us assume that $P, \mathtt{p} \models \Box^l \varphi$. For each $\mathtt{q} \in Proc(P_{\mathtt{p}})$, let $\chi_{\mathtt{q}}$ be an extended state formula capturing the set $S^R_{\mathtt{q}}$ (i.e., for each extended state (σ_{en}, σ) of q, we have $(\sigma_{en}, \sigma) \models \chi_{\mathtt{q}}$ iff $(\sigma_{en}, \sigma) \in S^R_{\mathtt{q}}$). By our assumption, these formulas exist. Now consider the pair of maps (I, Ψ), each assigning a formula to each q as above, such that for all such q, we have $I(\mathtt{q}) = \chi_{\mathtt{q}}$ and $\Psi(\mathtt{q}) = I(\mathtt{q}) \wedge (pc = \perp_{\mathtt{q}})$.

We claim that (I, Ψ) is an inductive pair for $P_{\mathtt{p}}$. To see why this is so, consider the conditions in Definition 1. Condition (1) holds because $(\sigma_{in}, \sigma_{in})$, where σ_{in} is an entry state of p belongs to $S^R_{\mathtt{p}}$. Condition (5) holds trivially from our choice of Ψ. Conditions (2), (3), and (4) follow from the definition of local reachability and predicate transformers, and the hypothesis that Ψ captures summaries.

Now note that $I(\mathtt{p}) \Rightarrow \varphi$. Recall that $(\sigma_{en}, \sigma) \models \varphi$ for all entry states σ_{en} of p and all σ such that σ is locally reachable from σ_{en}. As $I(\mathtt{p})$ (i.e., $\chi_{\mathtt{p}}$) precisely characterizes those pairs, (I, Ψ) satisfies the premises of L-SAFE. Thus, $P, \mathtt{p} \vdash \Box^l \varphi$. □

Now we show a way to encode the sets $S^R_{\mathtt{q}}$ using assertions, generalizing a technique in Manna and Pnueli's completeness proof [14] and proving that:

Theorem 3. L-SAFE *is relatively complete.*

Proof: We assume that our data domain can express records and *binary trees* of records; our assertions use auxiliary variables of these types. For a node u in a tree τ of records, let $lc(u)$ and $rc(u)$ respectively denote the left and right children of u (the right child may not exist, in which case we write $rc(u) = \perp$). The root of τ is denoted by $root(\tau)$; u satisfies the predicate $leaf(u, \tau)$ iff it is a leaf of τ.

The records u forming the tree nodes have fields indexed by the logical variables x_{en} and x of our state formulas. For an extended state formula ψ, the *application* $\psi(u)$ is obtained by substituting the free variables of ψ with the corresponding fields of u. The formula $\widetilde{V} = u$ has free variables x and x_{en} for every variable x of q, and states that each free variable has the value of the corresponding field in u. For each local or call edge e, $Post_e(u)$ refers to $Post_e(\psi_u)$, where ψ_u states that each variable has the value of the corresponding field in u. The application of $Post_e(u)$ to a node u' is denoted by $(u = Post_e(u'))$. If e is a summary edge, the formula $(u = Post_e(u', u''))$ (where u', u'' are records) is likewise defined.

The formula $\chi_{\mathtt{q}}$ is:

$$\chi_{\mathtt{q}} : \exists\tau.((|\tau| > 0) \wedge \lambda_{leaf} \wedge \lambda_{root} \wedge \forall u.(\neg leaf(u,\tau) \Rightarrow \delta_{loc} \vee \delta_{sum}))$$

where

$$\begin{aligned}
\lambda_{leaf} &: \forall u.\ leaf(u,\tau) \Rightarrow \textstyle\bigvee_{\mathtt{r}\in Proc}(\mathcal{I}_{\mathtt{r}} \wedge (pc = pc_{en} = First(\mathtt{r}))(u) \\
\lambda_{root} &: \widetilde{V} = root(\tau) \\
\delta_{loc} &: \ (rc(u) = \perp) \wedge \textstyle\bigvee_{e\in E_{loc}}(u = Post_e(lc(u))) \\
\delta_{sum} &: (rc(u) \neq \perp) \wedge \textstyle\bigvee_{e\in E_{sum}}(u = Post_e(lc(u), rc(u)))
\end{aligned}$$

The assertion $\chi_{\mathtt{p}}$ encodes a proof tree establishing local reachability between states σ_{en} and σ in p (also, σ_{en} is an entry state of p). The root of τ encodes variable values at these states. The leaves encode the fact that each state σ is locally reachable from itself. The children of a node $u = (\sigma'_{en}, \sigma')$ capture reachability facts that, together, imply that σ' is locally reachable from σ'_{en} (note that these states are not necessarily in p; also, if u has no right child, then only one premise is needed to derive it). For example, u may have a single child (σ'_{en}, σ''), where σ'' has a transition along a local edge to σ'. Thus, $\chi_{\mathtt{p}}$ captures $S^R_{\mathtt{p}}$. □

Local response. Now we extend our approach to liveness. We define *local response* as:

Definition 3. *Let $\varphi_1, \varphi_2 \in Assn(\mathtt{p})$ for a procedure* p. *The procedure* p *satisfies the local response property $f = \Box^l(\varphi_1 \Rightarrow \Diamond^l\varphi_2)$ if for each $w \in [\![\mathtt{p}]\!]^\omega$ and for each position i in the local path $\sigma_0\sigma_1\ldots$ such that $(\sigma_0, \sigma_i) \models \varphi_1$, there exists $j \geq i$ such that $(\sigma_0, \sigma_j) \models \varphi_2$. This fact is written as $P, \mathtt{p} \models f$.*

Note that the definition only considers the *infinite* executions of p.

Liveness properties as above are proved by generalizing techniques from classical verification using ranking functions. Let $(D, \preceq)$ be a well-founded preorder; for $a, b \in D$, we write $a = b$ if $a \preceq b$ and $b \preceq a$, and $a \prec b$ if $a \preceq b$ and $a \neq b$. Let a *ranking function* for the above preorder and the program P be a map $\delta : (\sigma_{en}, \sigma) \mapsto d$, where (σ_{en}, σ) is an extended state and $d \in D$. We use extended state formulas such as $(\delta \preceq d)$ and $(\delta = d)$ that are satisfied by an extended state (σ_{en}, σ) respectively when $\delta(\sigma_{en}, \sigma) \preceq d$ and $\delta(\sigma_{en}, \sigma) = d$. Ways to encode such assertions in a language like $\mathcal{A}$ may be found in [14].

Our rule L-Resp for local response is in Fig. 4. Intuitively, the obligation κ is asserted whenever φ_1 holds along a local path, and is "released" only when φ_2 holds on this path as well. In path fragments where κ is asserted, the ranking function decreases in value; as D has no infinite descending chain, this means that φ_2 will hold eventually.

Input: (1) Procedure $\mathtt{p}$ in program P; (2) Formulas $\varphi_1, \varphi_2 \in Assn(\mathtt{p})$

Rule: Find an inductive pair (I, Ψ) for the program $P_{\mathtt{p}}$, a ranking function from extended states of P to D, a formula $\kappa \in Assn(\mathtt{p})$ and, for each procedure $\mathtt{q} \in Proc(P_{\mathtt{p}})$, a formula $\beta_{\mathtt{q}} \in Assn(\mathtt{q})$, such that:

1. $\vdash \varphi_1 \Rightarrow \varphi_2 \vee \kappa$;
2. For each local edge e in $\mathtt{p}$,
   $\vdash \{\kappa \wedge (\delta = d)\}\ e\ \{\varphi_2 \vee (\kappa \wedge (\delta \prec d)\}$;
   for each local edge in a procedure $\mathtt{q}$,
   $\vdash \{\beta_{\mathtt{q}} \wedge (\delta = d)\}\ e\ \{(pc = \perp_{\mathtt{q}}) \vee (\beta_{\mathtt{q}} \wedge (\delta \prec d)\}$
3. For each call edge e from $\mathtt{p}$ to a procedure $\mathtt{q}$,
   $\vdash \{\kappa \wedge (\delta = d)\}\ e\ \{\beta_{\mathtt{q}} \wedge (\delta \prec d)\}$;
   for each call edge from a procedure $\mathtt{q}$ to a procedure $\mathtt{r}$,
   $\vdash \{\beta_{\mathtt{q}} \wedge (\delta = d)\}\ e\ \{\beta_{\mathtt{r}} \wedge (\delta \prec d)\}$
4. For each summary edge $e = (l, \mathtt{r}, m)$ in $\mathtt{p}$,
   $\vdash \{\kappa \wedge (\delta = d)\}\ (e, \Psi(\mathtt{r}))\ \{\varphi_2 \vee (\kappa \wedge (\delta \prec d))\}$;
   for each such edge in a procedure $\mathtt{q}$,
   $\vdash \{\beta_{\mathtt{q}} \wedge (\delta = d)\}\ (e, \Psi(\mathtt{r}))\ \{(pc = \perp_{\mathtt{q}}) \vee (\beta_{\mathtt{q}} \wedge (\delta \prec d))\}$

$$P, \mathtt{p} \vdash \square^l(\varphi_1 \Rightarrow \lozenge^l \varphi_2)$$

Fig. 4. Rule L-RESP for local response

Now, when the execution enters a new context via a call, the execution fragment from then on till the matching return is not part of the local path. Suppose κ was not released by the time the call happened. If the call never terminates, the local path will have ended at the call, and the response property will be violated. Consequently, we must ensure that all such calls eventually return. This is done using the properties $\beta_{\mathtt{q}}$ (split among procedures), which are just like κ, except they are released when the "terminal" label $\perp_{\mathtt{q}}$ is reached. Note that because of recursive calls, a procedure may be re-entered—e.g., we may have $\mathtt{q} = \mathtt{p}$.

Example 2. In the program in Fig. 2, suppose we want to show that `bar` satisfies the property $\square^l(cond \Rightarrow \lozenge^l(\neg flag \vee (n \geq n_{en} + 100)))$. This is done using a ranking function that maps each extended state (σ_{en}, σ) of `bar` to a pair (l, v), where l is the label of σ, and v is the value of $\max\{0, (n_{en} + 100 - n)\}$ in this extended state. The labels are partially ordered as $(L1 < L2 < L3)$, $(L4 < L3)$, and $(L5 < L3)$. We have $(l', v') \prec (l, v)$ iff either $(v' < v)$, or $(v' = v)$ and $(l' < l)$.

Now κ says: "pc is one of *L1*, *L2*, *L3*, *L4*, or *L5*, and $(n < n_{en} + 100)$." Clearly, this satisfies the rule's premises.

We can show that:

Theorem 4. *The rule* L-RESP *is sound and relatively complete.*

Global response. Local invariants may also be used to modularly prove properties of executions spanning multiple contexts. The simplest of these is *global*

Input: (1) Procedure $\mathtt{p}$ in program P; (2) Formulas $\varphi_1, \varphi_2 \in Assn(\mathtt{p})$

Rule: Find an inductive pair (I, Ψ) for the program $P_{\mathtt{p}}^{\varphi_2}$, a ranking function from extended states of P to D, and, for each procedure $\mathtt{q}$ in $P_{\mathtt{p}}^{\varphi_2}$, a formula $\kappa_{\mathtt{q}} \in Assn(P)$, such that:

1. $\vdash (pc = l) \wedge \varphi_1 \Rightarrow (\varphi_2 \vee \kappa_{\mathtt{q}})$, if the label l is in $\mathtt{q}$;
2. For each local edge e in a procedure $\mathtt{q}$,
   $\vdash \{\kappa_{\mathtt{q}} \wedge (\delta = d)\}\ e\ \{\varphi_2 \vee (\kappa_{\mathtt{q}} \wedge (\delta \prec d)\}$;
3. For each call edge from procedure $\mathtt{q}$ to procedure $\mathtt{r}$,
   $\vdash \{\kappa_{\mathtt{q}} \wedge (\delta = d)\}\ e\ \{\varphi_2 \vee (\kappa_{\mathtt{r}} \wedge (\delta \prec d))\}$
4. For each summary edge $e = (l, \mathtt{r}, m)$ in procedure $\mathtt{q}$,
   $\vdash \{\kappa_{\mathtt{q}} \wedge (\delta = d)\}\ (e, \Psi(\mathtt{r}))\ \{\neg \#_{\varphi_2} \Rightarrow (\varphi_2 \vee (\kappa_{\mathtt{q}} \wedge (\delta \prec d)))\}$

$$P, \mathtt{p} \vdash \Box^g(\varphi_1 \Rightarrow \Diamond^g \varphi_2)$$

Fig. 5. Rule G-RESP for global response

Input: (1) Procedure $\mathtt{p}$ in program P; (2) Formulas $\varphi_1, \varphi_2, \theta \in Assn(P)$
Rule: Find an inductive pair (I, Ψ) for the program $P_{\mathtt{p}}$, a ranking function from extended states of P to D, a formula $\kappa \in Assn(\mathtt{p})$ and, for each procedure $\mathtt{q} \in Proc(P_{\mathtt{p}})$, a formula $\beta_{\mathtt{q}} \in Assn(\mathtt{q})$, such that:

1. $\vdash \varphi_1 \Rightarrow \varphi_2 \vee \kappa$;
2. For each local edge e in $\mathtt{q}$,
   $\vdash \{\kappa \wedge \theta \wedge (\delta = d)\}\ e\ \{\varphi_2 \vee (\kappa \wedge (\delta \prec d)\}$ $\quad \vdash \{\kappa \wedge (\delta = d)\}\ e\ \{\varphi_2 \vee (\kappa \wedge (\delta \preceq d)\}$
   $\vdash \{\beta_{\mathtt{q}} \wedge \theta \wedge (\delta = d)\}\ e\ \{(pc = \perp_{\mathtt{q}}) \vee \varphi_2 \vee (\beta_{\mathtt{q}} \wedge (\delta \prec d)\}$
   $\vdash \{\beta_{\mathtt{q}} \wedge (\delta = d)\}\ e\ \{(pc = \perp_{\mathtt{q}}) \vee \varphi_2 \vee (\beta_{\mathtt{q}} \wedge (\delta \preceq d)\}$
3. For each call edge e from a procedure $\mathtt{q}$ to a procedure $\mathtt{r}$,
   $\vdash \{\kappa \wedge \theta \wedge (\delta = d)\}\ e\ \{\beta_{\mathtt{r}} \wedge (\delta \prec d)\}$ $\quad \vdash \{\kappa \wedge (\delta = d)\}\ e\ \{\beta_{\mathtt{r}} \wedge (\delta \preceq d)\}$
   $\vdash \{\beta_{\mathtt{q}} \wedge \theta \wedge (\delta = d)\}\ e\ \{\beta_{\mathtt{r}} \wedge (\delta \prec d)\}$ $\quad \vdash \{\beta_{\mathtt{q}} \wedge (\delta = d)\}\ e\ \{\beta_{\mathtt{r}} \wedge (\delta \preceq d)\}$
4. For each summary edge $e = (l, \mathtt{q}, m)$ in a procedure $\mathtt{r}$,
   $\vdash \{\kappa \wedge \theta \wedge (\delta = d)\}\ (e, \Psi(\mathtt{q}))\ \{\varphi_2 \vee (\kappa \wedge (\delta \prec d))\}$
   $\vdash \{\kappa \wedge (\delta = d)\}\ (e, \Psi(\mathtt{q}))\ \{\varphi_2 \vee (\kappa \wedge (\delta \preceq d))\}$
   $\vdash \{\beta_{\mathtt{r}} \wedge \theta \wedge (\delta = d)\}\ (e, \Psi(\mathtt{q}))\ \{(pc = \perp_{\mathtt{r}}) \vee \varphi_2 \vee (\beta_{\mathtt{r}} \wedge (\delta \prec d))\}$
   $\vdash \{\beta_{\mathtt{r}} \wedge (\delta = d)\}\ (e, \Psi(\mathtt{q}))\ \{(pc = \perp_{\mathtt{r}}) \vee \varphi_2 \vee (\beta_{\mathtt{r}} \wedge (\delta \preceq d))\}$

$$P, \mathtt{p} \vdash \Box^s((\varphi_1 \wedge \Box^s \Diamond^s \theta) \Rightarrow \Diamond^s \varphi_2)$$

Fig. 6. Rule S-REACT for staircase reactivity

safety. Here we consider the *global response property* $\Box^g(\varphi_1 \Rightarrow \Diamond^g \varphi_2)$, which is defined in exactly the same way as local response, except that it is interpreted on the global rather than the local path.

Our rule G-RESP for global response is in Fig. 5. To understand it, first consider the rule for local response and a state of procedure $\mathtt{p}$ that calls the procedure $\mathtt{q}$ and satisfies κ, but not φ_2. Clearly, this state was reached along a local path where φ_1 held at one point, but φ_2 has not held since. In local response, we had to ensure that this call terminates, and that φ_2 holds along the local path in the continuation. In global response, we do not need termination: a non-returning path is legitimate if φ_2 eventually holds in it. However, we must assert that in all executions that do reach the matching return without having satisfied φ_2 in the interim, an invariant like κ must be asserted at the matching return. This requires us to relate the fragment of the execution within q with the conditions that hold afterwards. It is possible to do this using an auxiliary program variable.

For an assertion φ and a program P, let us define the program P^{φ} obtained by modifying P as follows. To each procedure p of P, we add a local boolean variable $\#_{\mathtt{p},\varphi}$. Between every two commands in p, we add the command `if(`φ`) then (`$\#_{\mathtt{p},\varphi}$`:=true) else skip`. We also make p return the value of this variable. This is encoded using a global variable γ—the last command in p stores the value of $\#_{\mathtt{p},\varphi}$ in γ. Finally, after each procedure call from p to q, we add a statement $\#_{\mathtt{p},\varphi} = \gamma$.

This augmented program tracks if φ is satisfied within a procedure q called from p. As q returns the value of $\#_{\mathtt{q},\varphi}$ on termination, we can refer to this value to see if φ was satisfied within the called context.

The rule G-Resp uses such an augmentation of the input program P. The interesting premise concerns summary edges: we assert liveness at the target of such an edge only if the procedure's auxiliary variable is false at that point (i.e., if the property is not satisfied within the context summarized by the edge).

Example 3. Consider the program in Fig. 2 once again, and the global response property $\Box^g((n = 0) \Rightarrow \Diamond^g(n \geq 1))$. While the local version of this property is not satisfied by the procedure `main`, the global version is easily verified using G-Resp. As `bar` may or may not terminate or not increment n, the auxiliary variables are critical to the proof.

Soundness and completeness are obtained by slightly modifying the corresponding proofs for local response:

Theorem 5. G-Resp *is sound and relatively complete.*

Staircase reactivity. Now we prove the most general of our properties: *staircase reactivity*. A staircase reactivity property asserts: "Along the staircase path in any nested execution, if φ_1 holds infinitely often, then φ_2 also holds infinitely often." These properties can capture the parity acceptance condition of ω-automata. As automata operating on the staircase path can capture all ω-regular properties of nested words [5], a complete rule for staircase reactivity can prove all temporal properties of nested executions.

Following [14], we use a syntactic formulation of reactivity that involves an extra assertion θ. We define:

Definition 4. *Let* $\varphi_1, \varphi_2, \theta \in Assn(\mathtt{p})$ *for a procedure* p*. The procedure* p *satisfies the* staircase reactivity property $f = \Box^s(\varphi_1 \wedge \Box^s\Diamond^s\theta \Rightarrow \Diamond^s\varphi_2)$ *if for each* $w \in [\![\mathtt{p}]\!]$ *and for each position* i *in the staircase path* $\sigma_0\sigma_1\ldots$ *such that: (1)* $(\sigma_0, \sigma_i) \models \varphi_1$*, and (2) there exist infinitely many* $j \geq i$ *such that* $(\sigma_0, \sigma_j) \models \theta$*, there is some* $k \geq i$ *such that* $(\sigma_0, \sigma_k) \models \varphi_2$*.*

Our rule S-React for staircase reactivity is shown in Fig. 6. The rule combines features of proofs for local and global properties, and generalizes the rule for response.

Consider, first, the case where there are no procedure calls. As in local response, κ is asserted whenever an extended state satisfying φ_1 is reached along a local path, and continues to hold till the "goal" of reaching φ_2 is met. However, this time the rank decreases along a path fragment with invariant κ only when θ is satisfied (and it never increases along a path). If θ holds infinitely often, then either φ_2 holds eventually, or the rank must decrease unboundedly. The latter is impossible as D is well-founded.

If the program has procedure calls, we propagate two liveness conditions at each call. Along the call edge, we assert the property that along each path within the new context, either the reactivity condition is met, or the matching return of the present call is reached. Along the summary edge, we assert: "the reactivity condition is met eventually."

To see why, suppose a call terminates *after having satisfied the liveness obligation.* The part of this execution within the called context is not in the staircase path, but this is not an issue as liveness is asserted along the summary edge *regardless of* what happens within the called context. Now suppose this call never returns. In this case, using a strong summary, we rule out a continuation of the current execution along the summary edge in question. However, the condition for the call edge ensures that the context reached via the call satisfies the liveness obligation. In general, we can show that:

Theorem 6 (Soundness, completeness). *The rule* S-React *is sound and relatively complete.*

6 Conclusion

We have presented a set of rules to modularly verify temporal properties of procedural programs. Our approach uses a nested-word semantics of programs, and uses summaries and local invariants to perform modular reasoning. Our rules are sound and relatively complete, and can prove any temporal property of nested words.

In future work, we will mechanize these rules using recent techniques for automatic invariant generation [7,18]. Also, we did not permit assertions referring to the past in this paper—they will be dealt with in the journal version.

References

1. Alur, R., Arenas, M., Barceló, P., Etessami, K., Immerman, N., Libkin, L.: First-order and temporal logics for nested words. In: Proceedings of LICS, pp. 151–160 (2007)
2. Alur, R., Etessami, K., Madhusudan, P.: A temporal logic of nested calls and returns. In: Jensen, K., Podelski, A. (eds.) TACAS 2004. LNCS, vol. 2988, pp. 467–481. Springer, Heidelberg (2004)

3. Alur, R., Madhusudan, P.: Adding nesting structure to words. J. ACM (2009)
4. Apt, K.R.: Ten years of Hoare's logic: A survey—part I. ACM Transactions on Programming Languages and Systems 3(4), 431–483 (1981)
5. Arenas, M., Barceló, P., Libkin, L.: Regular languages of nested words: Fixed points, automata, and synchronization. In: Arge, L., Cachin, C., Jurdziński, T., Tarlecki, A. (eds.) ICALP 2007. LNCS, vol. 4596, pp. 888–900. Springer, Heidelberg (2007)
6. Ball, T., Rajamani, S.: The SLAM toolkit. In: Berry, G., Comon, H., Finkel, A. (eds.) CAV 2001. LNCS, vol. 2102, pp. 260–264. Springer, Heidelberg (2001)
7. Bradley, A., Manna, Z.: The Calculus of Computation. Springer, Heidelberg (2007)
8. Cook, B., Podelski, A., Rybalchenko, A.: Summarization for termination: no return! Formal Methods for System Design (2009)
9. Dillig, I., Dillig, T., Aiken, A.: Sound, complete and scalable path-sensitive analysis. In: PLDI, pp. 270–280 (2008)
10. Heizmann, M., Hoenicke, J., Podelski, A.: Nested interpolants. In: Proceedings of POPL (2010)
11. Henzinger, T.A., Jhala, R., Majumdar, R., Necula, G.C., Sutre, G., Weimer, W.: Temporal-safety proofs for systems code. In: Brinksma, E., Larsen, K.G. (eds.) CAV 2002. LNCS, vol. 2404, pp. 526–538. Springer, Heidelberg (2002)
12. Hoare, C.A.R.: An axiomatic basis for computer programming. Communications of the ACM 12(10), 576–580 (1969)
13. Löding, C., Madhusudan, P., Serre, O.: Visibly pushdown games. In: Lodaya, K., Mahajan, M. (eds.) FSTTCS 2004. LNCS, vol. 3328, pp. 408–420. Springer, Heidelberg (2004)
14. Manna, Z., Pnueli, A.: Completing the temporal picture. Theoretical Computer Science 83(1), 91–130 (1991)
15. Manna, Z., Pnueli, A.: The Temporal Logic of Reactive and Concurrent Systems: Safety. Springer, New York (1995)
16. Manna, Z., Pnueli, A.: The Temporal Logic of Reactive and Concurrent Systems: Progress (1996)
17. Pnueli, A.: The temporal logic of programs. In: Proceedings of FOCS, pp. 46–77 (1977)
18. Podelski, A., Rybalchenko, A.: A complete method for the synthesis of linear ranking functions. In: Steffen, B., Levi, G. (eds.) VMCAI 2004. LNCS, vol. 2937, pp. 239–251. Springer, Heidelberg (2004)
19. Podelski, A., Schaefer, I., Wagner, S.: Summaries for while programs with recursion. In: Sagiv, M. (ed.) ESOP 2005. LNCS, vol. 3444, pp. 94–107. Springer, Heidelberg (2005)
20. Reps, T., Horwitz, S., Sagiv, S.: Precise interprocedural dataflow analysis via graph reachability. In: Proc. of POPL, pp. 49–61 (1995)
21. Reps, T.W., Schwoon, S., Jha, S.: Weighted pushdown systems and their application to interprocedural dataflow analysis. In: Proceedings of SAS, pp. 189–213 (2003)
22. Sharir, M., Pnueli, A.: Two approaches to interprocedural dataflow analysis. Program Flow Analysis: Theory and Applications, 189–234 (1981)

Improved Model Checking of Hierarchical Systems

Benjamin Aminof[1,⋆], Orna Kupferman[1], and Aniello Murano[2,⋆⋆]

[1] Hebrew University, Jerusalem 91904, Israel
[2] Università degli Studi di Napoli "Federico II", 80126 Napoli, Italy

Abstract. We present a unified game-based approach for branching-time model checking of hierarchical systems. Such systems are exponentially more succinct than standard state-transition graphs, as repeated sub-systems are described only once. Early work on model checking of hierarchical systems shows that one can do better than a naive algorithm that "flattens" the system and removes the hierarchy.

Given a hierarchical system $\mathcal{S}$ and a branching-time specification ψ for it, we reduce the model-checking problem (does $\mathcal{S}$ satisfy ψ?) to the problem of solving a *hierarchical game* obtained by taking the product of $\mathcal{S}$ with an alternating tree automaton $\mathcal{A}_\psi$ for ψ. Our approach leads to clean, uniform, and improved model-checking algorithms for a variety of branching-time temporal logics. In particular, by improving the algorithm for solving hierarchical parity games, we are able to solve the model-checking problem for the μ-calculus in PSPACE and time complexity that is only polynomial in the depth of the hierarchy. Our approach also leads to an abstraction-refinement paradigm for hierarchical systems. The abstraction maintains the hierarchy, and is obtained by merging both states and sub-systems into abstract states.

1 Introduction

In model checking, we verify that a system meets its specification by translating the system to a finite state machine (FSM), translating the specification to a temporal-logic formula, and checking that the FSM satisfies the formula [6]. The translation of a high-level description of a system to an FSM involves a painful blow-up, and the size of the FSM is typically the computational bottleneck in model-checking algorithms.

There are several sources of the blow-up that the translation involves. A well-studied source is the ability of components in the system to work in parallel and communicate with each other, possibly using variables. Formally, *concurrent FSMs* are exponentially more succinct than *flat* (usual) ones [9]. This has led to extensive research on compositional model checking, where the goal is to reason about a system by reasoning about its underlying components and without constructing an equivalent flat system (c.f., [8,19]). Compositionality

⋆ This work was partially done while the author was visiting Università degli Studi di Napoli "Federico II", supported by ESF GAMES project, short visit grant n.2789.
⋆⋆ Partially supported by MIUR PRIN Project n.2007-9E5KM8.

G. Barthe and M. Hermenegildo (Eds.): VMCAI 2010, LNCS 5944, pp. 61–77, 2010.

methods are successfully applied in practice (c.f., [20]), but it is a known reality that they cannot always work. Formally, the system complexity of the model-checking problem (that is, the complexity in terms of the system, assuming a specification of a fixed length) for all common temporal logics is exponentially higher in the concurrent setting [15]. This exponential gap is carried over to other related problems such as checking language-containment and bisimulation — all are exponentially harder in the concurrent setting [13,21].

Another source of the blow-up in the translation of systems to FSMs has to do with the ability of a high-level description of a system to reuse the same component in different contexts (say, by calling a procedure). The sequential setting is that of *hierarchical FSMs*, where some of the states of the FSM are boxes, which correspond to nested FSMs. The naive approach to model checking such systems is to "flatten" them by repeatedly substituting references to sub-structures with copies of these sub-structures. However, this results in a flat system that is exponential in the nesting depth of the hierarchical system. In [5], Alur and Yannakakis show that for LTL model checking, one can avoid this blow-up altogether, whereas for CTL, one can trade it for an exponential blow-up in the (often much smaller) size of the formula and the maximal number of exits of sub-structures. In other words, while hierarchical FSMs are exponentially more succinct than flat FSMs [4], in many cases the system complexity of the model-checking problem is not exponentially higher in the hierarchical setting! Thus, even more than with the feature of concurrency, here there is clear motivation not to flatten the FSM before model checking it.

The results in [5] set the stage to further work on model-checking of hierarchical systems. As it so happened, however, this line of research has quickly been focused on *recursive systems*, which allow unbounded nesting of components. Having no bound on the nesting gives rise to infinite-state systems. The emergence of software model checking, the natural association of reusability with (possibly recursive) procedure calls, the challenge and abstraction that the infinite-state setting involves, and the neat connection to pushdown automata, have all put recursive systems in the central stage [1,2,3], leaving the hierarchical setting as a special case. This work hopes to shift some attention back to the hierarchical setting. We suggest a uniform game-based approach for model checking such systems, and argue that the game-based approach enjoys the versatility and advantages it has proven to have in the flat setting. In particular, the game-based approach leads to improved model-checking algorithms and to an abstraction-refinement framework for hierarchical systems and CTL formulas. An important conclusion of our work is that we should not hurry to give up the finite-state nature of the hierarchical setting, as it does lead to simpler algorithms, and better complexities than the recursive setting.

In the flat setting, the *game-based* approach reduces the model-checking problem (does a system $\mathcal{S}$ satisfy a branching temporal logic specification ψ?) to the problem of deciding a *two-player game* obtained by taking the product of $\mathcal{S}$ with an alternating tree automaton $\mathcal{A}_\psi$ for ψ [15]. The game-based approach separates the logic-related aspects of the model-checking problem, which are handled in the translation of the specifications to automata, and the combinatorial aspects, which are handled by the game-solving algorithm. Using the game-based approach, it was possible to tighten the time and space complexity of the branching-time model-checking problem [15]. We describe a unified game-based approach for branching-time model checking of hierarchical systems. We define *two-player hierarchical games*, and reduce model checking to deciding such games. In a hierarchical game, an arena may have boxes, which refer to nested sub-arenas. As in the flat setting, one can take the product of a hierarchical system with an alternating tree automaton for its specification, and model checking is reduced to solving the game obtained by taking this product. Now, however, the hierarchy of the system induces hierarchy in the game.

Having introduced the framework, we turn to the two main technical contributions of the paper: a new and improved algorithm for solving hierarchical parity games, and an abstraction-refinement paradigm for hierarchical systems. We now briefly describe both. Consider a hierarchical game $\mathcal{G}$. The idea behind our algorithm is that even though a sub-arena may appear in different contexts, it is possible to extract information about the sub-arena that is independent of the context in which it appears. Formally, for each strategy of one of the players, we can analyze the sub-arena and extract a *summary function*, mapping each exit of the sub-arena to the best color (of the parity condition) that the other player can hope for, given that the current play eventually leaves the sub-arena through this exit. The summary function is independent of the context and has to be calculated only once. The algorithm for solving the game $\mathcal{G}$ then solves a sequence of flat parity games, obtained by replacing sub-arenas by simple gadgets that implement the summary functions.

While hierarchical systems may be exponentially more succinct than flat ones, they are not immune to the "state explosion problem", which, in some circumstances, could completely absorb the flavor of using hierarchical state machines. For flat systems, a powerful solution to the state-explosion problem is based on reasoning about an abstraction of the concrete model. To guarantee preservation of the branching-time specification from abstract models to concrete models, two transition relations have been considered [7,17]: preservation of universal properties requires an over-approximation, whereas preservation of existential properties requires an under-approximation. This is accomplished by using Modal Transition Systems (MTS) [11,14]. We extend this approach to hierarchical state machines and introduce *hierarchical MTS* (HMTS) and *hierarchical 3-valued games*. We show how to abstract a hierarchical system and get an HMTS, and model check specifications in CTL. The abstraction technique fits into our game-based approach very naturally. Indeed, already in the flat setting, reasoning about abstractions has the flavor of solving games [22]. From a technical viewpoint, combining our algorithm for the concrete hierarchical setting and the abstraction-refinement solution for the flat setting [22], is not difficult, and is based on adding to the gadgets that capture the summary functions a layer in which the players can chose between winning and not losing (i.e., forcing the game to an unknown-winner value). We see this as a witness to the neatness of our framework.

Related work. As described above, the formulation of hierarchical systems as well as the observation that model-checking algorithms for them should not flatten the system, was done in [5]. The work since then was focused on recursive systems, with the exception of [12,16,18]. The closest to our work here is [12], which proved that the model-checking problem for the μ-calculus and hierarchical systems is PSPACE-complete (as opposed to the recursive setting, in which μ-calculus model checking is EXPTIME-complete). However, the μ-calculus model-checking algorithm that our approach induces enjoys several advantages with respect to the one in [12]. The first one is the complexity. Beyond having a polynomial space complexity, the time complexity of our algorithm is usually much better than the one that follows the "flattening" approach, and in all cases it is much better than the one in [12]. Second, recall that we reduce the μ-calculus model-checking to solving hierarchical parity games and our algorithm solves the latter by solving a sequence of (non-hierarchical) parity games. As such, it can benefit from existing and future algorithms and tools for solving parity games. Third, the algorithm presented in [12] does not deal directly with hierarchical systems. Rather, it considers *straight line programs* (SLP). Translating a hierarchical system to an SLP is not hard (indeed, it involves a quadratic blow-up), but it messes-up the direct relationship between the structure of the hierarchical system and the game. This relationship is crucial in understanding the output of the model-checking procedure, by means of counterexamples, and in describing an abstraction-refinement paradigm on top of the game.

Due to lack of space, many details are omitted from this version. A full version of the paper can be found in the authors URLs.

2 Preliminaries

A *hierarchical two-player game* is a game played between two players, referred to as Player 0 and Player 1. The game is defined by means of a hierarchical arena and a winning condition. The players move a token along the hierarchical arena, and the winning condition specifies the objectives of the players, which typically refer to the sequence of states traversed by the token. A *hierarchical arena* is a hierarchical FSM in which the state space of each of the underlying FSMs is partitioned into states belonging to Player 0 (that is, when the token is in these states, then Player 0 chooses a successor to which he moves the token) and states belonging to Player 1. We refer to the underlying FSMs as *sub-arenas*. Formally, a hierarchical two-player game is a pair $\mathcal{G} = (\mathcal{V}, \Gamma)$, where $\mathcal{V} = \langle \mathcal{V}_1, ..., \mathcal{V}_n \rangle$ is a hierarchical arena, and Γ is a winning condition. For every $1 \leq i \leq n$, the sub-arena $\mathcal{V}_i = \langle W_i^0, W_i^1, \mathcal{B}_i, in_i, exit_i, \tau_i, \mathcal{R}_i \rangle$ has the following elements:

- W_i^0 and W_i^1 are finite sets of *states*. States in W_i^0 belong to Player 0, and states in W_i^1 belong to Player 1. We assume that $W_i^0 \cap W_i^1 = \emptyset$, and let $W_i = W_i^0 \cup W_i^1$. The state $in_i \in W_i$ is an *initial state*[1], and $exit_i \subseteq W_i$ is a set of *exit-states*. We assume that $exit_1 = \emptyset$, i.e., the top-level arena $\mathcal{V}_1$ has no exits.

[1] We assume a single entry for each sub-arena. Multiple entries can be handled by duplicating sub-arenas.

- A finite set $\mathcal{B}_i$ of *boxes*. We assume that $W_1,\ldots,W_n,\mathcal{B}_1,\ldots,\mathcal{B}_n$ are pairwise disjoint.
- An indexing function $\tau_i : \mathcal{B}_i \to \{i+1,\ldots,n\}$ that maps each box of the i-th sub-arena to an index greater than i. If $\tau_i(b) = j$, we say that b *refers* to $\mathcal{V}_j$.
- An edge relation $\mathcal{R}_i \subseteq (\bigcup_{b\in\mathcal{B}_i}(\{b\} \times exit_{\tau_i(b)}) \cup W_i) \times (W_i \cup \mathcal{B}_i)$. Let the pair (u,v) be an edge in $\mathcal{R}_i$, with a source u and a target v. The source u is either a state of $\mathcal{V}_i$ or a pair (b,e), where b is a box of $\mathcal{V}_i$ and e is an exit-state of the sub-arenas that b refers to. The target v is either a state or a box of $\mathcal{V}_i$.

In a sub-arena, the edges connect states and boxes with one another. Edges entering a box implicitly lead to the unique initial state of the sub-arena that the box refers to. On the other hand, an edge exiting a box explicitly specifies the exit-state it comes out of. Note that the fact that boxes can refer only to sub-arenas of a greater index implies that the nesting depth of arenas is finite. In contrast, in the *recursive* setting such a restriction does not exist [1].

A parity winning condition Γ for the game maps all states (of all sub-arenas) to a finite set of colors $C = \{C_{\min},\ldots,C_{\max}\} \subset \mathbb{N}$. Thus, $\Gamma : \bigcup_i W_i \to C$. For technical convenience we allow Γ to be partial, but require that in every sub-arena every cycle, and every path from an entry to an exit, has at least one colored state.

A *hierarchical structure* (*hierarchical system*) can be viewed as a hierarchical arena with a single player. In addition, the structure is defined with respect to a set AP of *atomic propositions*, and each state of the structure is mapped to the set of propositions that hold in it. Formally, a hierarchical structure over AP is a tuple $\mathcal{K} = \langle \mathcal{K}_1,\ldots,\mathcal{K}_n\rangle$ of *structures*, where each $\mathcal{K}_i = \langle AP, \mathcal{V}_i, \sigma_i\rangle$ has a sub-arena $\mathcal{V}_i$ with $W_i^1 = \emptyset$, and a labeling function $\sigma_i : W_i \times AP \to \{tt, ff\}$ that assigns a truth value to a pair $(w,p) \in W_i \times AP$, which indicates whether the atomic proposition p holds or not in w. For convenience, we sometimes abuse notation and write $\sigma_i(w)$ to denote the set $\{p \in AP : \sigma_i(w,p) = tt\}$.

A sub-arena without boxes is *flat*, and a sub-arena which is flat and has no exits is *simple*. A game over a flat (resp. simple) arena is called a flat (resp. simple) game. The special case of a simple hierarchical structure is the classical Kripke structure. Each hierarchical arena $\mathcal{V}$ can be transformed to an equivalent flat arena $\mathcal{V}^f$ (called its *flat expansion*) by recursively substituting each box by a copy of the sub-arena it refers to. Since different boxes can refer to the same sub-arena, states may appear in different contexts. In order to obtain unique names for states in the flat arena, we prefix each copy of a sub-arena's state by the sequence of boxes through which it was reached. Thus, a state $(b_0,\ldots,b_k,w)$ of $\mathcal{V}^{\mathrm{f}}$ is a vector whose last component w is a state of $\mathcal{V}$, and the remaining components $(b_0,\ldots,b_k)$ are boxes that describe its context. For simplicity, we refer to vectors of length one as elements (that is, w, rather than (w)). Formally, given a hierarchical arena $\mathcal{V} = \langle \mathcal{V}_1,\ldots,\mathcal{V}_n\rangle$, for each sub-arena $\mathcal{V}_i$ we inductively define its flat expansion $\mathcal{V}_i^{\mathrm{f}} = \langle W_i^{0^{\mathrm{f}}}, W_i^{1^{\mathrm{f}}}, \emptyset, in_i, exit_i, \emptyset, \mathcal{R}_i^{\mathrm{f}}\rangle$ as follows.[2]

- For $\sigma \in \{0,1\}$, the set $W_i^{\sigma^{\mathrm{f}}} \subseteq W_i^{\sigma} \cup (\mathcal{B}_i \times (\bigcup_{j=i+1}^{n} W_j^{\sigma^{\mathrm{f}}}))$ is defined as follows:

[2] We note that, unlike the definition of flat structures in [5], our definition of flat arenas also refers to exits. This is useful in the solution of games.

  - If w is a state of W_i^σ, then w belongs to $W_i^{\sigma f}$;
  - If b is a box of $\mathcal{V}_i$ with $\tau_i(b) = j$, and the tuple $(u_1,..., u_h)$ is a state in $W_j^{\sigma f}$, then $(b, u_1,..., u_h)$ belongs to $W_i^{\sigma f}$.
- The transition relation $\mathcal{R}_i^f$ is defined as follows.
  - If $(u, v) \in \mathcal{R}_i$, where $u \in W_i$ or $u = (b, e)$, where $b \in \mathcal{B}_i$ and $e \in exit_{\tau_i(b)}$, then if the target v is a state then $(u, v) \in \mathcal{R}_i^f$; and if v is a box then $(u, (v, in_{\tau_i(v)})) \in \mathcal{R}_i^f$. Note that $(v, in_{\tau_i(v)})$ is indeed a state of W_i^f by the second item in the definition of states above.
  - If b is a box of $\mathcal{V}_i$, and $((u_1,..., u_h), (v_1,..., v_{h'}))$ is a transition of $\mathcal{V}_{\tau_i(b)}^f$, then $((b, u_1,..., u_h), (b, v_1,..., v_{h'}))$ belongs to $\mathcal{R}_i^f$.

The arena $\mathcal{V}_1^f$ is the required flat expansion $\mathcal{V}^f$ of $\mathcal{V}$. Let $W_i^f = W_i^{0f} \cup W_i^{1f}$. In case $\mathcal{K} = \langle \mathcal{K}_1,..., \mathcal{K}_n \rangle$ is a hierarchical structure, where each $\mathcal{K}_i = \langle AP, \mathcal{V}_i, \sigma_i \rangle$ is a structure over AP, then the flat expansion is $\mathcal{K}_i^f = \langle AP, \mathcal{V}_i^f, \sigma_i^f \rangle$, where the labels are induced by the innermost state. Thus, $\sigma_i^f : W_i^f \times AP \to \{tt, ff\}$ is such that for every $p \in AP$, if $w = (u_1,..., u_h)$, then $\sigma_i^f(w, p) = \sigma_j(u_h, p)$, where j is the index of the structure of which u_h is a state of. A hierarchical structure $\mathcal{K}$ satisfies a formula φ (denoted $\mathcal{K} \models \varphi$) iff its flat expansion $\mathcal{K}^f$does. The *hierarchical model-checking problem* is to decide, given a hierarchical structure $\mathcal{K}$ and temporal logic formula φ, whether $\mathcal{K}$ satisfies φ.

The semantics of a game over a hierarchical arena is defined by means of its flat expansion, and thus the definitions of a play, a strategy, etc. are essentially the classic definitions for flat games. However, for our purpose, it is convenient to also consider plays over arenas $\mathcal{V}_i$, for $1 < i \leq n$, which are not the top level arena $\mathcal{V}_1$. Such arenas may have exit nodes, and we adjust the definitions to deal with these exits. Intuitively, a play of a game over $\mathcal{V}_i$ proceeds by moving a token on the nodes of the flat expansion $\mathcal{V}_i^f$, starting at the initial node in_i. If the token is placed on a node $s \in W_i^{\sigma f}$ then Player σ chooses the next move. The available moves are as follows. If s has no successors in $\mathcal{V}_i^f$, and $s \notin exit_i$ (we call such a node a *terminal node*), then the play ends; Otherwise, the player chooses a successor of s and moves the token to this successor, or, if $s \in exit_i$, he may choose instead to move the token "outside" $\mathcal{V}_i^f$, in which case the play also ends. A *play* of the game is thus a (finite or infinite) sequence of nodes $\pi = \pi_0, \pi_1,...$, namely, the sequence of nodes the token has traversed during the play, with possibly the symbol *out* at the end of a finite sequence (indicating that the token was moved out of the arena). A play π is *initial* if $\pi_0 = in_i$; it is *maximal* if it is *(i)* initial, and *(ii)* it is infinite, or it is finite but it cannot be extended to a longer play. We sometimes refer to plays as words in $(W^f)^\omega + (W^f)^* + (W^f)^* \cdot \{out\}$.

Consider a parity winning condition Γ. For a play π, let $maxC(\pi)$ be the maximal color that appears infinitely often along π (recall that by our assumptions an infinite play must have infinitely many colored nodes), or appears at least once if π is finite and has at least one colored node. A play is winning for Player 0 if it ends in a terminal node $s \in W_i^{1f}$, i.e., if Player 1 cannot extend the play; or if the play is infinite and satisfies Γ, i.e., $maxC(\pi)$ is even. Similarly, a play is winning for Player 1 if it ends in a terminal node $s \in W_i^{0f}$, or if the play is infinite and does not satisfy the winning condition Γ. A play that ends with *out* (i.e., because the token was moved outside the arena) is not winning for either player, and has an undefined value.

A *strategy* for a player is a function from prefixes of plays ending in one of his nodes, to the set of nodes plus the action *out*, telling Player σ what move to make in order to extend the play. Thus, for $\sigma \in \{0,1\}$, a Player σ strategy is a partial function $\xi : (W^{\mathrm{f}})^* \cdot W_i^{\sigma \mathrm{f}} \to (W^{\mathrm{f}} \cup \{out\})$, such that for all $u \cdot v$, with $u \in (W^{\mathrm{f}})^*$ and $v \in W_i^{\sigma \mathrm{f}}$, we have that $\xi(u \cdot v) = out$ only if $v \in exit_i^{\mathrm{f}}$, and otherwise, $(v, \xi(u \cdot v)) \in \mathcal{R}_i^{\mathrm{f}}$. A prefix $\pi_0,\ldots,\pi_n$ is consistent with a strategy ξ of Player σ, if for all $j \geq 0$ it holds that if π_j is a Player σ node then $\pi_{j+1} = \xi(\pi_0,\ldots,\pi_j)$. The function is partial as there may be vertices in $W_i^{\sigma \mathrm{f}}$ with no successors, and since we do not require it to be defined over plays that are not consistent with it. A strategy ξ is *memoryless* if its output does not depend on the whole prefix of the play, but only on the last position, i.e, if for all $u, u' \in (W^{\mathrm{f}})^*$ and all $v \in W_i^{\sigma \mathrm{f}}$, we have that $\xi(u \cdot v) = \xi(u' \cdot v)$. We can thus abbreviate and think of a memoryless strategy for Player σ as a partial function $\xi : W_i^{\sigma \mathrm{f}} \to (W^{\mathrm{f}} \cup \{out\})$. Observe that if $b_1, b_2 \in \mathcal{B}_i$ are two boxes that refer to the same sub-arena $\mathcal{V}_j$, then it is normally *not* the case that ξ (even if it is memoryless) behaves in the same way, inside $\mathcal{V}_j$, in both cases. That is, the choice of how to move inside $\mathcal{V}_j$ depends on the context in which it appears.

It is easy to see that for every two strategies, ξ^0 for Player 0 and ξ^1 for Player 1, there is exactly one play consistent with both strategies. Thus, two strategies induce a play. We denote this play by $outcome(\xi^0, \xi^1)$. A strategy ξ^σ for Player σ is *winning*, if for all strategies $\xi^{1-\sigma}$ for Player $1-\sigma$, the play $outcome(\xi^0, \xi^1)$ is winning for Player σ. Dually, a strategy ξ^σ for Player σ is *losing*, if there exists a strategy $\xi^{1-\sigma}$ for Player $1-\sigma$, for which the play $outcome(\xi^0, \xi^1)$ is winning for Player $1-\sigma$. Note that since plays that end with *out* have an undefined value, a strategy ξ^σ may be neither winning nor losing. Also note that if ξ^σ is not a losing strategy for Player σ, then all plays agreeing with ξ^σ that do not end with *out* are winning for Player σ. If the arena $\mathcal{V}_i$ has no exits, i.e., if $exit_i = \emptyset$, then neither does $\mathcal{V}_i^{\mathrm{f}}$, and the semantics of a game over $\mathcal{V}_i$ coincides with the classic definition for parity games over simple arenas. By [10], parity games are *determined* with memoryless strategies over simple arenas, i.e., it is always the case that one of the players (called the *winner* of the game) has a memoryless winning strategy. To *solve* a game over an arena with no exits is to find the winner of the game.

Observe that an alternative way of looking at the semantics of a game over the hierarchical arena $\mathcal{V}_i$ is to think of the token as being moved directly on the nodes of the sub-arenas $\mathcal{V}_i,\ldots,\mathcal{V}_n$, using an auxiliary stack to keep track of the context. Recall that a node $s = (b_0,\ldots,b_k,w)$ of $\mathcal{V}_i^{\mathrm{f}}$ is a vector whose last component w is a node in $\bigcup_{j=i}^{n}(W_j)$, and the remaining components $b_0,\ldots,b_k$ are boxes in $\bigcup_{j=i}^{n}(\mathcal{B}_j)$ that give its context. Thus, a token that is on s can be represented by a token on w, with an auxiliary stack containing $b_1 \cdots b_k$. Since the arena is hierarchical (and not recursive) the depth of the stack is bounded.

The *size* $|\mathcal{V}_i|$ of a sub-arena $\mathcal{V}_i$ is the sum $|W_i| + |\mathcal{B}_i| + |\mathcal{R}_i|$, and the number of exits of $\mathcal{V}_i$ is $|exit_i|$. The size $|\mathcal{V}|$ of a hierarchical arena $\mathcal{V}$ is the sum of the sizes of all its sub-arenas $\mathcal{V}_i$, and the number of its exits $exits(\mathcal{V}) = \max_i(|exit_i|)$ is the maximal number of exits in any of its sub-arenas. The nesting depth of $\mathcal{V}$, denoted $nd(\mathcal{V})$, is the length of the longest chain $i_1, i_2,..., i_j$ of indices such that a box of $\mathcal{V}_{i_l}$ is mapped to i_{l+1}. Observe that each state of the expanded structure is a vector of length at most the nesting depth, and that the size of $\mathcal{V}^f$ can be exponential in the nesting depth, i.e., $\Omega(|\mathcal{V}|^{nd(\mathcal{V})})$.

We are going to take the product of hierarchical games with *alternating tree automata*. We work with *symmetric* automata with *ε-transitions*. In such automata, the state space is partitioned into four types of states: universal ($Q^\wedge$), existential ($Q^\vee$), ε-and ($Q^{(\varepsilon,\wedge)}$), and ε-or ($Q^{(\varepsilon,\vee)}$) states (we also write $Q^{\vee,\wedge} = Q^\vee \cup Q^\wedge$, and $Q^\varepsilon = Q^{(\varepsilon,\vee)} \cup Q^{(\varepsilon,\wedge)}$). The transition function $\delta : Q \times \Sigma \to (Q \cup 2^Q)$ is such that for all $\sigma \in \Sigma$, we have that $\delta(q, \sigma) \in Q$ for $q \in Q^{\vee,\wedge}$, and $\delta(q, \sigma) \in 2^Q$ for $q \in Q^\varepsilon$. When an automaton $\mathcal{A}$ runs on an input tree, it starts with a copy in the initial state q_0 that reads the root of the tree. It then follows the transition function δ in order to send further copies. For example, if a copy of $\mathcal{A}$ in state $q \in Q^{(\varepsilon,\wedge)}$ reads a node labeled σ, and $\delta(q, \sigma) = \{q_1, q_2\}$, then this copy splits into two copies, in states q_1 and q_2, and both copies read the current node. As another example, if $q \in Q^\vee$ and $\delta(q, \sigma) = q_1$, then $\mathcal{A}$ sends a copy in state q_1 to one of the successors of the current node. Note that, by using ε-transitions, different copies of $\mathcal{A}$ may be reading the same node of the input tree. We assume that $Q^\vee$ contains two states *ff* (*rejecting sink*) and *tt* (*accepting sink*), such that for all $a \in \Sigma$, we have $\delta(tt, a) = tt$ and $\delta(ff, a) = ff$.

3 The Hierarchical Model-Checking Game

The game-based approach to model checking a flat system $\mathcal{K}$, with respect to a branching-time temporal logic specification φ, reduces the model-checking problem to solving a game obtained by taking the product of $\mathcal{K}$ with the alternating tree automaton $\mathcal{A}_\varphi$ [15]. In this section, we extend this approach to hierarchical structures: given a hierarchical system $\mathcal{K}$ and an alternating tree automaton $\mathcal{A}$, we construct a game $\mathcal{G}_{\mathcal{K},\mathcal{A}}$, such that Player 0 wins the game iff the tree obtained by unwinding the flat expansion of $\mathcal{K}$ is accepted by $\mathcal{A}$. In particular, when $\mathcal{A}$ accepts exactly all the tree models of a branching-time formula φ, the above holds iff $\mathcal{K}$ satisfies φ. Note that a naive approach for doing this is to start by constructing the flat expansion of $\mathcal{K}$ and then applying [15]. The whole point, however, is to avoid the exponentially large flat system and work directly in the hierarchical setting. We focus on the case in which $\mathcal{A}$ is an alternating parity tree automaton (APT), to which μ-calculus formulas are translated.

Given a hierarchical system $\mathcal{K} = \langle \mathcal{K}_1,..., \mathcal{K}_n \rangle$ and an APT $\mathcal{A} = \langle \Sigma, Q, q_0, \delta, F \rangle$, the hierarchical two-player game $\mathcal{G}_{\mathcal{K},\mathcal{A}} = (\mathcal{V}, \Gamma)$ for $\mathcal{K}$ and $\mathcal{A}$ is defined as follows. The hierarchical arena $\mathcal{V}$ has a sub-arena $\mathcal{V}_{i,q}$ for every $2 \le i \le n$ and state $q \in Q$, which is essentially the product of the structure $\mathcal{K}_i$ with $\mathcal{A}$, where the initial state of $\mathcal{K}_i$ is paired with the state q of $\mathcal{A}$. For $i = 1$, we need only the sub-arena V_{1,q_0}. The hierarchical order of the sub-arenas is consistent with the one in $\mathcal{K}$. Thus, the sub-arena $\mathcal{V}_{i,q}$ can be referred to by boxes of sub-arena $\mathcal{V}_{j,p}$ only if $i > j$.

Let $\mathcal{K}_i = \langle AP, W'_i, \mathcal{B}'_i, in'_i, exit'_i, \tau'_i, \mathcal{R}'_i, \sigma'_i \rangle$ and let $\mathcal{A} = \langle 2^{AP}, Q, q_0, \delta, F \rangle$ be an APT with Q partitioned to $Q^{(\varepsilon,\wedge)}$, $Q^{(\varepsilon,\vee)}$, $Q^{\wedge}$, and $Q^{\vee}$. Then, the sub-arena $\mathcal{V}_{i,q} = \langle W^0_{i,q}, W^1_{i,q}, \mathcal{B}_{i,q} in_{i,q}, exit_{i,q}, \tau_{i,q}, \mathcal{R}_{i,q} \rangle$ is defined as follows.

- $W^0_{i,q} = W'_i \times (Q^{\vee} \cup Q^{(\varepsilon,\vee)})$, $W^1_{i,q} = W'_i \times (Q^{\wedge} \cup Q^{(\varepsilon,\wedge)})$, $in_{i,q} = (in'_i, q)$, and $exit_{i,q} = exit'_i \times Q^{\vee,\wedge}$.
- $\mathcal{B}_{i,q} = \mathcal{B}'_i \times Q$, and $\tau_{i,q}(b, q) = (\tau'_i(b), q)$.
- For a state $u = (w, \hat{q}) \in W'_i \times Q$, if $\hat{q} \in Q^{\varepsilon}$ and $\delta(\hat{q}, \sigma'_i(w)) = \{p_0, \ldots, p_k\}$, then $(u, v) \in \mathcal{R}_{i,q}$ iff $v \in \{(w, p_0), \ldots, (w, p_k)\}$; and if $\hat{q} \in Q^{\vee,\wedge}$, then $(u, v) \in \mathcal{R}_{i,q}$ iff $v = (w', \delta(\hat{q}, \sigma'_i(w)))$ and $(w, w') \in \mathcal{R}'_i$.
- For $(b, p) \in \mathcal{B}'_i \times Q$, and an exit $(e, \hat{q}) \in exit'_{\tau'_i(b)} \times Q^{\vee,\wedge}$ of this box, then $(((b, p), (e, \hat{q})), v) \in \mathcal{R}_{i,q}$ iff $v = (w', \delta(\hat{q}, \sigma'_{\tau'_i(b)}(e)))$ and $((b, e), w') \in \mathcal{R}'_i$.

The winning condition of the game $\mathcal{G}_{\mathcal{K},\mathcal{A}}$ is induced by the acceptance condition of $\mathcal{A}$. Formally, for each state (w, q) of $\mathcal{V}_{i,q}$, we have $\Gamma(w, q) = F(q)$.

We now argue that the model checking problem $\mathcal{K} \models \varphi$ can be reduced to solving the hierarchical game $\mathcal{G}_{\mathcal{K},\mathcal{A}_\varphi}$. For that, we show that $\mathcal{G}_{\mathcal{K},\mathcal{A}_\varphi}$ is equivalent to the flat game $\mathcal{G}_{\mathcal{K}^f_1,\mathcal{A}_\varphi}$. Since, by [15], the model-checking problem can be reduced to solving the latter, we are done. The proof of the equivalence between $\mathcal{G}_{\mathcal{K},\mathcal{A}_\varphi}$ and $\mathcal{G}_{\mathcal{K}^f_1,\mathcal{A}_\varphi}$ is based on a bijection between the strategies of the two games. In particular, for every winning strategy for one of the players in $\mathcal{G}_{\mathcal{K},\mathcal{A}}$, there is a corresponding winning strategy for the same player in $\mathcal{G}_{\mathcal{K}^f_1,\mathcal{A}}$, and vice versa.

Theorem 1. *Consider a hierarchical system $\mathcal{K}$ and a branching-time formula φ. The following are equivalent: (i) $\mathcal{K}$ satisfies φ. (ii) Player 0 has a winning strategy in the flat game $\mathcal{G}_{\mathcal{K}^f_1,\mathcal{A}_\varphi}$. (iii) Player 0 has a winning strategy in the hierarchical game $\mathcal{G}_{\mathcal{K},\mathcal{A}_\varphi}$.*

In Section 4, we solve hierarchical two-player games and show how Theorem 1 leads to optimal model-checking algorithms for hierarchical systems.

4 Solving Hierarchical Parity Games

In this section we present an algorithm for solving hierarchical parity games. Consider a game $\mathcal{G} = (\mathcal{V}, \Gamma)$. A naive algorithm for solving the game would generate the flat expansion of $\mathcal{V}$ and solve it. In the flat expansion, each sub-arena may appear in many different contexts. The idea behind our algorithm is that even though the sub-arena appears in different contexts, the effect of the strategies chosen by the players for the segment of the game inside the sub-arena is independent of the context and can be summarized efficiently. The effects of every strategy of Player 0 for the segment of the play inside a sub-arena $\mathcal{V}_i$, can be captured by a *summary function* mapping each exit of $\mathcal{V}_i$ to the best color that Player 1 can hope for, if he chooses to respond by directing the token to leave $\mathcal{V}_i$ through this exit. The algorithm for solving the game $\mathcal{G} = (\mathcal{V}, \Gamma)$ then solves a sequence of flat parity games, obtained by replacing sub-arenas by gadgets that represent the behavior of Player 0 as a choice among the possible summary functions, and the behavior of Player 1 as a choice of the exit through which he wants the token to exit the sub-arena. The gadgets also take into account the possibility that the game will stay forever in the sub-arena.

We now describe the concept of summary functions in detail. Consider first a play that enters a box that has a single exit. Each player has one goal that is independent of the context in which the box appears: to either win inside the box, or failing that, use a strategy that provides the biggest possible advantage over the segment of the play that goes through the box. In the case where the box has multiple exits, the situation is more involved: if a player cannot force a win inside the box, he is faced with the question of which exit he should try to force the play to exit through. Depending on the context in which the box appears, it may be beneficial to force the play to a specific exit even if that involves letting the other player gain the upper hand in the path leading to it. Also, in certain situations, none of the players may force the game to a specific exit, and the strategy a player chooses may reflect a certain tradeoff between the different colors achieved on the paths going to the different exits.

In order to describe the relative merit of colors, we define an ordering $\succeq_0$ on colors by letting $c \succeq_0 c'$ when c is better for Player 0 than c'. Formally, $c \succeq_0 c'$ if the following holds: if c' is even then c is even and $c \geq c'$; and if c' is odd then either c is even, or c is also odd and $c \leq c'$. We denote by $\min^{\succeq_0}$ ($\max^{\succeq_0}$) the operation of taking the minimal (maximal) color, according to $\succeq_0$, of a finite set of colors. Consider a strategy ξ of Player 0 for a sub-arena $\mathcal{V}_i$. We define a function $g_\xi : exit_i \to C \cup \{\dashv\}$, called the *summary function* of ξ, that summarizes the best responses of Player 1 to ξ. [3] Let $e \in exit_i$ be an exit node of $\mathcal{V}_i$. If ξ is such that no matter how Player 1 plays, the token never exits through e, then we set $g_\xi(e) = \dashv$. Otherwise, we set $g_\xi(e)$ to be the most beneficial color that Player 1 can achieve along all plays that agree with ξ and exit through e. Formally, let $plays(\xi, e)$ be the set of all plays in $\mathcal{V}_i$ that agree with ξ and exit through e. For every $e \in exit_i$ we define $g_\xi(e) = \dashv$ if $plays(\xi, e) = \emptyset$, and $g_\xi(e) = \min^{\succeq_0}\{maxC(\pi) : \pi \in plays(\xi, e)\}$.

Recall that if ξ is not a losing strategy for Player 0 then all plays that agree with ξ and remain inside $\mathcal{V}_i$ are winning for Player 0. Hence, if ξ is not a losing strategy then Player 1 will always direct the token to exit through some exit $e \in exit_i$. Note that Player 1 can only choose e for which $g_\xi(e) \neq \dashv$, and that the choice of e depends on the context in which the sub-arena $\mathcal{V}_i$ appears. A key point in our algorithm is that, for every game $\mathcal{G}$ in which the sub-arena $\mathcal{V}_i$ is used, and every Player 0 strategy ξ for $\mathcal{V}_i$, if ξ is not a losing strategy then g_ξ captures all the information needed to analyze the influence of the play inside $\mathcal{V}_i$ on $\mathcal{G}$.

Let $Summ(\mathcal{V}_i) = \{g : g$ is a function from $exit_i$ to $C \cup \{\dashv\}\}$ be the set of all summary functions[4] for strategies of Player 0 over $\mathcal{V}_i$. If $\mathcal{V}_i$ has no exits, then $Summ(\mathcal{V}_i)$ contains only the empty summary function ε. Based on the ordering $\succeq_0$ we defined for colors, we can define a partial order $\succeq$ on $Summ(\mathcal{V}_i)$, by letting $g \succeq g'$ if for every exit node e of $\mathcal{V}_i$ the following holds: $g(e) = \dashv$, or $g(e) \neq \dashv \neq g'(e)$

[3] Note that our choice to consider summary functions of Player 0 strategies is arbitrary, and we could have taken Player 1's point of view instead.

[4] We call every $g \in Summ(\mathcal{V}_i)$ a "summary function" even if there is no Player 0 strategy whose summary is g.

and $g(e) \succeq_0 g'(e)$. Observe that if ξ and ϱ are two Player 0 strategies that are not losing strategies, and $g_\xi \succeq g_\varrho$, then Player 0 can always choose ξ over ϱ. Given a summary function $g \in Summ(\mathcal{V}_i)$, we say that a strategy ξ of Player 0 *achieves* g if $g_\xi \succeq g$; we say that g is *feasible* if there is a strategy ξ that achieves it; and we say that g is *relevant* if it can be achieved by a memoryless strategy that is not losing. In particular, if $\mathcal{V}_i$ has no exits, deciding whether the empty summary function ε is relevant amounts to deciding if it is not losing, i.e., to solving the game over $\mathcal{V}_i$.

We now describe the algorithm for solving a hierarchical parity game. The outline of the algorithm is described in Algorithm 1. Given a hierarchical parity game $\mathcal{G} = (\mathcal{V}, \Gamma)$, where $\mathcal{V} = \langle \mathcal{V}_1,..., \mathcal{V}_n \rangle$, our algorithm solves $\mathcal{G}$ by working its way up the hierarchy, starting with the lowest level sub-arena $\mathcal{V}_n$. At iteration $n \geq i \geq 1$, the algorithm first calculates the set M_i of relevant summary functions for strategies of Player 0 over $\mathcal{V}_i$. It does so by going over all summary functions and checking their relevancy. In order to check whether a summary function g is relevant, the algorithm solves a simple parity game $\mathcal{G}^{\mathsf{s}}_{i,g} = (\mathcal{V}^{\mathsf{s}}_{i,g}, \Gamma^{\mathsf{s}}_{i,g})$, which is defined in such a way that g is relevant iff Player 0 has a winning strategy for $\mathcal{G}^{\mathsf{s}}_{i,g}$. The arena $\mathcal{V}^{\mathsf{s}}_{i,g}$ is built from $\mathcal{V}_i$ by applying to it two operations: simplify, and loop. Once the set M_i is found, the algorithm uses it in order to construct a 3-level DAG structure H_i that reflects Player 0's choice of strategy for the sub-arena $\mathcal{V}_i$, and Player 1's possible responses to this strategy.

```
Input: G = (V, Γ), where V = ⟨V_1,..., V_n⟩
Output: true iff Player 0 wins G
for i = n downto 1 do
    M_i = ∅
    forall g ∈ Summ(V_i) do
        G^s_{i,g} = loop(g, simplify(V_i, H_{i+1},..., H_n))
        if Player 0 wins G^s_{i,g} then M_i = M_i ∪ {g}
    end
    if i > 1 then construct H_i from V_i and M_i
end
return true iff M_1 ≠ ∅
```

Algorithm 1. Solving a Hierarchical Parity Game.

The gadget H_i, together with $H_{i+1},..., H_n$ which were constructed in previous iterations, is used in future iterations. Indeed, as detailed below, the essence of the simplify procedure is to replace a box that refers to a sub-arena $\mathcal{V}_j$ by the gadget H_j. Since the top-level arena $\mathcal{V}_1$ has no exits, the only summary function it has is the empty summary function ε, which, by definition, is relevant iff Player 0 wins $\mathcal{G}$. Hence, the algorithm reduces the problem of solving the hierarchical game $\mathcal{G}$ to the problem of solving the simple parity game $\mathcal{G}^{\mathsf{s}}_{1,\varepsilon}$.

We now describe the construction of the gadget H_i. Let M_i be the set of all relevant summary functions for $\mathcal{V}_i$. Then, H_i is the following 3-level DAG:

- The set of nodes of H_i is $\{p\} \cup M_i \cup (exit_i \times C)$. The node p is a Player 0 node, every $g \in M_i$ is a Player 1 node, and a node $(e, c) \in exit_i \times C$ belongs to the same player that e belongs to.
- The set of edges is $\bigcup_{g \in M_i}(\{(p, g)\} \cup \{(g, (e, g(e))) : e \in exit_i \wedge g(e) \neq \dashv\})$.
- A node $(e, c) \in exit_i \times C$ is colored by c. These are the only colored nodes.

Finally, we remove from H_i all the nodes that are not reachable from its root p. Thus, in particular, if $M_i = \emptyset$, then p is the only node that remains in H_i. Intuitively, when the token is at the root p of the gadget H_i, Player 0 chooses a relevant summary function g for $\mathcal{V}_i$, and moves the token to the node g. In response, Player 1 chooses an exit $e \in exit_i$ for which $g(e) \neq \dashv$, and moves the token to the node $(e, g(e))$. The color of $(e, g(e))$ is $g(e)$, which is the best possible color achievable by Player 1 in any play over $\mathcal{V}_i$ that exits through e, when playing against a Player 0 strategy that achieves g.

Observe that if $M_i = \emptyset$, then it must be that all the summary functions in $Summ(\mathcal{V}_i)$ are not relevant, i.e., that all Player 0 strategies for $\mathcal{V}_i$ are losing. Note that this behavior is preserved if we turn all exit nodes of $\mathcal{V}_i$ to non-exit nodes. Hence, from the determinacy of simple parity games it follows that Player 1 has a winning strategy for $\mathcal{V}_i$, which explains why in this case H_i is a single terminal Player 0 node. Recall that for every $g \in M_i$ there exists at least one non-losing Player 0 strategy ξ^g that achieves g, and that since ξ^g is not losing, every play that agrees with ξ^g and does not exit $\mathcal{V}_i$ is winning for Player 0. It follows that if for every $e \in exit_i$ we have $g(e) = \dashv$ (in particular, if $exit_i = \emptyset$), then every play that is consistent with ξ^g cannot exit $\mathcal{V}_i$, and is thus winning for Player 0. This explains why in such a case the node g is a terminal Player 1 node.

It is left to describe and explain the operations simplify and loop. We start with simplify, which *simplifies* a hierarchical arena $\mathcal{V}_i$ by replacing every box $b \in \mathcal{B}_i$ by a copy of the gadget $H_{\tau_i(b)}$. Observe that the hierarchical nesting of the sub-arenas guarantees that all the boxes in $\mathcal{B}_i$ refer to arenas with an index higher than i, and thus the gadgets required for replacing them were already constructed in previous iterations. We usually denote the resulting flat arena simplify$(\mathcal{V}_i, H_{i+1}, \ldots H_n)$ by the shorter notation $\mathcal{V}_i^{\mathsf{s}}$. We now formally define $\mathcal{V}_i^{\mathsf{s}}$. To prevent name clashes between copies of the same gadget, given a box $b \in \mathcal{B}_i$, let H^b be a copy of $H_{\tau_i(b)}$ with all nodes renamed by annotating them with b. Replacing b with the gadget H^b is done by replacing every transition $(u, b) \in \mathcal{R}_i$ that enters b with a transition (u, p^b) that goes to the root of H^b, and replacing every transition $((b, e), v) \in \mathcal{R}_i$ that exits b with one transition $((e, c)^b, v)$ for every color c for which $(e, c)^b$ is present in H^b. Formally, given $\mathcal{V}_i = \langle W_i^0, W_i^1, \mathcal{B}_i, in_i, exit_i, \tau_i, \mathcal{R}_i\rangle$, then $\mathcal{V}_i^{\mathsf{s}} = \langle W_i^{0^{\mathsf{s}}}, W_i^{1^{\mathsf{s}}}, \emptyset, in_i, exit_i, \emptyset, \mathcal{R}_i^{\mathsf{s}}\rangle$, and its coloring function $\Gamma_i^{\mathsf{s}} : W_i^{\mathsf{s}} \to C$ are as follows:

- For $\sigma \in \{0, 1\}$, we have that $W_i^{\sigma^{\mathsf{s}}} = W_i^\sigma \cup \bigcup_{b \in \mathcal{B}_i} H^{b,\sigma}$, where $H^{b,\sigma}$ is the set of Player σ nodes of H^b.
- $\mathcal{R}_i^{\mathsf{s}}$ is $(W_i^{\mathsf{s}} \times W_i^{\mathsf{s}}) \cap \langle \bigcup_{b \in \mathcal{B}_i}(\{(u, p^b) : (u, b) \in \mathcal{R}_i\} \cup \{((e, c)^b, v) : c \in C, e \in exit_{\tau_i(b)}, ((b, e), v) \in \mathcal{R}_i\} \cup R(H^b)) \cup \mathcal{R}_i\rangle$, with $R(H^b)$ being the set of transitions of H^b.
- $\Gamma_i^{\mathsf{s}}(s) = \Gamma(s)$ for $s \in W_i$ for which $\Gamma(s)$ is defined; for every $b \in \mathcal{B}_i$ and every $(e, c) \in exit_{\tau_i(b)} \times C$ we have $\Gamma_i^{\mathsf{s}}((e, c)^b) = c$; otherwise, $\Gamma_i^{\mathsf{s}}(s)$ is undefined.

We now briefly describe the operation loop. Given a summary function g over a sub-arena $\mathcal{V}_i$, the operation $\mathsf{loop}(g, \mathcal{V}_i^{\mathrm{s}})$ constructs a simple arena $\mathcal{V}_{i,g}^{\mathrm{s}}$ such that Player 0 wins the associated simple parity game $\mathcal{G}_{i,g}^{\mathrm{s}} = (\mathcal{V}_{i,g}^{\mathrm{s}}, \Gamma_{i,g}^{\mathrm{s}})$ iff g is relevant. To build $\mathcal{V}_{i,g}^{\mathrm{s}}$ from $\mathcal{V}_i^{\mathrm{s}}$, we add, for every exit node $e \in exit_i$, a new Player 0 node $(e, 0)$ which is colored by $g(e) + 1$ if $g(e)$ is odd, is colored by $g(e) - 1$ if $g(e)$ is even, and is uncolored if $g(e) = \dashv$. Also, if $g(e) \neq \dashv$, we add the edges $(e, (e, 0))$, and $((e, 0), in_i)$. Finally, we designate all states of $\mathcal{V}_{i,g}^{\mathrm{s}}$ as non-exits. Note that the operations loop and $\mathsf{simplify}$ commute. By first adding the above states and loops to $\mathcal{V}_i$, and then simplifying, the reader may find it easier to see why g is relevant iff Player 0 wins $\mathcal{G}_{i,g}^{\mathrm{s}}$.

Observe that the definition of a summary function of a strategy can also be applied to Player 0 strategies over $\mathcal{V}_i^{\mathrm{s}}$. Since $\mathcal{V}_i$ has the same exit nodes as $\mathcal{V}_i^{\mathrm{s}}$, then the sets of summary functions over $\mathcal{V}_i$ and $\mathcal{V}_i^{\mathrm{s}}$ coincide, and we can compare strategy functions over $\mathcal{V}_i$ with ones over $\mathcal{V}_i^{\mathrm{s}}$ using the relation $\succeq$. Given a strategy ξ of Player 0 for $\mathcal{V}_i$, we say that a strategy ξ', of Player 0 for $\mathcal{V}_i^{\mathrm{s}}$, is *as good as* ξ, when: *(i)* if ξ is a winning strategy then so is ξ'; and *(ii)* if ξ is not a losing strategy then so is ξ', and $g_{\xi'} \succeq g_{\xi}$. We define strategies over $\mathcal{V}_i$ that are as good as strategies over $\mathcal{V}_i^{\mathrm{s}}$ in a symmetric way.

Lemma 1. *For every $1 \leq i \leq n$, and every memoryless strategy ξ of Player 0 for $\mathcal{V}_i$, there is a memoryless strategy ξ' for $\mathcal{V}_i^{\mathrm{s}}$ that is as good as ξ; and viceversa.*

By applying Lemma 1 to the arenas $\mathcal{V}_1$ and $\mathcal{V}_1^{\mathrm{s}}$, we obtain the following result:

Theorem 2. *Given a hierarchical parity game $\mathcal{G} = (\mathcal{V}, \Gamma)$, Player 0 wins the game iff he wins the simple parity game $\mathcal{G}_{1,\varepsilon}^{\mathrm{s}} = (\mathcal{V}_{1,\varepsilon}^{\mathrm{s}}, \Gamma_{1,\varepsilon}^{\mathrm{s}})$.*

Analyzing the time and space requirements of the above algorithm for solving hierarchical parity games, we get the following.

Theorem 3. *Let $\mathcal{G} = (\mathcal{V}, \Gamma)$ be a hierarchical parity game with k colors, $m = |\mathcal{V}|$ and $e = exits(\mathcal{V})$. Solving $\mathcal{G}$ can be done in time $2^{k \cdot \log m + O(k \cdot e \cdot \log k)}$, and it is* PSPACE*-complete.*

We conclude this section with a theorem that specifies the model-checking complexity for various branching-time temporal logics. Given a hierarchical system $\mathcal{K}$ and a branching-time temporal logic formula φ, the time complexity of model checking $\mathcal{K}$ with respect to φ follows by applying our algorithm for solving hierarchical parity games to the game $\mathcal{G}_{\mathcal{K},\mathcal{A}_\varphi} = (\mathcal{V}, \Gamma)$, where A_φ is an APT accepting exactly the set of trees satisfying the formula φ. In particular, we recall that if φ is a CTL or an alternation-free μ-calculus formula, then $\mathcal{A}_\varphi$ has $O(|\varphi|)$ states and index 2, if φ is a CTL* formula, then $\mathcal{A}_\varphi$ has $2^{O(|\varphi|)}$ states and index 3, and if φ is a μ-calculus formula, then $\mathcal{A}_\varphi$ has $O(|\varphi|)$ states and index $O(|\varphi|)$ [15]. Let h be the number of states of $\mathcal{A}_\varphi$, observe that $|\mathcal{V}| = |\mathcal{K}| \cdot h$, $exits(\mathcal{V}) = exits(\mathcal{K}) \cdot h$ and the number of sub-arenas of $\mathcal{V}$ is h times the number of sub-structures of $\mathcal{K}$. As we show in Theorem 3 our algorithm for solving hierarchical parity games can be implemented in polynomial space, which gives an alternative proof of the PSPACE upper bound for the hierarchical μ-calculus model checking given in [12]. For the other logics, a PSPACE upper bound follows by simply flattening the system and applying the NLOGSPACE algorithm from [15]. The PSPACE lower-bound for all these logics follows from the known result about CTL [5]. Note that for the logic CTL, the time complexity of the model-checking problem was already known and our algorithm suggests an alternative to the one in [5]. For the other logics, our approach leads to improved time complexities. It is interesting to note that for all branching-time temporal logics we consider, the hierarchical setting is easier than the recursive one.

Theorem 4. *Consider a hierarcical system $\mathcal{K}$ and a specification φ for it. Let e be the number of exits of the system, and l be the alternation depth of φ.*

- *For the μ-calculus, the model checking problem is PSPACE-complete and can be solved in time $(|\mathcal{K}| \cdot |\varphi|)^l \cdot 2^{O(|\varphi|) \cdot e \cdot l \cdot \log l}$.*
- *For* CTL *and the alternation-free μ-calculus, the model-checking problem is PSPACE-complete and can be solved in time $2^{(2 \log |\mathcal{K}| + O(|\varphi|) \cdot e)}$.*
- *For* CTL**, the model-checking problem is PSPACE-complete and can be solved in time $2^{(3 \log |\mathcal{K}| + 2^{O(|\varphi|)} \cdot e)}$.*

5 An Abstraction-Refinement Paradigm

In [22], Shoham and Grumberg defined 3-valued games and used them to describe an abstraction-refinement framework for CTL. In this section, we lift their contribution to hierarchical systems. As we show, the idea of summary functions can be applied also for solving *hierarchical 3-valued games.* Due to the lack of space, we describe here in detail the new notions of hierarchical 3-valued games and abstractions, and give only the idea behind the algorithm. In fact, once the notions are defined, then combining the algorithm in Section 4 for the concrete hierarchical setting, and the game-based approach to abstraction-refinement for the flat setting [22], into a game-based approach to abstraction-refinement of hierarchical systems, is not technically difficult. Essentially, the idea is as follows. In a 2-valued game, the goal of a player is to win. In a 3-valued game, the goal of a player is to win or (in case he cannot win) not to lose (that is, force the game to an "unknown" winning value). Accordingly, the lifting of algorithm in Section 4 to the 3-valued setting is based on adding a layer to the gadgets H_i described there; a layer in which Player 0 chooses between winning and not losing.

As in the flat setting, abstraction is based on merging sets of states of the concrete system into abstract states. What makes the hierarchical setting interesting is the fact that now it is possible to merge also boxes. Consider a (concrete) hierarchical structure. A sub-structure typically stands for a function, and a call to a function g from within another function f is modeled by a box inside the sub-structure modeling f that refers to the sub-structure modeling g. The values of the local variables of f are typically different in different calls to g. Thus, the source of complexity is not the number of sub-structures, but rather the number of states and boxes in each sub-structure. Accordingly, our abstraction does not try to merge sub-systems and contains one abstract sub-system for each concrete sub-system. Our abstraction does merge sets of concrete states into a single abstract state and sets of concrete boxes (referring to the same structures) into a single abstract box.

A *hierarchical 3-valued game* is similar to a hierarchical game, only that there are two transition relations $Rmust_i$ and $Rmay_i$, referred to as the *must* and *may* transitions. The transitions are defined as $\mathcal{R}_i$ in a hierarchical game and satisfy $Rmust_i \subseteq Rmay_i$. A *hierarchical modal transition system* (HMTS) over AP is then similar to a hierarchical system, only that, again, there are both must and may transitions, and the labeling function $\sigma_i : W_i \times AP \rightarrow \{tt, ff, \bot\}$ can map an atomic proposition also to $\bot$ (unknown). Note that, equivalently, we could have defined HMTS by adding hierarchy to the MTS of [17].

Given a (concrete) hierarchical system $\mathcal{K} = \langle \mathcal{K}_1,..., \mathcal{K}_n \rangle$, with $\mathcal{K}_i = \langle AP, W_i, \mathcal{B}_i, in_i, exit_i, \tau_i, \mathcal{R}_i, \sigma_i \rangle$, an abstraction of $\mathcal{K}$ is an HMTS $\mathcal{M} = \langle \mathcal{M}_1^A,..., \mathcal{M}_n^A \rangle$, where for every $1 \leq i \leq n$, the sub-model $\mathcal{M}_i^A = \langle AP, W_i^A, \mathcal{B}_i^A, in_i^A, exit_i^A, \tau_i^A, Rmust_i, Rmay_i, \sigma_i^A \rangle$ of $\mathcal{M}$ is an abstraction of the sub-structure $\mathcal{K}_i$, defined as follows. The set of abstract states is $W_i^A \subseteq 2^{W_i}$, and it forms a partition of W_i. The set of abstract boxes is $\mathcal{B}_i^A$, it forms a partition of $\mathcal{B}_i$, and an abstract box contains only concrete boxes that refer to the same sub-structure. Thus, if $b, b' \in b^a \in \mathcal{B}_i^A$, then $\tau_i(b) = \tau_i(b')$. The latter guarantees that the indexing function $\tau_i^A : \mathcal{B}_i^A \rightarrow \{i+1,..., n\}$, defined by $\tau_i^A(b^a) = \tau_i(b)$, for some $b \in b^a$, is well defined. The initial state in_i^A is such that $in_i \in in_i^A$. The set of abstract exits $exit_i^A \subseteq W_i^A$ is such that $e^a \in exit_i^A$ iff $e^a \cap exit_i \neq \emptyset$. Thus, the abstract initial state contains the concrete initial state, and an abstract exit contains at least one concrete exit. The transition relations $Rmay_i$ and $Rmust_i$ are subsets of $(\bigcup_{b \in \mathcal{B}_i^A}(\{b\} \times exit_{\tau_i^A(b)}) \cup W_i^A) \times (W_i^A \cup \mathcal{B}_i^A)$, and are over- and under-approximations of the concrete transitions. Given $w^a = (b^a, e^a) \in \bigcup_{b^a \in \mathcal{B}_i^A}(\{b^a\} \times exit_{\tau_i^A(b^a)})$, we write $w_c \in w^a$ if $w_c = (b_c, e_c)$, $b_c \in b^a$, and $e_c \in e^a$. Using the above notation, we have that $(w^a, w^{a'}) \in Rmay_i$ if there exist $w_c \in w^a$ and $w_c' \in w^{a'}$ such that $(w_c, w_c') \in R_i$; and $(w^a, w^{a'}) \in Rmust_i$ only if for all $w_c \in w^a$ there exists $w_c' \in w^{a'}$ such that $(w_c, w_c') \in R_i$. Finally, an atomic proposition holds (does not hold) in an abstract state if it holds (does not hold) in all the concrete states in it; otherwise, its truth value is undefined.

As shown for hierarchical systems, an HMTS $\mathcal{M}$ can be translated to a flat modal transition system (MTS) $\mathcal{M}^f$ by means of the flattening operation (since we only consider abstractions in which all the concrete boxes in an abstract box refer to the same structure, the flattening described for concrete systems can indeed be applied). The semantics of a temporal logic formula φ over $\mathcal{M}$ is thus simply defined to be the semantics of φ over $\mathcal{M}^f$. For the latter, we use the 3-valued semantics introduced in [14]. The idea is that since may transitions over-approximate concrete transitions, they are used to verify universal formulas or to refute existential formulas. Dually, since must transitions under-approximate concrete transitions, they are used to verify existential formulas or to refute universal formulas. We use $[\mathcal{M}^A \models \varphi]$ to denote the truth value (in $\{tt, ff, \bot\}$) of φ in $\mathcal{M}^A$. Applying the same considerations applied to MTSs [11], it is not hard to see that if an HMTS $\mathcal{M}^A$ abstracts a hierarchical structure $\mathcal{K}$, then $[\mathcal{M}^A \models \varphi] = tt(ff)$ implies that $\mathcal{K} \models \varphi$ (resp. $\mathcal{K} \not\models \varphi$).

Given an HMTS $\mathcal{M}$, and a CTL formula φ, we reduce the problem of deciding the value of $[\mathcal{M}^A \models \varphi]$, to solving a 3-valued game $\mathcal{G}_{\mathcal{M},\mathcal{A}_\varphi}$ obtained by taking the product of $\mathcal{M}$ with the weak alternating tree automaton $\mathcal{A}_\varphi$. The reason we restrict attention to CTL formulas is that taking the product of an HMTS with a weak automaton that corresponds to a CTL formula, there is a distinction between information lost in $\mathcal{M}$ due to atomic propositions whose value is unknown and information lost due to may and must transitions. Indeed, the states of the weak automaton are associated with either atomic propositions (in which case only the first type of missed information should be taken into an account) or with a subformula of the form AX or EX (where only the second type should be taken into an account). Furthermore, in the second case, the game is in either a universal (AX) or existential (EX) mode, so players can proceed along the must and may transitions in their attempt to prove or refute φ.

Now, as in [22], both players try to either prove or refute φ, and winning strategies must be *consistent*: all transitions taken during a play are must transitions (note that the consistency requirement applies only to winning strategies; the opponent can take also may transitions). Also, a winning strategy cannot end in a state associated with an atomic proposition whose value is unknown. It may be that none of the players have a winning strategy, in which case the value of the game is $\perp$. As described in Section 3 for concrete systems, the hierarchy in the system induces the hierarchy in the product game.

Theorem 5. *Given an HMTS $\mathcal{M}$ and a CTL formula φ, let $\mathcal{G}_{\mathcal{M},\mathcal{A}_\varphi}$ be the product of $\mathcal{M}$ with $\mathcal{A}_\varphi$. Then: (i) Player 0 has a winning strategy in $\mathcal{G}_{\mathcal{M},\mathcal{A}_\varphi}$ iff $[\mathcal{M} \models \varphi] = tt$. (ii) Player 1 has a winning strategy in $\mathcal{G}_{\mathcal{M},\mathcal{A}_\varphi}$ iff $[\mathcal{M} \models \varphi] = ff$. (iii) None of the players have a winning strategy in $\mathcal{G}_{\mathcal{M},\mathcal{A}_\varphi}$ iff $[\mathcal{M} \models \varphi] = \perp$.*

It is left to solve the 3-valued game $\mathcal{G}_{\mathcal{M},\mathcal{A}_\varphi}$. We do this by adjusting the algorithm described in Section 4 to the 3-valued setting. Recall that while a winning strategy in the 3-valued game has to proceed only along must transitions, the strategy of the opponent may proceed also along may transitions. Consider a strategy ξ of Player 0 for an abstract sub-arena $\mathcal{V}_i$. In order to fully capture the possible responses of Player 1 to ξ, we have to associate with ξ two summary functions: g_ξ^{must} and g_ξ^{may}. The function g_ξ^{must} captures the possible responses of Player 1 if it only uses must transitions (i.e., it tries to win), while g_ξ^{may} captures the possible responses of Player 1 if it uses may transitions (i.e., it tries not to lose). Accordingly, the gadget H_j constructed by the algorithm consists of a 4-level DAG (rather than a 3-level DAG in the concrete setting), where the additional level serves to let the player choose between trying to win and trying not to lose. Once we transform an hierarchical arena into a simple one by means of the gadgets, we can continue to solve 3-valued games on these arenas as in [22].

References

1. Alur, R., Benedikt, M., Etessami, K., Godefroid, P., Reps, T.W., Yannakakis, M.: Analysis of recursive state machines. ACM TOPLAS 27(4), 786–818 (2005)
2. Alur, R., Chaudhuri, S., Etessami, K., Madhusudan, P.: On-the-fly reachability and cycle detection for recursive state machines. In: Halbwachs, N., Zuck, L.D. (eds.) TACAS 2005. LNCS, vol. 3440, pp. 61–76. Springer, Heidelberg (2005)

3. Alur, R., Etessami, K., Yannakakis, M.: Analysis of recursive state machines. In: Berry, G., Comon, H., Finkel, A. (eds.) CAV 2001. LNCS, vol. 2102, pp. 207–220. Springer, Heidelberg (2001)
4. Alur, R., Kannan, S., Yannakakis, M.: Communicating hierarchical state machines. In: Wiedermann, J., Van Emde Boas, P., Nielsen, M. (eds.) ICALP 1999. LNCS, vol. 1644, pp. 169–178. Springer, Heidelberg (1999)
5. Alur, R., Yannakakis, M.: Model checking of hierarchical state machines. ACM Trans. Program. Lang. Syst. 23(3), 273–303 (2001)
6. Clarke, E.M., Grumberg, O., Peled, D.: Model Checking. MIT Press, Cambridge (1999)
7. Dams, D., Gerth, R., Grumberg, O.: Abstract interpretation of reactive systems. ACM Trans. Program. Lang. Syst. 19(2), 253–291 (1997)
8. de Roever, W.-P., Langmaack, H., Pnueli, A. (eds.): COMPOS 1997. LNCS, vol. 1536. Springer, Heidelberg (1998)
9. Drusinsky, D., Harel, D.: On the power of bounded concurrency I: Finite automata. J. of the ACM 41(3), 517–539 (1994)
10. Emerson, E.A., Jutla, C.: Tree automata, μ-calculus and determinacy. In: FOCS 1991, pp. 368–377 (1991)
11. Godefroid, P., Jagadeesan, R.: Automatic abstraction using generalized model checking. In: Brinksma, E., Larsen, K.G. (eds.) CAV 2002. LNCS, vol. 2404, pp. 137–150. Springer, Heidelberg (2002)
12. Göller, S., Lohrey, M.: Fixpoint logics on hierarchical structures. In: Sarukkai, S., Sen, S. (eds.) FSTTCS 2005. LNCS, vol. 3821, pp. 483–494. Springer, Heidelberg (2005)
13. Harel, D., Kupferman, O., Vardi, M.Y.: On the complexity of verifying concurrent transition systems. J. of Inf. & Comp. 173, 1–19 (2002)
14. Huth, M., Jagadeesan, R., Schmidt, D.A.: Modal transition systems: A foundation for three-valued program analysis. In: Sands, D. (ed.) ESOP 2001. LNCS, vol. 2028, pp. 155–169. Springer, Heidelberg (2001)
15. Kupferman, O., Vardi, M.Y., Wolper, P.: An automata-theoretic approach to branching-time model checking. J. of the ACM 47(2), 312–360 (2000)
16. La Torre, S., Napoli, M., Parente, M., Parlato, G.: Verification of scope-dependent hierarchical state machines. Inf. Comput. 206(9-10), 1161–1177 (2008)
17. Larsen, K.G., Thomsen, B.: A modal process logic. In: LICS, pp. 203–210. IEEE Computer Society, Los Alamitos (1988)
18. Murano, A., Napoli, M., Parente, M.: Program complexity in hierarchical module checking. In: Cervesato, I., Veith, H., Voronkov, A. (eds.) LPAR 2008. LNCS (LNAI), vol. 5330, pp. 318–332. Springer, Heidelberg (2008)
19. Pnueli, A.: In transition from global to modular temporal reasoning about programs. In: Apt, K. (ed.) Logics and Models of Concurrent Systems. NATO Advanced Summer Institutes, vol. F-13, pp. 123–144. Springer, Heidelberg (1985)
20. Qadeer, S.: Taming concurrency: A program verification perspective. In: van Breugel, F., Chechik, M. (eds.) CONCUR 2008. LNCS, vol. 5201, p. 5. Springer, Heidelberg (2008)
21. Rabinovich, A.: Complexity of equivalence problems for concurrent systems of finite agents. J. of Inf. & Comp. 139(2), 111–129 (1997)
22. Shoham, S., Grumberg, O.: A game-based framework for CTL counterexamples and 3-valued abstraction-refinement. In: Hunt Jr., W.A., Somenzi, F. (eds.) CAV 2003. LNCS, vol. 2725, pp. 275–287. Springer, Heidelberg (2003)

Path-Oriented Reachability Verification of a Class of Nonlinear Hybrid Automata Using Convex Programming

Lei Bu, Jianhua Zhao, and Xuandong Li

State Key Laboratory for Novel Software Technology, Nanjing University
Department of Computer Science and Technology, Nanjing University
Nanjing, Jiangsu, P.R.China 210093
bl@seg.nju.edu.cn, {zhaojh,lxd}@nju.edu.cn

Abstract. Hybrid automata are well-studied formal models for dynamical systems. However, the analysis of hybrid automata is extremely difficult, and even state-of-the-art tools can only analyze systems with few continuous variables and simple dynamics. Because the reachability problem for general hybrid automata is undecidable, we give a path-oriented reachability analysis procedure for a class of nonlinear hybrid automata called *convex hybrid automata*. Our approach encodes the reachability problem along a path of a convex hybrid automaton as a convex feasibility problem, which can be efficiently solved by off-the-shelf convex solvers, such as CVX. Our path-oriented reachability verification approach can be applied in the frameworks of bounded model checking and counterexample-guided abstraction refinement with the goal of achieving significant performance improvement for this subclass of hybrid automata.

1 Introduction

Hybrid automata [15] are widely used as the modeling language for hybrid systems – dynamical systems with both discrete and continuous system variables. Due to the presence of continuous real-valued variables, model checking of hybrid automata is very difficult. Despite many years of active research, there is still a complete lack of practical techniques to check the reachability problem of high dimensional hybrid automata with relatively simple dynamics [1][11]. For nonlinear hybrid automata, the verification of systems with five variables usually requires several hours of computation [18]. Even for the very simple class of *linear hybrid automata*, the reachability problem is computationally intensive and the size of solvable problems is quite limited [11].

In our earlier study on linear hybrid automata [17], we have proposed a complementary approach to the polyhedra based model checking of linear hybrid automata. Our approach is an efficient method that encodes the reachability problem along a path of a linear hybrid automaton as the feasibility problem of a linear program. As linear programming has polynomial complexity, both the length of the path being checked and the size of the automaton can be large enough to tackle problems of practical interest. This approach to symbolic execution of paths can be used by design engineers to check critical paths, thereby increasing the confidence in the correctness of the system. In [17][6],

G. Barthe and M. Hermenegildo (Eds.): VMCAI 2010, LNCS 5944, pp. 78–94, 2010.

we have conducted a series of case studies to demonstrate the practical performance of this approach.

Nevertheless, most industrial examples are nonlinear; therefore, nonlinear hybrid automata are the models of choice for industrial plants and controllers. The state-of-the-art nonlinear model checkers such as CheckMate [5] and d/dt [9] use general polyhedral over-approximations to compute the reachable states. To the best of our knowledge, they can only handle systems with few continuous variables. In this paper, we extend the method in [17] to develop an efficient method for solving the path-oriented reachability problem for a class of nonlinear hybrid automata. With the method presented in this paper, we can check the correctness of a given path in a hybrid automaton, where the paths being checked can be quite long and both the dimension and the number of locations of the automaton can be large enough to handle problems of practical interest. Our proposed method is meant to analyze a special class of nonlinear hybrid automata called *convex hybrid automata* (CHA). A hybrid automaton is said to be a convex hybrid automaton if each flow (sequence of states) in such an automaton is inside a convex set. In this paper, we encode the path-oriented reachability problem of a CHA as the feasibility problem of a convex program. We also present several case studies to show the performance of this method when applied to systems of high dimensions.

This paper is organized as follows. In the next section, we define the convex hybrid automata and the path-oriented reachability discussed in this paper. In Sec. 3, we present a semi-decision procedure to transform a path-oriented reachability specification of a CHA into a convex program. If the convex program is not feasible, we can prove the path-oriented reachability specification is not satisfied. In Sec.4, we extend our semi-decision procedure such that this procedure can give exact answer for two special classes of CHA when the reacability specification is satisfiable. Sec. 5 describes several case studies to show the practical performance of our method with respect to both the length of the paths and the dimension of the systems being analyzed. Sec. 6 describes several potential future applications of the approach presented in this paper.

2 Convex Hybrid Automata

We introduce the notion of *convex hybrid automata* and discuss the notations needed to study the path-oriented reachability of such systems.

2.1 Definition of Convex Hybrid Automata

The set of hybrid automata considered in this paper is a special class of general nonlinear hybrid automata where the state space of each location is a convex set. In order to meet the convexity requirement, we take advantage of the idea of disciplined convex programming [13]. In disciplined convex programming, all the *convex constraints* of a convex program should fall into one of the two kinds below[1]:

- Equality (=) constraints: Both the left-hand and right-hand side of a constraint are affine linear functions of the optimization variables, for example $2x + 5z = 3y + 7$.

[1] We refer the reader to the book [4] for a detailed discussion on convex programming.

– Less-than ($\leq$, $<$) inequality constraints: The left-hand expression is convex and the right-hand expression is concave, for example $6y^4 + 7z^6 - 3 \leq -5x^2$.

Borrowing this idea from disciplined convex programming, we add conservative restrictions to the definition of a hybrid automaton and refer to the resulting automaton as a *Convex Hybrid Automaton*. Without loss of generality, the *convex hybrid automata* considered in this paper will have just one initial location with no initial conditions or transitions to the initial location, and each variable is reset to an initial convex set by the transitions from the initial location.

Definition 1. A *convex hybrid automaton* is a tuple $H = (X, V, E, v_I, \alpha, \beta)$, where

– X is a finite set of real-valued variables.
– V is a finite set of *locations*.
– E is the *transition* relation whose elements are of the form (v, ϕ, ψ, v'), where
  • $v, v' \in V$,
  • ϕ is a set of *transition guards* of the form:
    * $f(\boldsymbol{x}) \leq 0$ where f is a convex function, or
    * $f(\boldsymbol{x}) = 0$ where f is an affine linear function,
  • ψ is a set of *reset actions* of the form $x_i := c_i$ where $x_i \in X$ $(0 \leq i \leq m)$ and $c_i \in \mathbb{R}$.
– v_I is the *initial* location.
– α is a labeling function which maps each location in $V - \{v_I\}$ to a *location invariant* which is a set of constraints of the form:
  • $f(\boldsymbol{x}) \leq 0$ where f is a convex function, or
  • $f(\boldsymbol{x}) = 0$ where f is an affine linear function.
– β is a labeling function which maps each location in $V - \{v_I\}$ to a set of *flow conditions* which is of the form: $\dot{x}_i \in [k_i(t), l_i(t)]$ where $dk_i/dt \geq 0$ and $dl_i/dt \leq 0$, $k_i : \mathbb{R} \rightarrow \mathbb{R}$, $l_i : \mathbb{R} \rightarrow \mathbb{R}$. $k_i(t)$ and $l_i(t)$ are continuously differentiable over $\mathbb{R}$; at most one of $k_i(t)$ and $l_i(t)$ may be $-\infty$ (or ∞).
  For any location v and any $x_i \in X$, there is one and only one definition of the flow condition. □

Definition 2. Given a convex hybrid automaton $H = (X, V, E, v_I, \alpha, \beta)$, a *state* s of H is a pair (v, q) such that

– $v \in V$
– $q = (x_{1_q}, x_{2_q} \ldots x_{n_q})$ is a valuation of all the continuous variables in X, such that q satisfies the location invariant α_v of v .

The state space S of location v_i is a (possibly infinite) set of states $\{(v, q) \mid v = v_i\}$. □

2.2 Path and Path-Oriented Reachability

We use sequence of locations to represent the evolution of a convex hybrid automaton from one location to another. For a convex hybrid automaton $H = (X, V, E, v_I, \alpha, \beta)$, a *path segment* is a sequence of locations of the form

$$v_1 \xrightarrow{(\phi_1, \psi_1)} v_2 \xrightarrow{(\phi_2, \psi_2)} \ldots \xrightarrow{(\phi_{n-1}, \psi_{n-1})} v_n$$

which satisfies $(v_i, \phi_i, \psi_i, v_{i+1}) \in E$ for each i $(1 \le i \le n-1)$. A *path* in H is a path segment starting at v_I.

The *behavior* of a path $v_I \xrightarrow{(\phi_0,\psi_0)} v_1 \xrightarrow{(\phi_1,\psi_1)} v_2 \xrightarrow{(\phi_2,\psi_2)} \ldots \xrightarrow{(\phi_{n-1},\psi_{n-1})} v_n$ can be represented by a *timed sequence*. A timed sequence is a sequence of the form $(v_1, t_1)\hat{}(v_2, t_2)\hat{}\ldots\hat{}(v_n, t_n)$ where v_i $(1 \le i \le n)$ is a location and t_i $(1 \le i \le n)$ is a nonnegative real number. Such a timed sequence represents the execution of a path where the system starts at the initial location and jumps to location v_1, stays there for t_1 time units, then jumps to location v_2 and stays at v_2 for t_2 time units, and so on[2].

Definition 3. For a convex hybrid automaton $H = (X, V, E, v_I, \alpha, \beta)$, a path $p = v_I \xrightarrow{(\phi_0,\psi_0)} v_1 \xrightarrow{(\phi_1,\psi_1)} v_2 \xrightarrow{(\phi_2,\psi_2)} \ldots \xrightarrow{(\phi_{n-1},\psi_{n-1})} v_n$ in H, a timed sequence $(v_1, t_1)\hat{}(v_2, t_2)\hat{}\ldots\hat{}(v_n, t_n)$ represents a behavior corresponding to p in H if and only if the following conditions are satisfied:

1. There exists a valuation $\gamma_i(\boldsymbol{x})$ $(1 \le i \le n)$ of all the state variables $\boldsymbol{x}$ when the automaton has stayed at location v_i for t_i time units,such that
   (a) $\gamma_i(\boldsymbol{x})$ satisfies all the transition guards in ϕ_i , and
   (b) $\gamma_i(\boldsymbol{x})$ satisfies all the location invariants in α_{v_i}.
2. There exists a valuation $\delta_i(\boldsymbol{x})$ $(1 \le i \le n)$ of all the state variables $\boldsymbol{x}$ at the time when the automaton jumped from location v_{i-1} to location v_i, such that
   (a) $\delta_i(\boldsymbol{x})$ satisfies all the reset actions in ψ_{i-1} when applied to the valuation $\gamma_{i-1}(\boldsymbol{x})$,
   (b) $\delta_i(\boldsymbol{x})$ satisfies all the location invariants in α_{v_i}.
3. There exists a differentiable function $W_j : [0, t_i] \to \mathbb{R}$ for each variable $x_j \in X(1 \le i \le n, 1 \le j \le m)$, with the first derivative $w_j : [0, t_i] \to \mathbb{R}$, such that
   (a) $W_j(0) = \delta_i(x_j)$ and $W_j(t_i) = \gamma_i(x_j)$
   (b) for all reals $\varepsilon \in [0, t_i]$
      i. $W_j(\varepsilon)$ satisfies all the location invariants in α_i,
      ii. $w_j(\varepsilon) \in [k_j, l_j] \in \beta_{v_i}$

A path p of a hybrid automaton H is *feasible* if and only if there is a timed sequence ρ which corresponds to a behavior of p in H. □

For a convex hybrid automaton H, a reachability specification consists of a location v in H and a set φ of convex constraints, denoted by $\mathcal{R}(v, \varphi)$, as defined below.

Definition 4. For a CHA $H = (X, \Sigma, V, E, V_I, \alpha, \beta)$, a *reachability specification*, denoted by $\mathcal{R}(v, \varphi)$, consists of

- a location v in H, and
- a set φ of variable constraints of the form
  - $f(\boldsymbol{x}) \le 0$ where f is a convex function, or
  - $f(\boldsymbol{x}) = 0$ where f is an affine linear function. □

[2] Since the initial location v_I fires a transition immediately, the time spent at v_I is 0.

In this paper, we are concerned with the problem of checking whether a path in H satisfies a given reachability specification. The formal definition is presented below.

Definition 5. Let $H = (X, V, E, v_I, \alpha, \beta)$ be a convex hybrid automaton, and $\mathcal{R}(v, \varphi)$ be a reachability specification. A path ρ in H of the form $v_I \xrightarrow{(\phi_0,\psi_0)} v_1 \xrightarrow{(\phi_1,\psi_1)} \ldots \xrightarrow{(\phi_{n-1},\psi_{n-1})} v_n$ satisfies $\mathcal{R}(v, \varphi)$ if and only if there exists a behavior of H of the form $(v_1, t_1)\hat{}(v_2, t_2)\hat{} \ldots \hat{}(v_n, t_n)$ such that:

1. $v_n = v$, and
2. any variable constraint in φ is satisfied when the automaton stays at v_n with the delay t_n, i.e. for each variable constraint $f(\boldsymbol{x}) \geq 0$, $f(\gamma_n(\boldsymbol{x})) \geq 0$ where $\gamma_n(\boldsymbol{x})$ is a valuation of all the state variables $\boldsymbol{x}$ at the time when the automaton has stayed at v_n for t_n time units. □

Above all, given a path ρ in CHA H and a reachability specification $\mathcal{R}(v, \varphi)$, ρ satisfies $\mathcal{R}(v, \varphi)$ if and only if there exists a timed sequence $(v_1, t_1)\hat{}(v_2, t_2)\hat{} \ldots \hat{}(v_n, t_n)$ which satisfy all the conditions in Def.3 and Def.5.

3 Semi-decision Procedure for Path-Oriented Reachability Verification

Given a path ρ in a convex hybrid automaton H and a reachability specification $\mathcal{R}(v, \varphi)$, if there is a timed sequence corresponding to ρ in H which satisfies all the conditions in Def.3 and Def.5, then we say the path ρ satisfies $\mathcal{R}(v, \varphi)$.

3.1 Convex Encoding

In this section, we present our method to encode the conditions in Def. 3 (except 3(b)) and Def.5 into numerical constraints, and suggest the use of convex programming to solve these constraints. By using this method, we can prove the path does not satisfy the reachability specification when the convex program is not feasible.

Theorem 1. For a convex hybrid automaton $H = (X, V, E, v_I, \alpha, \beta)$ where $X = \{x_1, x_2, \ldots, x_m\}$, and $\mathcal{R}(v, \varphi)$ be a reachability specification, given a path $\rho = v_I \xrightarrow{(\phi_0,\psi_0)} v_1 \xrightarrow{(\phi_1,\psi_1)} v_2 \xrightarrow{(\phi_2,\psi_2)} \ldots \xrightarrow{(\phi_{n-1},\psi_{n-1})} v_n$ where $v_n = v$, ρ does not satisfy $\mathcal{R}(v, \varphi)$ if there does not exist a group of real numbers t_i $(1 \leq i \leq n)$ which satisfy the following conditions:

- $t_1, t_2, \ldots, t_n$ compose a timed sequence of $\mathcal{L}(R) : (v_1, t_1)\hat{}(v_2, t_2)\hat{} \ldots \hat{}(v_n, t_n)$.
- there exists a set of real numbers $\gamma_i(\boldsymbol{x})$ and $\delta_i(\boldsymbol{x})$ $(1 \leq i \leq n)$ where $\gamma_i(x_q)$ $(0 \leq q \leq m)$ denotes the value of variable x_q when the automaton has stayed at v_i for t_i time units. If $\dot{x_q}(t) \in [k_q(t), l_q(t)] \in \beta_i$ in location v_i $(1 \leq i \leq n)$, then

$$\gamma_i(x_q) - \delta_i(x_q) \geq \int_0^{t_i} k_q(t)dt, \gamma_i(x_q) - \delta_i(x_q) \leq \int_0^{t_i} l_q(t)dt$$

  where $\delta_i(x_q)$ denotes the value of variable x_q at the time when the automaton jumped to v_i. If there is reset action $x_q := b$ in ψ_{i-1}, then $\delta_i(x_q) = b$ otherwise $\delta_i(x_q) = \gamma_{i-1}(x_q)$.

- $t_1, t_2, \ldots, t_n$ satisfy all the transition guards in ϕ_i ($1 \leq i \leq n-1$), i.e. for each transition guard $f(\boldsymbol{x}) \leq 0$ or $f(\boldsymbol{x}) = 0$ in ϕ_i, we have

$$f(\gamma_i(\boldsymbol{x})) \leq 0 \;\; or \;\; f(\gamma_i(\boldsymbol{x})) = 0$$

- $t_1, t_2, \ldots, t_n$ satisfy the location invariant for each location v_i ($1 \leq i \leq n$), i.e. for each location invariant $f(\boldsymbol{x}) \leq 0$ in α_i, we have

$$f(\gamma_i(\boldsymbol{x})) \leq 0 \; and \; f(\delta_i(\boldsymbol{x})) \leq 0$$

- $t_1, t_2, \ldots, t_n$ satisfy all the constraints in reachability specification φ, i.e. for each constraint $f(\boldsymbol{x}) \leq 0$ or $f(\boldsymbol{x}) = 0$ in φ, we have

$$f(\gamma_n(\boldsymbol{x})) \leq 0 \;\; or \;\; f(\gamma_n(\boldsymbol{x})) = 0.$$

Proof. A discretized sequence of states, of the form $(v_1, \delta_1(\boldsymbol{x}))\hat{}(v_1, \gamma_1(\boldsymbol{x}))\hat{}\ (v_2, \delta_2(\boldsymbol{x}))$ $\hat{}(v_2, \gamma_2(\boldsymbol{x}))\hat{}\ldots\hat{}(v_n, \delta_n(\boldsymbol{x}))\hat{}(v_n, \gamma_n(\boldsymbol{x}))$, is restricted by all the conditions in this theorem, where $\delta_i(x_q)$ represents the value of variable x_q at the time when the automaton jumped to v_i, $\gamma_i(x_q)$ represents the value of variable x_q when the automaton has stayed at v_i for time t_i. This discretized sequence of states satisfy all the conditions in Def.5 and the conditions $1(a), 1(b), 2(a), 2(b)$ and $3(a)$ in Def. 3.

Clearly if there does not exist a group of real numbers t_i ($1 \leq i \leq n$) which satisfies all the conditions in Def. 3, then the timed sequence $(v_1, t_1)\hat{}(v_2, t_2)\hat{}\ldots\hat{}\ (v_n, t_n)$ can not be a behavior of CHA H definitely, thus, it cannot satisfy $\mathcal{R}(v, \varphi)$. On the other hand, if the group of real numbers t_i ($1 \leq i \leq n$) do not satisfy the conditions in Def.5 then the timed sequence $(v_1, t_1)\hat{}(v_2, t_2)\hat{}\ldots\hat{}\ (v_n, t_n)$ does not satisfy the reachability specification neither. □

Corollary 1. The set of constraints given in Theorem 1 forms a convex set.

Proof. From Theorem 1, the reachability analysis of a path can be encoded to the feasibility problem of a conjunction of numerical constraints which are in the following four forms:

1. $f(\gamma_i(\boldsymbol{x})) \leq 0$
2. $f(\gamma_i(\boldsymbol{x})) = 0$
3. $\gamma_i(x_q) - \delta_i(x_q) \geq \int_0^{t_i} k_q(t)dt$
4. $\gamma_i(x_q) - \delta_i(x_q) \leq \int_0^{t_i} l_q(t)dt$

Constraints in form 1 and 2 come from transition guards, location invariants and reachability specification. As shown in Def.1, all the constraints in transition guards, location invariants and reachability specification are convex constraints, so all the constraints in form 1 and 2 are convex constraints. Constraints in form 3 and 4 come from flow conditions in each location. As $dl_i/dt \leq 0$ and $dk_i/dt \geq 0$, $\int_0^{t_i} l_i(t)dt$ is a concave function and $\int_0^{t_i} k_i(t)dt$ is a convex function. As $\gamma_i(x_q) - \delta_i(x_q)$ is an affine linear function, so constraints in form 3 and 4 are all convex constraints as well. Thus, all the constraints generated in Theorem 1 are all convex constraints. As intersection of convex sets is still convex, the conjunction of these constraints form a convex set. □

Table 1. Decision Procedure for Path-oriented Reachability Analysis of CHA Based on Convex Programming

Verify (**CHA** H, **Path** ρ, **Spec** $\mathcal{R}(v,\varphi)$)

Process:
1. Encoding ρ and $\mathcal{R}(v,\varphi)$ to a group of convex constraints θ
2. Solving the feasibility of θ by CVX
3. **If** infeasible
   return ρ does not satisfy $\mathcal{R}(v,\varphi)$
4. **Else**
   return do not know

Based on this corollary, we can change the path-oriented reachability analysis problem into a convex feasibility problem, which can be determined by convex optimization technique efficiently. If the convex program is infeasible, then the corresponding path does not satisfy the given reachability specification. However, if the convex program is feasible, we can not say the path satisfy the reachability specification accordingly. Based on this argument, we give a semi-decision procedure for path-oriented reachability analysis of CHA in Table 1.

3.2 Problem Size

Using Theorem 1, we can prove a path $\rho = v_I \xrightarrow{(\phi_0,\psi_0)} v_1 \xrightarrow{(\phi_1,\psi_1)} v_2 \xrightarrow{(\phi_2,\psi_2)} \ldots \xrightarrow{(\phi_{n-1},\psi_{n-1})} v_n$ does not satisfy a reachability specification $\mathcal{R}(v,\varphi)$ by proving the infeasibility of a convex program Θ. The number of the variables and the constraints in the corresponding convex program Θ can be calculated as follows:

- Variables
  - For each location $v_i \in \{V - v_I\}$ in the path segment, there is one variable t_i in the convex program, which measures the time spent in that location. Since the initial location v_I fires a transition immediately, the time spent at v_I is 0.
  - For each variable $x_k \in X$, there are at most two variables, $\delta_i(x_k)$ and $\gamma_i(x_k)$, in the convex program for each location $v_i \in \{V - v_I\}$ in the path segment, where $\delta_i(x_k)$ denotes the value of variable x_k at the time when the automaton jumped to v_i, and $\gamma_i(x_k)$ denotes the value of variable x_k when the automaton has stayed at v_i for time t_i. If $\delta_{i+1}(x_k) = \gamma_i(x_k)$, which means there is no reset of x_k in the transition $v_i \rightarrow v_{i+1}$, we do not need to generate a new variable $\delta_{i+1}(x_k)$.
- Constraints
  - For each variable t_i, there is one constraint $t_i \geq 0$.
  - For each variable $x_k \in X$ occurring in a flow condition of a location $v_i \in \{V - v_I\}$ in the path segment, there are at most two constraints in the convex program, representing the relation between $\delta_i(x_k)$ and $\gamma_i(x_k)$.
  - For each constraint $f(\boldsymbol{x}) \leq 0$ in ϕ_i labeling a transition, there is one constraint $f(\gamma_i(\boldsymbol{x})) \leq 0$ in the convex program.

- For each constraint $f(\boldsymbol{x}) \leq 0$ in a location invariant α_i, there are two constraints, $f(\gamma_i(\boldsymbol{x})) \leq 0$ and $f(\delta_i(\boldsymbol{x})) \leq 0$ in the convex program.
- For each constraint $f(\boldsymbol{x}) \leq 0$ in φ of the reachability specification, there is one constraint $f(\gamma_i(\boldsymbol{x})) \leq 0$ in the convex program.

3.3 Illustration

We use a simple example to illustrate our technique. The automaton is shown in Fig.1. It consists of three locations, s_0, s_1 and s_2, where s_0 is the initial location. The automaton has two state variables x and y, with initial value $x \geq 2$ and $y \geq 1$. In location s_1, the flow condition of x is in the range of $[t, 10 - 2t]$, and flow condition of y is in the range of $[t, 9 - 3t]$. All other constraints are denoted in Fig.1. We want to check whether path $\rho = s_0 \rightarrow s_1 \rightarrow s_2$ satisfy reachability specification $\mathcal{R}(s_2, y \geq 5)$. Now we show how we generate the convex program:

- generate variable t_1 and constraint $t_1 \geq 0$ for location s_1,
- generate variables $x_{1_{in}}$, $x_{1_{out}}$, $y_{1_{in}}$, and $y_{1_{out}}$, for the evaluations of the variables in location s_1,
- according to the reset actions on initial transition $e_0 : x \geq 2$ and $y \geq 1$, generate constraints $x_{1_{in}} \geq 2$ and $y_{1_{in}} \geq 1$,
- for the flow condition $\dot{x} \in [t, 10-2t]$ in s_1, get two constraints $x_{1_{out}} - x_{1_{in}} - 0.5{t_1}^2 \geq 0$ and $x_{1_{in}} + 10t_1 - t_1^2 - x_{1_{out}} \geq 0$,
- similarly, for the flow condition $\dot{y} \in [t, 9 - 3t]$, obtain two constraints $y_{1_{out}} - y_{1_{in}} - 0.5{t_1}^2 \geq 0$ and $y_{1_{in}} + 9t_1 - 1.5t_1^2 - y_{1_{out}} \geq 0$,
- for the location invariant $x^2 + y^2 \leq 9$ in s_1, generate two constraints : $x_{1_{in}}^2 + y_{1_{in}}^2 \leq 9$ and $x_{1_{out}}^2 + y_{1_{out}}^2 \leq 9$,
- for the transition guard $0 < x - y < 2$ in e_1, generate two constraints $x_{1_{out}} - y_{1_{out}} < 2$ and $x_{1_{out}} - y_{1_{out}} > 0$,
- for the location invariant $x^2 + 2x \leq 3$ in s_2, generate one constraint : $x_{1_{out}}^2 + 2x_{1_{out}} \leq 3$,
- for the location invariant $y \geq 5$ in reachability specification, generate one constraint : $y_{1_{out}} \geq 5$.

This is a simple illustration of how our technique can be used and it produces a convex programming problem with 12 constraints and 5 variables, it took a convex programming solver CVX [12] only 0.6 seconds to prove that this path is infeasible.

Thanks to the revolutions in computing during the past decade, researchers have recognized that interior-point methods, which were originally developed in the 1980s to solve linear programming problems, can be used to solve convex optimization problems

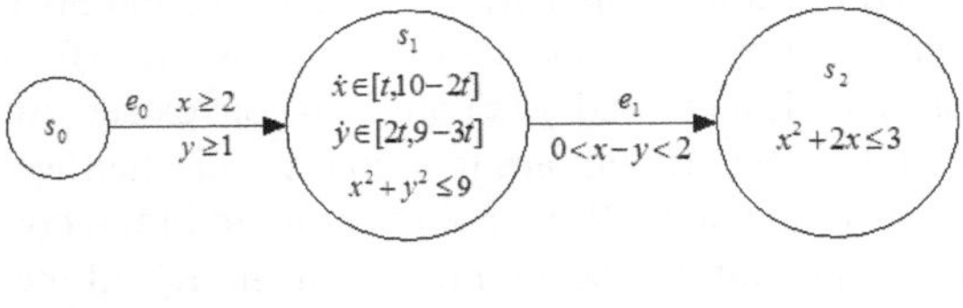

Fig. 1. Illustration Example

as well. Such interior-point methods allow convex problems to be solved both reliably and efficiently [4]. Utilizing the research on efficient solution of convex programs, we can develop an efficient tool to check one path of a convex hybrid automaton at a time, where the length of the path and the size of the automaton can both get closer to the practical problem sizes.

4 Extended Decision Procedure for Path-Oriented Reachability Verification

In the previous section, we give a semi-decision procedure to answer the reachability of a specification along a given path in a convex hybrid automaton. In that procedure, we give a convex encoding technique which transform the path and specification to a set of convex constraints. By determining the feasibility of the set of constraints, the specification can be proved to be unsatisfiable if the constraint set is infeasible. But in the other direction we cannot say the specification is satisfiable if the constraint set is feasible. Because all the constraints given in Theorem 1 do not concern the condition $3(b)$ given in Def.3.

In this section, we will extend our decision procedure by presenting two special classes of CHA, in which our analysis technique can also give an exact answer when the given specification is satisfiable.

4.1 Linear Flow Convex Hybrid Automata

In this subsection, we present a subclass of convex hybrid automata: linear flow convex hybrid automata (LF-CHA). The difference between LF-CHA and general CHA is that all the flow conditions of LF-CHA are linear, namely, the flow condition for each variable in LF-CHA is in the form of $\dot{x}_i \in [a_i, b_i]$, where $a_i, b_i \in R$.

Theorem 2. For a linear flow convex hybrid automaton $H = (X, V, E, v_I, \alpha, \beta)$ where $X = \{x_1, x_2, \ldots, x_m\}$, and $\mathcal{R}(v, \varphi)$ be a reachability specification, given a path $\rho = v_I \xrightarrow{(\phi_0,\psi_0)} v_1 \xrightarrow{(\phi_1,\psi_1)} v_2 \xrightarrow{(\phi_2,\psi_2)} \ldots \xrightarrow{(\phi_{n-1},\psi_{n-1})} v_n$ where $v_n = v$, ρ satisfies $\mathcal{R}(v, \varphi)$ if and only if all the conditions given in Theorem 1 are satisfied.

Proof. **(If)** Similar to the proof of Theorem 1, a discretized sequence of states, of the form $(v_1, \delta_1(\boldsymbol{x}))\hat{}(v_1, \gamma_1(\boldsymbol{x}))\hat{}\ (v_2,\ \delta_2(\boldsymbol{x}))\ \hat{}(v_2,\ \gamma_2(\boldsymbol{x}))\ \hat{}\ \ldots\hat{}(v_n, \delta_n(\boldsymbol{x}))\hat{}(v_n, \gamma_n(\boldsymbol{x}))$, is restricted by Theorem 1, where $\delta_i(x_q)$ represents the value of variable x_q at the time the automaton has just jumped to v_i, $\gamma_i(x_q)$ represents the value of variable x_q when the automaton has stayed at v_i for time t_i. This discretized sequence of states satisfy all the conditions in Def.5 and the conditions $1(a), 1(b), 2(a), 2(b)$ and $3(a)$ in Def. 3.

Now we prove this discretized sequence of states also satisfy the conditions $3(b)$ of Def. 3. From corollary 1, $\delta_i(\boldsymbol{x})$ and $\gamma_i(\boldsymbol{x})$ are in a convex set. According to convex theory, if $(v_i, \delta_i(\boldsymbol{x}))$ and $(v_i, \gamma_i(\boldsymbol{x}))$ both are in a convex set, then we can connect these two states by a straight line π, and all the points on π are in the convex set. Since this convex set is constrained by all the location invariants in α_{v_i}, all the states on π satisfy all the location invariants in α_{v_i} as well.(condition 3(b)i in Def. 3).

Furthermore, for any x_q $(1 \leq q \leq m)$, we can get the projection π_q of π on surface x_i, t. The slope of π_q is $(\delta_i(x_q) - \gamma_i(x_q))/t_i$. According to Theorem 1, $\gamma_i(x_q) - \delta_i(x_q) \geq \int_0^{t_i} k_q(t)dt$, $\gamma_i(x_q) - \delta_i(x_q) \leq \int_0^{t_i} l_q(t)dt$ where $k_q(t) = a_q$ and $l_q(t) = b_q$, so $t_i b_q \leq \gamma_i(x_q) - \delta_i(x_q) \geq t_i a_q \rightarrow ((\delta_i(x_q) - \gamma_i(x_q))/t_i \in [a_q, b_q]$. Thus, all the points on π_q satisfy the flow condition of $x_q \in [a_q, b_q]$ (condition 3(b)ii in Def. 3).

Above all, the discretized sequence of states $(v_1, \delta_1(\boldsymbol{x}))$ ^$(v_1, \gamma_1(\boldsymbol{x}))$ ^ $(v_2, \delta_2(\boldsymbol{x}))$ ^$(v_2, \gamma_2(\boldsymbol{x}))$ ^ ... ^$(v_n, \delta_n(\boldsymbol{x}))$^$(v_n, \gamma_n(\boldsymbol{x}))$ satisfy all the conditions in Def. 3 and Def. 5, which makes (v_1, t_1)^(v_2, t_2)^ ... ^(v_n, t_n) represents a behavior of $R = v_1$^v_2^ ... ^v_n and satisfies $\mathcal{R}(v, \varphi)$.

(Only If) This part of the proof follows from the definition of the behavior (Def. 3) corresponding to a path in the hybrid automaton. □

4.2 Monotonic Invariant Convex Hybrid Automata

In this subsection, we present another subclass of convex hybrid automata: monotonic invariant convex hybrid automata (MI-CHA). The difference between MI-CHA and general CHA is that all the invariants in MI-CHA are in the form of $f(\boldsymbol{x}) \leq 0$, where the value of $f(\boldsymbol{x})$ is monotonic over time t. Similarly to linear flow convex hybrid automata, we can use the conditions given in Theorem 1 to give the exact answer about whether a path in a MI-CHA is feasible or not.

Theorem 3. For a monotonic invariant convex hybrid automaton $H = (X, V, E, v_I, \alpha, \beta)$ where $X = \{x_1, x_2, \ldots, x_m\}$, and $\mathcal{R}(v, \varphi)$ be a reachability specification, given a path $\rho = v_I \xrightarrow{(\phi_0,\psi_0)} v_1 \xrightarrow{(\phi_1,\psi_1)} v_2 \xrightarrow{(\phi_2,\psi_2)} \ldots \xrightarrow{(\phi_{n-1},\psi_{n-1})} v_n$ where $v_n = v$, ρ satisfies $\mathcal{R}(v, \varphi)$ if and only if all the conditions given in Theorem 1 are satisfied.

Proof. **(If)** Similar to the proof of Theorem 1, a discretized sequence of states, of the form $(v_1, \delta_1(\boldsymbol{x}))$^$(v_1, \gamma_1(\boldsymbol{x}))$^ $(v_2, \delta_2(\boldsymbol{x}))$ ^$(v_2, \gamma_2(\boldsymbol{x}))$ ^ ... ^$(v_n, \delta_n(\boldsymbol{x}))$^$(v_n, \gamma_n(\boldsymbol{x}))$, is restricted by Theorem 1, where $\delta_i(x_q)$ represents the value of variable x_q at the time the automaton has just jumped to v_i, $\gamma_i(x_q)$ represents the value of variable x_q when the automaton has stayed at v_i for time t_i. This discretized sequence of states satisfy all the conditions in Def.5 and the conditions $1(a), 1(b), 2(a), 2(b)$ and $3(a)$ in Def. 3.

Now we prove this discretized sequence of states also satisfy the conditions $3(b)$ of Def. 3. First, as $\gamma_i(x_q) - \delta_i(x_q) \geq \int_0^{t_i} k_q(t)dt$, $\gamma_i(x_q) - \delta_i(x_q) \leq \int_0^{t_i} l_q(t)dt$, there must be a flow function $W_q : [0, t_i] \rightarrow \mathbb{R}$ for each variable $x_q \in X (1 \leq q \leq m)$, with the first derivative $w_q : [0, t_i] \rightarrow \mathbb{R}$, such that $W_q(0) = \delta_i(x_q)$, $W_q(t_i) = \gamma_i(x_q)$ and for all reals $\varepsilon \in [0, t_i]$ $w_q \in [k_q, l_q]$ (condition 3(b)ii in Def. 3).

As $\delta_i(\boldsymbol{x})$ and $\gamma_i(\boldsymbol{x})$ both satisfy all the location invariants $f(\boldsymbol{x}) \leq 0$ in α_i, and $f(\boldsymbol{x})$ is monotonic over time t, all the points on flow $W(t)$ between $\delta_i(\boldsymbol{x})$ and $\gamma_i(\boldsymbol{x})$ satisfy $f(\boldsymbol{x}) \leq 0$ (condition 3(b)i in Def. 3).

Above all, the discretized sequence of states $(v_1, \delta_1(\boldsymbol{x}))$^$(v_1, \gamma_1(\boldsymbol{x}))$^ $(v_2, \delta_2(\boldsymbol{x}))$ ^$(v_2, \gamma_2(\boldsymbol{x}))$ ^ ... ^$(v_n, \delta_n(\boldsymbol{x}))$^$(v_n, \gamma_n(\boldsymbol{x}))$ satisfy all the conditions in Def. 3 and Def. 5, which makes (v_1, t_1)^(v_2, t_2)^ ... ^(v_n, t_n) represents a behavior of $R = v_1$^v_2^ ... ^v_n and satisfies $\mathcal{R}(v, \varphi)$.

(Only If) This part of the proof follows from the definition of the behavior (Def. 3) corresponding to a path in the hybrid automaton. □

4.3 Extended Decision Procedure

Based on above discussion, we extend the semi-decision procedure for the path-oriented reachability analysis of CHA to a general framework. In this framework, we encode a path and a reachability specification into a set of convex constraints, which feasibility can be determined by convex programming technique efficiently. If the constraint set is infeasible, the specification is unreachable correspondingly. If the constraint set is feasible, we can also give an exact prove of the reachability of the specification when the given automaton falls into these two special classes of CHA:LF-CHA and MI-CHA[3]. The extended decision procedure is given in Table 2.

Table 2. Extended Decision Procedure for Path-oriented Reachability Analysis of CHA Based on Convex Programming

VERIFY (**CHA** H, **Path** ρ, **Spec** $\mathcal{R}(v, \varphi)$)

Process:
1. Encoding ρ and $\mathcal{R}(v, \varphi)$ to a group of convex constraints θ
2. Solving the feasibility of θ by CVX
3. **If** infeasible
   return ρ does not satisfy $\mathcal{R}(v, \varphi)$
4. **Else**
   If H is a LF-CHA
     return ρ satisfies $\mathcal{R}(v, \varphi)$
   If H is a MI-CHA
     return ρ satisfies $\mathcal{R}(v, \varphi)$
   Else
     return do not know

In the future, we will keep on identifying more subclasses of CHA, in which we can use the conditions given in Theorem 1 to give the exact answer about whether a path satisfies a given reachability specification, so that our algorithm can be extended accordingly.

5 Case Studies

Based on the technique presented in this paper, we conducted several experiments for the path-oriented reachability analysis of convex hybrid automata. The convex programming software package we use is CVX, a free package for specifying and solving convex programs [12].on a DELL workstation (Intel Core2 Quad CPU 2.4GHz /4GB RAM, Ubuntu 8.04.2, Matlab 7.4.0, CVX 1.2), we evaluated the potential of the technique presented in this paper by several case studies, which we now discuss in detail.

[3] The decision of whether a CHA is LF-CHA or MI-CHA can be done easily, which will not be described in detail here.

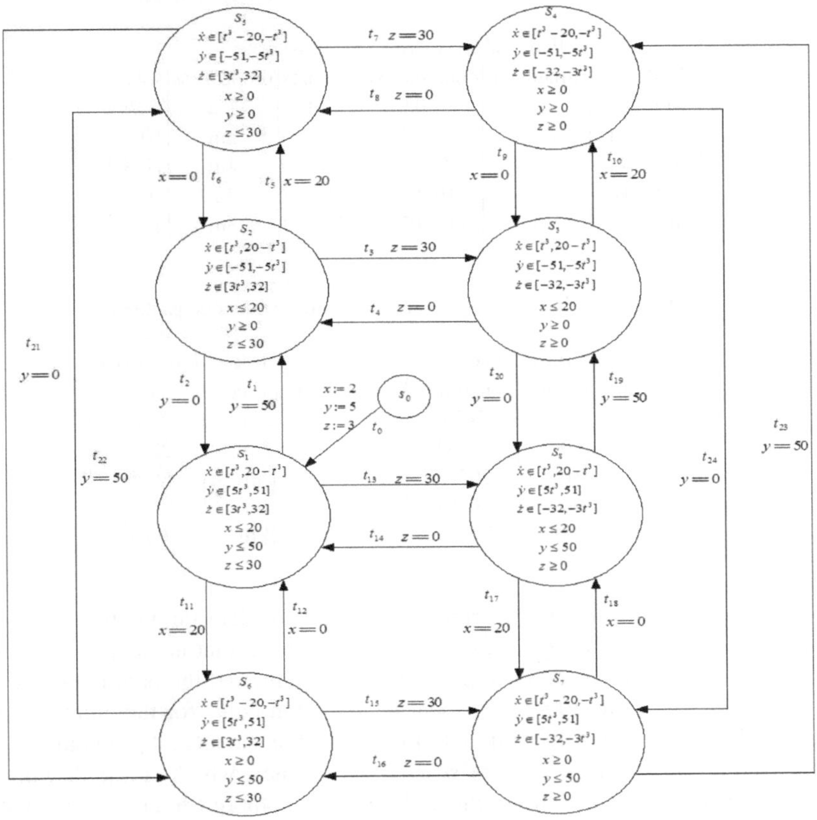

Fig. 2. 3D Shuttle Simulation

3D Shuttle Simulation. 3D shuttle simulation is an extension of the billiard game in [1]. This is a closed room (with three axes x, y and z) in which a shuttle is traveling. Each time the shuttle reaches a surface of the room, (for example, the surface yz perpendicular to the x axis), it will stop and then keep travelling with a new direction rebounding along the axis that is perpendicular to the striking surface but keeping the velocity in the other two axes (y and z) intact. The hybrid automaton for this example is shown in Fig. 2. It is easy to prove that this automaton is a MI-CHA.

The experimental result is shown in Table 3. All the columns are described as follows: "length" and "dimension" stand for the size of the path and automaton that we are checking, "constraints" and "variables" give the size of the convex program which describes the path, "preprocess" and "solve" give reports of the time the solver spent on preprocessing of the constraint set and solving of the problem.

The path[4] we choose to check is $s_0\hat{}\,(s_1\hat{}\,s_2\hat{}\,s_3\hat{}\,s_4\hat{}\,s_5\hat{}\,s_6\hat{}\,s_7\hat{}\,s_8)^k$. It is a trajectory which touches all the surfaces of the room k times. When k is set to 30, CVX spent 1

[4] For succinctly, in this section, we represent a path segment $p = v_1 \xrightarrow{(\phi_1,\psi_1)} v_2 \xrightarrow{(\phi_2,\psi_2)} \ldots \xrightarrow{(\phi_{n-1},\psi_{n-1})} v_n$ in H as a concise form $v_1\hat{}v_2\hat{}\ldots\hat{}v_n$.

Table 3. Experimental results on the 3D Shuttle Simulation

Path: $s_0\hat{}(s_1\hat{}s_2\hat{}s_3\hat{}s_4\hat{}s_5\hat{}s_6\hat{}s_7\hat{}s_8)^k$						
k	length	dimension	constraints	variables	preprocess	solve
30	241	3	2403	963	1m	5.7s
50	401	3	4003	1603	2m	10.2s
80	641	3	6403	2563	4m	18.3s
130	1041	3	10403	4163	7m	30.4s
140	1131	3	11203	4483	8m	N/A

Table 4. Experimental results on the Vehicle Sequence Example

Path: Initial ^ Cruise ^ Rec_1_2 ^ Cruise ^... ^ Rec_n-1_n ^ Error						
n	length	dimension	constraints	variables	preprocess	solve
20	40	40	5091	1598	2m	5.4s
30	60	60	11541	3598	5m	23.7s
40	80	80	20581	6398	15m	59.4s
45	90	90	26091	8098	20m	71.2s
50	100	100	32241	9998	29m	N/A

minute in preprocessing all the constraints, which include determining the convexity of each constraint and converting each constraint to the form that is compatible with the underlying solver, then 5.7 seconds to solve the problem, and the path is proved to be feasible. When k is set to 200, CVX spent nearly 60 minutes for the convexity judgment, then the underlying solver ran out of memory. For the largest problem we solve, we traversed the loop $(s_1\hat{}s_2\hat{}s_3\hat{}s_4\hat{}s_5\hat{}s_6\hat{}s_7\hat{}s_8)$ 130 times, which is a path with 1041 locations. This clearly demonstrates the ability of our technique to analyze long paths.

Motorcade. In order to show the ability of our technique to handle systems with high dimensions, we conducted another case study based on a nonlinear version of the automated highway model in [16]. The automaton we use is shown in Fig.3, which models a central arbiter that monitors a sequence of n vehicles. In this model, the distance between two consecutive vehicles v_i $(1 \leq i < n)$ and v_{i+1} can not exceed 10 units. Let x_i denote the x coordinate of vehicle i and y_i denote its y coordinate. If the distance between v_i and v_{i+1} is less than 4 units, then the arbiter will force all vehicles v_j before v_{i+1} $(1 \leq j \leq i+1)$ to accelerate and vehicle v_{i+1} to decelerate until the distance between v_i and v_{i+1} returns to the valid range. If the distance between both x and y coordinate of v_i and v_{i+1} is less than 1 unit, then we say that a crash has occurred. This state should not be reachable in a correct model of the arbiter. In the case study, we want to check whether the error location is reachable along path: Initial ^ Cruise ^ Recovery_1_2 ^ Cruise ^... ^ Recovery_n-1_n ^ Error, which traverses each recovery location one by one before it finally reaches the error location. Clearly, all the flow conditions in this automaton is in a linear range, so this automaton is a LF-CHA.

The experimental result is shown in Table 4. The largest example we ran is a system with 45 vehicles and hence, 90 system variables. When we set the number of vehicles to 50, CVX was unable to solve the convex programming problem.

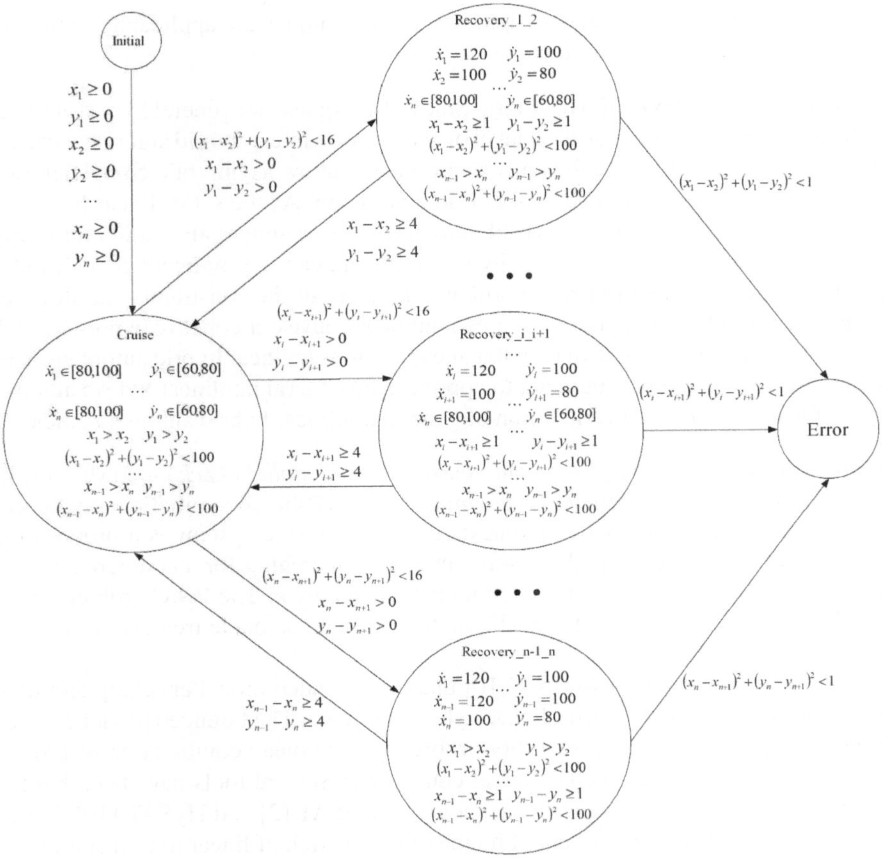

Fig. 3. Motorcade

To the best of our knowledge, there is no state-of-the-art tool that can perform reachability analysis of a *convex hybrid automaton*, so we do not have any opportunity to compare with other tools. But as widely reported in literature [18], the general verification of nonlinear systems with even five variables usually requires several hours of computation; if the dimension is larger than five, the state-of-the-art tools fail to analyze them. To the best of our knowledge, this status is not significant improved yet.

As we have shown in the experiments, our path-oriented technique can analyze *convex hybrid automata* systems with high dimensions. We also believe that the performance will be much better if a commercial convex optimization engine is employed.

6 Discussion on Potential Applications

To the best of our knowledge, there is no path-oriented technique for analyzing nonlinear hybrid automata. Although the path-oriented technique we present in this paper is restricted to *convex hybrid automata* and checks only a single path at a time, we still believe there are several related areas where our techniques are applicable. In this section, we discuss these applications.

General Nonlinear Hybrid Automata. Study [14] argues that general hybrid automata can be approximated to any desired level of accuracy by linear hybrid automata, because linear hybrid automata are sufficiently expressive to allow asymptotic completeness of the abstraction process for a general hybrid automaton. As the set of linear hybrid automata is a subclass of convex hybrid automata, this argument also holds for convex hybrid automata. Moreover, convex hybrid automata can approximate general hybrid automata more easily than linear hybrid automata, as all the constraints and flow conditions in convex hybrid automata can be nonlinear convex or concave expressions; the latter are much more expressive than linear expressions in linear hybrid automata. Thus, we can use convex hybrid automata to approximate general nonlinear hybrid automata and perform path-oriented verification of general nonlinear hybrid automata efficiently.

Bounded Model Checking. In recent years, *Bounded model checking* (BMC) [3] has been presented as a complementary technique for BDD-based symbolic model checking. The basic idea is to encode the next-state relation of a system as a propositional formula, and unroll this formula to some integer k, searching for a counterexample in the executions of the model, whose length is bounded by k. The BMC problem can be solved by Boolean Satisfiability (SAT) method, which has made tremendous progress in recent years [19].

There are several related works [2,10] that use bounded model checking and linear programming technique to verify linear hybrid automata. The bounded model checking problem is reduced to the satisfiability problem of a boolean combination of propositional variables and linear mathematical constraints. Several tools have been built for the analysis of linear hybrid automata, such as MathSAT [2] and HySAT [10]. We can take advantage of these studies about bounded verification of linear hybrid automata to develop an efficient tool to do bounded verification of *convex hybrid automata*, which allows us to analyze systems with richer dynamics than those analyzed by other state-of-art bounded model checkers, such as MathSAT and HySAT.

CEGAR. Counterexample guided abstraction refinement (CEGAR) has achieved great success in hardware and software verification [8]. The main idea of CEGAR is that when the original system is too big to handle, we perform over-approximation of the original system, and look for bad states in the new system. If we can not find a counterexample, the process terminates and the original system is correct. If we can find a counterexample, we try to analyze and concretize this counterexample. If the counterexample is true, the process terminates and reports the counterexample. If it is not true, we will build a new approximation of the original system that excludes this "counterexample", and keeps going until we cannot find a counterexample in the abstraction or we find a real counterexample in the concrete system.

Iterative Relaxation Abstraction (IRA) [16] is a technique to perform reachability analysis of linear hybrid automata by building several low dimensional abstractions of the original high dimensional linear hybrid automata. Then, IRA uses a state-of-the-art linear hybrid verification tool PHAVer [11] to perform reachability verification of the low dimensional abstract system. If PHAVer reports a spurious counterexample, which happens when a path reaches a bad state, IRA uses the path-oriented technique we proposed in study [17] to verify whether this counterexample really exists in the original high dimensional system. If the counterexample is present in the high dimensional system, IRA terminates and reports that the bad state is reachable; otherwise IRA uses the irreducible infeasible subset (IIS) technique [7] to analyze the spurious counterexample to get a new group of variables for the next low dimensional abstraction.

We are confident that the path-oriented technique suggested in this paper can be married to a state-of-the-art verification tool of general nonlinear hybrid automata (such as CheckMate) by using the IRA technique. Such an approach will greatly increase the dimension of the problems that the state-of-the-art tools can solve and make our technique contribute to the development of a model checker for nonlinear hybrid automata.

7 Conclusion

In this paper, we propose a class of nonlinear hybrid automata called *convex hybrid automata*. Based on convex programming, we develop an efficient technique for the path-oriented reachability analysis of convex hybrid automata. Our technique checks one path at a time where the path being checked can be made very long and both the dimension and number of locations of the hybrid automaton can be made large enough to handle problems of practical interest.

We conducted several case studies using a free convex solver CVX to show the ability of our technique to analyze problems with long paths and high dimensions. Since the existing techniques have not provided an efficient tool for checking all the paths in a general nonlinear hybrid automaton of practical size, we also present a general description of several areas where our technique can be used in a straightforward manner to improve the performance [18] of the state-of-the-art tools.

Acknowledgment

We are grateful to Professor Edmund M. Clarke and Mr. Sumit Jha for reading several drafts of this paper and contributing many helpful suggestions and corrections. We thank the anonymous reviewers for their valuable comments and suggestions. We also thank Dr. Michael Grant for his help with the CVX convex optimization engine. Furthermore, this work is supported by the National Natural Science Foundation of China (No.90818022 and No.60721002), the National 863 High-Tech Programme of China (No.2009AA01Z148 and No.2007AA010302), and by the National Grand Fundamental Research 973 Program of China (No.2009CB320702).

References

1. Alur, R., Courcoubetis, C., Halbwachs, N., Henzinger, T.A., Ho, P.-H., Nicollin, X., Olivero, A., Sifakis, J., Yovine, S.: The algorithmic analysis of hybrid systems. Theoretical Computer Science 138, 3–34 (1995)

2. Audemard, G., Bozzano, M., Cimatti, A., Sebastiani, R.: Verifying Industrial Hybrid Systems with MathSAT. Electronic Notes on Theoretical Computer Science 119, 17–32 (2005)
3. Biere, A., Cimatti, A., Clarke, E.M., Strichman, O., Zhu, Y.: Bounded Model Checking. Advance in Computers 58 (2003)
4. Boyd, S., Vandenberghe, L.: Convex Optimization. Cambridge University Press, Cambridge (2004)
5. Silva, B., Richeson, K., Krogh, B., Chutinan, A.: Modeling and verifying hybrid dynamic systems using checkmate. In: 4th International Conference on Automataion of Mixed Processes, pp. 323–328 (2000)
6. Bu, L., Li, Y., Wang, L., Li, X.: BACH: Bounded ReachAbility CHecker for Linear Hybrid Automata. In: 8th International Conference on Formal Methods in Computer Aided Design, pp. 65–68 (2008)
7. Chinneck, J., Dravnieks, E.: Locating minimal infeasible constraint sets in linear programs. ORSA Journal on Computing, 157–168 (1991)
8. Clarke, E.M., Grumberg, O., Jha, S., Lu, Y., Veith, H.: Counterexample-guided abstraction refinement. In: Emerson, E.A., Sistla, A.P. (eds.) CAV 2000. LNCS, vol. 1855, pp. 154–169. Springer, Heidelberg (2000)
9. Asarin, E., Dang, T., Maler, O.: d/dt, a Tool for Reachability Analysis of Continuous and Hybrid Systems. In: IFAC Nonlinear Control Systems, pp. 20–31 (2001)
10. Franzle, M., Herde, C.: Efficient Proof Engines for Bounded Model Checking of Hybrid Systems. Electronic Notes on Theoretical Computer Science 133, 119–137 (2005)
11. Frehse, G.: PHAVer: Algorithmic Verification of Hybrid Systems past HyTech. In: International Conference on Hybrid Systems: Computation and Control, pp. 258–273 (2005)
12. Grant, M., Boyd, S.: CVX: Matlab software for disciplined convex programming (web page and software) (2009), `http://stanford.edu/~boyd/cvx`
13. Grant, M., Boyd, S., Ye, Y.: Disciplined Convex Programming. In: Global Optimization: From Theory to Implementation, pp. 155–210 (2006)
14. Henzinger, T.A., Ho, P., Wong-Toi, H.: Algorithmic Analysis of Nonlinear Hybrid Systems. IEEE Transactions on Automatic Control, 540–554 (1998)
15. Thomas, A.: The Theory of Hybrid Automata. In: 11th Annual IEEE Symposium on Logic in Computer Science, pp. 278–292 (1996)
16. Jha, S., Krogh, B.H., Weimer, J.E., Clarke, E.M.: Reachability for Linear Hybrid Automata Using Iterative Relaxation Abstraction. In: 10th International Conference on Hybrid Systems: Computation and Control, pp. 287–300 (2007)
17. Li, X., Jha, S., Bu, L.: Towards an Efficient Path-Oriented Tool for Bounded Reachability Analysis of Linear Hybrid Systems using Linear Programming. Electronic Notes on Theoretical Computer Science 174(3), 57–70 (2007)
18. Silva, B.I., Stursberg, O., Krogh, B.H., Engell, S.: An Assessment of the Current Status of Algorithmic Approaches to the Verification of Hybrid Systems. In: 40th Conference on Decision and Control, pp. 2867–2874 (2001)
19. Zhang, L., Malik, S.: The Quest for Efficient Boolean Satifiability Solves. In: Brinksma, E., Larsen, K.G. (eds.) CAV 2002. LNCS, vol. 2404, pp. 17–36. Springer, Heidelberg (2002)

Complexity Bounds for the Verification of Real-Time Software

Rohit Chadha[1,*], Axel Legay[2,**], Pavithra Prabhakar[3,***], and Mahesh Viswanathan[3,†]

[1] LSV, ENS Cachan & CNRS & INRIA, France
[2] Dept. of Computer Science, University of Illinois at Urbana-Champaign, U.S.A
[3] IRISA, campus de Beaulieu, INRIA Rennes, France
chadha@lsv-ens.cachan.fr, alegay@irisa.fr, pprabha2@uiuc.edu, vmahesh@uiuc.edu

Abstract. We present uniform approaches to establish complexity bounds for decision problems such as reachability and simulation, that arise naturally in the verification of timed software systems. We model timed software systems as timed automata augmented with a data store (like a pushdown stack) and show that there is at least an exponential blowup in complexity of verification when compared with untimed systems. Our proof techniques also establish complexity results for boolean programs, which are automata with stores that have additional boolean variables.

1 Introduction

Timed automata [3] are a standard model for formally describing real-time systems. They are automata equipped with real-valued clocks that evolve continuously with time and which can be compared to integers, and reset during discrete transitions. When modelling concurrent real-time software systems, this basic model must be augmented with various data structures to capture different features — a program stack (visible [4] or otherwise) to model recursive procedure calls, a bag or buffer to model undelivered messages in a network, or a higher-order stack to capture safe higher-order functions. In this paper, we study the complexity of classical verification problems for such formal models of real-time software, namely, invariant verification, μ-calculus model checking, and simulation and bisimulation checking.

Our main thesis is that there is *at least* an exponential blowup in complexity for verifying real-time systems when compared with non-real-time systems. More precisely, the problem of verifying a property for automata with an auxiliary data store (like stack, bag or higher-order stack) and clocks is exponentially

* The research was carried out while Rohit Chadha was at University of Illinois at Urbana-Champaign. He was supported by NSF 0429639.
** Supported by European STREP-COMBEST 215543.
*** Supported by NSF 0448178.
† Supported by NSF 0448178.

G. Barthe and M. Hermenegildo (Eds.): VMCAI 2010, LNCS 5944, pp. 95–111, 2010.

harder than checking the same property for the automata model without clocks. In general, the increase in complexity could be worse than exponential. For example, (timed) language containment for timed automata is undecidable [3], but is decidable in PSPACE for finite automata (without clocks). However, we also show that for certain properties (specifically, invariant and μ-calculus model checking, simulation and bisimulation checking) the increase in complexity is *exactly* exponential by establishing upper bounds for solving timed games.

This increase in complexity has been implicitly observed through a series of results that established the complexity of verification problems for the basic timed automata model. It has also been explicitly observed in [19] again for timed automata. In this paper we extend this line of work for timed automata with an auxiliary store. However, there is an important difference in the proof techniques used in the earlier papers and the one we use here. While previous papers established lower bounds by coming up with new, non-trivial reductions for timed automata, we obtain our results by using a *uniform* method to lift lower bound proofs for automata without clocks to automata with clocks, *independent* of the verification problem and the auxiliary data store being considered.

More precisely, our main technical result is that if a verification problem for automata without clocks is hard for complexity class C_1 with respect to *poly-log-time* reductions then the same verification problem is hard for an exponentially larger class C_2 with respect to *polynomial time* reductions. In order to prove this, we rely on the following techniques. First, we draw on the ideas previously used in proving the complexity of problems whose input is succinctly represented as a circuit [14,23,6,28] to show that verifying boolean automata is exponentially harder. Boolean automata are automata with auxiliary data stores that have additional boolean variables. Such models arise when a program is abstracted using predicates [15] inferred through a process of counterexample-guided abstraction-refinement [11]. Thus, our observations about boolean automata are of independent interest. Next, we show that automata with clocks can mimic the behavior of automata with boolean variables, and hence establishing the main lemma for timed systems.

While poly-log-time reductions are a stricter class of reductions than polynomial time reductions, we observe that typically reductions satisfy these stronger conditions because they have a highly regular structure that depends only on certain local bits. We establish that this intuition does indeed hold when considering the reductions that establish lower bounds for the invariant and μ-calculus model checking, and simulation and bisimulation checking for finite state systems and pushdown systems. Thus, using our main technical lemma and our observations about reductions used in classical verification problems, we establish new complexity results for timed automata with data stores, and re-establish old results using new, uniform proof techniques.

Before concluding this introduction, we would like to make a couple of points about our new proofs. First, the new proofs are significantly easier to establish, as new reductions are not required. For the new proof, one needs to re-examine classical reductions for automata problem to check that they are poly-log-time,

but this requires much less creativity than constructing a new reduction. Second, and more importantly, from a philosophical standpoint the new proof is appealing since it highlights clearly some reasons why the verification of real-time and embedded systems is harder than that of non-real-time systems.
Our Results: We show the following complexity results.

1. The control state reachability problem for timed automata is PSPACE- complete and for pushdown timed automata is DEXPTIME-complete.
2. The bisimulation and simulation problems between timed automata is DEXPTIME-complete.
3. The bisimulation and simulation problems between two visibly pushdown timed automata is 2-DEXPTIME-complete.
4. The bisimulation and simulation problems between a timed automata and a pushdown timed automata is 2-DEXPTIME-complete.
5. Model checking μ-calculus properties for order n higher order pushdown timed systems is $(n+1)$-DEXPTIME-complete.

The first two results were previously known, but our proofs for them are new. The remaining three results are completely new[1].

1.1 Related Work

Verification problems for systems implicitly represented as a parallel composition of many processes, or using boolean variables has been studied since the work of Harel et al., and Rabinovich [17,24,25], where the exponential blow-up in complexity was first observed for model checking branching time modal logics. This observation was extended to process algebraic equivalences and to timed automata in [19]. All of these results were established through new reductions for automata without an additional data store. Alur and Dill [3], introduced the model of timed automata, and showed that the reachability problem is PSPACE-complete. Decidability of simulation and bisimulation was shown in [8], while tight lower bounds were established in [19]. Complexity of model checking μ-calculus was shown in [2]. For timed automata A and B, the language containment problem (i.e., whether $L(A) \subseteq L(B)$), was shown to be decidable when B has one clock [22], and undecidable otherwise; for infinite strings the language containment is undecidable even when B has one clock [1]. The model of pushdown timed systems was first studied in [7] where reachability was shown to be decidable; the decidability of binary reachability was demonstrated in [12]. The language containment problem for timed systems with pushdown stacks and visibly pushdown stacks [4], was studied in [13]. For systems A and B, the problem of whether $L(A) \subseteq L(B)$ was shown to be undecidable when both A and B have visibly pushdown stacks. They also conjectured that the problem is decidable when B is a simple timed automata (without stack) with one clock; however, this problem remains open.

[1] Due to lack of space, some proofs have been eliminated which can be found in [9].

2 Preliminaries

Transition Systems. Given a set of *edge labels* Σ_E, a *Σ_E-transition system* (transition system when Σ_E is clear from the context) $\mathbf{S}$ is a tuple $(\mathcal{S}, \longrightarrow, s_0)$ such that $\mathcal{S}$ is a set of *configurations*; Σ_E is a *finite* set of *labels*; $\longrightarrow \subseteq \mathcal{S} \times \Sigma_E \times \mathcal{S}$ is a set of *transitions* and $s_0 \in \mathcal{S}$ is the *initial configuration.* A transition system is said to be *finite* if Σ_E and $\mathcal{S}$ are finite. We often write $s \xrightarrow{a} s'$ instead of $(s, a, s') \in \longrightarrow$. As usual, we can define $s \xrightarrow{w} s'$ for all $w \in {\Sigma_E}^*$. We say that $s \longrightarrow^* s'$ if there exists $w \in \Sigma_E^*$ such that $s \xrightarrow{w} s'$. We assume the reader is familiar with the definitions of reachability, simulation and bisimulation for transition systems and the logic μ-calculus.

Decision problems, succinct and long representations. We assume that inputs to decision problems are encoded as finite words over the alphabet $\Gamma = \{0, 1\}$. A *problem* L over Γ is a subset of Γ^*. Following [6], a *succinct representation* of a word $w \in \Gamma^*$ is a boolean circuit that on input (the binary representation of) i outputs two boolean values, one indicating whether i is less than or equal to the length of w and the other indicating, in that case, the i-th bit of w. Given a problem L, the *succinct representation of* L, denoted $s(L)$, is the set of all boolean circuits which are succinct representations of words in L [6]. The set *long*(L) is the set of all strings whose length is equal to the number represented by some binary string $1w$ in L [6].

Indirect access Turing Machines and polylog-time computations. We recall the definition of *indirect access turing machines* [6] used to define complexity classes of low computational power. The Turing machines accepting languages in these classes do not have enough time to read the whole input. Hence *indirect access turing machines* are defined. The machine includes the following elements:

- an input tape;
- a fixed number of work tapes;
- a special tape (henceforth called the pointer tape) to point to a bit of the input, which may be subsequently read in;
- a special tape (henceforth called the symbol tape) on which the symbol just read from the input appears written;
- a "read" state.

The machine is otherwise standard. It reads its input in the following way: the machine can write on the pointer tape the number of position i of the input tape; whenever the "read" state is entered the machine gets (in one computation step) in the symbol tape the contents of the i-th position of the input tape. If the input has length less than i, then the machine does not get anything. The previous content of the symbol tape is overwritten, but the contents of the pointer tape and position of its head remain untouched.

We will denote by *LT*, the class of languages accepted by deterministic indirect access Turing machines within a computation time bounded by $O(log\ n)$. The class *PLT* is the class of languages accepted by deterministic indirect access Turing machines within a computation time bounded by $O((\log n)^k)$ for some natural number k and the class *FLT* is the class of all functions computable by such machines in $O((\log n)^k)$ time for some natural number k.

Polylog time and polynomial time reductions. Given two problems A and B, A is *polynomial time m-reducible* to B, denoted $A \leq_m^P B$, if and only if there is a polynomial time computable function f such that $w \in A \Leftrightarrow f(w) \in B$ for every string w. *Polylog time m-reducibility* (abbreviated as *PLT*-reducibility and denoted $\leq_m^{PLT}$) is defined as follows. A is *PLT*-reducible to B if and only if there is a function f such that i) $w \in A \Leftrightarrow f(w) \in B$ for every w; and ii) the following function φ is computable in polylogarithmic time: for $w \in \{0,1\}^*$ and $i \in N$, $\varphi(w,i)$ is the i-th bit of $f(w)$ if i is less than or equal to the length of $f(w)$ and is undefined otherwise.

We now present two results from [6]. The first result relates *PLT*-reducibility and polynomial-time m-reducibility[2]. The second result shows that the succinct version of $long(A)$ is at least as hard as A.

Lemma 1. *If* $A \leq_m^{PLT} B$, *then* $s(A) \leq_m^P s(B)$.

Lemma 2. $A \leq_m^P s(long(A))$.

Automata with auxiliary stores. An *automata with auxiliary store* [10] consists of a control and an auxiliary store. Formally, an *auxiliary store* is a tuple $\mathcal{D} = (D, \widetilde{pred}, \widetilde{op}, d_i)$ such that D is a set, elements of which are called *data values*; $\widetilde{op}$ is a finite collection of functions $f : D \to D$; $\widetilde{pred}$ is a finite collection of unary predicates on D; and d_i is an element of D, called the *initial data value.* It is assumed that the identity function $\mathsf{id} \in \widetilde{op}$ and the always true predicate $\mathsf{true} \in \widetilde{pred}$. Pushdown stores, visibly pushdown stores [5], and higher-order pushdown stores [16] can be seen as instances of auxiliary stores.

An automaton is defined over an auxiliary store and a *finite* alphabet (the alphabet is used to annotate the transitions of the automaton). Formally, given an auxiliary store $\mathcal{D} = (D, \widetilde{pred}, \widetilde{op}, d_i)$ and an alphabet Σ_E, a $(\mathcal{D}, \Sigma_E)$*-automaton* $\mathcal{A}$ is a tuple (Q, δ, q_i), where

- Q is a *finite* set of *control states.*
- $\delta \subseteq Q \times \widetilde{pred} \times \Sigma_E \times \widetilde{op} \times Q$ is a *transition relation.*
- q_i is the *initial state* of the automaton $\mathcal{A}$.

The semantics of $\mathcal{A}$ is described in terms of a Σ_E-labeled transition system $(\mathcal{S}, \longrightarrow_\delta, s_i)$. The set of configurations is $\{(q,d) \mid q \in Q \text{ and } d \in \mathcal{D}\}$ and (q_i, d_i) is the initial configuration. The transition relation $\longrightarrow_\delta$ is defined as follows– $(q,d) \xrightarrow{a}_\delta (q', d')$ iff there exists $p \in \widetilde{pred}$ and $g \in \widetilde{op}$ such that $(q, p, a, g, q') \in \delta$, $p(d)$ is true and $g(d) = d'$. We will assume the definition of *isomorphism* between automata.

For example, a pushdown store on an alphabet Γ in a pushdown automaton can be formalized as an auxiliary store in the following way. The set Γ^* (set

[2] The result in [6] is only shown for log time m-reducibility, but the extension is straightforward.

of all finite strings over Γ) can be taken as the set of data values with the empty string ϵ as the initial value. The set of predicates $\widetilde{pred}$ can be chosen as $\{\mathsf{empty}\} \cup \{\mathsf{top}_\gamma \mid \gamma \in \Gamma\} \cup \{\mathsf{true}\}$, where $\mathsf{empty} = \{\epsilon\}$, $\mathsf{top}_\gamma = \{w\gamma \mid w \in \Gamma^*\}$ (the top of stack is γ) and $\mathsf{true} = \Gamma^*$ (any stack). The set of functions $\widetilde{op}$ can be defined as $\{id\} \cup \{\mathsf{push}_\gamma \mid \gamma \in \Gamma\} \cup \{\mathsf{pop}_\gamma \mid \gamma \in \Gamma\}$ where push_γ and pop_γ are defined as follows. For all $w \in \Gamma^*$, $\mathsf{push}_\gamma(w) = w\gamma$ and $\mathsf{pop}_\gamma(w) = w_1$ if $w = w_1\gamma$ and w otherwise. In a pushdown system the function pop_γ will be enabled only when the store satisfies top_γ. The function push_γ is enabled when the store satisfies true.

We also consider *visibly pushdown automata* (*VPA*) [5]. A *VPA* is a special kind of pushdown automaton in which every symbol of the input alphabet is designated as a call, return or internal. Every transition labelled by a call pushes a symbol, those labelled by return pop a symbol and transitions labelled by internal symbols do not push or pop any symbols.

The other kind of automata that will be considered are *higher order pushdown systems.* First let us define a higher order store. Given an alphabet Σ, an order 1 store is a stack of elements from Σ, and an order n store for $n > 1$ is a stack of elements from the set of stores of order $n-1$. The different kinds of operation that can be performed on an order n store include push_w where w is a word of the input alphabet, push_l where $l \leq n$, pop_l where $l \leq n$. A stack is written with the top most element to the left. The first order 1 store in an order 2 store ABC, where A, B and C are order 1 stores, is A, and the first order 2 store is ABC itself. push_w pushes w onto the first order 1 stack in the store. push_l pushes a copy of the first element of the first order l store to the first order l store in the store, and pop_l pops the top element of the first order l store in the store. There is another operation *top* which returns the top element of the first order 1 store in the store. A higher order pushdown system of order n is an automaton equipped with an order n store. A transition can be taken only if the element returned by *top* matches the input symbol and the data store is modified according to the operation. A formal description can be found in [16].

Automaton Problem. A k-tuple of automata with auxiliary store has signature $\mathsf{Sig} = ((\mathcal{D}_1, \Sigma_{E1}), \cdots, (\mathcal{D}_k, \Sigma_{Ek}))$ if the i-th automaton in the tuple has auxiliary store $\mathcal{D}_i$ and alphabet Σ_{Ei}. A (k, Sig)-*automaton problem* is a set of k-tuples of automata having signature Sig. For the rest of the paper, we assume that an automaton problem is closed under isomorphism, *i.e.*, if $\mathcal{P}$ is a k-automaton problem, then for any k-tuple $(\mathcal{A}_1, \mathcal{A}_2, \cdots, \mathcal{A}_k)$, $1 \leq i \leq k$, and $\mathcal{A}'_i$ such that $\mathcal{A}_i$ is isomorphic to $\mathcal{A}'_i$, $(\mathcal{A}_1, \mathcal{A}_2, \cdots, \mathcal{A}_i, \cdots \mathcal{A}_k) \in \mathcal{P}$ iff $(\mathcal{A}_1, \mathcal{A}_2, \cdots, \mathcal{A}'_i, \cdots \mathcal{A}_k) \in \mathcal{P}$.

For example, the *simulation* poblem between pushdown automata over the same pushdown store over the same input alphabet Σ_E is the set of pairs $(\mathcal{A}_1, \mathcal{A}_2)$ such that $\mathcal{A}_1$ is simulated by $\mathcal{A}_2$.

Encoding of an automaton. We encode the automaton over an auxiliary store $\mathcal{D}$ and an alphabet Σ_E as a binary string. Let n_1, n_2, n_3 and n_4 be the least integers such that $|Q| \leq 2^{n_1}$, $|\Sigma_E| \leq 2^{n_2}$, $|\widetilde{pred}| \leq 2^{n_3}$ and $|\widetilde{op}| \leq 2^{n_4}$, respectively. We will assume some enumeration of the elements in Q (the initial state will always be numbered 0), Σ_E, $\widetilde{pred}$ and $\widetilde{op}$. The automaton is then encoded as a binary string w of length 2^n, where $n = n_2 + n_3 + n_4 + 2n_1$ as follows. We basically encode the transition function. Note that any position of the encoding can be represented by a binary number of length $n_2 + n_3 + n_4 + 2n_1$. The first n_2 bits index the edge symbol of a transition, the next n_3 bits index the predicate of the transition, the next n_4 bits index the operation and the next n_1 bits index the "current control state" and the final n_1 bits index the "next control state".

Before giving the formal encoding, let us fix some notation. Given a binary string $w \in \Gamma^*$, let $|w|$ denote the length of w and w_i denote its i-th symbol (counting from left to right) of w. Given a binary string w, $\hat{w}$ represents the natural number whose binary expansion is w.

Let w be the encoding of the automaton. Then $w_i = 1$ if and only if $i = \hat{s}$ and $s = xvyuz$ where $|x| = n_2$, $|v| = n_3$, $|y| = n_4$, $|u| = n_1$ and $|z| = n_1$, and $(q_1, p_1, e_1, o_1, q_2) \in \delta$, where q_1 is the $\hat{u}$-th symbol of $|Q|$, p_1 is the $\hat{v}$-th symbol of $\widetilde{pred}$, e_1 is the $\hat{x}$-th symbol of Σ_E, o_1 is the $\hat{y}$-th symbol of $\widetilde{op}$ and q_2 is the $\hat{z}$-th symbol of Q. $w_i = 0$, otherwise.

We now describe how a tuple $(\mathcal{A}_1, \mathcal{A}_2, \cdots, \mathcal{A}_n)$ of automata is encoded. Let $x_1, \cdots, x_n$ be the encoding of the automata $\mathcal{A}_1, \cdots, \mathcal{A}_n$, respectively as explained above. Let k be the length of the maximum of the lengths of x_is. We pad 0s to the end of the x_is if required so that their length is k. Let these new strings be $x'_1, \cdots, x'_n$. Let y_i be a string of length k with j_i 1s followed by 0s, where j_i is the number of bits required to index the states of $\mathcal{A}_i$ (which was n_1 in the encoding of the individual automaton). The encoding of the automata tuple would be $y_1 x'_1 y_2 x'_2 \cdots y_n x'_n$.

3 Boolean Automata with Stores

In this section, we establish complexity bounds for the verification of boolean automata, which we later use (in Section 4) to prove complexity bounds on the verification of real-time software. Boolean automata with stores are automata with auxiliary stores that are equipped with additional boolean variables that influence the enabling condition for transitions. We show that solving an automaton problem when the inputs are given as boolean automata is at least as hard as solving the same when the input automata are represented succinctly using circuits. This observation allows us to lift lower bound proofs for automata uniformly to those for boolean automata. Next we show that solving any problem on boolean automata is at most exponentially worse than solving the same problem for automata without boolean variables. We conclude this section by using these observations to establish the exact complexity for a variety of verification problems for boolean automata.

Definitions and notations. Let $Var = \{x_1, \cdots, x_n\}$ be a finite set of boolean variables. A *valuation* of Var is a function $v : Var \to \{0,1\}$. The set of boolean formulas over Var, denoted $BFor(Var)$ is defined inductively as: $\varphi := \top \mid x \mid \neg\varphi \mid \varphi \vee \varphi \mid \varphi \wedge \varphi$, where $x \in Var$. Given $\varphi \in BFor(Var)$, and a valuation v of Var, $(\varphi)_v$ is defined inductively as $(\top)_v = 1$, $(\neg\varphi)_v = 1 - (\varphi)_v$, $(\varphi_1 \vee \varphi_2)_v = \max((\varphi_1)_v, (\varphi_2)_v)$, and

$(\varphi_1 \wedge \varphi_2)_v = \min((\varphi_1)_v, (\varphi_2)_v)$. Next we define the set of reset expressions over *Var*, denoted *BReset*(*Var*), as the expressions of the form $x := y$, $x := 0$, $x := 1$, or *nondet*(x), where $x, y \in Var$. Let us fix $Var = \{x_1, \cdots, x_n\}$ with the ordering $x_1, \cdots, x_n$ for the rest of this section. We define *TReset*(*Var*) to be n-tuples over *BReset*(*Var*) where the i-th component of the tuple is of the form $x_i := x_j$, $x_i = 0$, $x_i = 1$ or *nondet*(x_i). Given $\eta \in TReset(Var)$ we denote by η_i, the i-th component of η. $(\eta)_v$ gives the valuations resulting from the application of η to v and is defined as follows. $(\eta)_v$ is the set of valuations v' such that for each i, $v'(x_i)$ is $v(x_j)$ if η_i is $x_i := x_j$, is 0 if η_i is $x_i := 0$, is 1 if η_i is $x_i := 1$, is either 0 or 1 if $\eta_i = nondet(x_i)$. Given a valuation v, $\bar{v}$ will denote the tuple $(v(x_1), \cdots, v(x_n))$.

We now define a boolean automaton as an automaton augmented with a finite set of boolean variables on which the transitions could depend. We have the following definition.

Boolean Automaton. Let $\mathcal{D}$ be a store and Σ_E be an alphabet. A $(\mathcal{D}, \Sigma_E)$-boolean automaton $\mathcal{B}$ is a tuple $(Q, Var, \delta, q_i, v_i)$, where

- Q is a finite set of *control states.*
- *Var* is a finite set of *control variables.*
- $\delta \subseteq Q \times BFor(Var) \times \widetilde{pred} \times \Sigma_E \times \widetilde{op} \times TReset(Var) \times Q$ is a finite set of *transitions.*
- q_i is the initial state of the automaton.
- v_i is the initial valuation of the variables.

The *semantics* of $\mathcal{B}$ is the same as that of the $(\mathcal{D}, \Sigma_E)$-automaton $[\![\mathcal{B}]\!] = (Q', \delta', q'_i)$, where $Q' = Q \times \{0,1\}^n$; $q'_i = (q_i, \bar{v_i})$; and $((q, \bar{v}), p, e, o, (q', \bar{v}')) \in \delta'$ iff there exists g and r such that $(q, g, p, e, o, r, q') \in \delta$, and $(g)_v = 1$ and $v' \in (r)_v$.

In order to avoid clutter, we do not give the binary encoding of a boolean automaton, but it follows the same lines as the encoding of an automaton. The signature of a k-tuple of Boolean automata with auxiliary stores is defined as for the case of automata. A k-boolean automaton problem is a set of k-tuples which have the same signature. The boolean version of a k-automaton problem $\mathcal{P}$, which we denote $b(\mathcal{P})$, is defined as $b(\mathcal{P}) = \{(B_1, B_2, \ldots B_k) \mid ([\![B_1]\!], [\![B_2]\!], \ldots [\![B_k]\!]) \in \mathcal{P}\}$.

3.1 Lower Bounds for Boolean Automata

We now show that the boolean version of an automaton problem is at least exponentially harder than the automaton problem itself. We first show that the boolean version of an automaton problem is at least as hard as its succinct version. This result will allow us to lift lower bound proofs uniformly. In order to carry out these steps, we need the technical definition of a *two-step automaton* which follows next.

Two-step automaton. Informally, a two-step of an automaton $\mathcal{A}$ is a collection of automata, where an automaton in this collection is obtained by replacing each transition of $\mathcal{A}$ by two consecutive transitions having the same label as the original transition. In addition there are one or more transitions out of every state to some dead states. Formally, given a $(\mathcal{D}, \Sigma_E)$-automaton $\mathcal{A} = (Q, \delta, \Sigma_E)$, an automaton $\mathcal{A}' = (Q', \delta', \Sigma'_E)$ is in *two-step*$(\mathcal{A})$, if there exists a set Y (disjoint from Q and δ) such that the following conditions hold. The states of Q' are $Q \cup \delta \cup Y$. For every transition $x = (q_1, p, e, o, q_2)$ in $\mathcal{A}$, there are transitions $(q_1, \mathsf{true}, e, id, x)$ and (x, p, e, o, q_2) in $\mathcal{A}'$. For every $q_1 \in Q$ and e, there are transitions $(q_1, \mathsf{true}, e, id, q_2)$ in $\mathcal{A}'$, for one or more $q_2 \in Y$. Y represents the dead states. There are no other transitions.

For a k-automaton problem $\mathcal{P}$, we define *two-step*$(\mathcal{P})$ to be $\{(\mathcal{A}'_1, \mathcal{A}'_2, \ldots, \mathcal{A}'_k) \mid \mathcal{A}'_i \in$ *two-step*$(\mathcal{A}_i)$ and $(\mathcal{A}_1, \mathcal{A}_2, \ldots, \mathcal{A}_k) \in \mathcal{P}\}$. Given an automaton problem $\mathcal{P}$, we say that $\mathcal{P}$ is *two-step expansion invariant* if *two-step*$(\mathcal{P}) \subseteq \mathcal{P}$. For example, consider an automaton problem $\mathcal{P}$ which corresponds to pairs of automata which are bisimilar. Then $\mathcal{P}$ is two-step expansion invariant, since whenever $\mathcal{A}$ and $\mathcal{B}$ are bisimilar and $\mathcal{A}' \in$ *two-step*$(\mathcal{A})$ and $\mathcal{B}' \in$ *two-step*$(\mathcal{B})$, $\mathcal{A}'$ and $\mathcal{B}'$ are bisimilar.

The following important lemma states that the succinct version of an automaton problem can be reduced to the boolean version of its two-step expansion.

Lemma 3. *Let $\mathcal{P}$ be an automaton problem, then $s(\mathcal{P}) \leq^P_m b($two-step$(\mathcal{P}))$.*

Proof (Sketch.) We show the reduction for a 1-automaton problem, the extension to the k-automaton problem is direct. Let $\mathcal{P}$ be an automaton problem. Let $\mathcal{A} \in \mathcal{P}$ be an automaton and C be its succinct representation. We construct in time polynomial in $|C|$, the boolean automaton $\mathcal{B}$ such that $[\![\mathcal{B}]\!] \in$ *two-step*$(\mathcal{A})$, i.e., $\mathcal{B} \in b($*two-step*$(\mathcal{A}))$.

The circuit C computes the encoding of the automaton $\mathcal{A}$. The first half of the encoding consists of n 1s followed by zero or more 0s where n is the number of bits used to represent the states in $\mathcal{A}$. The second half encodes the transition relation. Hence in time polynomial in the size of $|C|$, we can compute the value of n and also fix the most significant bit of the input of C to 1 to obtain the circuit C_δ which encodes only the transition relation. From now on by C we mean C_δ.

Let us name the inputs of C by variables in sets X, P, O, E and Y (will assume the sets are ordered) such that the inputs corresponding to variables X are used to index the current state; similarly the inputs labelled by P, O, E and Y are used to index the predicates, operations, edge labels and next states of a tuple (q_1, p, o, e, q_2), respectively. A valuation v to the variables corresponding to the tuple (q_1, p, o, e, q_2) when input to C evaluates to 1 if and only if (q_1, p, o, e, q_2) is a transition of $\mathcal{A}$. (Note the number of variables in X and Y are the same.)

The idea is to encode the states of $\mathcal{A}$ using boolean variables and use the circuit to somehow verify the transition relation. Since the boolean automaton can have boolean formulas as guards and not circuits, we verify the transition relation by converting the circuit $C(X, P, O, E, Y)$ to a boolean guard $\varphi(X, P, O, E, Y, I)$ such that for a transition $t = (q_1, p, o, e, q_2)$, $C(q_1, p, o, e, q_2) = 1$ iff $\varphi(q_1, p, o, e, q_2, I)$ is satisfiable, when I is a new set of variables.

However to check the satisfiability of $\varphi(X, P, O, E, Y, I)$ we need to guess the values of the variables in I. Hence the boolean automaton $\mathcal{B}$ we construct has two states, namely, the *current* and the *guess* state. There are six sets of variables X, P, O, E, Y and I. In the current state only the variables of X are non-zero and they correspond to an encoding of a state of the automaton $\mathcal{A}$. From the current state there is a transition to the guess state in which the variables in X remain intact but the variables in P, O, E, Y and I are all non-deterministically set to 0 or 1. The transition is labelled by the label encoded in E, the predicate is a boolean formula which checks that the edge label of the transition is same as that encoded by the variables in E, and the operation is the identity operation *id*. The values of the variables in P, O, E and Y are used to encode the predicate, operation, edge label and the next state, whereas the variables in I correspond to the intermediate variables which arise in the conversion from the circuit to the boolean guard. From the guess state there is a transition to the current state only if the variables satisfy the guard φ. Then the values of the variables in Y are copied to the corresponding variables of X and all variables other than those in X are set to 0. The edge label, predicate, operation of this transition are those encoded in E, P and O respectively.

This construction takes time polynomial in $|C|$ since the number of states is 2, the number of variables is less than the size of $|C|$ (it is just all the input variables and one intermediate variable for each gate in the circuit), and boolean formula is polynomial in the size of $|C|$ (in fact linear) and can be computed in time polynomial in $|C|$. Hence the boolean automaton constructed is polynomial in the size of $|C|$ and the reduction takes polynomial time.

It is easy to see that $[\![\mathcal{B}]\!]$ is in *two-step*($\mathcal{A}$). Different valuations in the current state correspond to different states of $\mathcal{A}$. Every transition of $\mathcal{A}$ is mimicked in $[\![\mathcal{B}]\!]$ by two consecutive transition, the first one going into the guess state and the other from the guess state to the current state. There are some transitions into the guess state which cannot be verified in the sense that the values of the variables do not satisfy the guard on the transition to the current state, these will occur as transitions from the current state to dead states (which are accommodated in the definition of *two-step*). □

The next theorem establishes the fact that the boolean version of an automaton problem is at least exponentially harder than the automaton problem.

Theorem 1. *Let C_1 and C_2 be arbitrary complexity classes such that for every problem $\mathcal{P}_1$ in C_1, long($\mathcal{P}_1$) is in C_2. Then for every automaton problem $\mathcal{P}_2$ which is two-step expansion invariant, if $\mathcal{P}_2$ is hard for C_2 under PLT-reducibility, then $b(\mathcal{P}_2)$ is hard for C_1 under polynomial time m-reducibility.*

Proof Let $\mathcal{P}_1 \in C_1$, we need to show that $\mathcal{P}_1 \leq_m^P b(\mathcal{P}_2)$. Since $long(\mathcal{P}_1) \in C_2$, and $long(\mathcal{P}_1) \leq_m^{PLT} \mathcal{P}_2$, we have from Lemma 1, that $s(long(\mathcal{P}_1)) \leq_m^P s(\mathcal{P}_2)$. But $\mathcal{P}_1 \leq_m^P s(long(\mathcal{P}_1))$, from Lemma 2. Hence $\mathcal{P}_1 \leq_m^P s(\mathcal{P}_2)$. Now from Lemma 3, we have $s(\mathcal{P}_2) \leq_m^P b(two\text{-}step(\mathcal{P}_2))$. But since $\mathcal{P}_2$ is expansion invariant we have $s(\mathcal{P}_2) \leq_m^P b(\mathcal{P}_2)$. Hence $\mathcal{P}_1 \leq_m^P b(\mathcal{P}_2)$. Therefore $b(\mathcal{P}_2)$ is hard for C_1 under m-reducibility. □

Note that if C_1 is an exponentially larger class than C_2, then they satisfy the condition in the above theorem. Hence if an automaton problem is hard for C_2, then its boolean version is at least exponentially harder.

3.2 Upper Bounds for Boolean Automata

We can also show that solving the boolean version of an automaton problem is at most exponentially harder than the automaton problem itself.

Proposition 1. *Let $\mathcal{P}$ be a k-automaton problem. If $t(n) \geq n$ and $\mathcal{P} \in \mathsf{DTIME}(t(n))$ (or $\mathcal{P} \in \mathsf{NTIME}(t(n))$) then the boolean automaton problem $b(\mathcal{P}) \in \mathsf{DTIME}(t(2^{O(n)}))$ (or $b(\mathcal{P}) \in \mathsf{NTIME}(t(2^{O(n)}))$, respectively). If $s(n) \geq \log(n)$ and $\mathcal{P} \in \mathsf{DSPACE}(s(n))$ (or $\mathcal{P} \in \mathsf{NSPACE}(s(n))$) then $b(\mathcal{P}) \in \mathsf{DSPACE}(s(2^{O(n)}))$ (or $b(\mathcal{P}) \in \mathsf{NSPACE}(s(2^{O(n)}))$, respectively).*

As an example of the application of this proposition, problem of deciding whether two boolean automata (with no store) are trace equivalent is easily seen to be in EXPSPACE as the trace equivalence problem between finite automata is in PSPACE.

3.3 Results

We demonstrate that Theorem 1 and Proposition 1 can be used to show that for a variety of automata problems, there is exactly an exponential blowup in complexity when we consider inputs that are boolean automata. For the rest of this section, by pushdown boolean automata we shall mean boolean automata with a pushdown stack as the auxiliary store and by boolean automata we shall mean a boolean automata with no store.[3]

We can extend the results on bisimulation and simulation between finite state machines [26], bisimulation and simulation between visibly pushdown automata [27], bisimulation and simulation between finite state systems and pushdown automata [20,18] and model-checking μ-calculus properties for higher order pushdown automata [21] to obtain the following result.

Theorem 2.

1. *The problem of control state reachability in boolean automata is* PSPACE-*complete.*
2. *The problem of bisimulation and simulation between boolean automata is* DEXPTIME-*complete.*
3. *The problem of bisimulation and simulation between two boolean VPAs is* 2-DEXPTIME-*complete.*
4. *The problem of bisimulation and simulation between boolean automata and pushdown boolean automata is* 2-DEXPTIME-*complete.*
5. *Model checking μ-calculus properties for order n higher order pushdown boolean automata is* $(n+1)$-DEXPTIME-*complete.*

The first two items have been established in [19,25], albeit by different methods. The last three items are new. The last item also implies that the μ-calculus satisfiability of boolean automata is DEXPTIME-complete and that of boolean pushdown automata is 2-DEXPTIME-complete since these correspond to order 0 and 1 higher order pushdown boolean systems respectively.

[3] No store is modeled by taking the set of data values to be a singleton.

4 Timed Automata

In this section we define timed automata with auxiliary stores and prove lower and upper bounds for problems on them. Let C be a finite set of symbols, henceforth called *clocks*. The set Φ_C of *clock constraints* over C is defined by $\phi ::= \mathsf{true} \mid x \sim k \mid x \sim y \mid \neg\phi \mid \phi \wedge \phi \mid \phi \vee \phi$, where $k \in N$ stands for any non-negative integer and $\sim \in \{=, <, >, \leq, \geq\}$ is a comparison operator. A *valuation* for C is a function from the set of clocks to the set of positive reals, *i.e.*, $v : C \to \mathbb{R}_{\geq 0}$. Let *ValSet(C)* be the set of all valuations of C. We say that v satisfies ϕ, denoted $v \models \phi$, if ϕ is true when the variables of ϕ are replaced by their values, i.e., x is replaced by $v(x)$. We denote by $v+t$ the function mapping x to $v(x)+t$, and by $v[X \to 0]$ the function which maps x to 0 if $x \in X$ and maps x to $v(x)$ otherwise.

Timed Automaton. Let $\mathcal{D}$ be an auxiliary store and Σ_E be an alphabet. A *($\mathcal{D}$,Σ_E)-timed automaton* is a tuple (Q, C, δ, q_i), where:

- Q is a finite set of *control states*,
- C is a finite set of clocks,
- $\delta \subseteq Q \times \Phi_C \times \widetilde{pred} \times \Sigma_E \times \widetilde{op} \times 2^C \times Q$ is a finite set of transitions, and
- $q_i \in Q$ is the *initial state*.

The semantics of a $(\mathcal{D}, \Sigma_E)$-timed automaton $\mathcal{T} = (Q, C, \delta, q_i)$ is described in terms of a $\Sigma_E \times \mathbb{R}_{\geq 0}$-labeled transition system $(\mathcal{S}, \longrightarrow_\delta, s_i)$, where $\mathcal{S} = Q \times D \times$ *ValSet(C)*; $s_i = (q_i, d_i, v[C \to 0])$; and $(q_1, d_1, v_1) \xrightarrow{(a,t)}_\delta (q_2, d_2, v_2)$ iff there exists a transition $(q_1, \phi, p, a, o, C_1, q_2) \in \delta$ such that $v_1 + t \models \phi$, $(v_1 + t)[C_1 \to 0] = v_2$, $p(d_1)$ is true, and $o(d_1) = d_2$.

4.1 Lower Bounds for Timed Automata with Store

Our goal is to show that solving a timed automaton problem with store is at least as hard as solving a corresponding boolean automaton problem with store. First, we will construct a timed automaton $Timed_k(\mathcal{B})$ for a boolean automaton $\mathcal{B}$ which has the following property. The construction of $Timed_k(\mathcal{B})$ is along the lines of [19], and is omitted here for lack of space.

Lemma 4. *Let $\mathcal{B}_1$ be a $(\mathcal{D}_1, \Sigma_{E1})$-boolean automata and $\mathcal{B}_2$ be a $(\mathcal{D}_2, \Sigma_{E2})$-boolean automata, and k be the maximum of the number of variables in $\mathcal{B}_1$ and $\mathcal{B}_2$. Then $Timed_k(\mathcal{B}_1)$ and $Timed_k(\mathcal{B}_2)$ are bisimilar iff $\mathcal{B}_1$ and $\mathcal{B}_2$ are bisimilar. Also $Timed_k(\mathcal{B}_1)$ is simulated by $Timed_k(\mathcal{B}_2)$ iff B_1 is simulated by B_2.*

The above lemma allows us to conclude the following results from the lower bound results of Theorem 2:

Theorem 3.

1. *The problem of control state reachability in timed automata is* PSPACE*-hard.*
2. *The problem of bisimulation and simulation between timed automata is* DEXPTIME*-hard.*

3. *The problem of simulation and bisimulation between two timed VPA is* 2-DEXPTIME*-hard.*
4. *The problem of bisimulation and simulation between timed automata and pushdown timed automata is* 2-DEXPTIME*-hard.*
5. *Model checking timed μ-calculus properties for order n higher order pushdown timed systems is* $(n+1)$-DEXPTIME*-hard.*

We note that the first result above has also been established in [3], while the second result was established in [19]. The last three results are however new and (to the best of our knowledge) do not appear in literature. As a byproduct we obtain that model-checking timed μ-calculus formulas for timed systems and pushdown timed systems is DEXPTIME-hard and 2-DEXPTIME-hard by instantiating n to 0 and 1 respectively in the last item.

4.2 Upper Bounds for Timed Automata with Store

We now show that the lower bounds for decision problems obtained in Section 4.1 are tight. As these decision problems are mainly concerned with simulation and bisimulation, they can be converted to decision problems on *game graphs* by standard techniques. The game graphs that will arise for timed automata will be infinitely branching and we shall appeal to the region construction [3] in order to deal with the "infinite-branching." We start by recalling the definition of regions and game graphs.

Regions. Regions were introduced in [3] in order to show that reachability in timed systems is decidable. Given a finite set of clocks $\mathcal{C}$ and a natural number n_{max}, we can define an equivalence class on the set of real-valuations $\mathit{ValSet}(\mathcal{C})$ as follows. For a real number r, let $\lfloor r \rfloor$ denote the integral value of r and $\mathit{frac}(r)$ the fractional value of r. We say that for valuations $v_1, v_2 \in \mathit{ValSet}(\mathcal{C})$, v_1 is equivalent to v_2 (denoted as $v_1 \equiv v_2$) iff for all $c, c_1, c_2 \in \mathcal{C}$:

1. $v_1(c) > n_{max}$ iff $v_2(c) > n_{max}$;
2. if $v_1(c), v_2(c) \leq n_{max}$, then $\lfloor v_1(c) \rfloor = \lfloor v_2(c) \rfloor$;
3. if $v_1(c), v_2(c) \leq n_{max}$, then $\mathit{frac}(v_1(c)) = 0$ iff $\mathit{frac}(v_2(c)) = 0$; and
4. if $v_1(c_1), v_1(c_2), v_2(c_1), v_2(c_2) \leq n_{max}$, then $\mathit{frac}(v_1(c_1)) \leq \mathit{frac}(v_1(c_2))$ iff $\mathit{frac}(v_2(c_1)) \leq \mathit{frac}(v_2(c_2))$.

The equivalence relation $\equiv$ is of finite index and the set of equivalence classes under $\equiv$ shall henceforth be denoted as $\mathsf{Reg}(n_{max}, \mathcal{C})$.

Game graphs. A game graph is a graph $\mathsf{G} = (V_P \cup V_O, E)$ such that $V_P \cap V_O = \emptyset$ and $E \subseteq (V_P \times V_O) \cup (V_O \times V_P)$. The nodes in the set V_P are called *proponent nodes* and the nodes in the set V_O are called *opponent nodes*. A binary relation $R \subseteq (V_P \times V_P) \cup (V_O \times V_O)$ is a *game bisimulation* if for every $(v_1, v_2) \in R$ the following two conditions hold:

1. For every $v_1' \in V_P \cup V_O$ such that $(v_1, v_1') \in E$, there is a $v_2' \in V_P \cup V_O$ such that $(v_1', v_2') \in R$ and $(v_2, v_2') \in E$.

2. For every $v_2' \in V_P \cup V_O$ such that $(v_2, v_2') \in E$, there is a $v_1' \in V_P \cup V_O$ such that $(v_1', v_2') \in R$ and $(v_1, v_1') \in E$.

The set of *plays* and *strategies* are defined in the standard way. It is well-known that simulation and bisimulation between transition systems can be stated as reachability games on appropriate game graphs.

Consider, for example, the problem of simulation of a timed transition system $\mathcal{G}_0$ by $\mathcal{G}_1$ (by a timed transition system we mean a transition system arising out of a timed automaton). A proponent node will correspond to a pair of configurations of $\mathcal{G}_0$ and $\mathcal{G}_1$. Since every move of $\mathcal{G}_0$ needs to be simulated by $\mathcal{G}_1$, the proponent moves are those of $\mathcal{G}_0$. Consider the proponent node (C_1, C_2) where C_1 is the configuration of $\mathcal{G}_0$ and C_2 the configuration of $\mathcal{G}_1$. Suppose $\mathcal{G}_0$ takes a transition (a, t) and moves to C_1'. Then, for $\mathcal{G}_0$ to be simulated by $\mathcal{G}_1$, $\mathcal{G}_1$ has to take a transition (a, t) from C_2 . Therefore, the proponent move corresponding to $\mathcal{G}_0$ transitioning to C_1' leads us to the opponent node (C_1', C_2, a, t). Now if $\mathcal{G}_2$ can take a (a, t) transition from C_2 to C_2' then we move from the opponent node (C_1', C_2, a, t) to the proponent node (C_1', C_2'). It is easy to see that $\mathcal{G}_0$ is simulated by $\mathcal{G}_1$, iff proponent does not have a strategy to reach an opponent node from which there is no transition. The case of bisimulation is similar except that the proponent must have moves corresponding to both $\mathcal{G}_0$ and $\mathcal{G}_1$, and a proponent move corresponding to $\mathcal{G}_0$ must be answered by a move of $\mathcal{G}_1$ (and vice-versa). We formalize these game graphs as *timed game graphs.*

Timed Game Graph. As already described above, simulation and bisimulation between timed automata can be cast as reachability games on game graphs. Given a $(\mathcal{D}_0, \Sigma_E)$-timed automaton $\mathcal{G}_0 = (Q_0, \mathcal{C}_0, \delta_0, \hat{q}_0)$ and a $(\mathcal{D}_1, \Sigma_E)$-timed automaton $\mathcal{G}_1 = (Q_1, \mathcal{C}_1, \delta_1, \hat{q}_1)$, let $(\mathsf{Conf}_0, \longrightarrow_{\delta_0}, s_{00})$ and $(\mathsf{Conf}_1, \longrightarrow_{\delta_1}, s_{01})$ be the timed transition systems associated with them. We assume that $\mathcal{C}_0 \cap \mathcal{C}_1 = \emptyset$ (we can always rename clocks). Let $\mathsf{Players}$ be a non-empty subset of $\{0, 1\}$ and $\mathsf{Moves} = \Sigma_E \times \mathbb{R}$. The *timed game graph* corresponding to $\mathcal{G}_0$, $\mathcal{G}_1$ and $\mathsf{Players}$ is given by the game graph $\mathsf{G} = (V_P \cup V_O, E)$ where:

1. $V_P = \{(\mathsf{Players}, Conf_0, Conf_1) \mid Conf_i \in \mathsf{Conf}_i \text{ for } i = 0, 1\}$.
2. Let $V_O^0 = (P \times \mathsf{Conf}_0 \times \mathsf{Conf}_1 \times \mathsf{Moves})$ where $P = \{1 - i \mid i \in \mathsf{Players}\}$.
3. For $(v, w) \in V_P \times V_O$, $(v, w) \in E$ iff $v = (\mathsf{Players}, Conf_0, Conf_1)$, $w = (P, Conf_0', Conf_1', (a, t))$ and there exists $i \in \mathsf{Players}$ such that $Conf_i \xrightarrow{(a,t)}_{\delta_0} Conf_i'$, $P = \{1 - i\}$ and $Conf_{1-i}' = Conf_{1-i}$.
   For $(w, v) \in V_O \times V_P$, $(w, v) \in E$ iff $w = (i, Conf_0, Conf_1, (a, t))$ and $v = (\mathsf{Players}, Conf_0', Conf_1')$, where $Conf_i \xrightarrow{(a,t)}_{\delta_0} Conf_i'$ and $Conf_{1-i}' = Conf_{1-i}$.

So the question of simulation can be cast as a question on the game graph G. Note that G is potentially *infinite-branching* and it is not immediately obvious as to how to solve the game problem. We appeal to the region construction to eliminate the infinite branching as follows.

The idea behind our construction is to use regions on clocks of both the systems (a similar strategy has been used in [8] to show that bisimulation between two timed systems without store is decidable). Let n_{max} be some integer such that n_{max} is greater than any integer occurring in the clock constraints of δ_0 and δ_1. Given $v_0 \in ValSet(\mathcal{C}_0)$ and $v_1 \in ValSet(\mathcal{C}_1)$, we use $\mathsf{Reg}(n_{max}, v_0, v_1)$ for the region $\mathsf{Reg}(n_{max}, v)$(the equivalence class of v), where $v \in ValSet(\mathcal{C}_0 \cup \mathcal{C}_1)$ is the valuation such that $v(c) = v_0(c)$ for $c \in \mathcal{C}_0$ and $v(c) = v_1(c)$ for $c \in \mathcal{C}_1$. Let $Conf_0 \in \mathsf{Conf}_0$ and $Conf_1 \in \mathsf{Conf}_1$ be configurations such that $Conf_0 = (q_0, d_0, v_0)$ and $Conf_1 = (q_1, d_1, v_1)$. For a proponent node $v = (\mathsf{Players}, Conf_0, Conf_1)$, let $\mathcal{H}(v) = (q_0, d_0, q_1, d_1, \mathsf{Reg}(n_{max}, v_1, v_2))$. For an opponent node $w = (i, Conf_0, Conf_1, (a, t))$, let $\mathcal{H}(w) = (i, a, q_0, d_0, q_1, d_1, \mathsf{Reg}(\ n_{max}, v_0', v_1'))$, where $v_i' = v_i + t$ and $v_{1-i}' = v_{1-i}$. We have the following result.

Theorem 4. *The relation $R = \{(u_1, u_2) \mid \mathcal{H}(u_1) = \mathcal{H}(u_2)\}$ is a game bisimulation on the timed game graph.*

Hence, while solving the problems of simulation and bisimulation between timed automata, one can appeal to Theorem 4 and reduce the timed game problem to one without time by constructing the $\mathcal{H}$-bisimulation quotient. Then a winning strategy for the proponent in the timed game graph is obtained by "mimicking" the strategy in the bisimulation quotient. For example, simulation between timed automata and pushdown timed automata can be converted to a game on pushdown graph by constructing the $\mathcal{H}$-bisimulation of the graph G. Note that the description of the resulting pushdown game however is exponential in size of the input as one needs to construct the regions on the clocks. Further, since the reachability game can be solved in PTIME for finite game graphs and DEXPTIME for pushdown games, we obtain the following results.

Theorem 5.

1. *The control state reachability problem of timed automata is in* PSPACE.
2. *The bisimulation and simulation problems between two timed automata is in* DEXPTIME.
3. *The problem of simulation and bisimulation between two timed VPA is in* 2-DEXPTIME.
4. *The bisimulation and simulation problems between a timed automaton and a pushdown timed automaton is in* 2-DEXPTIME.
5. *Model checking timed μ-calculus properties for order n higher order pushdown timed systems is* $(n+1)$-DEXPTIME-*complete.*

The first two results are known [3,19,2] and the last three are new.

5 Conclusions

We established the exact complexity of the problems of reachability, simulation, bisimulation, and μ-calculus model checking for timed automata, timed pushdown automata, and timed higher order pushdown automata. Our proof relied on ideas from succinct representations to uniformly lift lower bound proofs for finite automata, pushdown automata, and higher order pushdown automata to the corresponding timed versions. As an intermediate step we established complexity bounds on the verification of boolean automata (without stacks, with stacks, and with higher order stacks), which are also important models that arise in verification. Thus we re-established some previously known results for timed automata using new proof techniques, and proved many new results about timed pushdown automata and timed higher order pushdown automata.

References

1. Abdulla, P.A., Deneux, J., Ouaknine, J., Worrell, J.: Decidability and complexity results for timed automata via channel machines. In: Caires, L., Italiano, G.F., Monteiro, L., Palamidessi, C., Yung, M. (eds.) ICALP 2005. LNCS, vol. 3580, pp. 1089–1101. Springer, Heidelberg (2005)
2. Aceto, L., Laroussinie, F.: Is your model checker on time? In: Kutyłowski, M., Wierzbicki, T., Pacholski, L. (eds.) MFCS 1999. LNCS, vol. 1672, pp. 125–136. Springer, Heidelberg (1999)
3. Alur, R., Dill, D.: A theory of timed automata. Theoretical Computer Science 126, 183–235 (1994)
4. Alur, R., Madhusudan, P.: Visibly Pushdown Automata. In: ACM Symposium on Theory of Computation, pp. 202–211 (2004)
5. Alur, R., Madhusudan, P.: Visibly pushdown languages. In: Babai, L. (ed.) STOC, pp. 202–211. ACM, New York (2004)
6. Balcázar, J.L., Lozano, A., Torán, J.: The complexity of algorithmic problems on succinct instances. Computer Science, 351–377 (1992)
7. Bouajjani, A., Echahed, R., Robbana, R.: On the automatic verification of systems with continuous variables and unbounded discrete data structures. In: International Conference on Hybrid Systems: Computation and Control, pp. 64–85 (1994)
8. Cerans, K.: Decidability of bisimulation equivalence for parallel timer processes. In: Courcoubetis, C. (ed.) CAV 1993. LNCS, vol. 697, pp. 302–315. Springer, Heidelberg (1993)
9. Chadha, R., Legay, A., Prabhakar, P., Viswanathan, M.: Complexity bounds for the verification of real-time software. Technical report, University of Illinois at Urbana-Champaign (2009), `http://hdl.handle.net/2142/14134`
10. Chadha, R., Viswanathan, M.: Decidability results for well-structured transition systems with auxiliary storage. In: Caires, L., Vasconcelos, V.T. (eds.) CONCUR 2007. LNCS, vol. 4703, pp. 136–150. Springer, Heidelberg (2007)
11. Clarke, E., Grumberg, O., Jha, S., Lu, Y., Veith, H.: Counterexample-guided Abstraction-refinement. In: Emerson, E.A., Sistla, A.P. (eds.) CAV 2000. LNCS, vol. 1855, pp. 154–169. Springer, Heidelberg (2000)
12. Dang, Z.: Pushdown timed automata: A binary reachability characterization and safety verification. Theoretical Computer Science 302, 93–121 (2003)
13. Emmi, M., Majumdar, R.: Decision Problems for the Verification of Real-time Software. In: International Conference on Hybrid Systems: Computation and Control, pp. 200–211 (2006)
14. Galperin, H., Wigderson, A.: Succinct representations of graphs. Information and Computation 56, 183–198 (1983)
15. Graf, S., Saïdi, H.: Construction of abstract state graphs with PVS. In: Grumberg, O. (ed.) CAV 1997. LNCS, vol. 1254, pp. 72–83. Springer, Heidelberg (1997)

16. Hague, M., Ong, C.-H.L.: Symbolic backwards-reachability analysis for higher-order pushdown systems. In: Seidl, H. (ed.) FOSSACS 2007. LNCS, vol. 4423, pp. 213–227. Springer, Heidelberg (2007)
17. Harel, D., Kupferman, O., Vardi, M.Y.: On the complexity of verifying concurrent transition systems. In: International Conference on Concurrency Theory, pp. 258–272 (1997)
18. Kucera, A.: On simulation-checking with sequential systems. In: He, J., Sato, M. (eds.) ASIAN 2000. LNCS, vol. 1961, pp. 133–148. Springer, Heidelberg (2000)
19. Laroussinie, F., Schnoebelen, P.: The State Explosion Problem from Trace to Bisimulation Equivalence. In: Tiuryn, J. (ed.) FOSSACS 2000. LNCS, vol. 1784, pp. 192–207. Springer, Heidelberg (2000)
20. Mayr, R.: On the complexity of bisimulation problems for pushdown automata. In: Watanabe, O., Hagiya, M., Ito, T., van Leeuwen, J., Mosses, P.D. (eds.) TCS 2000. LNCS, vol. 1872, pp. 474–488. Springer, Heidelberg (2000)
21. Luke Ong, C.-H.: On model checking trees generated by higher order recursion schemes. In: IEEE Symposium on Logic in Computer Science, pp. 81–90 (2006)
22. Ouaknine, J., Worrell, J.: On the language inclusion problem for timed automata: Closing a decidability gap. In: IEEE Symposium on Logic in Computer Science, pp. 54–63 (2004)
23. Papadimitriou, C., Yannakakis, M.: A note on succinct representation of graphs. Information and Computation 71, 181–185 (1986)
24. Rabinovich, A.: Complexity of equivalence problems for concurrent finite agents. Information and Computation 139(2), 111–129 (1997)
25. Rabinovich, A.: Symbolic model checking for μ-calculus requires exponential time. Theoretical Computer Science 243(2), 467–475 (2000)
26. Sawa, Z., Jancar, P.: P-Hardness of Equivalence Testing on Finite-State Processes. In: Pacholski, L., Ružička, P. (eds.) SOFSEM 2001. LNCS, vol. 2234, pp. 326–335. Springer, Heidelberg (2001)
27. Srba, J.: Visibly pushdown automata: From language equivalence to simulation and bisimulation. In: International Workshop on Computer Science Logic, pp. 89–103 (2006)
28. Veith, H.: Succinct representation, leaf languages, and projection reductions. In: IEEE Conference on Computational Complexity, pp. 118–126 (1996)

An Abstract Domain to Discover Interval Linear Equalities*

Liqian Chen[1,2], Antoine Miné[1,3], Ji Wang[2], and Patrick Cousot[1,4]

[1] École Normale Supérieure, Paris, France
{chen,mine,cousot}@di.ens.fr
[2] National Laboratory for Parallel and Distributed Processing, Changsha, P.R.China
wj@nudt.edu.cn
[3] CNRS, France
[4] CIMS, New York University, New York, NY, USA

Abstract. We introduce a new abstract domain, namely the domain of *Interval Linear Equalities (itvLinEqs)*, which generalizes the affine equality domain with interval coefficients by leveraging results from interval linear algebra. The representation of *itvLinEqs* is based on a row echelon system of interval linear equalities, which natively allows expressing classical linear relations as well as certain topologically non-convex (even unconnected or non-closed) properties. The row echelon form limits the expressiveness of the domain but yields polynomial-time domain operations. Interval coefficients enable a sound adaptation of *itvLinEqs* to floating-point arithmetic. *itvLinEqs* can be used to infer and propagate interval linear constraints, especially for programs involving uncertain or inexact data. The preliminary experimental results are encouraging: *itvLinEqs* can find a larger range of invariants than the affine equality domain. Moreover, *itvLinEqs* provides an efficient alternative to polyhedra-like domains.

1 Introduction

In 1976, Karr [12] developed a polynomial-time algorithm to discover affine relationships among program variables ($\sum_k a_k x_k = b$). This algorithm is also understood as an abstract domain of affine equalities under the framework of abstract interpretation [5]. The affine equality domain features that the lattice of affine equalities has finite height, thus no widening is needed to ensure termination of the analysis, which makes it suitable for certain analyses, such as precise interprocedural analysis for affine programs [18]. Up to now, the affine equality domain is still one of the most efficient relational numerical abstract domains.

In recent related work [10,17,18], one difficulty observed associated with the affine equality domain is that a rational implementation of this domain can lead to exponentially large numbers. To alleviate this problem, in this paper we seek to implement the affine equality domain using floating-point numbers, as we did for the convex polyhedra domain in [2]. However, simply adapting the affine equality domain to floating-point arithmetic, both soundness and precision are difficult to guarantee due to pervasive

* This work is supported by the INRIA project "Abstraction" common to CNRS and ENS in France, and by the National Natural Science Foundation of China under Grant No.60725206.

G. Barthe and M. Hermenegildo (Eds.): VMCAI 2010, LNCS 5944, pp. 112–128, 2010.

rounding errors. E.g., in the floating-point world, when normalizing the coefficient of x to be 1 in the equality $3x + y = 1$, the only way to be sound is to throw this equality away, since the new coefficient $\frac{1}{3}$ is not a representable floating-point number. Thus, a proper and natural way is to extend the affine equality domain with interval coefficients, using intervals to enclose numbers not exactly representable in floating-point.

In the analysis and verification of real-life systems, the application data in the model, especially some physical quantities, may not be known exactly, e.g., elicited by inexact methods or by expert estimation. To handle such uncertainty, the application data are often provided in terms of intervals. Moreover, in program analysis, to cope with non-linearity in programs (such as multiplication/division of expressions, floating-point arithmetic), non-linear expressions may be abstracted into linear expressions with interval coefficients through certain abstraction techniques [16]. Thus, intervals appear naturally in program expressions during static analysis.

This paper introduces an abstract domain of *interval linear equalities (itvLinEqs)*, to infer relationships of the form $\sum_k [a_k, b_k] \times x_k = [c, d]$ over program variables x_k ($k = 1, \ldots, n$), where constants $a_k, b_k, c, d \in \mathbb{R} \cup \{-\infty, +\infty\}$ are automatically inferred by the analysis. Intuitively, *itvLinEqs* is an interval extension of the affine equality domain ($\sum_k a_k x_k = b$) [12] and a restriction to equalities of our previous work on the interval polyhedra domain ($\sum_k [a_k, b_k] x_k \leq c$) [3]. *itvLinEqs* maintains a row echelon system of interval linear equalities and its domain operations can be constructed analogously to those of the affine equality domain. Like the affine equality domain, both the time and space complexity of *itvLinEqs* is polynomial in the number of program variables (respectively quartic and quadratic in the worst case).

We illustrate *itvLinEqs* for invariant generation using a motivating example shown in Fig. 1. Both the affine equality domain [12] and the convex polyhedra domain [6] will obtain no information at ①, while *itvLinEqs* obtains $x + [-2, -1]y = 1$ at ① and proves $y = [-1, -0.5]$ at ②, which indicates that neither overflow nor division by zero happens in the statement $y := 1/y + 1$.

```
real x, y;
if random()
then   x := y + 1;
else   x := 2y + 1;
endif; ①
assume x == 0; ②
y := 1/y + 1;
```

Loc	Affine equalities/Convex polyhedra	*itvLinEqs*
①	$\top$(no information)	$x + [-2, -1]y = 1$
②	$x = 0$	$x = 0 \wedge y = [-1, -0.5]$

Fig. 1. A motivating example

The rest of the paper is organized as follows. Section 2 discusses related work. Section 3 reviews basic theory of interval linear systems. Section 4 presents the representation of *itvLinEqs*. Section 5 describes domain operations of *itvLinEqs*. Section 6 discusses reduction with the interval domain and the floating-point implementation of *itvLinEqs*. Section 7 presents initial experimental results before Section 8 concludes.

2 Related Work

Static Analysis. In the literature, the affine equality domain has been generalized in various ways, such as the domain of convex polyhedra ($\sum_k a_k x_k \leq b$) [6] and the domain of linear congruence equalities ($\sum_k a_k x_k = b \ \mathbf{mod}\ c$) [9]. Recently, Müller-Olm and Seidl have generalized the analysis of affine relations to polynomial relations of bounded degree [18]. In another direction, Gulwani and Necula [10] presented a polynomial-time randomized algorithm to discover affine equalities using probabilistic techniques.

The idea of using intervals to help the affine equality domain is not new. Feret has used a reduced product between the interval domain and the affine equality domain for the analysis of mobile systems [7]. Recently, the domain of SubPolyhedra [14] has been proposed based on delicate reductions between intervals and the affine equality domain, but allows only the constant term of the equality to be an interval.

More recently, we have proposed to use intervals in our domain of interval polyhedra ($\sum_k [a_k, b_k] x_k \leq c$) [3] which generalizes the convex polyhedra domain by using interval linear inequalities. *itvLinEqs* differs from it in the following respects:

1. *itvLinEqs* limits the constraint system to be in row echelon form, while the interval polyhedra domain has no such limit but restricts interval coefficients to be finite. E.g., $[-\infty, +\infty]x = 1$ (i.e., $x \neq 0$) is only representable in *itvLinEqs* while $\{x + y \leq 1, x + 2y \leq 1\}$ is only representable in the interval polyhedra domain.
2. Concerning the implementation, the interval polyhedra domain relies a lot on linear programming (LP). Since most state-of-the-art LP solvers are implemented using floating-point numbers, both soundness and "numerical instability" issues of floating-point LP should be carefully considered [2]. However, *itvLinEqs* avoids LP and is lightweight.

Interval Linear Algebra. The challenging problem of solving interval linear systems has received much attention in the community of interval analysis [19]. Both checking the solvability and finding the solution of an interval linear system are found to be NP-hard. Different semantics of solutions of an interval linear system have been considered, such as weak and strong solutions.

In contrast to the above community, we are interested in designing an abstract domain. Thus, we mainly focus on designing new operators for manipulating interval linear constraints according to program semantics. In addition, endpoints of interval coefficients are restricted to be finite in the above mentioned work but not in this paper, since infinite interval coefficients may appear naturally after operations such as linearization [16] and widening (Sect. 5.7) in static analysis.

3 Preliminaries

We first briefly recall basic theory and results on standard interval linear systems [19]. We extend interval linear systems with infinite interval coefficients. Let $\mathbf{x} = [\underline{x}, \overline{x}]$ be an interval with its bounds (endpoints) $\underline{x} \leq \overline{x}$. Let $\mathbb{IR}$ be the set of all real intervals $[\underline{a}, \overline{a}]$ where $\underline{a}, \overline{a} \in \mathbb{R}$. Let $\mathbb{IE}$ be the set of all intervals $[\underline{a}, \overline{a}]$ where $\underline{a} \in \mathbb{R} \cup \{-\infty\}, \overline{a} \in \mathbb{R} \cup \{+\infty\}$. Throughout the paper, intervals and other interval objects are typeset in boldface letters.

Let $\underline{A} \in (\mathbb{R} \cup \{-\infty\})^{m\times n}, \overline{A} \in (\mathbb{R} \cup \{+\infty\})^{m\times n}$ be two matrices with $\underline{A} \le \overline{A}$ where the order is defined element-wise. Then the set of matrices

$$\mathbf{A} = [\underline{A}, \overline{A}] = \{A \in \mathbb{R}^{m\times n} : \underline{A} \le A \le \overline{A}\}$$

is called an (extended) *interval matrix*, and the matrices $\underline{A}, \overline{A}$ are called its bounds. An *interval vector* is a one-column interval matrix $\mathbf{b} = \{b \in \mathbb{R}^m : \underline{b} \le b \le \overline{b}\}$, where $\underline{b} \in (\mathbb{R} \cup \{-\infty\})^m, \overline{b} \in (\mathbb{R} \cup \{+\infty\})^m$ and $\underline{b} \le \overline{b}$.

Let $\mathbf{A}$ be an interval matrix of size $m \times n$, $\mathbf{b}$ be an interval vector of size m, and x be a vector of variables in $\mathbb{R}^n$. The following system of interval linear equalities

$$\mathbf{A}x = \mathbf{b}$$

denotes an (extended) *interval linear system*, that is the family of all systems of linear equalities $Ax = b$ with data satisfying $A \in \mathbf{A}$, $b \in \mathbf{b}$.

Definition 1 (Weak solution). *A vector $x \in \mathbb{R}^n$ is called a* weak solution *of the interval linear system $\mathbf{A}x = \mathbf{b}$, if it satisfies $Ax = b$ for some $A \in \mathbf{A}$, $b \in \mathbf{b}$. And the set*

$$\Sigma_{\exists\exists}(\mathbf{A}, \mathbf{b}) = \{x \in \mathbb{R}^n : \exists A \in \mathbf{A}, \exists b \in \mathbf{b}. Ax = b\}$$

is said to be the weak solution set *of the system $\mathbf{A}x = \mathbf{b}$.*

The weak solution set $\Sigma_{\exists\exists}(\mathbf{A}, \mathbf{b})$ can be characterized by the following theorem.

Theorem 1. *Let $\Sigma_{j=1}^n [\underline{A}_{ij}, \overline{A}_{ij}]x_j = [\underline{b}_i, \overline{b}_i]$ be the i-th row of $\mathbf{A}x = \mathbf{b}$. Then a vector $x \in \mathbb{R}^n$ is a weak solution of $\mathbf{A}x = \mathbf{b}$ iff both linear inequalities*

$$\begin{cases} \sum_{j=1}^n A'_{ij}x_j \le \overline{b}_i \\ -\sum_{j=1}^n A''_{ij}x_j \le -\underline{b}_i \end{cases}$$

hold for all $i = 1, \ldots, m$ where A'_{ij}, A''_{ij} are defined through

$$A'_{ij} = \begin{cases} \underline{A}_{ij} & \text{if } x_j > 0 \\ 0 & \text{if } x_j = 0 \\ \overline{A}_{ij} & \text{if } x_j < 0 \end{cases} \qquad A''_{ij} = \begin{cases} \overline{A}_{ij} & \text{if } x_j > 0 \\ 0 & \text{if } x_j = 0 \\ \underline{A}_{ij} & \text{if } x_j < 0 \end{cases}$$

Theorem 1 can be derived from Theorem 2.11 in [19] that we extended to the case of infinite interval coefficients. Note that for the linear inequality $\sum_{j=1}^n A'_{ij}x_j \le \overline{b}_i$ in Theorem 1, each term $A'_{ij}x_j$ will never result in $+\infty$, since $A'_{ij} = -\infty$ may hold only when $x_j > 0$ and $A'_{ij} = +\infty$ may hold only when $x_j < 0$. Whenever one term $A'_{ij}x_j$ results in $-\infty$, the linear inequality $\sum_{j=1}^n A'_{ij}x_j \le \overline{b}_i$ defines the universal space and can be omitted from the system. The same argument holds for $-\sum_{j=1}^n A''_{ij}x_j \le -\underline{b}_i$.

Recall that a (closed) *orthant* is one of the 2^n subsets of an n-dimensional Euclidean space defined by constraining each Cartesian coordinate to be either nonnegative or nonpositive. In a given orthant, each component x_j of x keeps a constant sign, so the intersection of the weak solution set $\Sigma_{\exists\exists}(\mathbf{A}, \mathbf{b})$ with each orthant can be described as a not necessarily closed convex polyhedron. In fact, the possible non-closeness happens in a restricted way so that making it closed will add only a set of points satisfying $x_j = 0$ for some x_j. Particularly, if $\mathbf{A} \in \mathbb{IR}^{m\times n}$, the region in each closed orthant is a closed convex polyhedron [3]. In general, $\Sigma_{\exists\exists}(\mathbf{A}, \mathbf{b})$ can be *non-convex* and even *unconnected*, e.g., $[-1, 1]x = 1$ describes the set $\{x : x \in [-\infty, -1] \cup [1, +\infty]\}$.

Example 1. Given $[-\infty, +\infty]x = 1$, according to Theorem 1,

$$[-\infty, +\infty]x = 1 \Leftrightarrow \begin{cases} \{(-\infty)x \le 1, -(+\infty)x \le -1\} \Leftrightarrow \{-\infty \le 1, -\infty \le -1\} & \text{if } x > 0 \\ \{(+\infty)x \le 1, -(-\infty)x \le -1\} \Leftrightarrow \{-\infty \le 1, -\infty \le -1\} & \text{if } x < 0 \\ \{0x \le 1, -0x \le -1\} \Leftrightarrow \{0 \le 1, 0 \le -1\} & \text{if } x = 0 \end{cases}$$

To sum up, $[-\infty, +\infty]x = 1$ means $x \neq 0$ (since in the case of $x = 0$ the corresponding constraint system of $[-\infty, +\infty]x = 1$ is infeasible).

4 Representation

Now, we introduce the abstract domain of *interval linear equalities (itvLinEqs)*. The main idea of *itvLinEqs* is to use a row echelon system of interval linear equalities as its representation. The concretization of each element in *itvLinEqs* is defined as the weak solution set of the corresponding constraint system.

Constraint Normalization. Throughout this paper, we fix a variable ordering $x_1 \prec x_2 \prec \ldots \prec x_n$. $\Sigma_k[\underline{a}_k, \overline{a}_k]x_k = [\underline{b}, \overline{b}]$ is a *universal constraint* if $[\underline{b}, \overline{b}] = [-\infty, +\infty]$ or $0 \in [\underline{b}, \overline{b}] \wedge \forall k. 0 \in [\underline{a}_k, \overline{a}_k]$. We use $\Sigma_k[0, 0]x_k = [0, 0]$ as a normalized form for universal constraints. Let φ be a non-universal constraint $\Sigma_k[\underline{a}_k, \overline{a}_k]x_k = [\underline{b}, \overline{b}]$. Its *leading variable* x_i is the variable with the least index i such that $[\underline{a}_i, \overline{a}_i] \neq [0, 0]$. φ is said to be *normalized* if the interval coefficient of its leading variable x_i satisfies $[\underline{a}_i, \overline{a}_i] \in \{[0, 1], [0, +\infty], [1, c], [-1, c'], [-\infty, +\infty]\}$ where $c, c' \in \mathbb{R} \cup \{+\infty\}, c \ge 1, c' > 0$. Then, given φ which is not normalized, its normalized form can be obtained by dividing the whole constraint φ by either -1 (if $[\underline{a}_i, \overline{a}_i] = [-\infty, 0]$), $\pm\underline{a}_i$ (if $\underline{a}_i \notin \{0, -\infty\}$), or $\pm\overline{a}_i$ (if $\overline{a}_i \notin \{0, +\infty\}$). Note that this normalization operation is exact, i.e., it will cause no precision loss. For convenience sake, we enforce a normalized form on constraints throughout this paper.

Row Echelon Form. Let $\mathbf{A}x = \mathbf{b}$ be an interval linear system with $\mathbf{A} \in \mathbb{IE}^{m \times n}$ and $\mathbf{b} \in \mathbb{IE}^m$. The system $\mathbf{A}x = \mathbf{b}$ is said to be in *row echelon* form if

1) $m = n$, and
2) Either x_i is the leading variable of the i-th row, or the i-th row is filled with zeros.

***itvLinEqs* Elements.** Each domain element $\mathbf{P}$ in *itvLinEqs* is described as an interval linear system $\mathbf{A}x = \mathbf{b}$ in row echelon form, where $\mathbf{A} \in \mathbb{IE}^{n \times n}$ and $\mathbf{b} \in \mathbb{IE}^n$. It represents the set $\gamma(\mathbf{P}) = \Sigma_{\exists\exists}(\mathbf{A}, \mathbf{b}) = \{x \in \mathbb{R}^n : \exists A \in \mathbf{A}, \exists b \in \mathbf{b}. Ax = b\}$ where each point x is a possible environment (or state), i.e., an assignment of real values to abstract variables. Some examples of *itvLinEqs* elements are shown in Fig. 2.

Row Echelon Abstraction. A system of affine equalities can be equivalently converted into row echelon form via elementary matrix transformations. Unfortunately, not all systems of interval linear equalities can be exactly expressed in row echelon form. Let $\mathbf{P}$ be an arbitrary system of interval linear equalities. We seek a system in row echelon form $\rho(\mathbf{P})$ such that $\gamma(\mathbf{P}) \subseteq \gamma(\rho(\mathbf{P}))$. Unfortunately, row echelon abstraction $\rho(\mathbf{P})$ may not be uniquely defined and the best abstraction may not exist. A row echelon

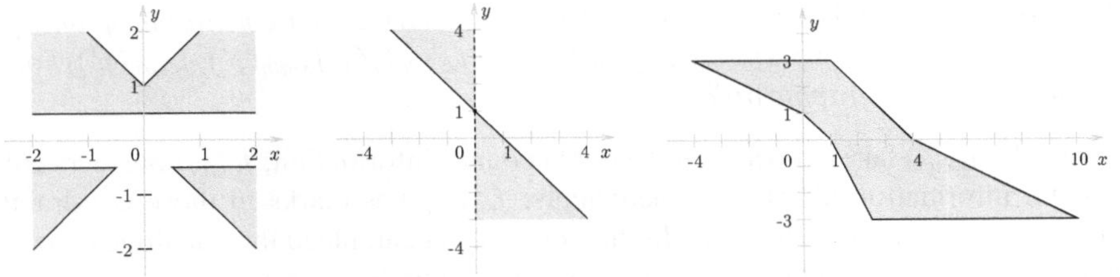

(a) (b) (c)

Fig. 2. Examples of *itvLinEqs* elements in 2 dimensions: (a) $\{[-1,1]x+y=[0,1],[-1,1]y=0.5\}$; (b) $\{[1,+\infty]x+y=1\}$; (c) $\{[1,2]x+[1,2]y=[2,4],y=[-3,3]\}$

abstraction $\rho(\mathbf{P})$ for $\mathbf{P}$ can be constructed based on constraint addition (Sect. 5.3), by "adding" the constraints in $\mathbf{P}$ one by one to a row echelon system initially filled with 0.

Although row echelon abstraction may cause some loss of precision, we enforce row echelon form in *itvLinEqs* since it yields polynomial-time domain operations and avoids the "exponential growth" problem (i.e., producing exponential output) [21]. Furthermore, row echelon form can still represent exactly any affine space. Finally, row echelon form also makes it easier for us to construct our new domain by following an analogous framework to the already known domain of affine equalities.

5 Domain Operations

In this section, we discuss the implementation of most common domain operations required for static analysis over *itvLinEqs*.

5.1 Constraint Comparison

To enforce a row echelon form, we often need to compare several candidate constraints and choose the best one to take the place of the i-th row of the system. We first use some heuristic metrics to estimate the precision of the information contained in a normalized constraint φ.

Definition 2. *Let* $\varphi : (\sum_k[\underline{a}_k,\overline{a}_k]x_k = [\underline{b},\overline{b}])$ *be a normalized constraint and* $[\underline{x}_k,\overline{x}_k]$ *be the bounds of* x_k*. Then metrics* $f_{weight}(\varphi), f_{width}(\varphi) \in \mathbb{R}\cup\{+\infty\}$*,* $f_{mark}(\varphi)\in\mathbb{R}$ *are defined as:*

1) $f_{weight}(\varphi) \stackrel{\text{def}}{=} \sum_k(\overline{a}_k-\underline{a}_k)\times(\overline{x}_k-\underline{x}_k)+(\overline{b}-\underline{b})$,

2) $f_{width}(\varphi) \stackrel{\text{def}}{=} \sum_k(\overline{a}_k-\underline{a}_k)+(\overline{b}-\underline{b})$,

3) $f_{mark}(\varphi) \stackrel{\text{def}}{=} \sum_k \delta(\underline{a}_k,\overline{a}_k)+\delta(\underline{b},\overline{b})$, where

$$\delta(\underline{d},\overline{d}) \stackrel{\text{def}}{=} \begin{cases} -1 & \text{if } \underline{d}=\overline{d}, \\ +200 & \text{else if } \underline{d}=-\infty \text{ and } \overline{d}=+\infty, \\ +100 & \text{else if } \underline{d}=-\infty \text{ or } \overline{d}=+\infty, \\ 0 & \text{otherwise.} \end{cases}$$

Definition 3 (Constraint comparison). *Given two normalized constraints φ and φ', we write $\varphi \preceq \varphi'$ if $(f_{weight}(\varphi), f_{width}(\varphi), f_{mark}(\varphi)) \leq (f_{weight}(\varphi'), f_{width}(\varphi'), f_{mark}(\varphi'))$ holds in the sense of lexicographic order.*

Specifically, f_{weight} takes into account variable bounds information; f_{width} considers only the width information of interval coefficients; f_{mark} gives marks to those constraints having infinite interval coefficients. In this sense, it is guaranteed that an affine equality is always smaller for $\preceq$ than other kinds of constraints. E.g., $(x + y = 1) \preceq (x + y = [1, 2]) \preceq (x + y = [1, +\infty])$. For convenience, we say that a non-universal constraint φ is *better* than φ' if $\varphi \preceq \varphi'$ or φ' is a universal constraint. (If $\varphi \preceq \varphi'$ and $\varphi' \preceq \varphi$, we choose the best one according to the context.) Constraint comparison requires $O(n)$ time.

5.2 Projection

In program analysis, projection is an important primitive to construct assignment transfer functions and interprocedural analysis. In *itvLinEqs*, it is also useful for constraint addition and join. We use $\{\boxplus, \boxminus, \boxtimes, \boxslash\}$ for interval arithmetic operations.

We first introduce a *partial linearization* operator $\zeta(\varphi, x_j)$ to linearize the interval coefficient of x_j in φ to be a scalar.

Definition 4 (Partial linearization). *Let φ: $(\sum_k [\underline{a}_k, \overline{a}_k] \times x_k = [\underline{b}, \overline{b}])$ be an interval linear equality and $[\underline{x}_j, \overline{x}_j]$ be the bounds of x_j.*

$$\zeta(\varphi, x_j) \stackrel{\text{def}}{=} \left(c \times x_j + \textstyle\sum_{k \neq j} [\underline{a}_k, \overline{a}_k] \times x_k = [\underline{b}, \overline{b}] \boxminus [\underline{a}_j - c, \overline{a}_j - c] \boxtimes [\underline{x}_j, \overline{x}_j]\right)$$

where c can be any real number.

A good choice of c that causes less precision loss depends on the values of $\underline{a}_j, \overline{a}_j, \underline{x}_j, \overline{x}_j$. In practice, when $[\underline{a}_j, \overline{a}_j]$ is finite, we often choose $c = (\underline{a}_j + \overline{a}_j)/2$ that is the midpoint of $[\underline{a}_j, \overline{a}_j]$, which gives good results in most cases. If one endpoint of the interval $[\underline{a}_j, \overline{a}_j]$ is infinite, we choose the other endpoint as c. When x_j has infinite bounds, we choose the best one w.r.t. $\preceq$ between resulting constraints given by $c = \underline{a}_j$ and by $c = \overline{a}_j$.

Theorem 2 (Soundness of the partial linearization operator). *Given an interval linear equality φ and a variable $x_j \in [\underline{x}_j, \overline{x}_j]$, $\zeta(\varphi, x_j)$ soundly over-approximates φ, that is, $\forall x.(x_j \in [\underline{x}_j, \overline{x}_j] \wedge x \in \gamma(\varphi)) \Rightarrow x \in \gamma(\zeta(\varphi, x_j))$.*

Now, we consider the problem of projecting out a variable from one constraint and from a pair of constraints.

Projection by Bounds. To project out x_j from one constraint φ: $(\sum_k [\underline{a}_k, \overline{a}_k] x_k = [\underline{b}, \overline{b}])$, we simply choose $c = 0$ in $\zeta(\varphi, x_j)$. Then $\sum_{k \neq j} [\underline{a}_k, \overline{a}_k] x_k = [\underline{b}, \overline{b}] \boxminus [\underline{a}_j, \overline{a}_j] \boxtimes [\underline{x}_j, \overline{x}_j]$ will be an overapproximation of φ which does not involve x_j any more.

Projection by Combination. Let φ: $(\sum_k [\underline{a}_k, \overline{a}_k] x_k = [\underline{b}, \overline{b}])$ and φ': $(\sum_k [\underline{a}'_k, \overline{a}'_k] x_k = [\underline{b}', \overline{b}'])$ be two constraints satisfying $[\underline{a}_j, \overline{a}_j] \neq [0, 0]$ and $[\underline{a}'_j, \overline{a}'_j] \neq [0, 0]$. To compute a constraint ϕ that does not involve x_j and satisfies $\gamma(\varphi) \cup \gamma(\varphi') \subseteq \gamma(\phi)$, we follow a similar way to Gaussian elimination. First, we convert the interval coefficient of x_j in φ to 1 (e.g., by $\zeta(\varphi, x_j)$ with $c = 1$). Assume that we get $x_j + \sum_{k \neq j} [\underline{a}''_k, \overline{a}''_k] x_k = [\underline{b}'', \overline{b}'']$.

Algorithm 1. PROJECT($\mathbf{P}, x_j$)

Input: $\mathbf{P}$: an *itvLinEqs* element $\mathbf{A}x = \mathbf{b}$;
x_j : a variable to be projected out;
Output: $\mathbf{P}'$: an *itvLinEqs* element that does not involve x_j and satisfies $\gamma(\mathbf{P}) \subseteq \gamma(\mathbf{P}')$.

$\mathbf{P}' \leftarrow \mathbf{P}$
for $i = 1$ to $j - 1$ **do**
  if $([\underline{A}_{ij}, \overline{A}_{ij}] \neq [0, 0])$ **then**
    $\varphi \leftarrow \zeta(\mathbf{P}'_i, x_j)$ with $c = 0$ // projection by bounds
    for $k = i + 1$ to j **do**
      if $([\underline{A}_{kj}, \overline{A}_{kj}] \neq [0, 0])$ **then**
        let φ' be the resulting constraint by combining $\mathbf{P}'_i$ and $\mathbf{P}'_k$ to project out x_j
        if $(\varphi' \preceq \varphi)$ **then** $\varphi \leftarrow \varphi'$
    $\mathbf{P}'_i \leftarrow \varphi$ // φ is the best constraint with leading variable x_i that does not involve x_j
$\mathbf{P}'_j \leftarrow [0, 0]^{1\times(n+1)}$
return $\mathbf{P}'$

Then by substituting x_j with $([\underline{b}'', \overline{b}''] - \sum_{k\neq j}[\underline{a}''_k, \overline{a}''_k]x_k)$ in φ', the combination of φ and φ' to eliminate x_j can be achieved as

$$\phi : \left(\textstyle\sum_{k\neq j}([\underline{a}'_k, \overline{a}'_k] \boxminus [\underline{a}'_j, \overline{a}'_j] \boxtimes [\underline{a}''_k, \overline{a}''_k])x_k = [\underline{b}', \overline{b}'] \boxminus [\underline{a}'_j, \overline{a}'_j] \boxtimes [\underline{b}'', \overline{b}'']\right).$$

Particularly, when $0 \notin [\underline{a}_j, \overline{a}_j]$, converting $[\underline{a}_j, \overline{a}_j]$ to 1 in φ can be also achieved by the following theorem.

Theorem 3. *Let φ be $\sum_k[\underline{a}_k, \overline{a}_k]x_k = [\underline{b}, \overline{b}]$ with $0 \notin [\underline{a}_j, \overline{a}_j]$. Then*

$$\varphi'' : \left(x_j + \textstyle\sum_{k\neq j}([\underline{a}_k, \overline{a}_k] \boxslash [\underline{a}_j, \overline{a}_j])x_k = [\underline{b}, \overline{b}] \boxslash [\underline{a}_j, \overline{a}_j]\right)$$

is an overapproximation of φ, that is, $\gamma(\varphi) \subseteq \gamma(\varphi'')$.

To convert $[\underline{a}_j, \overline{a}_j]$ to 1 in φ, the "division" method in Theorem 3 does not depend on the bounds of x_j but requires that $0 \notin [\underline{a}_j, \overline{a}_j]$, while $\zeta(\varphi, x_j)$ with $c = 1$ is more general but depends on the bounds of x_j. Both methods may cause some loss of precision. In practice, in most cases Theorem 3 gives more precise results, especially when the bounds of x_j are coarse or even infinite. E.g., given $\varphi : ([1, 2]x + y = 2)$ with no bounds information, converting the coefficient of x to be 1, $\zeta(\varphi, x_j)$ with $c = 1$ will give a universal constraint while Theorem 3 will result in $\varphi'' : (x + [0.5, 1]y = [1, 2])$. Note that some loss of precision happens here, e.g., point (0,1) satisfies φ'' but not φ.

Projection in *itvLinEqs*. We denote as $\mathbf{P}_i$ the i-th row of $\mathbf{P}$. Based on the above projection operations on constraints, we now propose Algorithm 1 to project out x_j from an *itvLinEqs* element $\mathbf{P}$, denoted as PROJECT($\mathbf{P}, x_j$). For each row, we try various elimination methods (by bounds and by combining with other constraints) and keep the best resulting constraint w.r.t. $\preceq$. E.g., given $\mathbf{P} = \{x - y = 0, [-1, 1]y = [2, +\infty]\}$, PROJECT($\mathbf{P}, y$) results in $\{[-1, 1]x = [2, +\infty]\}$. Note that the affine space of the result of PROJECT($\mathbf{P}, x_j$) is always as precise as that given by projecting out x_j from the affine space of $\mathbf{P}$ via Gaussian elimination. The worst-case complexity of Algorithm 1 is $O(n^3)$.

5.3 Constraint Addition

We now consider the problem of "adding" a new constraint $\varphi : (\sum_k [\underline{a}_k, \overline{a}_k]x_k = [\underline{b}, \overline{b}])$ to an *itvLinEqs* element **P**, denoted as $[\![\varphi]\!]^\#(\mathbf{P})$, i.e., to derive a row echelon abstraction $\mathbf{P}'$ such that $\gamma(\mathbf{P}) \cap \gamma(\varphi) \subseteq \gamma(\mathbf{P}')$. Let x_i be the leading variable of φ. We first initialize $\mathbf{P}'$ as **P**. Then, we compare φ with the i-th row φ' of $\mathbf{P}'$ (i.e., $\varphi' = \mathbf{P}'_i$).

1) If φ is parallel to φ', i.e., $\forall k.[\underline{a}_k, \overline{a}_k] = [\underline{a}'_k, \overline{a}'_k]$, $\mathbf{P}'_i$ will be updated as $\sum_k [\underline{a}'_k, \overline{a}'_k]x_k = [\max\{\underline{b}, \underline{b}'\}, \min\{\overline{b}, \overline{b}'\}]$. If $\max\{\underline{b}, \underline{b}'\} > \min\{\overline{b}, \overline{b}'\}$, then $\mathbf{P}'$ is infeasible.
2) Otherwise, we choose the best one for $\preceq$ between φ and φ' to replace $\mathbf{P}'_i$. Next, we combine φ with φ' to eliminate x_i (Sect.5.2) and recursively "add" the resulting constraint φ'' to the updated $\mathbf{P}'$. As the index of the leading variable of the constraint to add increases strictly, this process terminates when φ'' becomes universal.

Unfortunately, in general neither $\gamma(\mathbf{P}') \subseteq \gamma(\mathbf{P})$ nor $\gamma(\mathbf{P}') \subseteq \gamma(\varphi)$ holds.

Constraint addition is used as a primitive for operations such as transfer functions, row echelon abstraction, intersection. The intersection of two *itvLinEqs* elements **P** and $\mathbf{P}'$, denoted as $\mathbf{P} \sqcap_w \mathbf{P}'$, can be implemented via "adding" the constraints from $\mathbf{P}'$ to **P** one by one, from the first row to the last. Note that $\gamma(\mathbf{P}) \cap \gamma(\mathbf{P}') \subseteq \gamma(\mathbf{P} \sqcap_w \mathbf{P}')$, but the converse may not hold. Also, $\sqcap_w$ is not commutative. Constraint addition can be computed in time $O(n^2)$ and $\mathbf{P} \sqcap_w \mathbf{P}'$ in time $O(n^3)$.

5.4 Join

In order to abstract the control-flow join, we need to design a *join* operation that returns an *itvLinEqs* element which geometrically encloses the two input *itvLinEqs* elements. However, in general, there is no best join available for *itvLinEqs* that computes the smallest *itvLinEqs* element enclosing the input arguments. In this paper, we propose a cheap join operation that we call *weak join*, which can compute the exact affine hull of the affine spaces of the input arguments (i.e., no affine relation is missed) and performs well but without precision guarantee on general interval linear constraints.

5.4.1 Approximate Convex Combination

In the affine equality domain, the join of two affine spaces can be computed via affine hull that is based on affine combination.[1] In the convex polyhedra domain, the join of two convex polyhedra can be computed via polyhedral convex hull that is based on convex combination [21].[2] Following the same idea, we seek to construct a join operation for *itvLinEqs* based on an approximate convex combination.

Given two *itvLinEqs* elements $\gamma(\mathbf{P}) = \{x \mid \mathbf{A}x = \mathbf{b}\}$ and $\gamma(\mathbf{P}') = \{x \mid \mathbf{A}'x = \mathbf{b}'\}$, based on the convex combination of points respectively from **P** and $\mathbf{P}'$ we define a set of points

$$\gamma(\mathbf{P}) \uplus \gamma(\mathbf{P}') = \left\{ x \in \mathbb{R}^n \;\middle|\; \begin{array}{c} \exists \sigma_1, \sigma_2 \in \mathbb{R}, z, z' \in \mathbb{R}^n. \\ x = \sigma_1 z + \sigma_2 z' \wedge \sigma_1 + \sigma_2 = 1 \wedge \sigma_1 \geq 0 \wedge \\ \mathbf{A}z = \mathbf{b} \quad \wedge \quad \mathbf{A}'z' = \mathbf{b}' \;\; \wedge \sigma_2 \geq 0 \end{array} \right\}$$

[1] An *affine combination* of vectors $x_1, \ldots, x_n$ is a vector of the form $\Sigma_{i=1}^n \lambda_i x_i$ with $\Sigma_{i=1}^n \lambda_i = 1$.

[2] A *convex combination* of vectors $x_1, \ldots, x_n$ is a vector of the form $\Sigma_{i=1}^n \lambda_i x_i$ with $\Sigma_{i=1}^n \lambda_i = 1$ and $\forall i. \lambda_i \geq 0$.

It is obvious that $\gamma(\mathbf{P}) \Cup \gamma(\mathbf{P'})$ is an overapproximation of the union of $\gamma(\mathbf{P})$ (when $\sigma_1 = 1$) and $\gamma(\mathbf{P'})$ (when $\sigma_2 = 1$). To avoid the non-linear terms $\sigma_1 z$ and $\sigma_2 z'$, we introduce $y = \sigma_1 z$ as well as $y' = \sigma_2 z'$ and relax the system into

$$\left\{ x \in \mathbb{R}^n \;\middle|\; \begin{array}{l} \exists \sigma_1, \sigma_2 \in \mathbb{R}, y, y' \in \mathbb{R}^n. \\ x = y + y' \;\wedge \sigma_1 + \sigma_2 = 1 \;\wedge \sigma_1 \geq 0 \wedge \\ \mathbf{A}y = \sigma_1 \mathbf{b} \;\wedge\; \mathbf{A'}y' = \sigma_2 \mathbf{b'} \;\wedge \sigma_2 \geq 0 \end{array} \right\}$$

which can be rewritten as

$$\left\{ x \in \mathbb{R}^n \;\middle|\; \begin{array}{rl} \exists \sigma_1 \in \mathbb{R}, y \in \mathbb{R}^n. & \\ \mathbf{A'}x - \mathbf{A'}y + \mathbf{b'}\sigma_1 = \mathbf{b'} & \wedge \\ \mathbf{A}y - \mathbf{b}\sigma_1 = 0 & \wedge \\ \sigma_1 = [0, 1] & \end{array} \right\} \tag{1}$$

which is in row echelon form with respect to the variable ordering $x_1 \prec \ldots \prec x_n \prec y_1 \prec \ldots \prec y_n \prec \sigma_1$. Projecting out y, σ_1 from (1) in sequence (i.e., $y_1, \ldots, y_n, \sigma_1$) via the projection operation in *itvLinEqs* (see Algorithm 1) yields an *itvLinEqs* element, denoted as $\mathbf{P} \Cup_w \mathbf{P'}$. Then we have

$$\gamma(\mathbf{P}) \cup \gamma(\mathbf{P'}) \subseteq \gamma(\mathbf{P}) \Cup \gamma(\mathbf{P'}) \subseteq \gamma(\mathbf{P} \Cup_w \mathbf{P'}).$$

Note that $\mathbf{P} \Cup_w \mathbf{P'}$ which is computed via the projection operation in *itvLinEqs* is definitely an *itvLinEqs* element, while $\gamma(\mathbf{P}) \Cup \gamma(\mathbf{P'})$ which is a point set defined via exact existential quantifiers may not be exactly representable in *itvLinEqs*.

$\mathbf{P} \Cup_w \mathbf{P'}$ will not miss any affine equality that the affine equality domain will generate through affine combination, since an affine equality is always kept when compared with other non-affine equalities according to the definition of constraint comparison $\preceq$. Moreover, $\mathbf{P} \Cup_w \mathbf{P'}$ can also generate other kinds of interesting interval linear constraints, such as linear stripes (of the form $\sum_k a_k x_k = [\underline{b}, \overline{b}]$), to take the place of those rows where no affine relation holds anymore after the join operation. In contrast to polyhedral convex hull which is of exponential time in the worst case and the result of which is always convex, $\mathbf{P} \Cup_w \mathbf{P'}$ can be achieved in polynomial time $O(n^4)$ and can generate non-convex constraints (although it may miss some linear inequalities).

5.4.2 Interval Combination

Definition 5 (Interval combination). *Given two constraints* φ': $(\sum_k [\underline{a}'_k, \overline{a}'_k] \times x_k = [\underline{b}', \overline{b}'])$ *and* φ'': $(\sum_k [\underline{a}''_k, \overline{a}''_k] \times x_k = [\underline{b}'', \overline{b}''])$, *the* interval combination *of* φ' *and* φ'' *is defined as*

$$\varphi' \uplus \varphi'' : \left(\textstyle\sum_k [\min(\underline{a}'_k, \underline{a}''_k), \max(\overline{a}'_k, \overline{a}''_k)] \times x_k = [\min(\underline{b}', \underline{b}''), \max(\overline{b}', \overline{b}'')]\right).$$

This definition straightforwardly lifts to *itvLinEqs* elements. Given two elements in *itvLinEqs* $\mathbf{P'}$ and $\mathbf{P''}$, we define $\mathbf{P'} \uplus \mathbf{P''}$ as $\mathbf{P}$ such that $\mathbf{P}_i = \mathbf{P}'_i \uplus \mathbf{P}''_i$ for all $i = 1, \ldots, n$.

Theorem 4 (Soundness of the interval combination). *Given two interval linear equalities* φ' *and* φ'', *their interval combination* $\varphi' \uplus \varphi''$ *soundly over-approximates the union of* φ' *and* φ'', *that is,* $\gamma(\varphi') \cup \gamma(\varphi'') \subseteq \gamma(\varphi' \uplus \varphi'')$.

Theorem 4 implies the soundness of $\uplus$ on *itvLinEqs*, i.e., $\gamma(\mathbf{P'}) \cup \gamma(\mathbf{P''}) \subseteq \gamma(\mathbf{P'} \uplus \mathbf{P''})$. $\mathbf{P} \uplus \mathbf{P'}$ can be computed in time $O(n^2)$.

5.4.3 Weak Join

Definition 6 (Weak join). *Given two itvLinEqs elements* $\mathbf{P}$ *and* $\mathbf{P}'$*, we define a* weak join *operation for the itvLinEqs domain as*

$$\mathbf{P} \sqcup_w \mathbf{P}' \stackrel{\text{def}}{=} (\mathbf{P} \Cup_w \mathbf{P}') \sqcap_w (\mathbf{P} \uplus \mathbf{P}').$$

Intuitively, the part $\mathbf{P} \Cup_w \mathbf{P}'$ follows a similar way as the polyhedral convex hull of the convex polyhedra domain and thus can construct some important convex constraints (such as affine equalities and linear stripes). Especially, $\mathbf{P} \Cup_w \mathbf{P}'$ can calculate the exact affine hull of the affine spaces of the input. However, for non-affine relations, in general $\mathbf{P} \Cup_w \mathbf{P}'$ has no precision guarantee, since it is implemented based on a series of projections which often depend on the bounds of variables. Thus, we use the other part $\mathbf{P} \uplus \mathbf{P}'$ to recover some precision by generating non-convex constraints based on syntactic heuristics. $\mathbf{P} \uplus \mathbf{P}'$ does not depend on the bounds of variables and can be easily implemented via the join of the interval domain. $\mathbf{P} \sqcup_w \mathbf{P}'$ can be computed in time $O(n^4)$.

Example 2. Given two *itvLinEqs* elements $\mathbf{P} = \{I = 2, J - K = 5, [-1,1]K = 1\}$ and $\mathbf{P}' = \{I = 3, J - K = 8, [-1,4]K = 2\}$. $\mathbf{P} \Cup_w \mathbf{P}' = \{3I - J + K = 1, J - K = [5,8]\}$. $\mathbf{P} \uplus \mathbf{P}' = \{I = [2,3], J - K = [5,8], [-1,4]K = [1,2]\}$. Thus, $\mathbf{P} \sqcup_w \mathbf{P}' = \{3I - J + K = 1, J - K = [5,8], [-1,4]K = [1,2]\}$. Whereas, when considering only the join of their affine spaces $\{I = 2, J - K = 5\}$ and $\{I = 3, J - K = 8\}$, affine hull gives $\{3I - J + K = 1\}$ in the affine equality domain and polyhedral convex hull gives $\{3I - J + K = 1, J - K = [5,8]\}$ in the convex polyhedra domain.

Theorem 5 (Soundness of the weak join). *Given two itvLinEqs elements* $\mathbf{P}$ *and* $\mathbf{P}'$*, the weak join* $\mathbf{P} \sqcup_w \mathbf{P}'$ *overapproximates both* $\mathbf{P}$ *and* $\mathbf{P}'$*, i.e.,* $\gamma(\mathbf{P}) \cup \gamma(\mathbf{P}') \subseteq \gamma(\mathbf{P} \sqcup_w \mathbf{P}')$.

5.5 Assignment Transfer Function

The assignment of an interval linear expression e to a variable x_j can be modeled using constraint addition, projection and variable renaming as follows:

$$[\![x_j := e]\!]^\#(\mathbf{P}) \stackrel{\text{def}}{=} (\textsc{Project}([\![x'_j - e = 0]\!]^\#(\mathbf{P}), x_j))[x'_j/x_j]\,.$$

The fresh variable x'_j, introduced to hold the value of the expression e, is necessary when x_j appears in e, e.g., $x := [-1,1]x + 1$. The assignment transfer function $[\![x_j := e]\!]^\#(\mathbf{P})$ can be computed in time $O(n^3)$ and its soundness is obvious.

5.6 Inclusion Test

The best order relation $\sqsubseteq$ on *itvLinEqs* is defined as $\mathbf{P} \sqsubseteq \mathbf{P}'$ iff $\gamma(\mathbf{P}) \subseteq \gamma(\mathbf{P}')$. Theorem 1 shows that $\sqsubseteq$ can be in principle checked by checking the inclusion in each orthant in the convex polyhedra domain. However, it may be too expensive to compute (an exponential number of linear programs). To solve this problem, we introduce an approximate order relation $\sqsubseteq_s$ on *itvLinEqs*. Given $\varphi\colon (\Sigma_k[\underline{a}_k, \overline{a}_k]x_k = [\underline{b}, \overline{b}])$ and $\varphi'\colon (\Sigma_k[\underline{a}'_k, \overline{a}'_k]x_k = [\underline{b}', \overline{b}'])$, $\varphi \sqsubseteq_s \varphi'$ iff $[\underline{b}, \overline{b}] \subseteq [\underline{b}', \overline{b}']$ and $\forall k.[\underline{a}_k, \overline{a}_k] \subseteq [\underline{a}'_k, \overline{a}'_k]$. Given two *itvLinEqs* elements $\mathbf{P}$ and $\mathbf{P}'$, $\mathbf{P} \sqsubseteq_s \mathbf{P}'$ iff for each row $\mathbf{P}'_i$ of $\mathbf{P}'$, either $\mathbf{P}'_i$ is a universal constraint or $\mathbf{P}_i \sqsubseteq_s \mathbf{P}'_i$. Then, $\mathbf{P} \sqsubseteq_s \mathbf{P}'$ implies $\mathbf{P} \sqsubseteq \mathbf{P}'$, while the converse may not hold. Checking $\mathbf{P} \sqsubseteq_s \mathbf{P}'$ requires $O(n^2)$ time.

5.7 Widening

Unlike the affine equality domain, *itvLinEqs* does not satisfy the ascending chain condition. Thus, to cope with loops, a widening [5] operator is needed to ensure the convergence of fixpoint computations.

Definition 7. *Given two interval linear equalities* $\varphi' : (\sum_k [\underline{a}'_k, \overline{a}'_k] x_k = [\underline{b}', \overline{b}'])$ *and* $\varphi'' : (\sum_k [\underline{a}''_k, \overline{a}''_k] x_k = [\underline{b}'', \overline{b}''])$, *we define the* widening *on constraints* φ' *and* φ'' *as*

$$\varphi' \nabla_{row} \varphi'' : \left(\sum_k ([\underline{a}'_k, \overline{a}'_k] \nabla_{itv} [\underline{a}''_k, \overline{a}''_k]) x_k = ([\underline{b}', \overline{b}'] \nabla_{itv} [\underline{b}'', \overline{b}''])\right)$$

where ∇_{itv} *is any widening of the interval domain [4], such as:*

$$[\underline{a}, \overline{a}] \nabla_{itv} [\underline{b}, \overline{b}] = [\underline{a} \le \underline{b} \,?\, \underline{a} : -\infty,\ \overline{a} \ge \overline{b} \,?\, \overline{a} : +\infty]$$

Then we define the widening in the *itvLinEqs* domain as follows:

Definition 8 (Widening of *itvLinEqs*). *Given two itvLinEqs elements* $\mathbf{P}' \sqsubseteq \mathbf{P}''$, *we define the* widening *as* $\mathbf{P}' \nabla_{ile} \mathbf{P}'' \stackrel{\text{def}}{=} \mathbf{P}$ *where*

$$\mathbf{P}_i = \begin{cases} \mathbf{P}''_i & \text{if } \mathbf{P}''_i \text{ is an affine equality} \\ \mathbf{P}'_i \nabla_{row} \mathbf{P}''_i & \text{otherwise} \end{cases}$$

Note that if $\mathbf{P}' \sqsubseteq \mathbf{P}''$ does not hold, we use $\mathbf{P}' \nabla_{ile} (\mathbf{P}' \sqcup_w \mathbf{P}'')$ instead. The widening ∇_{ile} keeps all affine equalities from $\mathbf{P}''$, thus will not cause any precision loss on affine relations. When no affine relation holds at the i-th row, $\mathbf{P}'_i \nabla_{row} \mathbf{P}''_i$ recovers precision by capturing the stable information between a pair of evolving constraints $\mathbf{P}'_i$ and $\mathbf{P}''_i$. It is easy to check that the widening ∇_{ile} satisfies $\mathbf{P}' \sqsubseteq (\mathbf{P}' \nabla_{ile} \mathbf{P}'')$ and $\mathbf{P}'' \sqsubseteq (\mathbf{P}' \nabla_{ile} \mathbf{P}'')$. And the convergence of the widening ∇_{ile} can be guaranteed by the following two facts: 1) The lattice of affine equalities has finite height, and the number of affine equalities in $\mathbf{P}''$ is decreasing until it reaches the dimension of the affine space in the program; 2) The number of interval coefficients (including both variable coefficients and constant coefficients) in an *itvLinEq* element is at most $\frac{1}{2}n(n+3)$, and the interval widening ∇_{itv} at each position of these interval coefficients will guarantee the convergence of the non-affine part. The complexity of the widening ∇_{ile} is $O(n^2)$.

Widening with Thresholds. Widening with thresholds [1] ∇^T is a widening parameterized by a finite set of threshold values T, including $-\infty$ and $+\infty$. Widening with thresholds for the interval domain is defined as:

$$\begin{aligned}[\underline{a}, \overline{a}] \nabla^T_{itv} [\underline{b}, \overline{b}] = [&\underline{a} \le \underline{b} \,?\, \underline{a} : \max\{\ell \in T \mid \ell \le \underline{b}\}, \\ &\overline{a} \ge \overline{b} \,?\, \overline{a} : \min\{h \in T \mid h \ge \overline{b}\}]\end{aligned}$$

By replacing ∇_{itv} with ∇^T_{itv} in ∇_{row}, our widening with thresholds ∇^T_{row} lifts the interval widening with thresholds from individual variables to multiple variables in a natural way. Quite interestingly, it can guess not only the lower and upper bounds of the constant term (like augmenting the template polyhedra domain [20] with thresholds on the constant term), but also the shape (i.e., the $\sum_k [\underline{a}_k, \overline{a}_k] x_k$ part) of the stable invariants.

Example 3.

```
real x, y;
x := 0.75 * y + 1;
while true do
① if random()
   then   x := y + 1;
   else   x := 0.25 * x + 0.5 * y + 1;
done;
```

Given the above program, after the first iteration, the input arguments of the widening at ① are $\varphi : ([1, 1]x + [-0.75, -0.75]y = [1, 1])$ and $\varphi' : ([1, 1]x + [-1, -0.6875]y = [1, 1.25])$. $\varphi \nabla_{row} \varphi'$ results in $[1, 1]x + [-\infty, +\infty]y = [1, +\infty]$. However, if we use $\pm n \pm 0.5$ ($n \in \mathbb{N}$ and $n \leq 2$) together with $+\infty$ and $-\infty$ as the threshold set T, $\varphi \nabla^T_{row} \varphi'$ will result in $[1, 1]x + [-1, -0.5]y = [1, 1.5]$, which will be stable in the subsequent iterations.

6 Implementation

Reduction with the Interval Domain. Variable bounds play a very important role in our domain. E.g., both partial linearization (Def. 4) and constraint comparison (in Sect. 5.1) rely on variable bounds. However, *itvLinEqs* itself has limited ability to infer bounds information. Thus we employ the interval domain to maintain such information.

To avoid the well-known convergence problem of interaction between reduction and widening [15], we perform reduction between the interval domain and *itvLinEqs* only in one direction, i.e., from *itvLinEqs* to the interval domain. After certain domain operations (such as test/assignment transfer functions, meet), we propagate the information from *itvLinEqs* to the interval domain to tighten the bounds. Such bound tightening is performed through constraint propagation techniques, as in [2], by exploiting the fact that each constraint can be used to tighten the bounds of those variables involved.

Floating-Point Implementation. Up to now, the whole domain of *itvLinEqs* was considered in exact arithmetic. Now, we consider the problem of implementing *itvLinEqs* using floating-point numbers, since floating-point numbers are time and memory efficient. *itvLinEqs* is mainly based on interval arithmetic, which can be easily implemented soundly via interval arithmetic with outward rounding (i.e., rounding upper bounds upward and lower bounds downward). And this is sufficient to guarantee that all domain operations implemented in floating-point in this way are sound.

However, a floating-point implementation of *itvLinEqs* may also cause other issues. First, floating-point *itvLinEqs* may miss some affine equalities due to rounding errors, that is to say, floating-point *itvLinEqs* is not necessarily strictly more powerful than the exact (rational) affine equality domain. Normalizing an interval linear equality may not be exact any more in the floating-point world, e.g., normalizing $3x + y = 1$. Also, the analysis based on floating-point *itvLinEqs* may suffer from the known stabilization problem of floating-point iterations [1]. However, the widening with thresholds can partly alleviate this problem. E.g., we can choose thresholds like $\pm 2^{\pm n} (n \in \mathbb{N})$, as the division and multiplication by these threshold values are simply shifting binary bits and are exact in most cases.

Program name(#vars)	Analyzer #∇delay	*FP-itvLinEqs* #iter.	#=	#≃	time(ms)	*polkaeq* #iter.	#=	time(ms)	Result Invar.
Karr1(3)	1	4	1	1	13	4	1	8	>
Karr2(4)	1	1	2	1	10	1	2	7	>
GS1(4)	1	1	2	3	19	1	2	13	>
GS2(4)	1	1	2	0	9	1	2	7	=
MOS1(6)	1	8	1	1	66	8	1	33	>
MOS2(1)	1	1	1	0	3	1	1	5	=
policy1(2)	1	4	1	1	12	4	1	10	>
Karr1_f(3)	1	5	0	2	19	3	0	9	>
Deadcode(2)	1	1	1	1	4	1	0	11	>

Fig. 3. Experimental results comparing *FP-itvLinEqs* with a domain for affine equalities

7 Experiments

We have developed a prototype domain, *FP-itvLinEqs*, using double precision floating-point numbers. *FP-itvLinEqs* is interfaced to the APRON numerical abstract domain library [11]. Our experiments were conducted using the INTERPROC [13] static analyzer. In order to assess the precision and efficiency of *FP-itvLinEqs*, we compare the obtained invariants and the performance of *FP-itvLinEqs* with *polkaeq* [11] which is an implementation in exact arithmetic to infer affine equalities,[3] NewPolka [11] which is an implementation in exact arithmetic of the convex polyhedra domain, as well as *itvPol* [3] which is a sound floating-point implementation of our interval polyhedra domain.

We evaluated *FP-itvLinEqs* on three sets of examples. The results are summarized in Figs. 3-5. The column "#∇delay" specifies the value of the widening delay parameter for INTERPROC (i.e., the number of loop iterations performed before applying the widening operator). "#iter." gives the number of increasing iterations during the analysis. "Result Invar." compares as a whole the invariants obtained. A ">" ("<", "≠") indicates that the left analysis outputs stronger (weaker, incomparable) invariants than the right analysis. "time" presents the analysis times (where ">1h" indicates a timeout) when the analyzer is run on a 1.6GHz PC with 768MB of RAM running Fedora 9.

Comparison with a Domain for Affine Equalities. We first compare *FP-itvLinEqs* with *polkaeq* on a collection of small examples for discovering affine equalities, which were obtained from [12,18,10,8]. Fig. 3 summarizes the results on these examples. The number of discovered invariants is given by "#=" for affine equalities and "#≃" for other kinds of constraints. For these programs, *FP-itvLinEqs* can find all the affine relations that *polkaeq* finds, since indeed such programs involve only small integer values, thus the floating-point computation causes little or even no precision loss. *FP-itvLinEqs* also finds additional non-affine constraints. For the program Karr1_f which is the floating-point version of Karr1, the affine equalities that hold in Karr1 do not hold in Karr1_f any more, but *FP-itvLinEqs* can still find an interval linear invariant that involves 3 variables. For the program Deadcode (whose source code is $\{x := [0,1];$ if $(x{=}{=}2)$ then

[3] In fact, *polkaeq* is implemented on top of NewPolka convex polyhedra rather than Karr's algorithm [12], but *polkaeq* is as expressive as Karr's algorithm.

Program name(#vars)	Analyzer #∇delay	*FP-itvLinEqs* #iter.	#≤	#≃	time	NewPolka #iter.	#≤	time	*itvPol* #iter.	#≤	#≃	time	Result Invar.	
policy2(2)	1	5	3	1	20ms	6	2	22ms	5	3	0	46ms	>	>
policy3(2)	1	5	2	2	18ms	6	2	20ms	5	2	2	49ms	>	<
policy4(2)	1	5	3	1	19ms	7	1	24ms	6	2	1	59ms	>	≠
bubblesort(4)	1	3	3	3	87ms	8	2	58ms	8	1	3	123ms	>	≠
symmetricalstairs(2)	1	6	3	0	33ms	6	3	31ms	5	2	0	45ms	<	>
maccarthy91(3)	1	5	1	2	28ms	4	2	15ms	4	2	3	83ms	≠	<
incdec(32)	3	8	26	12	32s	×	×	>1h	×	×	×	>1h	>	>
mesh2X2(32)	5	8	24	18	20s	×	×	>1h	7	5	3	190s	>	≠
bigjava(44)	3	7	18	16	43s	×	×	>1h	6	6	4	1206s	>	≠

Fig. 4. Experimental results comparing *FP-itvLinEqs* with domains for inequalities

$y := 1$; else $y := x$;}), at the end of the program, *FP-itvLinEqs* proves $y = x$ whereas *polkaeq* can not find any affine equality.

Comparison with Domains for Inequalities. The second set of examples obtained from [8,2,20] is for discovering inequalities, as shown in Fig. 4. The number of discovered invariants is given by "#≤" for linear inequalities (including affine equalities and linear stripes, each of which is counted as two linear inequalities), and "#≃" for other kinds of constraints. The left sub-column of "Result Invar." compares *FP-itvLinEqs* with NewPolka while the right sub-column compares *FP-itvLinEqs* with *itvPol*. Compared with NewPolka, in most cases *FP-itvLinEqs* gives more precise results, since *FP-itvLinEqs* finds some non-convex interval linear invariants which make the overall feasible space of the invariants found (at each program point) smaller than that by NewPolka. Particularly, for large-dimension examples, NewPolka fails to complete the analysis in $1h$, while *FP-itvLinEqs* works well. Compared with *itvPol*, *FP-itvLinEqs* seems rather efficient. In fact, the efficiency difference becomes increasingly prominent when the number of variables increases. Besides, *FP-itvLinEqs* generates some invariants with infinite interval coefficients (e.g., 2 such constraints for policy3 and bubblesort, 5 for incdec and mesh2X2, 12 for bigjava) out of the reach of *itvPol*.

Widening with Thresholds. In Fig. 5, we compare *FP-itvLinEqs* using widening with thresholds and without thresholds (while we use only widening without thresholds in Figs. 3-4). Example3 corresponds to the previous example in Sect. 5.7. *ratelimiter_f* is a floating-point program extracted from a real-life system [2]. *nonlinear* is an example involving nonlinear expressions. When using widening with thresholds ($\{\pm n \pm 0.5 \mid n \in \mathbb{N}$,

Program name(#vars)	Analyzer #∇delay	*FP-itvLinEqs* without thresholds #iter.	time(ms)	with thresholds #iter.	#newinv.	time(ms)	Result Invar.
Example3(2)	1	4	12	4	1	18	<
ratelimiter_f(5)	2	5	88	5	2	91	<
nonlinear(3)	1	5	29	7	1	56	<

Fig. 5. Experimental results for widening with thresholds

$n \le 150\} \cup \{-\infty, +\infty\})$, *FP-itvLinEqs* finds tighter or new invariants, the number of which is given by "*#newinv.*" in Fig. 5.

8 Conclusion

We have presented an abstract domain of *interval linear equalities (itvLinEqs)*, which extends the affine equality domain with interval coefficients. *itvLinEqs* can represent and manipulate interval linear constraints, which natively allows expressing classical linear relations as well as certain non-convex properties. *itvLinEqs* enforces a row echelon form of the constraint system, which enables a polynomial-time implementation. We have shown through experiments that *itvLinEqs* can find interesting interval linear invariants in practice, including commonly used affine equalities, linear stripes, linear inequalities. *itvLinEqs* provides a time and space efficient alternative to polyhedra-like domains.

Future work will consider the variable ordering in *itvLinEqs*, since it has an impact on the precision of the overall analysis. In order to choose a proper variable ordering, data dependencies between variables need to be considered. It is also possible to maintain dynamic variable ordering, e.g., different orderings in different loops. It would be also interesting to consider other heuristic strategies to choose which constraint to keep and which to drop to maintain a row echelon form, e.g., to keep those constraints appearing syntactically in the program. We also plan to improve the prototype implementation (e.g., using a sparse representation for the constraint matrix) and use *itvLinEqs* for analyzing large realistic programs. Another direction of the work is to relax the row echelon form and allow several constraints per leading variable.

Acknowledgements. We would like to thank Axel Simon for useful discussions, and the reviewers for their helpful comments.

References

1. Blanchet, B., Cousot, P., Cousot, R., Feret, J., Mauborgne, L., Miné, A., Monniaux, D., Rival, X.: A static analyzer for large safety-critical software. In: ACM PLDI 2003, pp. 196–207. ACM Press, New York (2003)
2. Chen, L., Miné, A., Cousot, P.: A sound floating-point polyhedra abstract domain. In: Ramalingam, G. (ed.) APLAS 2008. LNCS, vol. 5356, pp. 3–18. Springer, Heidelberg (2008)
3. Chen, L., Miné, A., Wang, J., Cousot, P.: Interval polyhedra: An abstract domain to infer interval linear relationships. In: Palsberg, J., Su, Z. (eds.) SAS 2009. LNCS, vol. 5673, pp. 309–325. Springer, Heidelberg (2009)
4. Cousot, P., Cousot, R.: Static determination of dynamic properties of programs. In: Proc. of the 2nd International Symposium on Programming, Dunod, Paris, pp. 106–130 (1976)
5. Cousot, P., Cousot, R.: Abstract interpretation: a unified lattice model for static analysis of programs by construction or approximation of fixpoints. In: ACM POPL 1977, pp. 238–252. ACM Press, New York (1977)
6. Cousot, P., Halbwachs, N.: Automatic discovery of linear restraints among variables of a program. In: ACM POPL 1978, pp. 84–96. ACM Press, New York (1978)
7. Feret, J.: Occurrence counting analysis for the pi-calculus. In: GETCO 2000. Electr. Notes Theor. Comput. Sci., vol. 39(2), pp. 1–18. Elsevier, Amsterdam (2001)

8. Gaubert, S., Goubault, E., Taly, A., Zennou, S.: Static analysis by policy iteration on relational domains. In: De Nicola, R. (ed.) ESOP 2007. LNCS, vol. 4421, pp. 237–252. Springer, Heidelberg (2007)
9. Granger, P.: Static analysis of linear congruence equalities among variables of a program. In: Abramsky, S. (ed.) TAPSOFT 1991. LNCS, vol. 493, pp. 169–192. Springer, Heidelberg (1991)
10. Gulwani, S., Necula, G.: Discovering affine equalities using random interpretation. In: ACM POPL 2003, pp. 74–84. ACM Press, New York (2003)
11. Jeannet, B., Miné, A.: Apron: A library of numerical abstract domains for static analysis. In: Bouajjani, A., Maler, O. (eds.) CAV 2009. LNCS, vol. 5643, pp. 661–667. Springer, Heidelberg (2009)
12. Karr, M.: Affine relationships among variables of a program. Acta Inf. 6, 133–151 (1976)
13. Lalire, G., Argoud, M., Jeannet, B.: Interproc, `http://pop-art.inrialpes.fr/people/bjeannet/bjeannet-forge/interproc/`
14. Laviron, V., Logozzo, F.: Subpolyhedra: A (more) scalable approach to infer linear inequalities. In: Jones, N.D., Müller-Olm, M. (eds.) VMCAI 2009. LNCS, vol. 5403, pp. 229–244. Springer, Heidelberg (2009)
15. Miné, A.: The octagon abstract domain. Higher-Order and Symbolic Computation 19(1), 31–100 (2006)
16. Miné, A.: Symbolic methods to enhance the precision of numerical abstract domains. In: Emerson, E.A., Namjoshi, K.S. (eds.) VMCAI 2006. LNCS, vol. 3855, pp. 348–363. Springer, Heidelberg (2005)
17. Müller-Olm, M., Seidl, H.: A note on Karr's algorithm. In: Díaz, J., Karhumäki, J., Lepistö, A., Sannella, D. (eds.) ICALP 2004. LNCS, vol. 3142, pp. 1016–1028. Springer, Heidelberg (2004)
18. Müller-Olm, M., Seidl, H.: Precise interprocedural analysis through linear algebra. In: ACM POPL 2004, pp. 330–341. ACM Press, New York (2004)
19. Rohn, J.: Solvability of systems of interval linear equations and inequalities. In: Linear Optimization Problems with Inexact Data, pp. 35–77. Springer, Heidelberg (2006)
20. Sankaranarayanan, S., Sipma, H., Manna, Z.: Scalable analysis of linear systems using mathematical programming. In: Cousot, R. (ed.) VMCAI 2005. LNCS, vol. 3385, pp. 25–41. Springer, Heidelberg (2005)
21. Simon, A., King, A.: Exploiting sparsity in polyhedral analysis. In: Hankin, C., Siveroni, I. (eds.) SAS 2005. LNCS, vol. 3672, pp. 336–351. Springer, Heidelberg (2005)

Interpolant Strength

Vijay D'Silva[1,⋆], Daniel Kroening[1], Mitra Purandare[2,⋆⋆], and Georg Weissenbacher[1,2,⋆⋆⋆]

[1] Computing Laboratory, Oxford University
[2] Computer Systems Institute, ETH Zurich

Abstract. Interpolant-based model checking is an approximate method for computing invariants of transition systems. The performance of the model checker is contingent on the approximation computed, which in turn depends on the logical strength of the interpolants. A good approximation is coarse enough to enable rapid convergence but strong enough to be contained within the weakest inductive invariant. We present a system for constructing propositional interpolants of different strength from a resolution refutation. This system subsumes existing methods and allows interpolation systems to be ordered by the logical strength of the obtained interpolants. Interpolants of different strength can also be obtained by transforming a resolution proof. We analyse an existing proof transformation, generalise it, and characterise the interpolants obtained.

1 Introduction

Symbolic model checking techniques manipulate implicit representations of sets of states to verify correctness properties of transition systems. Image computation and fixed point detection, two essential steps in model checking, involve quantifier elimination, which is computationally expensive. Interpolant-based model checking of finite state systems uses approximate images to compute an inductive invariant that suffices to show correctness [11]. The approximate images are constructed from resolution refutations generated by a SAT solver, thereby avoiding quantifier elimination.

The performance of an interpolant-based model checker depends on the approximate images obtained. A coarse approximation typically contains spurious errors and causes the model checker to restart with a larger formula. Model checking with a larger formula is more resource intensive than with a smaller formula. On the other hand, a tight approximation delays convergence to a fixed point. If the property holds, the ideal approximate image is an inductive invariant that implies the property. If the property does not hold, the ideal approximation is one which enables the error to be detected efficiently. Thus, rather than strong

⋆ Supported by Microsoft Research's European PhD Scholarship Programme.
⋆⋆ Supported by the Semiconductor Research Corporation (SRC) under contract no. 2006-TJ-1539.
⋆⋆⋆ Supported by the EU FP7 STREP MOGENTES (project ID ICT-216679) and by Microsoft Research's European PhD Scholarship Programme.

G. Barthe and M. Hermenegildo (Eds.): VMCAI 2010, LNCS 5944, pp. 129–145, 2010.

or weak interpolants, procedures to compute interpolants of different strengths are required. A procedure for constructing interpolants from resolution refutations is called an *interpolation system* in this paper.

We study two orthogonal approaches to obtaining interpolants of different strengths. The first approach is to construct different interpolants from a refutation. This is a challenge because only two interpolation systems exist; a symmetric system, published independently by Huang [6], Krajíček [8] and Pudlák [13], and McMillan's system [11]. We are not aware of any results relating these two systems. The second approach, suggested by Jhala and McMillan [7], is to reorder the sequence of resolution steps in a proof to strengthen the interpolants obtained. Our implementation of their algorithm led us to find an error and was the motivation for much of this work. The effect of proof transformations has only been studied for McMillan's system [11]. It is not known if such transformations result in stronger interpolants in other systems.

Contributions. The contributions of this paper are as follows.

- An ordered family of linear-time interpolation systems. This family subsumes existing interpolation systems. An interpolation system Itp maps a resolution refutation R to an interpolant $\mathsf{Itp}(R)$. The order guarantees interpolant strength; if $\mathsf{Itp}_1 \preceq \mathsf{Itp}_2$ then $\mathsf{Itp}_1(R)$ implies $\mathsf{Itp}_2(R)$ for any refutation R.
- Operators for composing interpolation systems. The ordered family of interpolation systems with these operators forms a complete lattice with McMillan's systems being the strongest. Interpolation systems can be composed to obtain stronger and weaker interpolants as required.
- A study of the effect of pivot reordering on interpolant strength. A proof transformation due to Jhala and McMillan [7] is shown to produce invalid refutations and redundant interpolants in cases. These cases are analysed and characterised.

This paper is organised as follows. Background material on model checking and resolution proofs is covered in § 2. Existing interpolation systems are presented in § 3 and our parametrised interpolation system appears in § 4. Proof transformations that change interpolant strength are studied in § 5. We discuss related work in § 6 and conclude in § 7. The proofs of all statements in this paper are presented in the appendices of the supplemental technical report [5].

2 Preliminaries

2.1 Finite State Model Checking

A transition system $M = (S, T)$ is a finite set of states S and a transition relation $T \subseteq S \times S$. Fix the sets J and F, where $J \cap F = \emptyset$, as sets of initial and failure states respectively. A system is correct if no state in F is reachable from any state in J. The image operator $post : \wp(S) \rightarrow \wp(S)$ maps a set of states to its successors: $post(Q) = \{s' \in S | s \in Q \text{ and } (s, s') \in T\}$. Let $post^0(Q) = Q$ and

$post^{i+1}(Q) = post(post^i(Q))$. The pre-image operator $pre : \wp(S) \to \wp(S)$ maps a set of states to its predecessors: $pre(Q) = \{s \in S | s' \in Q \text{ and } (s, s') \in T\}$. A set of states P is *inductive* if $post(P) \subseteq P$. The set P is an *inductive invariant* if P is inductive and $J \subseteq P$. Given J and F, the *strongest inductive invariant* R_J is the set of states reachable from J. In a correct system, the *weakest inductive invariant* W_F is the largest set of states from which F is unreachable. These sets have the standard fixed point characterisations given below.

$$R_J = \mu Q.(J \cup post(Q)) \qquad W_F = S \setminus \mu Q.(F \cup pre(Q))$$

An approximate image operator $\hat{post} : \wp(S) \to \wp(S)$ satisfies that $post(Q) \subseteq \hat{post}(Q)$ for all $Q \in \wp(S)$. An approximation of the set of reachable states is the set:

$$\hat{R}_J = \bigcup_{i \geq 0} \hat{post}^i(J) .$$

Observe that if $\hat{R}_J \cap F = \emptyset$, then F is not reachable from J. Thus, it suffices to compute an approximation $\hat{R}_J$ to decide correctness.

2.2 Interpolant-Based Model Checking

Interpolant-based model checking is a method for computing an approximation $\hat{R}_J$ as above. An approximate operator $\hat{post}$ is implemented using a refutation generating SAT solver and an interpolation system. Finite sets and relations are encoded in propositional logic. We use sets or relations and their encoding interchangeably. For instance, the propositional encoding of $T \subseteq S \times S$ is written $T(\boldsymbol{x}, \boldsymbol{x}')$, where $\boldsymbol{x}$ and $\boldsymbol{x}'$ are vectors of propositional variables. Consider a set of states Q and $k \geq 0$. A Bounded Model Checking (BMC) instance is a formula $A(x_0, x_1) \wedge B(x_1, \ldots, x_k)$, where A and B are as below.

$$\begin{aligned} A(x_0, x_1) &\stackrel{\text{def}}{=} Q(x_0) \wedge T(x_0, x_1) \\ B(x_1, \ldots, x_k) &\stackrel{\text{def}}{=} T(x_1, x_2) \wedge \ldots \wedge T(x_{k-1}, x_k) \wedge (F(x_1) \vee \cdots \vee F(x_k)) \end{aligned} \tag{1}$$

If the BMC instance is satisfiable, F is reachable from a state in Q. The formula $P(x_1) \stackrel{\text{def}}{=} \exists x_0.A(x_0, x_1)$ encodes the image $post(Q)$. If the formula $Q(x_0)$ can be replaced by $Q(x_0) \vee P(x_0)$, we can repeatedly compute images until we obtain a formula encoding R_J. The formula $P(x_1)$ is quantified and quantifier elimination is necessarily expensive, so computing R_J in this manner is not feasible. Instead, an efficient procedure for computing a formula $I(x_1)$ such that $\exists x_0.A(x_0, x_1) \Rightarrow I(x_1)$ provides an implementation of $\hat{post}$ applicable to compute $\hat{R}_J$. An interpolation system is such a procedure.

Craig [4] showed that for a valid implication $A \Rightarrow B$, where A and B are first order formulae containing no free variables, there is a formula I such that $A \Rightarrow I$, $I \Rightarrow B$ and the non-logical symbols in I occur in both A and B. The formula I is called the *Craig interpolant*. Propositional logic has the Craig interpolation property as well [3,8]. The notion is stated differently to apply to CNF formulae. Let Var(A) be the set of propositional variables occurring in a formula A.

Definition 1 (Interpolant). *An* interpolant *for a pair of CNF formulae* (A, B)*, where* $A \wedge B$ *is unsatisfiable, is a propositional formula* I *such that* $A \Rightarrow I$*,* $I \wedge B$ *is unsatisfiable and* $\text{Var}(I) \subseteq \text{Var}(A) \cap \text{Var}(B)$.

If the CNF pair $(A(x_0, x_1), B(x_1, \ldots, x_k))$ in Equation 1 is unsatisfiable, an interpolant $I(x_1)$ is an approximate image. Successive images are computed by replacing $Q(x_0)$ in $A(x_0, x_1)$ with $I(x_0)$. The definition of an interpolant is not symmetric with respect to A and B; however, the following relationship holds.

Lemma 1. *If* I *is an interpolant for* (A, B)*,* $\neg I$ *is an interpolant for* (B, A).

2.3 Resolution Refutations

The procedures for checking if a BMC formula is satisfiable can be extended to generate resolution refutations. Interpolants are computed from resolution refutations. Let X be a set of propositional variables and $\texttt{Lit}_X = \{x, \overline{x} \mid x \in X\}$ be the set of literals over X, where $\overline{t}$ or equivalently $\neg t$ is the negation of t. Let F denote false and T denote true. We write $\text{var}(t)$ for the variable occurring in the literal t.

A clause C is a set of literals. The empty clause $\square$ contains no literals. The disjunction of two clauses C and D is their union, denoted $C \vee D$, which is further simplified to $C \vee t$ if D is the singleton $\{t\}$. A formula in Conjunctive Normal Form (CNF) is a conjunction of clauses, also represented as a set of clauses. For a clause C and a formula F, let $C|_F$ be the restriction of C to variables in F. That is, $C|_F \stackrel{\text{def}}{=} C \cap \{x, \overline{x} \mid x \in \text{Var}(F)\}$.

The *resolution principle* states that an assignment satisfying the clauses $C \vee x$ and $D \vee \overline{x}$ also satisfies $C \vee D$. The clauses $C \vee x$ and $D \vee \overline{x}$ are the *antecedents*, x is the *pivot*, and $C \vee D$ is the *resolvent*. Let $\text{Res}(C, D, x)$ denote the resolvent of the clauses C and D with the pivot x.

Definition 2. *A* resolution proof R *is a DAG* $(V_R, E_R, piv_R, \ell_R, \mathtt{s}_R)$*, where* V_R *is a set of vertices,* E_R *is a set of edges,* piv_R *is a pivot function,* ℓ_R *is the clause function, and* $\mathtt{s}_R \in V_R$ *is the sink vertex. An* initial vertex *has in-degree* 0*. All other vertices are* internal *and have in-degree* 2*. The sink has out-degree* 0*. The pivot function maps internal vertices to variables. For an internal vertex* v *and* $(v_1, v), (v_2, v) \in E_R$*,* $\ell_R(v) = \text{Res}(\ell_R(v_1), \ell_R(v_2), piv_R(v))$.

The subscripts above are dropped if clear. A vertex v_1 in R is a *parent* of v_2 if $(v_1, v_2) \in E_R$. Note that the value of ℓ at internal vertices is determined by that of ℓ at initial vertices and the pivot function. We write v^+ for the parent of v with $piv(v)$ in $\ell(v^+)$ and v^- for the parent with $\neg piv(v)$ in $\ell(v^-)$.

A proof R is a *resolution refutation* if $\ell(\mathtt{s}) = \square$. Henceforth, the words proof and refutation connote resolution proofs and resolution refutations. An (A, B)-*refutation* R of an unsatisfiable CNF pair (A, B), is one in which $\ell_R(v)$ is an element of A or B for each initial vertex $v \in V_R$. Note that an (A, B)-refutation is also a (B, A)-refutation.

3 Comparison of Interpolation Systems

In this section, we highlight issues related to interpolant strength using examples. We recall two interpolation systems from the literature. The examples show that they produce different results, that there are interpolants not obtained in either system, and that weaker interpolants can be beneficial for model checking.

3.1 Interpolation Systems

An *interpolation system* is a procedure for constructing an interpolant from an (A, B)-refutation. Different linear-time interpolation systems exist. The first system, which we call the *symmetric system*, was proposed by Huang [6], Krajíček [8] and Pudlák [13]. Another system was proposed by McMillan [11]. Both systems map vertices in a refutation to a formula called the *partial interpolant*.

Formally, an interpolation system Itp is a function that given an (A, B)-refutation R yields a function, denoted $\mathsf{Itp}(R, A, B)$, from vertices in R to formulae over $\mathrm{Var}(A, B)$. An interpolation system is *correct* if for every (A, B)-refutation R with sink $\mathtt{s}$, it holds that $\mathsf{Itp}(R, A, B)(\mathtt{s})$ is an interpolant for (A, B). We write $\mathsf{Itp}(R)$ for $\mathsf{Itp}(R, A, B)(\mathtt{s})$ when A and B are clear. Let v be a vertex in an (A, B)-refutation R. The pair $(\ell(v), \mathsf{Itp}(R, A, B)(v))$ is an *annotated clause* and is written $\ell(v) \quad [\mathsf{Itp}(R, A, B)(v)]$. An interpolation system can be presented as an extension of resolution using annotated clauses. This style of presentation was introduced by McMillan [12].

Definition 3 (Symmetric System). *The symmetric system Itp_S maps vertices in an (A, B)-refutation R to partial interpolants as defined below.*

For an initial vertex v with $\ell(v) = C$

$$(A\text{-clause})\ \frac{}{C \quad [\mathsf{F}]}\ \text{if } C \in A \qquad\qquad (B\text{-clause})\ \frac{}{C \quad [\mathsf{T}]}\ \text{if } C \in B$$

For an internal vertex v with $piv(v) = x$, $\ell(v^+) = C_1 \vee x$ and $\ell(v^-) = C_2 \vee \overline{x}$

$$\frac{C_1 \vee x \quad [I_1] \qquad C_2 \vee \overline{x} \quad [I_2]}{C_1 \vee C_2 \quad [I_3]}$$

$$\begin{array}{lll} (A\text{-Res}) & \text{if } x \in \mathrm{Var}(A) \setminus \mathrm{Var}(B), & I_3 \stackrel{\text{def}}{=} I_1 \vee I_2 \\ (AB\text{-Res}) & \text{if } x \in \mathrm{Var}(A) \cap \mathrm{Var}(B), & I_3 \stackrel{\text{def}}{=} (x \vee I_1) \wedge (\overline{x} \vee I_2) \\ (B\text{-Res}) & \text{if } x \in \mathrm{Var}(B) \setminus \mathrm{Var}(A), & I_3 \stackrel{\text{def}}{=} I_1 \wedge I_2 \end{array}$$

See [3,14] for proofs of correctness. The *inverse* of an interpolation system, denoted Itp', is defined as $\mathsf{Itp}'(R, A, B)(v) \stackrel{\text{def}}{=} \mathsf{Itp}(R, B, A)(v)$ vertices v in R. An interpolation system Itp is *symmetric* if $\mathsf{Itp}(R, A, B)(\mathtt{s}) = \neg\mathsf{Itp}'(R, A, B)(\mathtt{s})$. Huang has shown that Itp_S is symmetric [6, Lemma 13].

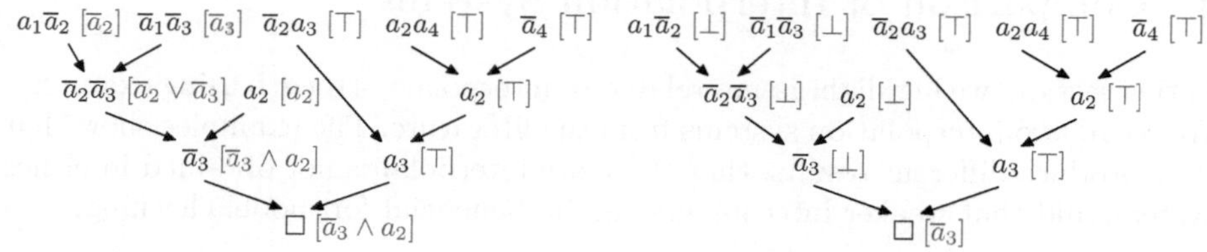

(a) McMillan's System (b) Symmetric System

Fig. 1. Refutation yielding different interpolants for different systems

Definition 4 (McMillan's System). *McMillan's system* Itp_M *maps vertices in an* (A, B)*-refutation* R *as to partial interpolants as defined below.*

For an initial vertex v *with* $\ell(v) = C$

(*A*-clause) $\dfrac{}{\mathrm{C} \quad [C|_B]}$ *if* $C \in A$ (*B*-clause) $\dfrac{}{\mathrm{C} \quad [\top]}$ *if* $C \in B$

For an internal vertex v *with* $piv(v) = x$, $\ell(v^+) = C_1 \vee x$ *and* $\ell(v^-) = C_2 \vee \overline{x}$

$$\frac{C_1 \vee x \quad [I_1] \qquad C_2 \vee \overline{x} \quad [I_2]}{C_1 \vee C_2 \quad [I_3]}$$

(*A*-Res) *if* $x \notin \mathrm{Var}(B)$, $I_3 \stackrel{\text{def}}{=} I_1 \vee I_2$
(*B*-Res) *if* $x \in \mathrm{Var}(B)$, $I_3 \stackrel{\text{def}}{=} I_1 \wedge I_2$

See [12] for McMillan's proof of correctness. Example 1 shows that the interpolants obtained from Itp_M and Itp_S are different and that Itp_M is not symmetric.

Example 1. Let A be the formula $(a_1 \vee \overline{a}_2) \wedge (\overline{a}_1 \vee \overline{a}_3) \wedge a_2$ and B be the formula $(\overline{a}_2 \vee a_3) \wedge (a_2 \vee a_4) \wedge \overline{a}_4$. An (A, B)-refutation R is shown in Figure 1. The partial interpolants in McMillan's system are shown in Figure 1(a) and those in the symmetric system in Figure 1(b). We have that $\mathsf{Itp}_M(R) = \overline{a}_3 \wedge a_2$ and $\mathsf{Itp}_S(R) = \overline{a}_3$. For the inverse systems, the interpolants are $\mathsf{Itp}'_M(R) = a_2 \wedge a_3$ and $\mathsf{Itp}'_S(R) = a_3$. Observe that $\mathsf{Itp}_M(R) \Rightarrow \mathsf{Itp}_S(R)$, $\mathsf{Itp}_S(R) \Leftrightarrow \neg\mathsf{Itp}'_S(R)$, and $\neg\mathsf{Itp}'_S(R) \Rightarrow \neg\mathsf{Itp}'_M(R)$. ◁

Example 2 below shows that there are interpolants that cannot be obtained by these systems and that the interpolants from Itp_M and Itp_S may coincide.

Example 2. Let A be the formula $\overline{a}_1 \wedge (a_1 \vee \overline{a}_2)$ and B be the formula $(\overline{a}_1 \vee a_2) \wedge a_1$. An (A, B)-refutation R is shown alongside. We obtain the following interpolants: $\mathsf{Itp}_M(R) = \overline{a}_1 \wedge \overline{a}_2$, $\mathsf{Itp}_S(R) = \overline{a}_1 \wedge \overline{a}_2$, and $\neg\mathsf{Itp}'_M(R) = \overline{a}_1 \vee \overline{a}_2$. In addition, $\overline{a}_1$ is an interpolant for $A \wedge B$, as is $\overline{a}_2$. However, we cannot obtain these interpolants from Itp_M, Itp_S Itp'_M or Itp'_S.

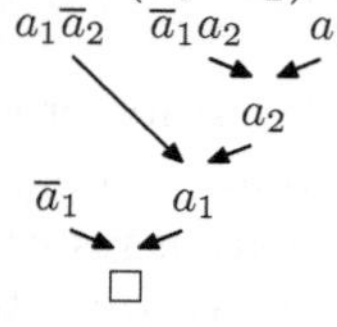

◁

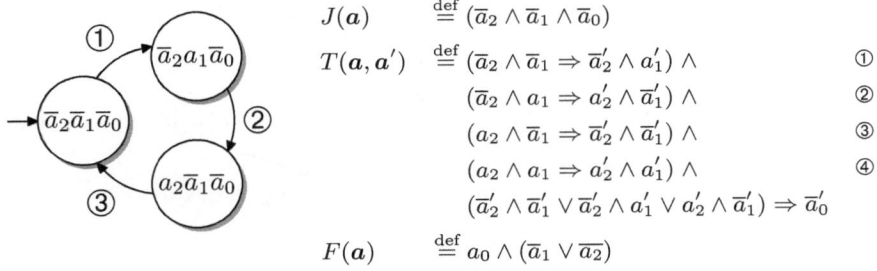

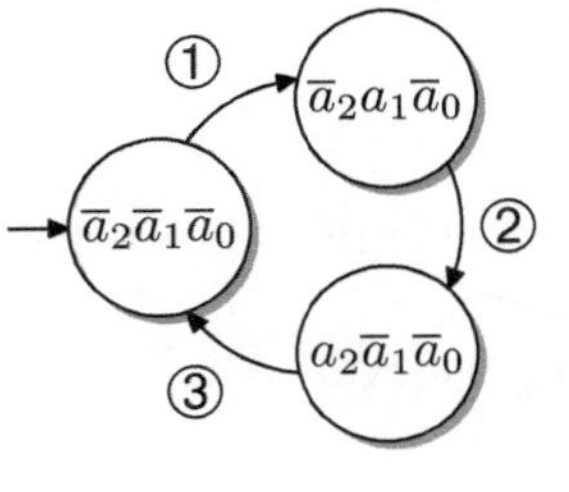

$$\begin{aligned}
J(\boldsymbol{a}) &\stackrel{\text{def}}{=} (\overline{a}_2 \wedge \overline{a}_1 \wedge \overline{a}_0) \\
T(\boldsymbol{a}, \boldsymbol{a}') &\stackrel{\text{def}}{=} (\overline{a}_2 \wedge \overline{a}_1 \Rightarrow \overline{a}_2' \wedge a_1') \wedge && \text{①} \\
&\quad (\overline{a}_2 \wedge a_1 \Rightarrow a_2' \wedge \overline{a}_1') \wedge && \text{②} \\
&\quad (a_2 \wedge \overline{a}_1 \Rightarrow \overline{a}_2' \wedge \overline{a}_1') \wedge && \text{③} \\
&\quad (a_2 \wedge a_1 \Rightarrow a_2' \wedge a_1') \wedge && \text{④} \\
&\quad (\overline{a}_2' \wedge \overline{a}_1' \vee \overline{a}_2' \wedge a_1' \vee a_2' \wedge \overline{a}_1') \Rightarrow \overline{a}_0' \\
F(\boldsymbol{a}) &\stackrel{\text{def}}{=} a_0 \wedge (\overline{a}_1 \vee \overline{a_2})
\end{aligned}$$

Fig. 2. A transition system implementing a binary counter

3.2 Interpolant Strength and Model Checking

In Examples 1 and 2, the interpolant obtained from Itp_M implies all other interpolants. In § 4, we prove that the interpolant from Itp_M implies the interpolants obtained from all the systems we propose. Stronger interpolants represent more precise approximations, so one may ask why other systems should be considered.

We make two arguments for studying other systems. First, the approximate image operator realised using interpolation is not monotone. Using a more precise approximation in one iteration does not guarantee a more precise approximation after two iterations. Second, a coarse approximation may converge to an inductive invariant faster than a precise one as Example 3 illustrates.

Example 3. The state machine in this example cycles through the sequence $0, 2, 4$. Let $S = \{0, \ldots, 7\}$ be the set of all states and $J = \{0\}$ be the initial state set. The formulae $J(\boldsymbol{a})$ and $T(\boldsymbol{a}, \boldsymbol{a}')$ over the variables $\boldsymbol{a} = (a_2, a_1, a_0)$ are shown in Figure 2. The transitions encoded by the conjuncts ①, ②, and ③ connect reachable states, whereas the transitions encoded by the conjunct ④ connect unreachable states. Failure states, encoded by the formula $F(\boldsymbol{a})$, are odd values less than 6.

Let A_1 be $J(\boldsymbol{a}) \wedge T(\boldsymbol{a}, \boldsymbol{a}')$ and B_1 be $F(\boldsymbol{a}')$. An (A_1, B_1)-refutation R_1 is shown in Figure 3 along with the partial interpolants obtained from Itp_M. The formula $I_1(\boldsymbol{a}') \stackrel{\text{def}}{=} \mathsf{Itp}_M(R_1) = \overline{a}_2' \wedge a_1' \wedge \overline{a}_0'$ is equivalent to the exact image $\exists \boldsymbol{a} \,.\, J(\boldsymbol{a}) \wedge T(\boldsymbol{a}, \boldsymbol{a}')$. In the next iteration of the model checker, a formula A_2 is constructed by replacing $J(\boldsymbol{a})$ with $J(\boldsymbol{a}) \vee I_1(\boldsymbol{a})$ in A_1. One can construct a sequence of pairs (A_i, B_i) and a sequence of (A_i, B_i)-refutations R_i so that $\mathsf{Itp}_M(R_i)$ is the set of states reachable from $J(\boldsymbol{a})$ in i steps. In contrast, the symmetric interpolant $\mathsf{Itp}_S(R_1) = \overline{a}_0'$ is an inductive invariant. Model checking with a weaker interpolation system converges more quickly in this case. $\lhd$

We do not claim that such proofs are generated by the SAT solvers used in practice. The example only shows that there are situations in which weaker interpolants lead to better performance.

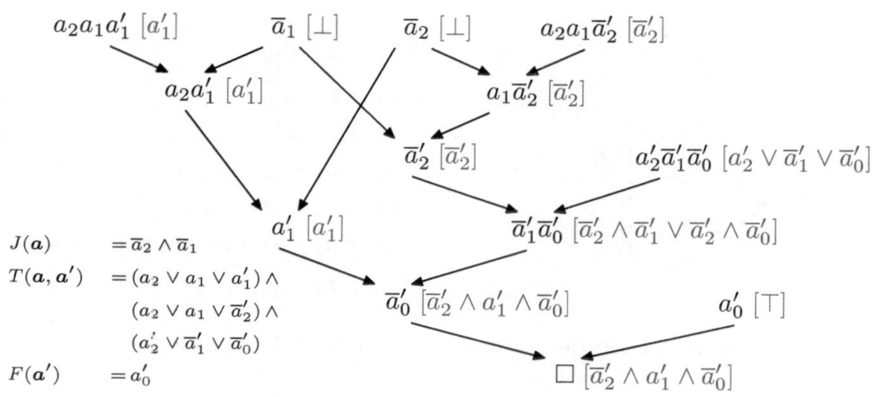

Fig. 3. Refutation with McMillan's interpolant of $J(\boldsymbol{a}) \wedge T(\boldsymbol{a}, \boldsymbol{a}')$ and $F(\boldsymbol{a}')$. The figure shows a contradictory subset of the clauses of a CNF encoding of the formulae.

4 Labelled Interpolation Systems

In this section, we introduce labelled interpolation systems. In § 4.1 we define labelled interpolation systems and show that they are strictly more general than the interpolation systems from § 3.1. In § 4.2 we show how labelled interpolation systems can be composed to obtain stronger and weaker interpolants.

4.1 Labelling Functions and Interpolation

Definition 5 (Labelling Function). *Let* $(\mathcal{S}, \sqsubseteq, \sqcap, \sqcup)$ *be the lattice below, where* $\mathcal{S} = \{\bot, \mathsf{a}, \mathsf{b}, \mathsf{ab}\}$ *is a set of symbols and* $\sqsubseteq$, $\sqcap$ *and* $\sqcup$ *are defined by the Hasse diagram. A* labelling function $L_R : V_R \times \texttt{Lit} \to \mathcal{S}$ *for a refutation* R *over a set of literals* $\texttt{Lit}$ *satisfies that for all* $v \in V_R$ *and* $t \in \texttt{Lit}$*:*

1. $L_R(v, t) = \bot$ *iff* $t \notin \ell_R(v)$
2. $L_R(v, t) = L_R(v^+, t) \sqcup L_R(v^-, t)$ *for an internal vertex* v *and literal* $t \in \ell_R(v)$.

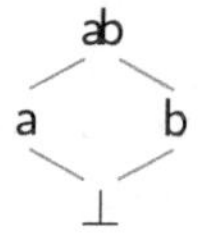

Due to condition (2) above, the labelling function for literals at internal vertices is completely determined by the labels of literals at initial vertices. A variable x is *A-local* in a pair (A, B) if $x \in \text{Var}(A) \setminus \text{Var}(B)$, *B-local* if $x \in \text{Var}(B) \setminus \text{Var}(A)$, *local* if it is either of these, and *shared* otherwise.

Definition 6 (Locality). *A labelling function for an* (A, B)*-refutation* R preserves locality *if for any initial vertex* v *and literal* t *in* R

1. $\mathsf{a} \sqsubseteq L(v, t)$ *implies that* $\text{var}(t) \in \text{Var}(A)$*, and*
2. $\mathsf{b} \sqsubseteq L(v, t)$ *implies that* $\text{var}(t) \in \text{Var}(B)$.

The locality condition ensures that literals over A-local variables are labelled a and literals over B-local variables are labelled b. Our system generalises existing ones by permitting arbitrary labels for literals over shared variables. We refer to locality-preserving labelling functions as labelling functions. Given a labelling function L, the downward *projection* of a clause at a vertex v with respect to $\mathsf{c} \in \mathcal{S}$ is: $\ell(v)\downharpoonright_{\mathsf{c},L} \stackrel{\text{def}}{=} \{t \in \ell(v) \mid L(v,t) \sqsubseteq \mathsf{c}\}$. The upward projection $\ell(v)\upharpoonright_{\mathsf{c},L}$ is similarly defined. The subscript L is omitted if clear.

Definition 7 (Labelled Interpolation System). *Let L be a locality preserving labelling function for an (A,B)-refutation R. The labelled interpolation system $\mathsf{Itp}(L)$ maps vertices in R to partial interpolants as defined below.*

For an initial vertex v with $\ell(v) = C$

$$(A\text{-clause})\ \frac{}{C \quad [C\downharpoonright_{\mathsf{b}}]}\ \textit{if } C \in A \qquad\qquad (B\text{-clause})\ \frac{}{C \quad [\neg(C\downharpoonright_{\mathsf{a}})]}\ \textit{if } C \in B$$

For an internal vertex v with $piv(v) = x$, $\ell(v^+) = C_1 \vee x$ and $\ell(v^-) = C_2 \vee \overline{x}$

$$\frac{C_1 \vee x \quad [I_1] \qquad C_2 \vee \overline{x} \quad [I_2]}{C_1 \vee C_2 \quad [I_3]}$$

$$\begin{array}{lll}
(A\text{-Res}) & \textit{if } L(v^+,x) \sqcup L(v^-,\overline{x}) = \mathsf{a}, & I_3 \stackrel{\text{def}}{=} I_1 \vee I_2 \\
(AB\text{-Res}) & \textit{if } L(v^+,x) \sqcup L(v^-,\overline{x}) = \mathsf{ab}, & I_3 \stackrel{\text{def}}{=} (x \vee I_1) \wedge (\overline{x} \vee I_2) \\
(B\text{-Res}) & \textit{if } L(v^+,x) \sqcup L(v^-,\overline{x}) = \mathsf{b}, & I_3 \stackrel{\text{def}}{=} I_1 \wedge I_2
\end{array}$$

The interpolant obtained from an (A,B)-refutation R with a labelling function L is written $\mathsf{Itp}(L,R)$. Example 4 illustrates the use of a labelled interpolation system. Our claim that labelled interpolation systems are strictly more general than existing systems is substantiated by constructing an interpolant that cannot be obtained from Itp_M, Itp_S, Itp'_S or Itp'_M.

Example 4. Let $A = \overline{a}_1 \wedge (a_1 \vee \overline{a}_2)$ and $B = (\overline{a}_1 \vee a_2) \wedge a_1$. An (A,B)-refutation is shown in Figure 4 with the symbol $L(v,t)$ above each literal. The interpolant obtained from $\mathsf{Itp}(L)$ is $\overline{a}_2$. Recall from Example 2 that this interpolant cannot be derived in existing systems. $\triangleleft$

Theorem 1 (Correctness). *For any (A,B)-refutation R and locality preserving labelling function L, $\mathsf{Itp}(L,R)$ is an interpolant for (A,B).*

Let v be a vertex in the refutation R in Theorem 1. Let C be $\ell(v)$ and I be the partial interpolant at v. We prove the theorem by showing that I and C satisfy the following conditions:

1. $A \wedge \neg(C\upharpoonright_{\mathsf{a},L}) \Rightarrow I$,
2. $B \wedge \neg(C\upharpoonright_{\mathsf{b},L}) \Rightarrow \neg I$, and
3. $\mathrm{Var}(I) \subseteq \mathrm{Var}(A) \cap \mathrm{Var}(B)$.

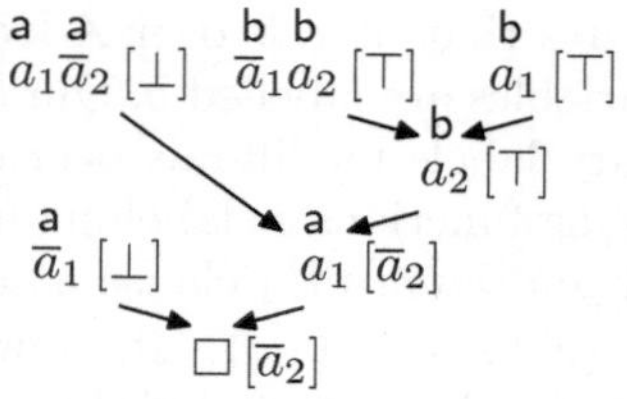

Fig. 4. A labelled interpolation system $\mathsf{Itp}(L)$ that can be used to obtain a different interpolant from Itp_M, Itp_S, Itp'_M or Itp'_S

For the sink $\mathtt{s}$, $C = \square$ and it follows that the partial interpolant at $\mathtt{s}$ is an interpolant for (A, B). Yorsh and Musuvathi use a similar invariant to prove that Itp_S is correct [14]. Lemma 2, which follows, shows that McMillan's system and the symmetric system are instances of labelled interpolation systems. Recall that the labelling function for literals at internal vertices is determined by the labelling function at initial vertices. Thus, it suffices to define the labelling functions corresponding to Itp_M, Itp'_M and Itp_S at initial vertices.

Lemma 2. *Let R be an (A, B)-refutation. The labelling functions L_S, L_M and $L_{M'}$ are defined for initial vertices v and literals $t \in \ell(v)$ as follows:*

var(t)	$L_M(v,t)$	$L_S(v,t)$	$L_{M'}(v,t)$
A-local	a	a	a
shared	b	ab	a
B-local	b	b	b

The following equalities hold: $\mathsf{Itp}_M(R) = \mathsf{Itp}(L_M, R)$, $\mathsf{Itp}_S(R) = \mathsf{Itp}(L_S, R)$ *and* $\mathsf{Itp}(L_{M'}, R) = \mathsf{Itp}'_M(R)$.

The the value, at an initial vertex, of each labelling function in Lemma 2 is determined only by whether a variable is A-local, B-local or shared. In contrast, other labelling functions may assign different symbols to different occurrences of the same literal (see, for instance, the literal a_1 in Figure 4).

4.2 Strength in Labelled Interpolation Systems

Labelled interpolation systems are useful because they allow different interpolants to be constructed from a refutation. We now show how these interpolants are related by strength. A labelled interpolation system $\mathsf{Itp}(L)$ is *stronger than* $\mathsf{Itp}(L')$ if for all refutations R, $\mathsf{Itp}(L, R) \Rightarrow \mathsf{Itp}(L', R)$. We define an order, denoted $\preceq$, on labelling functions that guarantees an ordering in strength. This order is different from the order on labelling functions induced by $\sqsubseteq$.

Definition 8 (Strength Order). *Define the total order $\preceq$ on $\mathcal{S} = \{\bot, \mathsf{a}, \mathsf{b}, \mathsf{ab}\}$, as: $\mathsf{b} \preceq \mathsf{ab} \preceq \mathsf{a} \preceq \bot$. Let L and L' be labelling functions for an (A, B)-refutation R. The function L is stronger than L', denoted $L \preceq L'$, if for all $v \in V_R$ and $t \in \ell(v)$, $L(v, t) \preceq L'(v, t)$.*

Note that $\preceq$ is not a total order on labelling functions. Lemma 3 simplifies the comparison of labelling functions by allowing us to compare the values of labelling functions at initial vertices. Theorem 2 shows that if L is a stronger labelling function than L', the interpolant obtained from $\mathsf{Itp}(L)$ is stronger than the one obtained from $\mathsf{Itp}(L')$.

Lemma 3. *Let L and L' be labelling functions for an (A, B)-refutation R. If $L(v, t) \preceq L'(v, t)$ for all initial vertices v and literals $t \in \ell(v)$, then $L \preceq L'$.*

Theorem 2. *If L and L' are labelling functions for an (A, B)-refutation R and $L \preceq L'$, then $\mathsf{Itp}(L, R) \Rightarrow \mathsf{Itp}(L', R)$.*

In the proof (presented in the technical report [5]), we show by structural induction that $I \Rightarrow I' \vee (\ell_R(v)|_A \cap \ell_R(v)|_B)$ for any vertex v, where I and I' are the partial interpolants at v due to $\mathsf{Itp}(L)$ and $\mathsf{Itp}(L')$. This establishes that $\mathsf{Itp}(L, R) \Rightarrow \mathsf{Itp}(L', R)$. By applying Theorem 2, we can show that McMillan's system produces stronger interpolants than the symmetric system.

Corollary 1. *Let R be an (A, B)-refutation and $L_M, L_S, L_{M'}$ be as in Lemma 2. It holds that $\mathsf{Itp}(L_M, R) \Rightarrow \mathsf{Itp}_S(L_S, R)$ and $\mathsf{Itp}(L_S, R) \Rightarrow \mathsf{Itp}_{M'}(L_{M'}, R)$.*

The strength order on labelling functions also suggests how interpolation systems can be combined to obtain stronger and weaker interpolants. One only has to strengthen or weaken the underlying labelling functions.

Definition 9. *Let $\max(\mathsf{c}_1, \mathsf{c}_2)$ and $\min(\mathsf{c}_1, \mathsf{c}_2)$ be the maximum and minimum, with respect to $\preceq$, of the symbols $\mathsf{c}_1, \mathsf{c}_2 \in \mathcal{S}$. Let R be an (A, B)-refutation and L_1 and L_2 be labelling functions. The labelling functions $L_1 \Uparrow L_2$ and $L_1 \Downarrow L_2$ are defined for any initial vertex v and literal $t \in \ell(v)$ as follows:*

- $(L_1 \Uparrow L_2)(v, t) = \max(L_1(v, t), L_2(v, t))$, *and*
- $(L_1 \Downarrow L_2)(v, t) = \min(L_1(v, t), L_2(v, t))$.

The label of an internal vertex v and $t \in \ell(v)$, is defined inductively as usual.

The final result of this section is that the set of labelling functions ordered by $\preceq$ and the two operators above is a complete lattice. Further, McMillan's system Itp_M is the least element of this lattice and the system $\mathsf{Itp}_{M'}$ is the greatest.

Theorem 3. *Let R be an (A, B)-refutation and $\mathbb{L}_R$ be the set of locality preserving labelling functions over R. The structure $(\mathbb{L}_R, \preceq, \Uparrow, \Downarrow)$ is a complete lattice with L_M as the least and $L_{M'}$ as the greatest element.*

5 Proof Transformations and Interpolation Systems

5.1 Proof Transformations

Labelled interpolation systems afford us a choice of interpolants given a refutation. Further interpolants can be obtained by modifying the structure of a proof

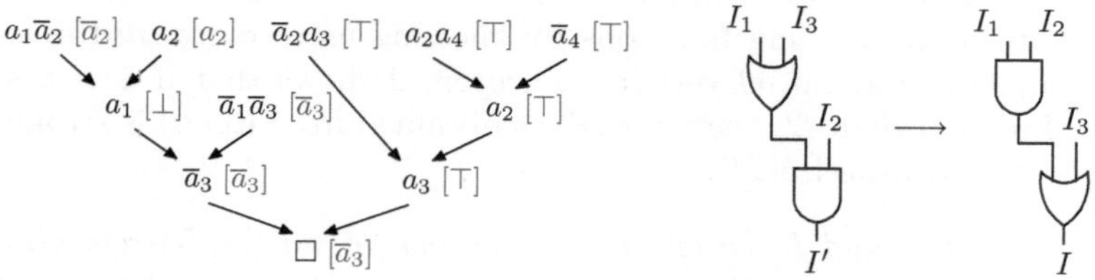

Fig. 5. An (A, B)-refutation that differs from Figure 1(a) and leads to a different interpolant. The two circuits show the structure of a partial interpolants at the vertex labelled $\overline{a}_3$ in Figure 1(a) and this figure, respectively.

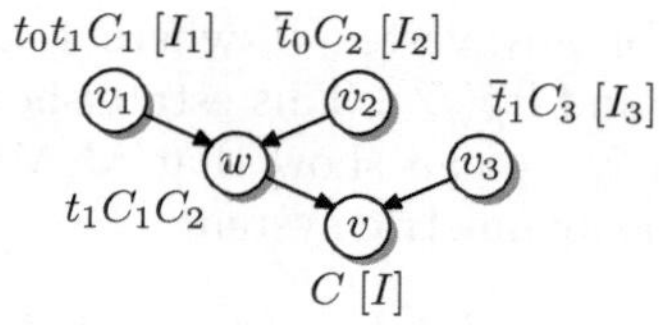

Fig. 6. Proof R

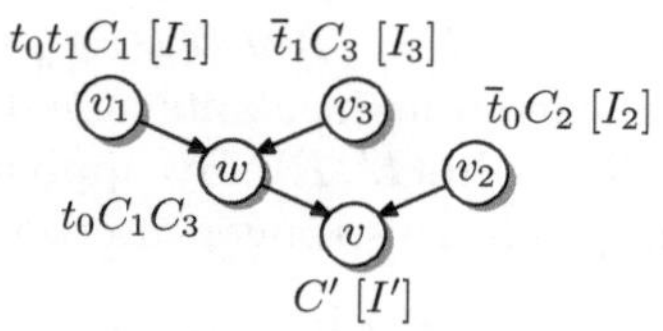

Fig. 7. Graph $R' \stackrel{\text{def}}{=} R[w \rightleftharpoons v]$

to obtain weaker and stronger interpolants. Jhala and McMillan report empirical findings that obtaining interpolants such as $(a_1 \wedge a_2) \Rightarrow (a_1' \wedge a_2')$ instead of the stronger formula $(a_1 \Rightarrow a_1') \wedge (a_2 \Rightarrow a_2')$ can retard convergence of a software model checker based on predicate-abstraction [7]. They show that changing the order of resolution steps in a proof leads to different interpolants. Example 5 illustrates such a transformation.

Example 5. Consider the formulae $A = (a_1 \vee \overline{a}_2) \wedge (\overline{a}_1 \vee \overline{a}_3) \wedge a_2$ and $B = (\overline{a}_2 \vee a_3) \wedge (a_2 \vee a_4) \wedge \overline{a}_4$ and the (A, B)-refutation R_1 in Figure 1(a). Another (A, B)-refutation R_2 is shown in Figure 5. The interpolant $\mathsf{Itp}_M(R_1)$ is $\overline{a}_3 \wedge a_2$ and $\mathsf{Itp}_M(R_2)$ is $\overline{a}_3$. Observe that $\mathsf{Itp}_M(R_1)$ implies $\mathsf{Itp}_M(R_2)$. The difference between R_1 and R_2 is that the clause $\{a_1, \overline{a}_2\}$ is first resolved with $\{a_2\}$ in R_2 but is first resolved with $\{a_1, \overline{a}_3\}$ in R_1. ◁

The change in interpolant strength is explained by viewing interpolants as circuits. Let I' be the partial interpolant at the vertex labelled $\overline{a}_3$ in Figure 1(a) and I be the partial interpolant at this vertex in Figure 5. The structure of I and I' is shown by the two circuits in Figure 5. If resolutions on local variables precede those on shared variables, the interpolant is closer to CNF, hence more constrained and stronger. We define a swap transformation for proof-graph vertices and study the effect of this swap on interpolant strength. To avoid notational tedium, the proof is assumed to be tree shaped. Let v and w be the vertices to be swapped. The ancestors of v and w are v_1, v_2 and v_3 and the edges between these vertices are as shown in Figure 6.

Definition 10 (Swap). *Let $R = (V_R, E_R, piv, \ell_R, \mathsf{s}_R)$ be a tree-shaped (A, B)-refutation with vertices v_1, v_2, v_3, v and w. The clauses and partial interpolants at*

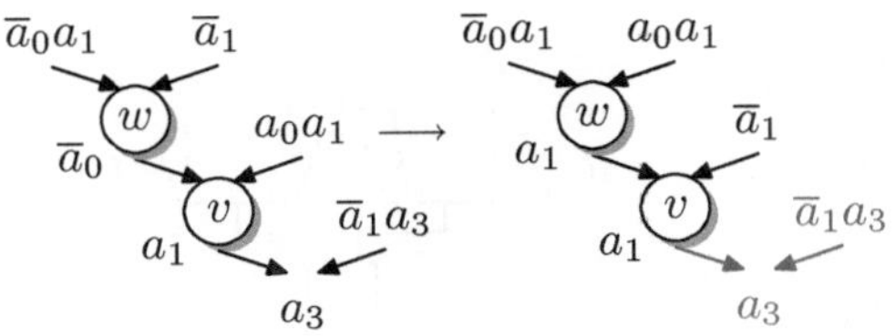

Fig. 8. The graph $R[w \rightleftharpoons v]$ is not a proof because a_1 becomes a merge literal

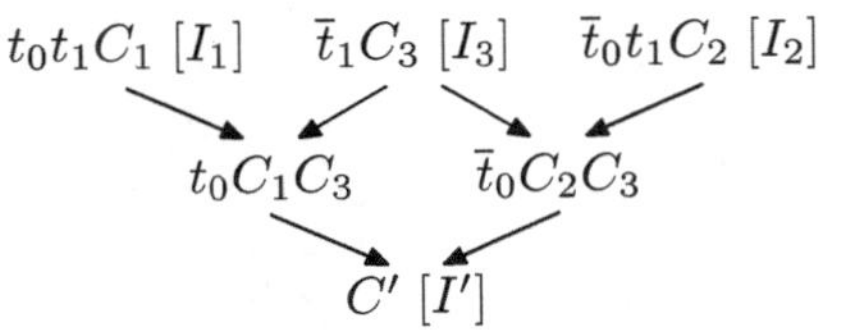

Fig. 9. Transformation for the case where t_0 is a merge literal

these vertices and edges between them are denoted as shown in Figure 6. The result of swapping w and v, denoted $R[w \rightleftharpoons v]$, is the graph $R' = (V', E', piv', \ell', \mathtt{s}')$ as depicted in Figure 7 where $V' \stackrel{\text{def}}{=} V_R$ and $E' \stackrel{\text{def}}{=} (E \setminus \{(v_2, w), (v_3, v)\}) \cup \{(v_3, w), (v_2, v)\}$. The pivot function is given by $piv'(w) \stackrel{\text{def}}{=} piv_R(v)$, $piv'(v) = piv(w)$ and for all $u \in V' \setminus \{v, w\}$, $piv'(u) \stackrel{\text{def}}{=} piv_R(u)$. For all vertices $u \in V'$, $\ell'(u) \stackrel{\text{def}}{=} \ell_R(u)$ if $u \neq w$ and $\ell'(u) \stackrel{\text{def}}{=} t_0 \vee C_1 \vee C_3$ otherwise.

The result of a swap is shown in Figure 7. The graph $R[w \rightleftharpoons v]$ has the same vertex set as R and all vertices except w have the same clause label as in R. However, $R[w \rightleftharpoons v]$ is not a resolution proof because the clause $\ell'(v)$ may not be the resolvent of $\ell(v^+)$ and $\ell(v^-)$. Clause labels may not be correct because of *merge literals*, a notion studied by Andrews [1]. A literal $t \in \ell(v)$ is a *merge literal* if $t \in \ell(v^+)$ and $t \in \ell(v^-)$. Let R and $R[w \rightleftharpoons v]$ be as in Figure 6 and Figure 7. The clause label $\ell'(v)$ as given in Definition 10 is incorrect in two cases.

- If $t_1 \in C_2$ then $t_1 \notin C$, so $t_1 \notin C'$ but $t_1 \in \text{Res}(\ell'(v^+), \ell'(v^-), piv'(v))$.
- If $t_0 \in C_3$ then $t_0 \in C$, so $t_0 \in C'$ but $t_0 \notin \text{Res}(\ell'(v^+), \ell'(v^-), piv'(v))$.

Jhala and McMillan claim in [7, page 11] that "*this transformation is valid when q occurs in v_1, but not in v_2.*" The transformation they refer to is $R[w \rightleftharpoons v]$, and the literal q is $piv(w)$. Figure 8 provides a counterexample to this claim. Observe that the clause at v is not the resolvent of its antecedents. Lemma 4 shows that in cases apart from two listed the above, $R[w \rightleftharpoons v]$ is a proof. Let R be a proof with vertices v and w connected and labelled as in Figure 6. An edge (w, v) in R is *merge-free* if $t_0 \notin \ell_R(v_3)$ and $t_1 \notin \ell_R(v_2)$.

Lemma 4. *Let R be a proof with vertices v and w connected and labelled as in Figure 6. If (w, v) is merge-free, then $R[w \rightleftharpoons v]$ is a resolution proof.*

Our counterexample is for the case when $t_0 \in C_3$ in Figure 6. If $t_1 \in C_2$, Jhala and McMillan transform the part of the proof in Figure 6 as shown in Figure 9. We show that this transformation does not change the interpolants in Itp_M. Assume that t_1 is A-local and t_0 is shared. The partial interpolants I and I', shown as circuits in the left of Figure 10, are $I = (I_1 \wedge I_2) \vee I_3$ and $I' = (I_1 \vee I_3) \wedge (I_2 \vee I_3)$. The transformation essentially distributes the disjunction. Now assume that t_0 is B-local and t_1 is shared. The circuits in the right of Figure 10 show that this transformation does not change the interpolants

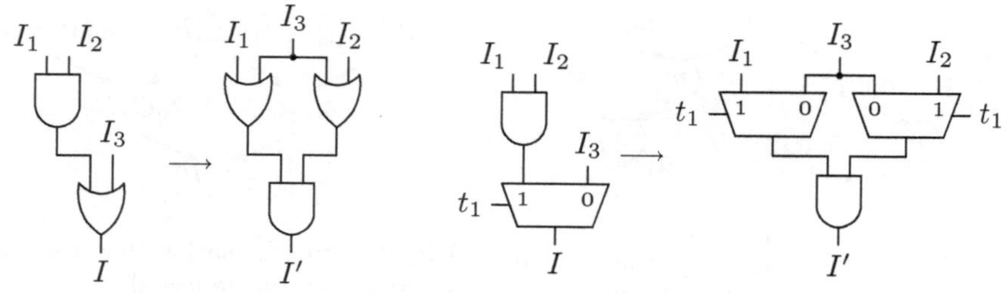

Fig. 10. Transforming R in Figure 6 as in Figure 9 does not change the interpolant

in Itp_S in this case. Lemma 5 in Appendix C of the technical report [5] shows that this transformation does not change the interpolants in Itp_M and Itp_S.

5.2 Proof Transformations and Interpolant Strength

Consider the sequence of pivot labels on a path in a proof. If pivots labelled a occur before those labelled ab, which in turn occur before b, the interpolant has conjunctions at the top-level. Such an interpolant is more constrained than one obtained from a proof which does not respect this order, hence stronger. To strengthen the interpolant obtained from a proof, we swap vertices so that the sequence of pivot labels is close to the sequence described above.

Let L_R be a labelling function for an (A, B)-refutation R, w an internal vertex and (w, v) a merge-free edge. Note that L_R is not a labelling function for the proof $R[w \rightleftharpoons v]$ because $R[w \rightleftharpoons v]$ has a different clause function from R. Nevertheless, $R[w \rightleftharpoons v]$ has the same initial vertices and clauses as R. Recall that labelling functions are determined by the labels of initial vertices, so we can derive a labelling function for $R[w \rightleftharpoons v]$, denoted $L_R[w \rightleftharpoons v]$, from L_R. Theorem 4 relates the swap transformation and interpolant strength.

Theorem 4. *Let R be an (A, B)-refutation, L be a labelling function, v and w be vertices with ancestors and partial interpolants, in particular I_2 and I_3, as in Figure 6, and (w, v) be a merge-free edge. Let $\mathsf{c} = L(w^+, piv(w)) \sqcup L(w^-, \neg piv(w))$ and $\mathsf{d} = L(v^+, piv(v)) \sqcup L(v^-, \neg piv(v))$.*

1. *If $\mathsf{c} \preceq \mathsf{d}$ and either $\mathsf{c} \neq \mathsf{d}$ or $\mathsf{c} \neq \mathsf{ab}$, $\mathsf{Itp}(L[w \rightleftharpoons v], R[w \rightleftharpoons v]) \Rightarrow \mathsf{Itp}(L, R)$.*
2. *In all other cases, if $I_2 \Rightarrow I_3$, then $\mathsf{Itp}(L[w \rightleftharpoons v], R[w \rightleftharpoons v]) \Rightarrow \mathsf{Itp}(L, R)$.*

Changing labelling functions and swapping vertices are two different methods for strengthening interpolants. Corollary 2 shows that these methods can be combined to obtain even stronger interpolants. The corollary follows from Lemma 3, Theorem 2 and Theorem 4. Corollary 2 is summarised in Figure 11.

Corollary 2. *Let R be an (A, B)-refutation and L and L' be labelling functions such that $L \preceq L'$. Let w be an internal vertex of R and (w, v) be a merge-free edge, such that for any L, $\mathsf{Itp}(L, R) \Rightarrow \mathsf{Itp}(L[w \rightleftharpoons v], R[w \rightleftharpoons v])$. Then, it holds that*

- $\mathsf{Itp}(L[w \rightleftharpoons v], R[w \rightleftharpoons v]) \Rightarrow \mathsf{Itp}(L'[w \rightleftharpoons v], R[w \rightleftharpoons v])$, *and*
- $\mathsf{Itp}(L', R) \Rightarrow \mathsf{Itp}(L'[w \rightleftharpoons v], R[w \rightleftharpoons v])$,

6 Related Work

Craig proved the interpolation theorem for first order logic in 1957 [4]. For a survey of the multitudinous applications and consequences of this theorem in mathematical logic, see [10]. Though the theorem has been known for a while, the study of interpolation algorithms is relatively recent. The first such algorithm is implicitly present in Maehara's constructive proof [9] of Craig's theorem. Maehara constructs interpolants from sequent calculus proofs and his algorithm does not apply to resolution proofs.

Interpolation algorithms for resolution proofs have been discovered several times. The first algorithm we are aware of is due to Huang [6], who constructs interpolants in a theorem prover that uses resolution, paramodulation and factoring [6]. Krajíček observed that lower bounds on interpolation algorithms for propositional proof systems have implications for separating certain complexity classes [8]. He constructs interpolants from *semantic derivations*; the latter being an inference system that subsumes resolution and the propositional sequent calculus. Pudlák [13] studies a similar problem and constructs a circuit representing the interpolant. Though the presentations in these papers differ, the interpolation systems are the same. This can be seen from the exposition of Krajíček's and Pudlák's methods by Buss [3].

McMillan proposed an interpolation algorithm for resolution refutations and applied it to obtain a purely SAT-based finite-state model checker [11]. We have shown that McMillan's algorithm is different from and produces stronger interpolants than the existing algorithm. Interpolant-based model checking has been extended to infinite-state systems [7] and other logical theories [12,14]. The impact of interpolant strength on the performance of a model checker was first highlighted by Jhala and McMillan [7] who proposed two proof transformations to strengthen interpolants. We have analysed these transformations in this paper and shown one of them to be redundant.

The labelled interpolation systems we propose are strictly more general than existing interpolation systems for resolution. Though much work in interpolant-based model checking uses McMillan's interpolation system from [11], Yorsh and Musuvathi [14] based their interpolating decision procedure on Pudlák's system and gave an elaborate proof of Pudlák's system [14]. Our generalisation arose from studying the difference between McMillan's system and Pudlák's system. Our proof of Theorem 1 is essentially Yorsh and Musuvathi's proof parametrised by a labelling function.

Proof transformations have been applied to reduce the size of unsatisfiable cores in [2]. These modifications may result in vertices being eliminated from a proof. Understanding the effect of such transformations on interpolant strength is an open problem.

7 Conclusion

In this paper, we presented a parametrised interpolation system capable of generating a family of interpolants. Our system is strictly more general than existing

$$\mathsf{Itp}(L'[w \rightleftharpoons v], R[w \rightleftharpoons v])$$

$$\mathsf{Itp}(L[w \rightleftharpoons v], R[w \rightleftharpoons v]) \qquad \mathsf{Itp}(L', R)$$

$$\mathsf{Itp}(L, R)$$

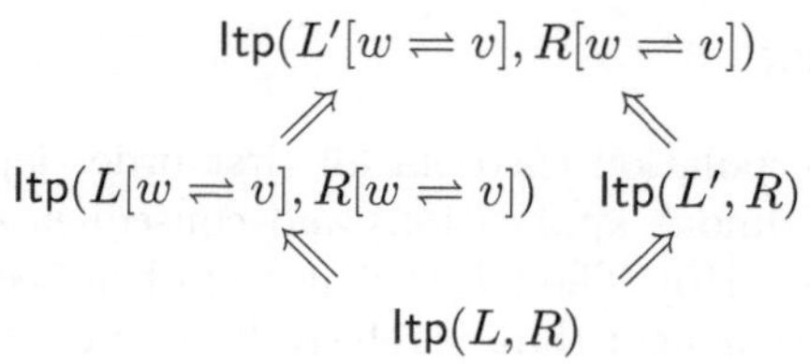

Fig. 11. Combining labelling functions and proof transformations (Corollary 2)

systems and was used to derive new results about existing systems. In addition, we studied two orthogonal methods for obtaining interpolants of different strength. The first method uses labelling functions and the second method is based on swapping vertices in a proof graph. The main results in this paper are summarised in Figure 11. We have shown that proof transformations and labelling functions can be combined to obtain interpolants of predictably different strength.

Two very important questions not answered in this paper are which strengthening techniques lead to performance improvements in model checking and how one can detect situations in which strengthening techniques are to be applied. Figuratively speaking, the methods we present can be viewed as constituting a dial for tuning interpolant strength. The next step is to empirically determine which settings to use for obtaining good performance in practice.

Acknowledgements. We thank our our colleagues Alastair Donaldson, Hristina Palikareva, and Phillip Rümmer and our anonymous reviewers for their helpful comments. Special recognition goes to our friend Ramon Granell for his unrestrained interest in our work.

References

1. Andrews, P.B.: Resolution with merging. Journal of the ACM 15(3), 367–381 (1968)
2. Bar-Ilan, O., Fuhrmann, O., Hoory, S., Shacham, O., Strichman, O.: Linear-time reductions of resolution proofs. Technical Report IE/IS-2008-02, Technion (2008)
3. Buss, S.R.: Propositional proof complexity: An introduction. In: Berger, U., Schwichtenberg, H. (eds.) Computational Logic. NATO ASI Series F: Computer and Systems Sciences, vol. 165, pp. 127–178. Springer, Heidelberg (1999)
4. Craig, W.: Linear reasoning. A new form of the Herbrand-Gentzen theorem. Journal of Symbolic Logic 22(3), 250–268 (1957)
5. D'Silva, V., Kroening, D., Purandare, M., Weissenbacher, G.: Interpolant strength. Technical Report 652, Institute for Computer Science, ETH Zurich (November 2009)
6. Huang, G.: Constructing Craig interpolation formulas. In: Li, M., Du, D.-Z. (eds.) COCOON 1995. LNCS, vol. 959, pp. 181–190. Springer, Heidelberg (1995)
7. Jhala, R., McMillan, K.L.: Interpolant-based transition relation approximation. Logical Methods in Computer Science (LMCS) 3(4) (2007)
8. Krajíček, J.: Interpolation theorems, lower bounds for proof systems, and independence results for bounded arithmetic. The Journal of Symbolic Logic 62(2), 457–486 (1997)

9. Maehara, S.: On the interpolation theorem of Craig (in Japanese). Sûgaku 12, 235–237 (1961)
10. Mancosu, P.: Interpolations. Essays in Honor of William Craig. Synthese, vol. 164:3. Springer, Heidelberg (2008)
11. McMillan, K.L.: Interpolation and SAT-based model checking. In: Hunt Jr., W.A., Somenzi, F. (eds.) CAV 2003. LNCS, vol. 2725, pp. 1–13. Springer, Heidelberg (2003)
12. McMillan, K.L.: An interpolating theorem prover. Theoretical Comput. Sci. 345(1), 101–121 (2005)
13. Pudlák, P.: Lower bounds for resolution and cutting plane proofs and monotone computations. The Journal of Symbolic Logic 62(3), 981–998 (1997)
14. Yorsh, G., Musuvathi, M.: A combination method for generating interpolants. In: Nieuwenhuis, R. (ed.) CADE 2005. LNCS (LNAI), vol. 3632, pp. 353–368. Springer, Heidelberg (2005)

Checking Bounded Reachability in Asynchronous Systems by Symbolic Event Tracing

Jori Dubrovin*

Helsinki University of Technology TKK
Department of Information and Computer Science
P.O.Box 5400, FI-02015 TKK, Finland
Jori.Dubrovin@tkk.fi

Abstract. This paper presents a new framework for checking bounded reachability properties of asynchronous systems by reducing the problem to satisfiability in difference logic. The analysis is bounded by fixing a finite set of potential events, each of which may occur at most once in any order. The events are specified using high-level Petri nets. The proposed logic encoding describes the space of possible causal links between events rather than possible sequences of states as in Bounded Model Checking. Independence between events is exploited intrinsically without partial order reductions, and the handling of data is symbolic. Experiments with a proof-of-concept implementation of the technique show that it has the potential to far exceed the performance of Bounded Model Checking.

1 Introduction

Design errors in concurrent hardware and software systems are notoriously difficult to find. This is due to the tremendous number of possible interleavings of events and combinations of data values. Symbolic model checking methods [7] attack the problem by expressing the actual and desired behavior of a system as formulas and using the tools of computational logic to search for a possible failure.

In this paper, we develop a new symbolic technique for verifying bounded reachability properties of asynchronous discrete-event systems. Instead of manipulating executions as sequences of states, we take an event-centered viewpoint. First, one fixes a collection of transitions, each of which describes one discrete step of execution. This collection is called an unwinding of the system. We only consider finite-length executions in which each transition of the unwinding occurs at most once, in whichever order. From the unwinding, we generate automatically a formula that is satisfiable if and only if a predefined condition, e.g. division by zero, can be reached within this bounded set of executions. For satisfiability checking, any SAT or SMT solver [18] can be used as long as it can handle the data constraints of transitions. If the reachability property holds within the bound, a witness execution can be extracted from an interpretation that satisfies the formula. Otherwise, longer executions can be covered by adding more transitions to the unwinding and generating a new formula. This technique will be called Bounded Event Tracing.

* Financial support from Hecse (Helsinki Graduate School in Computer Science and Engineering) and the Emil Aaltonen Foundation is gratefully acknowledged.

G. Barthe and M. Hermenegildo (Eds.): VMCAI 2010, LNCS 5944, pp. 146–162, 2010.

The approach is similar to Bounded Model Checking (BMC) [2]. Both methods can find bugs and report no false alarms, but they cannot be used as such to prove the absence of bugs in realistic systems. Unlike BMC, the new technique directly exploits the defining aspect of asynchronous systems: each transition accesses only a fraction of the global state of the system. Although the generation of optimal unwindings is not yet pursued in this work, Bounded Event Tracing is shown to be able to outperform BMC on several benchmarks.

In the next section, we will go through the central concepts with an extensive example. Section 3 defines unwindings as a class of high-level Petri nets [15] that allows concise modeling of concurrency and software features. The logic encoding is presented in Sect. 4, while Sect. 5 discusses the relationship to other approaches. In Sect. 6, we design one way to automatically generate unwindings for a class of state machine models and use these unwindings in an experimental comparison to BMC.

2 Bounded Event Tracing by Example

Figure 1a presents a system with three concurrent processes that run indefinitely. Suppose the reachability property in question is whether the system can ever print "equal". The execution in Fig. 1b shows that the property holds: after one cycle of process F and two cycles of G, both x and y have the value 9, and process H then runs the print statement. The circles represent the values of variables in states $M_1, M_2, \ldots$, and the rectangles f, g_1, g_2, and h represent the atomic execution of one cycle of process F, G, G, and H, respectively.

Figure 1c shows a related high-level Petri net. We can interpret Fig. 1b as a finite execution of the Petri net as follows. The *transition* (rectangle) named $init$ occurs first, producing a *token* in each of the *places* (circles) pj, px, and py, which correspond to the variables of the system. This leads to a state M_1, in which each place pj, px, and py contains one token that carries a value 3, 2, or 5, respectively. Transition f occurs next, consumes the token from place py and produces a new token with value 9. This results in a state M_2. Then, transition g_1 simultaneously consumes a token from each place pj and px, and uses their values to produce new tokens. Finally, the state M_5 is reached.

This is an example of a *one-off execution* of the Petri net. Generally, a one-off execution is a finite sequence that starts with a state in which no place contains a token. Then, a transition occurs, consuming exactly one token with each input arc (an arrow from a place to the transition) and producing exactly one token with each output arc (an arrow from the transition to a place) while fulfilling the data constraints. This leads to a new state and so on, as usual in Petri nets. The only distinctive requirement is that each transition occurs *at most once* in the sequence. The transitions that occur in a one-off execution are its *events*.

A Petri net whose set of one-off executions specifies a bounded portion of the behavior of a system is called an *unwinding* of the system. We assume that we are given an unwinding whose one-off executions map easily to finite-length executions of the original system. The unwinding of Fig. 1c has another one-off execution consisting of the sequence $init, g_2, h$ of events. This corresponds to process G running one cycle and then process H printing "equal". In total, this unwinding covers all executions of the

a) **Initially:** $j \leftarrow 3$; $x \leftarrow 2$; $y \leftarrow 5$

Process F:	**Process G:**	**Process H:**
while true:	while true:	while true:
$y \leftarrow 9$	$x \leftarrow x + j$; $j \leftarrow j + 1$	if $x = y$: print "equal"

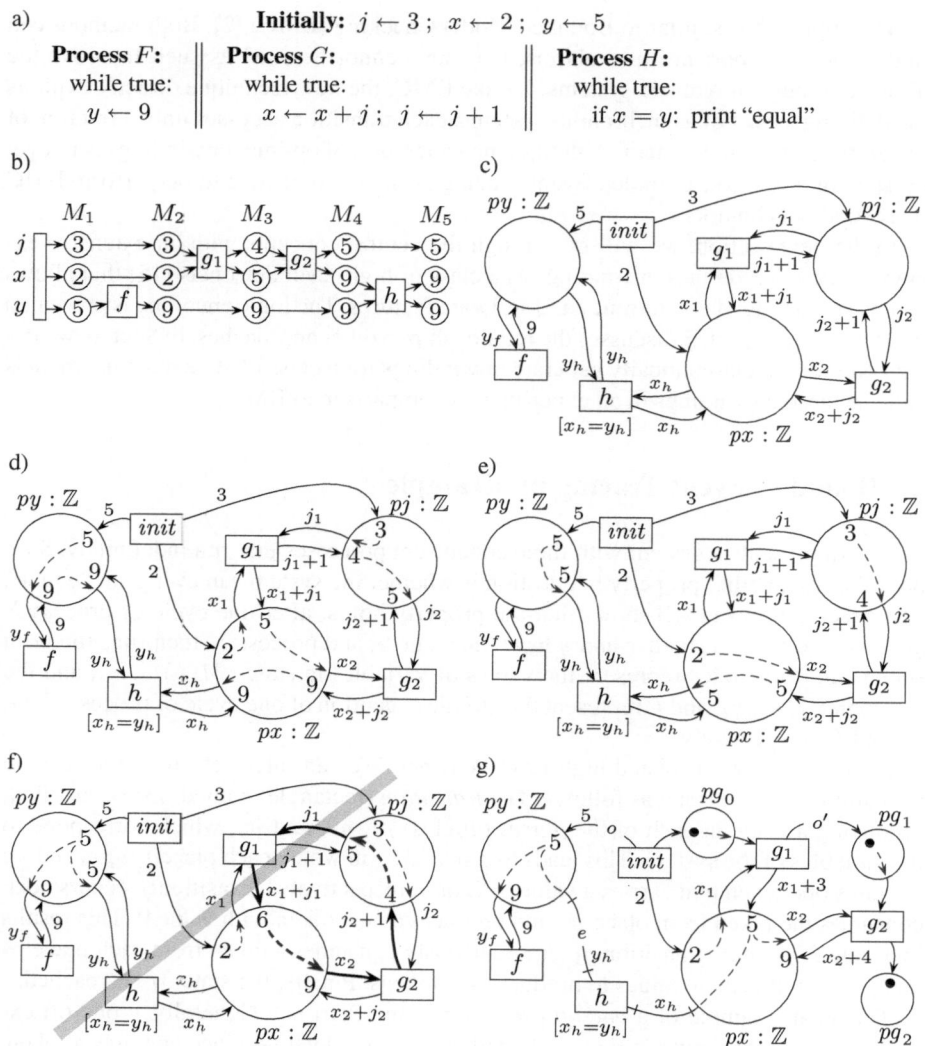

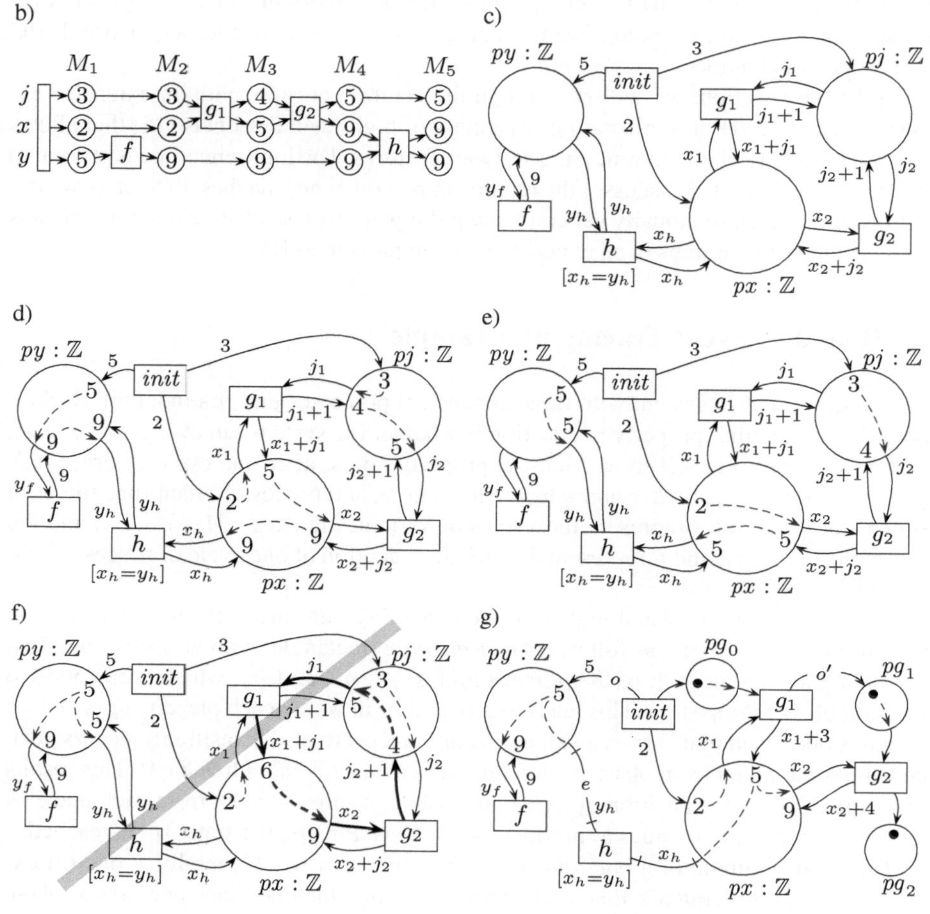

Fig. 1. An example system and illustrations of its behavior

system in which process F runs at most one cycle, process G at most two cycles, and H at most one cycle, in any possible order.

We observe that every token consumed during a one-off execution has been previously produced. Figure 1d illustrates this idea for the one-off execution of Fig. 1b. Transition g_1 consumes the token with value 2 produced by *init*, whereas the token with value 5 in place *pj* is not consumed at all. The numeric values and dashed arrows inside the big circles in Fig. 1d constitute an example of what we call a *token trace* of the unwinding. The token trace tells us some facts about the course of events. By following the arrows, we see that *init* occurs before g_1, which occurs before g_2, but we cannot infer whether f occurs before or after, say, g_2. A token trace generally fixes only a *partial order* of events. Figure 1e illustrates another token trace of the same unwinding. This time, transitions f and g_1 do not occur at all. We can check that this token trace describes the second one-off execution discussed above.

It turns out that by specifying a simple set of rules for constructing a token trace of a fixed unwinding, we can characterize the set of *all* one-off executions of the unwinding. In other words, an unwinding induces a set of one-off executions and a set of token traces, and there is a meaningful correspondence relation between the two sets. We can thus reduce the search for a one-off execution with a certain property to finding a corresponding token trace. Given an unwinding, its token traces are defined by the following rules.

1. A token trace consists of events, links (dashed arrows), and data values.
2. A subset of the transitions of the unwinding are chosen to be events.
3. Each output arc of each event is associated with a single token with a value.
4. Each input arc of each event is linked to an output arc of an event.
5. No two input arcs are linked to the same output arc.
6. The data constraints of all events are fulfilled by the values of tokens.
7. The links impose a partial order on the events.

Figure 1f contains a third attempt at a token trace of the same unwinding. However, there are several problems. First, transitions f and h are consuming the same token at place py. This breaks rule 5—an input arc denotes a destructive read operation. Second, transition h poses as an event although it gets no input from place px, breaking rule 4. Third, there is an illegal cycle, illustrated in thick arrows, that breaks rule 7: event g_1 produces a token with value 6, then g_2 consumes it and produces a token with value 4, which in turn is consumed by g_1. No chronological ordering of the occurrences agrees with the picture. Any of these three mistakes suffices to tell that Fig. 1f does not represent a valid token trace.

A model checking procedure. The discussion above suggests the following procedure for checking reachability properties of an asynchronous system. Generate an unwinding such that one-off executions of the unwinding map to finite executions of the system, and the property corresponds to the occurrence of a designated transition $t^{\diamond}$. Generate automatically a formula that encodes the rules for a token trace of the unwinding and add the constraint that $t^{\diamond}$ is an event. Feed the formula to an off-the-shelf satisfiability solver. If the formula is satisfiable, convert the satisfying interpretation to a token trace and further to an execution that witnesses the property. If the formula is unsatisfiable, expand the unwinding to cover more executions of the system, and start over.

Assembling unwindings. Figure 1c demonstrates a rudimentary way of obtaining unwindings, with a place for each variable and a transition or several identical transitions for each atomic action that the system can perform. However, we expect to gain better performance by further exploiting the versatility of Petri nets. In general, one can set up arcs in arbitrary configurations, and the number of tokens in a place needs not be fixed. With the multitude of possible design choices, it is generally not obvious how to find the best way to generate unwindings for a given class of systems.

Figure 1g shows another unwinding that covers the same set of executions as the previous one. The labels o, o', and e do not contribute to the semantics—they only name some arcs for later reference. A token in place pg_0, pg_1, or pg_2 denotes the fact that process G has executed 0, 1, or 2 cycles, respectively. The token carries a meaningless value denoted by •. This solution breaks the symmetry of transitions g_1 and g_2, and has allowed us to inline the fixed values $j_1 = 3$ and $j_2 = 4$ in g_1 and g_2 and to eliminate the place pj. In Sect. 6, we will use similar ideas in an automated unwinding scheme.

Another change in Fig. 1g is that transition h is incident to two *test arcs* (lines with cross bars close to each end). A test arc represents a non-destructive read operation. It is like an input arc but does not consume the token, and it is usually behaviorally equivalent to a pair of input and output arcs. The use of test arcs is optional, but they may result in a more efficient encoding. The following rules need to be added for token traces. Each test arc is linked to an output arc, and multiple test arcs plus at most one input arc can be linked to the same output arc. The partial order must be such that a transition that tests a token occurs after the transition that produces the token. A third transition can consume the token, but it must occur after the testing transition. The token trace of Fig. 1g imposes a partial order that obeys these rules. In particular, because of the links within place px, transition h occurs after g_1 and before g_2.

3 Semantics of Unwindings

We will use the following notations for formalizing unwindings and token traces. For a function $f : X \to Y$, sets $A \subseteq X$, $B \subseteq Y$, and an element $y \in Y$, we adopt the usual notation $f(A) := \{f(x) \mid x \in A\}$, $f^{-1}(B) := \{x \in X \mid f(x) \in B\}$, and $f^{-1}(y) := f^{-1}(\{y\})$. We will use *types*, *variables*, and *expressions* to model data manipulation in systems. Each type is identified with the set of elements of the type; in particular, the Boolean type is $\mathbb{B} = \{\text{false}, \text{true}\}$. Every variable v and expression ϕ has a type $type(v)$ or $type(\phi)$. The set of variables in an expression or a set of expressions ϕ is denoted by $vars(\phi)$. A *binding* of a set V of variables maps each variable $v \in V$ to a value $d \in type(v)$. If ϕ is an expression and b is a binding of (a superset of) $vars(\phi)$, the *value of* ϕ *in* b, denoted by ϕ^b, is obtained by substituting $b(v)$ for each occurrence of a variable $v \in vars(\phi)$ in the expression and evaluating the result. We will not fix a concrete language for expressions—the choice of a proper language depends on the problem domain and on the capabilities of the satisfiability solver used.

A *multiset* M over a set U is a function $U \to \mathbb{N}$, interpreted as a collection that contains $M(u)$ indistinguishable copies of each element $u \in U$. A multiset M is *finite* iff the sum $\sum_{u \in U} M(u)$ is finite. When the base set U is clear from the context, we will identify an ordinary set $A \subseteq U$ with the multiset χ_A over U, defined as $\chi_A(u) = 1$ if $u \in A$ and $\chi_A(u) = 0$ otherwise. If M_1 and M_2 are multisets over U, then M_1 is a *subset* of M_2, denoted $M_1 \leq M_2$, iff $M_1(u) \leq M_2(u)$ for all $u \in U$. A multiset M *contains* an element $u \in U$, denoted $u \in M$, iff $M(u) \geq 1$. We will use $M_1 + M_2$ and $M_2 - M_1$ with their usual meanings (as functions) to denote multiset union and multiset difference, respectively. The latter is defined only if $M_1 \leq M_2$.

A binary relation $\prec$ over a set X is a *strict partial order* iff it is irreflexive, asymmetric, and transitive, that is, iff for all $x, y, z \in X$ (i) $x \prec y$ implies not $y \prec x$ and (ii) $x \prec y$ and $y \prec z$ together imply $x \prec z$.

3.1 Colored Contextual Unweighted Petri Nets

Colored Petri Nets [15] are a powerful language for the design and analysis of distributed systems. In this work however, we use Petri nets with restricted semantics to specify a bounded portion of the behavior of a system. Our variant is called *Colored Contextual Unweighted Petri Nets*, or "nets" for short. The word *contextual* means that nets can contain test arcs [5], allowing compact modeling of non-destructive read operations. By *unweighted* we mean that each arc is associated with a single token instead of a multiset of tokens as in Colored Petri Nets. This restriction is crucial for the encoding, but does not seriously weaken the formalism. Places can still contain multisets of tokens, and multiple arcs can be placed in parallel to move several tokens at the same time.

Definition 1. *A* net *is a tuple* $N = \langle \Sigma, P, T, A_{in}, A_{test}, A_{out}, place, trans, colors, guard, expr\rangle$*, where*

1. Σ *is a set of non-empty* types *(sometimes called color sets),*
2. P *is a set of* places,
3. T *is a set of* transitions,
4. A_{in} *is a set of* input arcs,
5. A_{test} *is a set of* test arcs,
6. A_{out} *is a set of* output arcs,
7. P*,* T*,* A_{in}*,* A_{test}*, and* A_{out} *are all pairwise disjoint,*
8. $place$ *is a* place incidence function $A_{in} \cup A_{test} \cup A_{out} \rightarrow P$,
9. $trans$ *is a* transition incidence function $A_{in} \cup A_{test} \cup A_{out} \rightarrow T$,
10. *the set* $trans^{-1}(t)$ *is finite for all* $t \in T$,
11. $colors$ *is a* color function $P \rightarrow \Sigma$,
12. $guard$ *is a* guard function *over* T *such that for all* $t \in T$, $guard(t)$ *is an expression with* $type(guard(t)) = \mathbb{B}$ *and* $type(vars(guard(t))) \subseteq \Sigma$,
13. $expr$ *is an* arc expression function *over* $A_{in} \cup A_{test} \cup A_{out}$ *such that for all arcs* a*,* $expr(a)$ *is an expression with* $type(expr(a)) = colors(place(a))$ *and* $type(vars(expr(a))) \subseteq \Sigma$,

A net is *finite* iff P and T are finite sets. For a transition or a set of transitions t and a place or a set of places p, we use the shorthand notations

$$in(t) := A_{in} \cap trans^{-1}(t) \ , \qquad in(p) := A_{in} \cap place^{-1}(p) \ ,$$
$$test(t) := A_{test} \cap trans^{-1}(t) \ , \qquad test(p) := A_{test} \cap place^{-1}(p) \ ,$$
$$out(t) := A_{out} \cap trans^{-1}(t) \ , \qquad out(p) := A_{out} \cap place^{-1}(p) \ ,$$
$$vars(t) := vars(guard(t)) \cup \bigcup_{a \in trans^{-1}(t)} vars(expr(a)) \ .$$

In the net of Fig. 1g, we have $place(o) = py$, $trans(o) = init$, $test(py) = \{e\}$, $out(pg_1) = \{o'\}$, $place(in(g_2)) = \{px, pg_1\}$, $colors(py) = \mathbb{Z}$, $expr(e) = y_h$, $guard(h) = (x_h{=}y_h)$, $vars(h) = \{x_h, y_h\}$, and $vars(init) = \emptyset$. We omit vacuously true guards, so $guard(f) =$ true implicitly. Also, $colors(pg_1)$ is implicitly the type $\{\bullet\}$ with only one meaningless value, and $expr(o')$ is the constant expression $\bullet$.

A *token element* is a pair $\langle p, d\rangle$, where $p \in P$ is a place and $d \in colors(p)$ is a value. A *marking* M is a finite multiset over the set of token elements. Markings represent states of the system. The interpretation is that if $M(\langle p, d\rangle) = n$, then place p contains n tokens of value d in state M.

A *binding element* is a pair $\langle t, b\rangle$, where $t \in T$ is a transition and b is a binding of $vars(t)$. The shorthand $consumed_{\langle t,b\rangle} := \sum_{c\in in(t)} \{\langle place(c), expr(c)^b\rangle\}$ will mean the multiset of token elements consumed by a binding element, while $produced_{\langle t,b\rangle} := \sum_{o\in out(t)} \{\langle place(o), expr(o)^b\rangle\}$ means the multiset of produced token elements. A binding element $\langle t, b\rangle$ is *enabled* in a marking M iff the following conditions hold.

1. $consumed_{\langle t,b\rangle} \le M$,
2. $\langle place(e), expr(e)^b\rangle \in \left(M - consumed_{\langle t,b\rangle}\right)$ for all $e \in test(t)$, and
3. $guard(t)^b = \text{true}$.

The binding element can *occur* in the marking iff it is enabled in the marking, leading to a new marking $M' = M - consumed_{\langle t,b\rangle} + produced_{\langle t,b\rangle}$. We denote by $M\ [t, b\rangle\ M'$ the fact that the binding element is enabled in M and leads from M to M' if it occurs. A *finite occurrence sequence* of a net is a finite sequence $M_0\ [t_1, b_1\rangle\ M_1\ \cdots\ [t_k, b_k\rangle\ M_k$ such that $k \ge 0$ and $M_{i-1}\ [t_i, b_i\rangle\ M_i$ holds for each $1 \le i \le k$.

3.2 Unwindings and One-Off Executions

We define an *unwinding* to be any net $N = \langle \Sigma, P, T, \ldots, expr\rangle$ that fulfills the two constraints below.

1. Transitions do not share variables: when $t \in T$ and $u \in T$ are distinct, $vars(t) \cap vars(u) = \emptyset$. We can always achieve this by renaming variables if necessary, as done in Fig. 1c by using subscripts.
2. Every place is incident to an output arc: $out(p) \ne \emptyset$ for all $p \in P$. This is not a crucial restriction either: places with no incident output arcs are useless in unwindings and can be eliminated.

These constraints are just technicalities—the true restriction is that the transitions of an unwinding are treated as *potential events*: each of them occurs once or not at all. Thus, we define a *one-off execution* of an unwinding as a finite occurrence sequence $M_0\ [t_1, b_1\rangle\ M_1\ \cdots\ [t_k, b_k\rangle\ M_k$ such that $M_0 = \emptyset$ and $t_i \ne t_j$ for all $1 \le i < j \le k$. The set $\{t_1, \ldots, t_k\}$ is the *event set* of the one-off execution. A transition $t \in T$ is *one-off reachable* iff it is an event in some one-off execution. For example, the unwinding of Fig. 1c has a one-off execution $M_0\ [init, b_{init}\rangle\ M_1\ [f, b_f\rangle\ M_2$, where $M_2 = \{\langle pj, 3\rangle, \langle px, 2\rangle, \langle py, 9\rangle\}$, the binding b_{init} is empty, and ${y_f}^{b_f} = 5$. The initial marking M_0 is fixed to be empty, but we work around this by specifying the starting conditions with a transition *init* that necessarily occurs once in the beginning of any non-trivial one-off execution.

3.3 Token Traces

Let us formalize the rules presented in Sect. 2 for a token trace.

Definition 2. *A* token trace *of an unwinding* $N = \langle \Sigma, P, T, \ldots, expr \rangle$ *is a tuple* $R = \langle E, src, b \rangle$*, where*

1. $E \subseteq T$ *is a finite set of* events,
2. src *is a* source function $in(E) \cup test(E) \to out(E)$ *such that*
   (a) $place(a) = place(src(a))$ *for all arcs* $a \in in(E) \cup test(E)$ *and*
   (b) $src(c_1) \neq src(c_2)$ *for all input arcs* $c_1, c_2 \in in(E)$ *such that* $c_1 \neq c_2$,
3. b *is a binding of* $vars(E)$*, called the* total binding, *such that* $expr(a)^b = expr(src(a))^b$ *for all arcs* $a \in in(E) \cup test(E)$,
4. $guard(t)^b = \text{true}$ *for all events* $t \in E$,
5. *there exists a strict partial order* $\prec$ *over the set* E *such that*
   (a) $trans(src(a)) \prec trans(a)$ *for all arcs* $a \in in(E) \cup test(E)$ *and*
   (b) $trans(e) \prec trans(c)$ *for all test arcs* $e \in test(E)$ *and input arcs* $c \in in(E)$ *such that* $src(e) = src(c)$.

Relating to Sect. 2, the source function forms the links between the arcs, while the total binding takes care of the data constraints. According to item 3, the arc expression at each end of a link must evaluate to the same value, i.e. the value of the token. As $vars(E)$ is a *disjoint* union of the variables of each event, b can bind the variables of each event independently. Item 5 above says that the events can be ordered in such a way that each token is produced before any event consumes or tests it, and a token is not tested during or after its consumption. Any strict partial order over (a superset of) E that fulfills item 5 will be called a *chronological partial order* of the token trace.

Figure 1g portrays a token trace where $E = T$, ${y_f}^b = {x_h}^b = 5$, $src(e) = o$, $src(in(E)) \cap out(g_2) = \emptyset$, and necessarily $init \prec g_1 \prec h \prec g_2$. One of $f \prec g_2$ and $g_2 \prec f$ can be true, or both can be false, but not both true.

From a one-off execution $M_0\ [t_1, b_1\rangle\ M_1\ \cdots\ [t_k, b_k\rangle\ M_k$, we can construct a token trace by conjoining $b_1, \ldots, b_k$ to a total binding and tracing each consumed or tested token to its source. The interleaving $t_1 \prec t_2 \prec \cdots \prec t_k$ then gives a chronological partial order. Conversely, we can take a token trace and linearize its chronological partial order to obtain a one-off execution. These constructions constitute the proof of the following theorem. See the report [8] for details.

Theorem 1. *Given an unwinding* N *and a finite subset* E *of transitions, there is a one-off execution of* N *with event set* E *if and only if there is a token trace of* N *with event set* E.

4 Encoding Token Traces

Let $N = \langle \Sigma, P, T, \ldots, expr \rangle$ be a finite unwinding. We are interested in whether a transition $t^\diamond \in T$ is one-off reachable, or equivalently, whether there is a token trace of N whose event set contains $t^\diamond$. In this section, we will construct a formula that is satisfiable if and only if such a token trace exists.

A formula ϕ is satisfiable iff there is an interpretation I such that ϕ^I is true. In this context, an interpretation is a binding of the symbols in the formula. In propositional satisfiability (SAT), the formula only contains propositional (Boolean) symbols and Boolean connectives. Extensions known as SMT [18] also allow non-Boolean constraints. For example, an interpretation I satisfies the formula $\bigwedge_{j\in J}(\mathsf{X}_j < \mathsf{Y}_j)$, where the X_j and Y_j are symbols of real type, if and only if ${\mathsf{X}_j}^I$ is less than ${\mathsf{Y}_j}^I$ for all $j \in J$.

The formula will be built using the following set of symbols:

- for each $t \in T$, a propositional symbol Occur_t ("transition t occurs"),
- for each $t \in T$, a symbol Time_t of type $\mathbb{R}$ ("when transition t occurs"),
- for each pair $o \in A_{out}$, $a \in A_{in} \cup A_{test}$ such that $place(o) = place(a)$, a propositional symbol $\mathsf{Link}_{o,a}$ ("arc a is linked to arc o"), and
- for each $v \in vars(T)$, a symbol Val_v of type $type(v)$ ("the value of v").

We get an interpretation from a token trace $\langle E, src, b\rangle$ by setting ${\mathsf{Occur}_t}^I$ to true iff $t \in E$, setting ${\mathsf{Link}_{o,a}}^I$ to true iff $o = src(a)$, letting ${\mathsf{Val}_v}^I := v^b$, and assigning the values ${\mathsf{Time}_t}^I$ according to some chronological partial order $\prec$. Because the symbols Time_t are used for ordering and not arithmetic, we could as well type them as e.g. integers instead of reals. The detailed constructions from a token trace to a satisfying interpretation and vice versa are in the report version [8].

The formula ϵ below (denoted by $\epsilon_\emptyset$ in the report [8]) encodes the rules for a token trace in terms of the introduced symbols. Checking the existence of a token trace containing the event $t^\diamond$ then reduces to checking the satisfiability of the formula $\epsilon \wedge \mathsf{Occur}_{t^\diamond}$.

$$\epsilon := \bigwedge_{t\in T} \gamma_t \wedge \bigwedge_{a\in A_{in}\cup A_{test}} \Big(\beta_a \wedge \bigwedge_{o\in out(place(a))} \psi_{o,a}\Big) \wedge \bigwedge_{p\in P} \delta_p \ . \tag{1}$$

The subformulas γ_t and β_a encode items 4 and 2a of Definition 2. For a guard or arc expression ϕ, we use the special notation ϕ^{vals} to denote the substitution of each variable $v \in vars(T)$ with the symbol Val_v.

$$\gamma_t := \mathsf{Occur}_t \rightarrow guard(t)^{vals} \ ,$$
$$\beta_a := \mathsf{Occur}_{trans(a)} \rightarrow \bigvee_{o\in out(place(a))} \mathsf{Link}_{o,a} \ .$$

The subformula $\psi_{o,a}$ places constraints on linking arc a to output arc o, namely that $trans(o)$ must be an event, and items 5a and 3 of Definition 2 must hold.

$$\begin{aligned}\psi_{o,a} := &\big(\mathsf{Link}_{o,a} \rightarrow \mathsf{Occur}_{trans(o)}\big) \wedge \\ &\big(\mathsf{Link}_{o,a} \rightarrow (\mathsf{Time}_{trans(o)} < \mathsf{Time}_{trans(a)})\big) \wedge \\ &\big(\mathsf{Link}_{o,a} \rightarrow (expr(o)^{vals} = expr(a)^{vals})\big) \ .\end{aligned}$$

The constraints in δ_p are required to make sure that tokens consumed from a place p are indeed removed. We encode items 2b and 5b of Definition 2 as

$$\begin{aligned}\delta_p := &\bigwedge_{o\in out(p)} AtMostOne\left(\left\{\mathsf{Link}_{o,c} \;\middle|\; c \in in(p)\right\}\right) \wedge \\ &\bigwedge_{o\in out(p)} \bigwedge_{e\in test(p)} \bigwedge_{c\in in(p)} \big(\mathsf{Link}_{o,e} \wedge \mathsf{Link}_{o,c} \rightarrow (\mathsf{Time}_{trans(e)} < \mathsf{Time}_{trans(c)})\big) \ ,\end{aligned}$$

where $AtMostOne\,(\Phi)$ denotes a formula that is true iff exactly zero or one formulas in the finite set Φ are true. This can be expressed in size linear in $|\Phi|$.

4.1 Properties of the Encoding

The principal motivation for formula (1) is that it can be used for model checking reachability properties.

Theorem 2. *Let* $N = \langle \Sigma, P, T, \ldots, expr \rangle$ *be a finite unwinding and let* $t^\diamond \in T$ *be a transition. Then,* $t^\diamond$ *is one-off reachable if and only if the formula* $\epsilon \wedge \mathsf{Occur}_{t^\diamond}$ *is satisfiable.*

The proof [8], which is based on Theorem 1, is constructive and can be used to extract witness executions.

Concerning compactness, the formula ϵ contains *one* instance of each guard and arc expression of the unwinding, so there is no duplication involved here. The rest of the encoding adds a term $O(|out(p)|\,(1 + |in(p)|)(1 + |test(p)|))$ to the size for each place p. The encoding is thus *locally* cubic in the number of arcs incident to a place, or quadratic if there are no test arcs. We could generally avoid the cubic formulation by replacing every test arc with a behaviorally equivalent pair of input/output arcs. Such a transformation is always sound, except when it is possible that some transition accesses a single token with two different test arcs—a presumably rare construct. However, there are two reasons for not dropping test arcs out of the formalism. First, if the arcs incident to place p are mostly test arcs (the number of test arcs is at least of the order $|out(p)|\,|in(p)|$), then the quadratic encoding size obtained by eliminating test arcs can be actually larger than the original cubic size. Second, input/output arc pairs can introduce unnecessary orderings of successive non-destructive read operations. Consider duplicating transition h in Fig. 1g. In a token trace, several copies of h can have their test arcs linked to the same output arcs without imposing an ordering of the copies. If input/output arcs are used instead as in Fig. 1c, any token trace necessarily fixes an ordering of the copies of h because successive copies have to be linked to each other. Thus, a single token trace represents a smaller set of interleavings if test arcs have been eliminated. Further experiments are needed to determine whether the smaller encoding size compensates for the potentially larger search space in satisfiability solving.

Apart from the inner parts of guards and arc expressions, our encodings are examples of *difference logic* formulas. General difference logic allows inequalities of the form $var_i < var_j + constant$, but here the constant term is always zero. Such inequalities offer us a very compact way to rule out all illegal cycles of the form $t_1 \prec t_2 \prec \cdots \prec t_n \prec t_1$. Many SMT solvers support difference logic natively, and often the solver implementation is indeed based on illegal cycle detection [13]. Another possibility is to encode the inequalities in propositional logic [21] and use a SAT solver. As the constant term is always zero in our formulas, the size increment using the encoding [21] is $O(|T|^3)$ instead of exponential as in the worst case. The report [8] shows how to further reduce the size by exploiting the absence of inequalities under negations.

5 Comparison to Related Work

A straightforward way to apply Bounded Model Checking [2] to an asynchronous system is to unroll its interleaving transition relation k times to cover all executions of k steps [16]. Consider a system that performs one of n possible atomic actions in each step. The BMC view of executions corresponds to Fig. 1b. The long horizontal lines represent the realizations of frame conditions, which are parts of the formula that say when a variable must maintain its value. Because of unrolling, the BMC formula describes kn potential events, and only k of them are scheduled to occur. Furthermore, the notion of fixed time points means that insignificant reorderings of independent events, e.g. changing the order of Fig. 1b into $g_1 \rightarrow g_2 \rightarrow f \rightarrow h$, result in completely different interpretations of the SAT formula, potentially encumbering the solver.

In contrast, the encoding of token traces contains no frame conditions for conveying data over time steps, and no time points between independent transitions. Instead, the inputs and outputs of transitions are directly linked to each other. The selection of links is nondeterministic, which incurs some encoding overhead, and there are the potentially costly constraints for ordering the transitions. Using kn potential events, we can cover executions up to length kn instead of k, but this depends on the unwinding.

There have been several proposals for making BMC better suited to asynchronous systems. Using alternative execution semantics [16,9], several independent actions can occur in a single step of BMC, allowing longer executions to be analyzed without considerably increasing the size of the encoding. In [22], partial order reductions are implemented on top of BMC by adding a constraint that each pair of independent actions can occur at consecutive time steps only in one predefined order. An opposite approach [14] is to start BMC with some particular interleaving and then allow more behavior by iteratively removing constraints. As Bounded Event Tracing is inherently a partial order method, there is no need for retrofitted reductions.

Ganai and Gupta present a concurrent BMC technique [12] based on a similar kind of intuition as this paper. Individual BMC unrolling is applied to each thread of a multithreaded program, and all globally visible operations are potentially linked pairwise, with constraints that prevent cyclic dependencies. Lockset analysis is proposed for reducing the number of potential links. In the encodings of single threads, various BMC techniques are needed to avoid blowup. Bounded Event Tracing uses places to localize the communication between concurrent components, but [12] does not support this. Instead, operations in different threads can be linked even if there is no causal relation between them, and every thread has a local copy of all global variables. A similar, globally quadratic encoding would result from an unwinding where global communication goes through a single place that holds a vector of all global variables, with incident input arcs for accessing the vector and output arcs for restoring the possibly modified vector.

The CBMC approach [6] unwinds (up to a bound) the loops of a sequential C program, converts it to static single assignment form, and encodes the constraints on the resulting set of variables. A version for threaded programs [20] is based on bounding also the number of context switches. Each global read operation is conditioned on the number of context switches that have occurred so far, with the help of explicit symbols in the encoding for representing the value of each global variable x after i context switches. This value is in turn conditioned on the location where x is assigned the last time before the ith context switch. The encoding is geared towards the possibility of finding a witness with a low number of context switches. As in [12], a context switch involves copying all global variables to another thread. In contrast, the read operations in Bounded Event Tracing are conditioned directly on where the latest write operation occurred, with no intermediate encoding symbols that keep the data values between writing and reading.

CheckFence [4] is also based on CBMC-like unwinding of individual C threads and additional constraints for modeling the communication between threads. Although CheckFence is designed to find bugs specifically under relaxed memory models, an encoding of the ordinary sequential memory model is used as a baseline. Unlike in [12,20], context switches are not made explicit in the encoding. Instead, there are symbols encoding the potential causal relations between individual read and write operations, much like the potential links in Bounded Event Tracing. A global memory order plays the same role as the chronological partial order in this paper. The proposed encoding (details in [3]) is cubic in size and is in many ways similar to what we would obtain by consistently using test arcs for read operations and input/output arcs for write operations as in Fig. 1g. The possibility of a quadratic-size encoding or the decoupling of producing and consuming values are not discussed in [4,3].

A completely different symbolic technique for concurrent systems is based on unfoldings [11], which are partial-order representations of state spaces as (infinite) low-level Petri nets of a fixed form. Model checking is performed by taking a suitable finite prefix of an unfolding and encoding its behavior and the desired property in SAT. As unfoldings are acyclic, the encoding is simple. Although an unfolding represents interleavings implicitly, every possible control path and every nondeterministic choice of data is explicitly present, and in practice, the generation of the unfolding prefix is the most expensive part. We could obtain unwindings directly from unfoldings, but this would mean to abandon symbolic data and arbitrary connections between places and transitions.

6 Unwindings of State Machine Models

As a proof of concept, we will sketch a simple mechanical unwinding scheme for a class of state machine models and use it in an experimental comparison to Bounded Model Checking. Our input is a subset of the DVE modeling language, which is used e.g. by the model checking benchmark set Beem [19].

A DVE system consists of fixed sets of communication channels and processes, and the behavior of a process is defined by control locations connected with edges (Fig. 2a). An action of a system is either (i) the simultaneous firing of two edges in different processes such that one edge is labeled with $ch!$ and the other with $ch?$, where ch is the name of a channel, or (ii) the firing of a τ-edge, i.e. one not labeled with a channel. Edges can additionally be labeled with guard expressions (in square brackets) and assignments to local or global variables. The treatment of other important system features, such as arrays and buffered channels, is left for future work.

The first step is to obtain a new *unwound system* that contains cycle-free copies of the original processes. For each process, we perform a depth-first search from the initial location to identify a set of *retreating edges* [1], i.e. those that complete a control flow cycle (e.g. all edges leaving location wa in Fig. 2a). For each location s, the corresponding unwound process has the distinct locations $s_0, s_1, \ldots, s_L$ until some loop

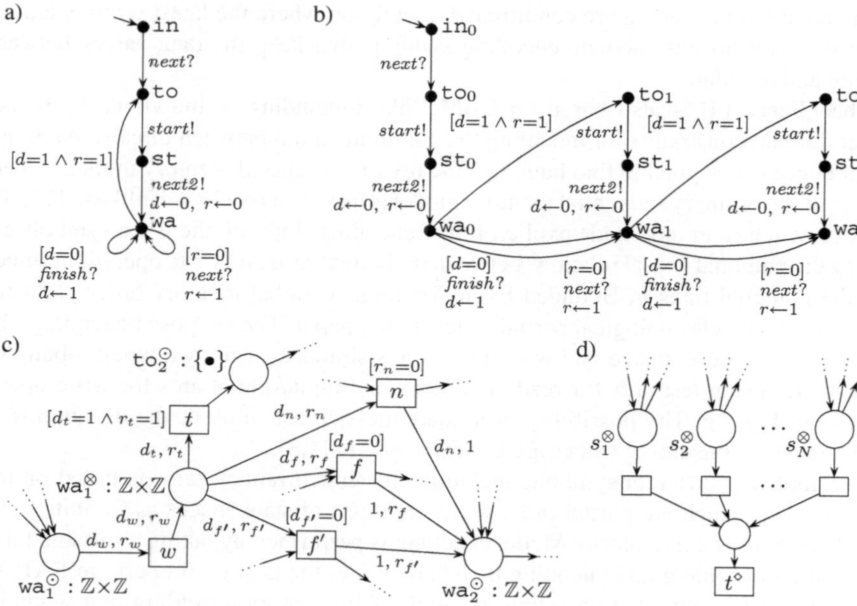

Fig. 2. Process `scheduler` and its unwinding

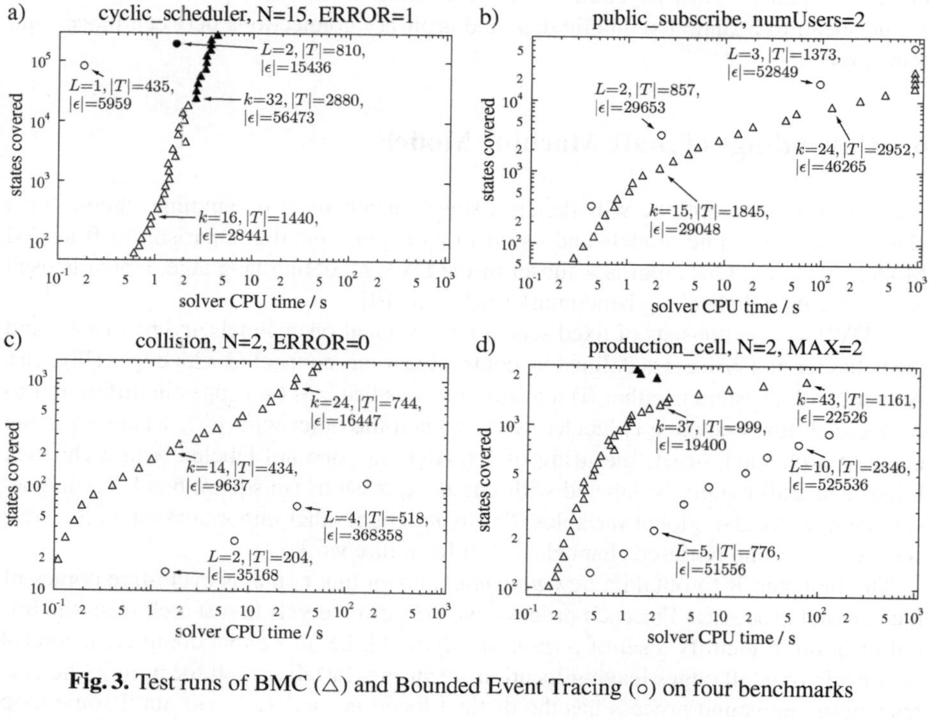

Fig. 3. Test runs of BMC (△) and Bounded Event Tracing (○) on four benchmarks

bound L. For each edge $s \rightarrow s'$, the unwound process has the edges $s_i \rightarrow s'_i$ for all i, or $s_i \rightarrow s'_{i+1}$ in the case of a retreating edge to guarantee acyclicity. Figure 2b illustrates the expansion. With these design choices, the unwound system behaves like the original one but the number of cycles executed in each process is bounded.

A Petri net unwinding (Fig. 2c) is then constructed from the unwound system by defining a pair of places $s^{\odot}, s^{\otimes}$ for each location s of each unwound process, and a transition for every possible action. The places contain the values of all local variables that are live (see [1]) in the corresponding location. For example, a token with value $(1, 0)$ in place $\mathtt{wa}_1^{\odot}$ or $\mathtt{wa}_1^{\otimes}$ in Fig. 2c means that the location $\mathtt{wa}_1$ is active with $d = 1$ and $r = 0$. A location s is always entered through $s^{\odot}$ and exited through $s^{\otimes}$, and we add a single trivial transition in the middle (transition w in Fig. 2c). This construct makes the encoding smaller by eliminating the quadratic number of potential links between the entering and exiting arcs. Transition t in the figure corresponds to the τ-edge from $\mathtt{wa}_1$ to $\mathtt{to}_2$. The edge labeled with *finish*? is modeled with several transitions (f and f' in Fig. 2c), one corresponding to each *finish*!-labeled edge elsewhere in the unwound system. These transitions thus also connect to places that belong to the other processes. In the resulting unwinding, two transitions associated with the same process either have a fixed mutual ordering, or they exclude one another. Global variables would be modeled as in Fig. 1g, using a single place for each variable. Assuming that the reachability property—like in many Beem benchmarks—is whether any location in some set $\{s_1, \ldots, s_N\}$ can become active, we add new places and transitions as in Fig. 2d and check whether $t^{\diamond}$ is a one-off reachable transition.

6.1 Experimental Evaluation

Bounded Event Tracing with the above unwinding scheme was applied to some of the Beem benchmarks [19] that fit in the described subset, possibly after minor modifications such as replacing arrays with multiple scalar variables or adding a reachability property. The same properties were also checked using Bounded Model Checking with a transition relation formula that follows the structure of the interleaving encoding in [9]. In both approaches, Yices 1.0.22 64-bit (`http://yices.csl.sri.com/`) was used for solving satisfiability modulo bit vectors and difference logic, running on one core of an Intel Xeon 5130 processor. The results for four benchmarks that exhibit typical behavior are plotted in Fig. 3. Each triangular marker corresponds to a BMC instance with bound k. Each circle marks a Bounded Event Tracing instance with loop bound L, using the same value of L for all processes for simplicity. Filled markers mean satisfiable cases, i.e. the discovery of a witness execution. The horizontal axes denote the (non-cumulative) median CPU time used by the solver over 11 runs. The range of fluctuation in CPU times was generally small compared to the difference between the methods; the exceptions are specified below. Some of the instances timed out at the limit of 900 seconds. The vertical axes show the number of states of the original system reachable within each unwinding or BMC bound. The states were counted by running an explicit-state model checker on an instrumented system. Selected instances are annotated with the bound k or L, the number of encoded potential events $|T|$, which in the case of BMC is k times the number of different actions the system can perform, and the circuit size $|\epsilon|$ of the formula given to the solver.

In Fig. 3a, an unwinding with loop bound 2 is sufficient for finding a witness of more than 30 steps, while using on average less CPU time (ranging from 1.0 to 4.9 seconds) and covering a larger number of states than the corresponding BMC instance. Figure 3b shows a benchmark where Bounded Event Tracing covers states faster than BMC, and the relative speed-up increases with the bound. In Figs. 3c and 3d, BMC is the faster method. In these cases, the number of transitions in the unwindings is much higher than the number of states reached, which indicates that the used unwinding scheme can result in the inclusion of many unnecessary transitions, mainly due to the design choices of a fixed system-wide loop bound L and quadratic-size modeling of channel synchronization. Furthermore, many of the resulting large number of transitions are connected to a common place that models a global variable, causing unwieldy growth in the formula size. Possibly because of this, there were also four individual Bounded Event Tracing runs of the production_cell benchmark that exceeded the median CPU time by a factor of more than 20.

The technical report [8] presents another set of experiments, in which Bounded Event Tracing with an alternative encoding is shown to outperform BMC on a family of models with very simple control flow but heavy dependence on a global variable.

7 Conclusions and Future Work

Bounded Event Tracing offers a new, well-defined framework for symbolically checking reachability properties of asynchronous systems. The analysis is bounded by a finite unwinding that fixes a collection of potential events that may occur but leaves the order of occurrences open. Unwindings are formalized as high-level Petri nets because the semantics of Petri nets rises naturally from the underlying concepts. The reachability problem is translated to a fragment of difference logic. The hard work is done by a SAT or SMT solver.

The technique incorporates ideas from Bounded Model Checking and unfoldings. Like in BMC, data handling is symbolic, but we avoid many pitfalls of BMC caused by viewing an execution of an asynchronous system as a sequence synchronized by fixed time steps. Like unfolding methods, Bounded Event Tracing has partial order reductions built in, but without the advance cost of explicit branching at every choice point.

Using a simple automated unwinding scheme, Bounded Event Tracing already performs better than interleaving BMC on a number of benchmark systems, but evident bottlenecks in the unwindings remain. In particular, the undirected expansion of unwindings easily becomes impractical when processes are tightly coupled with global variables. Interesting future research topics include better guidance of the expansion of unwindings e.g. using reachability information from smaller unwindings, integrating the expansion with incremental SAT solving [10], modeling interprocess communication more compactly, exploiting nested loops when unwinding control flow, modeling collections such as arrays or message queues using a place that contains a multiset of index-value pairs, and incorporating abstraction techniques [17] in some form to better cope with software features. The conjecture is that the construction of unwindings allows for much greater flexibility than, say, adjusting the bound or the transition relation formula in BMC, and that we can gain significant improvements in speed by using a sophisticated unwinding scheme.

Acknowledgements. The author gives many thanks to Tommi Junttila for discussions and inspiration.

References

1. Aho, A.V., Lam, M.S., Sethi, R., Ullman, J.D.: Compilers. Principles, Techniques, & Tools, 2nd edn. Addison-Wesley, Reading (2007)
2. Biere, A., Cimatti, A., Clarke, E.M., Zhu, Y.: Symbolic model checking without BDDs. In: Cleaveland, W.R. (ed.) TACAS 1999. LNCS, vol. 1579, pp. 193–207. Springer, Heidelberg (1999)
3. Burckhardt, S., Alur, R., Martin, M.M.K.: Bounded model checking of concurrent data types on relaxed memory models: a case study. In: Ball, T., Jones, R.B. (eds.) CAV 2006. LNCS, vol. 4144, pp. 489–502. Springer, Heidelberg (2006)
4. Burckhardt, S., Alur, R., Martin, M.M.K.: CheckFence: checking consistency of concurrent data types on relaxed memory models. In: PLDI 2007, pp. 12–21. ACM, New York (2007)
5. Christensen, S., Hansen, N.D.: Coloured Petri Nets extended with place capacities, test arcs and inhibitor arcs. In: Ajmone Marsan, M. (ed.) ICATPN 1993. LNCS, vol. 691, pp. 186–205. Springer, Heidelberg (1993)
6. Clarke, E.M., Kroening, D., Lerda, F.: A tool for checking ANSI-C programs. In: Jensen, K., Podelski, A. (eds.) TACAS 2004. LNCS, vol. 2988, pp. 168–176. Springer, Heidelberg (2004)
7. D'Silva, V., Kroening, D., Weissenbacher, G.: A survey of automated techniques for formal software verification. IEEE Trans. on Computer-Aided Design of Integrated Circuits and Systems 27(7), 1165–1178 (2008)
8. Dubrovin, J.: Checking bounded reachability in asynchronous systems by symbolic event tracing. Tech. Rep. TKK-ICS-R14, Helsinki University of Technology, Department of Information and Computer Science (2009)
9. Dubrovin, J., Junttila, T., Heljanko, K.: Symbolic step encodings for object based communicating state machines. In: Barthe, G., de Boer, F.S. (eds.) FMOODS 2008. LNCS, vol. 5051, pp. 96–112. Springer, Heidelberg (2008)
10. Eén, N., Sörensson, N.: Temporal induction by incremental SAT solving. Electronic Notes in Theoretical Computer Science 89(4) (2003)
11. Esparza, J., Heljanko, K.: Unfoldings — A Partial-Order Approach to Model Checking. Springer, Heidelberg (2008)
12. Ganai, M.K., Gupta, A.: Efficient modeling of concurrent systems in BMC. In: Havelund, K., Majumdar, R., Palsberg, J. (eds.) SPIN 2008. LNCS, vol. 5156, pp. 114–133. Springer, Heidelberg (2008)
13. Ganai, M.K., Talupur, M., Gupta, A.: SDSAT: Tight integration of small domain encoding and lazy approaches in solving difference logic. Journal on Satisfiability, Boolean Modeling and Computation 3(1-2), 91–114 (2007)
14. Grumberg, O., Lerda, F., Strichman, O., Theobald, M.: Proof-guided underapproximation-widening for multi-process systems. In: POPL 2005, pp. 122–131. ACM, New York (2005)
15. Jensen, K.: Coloured Petri Nets. Basic Concepts, Analysis Methods, and Practical Use, vol. 1. Springer, Heidelberg (1997)

16. Jussila, T., Heljanko, K., Niemelä, I.: BMC via on-the-fly determinization. Int. Journal on Software Tools for Technology Transfer 7(2), 89–101 (2005)
17. McMillan, K.L.: Lazy abstraction with interpolants. In: Ball, T., Jones, R.B. (eds.) CAV 2006. LNCS, vol. 4144, pp. 123–136. Springer, Heidelberg (2006)
18. de Moura, L.M., Dutertre, B., Shankar, N.: A tutorial on satisfiability modulo theories. In: Damm, W., Hermanns, H. (eds.) CAV 2007. LNCS, vol. 4590, pp. 20–36. Springer, Heidelberg (2007)
19. Pelánek, R.: BEEM: Benchmarks for explicit model checkers. In: Bošnački, D., Edelkamp, S. (eds.) SPIN 2007. LNCS, vol. 4595, pp. 263–267. Springer, Heidelberg (2007)
20. Rabinovitz, I., Grumberg, O.: Bounded model checking of concurrent programs. In: Etessami, K., Rajamani, S.K. (eds.) CAV 2005. LNCS, vol. 3576, pp. 82–97. Springer, Heidelberg (2005)
21. Strichman, O., Seshia, S.A., Bryant, R.E.: Deciding separation formulas with SAT. In: Brinksma, E., Larsen, K.G. (eds.) CAV 2002. LNCS, vol. 2404, pp. 209–222. Springer, Heidelberg (2002)
22. Wang, C., Yang, Z., Kahlon, V., Gupta, A.: Peephole partial order reduction. In: Ramakrishnan, C.R., Rehof, J. (eds.) TACAS 2008. LNCS, vol. 4963, pp. 382–396. Springer, Heidelberg (2008)

Invariant and Type Inference for Matrices*

Thomas A. Henzinger[1], Thibaud Hottelier[2], Laura Kovács[3], and Andrei Voronkov[4]

[1] IST Austria (Institute of Science and Technology Austria)
[2] UC Berkeley
[3] ETH Zürich
[4] University of Manchester

Abstract. We present a loop property generation method for loops iterating over multi-dimensional arrays. When used on matrices, our method is able to infer their shapes (also called types), such as upper-triangular, diagonal, etc. To generate loop properties, we first transform a nested loop iterating over a multi-dimensional array into an equivalent collection of unnested loops. Then, we infer quantified loop invariants for each unnested loop using a generalization of a recurrence-based invariant generation technique. These loop invariants give us conditions on matrices from which we can derive matrix types automatically using theorem provers. Invariant generation is implemented in the software package Aligator and types are derived by theorem provers and SMT solvers, including Vampire and Z3. When run on the Java matrix package JAMA, our tool was able to infer automatically all matrix types describing the matrix shapes guaranteed by JAMA's API.

1 Introduction

Static reasoning about unbounded data structures such as one- or multi-dimensional arrays is both interesting and hard [8,10,6,14,1,11,21,12,19,27]. Loop invariants over arrays can express relationships among array elements and properties involving array and scalar variables of the loop, and thus simplify program analysis and verification.

We present a method for an automatic inference of quantified invariants for loops iterating linearly over all elements of multi-dimensional (mD) arrays, demonstrated here for matrices. It is based on the following steps. First, we rewrite nested loops with conditional updates over matrices into equivalent collections of unnested loops over matrices without conditionals (Section 6). We call this step *loop synthesis*. In order to derive such a collection of loops automatically, we take into account each branch condition and construct a loop encoding this condition. This is done using symbolic summation together with constraint solving. After that, for each loop so derived we compute polynomial invariants using symbolic computation techniques, and then infer *quantified invariants over arrays* in the combined theory of scalars, arrays, and uninterpreted functions, by generalizing the recurrence-based invariant generation technique of [18] to mD arrays (Section 7). The conjunction of the generated quantified invariants can be used to find post-conditions of loops expressing properties of the matrices. From these post-conditions we can derive, using a theorem prover, shape properties

* The results presented here were obtained while the first three authors were at EPFL, Switzerland. The research was supported by the Swiss NSF.

G. Barthe and M. Hermenegildo (Eds.): VMCAI 2010, LNCS 5944, pp. 163–179, 2010.

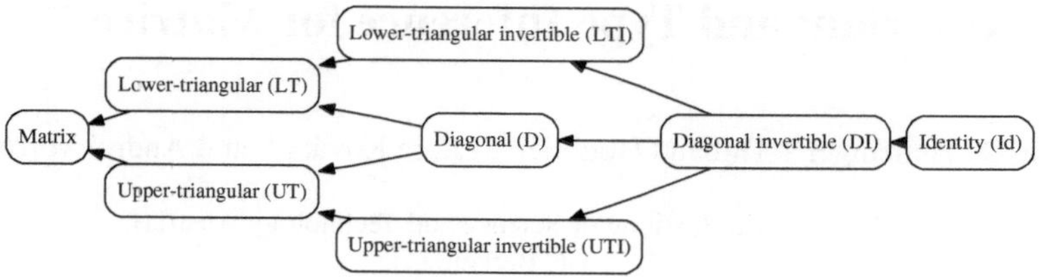

Fig. 1. Matrix type system. The arrows represent the subtyping relation.

of matrices, such as upper/lower-triangular matrices, identity matrices etc. (Section 9). We call these properties *matrix types* as they characterize particular types of matrices (Section 3).

Our method for invariant generation and deriving loop properties is sound. It is complete for generating invariants over scalars for a certain class of programs in which all branch conditions in loops are linear. In practice, all matrix loops in the Java matrix package JAMA [13] turned out to have linear branch conditions.

We implemented our approach to invariant generation in the Aligator software package [17] (Section 8). We have shown that the generated proof obligations can be proved automatically by modern theorem provers and SMT solvers. When run on the JAMA package, our technique is able to infer matrix properties which imply all matrix shapes guaranteed by JAMA's API and prove the implication automatically using theorem provers. We successfully ran our system on over 3,000 lines of JAMA code.

We are not aware of any other automated method that can automatically infer quantified properties for programs over mD (or even 2D) arrays without user guidance, such as providing templates, assertions or predicates. The novel features presented in this paper are as follows.

- The basis of our method is a new technique for transforming nested loops iterating over matrices into equivalent collections of unnested loops. This technique uses symbolic summation and constraint solving and improves our previous method [18] of invariant generation over scalars, which could only handle unnested loops over scalars. This technique is general and not specifically intended for programs handling matrices.
- We are able to generate invariants for programs over mD arrays such as matrices. We show that the generated invariants are strong enough to derive matrix types. We do not need a theorem prover as in [19] to generate these invariants.
- We require no user guidance, such as predefined predicates, templates, or annotations to automatically derive quantified loop properties for the class of loops we study.
- We show that the generated matrix properties are strong enough to prove that matrices have corresponding shapes completely automatically, by using SMT solvers or first-order theorem provers with suitably axiomatised subsets of arithmetic.

The long term goal of our work is to verify various properties of domain-specific packages, such as Mathematica [30], Matlab[4], or Mathcad [2], having explicit matrix types.

2 Related Work

Paper [6] addresses the problem of automatically inferring auxiliary annotations such as *invariants and post-conditions* for safety property verification of programs over *mD arrays*. The method relies on using code patterns for describing code constructs that require annotations, and templates to describe the annotations that are required by code patterns. For each program code and safety property some user-guidance is thus needed to identify the relevant code and template patterns. Annotation templates are then embedded in the code, resulting in the automatic generation of program annotations.

Our approach can also be compared to *quantified invariant generation* methods *over 1D arrays*, such as [8,14,1,11,21,27]. The methods used in the cited works combine inductive reasoning with predicate abstraction, constraint solving, and interpolation-based techniques, and require user guidance in providing necessary templates, assertions, or predicates. The various approaches differ in the extent of their required user guidance: papers [8,11,27] infer invariants by iteratively approximating the strongest boolean combination of a given set of predicates, whereas [14,1,21] search for appropriate invariant predicates using a given set of templates that define the boolean structure of the desired invariants.

Compared to the above mentioned work, our approach does not require a priori fixed templates and predicates. We derive quantified invariants directly from the loop description. Our technique allows one to generate properties of mD-arrays programs, which only the authors of [6] have done so far.

Papers [10,12] do not require user guidance and derive quantified array invariants by using abstract interpretation and partitioning array indexes into symbolic intervals. Our approach handles a richer subset of arithmetic over scalar variables and works for mD arrays.

In our previous paper [19] we derive quantified invariants by combining symbolic computation and first-order theorem proving. The approach requires no user guidance and allows one to infer quantified invariants with alternating quantifiers. In this paper we do not use theorem proving and cannot derive properties requiring quantifier alternations. It would be interesting to integrate the method of [19] into ours, in order to find more complex quantified invariants and properties, such as sortedness and permutation properties of arrays or matrices.

Since one ingredient of our method is numeric invariant generation, we also compare it with other *polynomial invariant generation* techniques [22,25,24]. Papers [22,25] compute polynomial equalities of fixed degree as invariants using the polynomial ideal theory. Unlike [22,25], our method does not impose bounds on polynomials: we derive polynomial invariants of an arbitrary degree from which any other polynomial invariant can be inferred. Our algorithm thus returns a finite representation of the polynomial invariant ideal, whereas [22,25] may only iteratively increase the polynomial degree to infer such a basis. Paper [24] derives polynomial invariants for loops with positive rational eigenvalues, by iteratively approximating the polynomial invariant ideal using Gröbner basis computation [3]. In contrast to [24], our approach generates polynomial invariants over scalars for polynomial loops with algebraic, and not just rational, eigenvalues.

3 Matrix Types

Figure 1 describes the matrix properties that we can infer for loops iterating over an $n \times n$ square matrix A. These properties are expressed by first-order formulas. We will refer to these properties and the formulas expressing them as *matrix types*. We only give the types for the lower-triangular (LT), lower-triangular invertible (LTI), diagonal (D), diagonal invertible (DI) and identity (Id) matrices, leaving the upper-triangular (UT) and upper-triangular invertible (UTI) types to the reader.

LT: $\forall i, j.\ 1 \le i < j \le n \Rightarrow A[i, j] = 0$
LTI: $\forall i, j.\ 1 \le i \le j \le n \Rightarrow (i < j \Rightarrow A[i, j] = 0) \wedge (i = j \Rightarrow A[i, j] \neq 0)$
D: $\forall i, j.\ 1 \le i, j \le n \Rightarrow (i \neq j \Rightarrow A[i, j] = 0)$
DI: $\forall i, j.\ 1 \le i, j \le n \Rightarrow (i \neq j \Rightarrow A[i, j] = 0) \wedge (i = j \Rightarrow A[i, j] \neq 0)$
Id: $\forall i, j.\ 1 \le i, j \le n \Rightarrow (i \neq j \Rightarrow A[i, j] = 0) \wedge (i = j \Rightarrow A[i, j] = 1)$

For checking invertibility, we use the fact that triangular and diagonal matrices are invertible if and only if every element on the main diagonal is non-zero.

To check whether a matrix is of a given type, we first infer quantified loop properties for a loop iterating over the matrix, as described in Sections 6 and 7, and then prove that the inferred properties imply the matrix type (Section 9).

4 Motivating Example

We give an example illustrating for what kind of loop we would like to infer quantified properties sufficient to derive matrix types.

Consider the program of Figure 2. This program is taken from the JAMA library [13]. We will use this example as our running example throughout the paper. The program computes the lower unit triangular part of an $n \times n$ square matrix LU [9]. This means that the resulting matrix L has only 0s above the main diagonal, only 1s on the main diagonal, and all entries of L below the main diagonal are equal to the corresponding entries of the matrix LU. We need invariants for this program that would help us to prove matrix types of L by using quantifiers over the matrix indexes. The difficulties for automatically finding such loop invariants come from the presence of nested loops, the use of scalar and matrix variables, and the nested conditional used in the loop. We overcome these difficulties as follows.

1. We rewrite the nested loop with conditional updates over L and LU into an equivalent, in some sense, collection of unnested loops without conditionals over matrices L and LU as shown in Figure 3. In this figure the constant c ranges over

```
for (i:=1; i ≤ n; i++) do
  for (j:=1; j ≤ n; j++) do
    if (i > j)
      then L[i,j]:=LU[i,j];
      else if (i = j)
        then L[i,j]:=1;
        else L[i,j]:=0;
  end do
end do
```

Fig. 2. Lower unit triangular part computation [12]

```
% Guard: i > j              % Guard: i = j              % Guard: i < j
i := c; j := 0;             i := 0; j := 0;             i := 0; j := c;
while (j < n) do            while (j < n) do            while (i < n) do
  i := i + 1; j := j+1;       i := i + 1; j := j+1;       i := i + 1; j := j+1;
  L[i,j] := LU[i,j]           L[i,j] := 1                 L[i,j] := 0
end do                      end do                      end do
```

Here c ranges over $\{1, \ldots, n-1\}$

Fig. 3. Loop sequence for Fig.2

$\{1, \ldots, n-1\}$ and appears from the fact that $i > j \iff \exists c(c > 0 \wedge i = c + j)$ (respectively, $i < j \iff \exists c(c > 0 \wedge j = c + i)$), see Section 6 for details.

2. We infer scalar invariants and quantified array invariants for each unnested loop using symbolic computation methods. The conjunction of the inferred quantified invariants of the unnested loops expresses matrix loop properties as postconditions of the nested loop with conditionals.

The matrix loop property derived for the loop of Figure 2 is given below.

$$\bigwedge \begin{cases} \forall i, j.\, 1 \leq i, j \leq n \Rightarrow (\, \forall c.\, c > 0 \;\wedge\; i = j + c \Rightarrow \\ \quad (\forall k.\, 1 \leq k \leq j \Rightarrow L[k+c, k] = LU[k+c, k]) \,) \\ \forall i, j.\, 1 \leq i, j \leq n \Rightarrow (\forall k.\, 1 \leq k \leq j \Rightarrow L[k, k] = 1) \\ \forall i, j.\, 1 \leq i, j \leq n \Rightarrow (\, \forall c.\, c > 0 \;\wedge\; j = i + c \Rightarrow \\ \quad (\forall k.\, 1 \leq k \leq i \Rightarrow L[k, k+c] = 0) \,) \end{cases} \tag{1}$$

Here the first quantified conjunct expresses that the lower part of L is updated by elements of LU; the second conjunct describes that the elements of L from its main diagonal are 1s; and the third conjunct expresses that the elements of L above its main diagonal are 0s. The LTI-type of L can be proved from this inferred property.

Note that executing the loops of Figure 3 might access matrix elements which are actually out of the bounds of the $n \times n$ matrices L and LU (for example, when $c = n-1$, $i = n$, $j = n$). However, Figure 3 will never be executed in our work. In our approach, the unnested loops of Figure 3 are "only" used to generate invariant properties. These invariants, together with the property capturing the relation between the constant c and the matrix bounds i and j, are then further used to derive matrix loop properties of Figure 2. Access to matrix elements in the loop properties used for proving matrix types are thus between valid matrix bounds.

In this paper we derive two kinds of loop properties. One kind expresses conditions on scalar and mD-array variables used in the loop. These conditions are loop invariants, and we refer to them as, respectively, *scalar and quantified array invariants*. Another kind of property is a quantified condition on the values of the arrays at the loop exit, cf. formula (1). This condition is a *valid postcondition* of the loop, however, it is not a loop invariant. In the rest of the paper we will make a distinction between invariants and valid postconditions and refer to the latter as (quantified) *loop properties*, (quantified) *matrix loop properties*, or *matrix properties*.

The rest of the paper discusses in detail how we automatically infer scalar invariants, array invariants and matrix properties, and prove matrix types from these matrix properties.

5 Programming Model

This section fixes the relevant notation and introduces our model of programs.

Algebraic notation. Let $\mathbb{N}$ and $\mathbb{Z}$ denote respectively the sets of natural and integer numbers, and $\mathbb{Z}[x]$ denote the ring of polynomial relations in indeterminate x over $\mathbb{Z}$.

Variables. We assume that programs contain *scalar variables* denoted by lower-case letters $a, b, c, \ldots$ and *matrix variables* denoted by capital-case letters $A, B, C, \ldots$. All notations may have indices. W.l.o.g. we assume that matrices are square and reserve the lower-case letter n for their dimension.

Expressions and their semantics. We assume that expressions contain integer constants, variables over scalars and matrices, logical variables, and some function and predicate symbols. We only consider the arithmetical function symbols $+$, $-$, and $\cdot$ as interpreted, all other function symbols are uninterpreted. Similarly, only the arithmetical predicate symbols $=$, $\neq$, $\leq$, $\geq$, $<$ and $>$ are interpreted, all other predicate symbols are treated as uninterpreted.

Programs and their semantics. We consider programs of the following form, iterating over matrices.

$$\begin{array}{l} \underline{\textbf{for}}\ (i := l_i;\ i \leq n;\ i := i + u_i)\underline{\textbf{do}} \\ \quad \underline{\textbf{for}}\ (j := l_j;\ j \leq n;\ j := j + u_j)\underline{\textbf{do}} \\ \quad\quad \ldots \text{ loop body } \ldots \\ \quad \underline{\textbf{end do}} \\ \underline{\textbf{end do}} \end{array} \tag{2}$$

with $l_i, l_j, u_i, u_j \in \mathbb{Z}$, and the loop body consists of (nested) conditionals, sequencing, and assignments over scalar and matrix variables satisfying some properties formulated below in this section. For the moment, we restrict ourselves to the case when $l_i = l_j = u_i = u_j = 1$. Such programs contain a nested for-loop iterating linearly (row-by-row or column-by-column) over the matrix content by incrementing or decrementing the matrix row and column indices. Let $\mathcal{P}$ be such a program. In the sequel we assume that $\mathcal{P}$ is fixed and present our approach relative to it.

We denote respectively by *Var* and *Matr* the sets of scalar and matrix variables of $\mathcal{P}$, where $Matr = RMatr \cup WMatr$ is a disjoint union of the sets *RMatr* of *read-only* and *WMatr* of *write-only* matrix variables. Throughout this paper, we assume that $i, j \in Var$ are the loop iteration/index variables of (2). As usual, the expression $A[k, l]$ is used to denote the element of an array A at the row k and column l.

Guarded assignments. Since the loop body of (2) is loop-free, we can equivalently consider it as the collection of all its paths. Every path can be written as a guarded *guarded assignments* [7] of the form

$$G \to \alpha_1; \ldots; \alpha_s, \tag{3}$$

where G is a formula, called the *guard* of this guarded assignments, and each of the α_k's is an assignment over $Var \cup Matr$. To turn a path into a guarded assignment, we collect all the tests satisfied on the path in the guard and write all assignments on the right of $\to$ keeping their relative order. This gives us an equivalent representation of the innermost loop body of $\mathcal{P}$ as a collection of guarded assignments of the form given below.

$$\begin{array}{rcl} G_1 & \to & \alpha_{11}; \ldots; \alpha_{1s_1}, \\ & \ldots & \\ G_d & \to & \alpha_{d1}; \ldots; \alpha_{ds_d}. \end{array} \tag{4}$$

Since each guard corresponds to a different path, in every state *exactly one guard holds.* That is, the formula $G_k \wedge G_l$ is unsatisfiable for $k \neq l$ and the formula $G_1 \vee \cdots \vee G_d$ is true in all states.

Conditions on loop bodies. After we rewrite loop bodies as collections of guarded assignments as given above, we require the following conditions to hold:

1. Each guard G_k is equivalent to an integer polynomial relation of the form

$$i \mathcal{R} P(j) \quad \text{or} \quad j \mathcal{R} Q(i), \tag{5}$$

where $\mathcal{R} \in \{=, \neq, <, >, \leq, \geq\}$, $P \in \mathbb{Z}[j]$ with $1 \leq \text{degree}(P) \leq 2$, and $Q \in \mathbb{Z}[i]$ with $1 \leq \text{degree}(Q) \leq 2$.
2. If some α_{ku} updates a matrix variable $A_u \in \mathit{WMatr}$, and some α_{kv} for $u \neq v$ in the *same guarded assignment* updates a matrix variable $A_v \in \mathit{WMatr}$, then A_u and A_v are different matrices.
3. The assignments α_{ku}'s have one of the forms given below.
   (a) Matrix assignments:

$$A[i, j] \; := \; f(\mathit{Var} \cup \mathit{RMatr}), \tag{6}$$

   where $A \in \mathit{WMatr}$ and $f(\mathit{Var} \cup \mathit{RMatr})$ is an arbitrary expression over the variables $\mathit{Var} \cup \mathit{RMatr}$. That is, this expression may contain arbitrary interpreted or uninterpreted functions but does not contain write-arrays.
   (b) Scalar assignments over $x_l \in \mathit{Var}$:

$$x_l := c_0 + c_l \cdot x_l + \sum_{\sigma \in M(\mathit{Var} \setminus \{x_l\})} c_\sigma \cdot \sigma, \tag{7}$$

   where
   - $c_0, c_l, c_\sigma \in \mathbb{Z}$ and $c_l \neq 0$;
   - $c_l \neq 1$ or $c_0 \neq 0$ or $c_\sigma \neq 0$ for some σ.
   - $M(\{x_1, \ldots, x_k\}) = \{x_1^{r_1} \cdots x_k^{r_k} \mid 1 \leq r_1 + \cdots + r_k \leq 2, r_1, \ldots, r_k \in \{0, 1\}\}$ is a subset of monomials over $\{x_1, \ldots, x_k\} \subseteq \mathit{Var}$.

The program of Figure 2 trivially satisfies conditions 2 and 3. Its transformation to guarded assignments does not immediately satisfy condition 1, despite that all tests in the program are of the required form $i \mathcal{R} P(j)$. The problem is that having more than one if-then-else expression results in guards that are *conjunctions* of formulas $i \mathcal{R} P(j)$, while property 1 requires to have a single formula instead of a conjunction.

Example 1. The loop body of the program of Figure 2 gives rise to the collection of guarded assignments shown below on the left. On the right we give its equivalent representation in which the guards satisfy condition 1.

$i > j \rightarrow L[i, j] := LU[i, j]$	$i > j \rightarrow L[i, j] := LU[i, j]$
$\neg(i > j) \wedge i = j \rightarrow L[i, j] := 1$	$i = j \rightarrow L[i, j] := 1$
$\neg(i > j) \wedge i < j \rightarrow L[i, j] := 0$	$i < j \rightarrow L[i, j] := 0$

The matrix L is conditionally updated at different positions (i, j). Updates over L involve initializations by 0 or 1, and copying from LU.

It is worth mentioning that our experiments over the JAMA library show that (i) in matrix programs nonlinear polynomial expressions over scalars are relatively rare and are of degree at most 2; (ii) polynomial tests on matrix indices are usually linear or otherwise of degree 2; (iii) the operations used for constructing matrices of specific shapes only involve initialization or copying from another matrix. Therefore, we believe that the restrictions on (5)-(7) cover a significant part of practical applications. It is also worth noting that properties 2 and 3a can be easily generalised so that our method still works: we only need to guarantee that matrices are never updated twice at the same positions.

One can relax and/or modify some of the conditions on the loops formulated here, however, the page limit prevents us from discussing possible modifications.

6 Loop Synthesis

Our aim is to find an explicit representation of the loop scalar variables in terms of the loop counters i and j. Conditions in if-then-else expressions are a main obstacle for doing that. In order to solve the problem, we transform $\mathcal{P}$ into an equivalent, in some sense, collection of unnested while-loops without conditionals, so that each unnested loop encodes the behavior of one conditional branch of $\mathcal{P}$. The unnested loops will be parametrised by new constants, similar to the constant c in Section 4, so that every suitable value of these constants, gives a separate unnested loop.

The transformation is performed separately for each guarded assignment $G \rightarrow \alpha_1; \ldots; \alpha_s$ from (4) and described below.

The general shape of the desired loop is

$$\underline{\textbf{while}}\ (index_{i,j} < n)\ \underline{\textbf{do}}\ \beta_i; \beta_j; \alpha_1; \ldots; \alpha_s\ \underline{\textbf{end do}},$$

where β_i and β_j are respectively the assignments to be constructed for i and j, and $index_{i,j}$ is either i or j.

To infer such a loop automatically, a case analysis on the shape of G is performed, as given below. We only present the case when G is $i\ \mathcal{R}\ P(j)$. In what follows, we denote by m the iteration counter of the loop being constructed. For a variable x, we denote by $x^{(m)}$ the value of x at the iteration m, whereas $x^{(0)}$ will stand for the initial value of x (i.e. its value before entering the loop). Note that $1 \leq i^{(m)}, j^{(m)} \leq n$.

Case 1: G is $i = P(j)$. While-loop condition. The guard G describes the values of i as polynomial expressions of degree at most 2 in j, and leaves j as an "independent" variable. For this reason, we take $index_{i,j} = j$ and construct a while-loop iterating over values i and j such that at each loop iteration G is a valid polynomial relation (i.e. loop invariant) among i and j.

While-loop body. The scalar assignments to i and j of the while-loop being constructed should satisfy the structural constraints of (7). For inferring these assignments, we use symbolic summation and constraint solving as described below.

As the while-loop condition depends on the values of $index_{i,j} = j$, we identify j to be in a linear correspondence with m. The generic assignments for i and j are built as given in (7), and the coefficients c_0, c_l and c_σ are treated as unknowns. As G involves only the variables i and j, the assignments of i and j need to be constructed only over i and j. We thus have

$$i := c_4 \cdot i + c_3 \cdot j + c_2;\ j := c_1 \cdot j + c_0,$$

where $(c_1 \neq 0) \wedge (c_1 \neq 1 \vee c_0 \neq 0) \wedge (c_4 \neq 0) \wedge (c_4 \neq 1 \vee c_3 \neq 0 \vee c_2 \neq 0)$.

Moreover, as G is a polynomial expression in i and j, the multiplicative coefficients c_4 and c_1 of i and j can be considered w.l.o.g. to be 1. We then have

$$i := i + c_3 \cdot j + c_2;\ j := j + c_0, \text{ with} \tag{8}$$

$$c_0 \neq 0 \wedge (c_3 \neq 0 \vee c_2 \neq 0). \tag{9}$$

From (8), we next derive the *system of recurrences* of i and j over m:

$$\begin{cases} i^{(m+1)} = i^{(m)} + c_3 \cdot j^{(m)} + c_2 \\ j^{(m+1)} = j^{(m)} + c_0 \end{cases}$$

Further, we compute the generic closed forms $i^{(m)}$ and $j^{(m)}$ as polynomial functions of m, $i^{(0)}$, and $j^{(0)}$, by symbolic summation and computer algebra techniques as discussed in [18]. We hence obtain:

$$\begin{cases} i^{(m)} = i^{(0)} + (c_2 + c_3 \cdot j^{(0)}) \cdot m + \frac{c_0 \cdot c_3}{2} \cdot m \cdot (m-1) \\ j^{(m)} = j^{(0)} + c_0 \cdot m \end{cases} \tag{10}$$

Next, closed forms $i^{(m)}$ and $j^{(m)}$ from (10) are substituted for variables i and j in G, and a polynomial relation in the indeterminate m is derived, as given below:

$$\sum_{k=0}^{2} q_k \cdot m^k = 0, \tag{11}$$

where the coefficients $q_k \in \mathbb{Z}$ are expressions over c_0, c_2, c_3, $i^{(0)}$, and $j^{(0)}$. Using properties of null-polynomials, we conclude that each q_k must equal to 0, obtaining a system of polynomial equations on c_0, c_2, c_3, $i^{(0)}$, and $j^{(0)}$. Such a system can be algorithmically solved by linear algebra or polynomial ideal theory [3], as discussed below.

Linear algebra methods (e.g. Gaussian elimination) offer an algorithmic way to derive integer solutions to a system of linear equations over integers. When G is *linear*, equations (9) and (11) yield a linear [1] constraint system over $c_0, c_2, c_3, i^{(0)}, j^{(0)}$. Hence, a finite representation of the sets of integers solutions for $c_0, c_2, c_3, i^{(0)}, j^{(0)}$ can be always constructed explicitly[2]. The loop assignments over i and j, such that the ideal of all polynomial invariant relations among i and j is generated by G, are thus always derived. Our loop synthesis method is hence complete in transforming nested loops over matrices with linear guards (e.g. JAMA benchmarks) into an equivalent collection of unnested loops.

When G is a *non-linear polynomial* relation (i.e. of degree 2), (11) yields a system of non-linear polynomial equations. Solving this system is done using Gröbner basis computation, which however may yield non-integer (and not even rational) solutions for $c_0, c_2, c_3, i^{(0)}, j^{(0)}$. In such cases, as matrix indices need to be integer valued, our method fails constructing unnested loops over matrix and scalar variables. It is worth to be mentioned though that for all examples we have tried (see Section 8), integer solutions for $c_0, c_2, c_3, i^{(0)}, j^{(0)}$ have successfully been inferred.

Example 2. Consider the condition $i = j$ from Figure 2. The condition of the while-loop being constructed is $j < n$. Substituting generic closed forms (10) into $i = j$, we derive the polynomial relation

$$2 \cdot (i^{(0)} - j^{(0)}) + (2 \cdot c_2 - 2 \cdot c_0 - c_0 \cdot c_3 + 2 \cdot c_3 \cdot j^{(0)}) \cdot m + c_0 \cdot c_3 \cdot m^2 = 0$$

[1] Linearity of G, together with (9) and (11), implies $c_0 \neq 0$, $c_3 = 0$ and $c_2 \neq 0$.

[2] In our work, we take the smallest integer solution for $c_0, c_2, c_3, i^{(0)}, j^{(0)}$.

Table 1. Experimental results using Aligator on JAMA programs

Program	Branch ♯	$[d, \mathcal{R}]$	Time (s)	Matrix Types
LU decomposition.getL	3	$[1,>], [1,=], [1,<]$	0.52	LT, LTI
LU decomposition.getU	2	$[1,\leq], [1,>]$	0.37	UT
QR decomposition.getR	3	$[1,<], [1,=], [1,>]$	0.57	UT, UTI
QR decomposition.getH	2	$[1,\geq], [1,<]$	0.37	LT
Matrix.identity	2	$[1,=], [1,\neq]$	0.32	LT, UT, LTI, UTI, D, DI, Id

The coefficients of m now must equal to 0. This gives us the system

$$\begin{cases} i^{(0)} - j^{(0)} & = 0 \\ 2 \cdot c_2 - 2 \cdot c_0 - c_0 \cdot c_3 + 2 \cdot c_3 \cdot j^{(0)} & = 0 \\ c_0 \cdot c_3 & = 0 \end{cases}$$

Solving this system of equations and considering also constraints (9), we obtain $c_2 = c_0$, $i^{(0)} = j^{(0)}$, and $c_3 = 0$. We conclude that $c_2 = c_0 = 1$, $c_3 = 0$, and $i^{(0)} = j^{(0)} = 0$ are (up to constant multipliers) the desired solutions, yielding the loop assignments $i := i + 1; j := j + 1$, with the initial value assignments $i := 0; j := 0$.

The while-loop corresponding to the condition $i = j$ is given in Figure 3.

Case 2: G is $i\ \mathcal{R}\ P(j)$, where $\mathcal{R} \in \{<, >, \leq, \geq, \neq\}$. We only present the case when $\mathcal{R}$ is $>$, all other cases are handled in a similar manner.

Since G is $i > P(j)$, G is equivalent to the existentially quantified formula

$$\exists c \in \mathbb{N}.\ (c > 0\ \wedge\ i = P(j) + c).$$

Thus, we apply the approach discussed in Case 1 for deriving a while-loop *parameterized by c*, yielding $i = P(j) + c$ as one of its invariants.

Example 3. Consider the condition $i > j$ from Figure 2. Introducing an integer skolem constant $c > 0$, we first rewrite this condition into $i = j + c$. The condition of the while-loop being constructed is then $j < n$.

Substituting generic closed forms (10) into $i = j + c$, we derive

$$2 \cdot (i^{(0)} - j^{(0)} - c) + (2 \cdot c_2 - 2 \cdot c_0 - c_0 \cdot c_3 + 2 \cdot c_3 \cdot j^{(0)}) \cdot m + c_0 \cdot c_3 \cdot m^2 = 0$$

The coefficients of m must equal to 0. Considering also constraints (9), we obtain a linear constraint system over c_0, c_2, c_3, $i^{(0)}$, and $j^{(0)}$, yielding $c_2 = c_0$, $i^{(0)} = j^{(0)} + c$ and $c_3 = 0$. We conclude that $c_2 = c_0 = 1$, $c_3 = 0$, $i^{(0)} = c$, and $j^{(0)} = 0$, yielding the loop assignments $i := i + 1; j := j + 1$, with the initial values given by $i := c; j := 0$.

The while-loop corresponding to the condition $i > j$ (respectively, $i < j$) is given in Figure 3.

Example 4. To illustrate the power of our synthesis method, consider the property $i = j^2$. We want to infer a loop yielding the invariant $i = j^2$. Applying our approach, the condition of the while-loop being constructed is $j < n$. The polynomial equation derived after substituting generic closed forms (10) into $i = j^2$ is

$$2 \cdot (i^{(0)} - {j^{(0)}}^2) + (2 \cdot c_2 - c_0 \cdot c_3 - 4 \cdot c_0 \cdot j^{(0)} + 2 \cdot c_3 \cdot j^{(0)}) \cdot m + (c_0 \cdot c_3 - c_0^2) \cdot m^2 = 0$$

We next solve the system of equations obtained by making the coefficients of m of the above polynomial equal to 0. Together with (9), we get $4 \cdot c_2 = c_3^2$, $i^{(0)} = {j^{(0)}}^2$, and

$2 \cdot c_0 = c_3$. We conclude that $c_0 = 1$, $c_2 = 1$, $c_3 = 2$, and $i^{(0)} = j^{(0)} = 0$, yielding the loop assignments $i := i + 2 \cdot j + 1; j := j + 1$, with the initial value assignments $i := 0; j := 0$.

7 Generation of Loop Invariants and Properties

For each while-loop derived in Section 6, loop invariants and properties are inferred in the combined theory of scalars, arrays, and uninterpreted function symbols, by generalizing the technique described in [18] to arrays. To this end, we first compute numeric invariants over scalars and then use them to generate quantified array invariants. The conjunction of these invariants is an invariant of the while-loop. Finally, the conjunction of the inferred quantified array invariants of the while-loops expresses matrix loop properties as postconditions of the nested loop $\mathcal{P}$ with conditionals.

Invariant generation over scalars. We infer scalar (numeric) invariants by combining symbolic summation and computer algebra, as described in [18]. Namely, (i) we build recurrence equations for scalars over the loop iteration counter m, (2) compute closed forms of scalars as functions of m, and (3) eliminate variables in m from the system of closed forms. The generators of the polynomial invariant ideal of the loop are thus inferred.

Example 5. The closed form system of the second inner loop from Figure 3 is

$$\begin{cases} i^{(m)} &= i^{(0)} + m \\ j^{(m)} &= j^{(0)} + m \end{cases}$$

After eliminating m, and substituting the initial values $i^{(0)} = j^{(0)} = 0$, the derived polynomial invariant is $i = j$. Proceeding in a similar manner, we obtain the scalar invariant $i = j + c$ for the first loop of Figure 3, whereas the third loop of Figure 3 yields the scalar invariant $j = i + c$.

Invariant generation over mD arrays. We generalize the method described in [18] to infer quantified array invariants. Recall that we only handle array assignments of the form (6) with $A \in \mathit{WMatr}$. For inferring universally quantified array invariants over the content of A, we make use of the already computed closed forms of scalars. The closed forms of the matrix indices i and j describe the positions at which A is updated as functions of m. We note that array updates are performed by iterating over the array positions, where the update expressions involve only scalars, read-only array variables, and interpreted and uninterpreted function symbols. Thus the closed form of an array element is given by substituting the closed form solutions for each scalar variable in (6), and is expressed as a function of m as follows:

$$A[i^{(m)}, j^{(m)}] = f(\mathit{Var}^{(m)} \cup \mathit{RMatr}), \tag{12}$$

where $\mathit{Var}^{(m)} = \{x^{(m)} | x \in \mathit{Var}\}$.

Further, we rely on the following fact. For all loop iterations up to the current one given by m, the array update positions and array update expressions can be expressed as functions of m. As m is a new variable not appearing elsewhere in the loop, we treat it symbolically, noting that every possible value of m corresponds to a single loop

Table 2. Other loop properties inferred by Aligator on JAMA programs

Program	Time (s)
Matrix.copy	< 0.1
Matrix.getMatrix	< 0.1
Matrix.constructWithCopy	< 0.1
Matrix.arrayLeftDivide	< 0.1
Matrix.arrayRightDivide	< 0.1
Matrix.times	< 0.1
Matrix.arrayTimes	< 0.1
Matrix.plus	< 0.1
Matrix.minus	< 0.1

Program	Time (s)
Matrix.getArrayCopy	< 0.1
Matrix.setMatrix	< 0.1
Matrix.uminus	< 0.1
Matrix.arrayLeftDivideEquals	< 0.1
Matrix.arrayRightDivideEquals	< 0.1
Matrix.timesEquals	< 0.1
Matrix.arrayTimesEquals	< 0.1
Matrix.plusEquals	< 0.1
Matrix.minusEquals	< 0.1

iteration. Therefore we can strengthen (12) to the formula universally quantified over loop iterations up to m as follows:

$$\forall k.\ 1 \leq k \leq m \Rightarrow A[i^{(k)}, j^{(k)}] = f(Var^{(k)} \cup RMatr). \tag{13}$$

We finally rewrite (13) as a quantified formula over $Var \cup Arr$, by eliminating m. For doing so, we rely once more on the closed forms of scalar variables, and express m as a linear function $g(Var) \in \mathbb{Z}[Var]$. This formula is given below:

$$\forall k.\ 1 \leq k \leq g(Var) \Rightarrow A[i^{(k)}, j^{(k)}] = f(Var^{(k)} \cup RMatr). \tag{14}$$

Formula (14) is a quantified array invariant over the content of A.

Example 6. Using the closed forms $i^{(m)} = i^{(0)} + m$ and $j^{(m)} = j^{(0)} + m$, the array assignment corresponding to the second loop of Figure 3 can be expressed as a function of the iteration counter m, as follows: $L[i^{(0)} + m, j^{(0)} + m] = 1$.

From Example 5, we have $m = j$, $i^{(0)} = 0$, and $j^{(0)} = 0$. The corresponding quantified array invariant of the second loop of Figure 3 is: $\forall k.\ (1 \leq k \leq j) \Rightarrow L[k, k] = 1$.

Similarly, we derive the following quantified array invariant of the first loop of Figure 3 as: $\forall k.\ (1 \leq k \leq j) \Rightarrow L[k + c, k] = LU[k + c, k]$.

Finally, the third loop of Figure 3 yields the array invariant: $\forall k.\ (1 \leq k \leq i) \Rightarrow L[k, k + c] = 0$.

Matrix loop properties of $\mathcal{P}$. We can now derive the following matrix loop property of $\mathcal{P}$:

$$\forall i, j.\ (1 \leq i, j \leq n) \Rightarrow \bigwedge_{k=1}^{d} \phi_k, \tag{15}$$

where ϕ_k satisfies one of the following conditions.

1. ϕ_k is a quantified array invariant (14) inferred for the while-loop corresponding to the guarded assignment from (4) with the guard $G_k \equiv i = P(j)$, or respectively with the guard $G_k \equiv j = Q(i)$.
2. ϕ_k is

   $\forall c.\ (c > 0 \wedge i = P(j) \pm c) \Rightarrow \phi_k^c$ or $\forall c.\ (c > 0 \wedge j = Q(i) \pm c) \Rightarrow \phi_k^c$

   where ϕ_k^c is a quantified array invariant (14) inferred for the while-loop corresponding to the guarded assignment from (4) with the guard $i = P(j) \pm c$, or respectively with the guard $j = Q(i) \pm c$. The formula ϕ_k is thus a quantified loop property of the while-loop corresponding to the guarded assignment from (4) with the guard $G_k \equiv i\ \mathcal{R}\ P(j)$, or respectively with the guard $G_k \equiv j\ \mathcal{R}\ Q(j)$, where $\mathcal{R} \in \{<, >, \leq, \geq, \neq\}$.

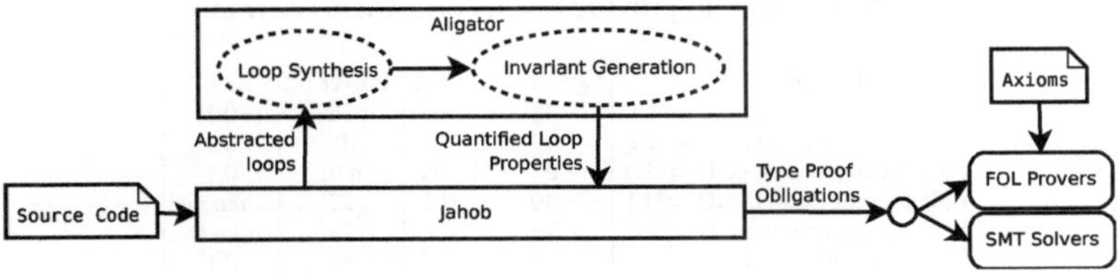

Fig. 4. Overview of our Implementation

The appropriate type of A can be proved from (15), as discussed in Section 9.

Example 7. The quantified array invariant ϕ_1 of the first loop of Figure 3 is:

$$\forall c.\, c > 0 \wedge i = j + c \Rightarrow (\forall k.\, 1 \leq k \leq j \Rightarrow L[k+c,k] = LU[k+c,k])$$

The corresponding matrix loop property of the nested loop from Figure 2 is shown in (1). The LTI-type of L is a logical consequence of the formula given above and the lower-triangular invertible shape property of L can be thus inferred, as presented in Section 9.

8 Implementation and Experiments

Implementation. We implemented a tool that infers matrix loop properties as described in Sections 6 and 7. Our tool is implemented in the Jahob verification system [20]. It takes a Java program as its input, and returns a quantified matrix loop property for each loop from its input. In more detail, the main features of our tool are as follows.

(i) It extends the Jahob framework [20] by handling mD arrays and floating point numbers;

(ii) It performs all the preprocessing steps needed for translating loops in the format described in Section 5, for instance, finding read- and write-only arrays and checking that the guards are pairwise disjoint using the SMT solver Z3 [5].

(iii) Most importantly, it integrates the software package Aligator [17] for synthesizing loops and generating quantified array invariants and loop properties. To this end, we extended Aligator with constraint solving over integers and loop synthesis, and generalized the recurrence-based invariant generation algorithm of [17] over scalars to mD arrays.

Finally, using the derived matrix properties returned by our tool, matrix types for loops are inferred by running theorem provers on the resulting proof obligations induced by type checking, as described in Section 9.

The overall workflow of our implementation is illustrated in Figure 4.

Experiments. We ran our tool on the JAMA linear algebra package [13], which provides user-level classes for constructing and manipulating matrices in Java. All matrix types guaranteed by JAMA's API, which fall into our type system, have successfully been derived from the matrix loop properties generated by our tool. We summarize some of our results, obtained on a machine with a 2.0GHz CPU and 2GB of RAM, in Table 1. The first column of the table contains the name of the JAMA program, the second specifies the number of conditional branches in the innermost loop, whereas the

Table 3. Theorem proving results on JAMA programs

Proof obligations	Vampire (s)	E (s)	iProver (s)	Z3 (s)
LU decomposition.getL ⇒ LT	48	105	98	0.1
LU decomposition.getL ⇒ LTI	49	107	101	0.1
QR decomposition.getR ⇒ UT	53	109	410	0.1
QR decomposition.getH ⇒ LT	49	0.2	22	Unknown
LU decomposition.getU ⇒ UT	49	0.2	23	Unknown
Matrix.identity ⇒ LT	48	102	84	0.1
Matrix.identity ⇒ UT	49	112	6	0.1
Matrix.identity ⇒ LTI	48	103	86	0.1
Matrix.identity ⇒ UTI	49	112	8	0.1
Matrix.identity ⇒ D	97	214	90	0.1
Matrix.identity ⇒ DI	98	215	94	0.1
Matrix.identity ⇒ I	97	215	91	0.1
Average time	58.7	116.2	92.8	0.1

third columns gives the degree d and relation $\mathcal{R}$ (equality, inequality or disequality) of the polynomial guard for each branch. The fourth column shows timing (in seconds) needed by Aligator to infer quantified matrix loop invariants and properties. The fifth column specifies which types we could automatically prove from the matrix loop properties using theorem provers. Theorem proving experiments are described in more detail in Section 9.

It is worth mentioning that our tool automatically inferred quantified array invariants and loop properties also for those JAMA programs which perform simple operations or provide access to submatrices or copies of given matrices. Such programs are e.g. Matrix.copy, Matrix.getMatrix, etc; the timings are shown by Table 2. The quantified properties of these loops do not explicitly describe matrix types, but they are strong enough so that a theorem prover can prove type-related properties, for instance, that a shape is preserved through a matrix copy, see Section 9.

We have also run our tool successfully on the JAMPACK library [28]. Results and timings are nearly identical to the ones in Table 1 and Table 2.

Aligator cannot yet handle programs with more complex matrix arithmetic. For example, JAMA loops implementing the Gaussian elimination algorithm involve various column and row switching and multiplying operations. We cannot generate loop properties implying that the resulting matrix is triangular. Handling such programs is beyond the scope of our technique but is an interesting subject for further research.

9 Type Checking Matrices

For automatic derivation of matrix loop properties one should be able to prove automatically formulas expressing that the derived loop properties imply corresponding matrix types. In this section we present experimental results showing that such formulas can be proved automatically by modern theorem provers.

Note that both the loop properties and matrix types are complex formulas with quantifiers and integer linear arithmetic. Combining first-order reasoning and linear arithmetic is very hard, for example, some simple fragments of this combination are Π_1^1-complete [16]. A calculus that integrates linear arithmetic reasoning into the superposition calculus is described in [16] but it is not yet implemented. There two kinds of tools that can be used for proving such formulas automatically.

First-order theorem provers. Such provers are very good in performing first-order reasoning with quantifiers but have no support for arithmetic. Partial and incomplete axiomatisations of fragments of arithmetic can be added to it. For example, this approach was used in generating loop invariants for programs over arrays in [19], and this is the approach we used in our experiments. Namely, we added the following formulas as axioms:

$$
\begin{array}{ll}
\forall i,j.\ (i \leq j \iff i < j \vee i = j); & \forall i,j,k.\ (i < j \wedge j < k \Rightarrow i < k); \\
\forall i,j.\ (i < j \Rightarrow i \neq j); & \forall i,j.\ (i < j \vee j \leq i); \\
0 < 1; & \forall i.\ (0 < i \iff 1 \leq i); \\
\forall i,j.\ (i + j = j + i); & \forall i.\ (i + 0 = i); \\
\multicolumn{2}{l}{\forall i_1, j_1, i_2, j_2.\ (i_1 \leq j_1 \wedge i_2 \leq j_2 \Rightarrow i_1 + i_2 \leq j_1 + j_2);} \\
\multicolumn{2}{l}{\forall i,j,k.\ (i < j \iff \exists k(i + k = j \wedge 0 < k)).}
\end{array}
$$

These formulas axiomatise inequalities and addition. We used the following first-order theorem provers: Vampire [23], E [26] and iProver [15], the three fastest first-order provers at the last CASC competitions [29]. Vampire and E are based on the superposition calculus, iProver is an instantiation-based prover.

SMT solvers. Contrary to first-order theorem provers, SMT solvers are good in (quantifier-free) theory reasoning, including reasoning with linear arithmetic. To work with quantifiers, they instantiate universally quantified variables by ground terms using various heuristics. If a problem requires few such instances to be proved (which is the case for the proof obligations generated), SMT solvers can be very good in solving this problem. Among SMT solvers, we used Z3 [5] that has a good support for quantifiers.

The results of running the four systems on the hardest generated problems are summarised in Table 3. An example of a hard problem is given in Example 7: it is not immediately obvious how one should instantiate quantifiers in the generated loop property to prove that it implies the lower-triangular-invertible type. The results of Table 3 were obtained on a machine with eight 2.8GHz CPU and 16GB of RAM. For each run, the provers were limited to a single CPU and 2GB of RAM. It turned out that the three first-order theorem provers were able to prove all the proof obligations, while Z3 was unable to solve two of them. On the solved problems Z3 spent essentially no time while the first-order provers spent between 58.7s and 116.2s on the average.

We also ran Vampire on simpler problems. The simplest problems of this kind are that Matrix.copy preserves all types. Other simple properties involve loops applying the same operation to all element of a matrix, for example, that Matrix.uminus preserves all types apart from Identity. All these problems were proved by Vampire in essentially no time. It also turned out that many problems involving element-wise operations on more than one matrix are easy and proved in no time as well. One example is that Matrix.plus preserves the LTI property.

One conclusion of our experiments is that our method can be fully automated. On the other hand, some of the generated problems turned out to be highly non-trivial. This suggests that this and similar experiments may also help to improve theorem proving with quantifiers and theories, and therefore improve theorem proving support for program analysis and program verification. The generated problems have been added to the TPTP library [29].

10 Conclusions and Future Work

We address the problem of automatically inferring quantified invariants for programs iterating over mD arrays, such as matrices. For doing so, we combine symbolic summation with constraint solving to derive unnested loops iterating over mD arrays, and use symbolic summation to generate loop invariants and properties in the combined theory of scalars, arrays, and uninterpreted functions. The inferred quantified loop invariants give us conditions on matrices from which we can derive matrix types using a first-order theorem prover. We implemented our approach to invariant generation in the Aligator package [17], successfully derived many matrix properties for all examples taken from the JAMA library [13], and used theorem provers and SMT solvers to prove automatically that these matrix properties imply matrix shapes guaranteed by the library.

We believe that the technique of generating invariants for loops with linear conditions introduced in Sections 6 and 7 has an independent value and can be used in other programs as well. Future work includes integrating our approach to loop property generation with techniques using predicate abstraction [11] and first order theorem proving [19], and extending our method to handle programs with more complex matrix arithmetic [13,2,30,4].

References

1. Beyer, D., Henzinger, T., Majumdar, R., Rybalchenko, A.: Invariant Synthesis for Combined Theories. In: Cook, B., Podelski, A. (eds.) VMCAI 2007. LNCS, vol. 4349, pp. 346–362. Springer, Heidelberg (2007)
2. Birkeland, B.: Calculus and Algebra with MathCad 2000. Haeftad. Studentlitteratur (2000)
3. Buchberger, B.: An Algorithm for Finding the Basis Elements of the Residue Class Ring of a Zero Dimensional Polynomial Ideal. J. of Symbolic Computation 41(3-4), 475–511 (2006)
4. Danaila, I., Joly, P., Kaber, S.M., Postel, M.: An Introduction to Scientific Computing: Twelve Computational Projects Solved with MATLAB. Springer, Heidelberg (2007)
5. de Moura, L., Bjorner, N.: Z3: An Efficient SMT Solver. In: Ramakrishnan, C.R., Rehof, J. (eds.) TACAS 2008. LNCS, vol. 4963, pp. 337–340. Springer, Heidelberg (2008)
6. Denney, E., Fischer, B.: A Generic Annotation Inference Algorithm for the Safety Certification of Automatically Generated Code. In: GPCE, pp. 121–130 (2006)
7. Dijkstra, E.W.: Guarded Commands, Nondeterminacy and Formal Derivation of Programs. Communications of the ACM 18(8), 453–457 (1975)
8. Flanagan, C., Qadeer, S.: Predicate Abstraction for Software Verification. In: Proc. of POPL, pp. 191–202 (2002)
9. Golub, G.H., van Loan, C.F.: Matrix Computations. Johns Hopkins Univ. Press (1996)
10. Gopan, D., Reps, T.W., Sagiv, M.: A Framework for Numeric Analysis of Array Operations. In: Proc. of POPL, pp. 338–350 (2005)
11. Gulwani, S., McCloskey, B., Tiwari, A.: Lifting Abstract Interpreters to Quantified Logical Domains. In: Proc. of POPL, pp. 235–246 (2008)
12. Halbwachs, N., Peron, M.: Discovering Properties about Arrays in Simple Programs. In: Proc. of PLDI, pp. 339–348 (2008)

13. Hicklin, J., Moler, C., Webb, P., Boisvert, R.F., Miller, B., Pozo, R., Remington, K.: JAMA: A Java Matrix Package (2005), `http://math.nist.gov/javanumerics/jama/`
14. Jhala, R., McMillan, K.L.: Array Abstractions from Proofs. In: Damm, W., Hermanns, H. (eds.) CAV 2007. LNCS, vol. 4590, pp. 193–206. Springer, Heidelberg (2007)
15. Korovin, K.: iProver - An Instantiation-based Theorem Prover for First-order Logic. In: Proc. of IJCAR, pp. 292–298 (2009)
16. Korovin, K., Voronkov, A.: Integrating Linear Arithmetic into Superposition Calculus. In: Duparc, J., Henzinger, T.A. (eds.) CSL 2007. LNCS, vol. 4646, pp. 223–237. Springer, Heidelberg (2007)
17. Kovacs, L.: Aligator: A Mathematica Package for Invariant Generation. In: Armando, A., Baumgartner, P., Dowek, G. (eds.) IJCAR 2008. LNCS (LNAI), vol. 5195, pp. 275–282. Springer, Heidelberg (2008)
18. Kovacs, L.: Reasoning Algebraically About P-Solvable Loops. In: Ramakrishnan, C.R., Rehof, J. (eds.) TACAS 2008. LNCS, vol. 4963, pp. 249–264. Springer, Heidelberg (2008)
19. Kovacs, L., Voronkov, A.: Finding Loop Invariants for Programs over Arrays Using a Theorem Prover. In: Chechik, M., Wirsing, M. (eds.) FASE 2009. LNCS, vol. 5503, pp. 470–485. Springer, Heidelberg (2009)
20. Kuncak, V., Rinard, M.: An overview of the Jahob analysis system: Project goals and current status. In: NSF Next Generation Software Workshop (2006)
21. McMillan, K.L.: Quantified Invariant Generation Using an Interpolating Saturation Prover. In: Ramakrishnan, C.R., Rehof, J. (eds.) TACAS 2008. LNCS, vol. 4963, pp. 413–427. Springer, Heidelberg (2008)
22. Müller-Olm, M., Seidl, H.: Computing Polynomial Program Invariants. Indormation Processing Letters 91(5), 233–244 (2004)
23. Riazanov, A., Voronkov, A.: The Design and Implementation of Vampire. AI Communications 15(2-3), 91–110 (2002)
24. Rodriguez-Carbonell, E., Kapur, D.: Generating All Polynomial Invariants in Simple Loops. J. of Symbolic Computation 42(4), 443–476 (2007)
25. Sankaranaryanan, S., Sipma, H.B., Manna, Z.: Non-Linear Loop Invariant Generation using Gröbner Bases. In: Proc. of POPL, pp. 318–329 (2004)
26. Schulz, S.: E — a brainiac theorem prover. AI Communications 15(2-3), 111–126 (2002)
27. Srivastava, S., Gulwani, S.: Program Verification using Templates over Predicate Abstraction. In: Proc. of PLDI, pp. 223–234 (2009)
28. Stewart, G.W.: JAMPACK: A Java Package For Matrix Computations, `http://www.mathematik.hu-berlin.de/~lamour/software/JAVA/Jampack/`
29. Sutcliffe, G.: The TPTP Problem Library and Associated Infrastructure. The FOF and CNF Parts, v3.5.0. J. of Automated Reasoning (to appear, 2009)
30. Wolfram, S.: The Mathematica Book. Version 5.0. Wolfram Media (2003)

Deriving Invariants by Algorithmic Learning, Decision Procedures, and Predicate Abstraction*

Yungbum Jung[1], Soonho Kong[1], Bow-Yaw Wang[2], and Kwangkeun Yi[1]

[1] School of Computer Science and Engineering, Seoul National University
{dreameye,soon,kwang}@ropas.snu.ac.kr
[2] Institute of Information Science, Academia Sinica
bywang@iis.sinica.edu.tw

Abstract. By combining algorithmic learning, decision procedures, and predicate abstraction, we present an automated technique for finding loop invariants in propositional formulae. Given invariant approximations derived from pre- and post-conditions, our new technique exploits the flexibility in invariants by a simple randomized mechanism. The proposed technique is able to generate invariants for some Linux device drivers and SPEC2000 benchmarks in our experiments.

1 Introduction

Algorithmic learning has been applied to assumption generation in compositional reasoning [9]. In contrast to traditional techniques, the learning approach does not derive assumptions in an off-line manner. It instead finds assumptions by interacting with a model checker progressively. Since assumptions in compositional reasoning are generally not unique, algorithmic learning can exploit the flexibility in assumptions to attain preferable solutions. Applications in formal verification and interface synthesis have also been reported [1,2,7,9,18].

Finding loop invariants follows a similar pattern. Invariants are often not unique. Indeed, programmers derive invariants incrementally. They usually have their guesses of invariants in mind, and gradually refine their guesses by observing program behavior more. Since in practice there are many invariants for given pre- and post-conditions, programmers have more freedom in deriving invariants. Yet traditional invariant generation techniques do not exploit the flexibility. They have a similar impediment to traditional assumption generation.

This article reports our first findings in applying algorithmic learning to invariant generation. We show that the three technologies (algorithmic learning, decision procedures, and predicate abstraction) can be arranged in concert to

* This work was supported by (A) the Engineering Research Center of Excellence Program of Korea Ministry of Education, Science and Technology(MEST) / Korea Science and Engineering Foundation(KOSEF) Grant Number R11-2008-007-01002-0, (B) the Brain Korea 21 Project, School of Electrical Engineering and Computer Science, Seoul National University, (C) SK Telecom, and (D) National Science Council of Taiwan Grant Numbers 95-2221-E-001-024-MY3 and 97-2221-E-001-006-MY3.

G. Barthe and M. Hermenegildo (Eds.): VMCAI 2010, LNCS 5944, pp. 180–196, 2010.

derive loop invariants in propositional (or, quantifier-free) formulae. The new technique is able to generate invariants for some Linux device drivers and SPEC2000 benchmarks without any help from static or dynamic analyses.

For a while loop, an exact learning algorithm for Boolean formulae searches for invariants by asking queries. Queries can be resolved (not always, see below) by decision procedures automatically. Recall that the learning algorithm generates only Boolean formulae but decision procedures work in propositional formulae. We thus perform predicate abstraction and concretization to integrate the two components.

In reality, information about loop invariant is incomplete. Queries may not be resolvable due to insufficient information. One striking feature of our learning approach is to exploit the flexibility in invariants. When query resolution requires information unavailable to decision procedures, we simply give a random answer. We surely could use static analysis to compute soundly approximated information other than random answers. Yet there are so many invariants for the given pre- and post-conditions. A little bit of random information does not prevent algorithmic learning from inferring invariants. Indeed, the learning algorithm is able to derive invariants in our experiments by coin tossing.

Example

$$\{i = 0\}\ \texttt{while}\ i < 10\ \texttt{do}\ b := \texttt{nondet};\ \texttt{if}\ b\ \texttt{then}\ i := i + 1\ \texttt{end}\ \{i = 10\ \wedge\ b\}$$

The while loop assigns a random truth value to the variable b in the beginning of its body. It increases the variable i by 1 if b is true. Observe that the variable b must be true after the while loop. We would like to find an invariant which proves the postcondition $i = 10 \wedge b$. Heuristically, we choose $i = 0$ and $(i = 10 \wedge b) \vee i < 10$ as under- and over-approximations to invariants respectively. With the help of a decision procedure, these invariant approximations are used to resolve queries made by the learning algorithm. After resolving a number of queries, the learning algorithm asks whether $i \neq 0 \wedge i < 10 \wedge \neg b$ should be included in the invariant. Note that the query is not stronger than the under-approximation, nor weaker than the over-approximation. Hence decision procedures cannot resolve it due to lack of information. At this point, one could apply static analysis and see that it is possible to have this state at the beginning of the loop. Instead of employing static analysis, we simply give a random answer to the learning algorithm. For this example, this information is crucial: the learning algorithm will ask us to give a counterexample to its best guess $i = 0 \vee (i = 10 \wedge b)$ after it processes the incorrect answer. Since the guess is not an invariant and flipping coins does not generate a counterexample, we restart the learning process. If the query $i \neq 0 \wedge i < 10 \wedge \neg b$ is answered correctly, the learning algorithm infers the invariant $(i = 10 \wedge b) \vee i < 10$ with two more resolvable queries.

Contribution

- We prove that algorithmic learning, decision procedures, and predicate abstraction in combination can automatically infer invariants in propositional formulae for programs in our simple language.

- We demonstrate that the technique works in realistic settings: we are able to generate invariants for some Linux device drivers and SPEC2000 benchmarks in our experiments.
- The technique can be seen as a framework for invariant generation. Static analyzers can contribute by providing information to algorithmic learning. Ours is hence orthogonal to existing techniques.

We organize this paper as follows. After preliminaries (Section 2), we present an overview of the framework in Section 3. In Section 4, we review the exact learning algorithm introduced in [6]. Section 5 gives the details of our learning approach. We report experiments in Section 6. Section 7 briefly discusses our learning approach, future work, and related work. Section 8 concludes our work.

2 The Target Language and Notation

The syntax of statements in our simple imperative language is as follows.

$$\begin{aligned}\mathsf{Stmt} \triangleq\ & \mathtt{nop} \mid \mathtt{assume}\ \mathsf{Prop} \mid \mathsf{Stmt};\ \mathsf{Stmt} \mid \\ & x := \mathsf{Exp} \mid x := \mathtt{nondet} \mid b := \mathsf{Bool} \mid b := \mathtt{nondet} \mid \\ & \mathtt{if}\ \mathsf{Prop}\ \mathtt{then}\ \mathsf{Stmt}\ \mathtt{else}\ \mathsf{Stmt} \mid \mathtt{switch}\ \mathsf{Exp}\ \mathtt{do}\ \mathtt{case}\ \mathsf{Exp} :\ \mathsf{Stmt} \cdots \mid \\ & \{\ \mathsf{Prop}\ \}\ \mathtt{while}\ \mathsf{Prop}\ \mathtt{do}\ \mathsf{Stmt}\ \{\ \mathsf{Prop}\ \}\end{aligned}$$

Natural number variables and Boolean variables are allowed. They assign to arbitrary values in their respective domains by the keyword `nondet`. Note that `while` statements are annotated. Programmers are asked to specify a *precondition* before a `while` statement, and a *postcondition* after the statement.

An *expression* Exp is a natural number ($n \in \mathbb{N}$), a variable (x), or a summation or the difference of two expressions. Due to the limitation of decision procedures, only linear arithmetic is allowed. It ensures complete answers from decision procedures.

$$\mathsf{Exp} \triangleq n \mid x \mid \mathsf{Exp} + \mathsf{Exp} \mid \mathsf{Exp} - \mathsf{Exp}$$

A *propositional formula* Prop is either: the falsehood symbol (F), a Boolean variable (b), the negation of a propositional formula, the conjunction of two propositional formulae, or comparisons ($E_0 < E_1$ or $E_0 = E_1$).

$$\mathsf{Prop} \triangleq \mathtt{F} \mid b \mid \neg\mathsf{Prop} \mid \mathsf{Prop} \wedge \mathsf{Prop} \mid \mathsf{Exp} < \mathsf{Exp} \mid \mathsf{Exp} = \mathsf{Exp}$$

Let ρ_0 and ρ_1 be propositional formulae, π_0 and π_1 be expressions. We write T for $\neg\mathtt{F}$, $\rho_0 \vee \rho_1$ for $\neg(\neg\rho_0 \wedge \neg\rho_1)$, $\rho_0 \Rightarrow \rho_1$ for $\neg\rho_0 \vee \rho_1$, $\rho_0 \Leftrightarrow \rho_1$ for $(\rho_0 \Rightarrow \rho_1) \wedge (\rho_1 \Rightarrow \rho_0)$, $\rho_0 \oplus \rho_1$ for $\neg(\rho_0 \Leftrightarrow \rho_1)$, $\pi_0 \leq \pi_1$ for $\pi_0 < \pi_1 \vee \pi_0 = \pi_1$, and $\pi_0 \neq \pi_1$ for $\neg(\pi_0 = \pi_1)$. Propositional formulae of the forms b, $\pi_0 < \pi_1$, and $\pi_0 = \pi_1$ are called *atomic propositions*. If A is a set of atomic propositions, Prop_A denotes the set of propositional formulae generated from A.

A *Boolean formula* Bool is a restricted propositional formula constructed from truth values and Boolean variables.

$$\mathsf{Bool} \triangleq \mathtt{F} \mid b \mid \neg\mathsf{Bool} \mid \mathsf{Bool} \land \mathsf{Bool}$$

A *valuation* ν is an assignment of natural numbers to variables and truth values to Boolean variables. A *Boolean valuation* μ is an assignment of truth values to Boolean variables. If A is a set of atomic propositions and $Var(A)$ is the set of variables occurred in A, $Val_{Var(A)}$ denotes the set of valuations for $Var(A)$. Let ρ be a propositional formula. The valuation ν is a *model* of ρ (written $\nu \models \rho$) if ρ evaluates to T under the valuation ν. Similarly, the Boolean valuation μ is a *Boolean model* of the Boolean formula β (written $\mu \models \beta$) if β evaluates to T under μ. If B is a set of Boolean variables, the set of Boolean valuations for B is denoted by Val_B. Given a propositional formula ρ, a *satisfiability modulo theories (SMT) solver* returns a model of ρ if it exists (written $SMT(\rho) \rightarrow \nu$); otherwise, it returns $UNSAT$ (written $SMT(\rho) \rightarrow UNSAT$) [11,22].

A *precondition* $Pre(\phi, S)$ for $\phi \in \mathsf{Prop}$ with respect to a statement S is a universally quantified formula that guarantees ϕ after the execution of the statement S.

$$\begin{aligned}
Pre(\phi, \mathtt{nop}) &= \phi \\
Pre(\phi, \mathtt{assume}\ \theta) &= \theta \Rightarrow \phi \\
Pre(\phi, S_0;\ S_1) &= Pre(Pre(\phi, S_1), S_0) \\
Pre(\phi, x := \pi) &= \begin{cases} \forall x.\phi & \text{if } \pi = \mathtt{nondet} \\ \phi[x \mapsto \pi] & \text{otherwise} \end{cases} \\
Pre(\phi, b := \rho) &= \begin{cases} \forall b.\phi & \text{if } \rho = \mathtt{nondet} \\ \phi[b \mapsto \rho] & \text{otherwise} \end{cases} \\
Pre(\phi, \mathtt{if}\ \rho\ \mathtt{then}\ S_0\ \mathtt{else}\ S_1) &= (\rho \Rightarrow Pre(\phi, S_0)) \land (\neg\rho \Rightarrow Pre(\phi, S_1)) \\
Pre(\phi, \mathtt{switch}\ \pi\ \mathtt{case}\ \pi_i\colon S_i) &= \bigwedge_i (\pi = \pi_i \Rightarrow Pre(\phi, S_i)) \\
Pre(\phi, \{\delta\}\ \mathtt{while}\ \rho\ \mathtt{do}\ S\ \{\epsilon\}) &= \begin{cases} \delta \text{ if } \epsilon \text{ implies } \phi \\ \mathtt{F} \text{ otherwise} \end{cases}
\end{aligned}$$

Observe that all universal quantifiers occur positively in $Pre(\phi, S)$ for any S. They can be eliminated by Skolem constants [12,23].

3 Framework Overview

We combine algorithmic learning, decision procedures [11], and predicate abstraction [13] in our framework. Figure 1 illustrates the relation among these technologies. In the figure, the left side represents the concrete domain; the right side represents the abstract domain. Assume there is an invariant for a `while` statement with respect to the given pre- and post-conditions in the concrete domain. We would like to apply algorithmic learning to find such an invariant.

To this purpose, we use the CDNF algorithm [6]. The CDNF algorithm is an exact learning algorithm for Boolean formulae. It is an active learning algorithm that makes queries about an unknown Boolean formula and outputs a Boolean formula that is equivalent to the unknown one [3,6]. We perform predicate

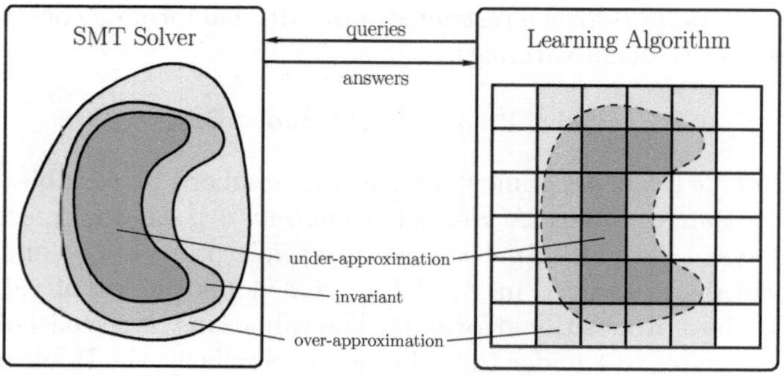

Fig. 1. Overview

abstraction to represent propositional formulae as Boolean formulae in the abstract domain. Since the CDNF algorithm is able to learn arbitrary Boolean formulae, our technique can infer arbitrary invariants in propositional formulae by answering queries.

To realize this idea, we devise a mechanism (a teacher) to resolve queries in the abstract domain. There are two types of queries: membership queries ask whether a Boolean valuation is a model of an invariant; equivalence queries ask whether a Boolean formula is an invariant and demand a counterexample if it is not. It is not difficult to concretize queries in the abstract domain. Answering queries however requires information about invariants yet to be computed.

Although an invariant is unknown, its approximations can be derived from the pre- and post-conditions, or computed by static analysis. Hence, we estimate invariant approximations heuristically and adopt decision procedures for query resolution. For a membership query, we check if its concretization is in the under-approximation or outside the over-approximation by an SMT solver. If it is in the under-approximation, the answer is affirmative; if it is out of the over-approximation, the answer is negative. Otherwise, we simply give a random answer. Equivalence queries are resolved similarly, but we restart the learning process when equivalence queries are not resolvable. If the concretization is not weaker than the under-approximation or not stronger than the over-approximation, a counterexample can be generated by an SMT solver. Otherwise, the learning process is restarted instead of giving random answers.

4 The CDNF Algorithm

In [6], an exact learning algorithm for Boolean formulae over a finite set B of Boolean variables is introduced. The CDNF algorithm generates a conjunction of formulae in disjunctive normal form equivalent to the unknown Boolean formula λ. It assumes a teacher to answer the following queries:

1. *Membership queries.* Let μ be a Boolean valuation for B. The membership query $MEM(\mu)$ asks if μ is a model of the unknown Boolean formula λ. If

$\mu \models \lambda$, the teacher answers *YES* (denoted by $MEM(\mu) \rightarrow YES$). Otherwise, the teacher answers *NO* (denoted by $MEM(\mu) \rightarrow NO$).

2. *Equivalence queries.* Let $\beta \in \mathsf{Bool}_B$. The equivalence query $EQ(\beta)$ asks if β is equivalent to the unknown Boolean formula λ. If so, the teacher answers *YES* (denoted by $EQ(\beta) \rightarrow YES$). Otherwise, the teacher returns a Boolean valuation μ for B such that $\mu \models \beta \oplus \lambda$ as a counterexample (denoted by $EQ(\beta) \rightarrow \mu$).

(* $B = \{b_1, b_2, \ldots, b_m\}$: a finite set of Boolean variables *)
Input: A teacher answers membership and equivalence queries for an unknown Boolean formula λ
Output: A Boolean formula equivalent to λ
$t := 0$;
if $EQ(\mathtt{T}) \rightarrow YES$ **then return** T;
let μ be such that $EQ(\mathtt{T}) \rightarrow \mu$;
0 $t := t + 1$; $(H_t, S_t, a_t) := (\mathtt{F}, \emptyset, \mu)$;
1 **if** $EQ(\bigwedge_{i=1}^{t} H_i) \rightarrow YES$ **then return** $\bigwedge_{i=1}^{t} H_i$;
let μ be such that $EQ(\bigwedge_{i=1}^{t} H_i) \rightarrow \mu$;
$I := \{i : \mu \not\models H_i\}$;
2 **if** $I = \emptyset$ **then goto 0**;
foreach $i \in I$ **do**
  $\mu_i := \mu$;
  walk from μ_i towards a_i while keeping $\mu_i \models \lambda$;
  $S_i := S_i \cup \{\mu_i \oplus a_i\}$;
end
$H_i := M_{DNF}(S_i)[B \mapsto B \oplus a_i]$ for $i = 1, \ldots, t$;
3 **goto 1**;

Algorithm 1. The CDNF Algorithm [6]

Let μ and a be Boolean valuations for B. The Boolean valuation $\mu \oplus a$ is defined by $(\mu \oplus a)(b_i) = \mu(b_i) \oplus a(b_i)$ for $b_i \in B$. For any Boolean formula β, $\beta[B \mapsto B \oplus a]$ is the Boolean formula obtained from β by replacing $b_i \in B$ with $\neg b_i$ if $a(b_i) = \mathtt{T}$. For a set S of Boolean valuations for B, define

$$M_{DNF}(\mu) = \bigwedge_{\mu(b_i)=\mathtt{T}} b_i \quad \text{and} \quad M_{DNF}(S) = \bigvee_{\mu \in S} M_{DNF}(\mu).$$

For the degenerate cases, $M_{DNF}(\mu) = \mathtt{T}$ when $\mu \equiv \mathtt{F}$ and $M_{DNF}(\emptyset) = \mathtt{F}$. Algorithm 1 shows the CDNF algorithm [6]. In the algorithm, the step "walk from μ towards a while keeping $\mu \models \lambda$" takes two Boolean valuations μ and a. It flips the assignments in μ different from those of a and maintains $\mu \models \lambda$. Algorithm 2 implements the walking step by membership queries.

Intuitively, the CDNF algorithm computes the conjunction of approximations to the unknown Boolean formula. In Algorithm 1, H_i records the approximation generated from the set S_i of Boolean valuations with respect to the Boolean valuation a_i. The algorithm checks if the conjunction of approximations H_i's

```
(* B = {b1,b2,...,bm}: a finite set of Boolean variables *)
Input: valuations μ and a for B
Output: a model μ of λ by walking towards a
i := 1;
while i ≤ m do
    if μ(bi) ≠ a(bi) then
        μ(bi) := ¬μ(bi);
        if MEM(μ) → YES then i := 0 else μ(bi) := ¬μ(bi);
    end
    i := i + 1;
end
return μ
```

Algorithm 2. Walking towards a

is the unknown Boolean formula (line **1**). If it is, we are done. Otherwise, the algorithm tries to refine H_i by expanding S_i. If none of H_i's can be refined (line **2**), another approximation is added (line **0**). The algorithm reiterates after refining the approximations H_i's (line **3**). Let λ be a Boolean formula, $|\lambda|_{DNF}$ and $|\lambda|_{CNF}$ denote the minimum sizes of λ in disjunctive and conjunctive normal forms respectively. The CDNF algorithm learns any Boolean formula λ with a polynomial number of queries in $|\lambda|_{DNF}$, $|\lambda|_{CNF}$, and the number of Boolean variables [6]. Appendix A gives a sample run of the CDNF algorithm.

5 Learning Invariants

Consider the `while` statement

$$\{\delta\}\ \texttt{while}\ \rho\ \texttt{do}\ S\ \{\epsilon\}.$$

The propositional formula ρ is called the *guard* of the `while` statement; the statement S is called the *body* of the `while` statement. The annotation is intended to denote that if the precondition δ holds, then the postcondition ϵ must hold after the execution of the `while` statement. The *invariant generation problem* is to compute an invariant to justify the pre- and post-conditions.

Definition 1. *Let* $\{\delta\}$ `while` ρ `do` S $\{\epsilon\}$ *be a* while *statement. An* invariant ι *is a propositional formula such that*

(a) $\delta \Rightarrow \iota$ *(b)* $\rho \wedge \iota \Rightarrow Pre(\iota, S)$ *(c)* $\neg\rho \wedge \iota \Rightarrow \epsilon$.

An invariant allows us to prove that the `while` statement fulfills the annotated requirements. Observe that Definition 1 (c) is equivalent to $\iota \Rightarrow \epsilon \vee \rho$. Along with Definition 1 (a), we see that any invariant must be weaker than δ but stronger than $\epsilon \vee \rho$. Hence δ and $\epsilon \vee \rho$ are called the *strongest* and *weakest* approximations to invariants for $\{\delta\}$ `while` ρ `do` S $\{\epsilon\}$ respectively.

Our goal is to apply the CDNF algorithm (Algorithm 1) to "learn" an invariant for an annotated `while` statement. To achieve this goal, we first lift the invariant generation problem to the abstract domain by predicate abstraction. Moreover, we need to devise a mechanism to answer queries from the learning algorithm in the abstract domain. In the following, we show how to answer queries by an SMT solver and invariant approximations.

5.1 Predicate Abstraction to Connect Algorithmic Learning and SMT Solvers

Domains for an SMT solver and algorithmic learning are adjoined via the predicate abstraction [13]. The α, α^*, γ, and γ^* are the abstraction (α, α^*) and concretization (γ, γ^*) maps between the two domains. SMT solvers work in propositional formulae. Algorithmic learning works in Boolean formulae.

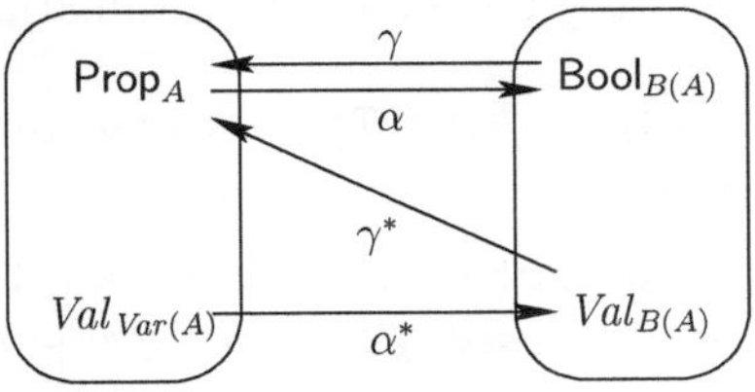

Let A be a fixed set of atomic propositions. For each atomic proposition $p \in A$, we use a Boolean variable b_p to represent p. Let $B(A) = \{b_p : p \in A\}$ be the set of Boolean variables corresponding to the atomic propositions in A. Consider the *concrete domain* Prop_A and the *abstract domain* $\mathsf{Bool}_{B(A)}$. A Boolean formula $\beta \in \mathsf{Bool}_{B(A)}$ is called a *canonical monomial* if it is a conjunction of literals such that each Boolean variable in $B(A)$ appears exactly once. Define the mappings $\gamma : \mathsf{Bool}_{B(A)} \to \mathsf{Prop}_A$ and $\alpha : \mathsf{Prop}_A \to \mathsf{Bool}_{B(A)}$:

$\gamma(\beta) = \beta[\overline{b}_p \mapsto \overline{p}]$; and
$\alpha(\theta) = \bigvee\{\beta \in \mathsf{Bool}_{B(A)} : \beta \text{ is a canonical monomial and } \theta \wedge \gamma(\beta) \text{ is satisfiable}\}$.

where $\overline{b}_p$ and $\overline{p}$ are the Boolean variables in $B(A)$ and their corresponding atomic propositions respectively.

The following lemmas are useful in proving our technical results:

Lemma 1. *Let A be a set of atomic propositions, $\theta, \rho \in \mathsf{Prop}_A$. Then*

$$\theta \Rightarrow \rho \textit{ implies } \alpha(\theta) \Rightarrow \alpha(\rho).$$

Lemma 2. *Let A be a set of atomic propositions, $\theta \in \mathsf{Prop}_A$, and β a canonical monomial in $\mathsf{Bool}_{B(A)}$. Then $\theta \wedge \gamma(\beta)$ is satisfiable if and only if $\gamma(\beta) \Rightarrow \theta$.*[1]

Recall that a teacher for the CDNF algorithm answers queries in the abstract domain, and an SMT solver computes models in the concrete domain. In order to let an SMT solver play the role of a teacher, more transformations are needed.

[1] Complete proofs are in [20]

A valuation induces a natural Boolean valuation. Precisely, define the Boolean valuation $\alpha^*(\nu)$ for the valuation ν as follows.

$$(\alpha^*(\nu))(b_p) = \begin{cases} \mathtt{T} & \text{if } \nu \models p \\ \mathtt{F} & \text{otherwise} \end{cases}$$

Lemma 3. *Let A be a set of atomic propositions, $\theta \in \mathsf{Prop}_A$, $\beta \in \mathsf{Bool}_{B(A)}$, and ν a valuation for $Var(A)$. Then*

1. *$\nu \models \theta$ if and only if $\alpha^*(\nu) \models \alpha(\theta)$; and*
2. *$\nu \models \gamma(\beta)$ if and only if $\alpha^*(\nu) \models \beta$.*

A Boolean valuation on the other hand induces a propositional formula. Define the propositional formula $\gamma^*(\mu)$ for the Boolean valuation μ as follows.

$$\gamma^*(\mu) = \bigwedge_{p \in A} \{p : \mu(b_p) = \mathtt{T}\} \wedge \bigwedge_{p \in A} \{\neg p : \mu(b_p) = \mathtt{F}\}$$

Lemma 4. *Let A be a set of atomic propositions, $\theta \in \mathsf{Prop}_A$, and μ a Boolean valuation for $B(A)$. Then $\gamma^*(\mu) \Rightarrow \theta$ if and only if $\mu \models \alpha(\theta)$.*

5.2 Answering Queries from Algorithmic Learning

Suppose $\iota \in \mathsf{Prop}_A$ is an invariant for the statement $\{\delta\}$ `while` ρ `do` S $\{\epsilon\}$. Let $\underline{\iota}, \overline{\iota} \in \mathsf{Prop}_A$. We say $\underline{\iota}$ is an *under-approximation* to an invariant ι if $\delta \Rightarrow \underline{\iota}$ and $\underline{\iota} \Rightarrow \iota$. Similarly, $\overline{\iota}$ is an *over-approximation* to an invariant ι if $\iota \Rightarrow \overline{\iota}$ and $\overline{\iota} \Rightarrow \epsilon \vee \rho$. The strongest ($\delta$) and weakest ($\epsilon \vee \rho$) approximations are trivial under- and over-approximations to any invariant respectively.

Recall that the CDNF algorithm makes the following queries: (1) membership queries $MEM(\mu)$ where $\mu \in Val_{B(A)}$, and (2) equivalence queries $EQ(\beta)$ where $\beta \in \mathsf{Bool}_{B(A)}$. In the following, we show how to resolve these queries by means of an SMT solver and the invariant approximations ($\underline{\iota}$ and $\overline{\iota}$).

Membership Queries. In the membership query $MEM(\mu)$, the teacher is required to answer whether $\mu \models \alpha(\iota)$. We concretize the Boolean valuation μ and check it against the approximations. If the concretization $\gamma^*(\mu)$ is inconsistent (that is, $\gamma^*(\mu)$ is unsatisfiable), we simply answer *NO* for the membership query. Otherwise, there are three cases:

1. $\gamma^*(\mu) \Rightarrow \underline{\iota}$. Thus $\mu \models \alpha(\underline{\iota})$ (Lemma 4). And $\mu \models \alpha(\iota)$ by Lemma 1.
2. $\gamma^*(\mu) \not\Rightarrow \overline{\iota}$. Thus $\mu \not\models \alpha(\overline{\iota})$ (Lemma 4). That is, $\mu \models \neg\alpha(\overline{\iota})$. Since $\iota \rightarrow \overline{\iota}$, we have $\mu \not\models \alpha(\iota)$ by Lemma 1.
3. Otherwise, we cannot determine whether $\mu \models \alpha(\iota)$ by the approximations.

Algorithm 3 shows our membership query resolution algorithm. Note that when a membership query cannot be resolved by an SMT solver given invariant approximations, one can use better approximations from static analyzers. Our framework is therefore orthogonal to existing static analysis techniques.

(* $\underline{\iota}$: an under-approximation; $\overline{\iota}$: an over-approximation *)
Input: a valuation μ for $B(A)$
$\theta := \gamma^*(\mu)$;
if $SMT(\theta) \rightarrow UNSAT$ **then return** NO;
if $SMT(\theta \wedge \neg\underline{\iota}) \rightarrow UNSAT$ **then return** YES;
if $SMT(\theta \wedge \neg\overline{\iota}) \rightarrow \nu$ **then return** NO;
abort with θ;

Algorithm 3. Resolving Membership Queries

Equivalence Queries. To answer the equivalence query $EQ(\beta)$, we concretize the Boolean formula β and check if $\gamma(\beta)$ is indeed an invariant of the `while` statement for the given pre- and post-conditions. If it is, we are done. Otherwise, we use an SMT solver to find a witness to $\alpha(\iota) \oplus \beta$. There are three cases:

1. There is a ν such that $\nu \models \neg(\underline{\iota} \Rightarrow \gamma(\beta))$. Then $\nu \models \underline{\iota} \wedge \neg\gamma(\beta)$. By Lemma 3 and 1, we have $\alpha^*(\nu) \models \alpha(\iota)$ and $\alpha^*(\nu) \models \neg\beta$. Thus, $\alpha^*(\nu) \models \alpha(\iota) \wedge \neg\beta$.
2. There is a ν such that $\nu \models \neg(\gamma(\beta) \Rightarrow \overline{\iota})$. Then $\nu \models \gamma(\beta) \wedge \neg\overline{\iota}$. By Lemma 3, $\alpha^*(\nu) \models \beta$. $\alpha^*(\nu) \models \neg\alpha(\iota)$ by Lemma 3 and 1. Hence $\alpha^*(\nu) \models \beta \wedge \neg\alpha(\iota)$.
3. Otherwise, we cannot find a witness to $\alpha(\iota) \oplus \beta$ by the approximations.

(* $\{\delta\}$ while ρ do S $\{\epsilon\}$ *)
(* $\underline{\iota}$: an under-approximation; $\overline{\iota}$: an over-approximation *)
Input: $\beta \in \mathsf{Bool}_{B(A)}$
$\theta := \gamma(\beta)$;
if $SMT(\underline{\iota} \wedge \neg\theta) \rightarrow UNSAT$ **and** $SMT(\theta \wedge \neg\overline{\iota}) \rightarrow UNSAT$ **and**
$SMT(\rho \wedge \theta \wedge \neg Pre(\theta, S)) \rightarrow UNSAT$ **then**
  return YES;
if $SMT(\underline{\iota} \wedge \neg\theta) \rightarrow \nu$ **then return** $\alpha^*(\nu)$;
if $SMT(\theta \wedge \neg\overline{\iota}) \rightarrow \nu$ **then return** $\alpha^*(\nu)$;
abort with θ;

Algorithm 4. Resolving Equivalence Queries

Algorithm 4 shows our equivalence query resolution algorithm. Note that Algorithm 4 returns *YES* only if an invariant is found.

Similar to membership query resolution, one can refine approximations by static analysis when an equivalence query is not resolvable by an SMT solver given invariant approximations. For simplicity, Algorithm 4 aborts the learning algorithm with the unresolved equivalence query.

5.3 Main Loop of Our Approach

Algorithm 5 gives the top-level loop of our framework. Initially, we use the disjunction of strongest approximation and the postcondition as the under-approximation; the weakest approximation is the over-approximation. The under-approximation aims to find an invariant that establishes the postcondition. This heuristic is proved very useful in practice.

```
(* {δ} while ρ do S {ε} *)
function randomized_membership μ =
   try Algorithm 3 with input μ when abort → return YES or NO randomly;

ι̲ := δ ∨ ε; ῑ := ε ∨ ρ;
repeat
   try ι := Algorithm 1 with randomized_membership and Algorithm 4
   when abort → continue
until an invariant ι is found ;
```

Algorithm 5. Main Loop

After determining the approximations, Algorithm 1 is used to find an invariant. We use Algorithms 3 and 4 to resolve queries with an SMT solver given the invariant approximations. If Algorithm 3 aborts with an unresolved membership query, a random answer is returned by *randomized_membership*. If Algorithm 4 aborts with an unresolved equivalence query, the learning algorithm is restarted.

Since algorithmic learning does not commit to any specific target, it always finds an invariant consistent with answers to previous queries. In other words, the learning algorithm will always generate an invariant if there is one consistent with our random answers. Although our random answers may exclude certain invariants, an invariant can still be inferred. Verifying whether a formula is an invariant is done by checking the sufficient conditions of Definition 1 in our equivalence query resolution algorithm (Algorithm 4).

6 Experiments

We have implemented a prototype in OCaml. In our implementation, we use YICES as the SMT solver to resolve queries (Algorithm 3 and 4). From SPEC2000 benchmarks and Linux device drivers we chose five `while` statements. We translated them into our language and added postcondition manually. Table 1 shows the performance numbers of our experiments. Among five `while` statements, the cases `parser` and `vpr` are extracted from PARSER and VPR in SPEC2000 benchmarks respectively. The other three cases are extracted from Linux 2.6.28 device drivers: both `ide-ide-tape` and `ide-wait-ireason` are from IDE driver; `usb-message` is from USB driver. For each case, we report the number of language constructs in the loop ($SIZE$), the number of atomic propositions (AP), the number of membership queries (MEM), the number of equivalence queries (EQ), the number of randomly resolved membership queries (coin tossing), the number of the CDNF algorithm invocations (iterations), and the execution time. The data are the average of 500 runs and collected on a 2.6GHz Intel E5300 Duo Core with 3GB memory running Linux 2.6.28.

Our technique is able to find invariants for four cases within 1 second. Most interestingly, the learning algorithm is able to find an invariant for `usb-message` regardless of the outcomes of coin tossing. For the most complicated case `parser`, our technique is able to generate an invariant with 991 random membership resolutions in about 33 seconds.

Table 1. Performance Numbers

case	$SIZE$	AP	MEM	EQ	coin tossing	iterations	time (sec)
`ide-ide-tape`	16	6	18.2	5.2	4.1	1.2	0.055
`ide-wait-ireason`	9	6	216.1	111.8	47.2	9.9	0.602
`parser`	37	20	6694.5	819.4	990.3	12.5	32.120
`usb-message`	18	10	20.1	6.8	1.0	1.0	0.128
`vpr`	8	7	14.5	8.9	11.8	2.9	0.055

```
{ ret = 0 ∧ bh_b_count ≤ bh_b_size }
while n > 0 do
  if (bh_b_size − bh_b_count) < n then count := bh_b_size − bh_b_count
  else count := n;
  b := nondet;
  if b then ret := 1;
  n := n − count; bh_b_count := bh_b_count + count;
  if bh_b_count = bh_b_size then
    bh_b_size := nondet; bh_b_count := nondet; bh_b_count := 0;
end
{ n = 0 ∧ bh_b_count ≤ bh_b_size }
```

Fig. 2. A Sample Loop in Linux IDE Driver

6.1 `ide-ide-tape` from Linux IDE Driver

Figure 2 is a `while` statement extracted from Linux IDE driver.[2] It copies data of size n from tape records. The variable *count* contains the size of the data to be copied from the current record (*bh_b_size* and *bh_b_count*). If the current tape record runs out of data, more data are copied from the next record. The flexibility in invariants can be witnessed in the following run. After successfully resolving 3 equivalence and 7 membership queries, the CDNF algorithm makes the following membership query unresolvable by the invariant approximations:

$$\overbrace{n > 0 \wedge (bh\_b\_size - bh\_b\_count) < n \wedge ret \neq 0}^{\rho} \wedge bh\_b\_count = bh\_b\_size$$

Answering *NO* to this query leads to the following unresolvable membership query after successfully resolving two more membership query:

$$\rho \wedge bh\_b\_count \neq bh\_b\_size \wedge bh\_b\_count \leq bh\_b\_size$$

We proceed with a random answer *YES*. After successfully resolving one more membership queries, we reach the following unresolvable membership query:

$$\rho \wedge bh\_b\_count \neq bh\_b\_size \wedge bh\_b\_count > bh\_b\_size$$

For this query, both answers lead to invariants. Answering *YES* yields the following invariant:

[2] The source code can be found in function `idetape_copy_stage_from_user()` of `drivers/ide/ide-tape.c` in Linux 2.6.28.

$$n \neq 0 \vee (bh\_b\_size - bh\_b\_count) \geq n$$

Answering *NO* yields the following invariant:

$$(bh\_b\_count \leq bh\_b\_size \wedge n \neq 0) \vee (bh\_b\_size - bh\_b\_count) \geq n$$

Note that they are two different invariants. The equivalence query resolution algorithm (Algorithm 4) ensures that both fulfill the conditions in Definition 1.

6.2 parser from VPR in SPEC2000 Benchmarks

Figure 3 shows a sample `while` statement from the `parser` program in SPEC2000 benchmark.[3] In the `while` body, there are three locations where *give_up* or *success* is set to T. Thus one of these conditions in the `if` statements must hold (the first conjunct of postcondition). Variable *valid* may get an arbitrary value if *linkages* is not zero. But it cannot be greater than *linkages* by the `assume` statement (the second conjunct of postcondition). The variable *linkages* gets an arbitrary value near the end of the `while` body. But it cannot be greater than 5000 (the fourth conjunct), and always equal to the variable *canonical* (the third

---

{ *phase* = F $\wedge$ *success* = F $\wedge$ *give_up* = F $\wedge$ *cutoff* = 0 $\wedge$ *count* = 0 }
```
 1 while ¬(success ∨ give_up) do
 2     entered_phase := F;
 3     if ¬phase then
 4         if cutoff = 0 then cutoff := 1;
 5         else if cutoff = 1 ∧ maxcost > 1 then cutoff := maxcost;
 6             else phase := T; entered_phase := T; cutoff := 1000;
 7         if cutoff = maxcost ∧ ¬search then give_up := T;
 8     else
 9         count := count + 1;
10         if count > words then give_up := T;
11     if entered_phase then count := 1;
12     linkages := nondet;
13     if linkages > 5000 then linkages := 5000;
14     canonical := 0; valid := 0;
15     if linkages ≠ 0 then
16         valid := nondet; assume 0 ≤ valid ∧ valid ≤ linkages;
17         canonical := linkages;
18     if valid > 0 then success := T;
19 end
```
{ (*valid* > 0 $\vee$ *count* > *words* $\vee$ (*cutoff* = *maxcost* $\wedge$ ¬*search*))$\wedge$
valid $\leq$ *linkages* $\wedge$ *canonical* = *linkages* $\wedge$ *linkages* $\leq$ 5000 }

Fig. 3. A Sample Loop in SPEC2000 Benchmark PARSER

---

[3] The source code can be found in function `loop()` of `CINT2000/197.parser/main.c` in SPEC2000.

conjunct of postcondition). Despite the complexity of the postcondition and the `while` body, our approach is able to compute an invariant in 13 iterations on average. The execution time and number of iterations vary significantly. They range from 2.22s to 196.52s and 1 to 84 with standard deviations 31.01 and 13.33 respectively. By Chebyshev's inequality [27], our technique infers an invariant within two minutes with probability 0.876.

One of the found invariants is the following:

$$
\begin{array}{l}
success \Rightarrow (valid \leq linkages \land linkages \leq 5000 \land canonical = linkages) \bigwedge \\
success \Rightarrow (\neg search \lor count > words \lor valid \neq 0) \bigwedge \\
success \Rightarrow (count > words \lor cutoff = maxcost \lor (canonical \neq 0 \land valid \neq 0 \land linkages \neq 0)) \bigwedge \\
give\_up \Rightarrow ((valid = 0 \land linkages = 0 \land canonical = linkages) \lor \\
\qquad\qquad (canonical \neq 0 \land valid \leq linkages \land linkages \leq 5000 \land canonical = linkages)) \bigwedge \\
give\_up \Rightarrow (cutoff = maxcost \lor count > words \lor \\
\qquad\qquad (canonical \neq 0 \land valid \neq 0 \land linkages \neq 0)) \bigwedge \\
give\_up \Rightarrow (\neg search \lor count > words \lor valid \neq 0)
\end{array}
$$

This invariant describes the conditions when *success* or *give_up* are true. For instance, it specifies that $valid \leq linkages \land linkages \leq 5000 \land canonical = linkages$ should hold if *success* is true. In Figure 3, we see that *success* is assigned to `T` at line 18 when *valid* is positive. Yet *valid* is set to 0 at line 14. Hence line 16 and 17 must be executed. Thus, the first ($valid \leq linkages$) and the third ($canonical = linkages$) conjuncts hold. Moreover, line 13 ensures that the second conjunct ($linkages \leq 5000$) holds as well.

7 Discussion and Future Work

The complexity of our technique depends on the distribution of invariants. It works most effectively if invariants are abundant. The number of iterations depends on the outcomes of coin tossing. The main loop may reiterate several times or not even terminate. Our experiments suggest that there are sufficiently many invariants in practice. For each of the 2500 ($= 5 \times 500$) runs, our technique always generates an invariant. On average, it takes 12.5 iterations for the most complicated case `parser`.

Since plentiful of invariants are available, it may appear that one of them can be generated by merely coin tossing. But this is not the case. In `parser`, our technique does not terminate if the under- and over-approximations are the strongest and weakest approximations respectively. Indeed, 6695 membership and 820 equivalence queries are resolved by invariant approximations in this case. Invariant approximations are essential to our framework.

For simplicity, predicates are collected from program texts, pre- and post-conditions in our experiments. Existing predicate discovery techniques can certainly be deployed. Better invariant approximations ($\underline{\iota}$ and $\overline{\iota}$) computed by static analysis can be used in our framework. More precise approximations of $\underline{\iota}$ and $\overline{\iota}$ will improve the performance by reducing the number of iterations via increasing the number of resolvable queries. Also, a variety of techniques from static analysis or loop invariant generation [12,17,28,16,19,21,23,25] in particular can be integrated to resolve queries in addition to one SMT solver with coin tossing. Such a set of multiple teachers will increase the number of resolvable queries because it suffices to have just one teacher to answer the query to proceed.

In comparison with previous invariant generation techniques [12,16,17,19,21] [23,25,28], we have the following distinguishing features. (1) We do not use fixed point computation nor any static or dynamic analyses. Instead, we use algorithmic learning [6] to search for loop invariants. (2) Templates for invariants are not needed. Our approach does not restrict to specific forms of invariants imposed by templates. (3) We employ SMT solvers instead of theorem provers in our technique. This allows us to take advantages of recent development in efficient SMT algorithms. (4) Our method can be extended and combined with the existing loop invariant techniques.

Related Work. Existing impressive techniques for invariant generation can be adopted as the query resolution components (teachers) in our algorithmic learning-based framework. Srivastava and Gulwani [28] devise three algorithms, two of them use fixed point computation and the other uses a constraint based approach [17,16] to derive quantified invariants. Gupta and Rybalchenko [19] present an efficient invariant generator. They apply dynamic analysis to make invariant generation more efficient. Flanagan and Qadeer use predicate abstraction to infer universally quantified loop invariants [12]. Predicates over Skolem constants are used to handle unbounded arrays. McMillan [25] extends a paramodulation-based saturation prover to an interpolating prover that is complete for universally quantified interpolants. He also solves the problem of divergence in interpolated-based invariant generation.

8 Conclusions

By combining algorithmic learning, decision procedures, and predicate abstraction, we introduced a technique for invariant generation. The new technique finds invariants guided by query resolution algorithms. Algorithmic learning gives a platform to integrate various techniques for invariant generation; it suffices to design new query resolution algorithms based on existing techniques. The learning algorithm will utilize the information provided by these techniques.

To illustrate the flexibility of algorithmic learning, we deploy a randomized query resolution algorithm. When a membership query cannot be resolved, a random answer is returned to the learning algorithm. Since the learning algorithm does not commit to any specific invariant beforehand, it always finds a solution consistent with query results. Our experiments indeed show that algorithmic learning is able to infer non-trivial invariants with this naïve membership resolution. It is important to exploit the power of coin tossing in our technique.

Acknowledgment We would like to thank anonymous referees for their comments and suggestions. We are grateful to Wontae Choi, Deokhwan Kim, Will Klieber, Sasa Misailovic, Bruno Oliveira, Corneliu Popeea, Hongseok Yang, and Karen Zee for their detailed comments and helpful suggestions. We also thank Heejae Shin for implementing OCaml binding for Yices.

References

1. Alur, R., Cerný, P., Madhusudan, P., Nam, W.: Synthesis of interface specifications for java classes. In: POPL, pp. 98–109. ACM, New York (2005)
2. Alur, R., Madhusudan, P., Nam, W.: Symbolic compositional verification by learning assumptions. In: Etessami, K., Rajamani, S.K. (eds.) CAV 2005. LNCS, vol. 3576, pp. 548–562. Springer, Heidelberg (2005)
3. Angluin, D.: Learning regular sets from queries and counterexamples. Information and Computation 75(2), 87–106 (1987)
4. Balaban, I., Pnueli, A., Zuck, L.: Shape analysis by predicate abstraction. In: Cousot, R. (ed.) VMCAI 2005. LNCS, vol. 3385, pp. 164–180. Springer, Heidelberg (2005)
5. Ball, T., Cook, B., Das, S., Rajamani, S.K.: Refining approximations in software predicate abstraction. In: Jensen, K., Podelski, A. (eds.) TACAS 2004. LNCS, vol. 2988, pp. 388–403. Springer, Heidelberg (2004)
6. Bshouty, N.H.: Exact learning boolean functions via the monotone theory. Information and Computation 123, 146–153 (1995)
7. Chen, Y.F., Farzan, A., Clarke, E.M., Tsay, Y.K., Wang, B.Y.: Learning minimal separating DFA's for compositional verification. In: Kowalewski, S., Philippou, A. (eds.) TACAS 2009. LNCS, vol. 5505, pp. 31–45. Springer, Heidelberg (2009)
8. Clarke, E.M., Grumberg, O., Jha, S., Lu, Y., Veith, H.: Counterexample-guided abstraction refinement. In: Emerson, E.A., Sistla, A.P. (eds.) CAV 2000. LNCS, vol. 1855, pp. 154–169. Springer, Heidelberg (2000)
9. Cobleigh, J.M., Giannakopoulou, D., Păsăreanu, C.S.: Learning assumptions for compositional verification. In: Garavel, H., Hatcliff, J. (eds.) TACAS 2003. LNCS, vol. 2619, pp. 331–346. Springer, Heidelberg (2003)
10. Cousot, P., Halbwachs, N.: Automatic discovery of linear restraints among variables of a program. In: POPL, pp. 84–96. ACM, New York (1978)
11. Dutertre, B., Moura, L.D.: The Yices SMT solver. Technical report, SRI International (2006)
12. Flanagan, C., Qadeer, S.: Predicate abstraction for software verification. In: POPL, pp. 191–202. ACM, New York (2002)
13. Graf, S., Saïdi, H.: Construction of abstract state graphs with PVS. In: Grumberg, O. (ed.) CAV 1997. LNCS, vol. 1254, pp. 72–83. Springer, Heidelberg (1997)
14. Gulwani, S., Jain, S., Koskinen, E.: Control-flow refinement and progress invariants for bound analysis. In: PLDI, pp. 375–385. ACM, New York (2009)
15. Gulwani, S., McCloskey, B., Tiwari, A.: Lifting abstract interpreters to quantified logical domains. In: POPL, pp. 235–246. ACM, New York (2008)
16. Gulwani, S., Srivastava, S., Venkatesan, R.: Program analysis as constraint solving. In: PLDI, pp. 281–292. ACM, New York (2008)
17. Gulwani, S., Srivastava, S., Venkatesan, R.: Constraint-based invariant inference over predicate abstraction. In: Jones, N.D., Müller-Olm, M. (eds.) VMCAI 2009. LNCS, vol. 5403, pp. 120–135. Springer, Heidelberg (2009)
18. Gupta, A., McMillan, K.L., Fu, Z.: Automated assumption generation for compositional verification. In: Damm, W., Hermanns, H. (eds.) CAV 2007. LNCS, vol. 4590, pp. 420–432. Springer, Heidelberg (2007)
19. Gupta, A., Rybalchenko, A.: Invgen: An efficient invariant generator. In: Bouajjani, A., Maler, O. (eds.) CAV 2009. LNCS, vol. 5643, pp. 634–640. Springer, Heidelberg (2009)
20. Jung, Y., Kong, S., Bow-Yaw, W., Yi, K.: Deriving invariants by algorithmic learning, decision procedures, and predicate abstraction. Technical Memorandum ROSAEC-2009-004, Research On Software Analysis for Error-Free Computing (2009)

21. Kovács, L., Voronkov, A.: Finding loop invariants for programs over arrays using a theorem prover. In: FASE 2009. LNCS, pp. 470–485. Springer, Heidelberg (2009)
22. Kroening, D., Strichman, O.: Decision Procedures an algorithmic point of view. EATCS. Springer, Heidelberg (2008)
23. Lahiri, S.K., Bryant, R.E., Bryant, A.E.: Constructing quantified invariants via predicate abstraction. In: Steffen, B., Levi, G. (eds.) VMCAI 2004. LNCS, vol. 2937, pp. 267–281. Springer, Heidelberg (2004)
24. Lahiri, S.K., Bryant, R.E., Bryant, A.E., Cook, B.: A symbolic approach to predicate abstraction. In: Hunt Jr., W.A., Somenzi, F. (eds.) CAV 2003. LNCS, vol. 2725, pp. 141–153. Springer, Heidelberg (2003)
25. McMillan, K.L.: Quantified invariant generation using an interpolating saturation prover. In: Ramakrishnan, C.R., Rehof, J. (eds.) TACAS 2008. LNCS, vol. 4963, pp. 413–427. Springer, Heidelberg (2008)
26. Podelski, A., Wies, T.: Boolean heaps. In: Hankin, C., Siveroni, I. (eds.) SAS 2005. LNCS, vol. 3672, pp. 268–283. Springer, Heidelberg (2005)
27. Rosen, K.H.: Discrete Mathematics and Its Applications. McGraw-Hill Higher Education, New York (2006)
28. Srivastava, S., Gulwani, S.: Program verification using templates over predicate abstraction. In: PLDI, pp. 223–234. ACM, New York (2009)
29. Zee, K., Kuncak, V., Rinard, M.: Full functional verification of linked data structures. In: PLDI, pp. 349–361. ACM, New York (2008)
30. Zee, K., Kuncak, V., Rinard, M.C.: An integrated proof language for imperative programs. In: PLDI, pp. 338–351. ACM, New York (2009)

A An Example of the CDNF Algorithm

Let us apply Algorithm 1 to learn the Boolean formula $b_0 \oplus b_1$. The algorithm first makes the query $EQ(\mathtt{T})$ (Figure 4). The teacher responds by giving the valuation $\mu_1(b_0) = \mu_1(b_1) = 0$ (denoted by $\mu_1(b_0 b_1) = 00$). Hence Algorithm 1 assigns $\emptyset$ to S_1, $\mathtt{F}$ to H_1, and μ_1 to a_1. Next, the query $EQ(H_1)$ is made and the teacher responds with the valuation $\mu_2(b_0 b_1) = 01$. Since $\mu_2 \not\models \mathtt{F}$, we have $I = \{1\}$. Algorithm 1 now walks from μ_2 towards a_1. Since flipping $\mu_2(b_1)$ would not give us a model of $b_0 \oplus b_1$, we have $S_1 = \{\mu_2\}$ and $H_1 = b_1$. In this example, Algorithm 1 generates $(b_1 \vee b_0) \wedge (\neg b_0 \vee \neg b_1)$ as a representation for the unknown Boolean formula $b_0 \oplus b_1$. Observe that the generated Boolean formula is a conjunction of two Boolean formulae in disjunctive normal form.

equivalence query	answer	I	S_i	H_i	a_i
$\mathtt{T}$	$\mu_1(b_0 b_1) = 00$		$S_1 = \emptyset$	$H_1 = \mathtt{F}$	$a_1 = \mu_1$
$\mathtt{F}$	$\mu_2(b_0 b_1) = 01$	$\{1\}$	$S_1 = \{\mu_2\}$	$H_1 = b_1$	
b_1	$\mu_3(b_0 b_1) = 11$	$\emptyset$	$S_2 = \emptyset$	$H_2 = \mathtt{F}$	$a_2 = \mu_3$
$b_1 \wedge \mathtt{F}$	$\mu_4(b_0 b_1) = 01$	$\{2\}$	$S_2 = \{\mu_5\}^\dagger$	$H_2 = \neg b_0$	
$b_1 \wedge \neg b_0$	$\mu_6(b_0 b_1) = 10$	$\{1, 2\}$	$S_1 = \{\mu_2, \mu_6\}$ $S_2 = \{\mu_5, \mu_7\}^\dagger$	$H_1 = b_1 \vee b_0$ $H_2 = \neg b_0 \vee \neg b_1$	
$(b_1 \vee b_0) \wedge (\neg b_0 \vee \neg b_1)$	*YES*				

† $\mu_5(b_0 b_1) = 10$ and $\mu_7(b_0 b_1) = 01$

Fig. 4. Learning $b_0 \oplus b_1$

Automatic Abstraction for Congruences

Andy King[1,*] and Harald Søndergaard[2]

[1] Portcullis Computer Security Limited, Pinner, HA5 2EX, UK
[2] The University of Melbourne, Victoria 3010, Australia

Abstract. One approach to verifying bit-twiddling algorithms is to derive invariants between the bits that constitute the variables of a program. Such invariants can often be described with systems of congruences where in each equation $\boldsymbol{c} \cdot \boldsymbol{x} = d \mod m$, m is a power of two, $\boldsymbol{c}$ is a vector of integer coefficients, and $\boldsymbol{x}$ is a vector of propositional variables (bits). Because of the low-level nature of these invariants and the large number of bits that are involved, it is important that the transfer functions can be derived automatically. We address this problem, showing how an analysis for bit-level congruence relationships can be decoupled into two parts: (1) a SAT-based abstraction (compilation) step which can be automated, and (2) an interpretation step that requires no SAT-solving. We exploit triangular matrix forms to derive transfer functions efficiently, even in the presence of large numbers of bits. Finally we propose program transformations that improve the analysis results.

1 Introduction

Recently there has been a resurgence of interest in inferring numeric relations between program variables, most notably with congruences [1,8,11]. In this abstract domain, each description is a system of congruence equations (over n variables), each taking the form $\boldsymbol{c} \cdot \boldsymbol{x} = d \mod m$, with $\boldsymbol{c} \in \mathbb{Z}^n$, $d, m \in \mathbb{Z}$ and $\boldsymbol{x}$ an n-ary vector of variables. The congruence $\boldsymbol{c} \cdot \boldsymbol{x} = d \mod m$, henceforth abbreviated to $\boldsymbol{c} \cdot \boldsymbol{x} \equiv_m d$, expresses that there exists a multiplier $k \in \mathbb{Z}$ of m such that $\boldsymbol{c} \cdot \boldsymbol{x} = d + km$. Quite apart from their expressiveness [5], such systems are attractive computationally since, if the values in $[0, m-1]$ can be represented with machine integers then arbitrary precision arithmetic can be avoided in abstract operations, and at the same time, polynomial performance guarantees are obtained [11]. This compares favourably with systems of inequalities that present, among other problems, the issue of how to curb the growth of coefficients [6,9,15].

Of particular interest are congruences where m is a power of two, since these can express invariants that hold at the level of machine words [11] or bits [8]. The central idea of [8] is *congruent closure* which computes a system of congruences c to describe all the solutions of a given Boolean function f. To see the motivation for this, consider bit-twiddling programs such as those in Figure 1 (we return to the two programs in later sections). Such programs often establish important

* Andy King is on secondment from the University of Kent, CT2 7NF, UK.

G. Barthe and M. Hermenegildo (Eds.): VMCAI 2010, LNCS 5944, pp. 197–213, 2010.

```
ℓ0: p := 0; y := x;              ℓ0: y := x;
ℓ1: while (y ≠ 0)                    y := ((y ≫ 1) & 0x5555) | ((y & 0x5555) ≪ 1);
        y := y & (y − 1);            y := ((y ≫ 2) & 0x3333) | ((y & 0x3333) ≪ 2);
        p := 1 - p;                  y := ((y ≫ 4) & 0x0F0F) | ((y & 0x0F0F) ≪ 4);
ℓ2: skip                             y := (y ≫ 8)            | (y ≪ 8);
                                 ℓ1: skip

            (a)                                        (b)
```

Fig. 1. Computing the parity of x and reversing the 16-bit word x

but obscure invariants. Performing a complete bit-precise analysis is infeasible for all but the simplest loop-free programs. At the same time, the invariants can often be captured succinctly as a system of congruence equations. However, as the assignments involved are not linear, traditional congruence analyses will not work. An alternative is to summarise basic program blocks bit-precisely and apply congruent closure judiciously. This allows us to reveal "numeric" invariants amongst bits, even for flowchart programs with loops, such as in Figure 1(a). Congruences satisfy the ascending chain condition: no infinite chain $c_1, c_2, \ldots$ with $[\![c_i]\!] \subset [\![c_{i-1}]\!]$ exists. We exploit this to compute congruent closure symbolically, by solving a finite number of SAT instances [8].

Congruent closure connects with work on how to compute most precise transfer functions for a given abstract domain. A transfer function simulates the effect of executing an operation where the possible input values are summarised by an element in the abstract domain. The problem is how to find, in the domain, the most precise element that summarises all outputs that can result from the summarised inputs. In predicate abstraction, when the abstract domain is a product of Boolean values, decision procedures have been used to solve this problem [4]. More generally, a decision procedure can also be applied to compute the most precise transfer function when the domain satisfies the ascending chain condition [13]. The idea is to translate the input summary into a formula which is conjoined with another that expresses the semantics of the operation as a relationship between input values and output values. An output summary is then extracted from the conjoined formula by repeatedly calling the decision procedure. Reps et al [13] illustrate this construction for constant propagation, and the technique is equally applicable to congruences. In this context, the semantics of an operation can be expressed propositionally [8]. The state of each integer variable is represented by a vector of propositional variables, one propositional variable for each bit. A formula is then derived [2,7], that is propositional, which specifies how the output bits depend on the input bits. Given an input summary that is congruent, a congruent output summary can be derived by: (1) converting the input summary to a propositional formula; (2) conjoining it with the input-output formula; (3) applying congruent closure to the conjunction. The advantage of this formulation is that it can derive invariants down to the level of bits, which enables the correctness of bit-twiddling code to be verified [8].

Congruent closure may require many calls to a SAT solver. As sketched, it is computed each time a transfer function is applied. A critical observation in this paper is that it is possible, and simpler, to summarise the input-output formula as a linear system that prescribes a transfer function. Once all transfer functions have been derived, it is only necessary to manipulate linear systems. In this new scheme, the application of a SAT solver is limited to the compilation step: the derivation of the transfer function. With this paper we:

– Consider an unrestricted flowchart language with various non-linear, bit-manipulating operations and provide it with a relational semantics. The semantic definition lets us dovetail bit-blasting with congruent closure, and avoids the need for a separate collecting semantics.
– Show that congruent closure is only needed in the derivation, from the bit-blasted relational semantics, of a certain transition system; thereafter congruence invariants can be inferred by repeatedly applying linear operations to the transition system. As well as allowing separation of concerns, this avoids the overhead of repeated closure calculation.
– Present a new algorithm for congruent closure. Its use of (upper triangular) matrices for congruence systems makes it considerably faster than a previous algorithm [8].
– Show how an input program can be transformed so that range information can be inferred for variables occurring in loops. This is possible since bit-level (rather than word-level) congruences can express the non-negativity of a variable, which is sufficient to verify that inequalities hold.

Analyses using congruences modulo 2^k have previously been designed [8,11]. Our main contribution here is the automated derivation of transfer functions for these analyses. This complements recent work [10] on automatically deriving transfer functions for linear template domains [14] (which can realise octagons and intervals) where the semantics of instructions is modelled with piecewise linear functions. However, our approach does not impose this semantic restriction and is not based on quantifier elimination.

The paper is structured as follows: The new algorithm for congruent closure is given in Section 2. Section 3 presents a relational semantics for flowchart programs over machine integers and Section 4 develops a bit-level relational semantics that encapsulates the spirit of bit-blasting. Section 5 shows how these semantics can be abstracted to derive transition systems over congruences. Section 6 explains how programs can be transformed to derive range information. Section 7 concludes.

2 Congruent Closure

This section introduces a new algorithm for computing the congruent closure of a Boolean function. Let $\mathbb{B} = \{0, 1\}$ and let $\mathbb{Z}_m = [0, m-1]$. If $\boldsymbol{x}, \boldsymbol{y} \in \mathbb{Z}^k$ then we write $\boldsymbol{x} \equiv_m \boldsymbol{y}$ for $\bigwedge_{i=1}^{k} x_i \equiv_m y_i$ where $\boldsymbol{x} = \langle x_1, \ldots, x_k \rangle$ and $\boldsymbol{y} = \langle y_1, \ldots, y_k \rangle$.

Definition 1. The (modulo m) *affine hull* of $S \subseteq \mathbb{Z}_m^k$ is defined:

$$\mathsf{aff}_m^k(S) = \left\{ \boldsymbol{x} \in \mathbb{Z}_m^k \,\middle|\, \begin{array}{l} \boldsymbol{x}_1, \ldots, \boldsymbol{x}_\ell \in S \;\wedge\; \lambda_1, \ldots, \lambda_\ell \in \mathbb{Z} \;\wedge \\ \sum_{i=1}^{\ell} \lambda_i \equiv_m 1 \;\wedge\; \boldsymbol{x} \equiv_m \sum_{i=1}^{\ell} \lambda_i \boldsymbol{x}_i \end{array} \right\}$$

Example 1. If $S = \emptyset$, $S = \mathbb{Z}_m^k$ or $S = \{\boldsymbol{x}\}$ for some $\boldsymbol{x} \in \mathbb{Z}_m^k$ then $\mathsf{aff}_m^k(S) = S$. Now consider $S = \{\langle 0, 3\rangle, \langle 1, 5\rangle\}$. We have

$$\begin{aligned} \mathsf{aff}_8^2(S) &= \{\boldsymbol{x} \in \mathbb{Z}_8^2 \mid \lambda_1 + \lambda_2 \equiv_8 1 \wedge \boldsymbol{x} \equiv_8 \lambda_1\langle 0,3\rangle + \lambda_2\langle 1,5\rangle\} \\ &= \{\boldsymbol{x} \in \mathbb{Z}_8^2 \mid \boldsymbol{x} \equiv_8 \langle k, 3+2k\rangle \wedge k \in \mathbb{Z}\} \end{aligned}$$

Let $\mathsf{Aff}_m^k = \{S \subseteq \mathbb{Z}_m^k \mid \mathsf{aff}_m^k(S) = S\}$. Suppose $S_i \in \mathsf{Aff}_m^k$ for all $i \in I$ where I is some index set. Put $S = \bigcap_{i \in I} S_i$. It is not difficult to see that $\mathsf{aff}_m^k(S) = S$. In other words, $\langle \mathsf{Aff}_m^k, \subseteq, \bigcap\rangle$ is a Moore family [3], and we obtain a complete lattice $\langle \mathsf{Aff}_m^k, \subseteq, \bigcap, \bigsqcup\rangle$ by defining $\bigsqcup_{i \in I} S_i = \bigcap\{S' \in \mathsf{Aff}_m^k \mid \forall i \in I. S_i \subseteq S'\}$. This gives rise to a notion of abstraction in the following sense:

Definition 2. The abstraction map $\alpha_m^k : \wp(\mathbb{B}^k) \to \mathsf{Aff}_m^k$ and concretisation map $\gamma_m^k : \mathsf{Aff}_m^k \to \wp(\mathbb{B}^k)$ are defined: $\alpha_m^k(S) = \mathsf{aff}_m^k(S)$ and $\gamma_m^k(S) = S \cap \mathbb{B}^k$.

For any k and m we call α_m^k the (modulo m) *congruent closure*[1] of its argument.

Example 2. Let us denote the set of solutions (models) of a Boolean function f by $[\![f]\!]$ thus, for example, $[\![x_1 \wedge x_2]\!] = \{\langle 1,1\rangle\}$ and $[\![x_1 \oplus x_2]\!] = \{\langle 0,1\rangle, \langle 1,0\rangle\}$ where $\oplus$ denotes exclusive-or. Likewise, let us denote the set of solutions of a system of congruences c by $[\![c]\!]$. For instance, if $c = (x_1 + x_2 \equiv_4 3 \wedge 3x_2 \equiv_4 2)$ then $[\![c]\!] = \{\langle 4k_1+1, 4k_2+2\rangle \in \mathbb{Z}_4^2 \mid k_1, k_2 \in \mathbb{Z}\}$ where $\mathbb{Z}_m = [0, m-1]$. Given f over n (propositional) variables $\boldsymbol{x}$ and a modulus m, congruent closure computes the strongest congruence system c over n (integer) variables such that $[\![f]\!] \subseteq [\![c]\!]$, or equivalently, $[\![f]\!] \subseteq [\![c]\!] \cap \mathbb{B}^n$ where $\mathbb{B} = \{0,1\}$. For example, given $m = 4$, $f_1 = (\neg x_1) \wedge (x_1 \oplus x_2 \oplus x_3)$, and $f_2 = x_1 \wedge (x_2 \vee x_3)$, congruent closure computes $c_1 = (x_1 \equiv_4 0 \wedge x_2 + x_3 \equiv_4 1)$ and $c_2 = (x_1 \equiv_4 1)$ respectively. The congruences c_1 and c_2 describe all solutions of f_1 and f_2, as

$$\begin{aligned} [\![f_1]\!] = \{\langle 0,0,1\rangle, \langle 0,1,0\rangle\} &= [\![c_1]\!] \cap \mathbb{B}^3 \\ [\![f_2]\!] = \{\langle 1,0,1\rangle, \langle 1,1,0\rangle, \langle 1,1,1\rangle\} \subseteq \{\langle 1, x_2, x_3\rangle \mid x_2, x_3 \in \mathbb{B}\} &= [\![c_2]\!] \cap \mathbb{B}^3 \end{aligned}$$

Note that c_2 additionally contains a non-solution $\langle 1,0,0\rangle$ of f_2 and hence, in general, congruent closure upper-approximates the set of models of a Boolean function.

It is straightforward to verify that α_m^k and γ_m^k form a Galois connection between the complete lattices $\langle \wp(\mathbb{B}^k), \subseteq, \bigcap, \bigcup\rangle$ and $\langle \mathsf{Aff}_m^k, \subseteq, \bigcap, \bigsqcup\rangle$.

[1] The notion should not be confused with congruence closure as used in the automated deduction community for the computation of equivalence relations over the set of nodes of a graph a la Nelson and Oppen [12].

```
function closure(input: S ⊆ B^k and modulus m ∈ N)
    [A|b] := [0, ..., 0, 1];                      – the unsatisfiable system
    i := 0; r := 1;
    while (i < r)
        ⟨a_1, ..., a_k, b⟩ := row([A|b], r − i);    – last non-stable row
        S' := {x ∈ S | ⟨a_1, ..., a_k⟩ · x ≢_m b}; – impose disequality
        if (there exists x ∈ S') then             – solve new SAT instance
            [A'|b'] := [A|b] ⊔ [Id|x];            – merge with new solution x
            [A|b] := triangular([A'|b']);
            r := rows([A|b]);
        else
            i := i + 1;                           – a · x ≡_m b is invariant so move on
    return [A|b];
```

Fig. 2. Calculating Congruent Closure Based on Triangularisation

Example 3. Suppose $S_{b_0b_1b_2b_3} = \{\langle 0,0\rangle \mid b_0 = 1\} \cup \{\langle 0,1\rangle \mid b_1 = 1\} \cup \{\langle 1,0\rangle \mid b_2 = 1\} \cup \{\langle 1,1\rangle \mid b_3 = 1\}$ where $b_0, b_1, b_2, b_3 \in \mathbb{B}$. Then

$$\begin{array}{ll}
\alpha^2_{16}(S_{0000}) = \emptyset & \alpha^2_{16}(S_{1000}) = \{\langle 0,0\rangle\} \\
\alpha^2_{16}(S_{0001}) = \{\langle 1,1\rangle\} & \alpha^2_{16}(S_{1001}) = \{\langle k,k\rangle \mid k \in [0,15]\} \\
\alpha^2_{16}(S_{0010}) = \{\langle 1,0\rangle\} & \alpha^2_{16}(S_{1010}) = \{\langle k,0\rangle \mid k \in [0,15]\} \\
\alpha^2_{16}(S_{0011}) = \{\langle 1,k\rangle \mid k \in [0,15]\} & \alpha^2_{16}(S_{1011}) = \mathbb{Z}^2_{16} \\
\alpha^2_{16}(S_{0100}) = \{\langle 0,1\rangle\} & \alpha^2_{16}(S_{1100}) = \{\langle 0,k\rangle \mid k \in [0,15]\} \\
\alpha^2_{16}(S_{0101}) = \{\langle k,1\rangle \mid k \in [0,15]\} & \alpha^2_{16}(S_{1101}) = \mathbb{Z}^2_{16} \\
\alpha^2_{16}(S_{0110}) = \{\langle k_1,k_2\rangle \in \mathbb{Z}^2_{16} \mid k_1 + k_2 \equiv_{16} 1\} & \alpha^2_{16}(S_{1110}) = \mathbb{Z}^2_{16} \\
\alpha^2_{16}(S_{0111}) = \mathbb{Z}^2_{16} & \alpha^2_{16}(S_{1111}) = \mathbb{Z}^2_{16}
\end{array}$$

From this we conclude that, in general, α^k_m is not surjective and therefore α^k_m and γ^k_m do not form a Galois insertion.

Example 4. Let f be the Boolean function $c'_0 \leftrightarrow (c_0 \oplus 1) \wedge c'_1 \leftrightarrow (c_1 \oplus c_0) \wedge c'_2 \leftrightarrow (c_2 \oplus (c_0 \wedge c_1)) \wedge c'_3 \leftrightarrow (c_3 \oplus (c_0 \wedge c_1 \wedge c_2))$. Then $\alpha^8_{16}([\![f]\!]) = [\![c]\!]$, where c is the conjunction of two equations $c_0 + 2c_1 + 4c_2 + 8c_3 + 1 \equiv_{16} c'_0 + 2c'_1 + 4c'_2 + 8c'_3$ and $c_0 + c'_0 \equiv_{16} 1$. This illustrates how congruent closure can extract numeric relationships from a Boolean function.

Figure 2 presents a new algorithm for finding the congruent closure of a Boolean function. For the purpose of presentation, it is convenient to pretend the function is given as a set S of models, although we assume it given in conjunctive normal form. If A is an $m \times n$ matrix and $\boldsymbol{b} = (b_1, \ldots, b_m)$ is a vector, we denote by $[A|\boldsymbol{b}]$ the $m \times (n+1)$ matrix B defined by

$$B_{ij} = \begin{cases} A_{ij} & \text{if } 1 \le i \le m \text{ and } 1 \le j \le n \\ b_i & \text{if } 1 \le i \le m \text{ and } j = n+1 \end{cases}$$

Given a matrix A, we write 'row(A, i)' for its ith row, and 'rows(A)' for the number of rows. We use 'triangular(A)' for the result of bringing A into upper

Step	i	Response from SAT solver	$\boldsymbol{Ax} \equiv_m \boldsymbol{b}$
0	0	$x_0 = 0, x_1 = 0, x_2 = 1, x_3 = 0, x'_0 = 1, x'_1 = 0, x'_2 = 0, x'_3 = 0$	s_1
1	0	$x_0 = 0, x_1 = 0, x_2 = 0, x_3 = 1, x'_0 = 1, x'_1 = 1, x'_2 = 1, x'_3 = 1$	s_2
2	0	UNSATISFIABLE	s_2
3	1	UNSATISFIABLE	s_2
4	2	$x_0 = 0, x_1 = 0, x_2 = 0, x_3 = 0, x'_0 = 0, x'_1 = 0, x'_2 = 0, x'_3 = 0$	s_3
5	2	UNSATISFIABLE	s_3
6	3	$x_0 = 0, x_1 = 1, x_2 = 0, x_3 = 0, x'_0 = 1, x'_1 = 0, x'_2 = 0, x'_3 = 0$	s_4
7	3	$x_0 = 0, x_1 = 1, x_2 = 1, x_3 = 0, x'_0 = 1, x'_1 = 0, x'_2 = 0, x'_3 = 0$	s_5
8	3	$x_0 = 1, x_1 = 0, x_2 = 0, x_3 = 0, x'_0 = 1, x'_1 = 0, x'_2 = 0, x'_3 = 0$	s_6

s_1 :

$$\left\{\begin{array}{l} x_0 \equiv_4 0 \\ x_1 \equiv_4 0 \\ x_2 \equiv_4 1 \\ x_3 \equiv_4 0 \\ x'_0 \equiv_4 1 \\ x'_1 \equiv_4 0 \\ x'_2 \equiv_4 0 \\ x'_3 \equiv_4 0 \end{array}\right\}$$

s_2 :

$$\left\{\begin{array}{l} x_0 \equiv_4 0 \\ x_1 \equiv_4 0 \\ x_2\ x_3 \equiv_4 1 \\ x_3\ -x'_1 \equiv_4 0 \\ x'_0 \equiv_4 1 \\ x'_1\ -x'_2 \equiv_4 0 \\ x'_2\ -x'_3 \equiv_4 0 \end{array}\right\}$$

s_3 :

$$\left\{\begin{array}{l} x_0 \equiv_4 0 \\ x_1 \equiv_4 0 \\ x_2\ x_3\ -x'_0 \equiv_4 0 \\ x_3\ -x'_1 \equiv_4 0 \\ x'_1\ -x'_2 \equiv_4 0 \\ x'_2\ -x'_3 \equiv_4 0 \end{array}\right\}$$

s_4 :

$$\left\{\begin{array}{l} x_0 \equiv_4 0 \\ x_1\ x_2\ x_3\ -x'_0 \equiv_4 0 \\ x_3\ -x'_1 \equiv_4 0 \\ x'_1\ -x'_2 \equiv_4 0 \\ x'_2\ -x'_3 \equiv_4 0 \end{array}\right\}$$

s_5 :

$$\left\{\begin{array}{l} x_0 \equiv_4 0 \\ x_3\ -x'_1 \equiv_4 0 \\ x'_1\ -x'_2 \equiv_4 0 \\ x'_2\ -x'_3 \equiv_4 0 \end{array}\right\}$$

s_6 :

$$\left\{\begin{array}{l} x_3\ -x'_1 \equiv_4 0 \\ x'_1\ -x'_2 \equiv_4 0 \\ x'_2\ -x'_3 \equiv_4 0 \end{array}\right\}$$

Fig. 3. SAT responses and the six congruence systems that arise for Example 5

triangular form—Müller-Olm and Seidl [11] provide an algorithm for this. The join operation $\sqcup$ can be implemented in terms of projection which in turn has a simple implementation utilising the maintenance of upper-triangular form [8]. Space constraints prevent us from repeating the join algorithm here.

It is important to observe that S' can be expressed propositionally by augmenting S with a propositional encoding of the *single* disequality constraint $\langle a_1, \ldots, a_k \rangle \cdot \boldsymbol{x} \not\equiv_m b$. This ensures that the propositional encoding of S' does not grow without bound, which is vital for tractability. A chain length result for congruences [11] ensures that the total number of calls to the SAT solver is $O(wk)$ when $m = 2^w$.

Example 5. Suppose $f = (\neg x_3 \wedge \neg x_2 \wedge \neg x_1 \wedge \neg x_0 \wedge \neg x'_3 \wedge \neg x'_2 \wedge \neg x'_1 \wedge \neg x'_0) \vee (x_3 \wedge x'_3 \wedge x'_2 \wedge x'_1 \wedge x'_0) \vee (\neg x_3 \wedge (x_2 \vee x_1 \vee x_0) \wedge \neg x'_3 \wedge \neg x'_2 \wedge \neg x'_1 \wedge x'_0)$.

(This function could appear in an attempt to reason about an assignment $x := \text{sign}(x)$ for a machine with 4-bit words.) The table given in Figure 3 shows how the algorithm proceeds when computing the congruent closure of f, assuming a particular sequence of results being returned from a SAT solver. The responses from the solver are shown. In step 0, a single model of f produces the equation system s_1. This, and the subsequent congruence systems, are also shown. Each system s_i is produced from its predecessor s_{i-1} by identifying some model $\boldsymbol{x}$ of f that is not covered by s_{i-1} and calculating the strongest congruence system covering both, that is, s_i is the join of s_{i-1} and the system expressing the fact that $\boldsymbol{x}$ is a model. The congruent closure of f is finally given by s_6.

The following proposition states the correctness of the algorithm: the result is independent of the order in which a SAT/SMT solver finds solutions. A proof sketch has been relegated to the appendix.

Proposition 1. Let $S \subseteq \mathbb{B}^k$ and $m \in \mathbb{N}$, and let $[A|\boldsymbol{b}] = \text{closure}(S, m)$. Then $\mathsf{aff}^k_m(S) = \{\boldsymbol{x} \in \mathbb{Z}^k_m \mid A\boldsymbol{x} \equiv_m \boldsymbol{b}\}$.

3 Relational Semantics

Flowchart programs are defined over a finite set of labels L and a set of variables $X = \{x_1, \ldots, x_k\}$ that range over values drawn from $R = [-2^{w-1}, 2^{w-1} - 1]$. A flowchart program P is a quadruple $P = \langle L, X, \ell_0, T\rangle$ where $\ell_0 \in L$ indicates the program entry point and $T \subseteq L \times L \times \mathsf{Guard} \times \mathsf{Stmt}$ is a finite set of transitions.

3.1 Syntax of Flowchart Programs

The classes of well-formed expressions, guards and statements are defined by:

$$\begin{aligned} \mathsf{Expr} &::= X \mid R \mid -\mathsf{Expr} \mid \mathsf{Expr\ bop\ Expr} \\ \mathsf{Guard} &::= \mathsf{true} \mid \mathsf{false} \mid \mathsf{Expr\ rop\ Expr} \mid \mathsf{Guard\ lop\ Guard} \\ \mathsf{Stmt} &::= \mathsf{skip} \mid X := \mathsf{Expr} \mid \mathsf{Stmt; Stmt} \end{aligned}$$

where the sets of binary operators bop, logical operators lop and relational operators rop are defined thus $\mathsf{rop} = \{=, \neq, <, \leq\}$, $\mathsf{bop} = \{+, -, \&, \mid, \ll, \gg\}$, $\mathsf{lop} = \{\wedge, \vee\}$ and the $\&, \mid, \ll, \gg$ symbols denote C-style bitwise operations.

Example 6. The program in Figure 1(a) can be expressed as the flowchart $\langle\{\ell_0, \ell_1, \ell_2\}, \{p, x, y\}, \ell_0, T\rangle$ where $T = \{t_1, t_2, t_3\}$ and $t_1 = \langle \ell_0, \ell_1, true,\ p = 0; y = x\rangle$, $t_2 = \langle \ell_1, \ell_1, y \neq 0, y := y \,\&\, (y-1); p := 1 - p\rangle$, $t_3 = \langle \ell_1, \ell_2, y = 0, \mathsf{skip}\rangle$.

Example 7. The program in Figure 1(b) is expressed as

$$\langle\{\ell_0, \ell_1\}, \{x, y\}, \ell_0, \{\langle \ell_0, \ell_1, true, y := x; y := e_1; y := e_2; y := e_3; y := e_4\rangle\}\rangle$$

where e_1, e_2, e_3 and e_4 are the RHSs of the assignments that follow $y := x$.

3.2 Semantics of Flowchart Programs

All variables are of limited-precision integer signed type, based on some word length w. The semantics can be formulated denotationally in terms of functions: The set of states is the function space $\Sigma = X \to R$ and each state $\sigma \in \Sigma$ maps a variable to a value of R; the function $\mathcal{E} : \mathsf{Expr} \to \Sigma \to R$ evaluates an expression; and the function $\mathcal{S} : \mathsf{Stmt} \to \Sigma \to \Sigma$ transforms one state to another. However, we prefer to give a relational semantics, for a number of reasons. First, we consider programs to take input via the program variables, so the semantics needs to express how, at different points, program states are related to initial states. Second, the relational semantics can be bit-blasted in a natural way, and this is essential to the program analysis that we discuss. Third, we avoid a need to lift a standard semantics to a so-called collecting semantics. Hence we wish to express the effect of a program statement as a relation $r \subseteq R^{2k}$ that captures the values of the k variables before and after the statement is executed. Compared to the denotational approach, in our relational viewpoint a state transformer $\mathcal{S}[\![s]\!] : \Sigma \to \Sigma$ is replaced by a relation $r = \{\langle \sigma(x_1), \ldots, \sigma(x_k), \tau(x_1), \ldots, \tau(x_k) \rangle \mid \sigma \in \Sigma \wedge \tau = \mathcal{S}[\![s]\!](\sigma)\}$. Henceforth $\mathcal{S}[\![s]\!]$ will denote a relation $\mathcal{S}[\![s]\!] \subseteq R^{2k}$.

3.3 Semantic Machinery: Composition and Bit Manipulation

To formulate a relational semantics, if $\boldsymbol{a}, \boldsymbol{b} \in R^k$ then let $\boldsymbol{a} \cdot \boldsymbol{b} \in R^{2k}$ denote the concatenation of $\boldsymbol{a}$ and $\boldsymbol{b}$. The identity relation is then $\mathsf{Id} = \{\boldsymbol{a} \cdot \boldsymbol{a} \mid \boldsymbol{a} \in R^k\}$. If $r_1, r_2 \subseteq R^{2k}$ then the composition of r_1 and r_2 is defined $r_1 \circ r_2 = \{\boldsymbol{a} \cdot \boldsymbol{c} \mid \boldsymbol{b} \in R^k \wedge \boldsymbol{a} \cdot \boldsymbol{b} \in r_1 \wedge \boldsymbol{b} \cdot \boldsymbol{c} \in r_2\}$. Furthermore, if $r_1 \subseteq R^k$ and $r_2 \subseteq R^{2k}$ then let $r_1 \circ r_2 = \{\boldsymbol{b} \mid \boldsymbol{a} \in r_1 \wedge \boldsymbol{a} \cdot \boldsymbol{b} \in r_2\}$. If $\boldsymbol{a} = \langle a_1, \ldots, a_k \rangle \in R^k$ let $\boldsymbol{a}[i] = a_i$ and if $b \in R$ let $\boldsymbol{a}[i \mapsto b] = \langle a_1, \ldots, a_{i-1}, b, a_{i+1}, \ldots, a_k \rangle$.

To specify bit-twiddling operations, let $\langle\!\langle . \rangle\!\rangle : [-2^{w-1}, 2^{w-1} - 1] \to \mathbb{B}^w$ and $\langle . \rangle : [0, 2^w - 1] \to \mathbb{B}^w$ denote the signed and unsigned w-bit representation of an integer. Thus let $\langle\!\langle n \rangle\!\rangle = \langle x_0, \ldots, x_{w-1} \rangle$ where $n = (\sum_{i=0}^{w-2} 2^i x_i) - 2^{w-1} x_{w-1}$ and let $\langle m \rangle = \langle x_0, \ldots, x_{w-1} \rangle$ where $m = \sum_{i=0}^{w-1} 2^i x_i$. Let $n_1, n_2 \in R$. To define $n_1 \mid n_2 = n$ let $\langle\!\langle n \rangle\!\rangle = \langle x_0^1 \vee x_0^2, \ldots, x_{w-1}^1 \vee x_{w-1}^2 \rangle$ where $\langle\!\langle n_i \rangle\!\rangle = \langle x_0^i, \ldots, x_{w-1}^i \rangle$. To define $n_1 \ll n_2 = n$ let $\langle\!\langle n \rangle\!\rangle = \langle 0, \ldots, 0, x_0^1, \ldots, x_{w-1-n_2}^1 \rangle$ if $n_2 \in [0, w-1]$ otherwise $n = 0$ (which handles the normally unspecified case of when $n_2 < 0$). To define $n_1 + n_2 = n$ let $n \in R$ such that $n_1 + n_2 \equiv_{2^w} n$. Bitwise conjunction, rightshift and subtraction are analogously defined.

3.4 Semantic Equations

The relational semantics of a guard $g \in \mathsf{Guard}$ is then given by $\mathcal{S}[\![g]\!] = \{\boldsymbol{a} \cdot \boldsymbol{a} \mid \boldsymbol{a} \in R^k \wedge \mathcal{G}[\![g]\!]\boldsymbol{a}\}$. The effect of a statement $s \in \mathsf{Stmt}$ is defined thus:

$$
\begin{aligned}
\mathcal{S}[\![\mathsf{skip}]\!] &= \mathsf{Id} \\
\mathcal{S}[\![x_i := e]\!] &= \{\boldsymbol{a} \cdot \boldsymbol{a}[i \mapsto \mathcal{E}[\![e]\!]\boldsymbol{a}] \mid \boldsymbol{a} \in R^k\} \\
\mathcal{S}[\![s_1; s_2]\!] &= \mathcal{S}[\![s_1]\!] \circ \mathcal{S}[\![s_2]\!]
\end{aligned}
$$

where $\mathcal{E}$ and $\mathcal{G}$ are defined:

$$\begin{aligned}
\mathcal{E}[\![x_i]\!]\boldsymbol{a} &= \boldsymbol{a}[i] \\
\mathcal{E}[\![n]\!]\boldsymbol{a} &= n \\
\mathcal{E}[\![-e]\!]\boldsymbol{a} &= r \in R && \text{where } r \equiv_{2^w} -(\mathcal{E}[\![e]\!]\boldsymbol{a}) \\
\mathcal{E}[\![e_1 \odot e_2]\!]\boldsymbol{a} &= (\mathcal{E}[\![e_1]\!]\boldsymbol{a}) \odot (\mathcal{E}[\![e_2]\!]\boldsymbol{a}) && \text{where } \odot \in \mathsf{bop}
\end{aligned}$$

$$\begin{aligned}
\mathcal{G}[\![\mathsf{true}]\!]\boldsymbol{a} &= 1 \\
\mathcal{G}[\![\mathsf{false}]\!]\boldsymbol{a} &= 0 \\
\mathcal{G}[\![e_1 \otimes e_2]\!]\boldsymbol{a} &= (\mathcal{E}[\![e_1]\!]\boldsymbol{a}) \otimes (\mathcal{E}[\![e_2]\!]\boldsymbol{a}) && \text{where } \otimes \in \mathsf{rop} \\
\mathcal{G}[\![g_1 \ominus g_2]\!]\boldsymbol{a} &= (\mathcal{G}[\![g_1]\!]\boldsymbol{a}) \ominus (\mathcal{G}[\![g_2]\!]\boldsymbol{a}) && \text{where } \ominus \in \mathsf{lop}
\end{aligned}$$

The semantics of a program $P = \langle L, X, \ell_0, T\rangle$ is then defined as the set of smallest relations $\{r_\ell \in R^{2k} \mid \ell \in L\}$ such that $\mathsf{Id} \subseteq r_{\ell_0}$ and $r_{\ell_i} \circ \mathcal{S}[\![g]\!] \circ \mathcal{S}[\![s]\!] \subseteq r_{\ell_j}$ for all $\langle \ell_i, \ell_j, g, s\rangle \in T$. Each relation r_ℓ is finite and relates states at ℓ_0 to states at ℓ. The set of reachable states at ℓ is given by the composition $R^k \circ r_\ell$.

4 Symbolic Relational Semantics over Boolean Functions

This section shows how a flowchart program can be bit-blasted, that is, described symbolically with Boolean formulae. First, two disjoint sets of propositional variables are introduced: $\mathbf{X} = \{x_{i,j} \mid x_i \in X \wedge j \in [0, w-1]\}$ and $\mathbf{X}' = \{x'_{i,j} \mid x_i \in X \wedge j \in [0, w-1]\}$. Second, each relation $r_\ell \subseteq R^{2k}$ for $\ell \in L$, is encoded symbolically as a formula $f_\ell \in \mathcal{B}_{\mathbf{X}\cup\mathbf{X}'}$, where $\mathcal{B}_Y$ denotes the class of propositional formulae that can be defined over the propositional variables Y. Third, operations over relations are simulated by operations over formulae.

4.1 Semantic Machinery: Encoding and Composition

We introduce a map $\mathsf{sym} : \wp(R^{2k}) \to \mathcal{B}_{\mathbf{X}\cup\mathbf{X}'}$ that specifies the symbolic encoding:

$$\mathsf{sym}(r) = \bigvee\{ \bigwedge_{x_i \in X, j \in [0,w-1]} (x_{i,j} \leftrightarrow \langle\!\langle \boldsymbol{a}[i]\rangle\!\rangle[j] \wedge x'_{i,j} \leftrightarrow \langle\!\langle \boldsymbol{b}[i]\rangle\!\rangle[j]) \mid \boldsymbol{a}\cdot\boldsymbol{b} \in r\}$$

For example, $\mathsf{sym}(\mathsf{Id}) = \bigwedge_{x_i \in X, j\in[0,w-1]} x_{i,j} \leftrightarrow x'_{i,j}$. To handle expressions and guards, we introduce a variant of the encoding map $\mathsf{sym} : \wp(R^k) \to \mathcal{B}_{\mathbf{X}}$ defined

$$\mathsf{sym}(r) = \bigvee\{ \bigwedge_{x_i \in X, j \in [0,w-1]} x_{i,j} \leftrightarrow \langle\!\langle \boldsymbol{a}[i]\rangle\!\rangle[j] \mid \boldsymbol{a} \in r\}.$$

Different formulae can represent the same Boolean function, but if we identify equivalent formulae (implicitly working with equivalent classes of formulae), then functions and formulae can be used interchangeably. With this understanding, sym is bijective so that a relation $r \subseteq R^{2k}$ uniquely defines a function $f \in \mathcal{B}_{\mathbf{X}\cup\mathbf{X}'}$, and vice versa. Moreover, if $r_1, r_2 \in R^{2k}$ then $r_1 \subseteq r_2$ iff $\mathsf{sym}(r_1) \models \mathsf{sym}(r_2)$ where $\models$ denotes logical consequence.

To simulate composition with operations on formulae, let $r_1, r_2 \subseteq R^{2k}$ and suppose $\mathsf{sym}(r_1) = f_1$ and $\mathsf{sym}(r_2) = f_2$, hence $f_1, f_2 \in \mathcal{B}_{\mathbf{X} \cup \mathbf{X}'}$. A formula $f \in \mathcal{B}_{\mathbf{X} \cup \mathbf{X}'}$ such that $\mathsf{sym}(r_1 \circ r_2) = f$ can be derived as follows: Let $\mathbf{X}'' = \{x''_{i,j} \mid x_i \in X \wedge j \in [0, w-1]\}$ so that $\mathbf{X} \cap \mathbf{X}'' = \mathbf{X}' \cap \mathbf{X}'' = \emptyset$. Put $f'_1 = f_1 \wedge \bigwedge_{x_i \in X, j \in [0,w-1]} x'_{i,j} \leftrightarrow x''_{i,j}$ and $f'_2 = f_2 \wedge \bigwedge_{x_i \in X, j \in [0,w-1]} x_{i,j} \leftrightarrow x''_{i,j}$. Define $f' = \exists_{\mathbf{X}'}(f'_1) \wedge \exists_{\mathbf{X}}(f'_2)$ and then put $f = \exists_{\mathbf{X}''}(f')$ where the operations $\exists_{\mathbf{X}'}(f'_1)$, $\exists_{\mathbf{X}}(f'_2)$ and $\exists_{\mathbf{X}''}(f')$ eliminate the variables $\mathbf{X}'$, $\mathbf{X}$ and $\mathbf{X}''$ from f'_1, f'_2 and f' respectively. Henceforth, denote $f_1 \circ_b f_2 = f$.

4.2 Semantic Equations

Analogues of $\mathcal{S}[\![s]\!] \subseteq R^{2k}$, $\mathcal{E}[\![e]\!] : R^k \to R$ and $\mathcal{G}[\![g]\!] \subseteq R^k$ over Boolean formulae, namely, $\mathcal{S}_b[\![s]\!] \in \mathcal{B}_{\mathbf{X} \cup \mathbf{X}'}$, $\mathcal{E}_b[\![e]\!] \in \mathcal{B}^w_{\mathbf{X}}$ and $\mathcal{G}_b[\![g]\!] \in \mathcal{B}_{\mathbf{X}}$ can now be constructed. The symbolic bit-level semantics for a guard $g \in \mathsf{Guard}$ is given by

$$\mathcal{S}_b[\![g]\!] = \mathcal{G}_b[\![g]\!] \wedge \bigwedge_{x_i \in X, j \in [0,w-1]} (x'_{i,j} \leftrightarrow x_{i,j})$$

whereas the semantics for a statement $s \in \mathsf{Stmt}$ is given as follows:

$$\begin{aligned}
\mathcal{S}_b[\![\mathsf{skip}]\!] &= \textstyle\bigwedge_{x_i \in X, j \in [0,w-1]} (x'_{i,j} \leftrightarrow x_{i,j}) \\
\mathcal{S}_b[\![x_i := e]\!] &= \textstyle\bigwedge_{j \in [0,w-1]} (x'_{i,j} \leftrightarrow \mathcal{E}_b[\![e]\!][j]) \wedge \bigwedge_{x_k \in X \setminus \{x_i\}, j \in [0,w-1]} (x'_{k,j} \leftrightarrow x_{k,j}) \\
\mathcal{S}_b[\![s_1; s_2]\!] &= \mathcal{S}_b[\![s_1]\!] \circ_b \mathcal{S}_b[\![s_2]\!]
\end{aligned}$$

The second conjunct of $\mathcal{S}_b[\![g]\!]$ expresses that variables remain unchanged. As before, $\mathcal{S}_b$ is defined in terms of $\mathcal{G}_b$ and $\mathcal{E}_b$. The semantic function $\mathcal{E}_b : \mathsf{Expr} \to [0, w-1] \to \mathcal{B}_{\mathbf{X}}$ takes an expression and a bit position and returns the value of that bit, expressed in terms of a Boolean formula. The function $\mathcal{G}_b : \mathsf{Guard} \to \mathcal{B}_{\mathbf{X}}$ takes a guard and returns its (Boolean) value. In what follows, $\boldsymbol{f}_1 \in \mathcal{B}^w_{\mathbf{X}}$ and $\boldsymbol{f}_2 \in \mathcal{B}^w_{\mathbf{X}}$ abbreviate $\mathcal{E}_b[\![e_1]\!]$ and $\mathcal{E}_b[\![e_2]\!]$, respectively.

$$\begin{aligned}
\mathcal{E}_b[\![x_i]\!][j] &= x_{i,j} \\
\mathcal{E}_b[\![n]\!][j] &= \langle\!\langle n \rangle\!\rangle[j] \\
\mathcal{E}_b[\![-e]\!][j] &= \mathcal{E}_b[\![e]\!][j] \oplus \textstyle\bigvee_{j=0}^{i-1} \mathcal{E}_b[\![e]\!][j] \\
\mathcal{E}_b[\![e_1 + e_2]\!][j] &= \boldsymbol{f}_1[j] \oplus \boldsymbol{f}_2[j] \oplus \textstyle\bigoplus_{k=0}^{j-1} (\boldsymbol{f}_1[k] \wedge \boldsymbol{f}_2[k] \wedge \bigwedge_{m=k+1}^{j-1} (\boldsymbol{f}_1[m] \oplus \boldsymbol{f}_2[m])) \\
\mathcal{E}_b[\![e_1 - e_2]\!][j] &= \mathcal{E}_b[\![e_1 + (-e_2)]\!][j] \\
\mathcal{E}_b[\![e_1 \,\&\, e_2]\!][j] &= \boldsymbol{f}_1[j] \wedge \boldsymbol{f}_2[j] \\
\mathcal{E}_b[\![e_1 \mid e_2]\!][j] &= \boldsymbol{f}_1[j] \vee \boldsymbol{f}_2[j]
\end{aligned}$$

$$\begin{aligned}
\mathcal{G}_b[\![\mathsf{true}]\!] &= 1 \\
\mathcal{G}_b[\![\mathsf{false}]\!] &= 0 \\
\mathcal{G}_b[\![g_1 = g_2]\!] &= \textstyle\bigwedge_{i=0}^{w-1} (\boldsymbol{f}_1[j] \leftrightarrow \boldsymbol{f}_2[j]) \\
\mathcal{G}_b[\![g_1 \neq g_2]\!] &= \neg(\mathcal{G}_b[\![g_1 = g_2]\!]) \\
\mathcal{G}_b[\![g_1 < g_2]\!] &= \neg(\mathcal{G}_b[\![g_2 \leq g_1]\!]) \\
\mathcal{G}_b[\![g_1 \leq g_2]\!] &= (\boldsymbol{f}_1[w-1] \wedge \neg \boldsymbol{f}_2[w-1]) \\
&\quad \vee \textstyle\bigvee_{j=0}^{w-2} (\neg \boldsymbol{f}_1[j] \wedge \boldsymbol{f}_2[j] \wedge \bigwedge_{k=j+1}^{w-1} \boldsymbol{f}_1[k] \leftrightarrow \boldsymbol{f}_2[k]) \\
\mathcal{G}_b[\![g_1 \wedge g_2]\!] &= (\mathcal{G}_b[\![g_1]\!]) \wedge (\mathcal{G}_b[\![g_2]\!]) \\
\mathcal{G}_b[\![g_1 \vee g_2]\!] &= (\mathcal{G}_b[\![g_1]\!]) \vee (\mathcal{G}_b[\![g_2]\!])
\end{aligned}$$

The formula for $e_1 + e_2$ is derived by considering a cascade of full adders with w carry bits $\boldsymbol{c}$. Then $\mathcal{G}_b[\![e_1 + e_2]\!][j] = (\boldsymbol{f}_1[j] \oplus \boldsymbol{f}_2[j] \oplus \boldsymbol{c}[j]) \wedge (\neg\boldsymbol{c}[0]) \wedge f$ where $f = \bigwedge_{j=1}^{w-1} \boldsymbol{c}[j] \leftrightarrow ((\boldsymbol{f}_1[j-1] \wedge \boldsymbol{f}_2[j-1]) \vee (\boldsymbol{f}_1[j-1] \wedge \boldsymbol{c}[j-1]) \vee (\boldsymbol{f}_2[j-1] \wedge \boldsymbol{c}[j-1]))$. By eliminating the $\boldsymbol{c}$ variables and simplifying, the above formula is obtained. The equation for $\mathcal{E}_b[\![e_1 \ll e_2]\!][j]$ can be straightforwardly defined with $w + 2$ cases that handle the various classes of shift. Likewise for $\mathcal{E}_b[\![e_1 \gg e_2]\!][j]$. Both equations are omitted for brevity.

4.3 Semantic Equivalence

The semantics of a program $P = \langle L, X, \ell_0, T\rangle$ can then be prescribed as the set of least Boolean functions $\{f_\ell \in \mathcal{B}_{\mathbf{X}\cup\mathbf{X}'} \mid \ell \in L\}$ such that $\mathsf{sym}(\mathsf{Id}) \models f_{\ell_0}$ and $f_{\ell_i} \circ_b \mathcal{S}[\![g]\!] \circ_b \mathcal{S}[\![s]\!] \models f_{\ell_j}$ for all $\langle \ell_i, \ell_j, g, s\rangle \in T$. The semantics can be equivalently stated as the least fixed point of a system of equations of the form $f_{\ell_j} = \bigvee\{f_{\ell_i} \circ_b \mathcal{S}[\![g]\!] \circ_b \mathcal{S}[\![s]\!] \mid \langle \ell_i, \ell_j, g, s\rangle \in T\}$, where the equation for f_{ℓ_0} includes the additional disjunction $\mathsf{sym}(\mathsf{Id})$. The semantics of the previous section can likewise be expressed as a fixed point. This allows induction to be applied to argue $\mathsf{sym}(r_\ell) = f_\ell$ for all $\ell \in L$. However this itself requires the use of induction to show $\mathsf{sym}(\mathcal{G}[\![g]\!]) = \mathcal{G}_b[\![g]\!]$ for all $g \in \mathsf{Guard}$ and $\mathsf{sym}(\mathcal{E}[\![e]\!][j]) = \mathcal{E}_b[\![e]\!][j]$ for all $e \in \mathsf{Expr}$ and $j \in [0, w-1]$. The key point is that the semantics of this section is equivalent to that introduced previously in that $\mathsf{sym}(r_\ell) = f_\ell$ for all $\ell \in L$. The difference is the latter semantics provides a basis suitable for deriving transition systems over congruences.

5 Abstract Relational Semantics over Congruences

Abstract interpretation [3] is a systematic way of deriving invariants by considering all paths through a program. Each atomic operation over the concrete data values is simulated with an abstract version manipulating abstract data values drawn from an abstract domain. The semantics of a transition $t = \langle \ell_i, \ell_i, g, s\rangle$ is expressed by the Boolean function $f = \mathcal{S}[\![g]\!] \circ_b \mathcal{S}[\![s]\!] \in \mathcal{B}_{\mathbf{X}\cup\mathbf{X}'}$, which permits t to be viewed as a single atomic operation. Once the modulus m is chosen, congruent closure provides a way to map f to a system of congruence equations that define an abstract version of t.

5.1 Deriving Abstract Transitions

Since f is a Boolean formula on $\mathbf{X} \cup \mathbf{X}'$, we let $\mathsf{Aff}_m^{\mathbf{X}\cup\mathbf{X}'}$ denote the set of systems of equations modulo m that can be defined over $\mathbf{X} \cup \mathbf{X}'$. Thus if $c \in \mathsf{Aff}_m^{\mathbf{X}\cup\mathbf{X}'}$ then c is a system of implicitly conjoined equations (rather than a single equation). Then the abstraction map $\alpha_m^{2kw} : \wp(\mathbb{B}^{2kw}) \to \mathsf{Aff}_m^{2kw}$ can be extended to $\alpha_m : \mathcal{B}_{\mathbf{X}\cup\mathbf{X}'} \to \mathsf{Aff}_m^{\mathbf{X}\cup\mathbf{X}'}$ in the natural way. This leads to the notion of an abstract flowchart program $\langle L, X, \ell_0, T'\rangle$ where $T' = \{\langle \ell_i, \ell_j, \alpha_m(\mathcal{S}[\![g]\!] \circ_b \mathcal{S}[\![s]\!])\rangle \mid \langle \ell_i, \ell_j, g, s\rangle \in T\}$. Enlarging m preserves more of f at the expense of a more complicated abstract program. Note how $\alpha_m(\mathcal{S}[\![g]\!] \circ_b \mathcal{S}[\![s]\!])$ summarises both g and s (even when s is itself compound) with a *single* system of congruences.

Example 8. Observe $\alpha_m(\mathsf{sym}(\mathsf{Id})) = \bigwedge_{x_i \in X, j \in [0,w-1]} x_{i,j} \equiv_m x'_{i,j}$.

Example 9. Consider again the parity program and suppose $w = 16$. Then computing $\alpha_m(\mathcal{S}[\![g]\!] \circ_b \mathcal{S}[\![s]\!])$ for $m = 2$ and each transition $\langle \ell_i, \ell_j, g, s \rangle \in T$ given in Example 6, we derive the abstract transitions $t'_1 = \langle \ell_0, \ell_1, c_1 \rangle$, $t'_2 = \langle \ell_1, \ell_1, c_2 \rangle$ and $t'_3 = \langle \ell_1, \ell_2, c_3 \rangle$ where

$$c_1 = (\textstyle\bigwedge_{i=0}^{15} p'_i \equiv_2 0) \wedge (\bigwedge_{i=0}^{15} y'_i \equiv_2 x_i) \wedge (\bigwedge_{i=0}^{15} x'_i \equiv_2 x_i)$$

$$\begin{aligned} c_2 = \;& p_0 + p'_0 \equiv_2 1 \;\wedge\; (\textstyle\bigwedge_{i=1}^{15} p_i \equiv_2 p'_i) \wedge (\bigwedge_{i=0}^{15} x_i \equiv_2 x'_i) \\ & \wedge\; y'_0 \equiv_2 0 \;\wedge\; 1 + \textstyle\sum_{i=1}^{15} y'_i \equiv_2 \sum_{i=0}^{15} y_i \end{aligned}$$

$$c_3 = (\textstyle\bigwedge_{i=0}^{15} p'_i \equiv_2 p_i) \wedge (\bigwedge_{i=0}^{15} x'_i \equiv_2 x_i) \wedge (\bigwedge_{i=0}^{15} y_i \equiv_2 0) \wedge (\bigwedge_{i=0}^{15} y'_i \equiv_2 0)$$

Of course, such translation cannot be performed manually and therefore we have written a Java application that derives abstract transition systems. It applies the congruent closure algorithm presented in Section 2 and uses the MiniSat solver through the Kodkod Java bindings. The most complicated system, c_2, requires 97 SAT instances to be derived taking 3s overall. A modulus of 2 is sufficient to verify the correctness of parity, but in general, the behaviour of the program is unknown and then it is more appropriate to use a modulus that reflects the size of machine words. Using a modulus of, say, 2^{32} does not increase the number of SAT instances but does double the time required to compute c_2. Interestingly, if c_2 is derived without the guard $y \neq 0$ (which accidentally happened when this experiment was conducted), then the equation $1 + \sum_{i=0}^{15} y'_i \equiv_2 \sum_{i=0}^{15} y_i$ cannot be inferred. Note too that $y'_0 \equiv_2 0$ asserts that the low bit of y is reset.

Example 10. Consider the word reversal program of Example 7, with $w = 16$. Thus put $m = 2^{16}$. Then the abstract flowchart has a single transition $\langle \ell_0, \ell_1, c \rangle$ where $c = \bigwedge_{i=0}^{15}(x'_i \equiv_{2^{16}} x_i \wedge y'_{15-i} \equiv_{2^{16}} x_i)$. This can be derived in 0.8s and requires 33 calls to the SAT solver. Note how c precisely summarises program behaviour, despite the use of devious bit-twiddling operations.

5.2 Applying Abstract Transitions

Once an abstract transition system has been derived, existing techniques can be used to compute congruences that hold at each $\ell \in L$. Efficient algorithms have been reported elsewhere [1,8,11] for checking entailment $c_1 \models c_2$, calculating join $c_1 \sqcup c_2$, and eliminating variables $\exists_Y(c_1)$ for $c_1, c_2 \in \mathsf{Aff}_m^{\mathbf{X} \cup \mathbf{X}'}$. We make no contribution in this area, but to keep the paper self-contained, we present a semantics for abstract flowchart programs which specifies a program analysis. The semantics is formulated in terms of a composition operator, $\circ_c$, that mirrors $\circ_b$. To define this operator, let $c_1, c_2 \subseteq \mathsf{Aff}_m^{\mathbf{X} \cup \mathbf{X}'}$. Put $c'_1 = c_1 \wedge \bigwedge_{x_i \in X, j \in [0,w-1]} x'_{i,j} \equiv_m x''_{i,j}$ and $c'_2 = c_2 \wedge \bigwedge_{x_i \in X, j \in [0,w-1]} x_{i,j} \equiv_m x''_{i,j}$, and then proceed by analogy with the $\circ_b$ construction to define $c_1 \circ_c c_2 = c$.

The semantics of an abstract flowchart program $\langle L, X, \ell_0, T'\rangle$ can then be defined as the set of least congruence systems $\{c_\ell \in \mathsf{Aff}_m^{\mathbf{X}\cup\mathbf{X}'} \mid \ell \in L\}$ such that $\alpha_m(\mathsf{sym}(\mathsf{Id})) \models c_{\ell_0}$ and $c_{\ell_i} \circ_c c \models c_{\ell_j}$ for all $\langle \ell_i, \ell_j, c\rangle \in T'$. As before, the semantics can be equivalently stated as the least fixed point of a system of equations, which leads to an iterative approach for computing congruence invariants.

Example 11. Returning to Example 9, the invariants $c_{\ell_0}, c_{\ell_1}, c_{\ell_2}$ can be computed iteratively since they are the least solutions to the equations: $c_{\ell_0} = \alpha_m(\mathsf{sym}(\mathsf{Id}))$, $c_{\ell_1} = (c_{\ell_0} \circ_c c_1) \sqcup (c_{\ell_1} \circ_c c_2)$ and $c_{\ell_2} = c_{\ell_1} \circ_c c_3$. To solve these equations, first assign $c_{\ell_0} = c_{\ell_1} = c_{\ell_2} = \mathsf{false}$ where false is the unsatisfiable congruence system. Application of the first equation then yields

$$c_{\ell_0} = (\bigwedge_{j\in[0,15]} p'_j \equiv_2 p_j) \wedge (\bigwedge_{j\in[0,15]} x'_j \equiv_2 x_j) \wedge (\bigwedge_{j\in[0,15]} y'_j \equiv_2 y_j).$$

Thereafter c_{ℓ_0} is stable. For brevity, let

$$c = (\bigwedge_{j\in[1,15]} p'_j \equiv_2 p_j) \wedge (\bigwedge_{j\in[0,15]} x'_j \equiv_2 x_j).$$

An application of the second equation gives

$$c_{\ell_1} = c \wedge p'_0 \equiv_2 0 \wedge (\bigwedge_{j\in[0,15]} y'_i \equiv_2 x_i).$$

Then

$$c_{\ell_1} \circ_c c_2 = c \wedge (p'_0 \equiv_2 1) \wedge (y_0 \equiv_2 0) \wedge (1 \equiv_2 \sum_{j\in[0,15]} x_i - \sum_{j\in[1,15]} y'_i),$$

so reapplying the second equation gives

$$c_{\ell_1} = c \wedge (y_0 \equiv_2 0) \wedge (p'_0 \equiv_2 \sum_{j\in[0,15]} x_i - \sum_{j\in[1,15]} y'_i).$$

Thereafter c_{ℓ_1} is also stable. Finally, the third equation then gives

$$c_{\ell_2} = c \wedge (\bigwedge_{j\in[0,15]} y_0 \equiv_2 0) \wedge (\bigwedge_{j\in[0,15]} y'_0 \equiv_2 0) \wedge (p'_0 \equiv_2 \sum_{j\in[0,15]} x_i).$$

Then c_{ℓ_2} is stable too, and the fixed point has been reached. Correctness of parity follows from the invariant $p'_0 \equiv_2 \sum_{j\in[0,15]} x_i$ that holds at ℓ_2.

6 Transformation for Range Information

Consider the program in Figure 4(a) where n, x and y are signed w bit variables. Bit-level congruences cannot directly represent the inequality $(\sum_{i=0}^{w-2} 2^i x_i) - 2^{w-1}x_{w-1} \leq (\sum_{i=0}^{w-2} 2^i n_i) - 2^{w-1}n_{w-1}$ that holds at ℓ_2, which is crucial for inferring that x and n are bit-wise equivalent at ℓ_2.

(a)

$$
\begin{array}{ll}
\ell_0: & \mathsf{assume}(0 \le n); \\
 & x := 0;\ y := 0; \\
\ell_1: & \text{while } (x < n) \\
 & \quad y := y + 2; \\
 & \quad x := x + 1; \\
\ell_2: & \text{skip}
\end{array}
$$

(b)

$$
\begin{array}{ll}
\ell_0: & \mathsf{assume}(0 \le n); \\
 & x := 0;\ y := 0;\ \delta := n - x; \\
\ell_1: & \text{while } (0 < \delta) \\
 & \quad y := y + 2; \\
 & \quad x := x + 1; \\
 & \quad \delta := n - x; \\
\ell_2: & \text{skip}
\end{array}
$$

Fig. 4. Inferring $x \le n$ by using a witness variable δ

6.1 Adding Witness Variables

However, bit-level congruences can express the non-negativity of a variable, which suggests augmenting the program with a variable δ that witnesses the non-negativity of $n - x$. The program in Figure 4(b) illustrates the tactic, and the flow-graph for this program is given below:

$$
\begin{array}{l}
\langle \ell_0, \ell_1, 0 \le n, x := 0; y := 0; \delta := n - x \rangle \\
\langle \ell_1, \ell_1, 0 < \delta, y := y + 2; x := x + 1; \delta := n - x \rangle \\
\langle \ell_1, \ell_2, \delta \le 0, \mathsf{skip} \rangle
\end{array}
$$

Generating the abstract transitions as previously described gives $t'_1 = \langle \ell_0, \ell_1, c_1 \rangle$ and $t'_2 = \langle \ell_1, \ell_1, c_2 \rangle$ where

$$
c_1 = \bigwedge \left\{ \begin{array}{llll}
x'_0 \equiv_{16} 0, & x'_1 \equiv_{16} 0, & x'_2 \equiv_{16} 0, & x'_3 \equiv_{16} 0, \\
y'_0 \equiv_{16} 0, & y'_1 \equiv_{16} 0, & y'_2 \equiv_{16} 0, & y'_3 \equiv_{16} 0, \\
n'_0 \equiv_{16} n_0, & n'_1 \equiv_{16} n_1, & n'_2 \equiv_{16} n_2, & n'_3 \equiv_{16} n_3, \\
\delta'_0 \equiv_{16} n_0, & \delta'_1 \equiv_{16} n_1, & \delta'_2 \equiv_{16} n_2, & \delta'_3 \equiv_{16} n_3
\end{array} \right\}
$$

$$
c_2 = \bigwedge \left\{ \begin{array}{lll}
\delta_0 + \delta'_0 \equiv_{16} 1, & \delta_1 + 2\delta_2 \equiv_{16} \delta'_0 + \delta'_1 + 2\delta'_2, & 0 \equiv_{16} \delta_3, \\
0 \equiv_{16} \delta'_3, & n'_0 \equiv_{16} n_0, & n'_1 \equiv_{16} n_1, \\
n'_2 \equiv_{16} n_2, & n_3 \equiv_{16} n'_3, & 1 \equiv_{16} x_0 + x'_0, \\
y_0 \equiv_{16} y'_0, & 1 \equiv_{16} y_1 + y'_1, & \\
\multicolumn{3}{l}{\delta'_0 + 8(n_3 + x_3 + x'_2) + 1 \equiv_{16}} \\
\multicolumn{3}{l}{\qquad n_0 + 2(n_1 + x_1 - \delta'_1) + 4(n_2 + x_2 - \delta'_2 - x'_1) + 3x_0,} \\
\multicolumn{3}{l}{2x'_0 + 2x'_1 + 4x'_2 \equiv_{16} 2x_1 + 4x_2 + 8x_3 + 8x'_3 + 2,} \\
\multicolumn{3}{l}{4y_2 + 4 \equiv_{16} 8y_3 + 4y'_1 + 4y'_2 + 8y'_3}
\end{array} \right\}
$$

The width is set to $w = 4$ merely for presentational purposes. The key point is that c_2 asserts that $0 \equiv_{16} \delta'_3$ indicating that δ is non-negative at the end of the loop, as required. In general, a loop condition that is a single inequality $e_1 < e_2$ (resp. $e_1 \le e_2$) can be replaced with $0 < \delta$ where $\delta = e_2 + (-e_1)$ (respectively $\delta = e_2 + (-e_1) + 1$) so the transformation can be automated.

6.2 Decomposing Guards

Interestingly, introducing a witness variable is not by itself sufficient to deduce $x_i \equiv_{2^w} n_i$ for all $i \in [0, w-1]$ at ℓ_2. The semantics of abstract transition systems can be applied to derive:

$$c_{\ell_1} = \bigwedge \left\{ \begin{array}{l} \delta_3 \equiv_{16} 0, \\ y_0 \equiv_{16} 0, \quad y_1 \equiv_{16} x_0, \quad y_2 \equiv_{16} x_1, \quad y_3 \equiv_{16} x_2, \\ \sum_{i=0}^{3} 2^i \delta_i + \sum_{i=0}^{3} 2^i x_i \equiv_{16} \sum_{i=0}^{3} 2^i n_i \end{array} \right\}$$

which, although unexpected, is not in error since $8\delta_3 \equiv_{16} -8\delta_3$ and likewise for x_3 and n_3. But to infer the equivalence of x and n at ℓ_2 it is necessary to additionally impose the constraint $\delta \leq 0$. However, such a constraint is not captured in the abstract transition $t_3 = \langle \ell_1, \ell_2, c \rangle$ where

$$c = \bigwedge \left\{ \begin{array}{llll} n_0 \equiv_{16} n'_0, & n_1 \equiv_{16} n'_1, & n_2 \equiv_{16} n'_2, & n_3 \equiv_{16} n'_3, \\ x_0 \equiv_{16} x'_0, & x_1 \equiv_{16} x'_1, & x_2 \equiv_{16} x'_2, & x_3 \equiv_{16} x'_3, \\ y_0 \equiv_{16} y'_0, & y_1 \equiv_{16} y'_1, & y_2 \equiv_{16} y'_2, & y_3 \equiv_{16} y'_3, \\ \delta_0 \equiv_{16} \delta'_0, & \delta_1 \equiv_{16} \delta'_1, & \delta_2 \equiv_{16} \delta'_2, & \delta_3 \equiv_{16} \delta'_3 \end{array} \right\}$$

since c does not preserve any information pertaining to the $\delta \leq 0$ constraint. However, observe that $\delta \leq 0$ holds iff $\delta < 0 \vee \delta = 0$ and both $\delta < 0$ and $\delta = 0$ can be represented with bit-level congruences. This suggests transforming the third transition into $\langle \ell_1, \ell_2, \delta < 0, \mathsf{skip} \rangle$ and $\langle \ell_1, \ell_2, \delta = 0, \mathsf{skip} \rangle$. Then these rules respectively yield the abstract transitions $\langle \ell_1, \ell_2, c_1 \rangle$ and $\langle \ell_1, \ell_2, c_2 \rangle$ where $c_1 = c \wedge (\delta_3 \equiv_{16} 1)$ and $c_2 = c \wedge (\bigwedge_{j \in [0,3]} \delta_j \equiv_{16} 0)$. Only the second transition is applicable since c_{ℓ_1} asserts $\delta_3 \equiv_{16} 0$. Thus the following constraints hold at ℓ_2:

$$c_{\ell_2} = \bigwedge \left\{ \begin{array}{llll} \delta_0 \equiv_{16} 0, & \delta_1 \equiv_{16} 0, & \delta_2 \equiv_{16} 0, & \delta_3 \equiv_{16} 0, \\ y_0 \equiv_{16} 0, & y_1 \equiv_{16} x_0, & y_2 \equiv_{16} x_1, & y_3 \equiv_{16} x_2, \\ x_0 \equiv_{16} n_0, & x_1 \equiv_{16} n_1, & x_2 \equiv_{16} n_2, & x_3 \equiv_{16} n_3 \end{array} \right\}$$

Thus, even if a guard is not amenable to an exact bit-level representation, its transition may still be decomposed to circumvent this problem.

7 Concluding Discussion

We have shown how a SAT/SMT solver can be employed to derive abstract transition systems over linear congruences. The resulting invariants can express congruence relationships amongst the individual bits that comprise variables and, as a consequence, the abstract transition systems can calculate relationships even at the granularity of bit-twiddling. The advantage of the scheme presented in this paper is that SAT solving is confined to the derivation of the abstract transition system; only linear operations of polynomial complexity are required thereafter. We also proposed program transformations to improve the analysis through the use of witness variables that can help observe range information.

One may wonder how the efficiency of congruence closure depends on the SAT (or SMT) engine. Thus, as an experiment, MiniSat was replaced with ZChaff. This had little discernible impact on the overall time to compute the closure (transfer functions) for transition relations that formalised a number of bit-twiddling algorithms given in Warren's book [16]. Rather surprisingly, only a modest slow-down was found when MiniSat was replaced by SAT4J which is a solver that is implemented in Java itself. To understand why, consider Wegner's fast bit counting algorithm [16]. Deriving the transfer functions for the 16 bit version involves 98 SAT instances. Solving the instances takes 0.5s overall but 5.6s is spent computing all the joins. In this example, many joins involve matrices of size 129×129 arising from a relation over 129 bits. The effect is more pronounced for a 32 bit version of the algorithm which has one relation over 259 bits. To solve the 195 SAT instances requires 11.4s overall, but the join operation takes up 149.5s, partly because it manipulates matrices of size 259×259. The bias towards join is least in an example that computes the sign operation by bit-twiddling. For the 32 bit version of the algorithm, the timings are 0.1s and 0.4s for the SAT and join components. We conclude that SAT is not the bottleneck, and that future effort should focus on how to exploit the sparsity of the matrices that arise.

Acknowledgements. This work was funded by the EPSRC project EP/F012896, a Royal Society Industrial Fellowship, and a Tewksbury Fellowship that enabled the first author to visit the University of Melbourne. Discussions with Paul Docherty provided impetus for this work. We have been greatly helped by discussions with Mike Codish and Kristy Siu (on Boolean encoding) and with Tom Reps (on the notion of a best symbolic transformer). We also thank the referees for their helpful suggestions.

References

1. Bagnara, R., Dobson, K., Hill, P.M., Mundell, M., Zaffanella, E.: Grids: A domain for analyzing the distribution of numerical values. In: Puebla, G. (ed.) LOPSTR 2006. LNCS, vol. 4407, pp. 219–235. Springer, Heidelberg (2007)
2. Clarke, E., Kroening, D., Lerda, F.: A tool for checking ANSI-C programs. In: Jensen, K., Podelski, A. (eds.) TACAS 2004. LNCS, vol. 2988, pp. 168–176. Springer, Heidelberg (2004)
3. Cousot, P., Cousot, R.: Abstract interpretation: A unified lattice model for static analysis of programs by construction or approximation of fixpoints. In: Principles of Programming Languages, pp. 238–252. ACM, New York (1977)
4. Graf, S., Saïdi, H.: Construction of abstract state graphs with PVS. In: Grumberg, O. (ed.) CAV 1997. LNCS, vol. 1254, pp. 72–83. Springer, Heidelberg (1997)
5. Granger, P.: Static analyses of linear congruence equalities among variables of a program. In: Abramsky, S. (ed.) TAPSOFT 1991. LNCS, vol. 493, pp. 167–192. Springer, Heidelberg (1991)
6. Howe, J.M., King, A.: Logahedra: A new weakly relational domain. In: Liu, Z., Ravn, A.P. (eds.) Automated Technology for Verification and Analysis. LNCS, vol. 5799, pp. 306–320. Springer, Heidelberg (2009)
7. Jackson, D., Vaziri, M.: Finding bugs with a constraint solver. In: International Symposium on Software Testing and Analysis, pp. 14–25. ACM, New York (2000)
8. King, A., Søndergaard, H.: Inferring congruence equations using SAT. In: Gupta, A., Malik, S. (eds.) CAV 2008. LNCS, vol. 5123, pp. 281–293. Springer, Heidelberg (2008)

9. Laviron, V., Logozzo, F.: Subpolyhedra: A (more) scalable approach to infer linear inequalities. In: Jones, N.D., Müller-Olm, M. (eds.) VMCAI 2009. LNCS, vol. 5403, pp. 229–244. Springer, Heidelberg (2009)
10. Monniaux, D.: Automatic modular abstractions for linear constraints. In: Principles of Programming Languages, pp. 140–151. ACM, New York (2009)
11. Müller-Olm, M., Seidl, H.: Analysis of modular arithmetic. ACM Transactions on Programming Languages and Systems, article 29, 29(5) (August 2007)
12. Nelson, G., Oppen, D.C.: Fast decision procedures based on congruence closure. Journal of the ACM 27(2), 356–364 (1980)
13. Reps, T., Sagiv, M., Yorsh, G.: Symbolic implementation of the best transformer. In: Steffen, B., Levi, G. (eds.) VMCAI 2004. LNCS, vol. 2937, pp. 252–266. Springer, Heidelberg (2004)
14. Sankaranarayanan, S., Sipma, H.B., Manna, Z.: Scalable analysis of linear systems using mathematical programming. In: Cousot, R. (ed.) VMCAI 2005. LNCS, vol. 3385, pp. 25–41. Springer, Heidelberg (2005)
15. Simon, A., King, A.: Exploiting sparsity in polyhedral analysis. In: Hankin, C., Siveroni, I. (eds.) SAS 2005. LNCS, vol. 3672, pp. 336–351. Springer, Heidelberg (2005)
16. Warren Jr., H.S.: Hacker's Delight. Addison Wesley, Reading (2003)

Shape Analysis of Low-Level C with Overlapping Structures

Jörg Kreiker, Helmut Seidl, and Vesal Vojdani*

Fakultät für Informatik, Technische Universität München
Boltzmannstraße 3, D-85748 Garching b. München, Germany
{kreiker,seidl,vojdanig}@in.tum.de

Abstract. Device drivers often keep data in multiple data structures simultaneously while embedding list or tree related records into the records containing the actual data; this results in *overlapping* structures. Shape analyses have traditionally relied on a graph-based representation of memory where a node corresponds to a whole record and edges to pointers. As this is ill-suited for encoding overlapping structures, we propose and formally relate two refined memory models. We demonstrate the appropriateness of these models by implementing shape analyses based on them within the TVLA framework. The implementation is exemplified using code extracted from cache managing kernel modules.

1 Introduction

Shape analysis of heap-manipulating programs is a very active field of research; however, the focus of most work has been devoted to Java-like data-structures, where pointers are not as heavily manipulated and computed with as in low-level C. While shape analyses addressing pointer arithmetic in a broad sense have recently been designed, e.g., [7,3,10,19,16,9,18], we address a related and particularly difficult problem: *overlapping structures.* The term was coined in [3], where the shape analysis of such structures was stated as an open problem.

Overlap is often found in device drivers where data is kept in several data-structures at the same time by means of embedding list or tree related records into the records containing the actual data. An example of such code is shown in Figure 1, where a `node` record (we shall consequently use the more general term record to denote C structs) contains data as well as two list-related components. The first, `hlist_node`, is the record type which embeds the forward and backward pointers of an hlist (see below) into a node; the second, `list_head`, is a record type which serves both as the list head and as the record that embeds standard cyclic doubly-linked lists into nodes.

Hlists (or pprev lists) are in themselves quite tricky data-structures. In order to save memory while maintaining efficient implementation of insertion and deletion, Linux developers use these doubly linked lists with a pointer to the `next` component of the previous element rather than to the element itself. (This is visualized in a memory snapshot in Figure 2, where the edges from pprev boxes

* On leave from the University of Tartu; partially supported by EstSF grant 6713.

G. Barthe and M. Hermenegildo (Eds.): VMCAI 2010, LNCS 5944, pp. 214–230, 2010.

```
struct hlist_head { struct hlist_node *first; };
struct hlist_node { struct hlist_node *next, **pprev; };
struct  list_head { struct  list_head *next, *prev; };

struct node { int data; struct hlist_node list;
                        struct  list_head queue; };

struct hlist_head ht[512];  struct mutex hlock;
struct  list_head cq;

void cleanup_task(void *arg) {
    struct hlist_head garbage; struct node *pos;
    lock(&hlock);
    list_for_each(pos, &cq) {
        hlist_del(&pos→list);
        list_del(&pos→queue);
        hlist_add(&pos→list, &garbage); }
    unlock(&hlock);
    hlist_for_each(pos, &garbage, list) {
        access(pos→data);
        hlist_del(&pos→list); } }
```

Fig. 1. Overlapping data-structures from the Linux kernel

end at the smallest boxes rather than at the medium-sized ones as is the case for edges originating in prev boxes.) Hlists are used in hash-tables where having only a single pointer in the list head can be a significant gain.

The code given in Figure 1 shall serve as a basis for our case study. We use a syntax close to the original code, but abbreviate function names and eliminate some of the parameters to the list-traversal macros. These macros expand into for-loops and use pointer-arithmetic to move from a record embedded within a node to the containing record. The example is based on code for maintaining a cache where the least recently used items are tagged and added to the cleanup queue. This queue is processed asynchronously by a cleanup task whose code is given in the figure. As this task may be executing concurrently with code that accesses the cache, elements in the queue are moved to the thread-local list `garbage` for statistical processing before being deallocated. This minimizes the time that the cleanup task must keep the lock on the cache.

When an object is removed from *all* thread-shared data-structures, the subsequent post-processing of the *privatized* object no longer requires protection through the acquisition of locks. However, if an element resides in two lists simultaneously, traversing these distinct lists may cause a race when accessing the data of the shared element. To prove absence of races in the example, we must infer that an element is in the queue but no longer in the list, although both queue- and list-related records are embedded into the same `node`.

Shape analyses often rely on graph-based representations of memory where a node corresponds to a whole record and edges to pointers. For these, it is not

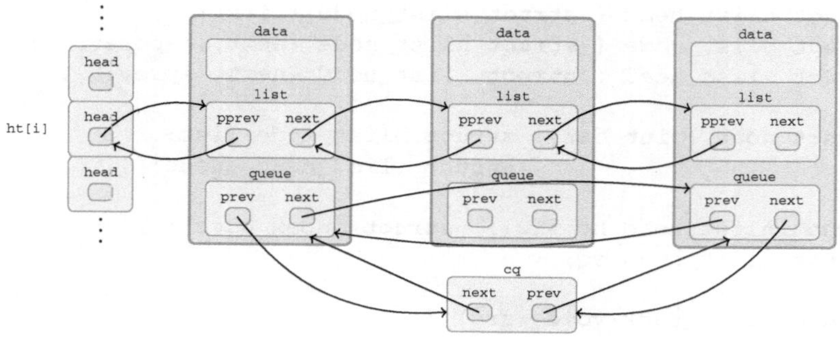

Fig. 2. Overlapping Structures

immediate how to encode pointers between components. Therefore, we propose two refined memory models which exhibit the low-level details required to reason about overlapping structures. Both memory models are formulated in terms of the TVLA framework [27]. Using the TVLA framework is not necessary but allows for a quick prototype implementation. Since our refinement is conservative, we can also benefit from knowledge and developments in the TVLA realm.

The model of Section 3 uses a one-node-per-component approach, i.e., each box of Figure 2 becomes a single node in the shape graph, and the hierarchy induced by the box nesting is translated into a tree structure. We design a program analysis based on this model and demonstrate its potential on a list element deletion procedure that uses unorthodox pointer manipulations.

Alternatively in Section 4, we propose a coarser and possibly more efficient model that employs a one-node-per-outermost-record paradigm. This approach annotates edge dereferences with access paths into the finer structure of the records, making sources and targets of dereferencing explicit. We exemplify shape analyses based on this coarser semantics by verifying deletion from an hlist. In Section 5, we characterize the relationship between the two models.

In Section 6, we revisit our motivating example of Figure 1. The analysis is conducted w.r.t. the coarse-grained semantics and enables us to verify race detection properties for it. Sections 7 and 8 present related work and conclude.

2 Preliminaries

We begin by introducing the syntax of the C subset under consideration. Our aim is to cover the part of the C language crucial to most low-level programs like kernel code and drivers. We support arbitrarily nested named records and pointers to named types only; integers are not considered. This implies that we have both records and pointers as values. We use the domain **Id** of *variables* ranged over by x, y, and z, and the domain **Sel** of component *selectors* ranged over by s. Type names are ranged over by t. We consider the following languages of types τ and pointer expressions e:

$$\tau ::= \textbf{struct}\ t\ \{\tau_1\ s_1, \ldots, \tau_k\ s_k\} \mid \tau\ *$$
$$e ::= \mathbf{0} \mid x \mid *e \mid \&e \mid e \rightarrow s \mid \textbf{malloc}(t) \mid \textbf{up}(x, t, s)$$

We omit arbitrary pointer arithmetic, unions, and type-casts; rather, we restrict pointer manipulation to component selection and the expression $\textbf{up}(x, t, s)$ used as a primitive to model the `container_of` macro which computes the address of a record of type t from a pointer x to its s component. Since recent versions of the Linux kernel rely on *built-in* support by the compiler to implement this macro, a primitive treatment of the container-of idiom is sensible.

In the presence of overlap the $\textbf{up}()$-operator is crucial to *change views*. For instance, in the example of Figure 1 one could traverse the cleanup queue, use the operator $\textbf{up}()$ to jump to the data component of a node, and then continue traversing the `list` components.

As for statements we only consider assignments between pointer expressions. We assume that programs are compiled into a control-flow graph where assignments are attached to edges and where pointer comparisons may serve as guards. Two different semantics will be provided in Sections 3 and 4 in the framework of the *Three-valued Logic Based Shape Analysis (TVLA)* [27]. We therefore briefly recapitulate the basics of the TVLA approach in order to have the necessary notation at hand.

TVLA builds on the notion of logical structures over a certain signature $\mathcal{P}$. A logical structure $S = (U, \iota)$ is a pair of a set of individuals U ranged over by u and an interpretation, ι. Each predicate symbol $p/k \in \mathcal{P}$ of arity k is mapped by ι to a boolean-valued function $\iota(p/k) : U^k \rightarrow \mathbb{B}$. The set of all structures over a $\mathcal{P}$ is written $\mathcal{S}[\mathcal{P}]$. We evaluate formulas of first-order logic with transitive closure, FO(TC), on logical structures. Formulas are defined by:

$$\varphi = 0 \mid p(v_1, \ldots, v_k) \mid \neg\varphi \mid \varphi \wedge \varphi \mid \exists v : \varphi \mid TC(v_1, v_2 : \varphi)(v_1', v_2')$$

where $v \in \mathsf{Var}$ is a logical variable. The transitive closure operator, $TC(v_1, v_2 : \varphi)(v_1', v_2')$ defines a binary relation by φ using free variables v_1 and v_2. The transitive closure of this relation is then evaluated on v_1' and v_2'. The evaluation of a formula φ in structure S and assignment Z (of free variables to individuals) is written $[\![\varphi]\!]^S(Z)$.

Logical structures are used to encode heap graphs. Traditionally, an individual corresponds to a record and a binary predicate s holds of individuals u and u', if there is a pointer-valued component s of the record modeled by u which points to (the head of) the record modeled by u'. The predicates used to encode a heap are essentially the binary selectors, **Sel**, and the unary program variables, **Id**, that hold of records pointed to by the corresponding variables. These predicates are called *core predicates*, the set of which is denoted by $\mathcal{C}$.

The semantics of an assignment *st* is a mapping $[\![st]\!] : \mathcal{S}[\mathcal{C}] \rightarrow \mathcal{S}[\mathcal{C}]$ This is given in terms of *predicate update formulas* that update the value of predicates affected by the statement. Given for each k-ary predicate $p \in \mathcal{C}$ an update formula φ_p^{st} with free variables $v_1, \ldots, v_k$, the semantics of *st* is defined as $[\![st]\!](S) = (U', \lambda p.\lambda u_1, \ldots, u_k.[\![\varphi_p^{st}]\!]^S(Z))$ where $Z = [v_1 \mapsto u_1, \ldots, v_k \mapsto u_k]$ and the universe U' is either the same as before or (in the case of memory allocation) extended with fresh individuals.

Abstract states in the TVLA framework are *three-valued logical structures* based on Kleene's three-valued logic. Abstract states are obtained by *canonical abstraction*, an abstraction that summarizes individuals that are indistinguishable under a set of abstraction predicates to *summary nodes*. Due to summarization, knowledge about certain predicates may become indefinite, in which case the logical value 1/2 is introduced. To avoid serious loss of precision, *instrumentation predicates* are employed; these are additional predicates defined through formulas of FO(TC) using the core predicates $\mathcal{C}$. Instrumentation predicates allow to better distinguish abstract nodes by annotating logical structures with additional information such as reachability, sharing, or cyclicity. Update formulas for instrumentation predicates can be automatically inferred using differencing [25].

As abstract states are still logical structures, the concrete semantics in terms of predicate update formulas is easily lifted to three-valued logical structures, too. As a consequence, it is sufficient to specify predicate update formulas and a set of instrumentation predicates to define a program analysis in the TVLA framework. Soundness then is immediate.

3 Fine-Grained Semantics and Analysis

We now present our first refinement of the one-node-per-record paradigm by adopting a *one-node-per-component* representation. More precisely, a record of type **struct** t $\{\tau_1 * s_1, \ldots, \tau_k * s_k\}$ is represented by $k + 1$ nodes, one being the head and one for each pointer component. If the component types are records again, additional nodes for the subcomponents are introduced, until finally pointer types are reached. This corresponds to transforming the hierarchy of boxes in Figure 2 into a tree.

This memory model is both more explicit and more abstract than that of real C. While in C the address of a record and the address of its first component coincide, they are considered as different here. On the other hand, we do not model the order of components or padding between each two of them. In our model, the operation **up**() amounts to moving from a component node to the head of its enclosing record.

Since we rely on the TVLA framework, we aim at encoding a state as a logical structure. Here we use the signature

$$\mathcal{C} = \{x/1 \mid x \in \mathbf{Id}\} \cup \{s/2 \mid s \in \mathbf{Sel}\} \cup \{*/2\}$$

In order to reason about expressions of the form $\&x$, the corresponding predicate x holds of an individual representing the stack location where x's value is stored. In standard TVLA the predicate x holds of the element *pointed to* by x.

The key predicate in our formulation is the binary $*$ for dereferencing. In particular, it holds between the location of a pointer variable and the value the variable points to. An interesting feature of our model is that the only predicate

Table 1. Predicate update formulas for nullification and assignments. The latter assume that $*x$, x, and $x \rightarrow s$ have been nullified.

st	$\varphi_*^{st}(v_1, v_2) =$
$x = \mathbf{0}$	$*(v_1, v_2) \wedge \neg x(v_1)$
$*x = \mathbf{0}$	$*(v_1, v_2) \wedge \neg\exists\, v' : \; x(v') \wedge *(v', v_1)$
$x \rightarrow s = \mathbf{0}$	$*(v_1, v_2) \wedge \neg\exists\, v', v'' : \; x(v') \wedge *(v', v'') \wedge s(v'', v_1)$
$x = y$	$*(v_1, v_2) \vee x(v_1) \wedge \exists\, v' : \; y(v') \wedge *(v', v_2)$
$x = *y$	$*(v_1, v_2) \vee x(v_1) \wedge \exists\, v', v'' : \; y(v') \wedge *(v', v'') \wedge *(v'', v_2)$
$x = \&y$	$*(v_1, v_2) \vee x(v_1) \wedge y(v_2)$
$x = \&y \rightarrow s$	$*(v_1, v_2) \vee x(v_1) \wedge \exists\, v', v'' : \; y(v') \wedge *(v', v'') \wedge s(v'', v_2)$
$x = y \rightarrow s$	$*(v_1, v_2) \vee x(v_1) \wedge \exists\, v', v'', v''' : y(v') \wedge *(v', v'') \wedge s(v'', v''') \wedge *(v''', v_2)$
$x = \mathbf{up}(y, t, s)$	$*(v_1, v_2) \vee x(v_1) \wedge \exists\, v', v'' : \; y(v') \wedge *(v', v'') \wedge s(v_2, v'')$
$*x = y$	$*(v_1, v_2) \vee \exists\, v', v'' : \; x(v') \wedge *(v', v_1) \wedge y(v'') \wedge *(v'', v_2)$
$x \rightarrow s = y$	$*(v_1, v_2) \vee \exists\, v', v'', v''' : x(v') \wedge *(v', v'') \wedge s(v'', v_1) \wedge y(v''') \wedge *(v''', v_2)$

that is affected by assignments is the $*$ predicate: once allocated, the nodes representing a record and its components do not change and neither does the location of a variable.

We now formalize the semantics of our programming language. Each basic statement gives rise to an *update formula.* The update formulas, except for allocation, are given in Table 1. As is often done, we consider only one pointer operation per assignment, and we assume that pointers which are assigned to are always explicitly nullified before-hand, so that updates for assignments only introduce a single new points-to relationship. For example, in the case of $x = \mathbf{up}(y, t, s)$, we have that $*(u_1, u_2)$ holds after the assignment if it either held before, or if u_1 is the individual hosting x and u_2 has an s-component which is pointed to by the individual hosting y.

As for memory allocation, we expand the universe by a set of new individuals depending on the type of the record to be allocated. Recall that we require one individual per (sub)component of each non-pointer type. To this end, we introduce the notion of an *access path.* Such paths are not to be confused with access paths found in storeless semantics [20, 15]. Here, they merely reflect the static structure of a (possibly nested) record. Intuitively, there is a path for each component of a record. Formally, we define the set Π of access paths to be a union over all record types t occurring in the program, $\Pi = \bigcup_t \Pi(t)$, where

$$\Pi(\tau\ *) = \{\varepsilon\}$$

$$\Pi(\mathbf{struct}\ t\ \{\tau_1\ s_1, \ldots, \tau_k\ s_k\}) = \textstyle\bigcup_{i=1}^{k} \{s_i\}.\Pi(\tau_i) \cup \{s_i\}$$

As t ranges over record types, $\varepsilon \notin \Pi$; we write $\Pi_\varepsilon = \Pi \cup \{\varepsilon\}$.

Using the access paths from Π, we define the semantics of malloc as $[\![x = \mathbf{malloc}(t)]\!](U, \iota) = (U', \iota')$ where $U' = U \uplus \{u_\pi \mid \pi \in \Pi_\varepsilon(t)\}$ and

$$\iota'(s)(u_1,u_2) = \begin{cases} \iota(s)(u_1,u_2) & \text{if } u_1,u_2 \in U \\ 1 & \text{if } u_1 = u_\pi \wedge u_2 = u_{\pi.s} \\ 0 & \text{otherwise} \end{cases}$$

$$\iota'(*)(u_1,u_2) = \begin{cases} \iota(*)(u_1,u_2) & \text{if } u_1,u_2 \in U \\ 1 & \text{if } \iota(x)(u_1) \wedge u_2 = u_\varepsilon \\ 0 & \text{otherwise} \end{cases}$$

Analysis. As first example which goes beyond the one-node-per-record memory model, we consider a program which iterates over a singly-linked list pointed to by `x` using a pointer, `lpp`, to the `next` *component* of list elements, rather than to the elements themselves. The iteration is driven by the loop

```
for (lpp = &x; *lpp != NULL; lpp = &(*lpp)→next)
```

In the beginning `lpp` points to the *address* of `x`. It is advanced by dereferencing and taking the address of the `next` component of the next element. Once an element to be deleted is found, the assignment `*lpp = (*lpp)→next` removes it from the list. This routine is quite elegant in that it needs only one iterator and no check whether the iterator points to the first element or not. Also it uses pointers to components of records.

We implemented the creation of a fine-grained singly-linked list, the iteration over it, and the deletion of an element from it as outlined above in TVLA.[1] The encoding of the fine-grained model into TVLA amounted in representing the $*$ predicate together with its update formulas for the basic statements. Through this encoding, we could re-use instrumentation predicates like sharing and reachability (`r[z]`: reachability from program variable `z`) to make the analysis go through and prove memory safety and well-formedness. Essentially, these come for free from TVLA. Additional instrumentation that we had to provide concerned type information (`lnode`, `lnodep`), the location to which pointer variables point (`ptr[z]`), and the fact that each record always has a `next` component (`hasn`).

In Figure 3, we show a sample shape graph, where summary nodes are denoted by double lines, definite edges by solid arrows, and 1/2 edges, which may or may not be there, by dotted arrows. Variable `t` points to an element in the middle of the list and is to be deleted using the code above. The snapshot is taken after the first iteration of the loop, where `lpp` was advanced once. The two *pairs* of summary nodes (double circles) represent any number (at least 1) of list elements before and after `t`. Each pair would be a single node in the standard TVLA memory model. Also observe, that `lpp` indeed points to the `n` *component* of the list element pointed to by `x`.

[1] All our TVLA analysis specification files are provided online at `http://www7.in.tum.de/~joba/overlap.tgz`. These files also contain the precise definitions of instrumentation predicates and integrity constraints.

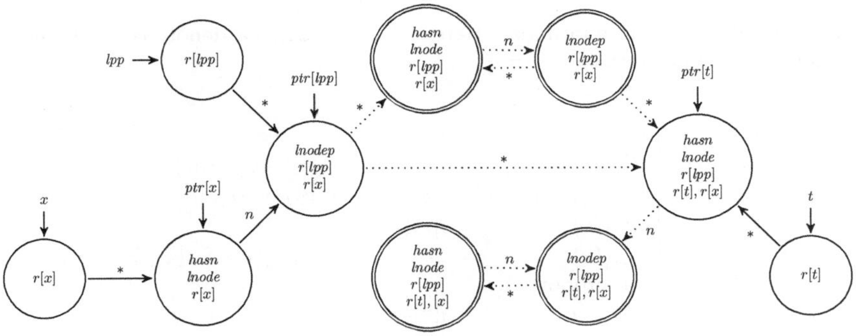

Fig. 3. Shape graph during list traversal with indirect pointer. Double lines indicate summary nodes, solid arrows indicate definite edges, and dotted ones 1/2-edges. Predicates within a node do hold for this node.

4 Coarse-Grained Semantics and Analysis

The fine-grained model from the last section has a very explicit view of the heap and allows for very detailed modelling. The number of individuals, though, in a logical structure is a multiple of the number occurring in standard TVLA based analyses because each component of a record is modeled by a separate individual. On top of that, care must be taken that individuals belonging to the same record — encoded as the outermost boxes in Figure 2 — are kept together, something not supported by standard TVLA.

Fortunately, we can atone for these drawbacks by exploiting the fact that the structure of a record is completely static. Once allocated, the interpretation of predicates in **Sel** never changes, only the $*$ predicate does. This observation suggests an encoding of records as single nodes after all, rather than representing them explicitly through a linked set of nodes — as in the one-node-per-record paradigm. Still, pointers to the head of a record need be distinguished from pointers to components. We do so by *parameterizing* the $*$ predicate. For example, if $*[p, n]$ is true of two individuals u and u', it means that the p-component of the record modeled by u holds a pointer to the n-component of the record modeled by u'. Analogously, we parameterize the unary predicates encoding pointer variables: if $x[n]$ holds of individual u, it means that x holds a pointer to the n-component of the record modeled by u. In the special case (which in practice is the most common) of a pointer to the head of a record, we write $x[\varepsilon]$.

Addresses of variables can be handled by adding one individual per variable exactly like in the fine-grained model. In order to simplify the presentation, though, we here omit addresses of pointer variables. Unlike in the fine-grained semantics, the unary predicate $x[\varepsilon]$ now holds for the individual pointed to by the pointer x, rather than for the location of x itself. Thus, the standard TVLA model is obtained from this version of the coarse-grained model by restricting predicates to the forms $*[s, \varepsilon]$ and $x[\varepsilon]$, i.e., all pointers point to the *heads* of records.

Table 2. Predicate update formulas. Here, $\varphi_{x[\pi]}$ and $\varphi_{*[\pi,\pi']}$ denote rule schemes and stand for one rule per instance of π.

st	φ_p^{st}
$x = \mathbf{0}$	$\varphi^{st}_{x[\pi]}(v) = 0$
$*x = \mathbf{0}$	$\varphi^{st}_{*[\pi,\pi']}(v_1, v_2) = *[\pi, \pi'](v_1, v_2) \wedge \neg x[\pi](v_1)$
$x \rightarrow s = \mathbf{0}$	$\varphi^{st}_{*[\pi.s,\pi']}(v_1, v_2) = *[\pi.s, \pi'](v_1, v_2) \wedge \neg x[\pi](v_1)$
$x = y$	$\varphi^{st}_{x[\pi]}(v) = y[\pi](v)$
$x = *y$	$\varphi^{st}_{x[\pi]}(v) = \exists v' : \bigvee_{\pi' \in \Pi} y[\pi'](v') \wedge *[\pi', \pi](v', v)$
$x = \&y$	not supported
$x = \&y \rightarrow s$	$\varphi^{st}_{x[\pi.s]}(v) = y[\pi](v)$
$x = y \rightarrow s$	$\varphi^{st}_{x[\pi]}(v) = \exists v' : \bigvee_{\pi' \in \Pi} y[\pi'](v') \wedge *[\pi'.s, \pi](v', v)$
$x = \mathbf{up}(y, t, s)$	$\varphi^{st}_{x[\pi]}(v) = y[\pi.s](v)$
$*x = y$	$\varphi^{st}_{*[\pi,\pi']}(v_1, v_2) = *[\pi, \pi'](v_1, v_2) \vee x[\pi](v_1) \wedge y[\pi'](v_2)$
$x \rightarrow s = y$	$\varphi^{st}_{*[\pi.s,\pi']}(v_1, v_2) = *[\pi.s, \pi'](v_1, v_2) \vee x[\pi](v_1) \wedge y[\pi'](v_2)$

Recall the notion of an access path of the previous section. Using access paths, we define coarse-grained states as logical structures over the following signature, $\mathcal{D}$, serving as our set of core predicates.

$$\mathcal{D} = \{x[\pi]/1 \mid x \in \mathbf{Id}, \pi \in \Pi_\varepsilon\} \cup \{*[\pi_1, \pi_2]/2 \mid \pi_1 \in \Pi, \pi_2 \in \Pi_\varepsilon\}$$

In order to complete the coarse-grained semantics, we provide the predicate update formulas for the predicates in $\mathcal{D}$. The update formulas shown in Table 2 constitute the state transformers both for the concrete and for the abstract semantics. These formulas are more concise than those of the fine-grained model. The update for the **up**() operation, e.g., only requires updating the predicates $x[\pi]$ to be true whenever the corresponding $y[\pi.s]$ used to be true. In the case of memory allocation, the effect of $x = \mathbf{malloc}(t)$ is to extend the universe with one fresh individual for which only the predicate $x[\varepsilon]$ holds.

Analysis. As for the fine-grained semantics, we implemented the coarse-grained transformers inside TVLA. As an example, we analyzed a program that first generates an hlist using the expanded `hlist_add` macro, which was already used in Figure 1, then iterates to some arbitrary point, and then deletes the element there using the `hlist_del` macro. The concrete C code of these macros is available from the `list.h` file of the current Linux distribution.

Being able to handle hlists is mandatory for verifying absence of races in programs such as in Figure 1. In our TVLA implementation, we parameterized the $*$ predicate with source and target components as described in the semantics. Other than that, we could migrate existing analysis specifications for doubly-linked lists to hlists. The analysis of doubly linked lists uses, e.g., the instrumentation predicate which says that first following the pointers n and then p yields the same element. This predicate now is migrated to a predicate $c[n, p]$ stating that following $*[n, \varepsilon]$ and then $*[p, n]$ results in the same individual.

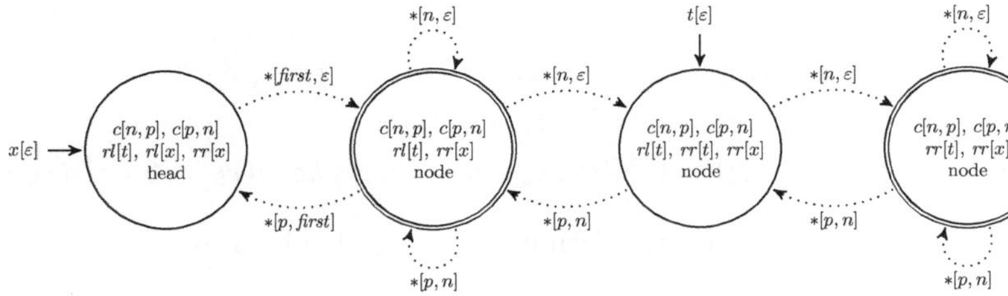

Fig. 4. Shape graph obtained during hlist traversal

The sample shape of Figure 4 shows a situation where `t` points to the middle of an hlist. Note that there are two sorts of reachability: forward (`tr`, `rr[z]`) and backward (`tl` and `rl[z]`). This shows that `t` is indeed in the middle, well-formedness follows from the `c[]` predicates. Finally, observe that the back pointers either point to the `first` component of the head `x`, `*[p,first]`, or to the `n` component of a predecessor element (`*[p,n]`). In contrast, the forward pointer always points to the head of a record (`*[n,`ε`]`).

We successfully verified well-formedness and memory safety for the hlist example. Before we proceed to the example program of Figure 1, we investigate the formal relation between the fine-grained and the coarse-grained model in terms of expressiveness.

5 Fine-Grained versus Coarse-Grained

Since the fine-grained model is more detailed, it is able to simulate the coarser one in a sense to be made explicit now.

We start by defining a mapping g from a coarse-grained structure $S_c = (U_c, \iota_c)$ into a fine-grained structure $g(S_c) = (U_f, \iota_f)$. The set of individuals of $g(S_c)$ is given by

$$U_f = \mathbf{Id} \cup \{u_\pi \mid u \in U_c, \pi \in \Pi_\varepsilon(\mathbf{type}(u))\}$$

The interpretation function ι_f then is given by:

$$\begin{aligned}
\iota_f(*)(u_\pi, u'_{\pi'}) &\text{ iff } \iota_c(*[\pi,\pi'])(u,u') \\
\iota_f(*)(x, u_\pi) &\text{ iff } \iota_c(x[\pi])(u) \\
\iota_f(x)(v) &\text{ iff } v = x \\
\iota_f(s)(v,v') &\text{ iff } \exists u_{\pi.s} \in U_f.\ v = u_\pi \wedge v' = u_{\pi.s}
\end{aligned}$$

where $\mathbf{type}(u) = t$ if u was created by $\mathbf{malloc}(t)$. Also we assume that S_c *respects types*, i.e., there are no pointers from or to a π component of node u if $\pi \notin \Pi(\mathbf{type}(u))$.

Since we deal with two different vocabularies, $\mathcal{C}$ and $\mathcal{D}$, on top of the mapping g between structures, a mapping $\mathcal{T}$ is required which translates formulas. Let φ be a FO(TC) formula over $\mathcal{D}$. The translation $\mathcal{T}$ commutes with boolean connectives and additionally is defined by:

$$\mathcal{T}(*[\pi_1, \pi_2](v_1, v_2)) = \exists v_1', v_2', v : \pi_1(v_1, v_1') \wedge \pi_2(v_2, v_2') \wedge *(v_1', v_2')$$
$$\mathcal{T}(x[\pi](v)) = \exists v', v'' : x(v') \wedge \pi(v, v'') \wedge *(v', v'')$$
$$\mathcal{T}(\exists v : \varphi) = \exists v : \mathit{head}(v) \wedge \mathcal{T}(\varphi)$$
$$\mathcal{T}((TC\, v_1, v_2 : \varphi)(v_3, v_4)) = (TC\, v_1, v_2 : \mathit{head}(v_1) \wedge \mathit{head}(v_2) \wedge \mathcal{T}(\varphi))(v_3, v_4)$$

where for $\pi = s_1. \cdots .s_k \in \Pi$, the formula $\pi(v_0, v_k)$ is given by

$$\exists v_1, \ldots, v_{k-1} : s_1(v_0, v_1) \wedge \ldots \wedge s_k(v_{k-1}, v_k)$$

and where *head* holds for heads of records in a fine-grained structure only. A node is a head, if it is not the location of a variable and if it has no incoming **Sel** edge. The following theorem states that this translation preserves the valuation of formulas and that it commutes with state transformers, i.e., with predicate update formulas.

Theorem 1. *Let S_c be a type-respecting, coarse-grained logical structure and $S_f = g(S_c)$ the corresponding fine-grained structure. Then we have:*

1. *For every closed FO(TC) formula φ over $\mathcal{D}$, $[\![\varphi]\!]^{S_c} = [\![\mathcal{T}(\varphi)]\!]^{S_f}$.*
2. *For every basic statement st, $g([\![st]\!]_c(S_c)) = [\![st]\!]_f(S_f)$.*

Proof. For an induction argument, we prove the statement for open formulas. Let $Z_c\colon \mathsf{Var} \to U_c$ be an assignment of logical variables to individuals in the coarse-grained universe; we define $Z_f = g(Z_c)\colon \mathsf{Var} \to U_f$ as an assignment selecting the head u_ε for each record u. We show $[\![\varphi]\!]^{S_c}(Z_c) = [\![\mathcal{T}(\varphi)]\!]^{S_f}(Z_f)$ by induction on φ. For the core predicates, we compute for $u = Z_c(v)$:

$$\begin{aligned}[\![x[\pi](v)]\!]^{S_c}(Z_c) &= \iota_c(x[\pi])(u) = \iota_f(*)(x, u_\pi)\\ &= \exists u' \in U_f : \pi(u_\varepsilon, u') \wedge \iota_f(*)(x, u')\\ &= [\![\mathcal{T}(x[\pi](v))]\!]^{S_f}(Z_f)\end{aligned}$$

And analogously for the binary predicates. We need to further consider cases for $\wedge$, $\exists$, $\neg$, and TC (as the rest follows from DeMorgan's Laws). Conjunction and negation are obvious, while existential quantification and transitive closure rely on the restriction of quantification to heads of records. We consider existential quantification, for which we observe:

$$\begin{aligned}[\![\exists v : \varphi]\!]^{S_c}(Z_c) &= \exists u \in U_c : [\![\varphi]\!]^{S_c}(Z_c[v \mapsto u]) = \exists u \in U_c : [\![\mathcal{T}(\varphi)]\!]^{S_f}(Z_f[v \mapsto u_\varepsilon])\\ &= \exists u' \in U_f : \mathit{head}(u') \wedge [\![\mathcal{T}(\varphi)]\!]^{S_f}(Z_f[v \mapsto u'])\\ &= [\![\exists v : \mathit{head}(v) \wedge \mathcal{T}(\varphi)]\!]^{S_f}(Z_f) = [\![\mathcal{T}(\exists v : \varphi)]\!]^{S_f}(Z_f)\end{aligned}$$

This completes the proof of the first statement. For the second statement, let $S_c = (U_c, \iota_c)$ denote a coarse-grained logical structure. We do a case distinction on the form of basic statements.

Consider, e.g., the statement *st* given by $x = \mathbf{up}(y, t, s)$. If it exists, let $u \in U_c$ denote the unique individual for which $\iota_c(y[\pi.s])$ holds for some access path π.

Then $[\![st]\!]_c(S_c) = S'_c = (U'_c, \iota'_c)$ where $U'_c = U_c$ and ι'_c equals ι_c up to the predicate $x[\pi]$, which is updated such that $\iota'_c(x[\pi])(u')$ holds iff $u' = u$. Let $S_f = g(S_c)$ denote the fine-grained structure corresponding to S_c. This generates for $u \in U_c$ the head $u_\varepsilon \in U_f$ as well as its components, including u_π and $u_{\pi.s}$. Since we assumed that $\iota_c(y[\pi.s])(u)$ is true in S_c, we know that $\iota_f(*)(y, u_{\pi.s})$ must hold in S_f. Thus, $[\![st]\!]_f(S_f) = S'_f = (U'_f, \iota'_f)$ where the set of individuals are the same as S_f and ι'_f equals ι_f up to the predicate $*$ which now additionally holds for the pair (x, u_π). Ultimately, the only change to S_f and S_c is that $\iota'_c(x[\pi])(u)$ holds in S'_c and $\iota'_f(*)(u, u_\pi)$ holds in S'_f. As this is in accord with the definition of g, we conclude that $g(S'_c) = S'_f$. This holds also if $\iota_c(y[\pi.s])$ is false everywhere, in which case $S'_c = S_c$ and $S'_f = S_f$. □

The theorem effectively constitutes a simulation result between fine-grained and coarse-grained semantics. Notice that the restriction of quantified variables to heads of records in the translation $\mathcal{T}$ is an important one. It also demonstrates exactly *how* fine-grained structures are finer: they can talk about record components explicitly and quantify over them, while components occur only implicitly in the coarse-grained model.

Part 1 of Theorem 1 can be lifted to abstract states as well. Assume an abstract, three-valued coarse-grained structure S_c^3 and any two-valued coarse-grained structure S_c^2 such that $S_c^2 \sqsubseteq S_c^3$ using the embedding order of [27]. Then any formula ψ of FO(TC) that holds for S_c^3 also holds for S_c^2 by the Embedding Theorem. By Theorem 1, $\mathcal{T}(\psi)$ holds in $S_f = g(S_c^2)$. If S_c^3 was obtained by the set A of abstraction predicates, then ψ will also hold in the canonical abstraction of S_f using $\mathcal{T}(A)$ as abstraction predicates. Lifting part 2 of Theorem 1 is far more involved, because it needs to take materialization strategies into account.

6 Application

Let us finally consider the motivating program from the Introduction. Its code is shown in Figure 1 and a typical memory configuration in Figure 2. In order to argue about data races in the presence of privatization, reachability information is crucial. In particular, one must reason about reachability along different embedded lists. For instance, in Figure 2, only the first and the third node are in the queue, whereas all three are in the list.

The TVLA tool does not natively support computations on predicates as necessary to conveniently express the string manipulation on access paths as used in the update formulas of Table 2. This makes the implementation cumbersome and look clumsy in places. Also, it introduces a lot of superfluous predicates and coercion constraints greatly slowing down the tool. This, however, is not a principal restriction of our memory model but the lack of tool support. Therefore, we had to settle for a proof of concept implementation where the cleanup queue is actually a singly-linked list.

First, we analyzed a program creating a structure like that of Figure 2 from scratch. This amounts to iterating the code

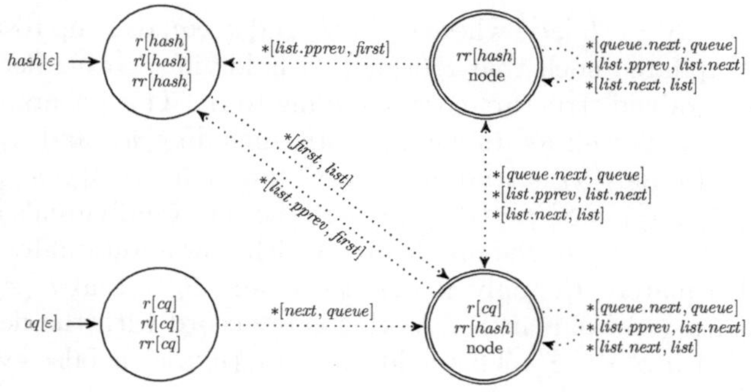

Fig. 5. Shape graph obtained while analyzing overlapping data-structure

```
n = malloc(sizeof(node));
hlist_add_head(&n→list,&hash);
if (?) list_add(&n→queue, &cq);
```

After this loop, four shapes are obtained, the most general of which is shown in Figure 5. It shows that (i) all nodes are reachable from `hash`, which is the head of the hlist component, a fact indicated by `rr[hash]`; and (ii) only some nodes are reachable from `cq`, indicated by `r[cq]`. This is the arbitrary subset of nodes added to the cleanup queue. Also it shows the $*$ predicates with parameters like `list.pprev`, denoting the pprev component of the hlist component of a node. Recall that `rr[x]` (`rl[x]`) means reachability from x along forward (backward) pointers in a doubly-linked list, while `r[x]` is just singly-linked list reachability — which is how we implement the cleanup queue. The precise definitions can be found at `http://www7.in.tum.de/~joba/overlap.tgz`.

Subsequently, the elements of the queue are to be removed from the hlist component using

```
list_for_each_entry(n, &cq, queue) { hlist_del(&n→list); }
```

Here, the challenge for the analysis is the *change of views* implied by traversing the queue and then removing from the hlist. A lot of reachability information is lost; in fact, properties like absence of memory leaks cannot be guaranteed by this analysis. Still, we are able to prove that an element is deleted from the queue using the very same routine that was used in a non-embedded record in Section 4. Thus, we can infer that the element is no longer reachable from the thread-shared data.

Again, the analysis specifications are available online. Even in this most complicated scenario, the analysis time was just a few seconds.

7 Related Work

The body of work on shape analysis is too large to do equal justice to all techniques. Approaches based on regular model checking [5], symbolic backwards reachability analysis [1], or decision procedures such as [6] seem not to have dealt with the analysis of low-level system code, much less with overlapping records. There are a number of approaches that make use of numeric reasoning to deal with pointer arithmetic. While pioneered by Deutsch [15], who used numeric domains to constrain access paths, Gulwani and Tiwari [19] provide a C semantics which perhaps is even more explicit about blocks and offsets as ours. However, it is unable to deal with structures such as doubly-linked lists. Recent work [18] combines numeric and shape domains. It is focused on tracking partition sizes to prove memory safety and sometimes even termination in presence of arrays of dynamically allocated structures. So far, however, none of the above treats overlapping records.

More direct approaches to shape analysis are based on either TVLA [27] or separation logic [26]. As stated before, most work in the TVLA setting focuses on higher-level programming languages; however, Dor's thesis [16] and subsequent work provided a semantics of low-level C similar to our fine-grained semantics and program analyses based on this semantics. These analyses are mostly concerned with string manipulations.

As for separation logic based approaches which deal with a low-level C semantics and with pointer arithmetic, one early work is [7], which however specifically targets the data-structure of multiword lists. Berdine et al. [3] present a shape analysis of composite data-structures which can reason about lists of lists. They explicitly identify shape analysis of overlapping or embedded structures as presented here as a limitation to their approach. Also, Chang and Rival [9] present a shape analysis based on separation logic and user-specified data-structure specifications called checkers. It also treats combinations of numerical and shape domains, but overlapping records are not considered. Despite some impressive improvements recently [31, 8], in particular concerning scalable shape analyses of real code, a formal treatment of overlapping records has yet to be reported. In addition, most of that work focuses exclusively on memory safety rather than on subtle reachability problems as we face.

Separation logic is also used in the broader context of modular verification and extended static checking. There, one relies on specifications of components, and the analysis operates under the assumption that other components behave as specified [17, 2, 14]. The fine-grained memory model we use for shape analysis is also used by the VCC C verifier [12]; in particular, it uses an implicit type-system to verify that distinct pointers do not reference overlapping objects [13]. In the HAVOC verifier [10], a particular reachability predicate is employed which also works on a semantics resembling ours, but is much more numeric in nature, focused on pointer arithmetic. Other techniques exist for dealing with the heap in modular verification, including ownership [11], which is used by Spec# and Java/JML; dynamic frames [21, 29], which is used by VeriCool 1 and Dafny; and implicit dynamic frames [30], which are used in VeriCool 3 and Chalice.

Our interest in shape analysis of overlapping records is derived from attempts to verify absence of data races in low-level C. In static race detection, dynamic memory is treated at a fairly superficial level by *blobbing* together objects into static allocation sites. There are techniques for verifying mutually exclusive access to heap objects when each record contains its own dedicated lock [24]; and analyses relying on reachability information, such as *disjoint reachability analysis* [23] and *region analysis* [28], have been employed to ensure correct synchronization of accesses to disjoint regions of dynamically allocated memory. These analyses, however, cannot deal with object privatization and overlapping structures as occur in our example. On the other hand, by virtue of not tracking the state of the heap at each program point, such analyses can be directly used in a concurrent setting, while our approach requires adaptations of the TVLA approach to handle concurrency [22, 4].

8 Conclusion

We presented a shape analysis for overlapping data-structures, which are ubiquitous in low-level systems code. Using our prototype implementation we were able to establish subtle reachability properties as required, e.g., for reasoning about data races in system code with overlapping records.

For that, we introduced two refinements of existing memory models. This enabled us to implement both approaches within the TVLA framework. Accordingly, our analysis will benefit from any future improvements of the TVLA tool. However, as dynamic manipulation of predicates is not natively supported by the TVLA tool, a new front-end and/or tool extension is desirable as future work.

The step from fine-grained to coarse-grained semantics is essentially a technique of encoding statically known parts of graph structures like the internal structure of records into syntax. Somehow similar, separation logic based approaches rely on inductively defined predicates capturing data-structures. This connection might be exploited to enable the use of different formalisms for different parts of the heap in a common setting.

References

1. Abdulla, P.A., Bouajjani, A., Cederberg, J., Haziza, F., Rezine, A.: Monotonic abstraction for programs with dynamic memory heaps. In: Gupta, A., Malik, S. (eds.) CAV 2008. LNCS, vol. 5123, pp. 341–354. Springer, Heidelberg (2008)
2. Barnett, M., Chang, B., DeLine, R., Jacobs, B., Leino, K.: Boogie: A modular reusable verifier for Object-Oriented programs. In: de Boer, F.S., Bonsangue, M.M., Graf, S., de Roever, W.-P. (eds.) FMCO 2005. LNCS, vol. 4111, pp. 364–387. Springer, Heidelberg (2006)
3. Berdine, J., Calcagno, C., Cook, B., Distefano, D., O'Hearn, P.W., Wies, T., Yang, H.: Shape analysis for composite data structures. In: Damm, W., Hermanns, H. (eds.) CAV 2007. LNCS, vol. 4590, pp. 178–192. Springer, Heidelberg (2007)
4. Berdine, J., Lev-Ami, T., Manevich, R., Ramalingam, G., Sagiv, M.: Thread quantification for concurrent shape analysis. In: Gupta, A., Malik, S. (eds.) CAV 2008. LNCS, vol. 5123, pp. 399–413. Springer, Heidelberg (2008)
5. Bouajjani, A., Jonsson, B., Nilsson, M., Touili, T.: Regular model checking. In: Emerson, E.A., Sistla, A.P. (eds.) CAV 2000. LNCS, vol. 1855, pp. 403–418. Springer, Heidelberg (2000)

6. Bouillaguet, C., Kuncak, V., Wies, T., Zee, K., Rinard, M.C.: Using first-order theorem provers in the Jahob data structure verification system. In: Cook, B., Podelski, A. (eds.) VMCAI 2007. LNCS, vol. 4349, pp. 74–88. Springer, Heidelberg (2007)
7. Calcagno, C., Distefano, D., O'Hearn, P., Yang, H.: Beyond reachability: Shape abstraction in the presence of pointer arithmetic. In: Yi, K. (ed.) SAS 2006. LNCS, vol. 4134, pp. 182–203. Springer, Heidelberg (2006)
8. Calcagno, C., Distefano, D., O'Hearn, P., Yang, H.: Compositional shape analysis by means of bi-abduction. In: POPL 2009, pp. 289–300. ACM Press, New York (2009)
9. Chang, B.Y.E., Rival, X.: Relational inductive shape analysis. In: POPL 2008, pp. 247–260. ACM Press, New York (2008)
10. Chatterjee, S., Lahiri, S., Qadeer, S., Rakamarić, Z.: A low-level memory model and an accompanying reachability predicate. Int. J. Softw. Tools Technol. Transfer 11(2), 105–116 (2009)
11. Clarke, D.G., Potter, J.M., Noble, J.: Ownership types for flexible alias protection. In: OOPSLA 1998, pp. 48–64. ACM Press, New York (1998)
12. Cohen, E., Dahlweid, M., Hillebrand, M., Leinenbach, D., Moskal, M., Santen, T., Schulte, W., Tobies, S.: VCC: a practical system for verifying concurrent C. In: Urban, C. (ed.) TPHOLs 2009. LNCS, vol. 5674, pp. 23–42. Springer, Heidelberg (2009)
13. Cohen, E., Moskal, M., Tobies, S., Schulte, W.: A precise yet efficient memory model for C. In: SSV 2009. ENTCS, vol. 254, pp. 85–103. Elsevier, Amsterdam (2009)
14. Condit, J., Hackett, B., Lahiri, S.K., Qadeer, S.: Unifying type checking and property checking for low-level code. In: POPL 2009, pp. 302–314. ACM Press, New York (2009)
15. Deutsch, A.: Interprocedural alias analysis for pointers: beyond k-limiting. In: PLDI 1994, pp. 230–241. ACM Press, New York (1994)
16. Dor, N.: Automatic Verfication of Program Cleanness. Master's thesis, Tel Aviv University (2003)
17. Flanagan, C., Leino, K.R.M., Lillibridge, M., Nelson, G., Saxe, J.B., Stata, R.: Extended static checking for Java. In: PLDI 2002, pp. 234–245. ACM Press, New York (2002)
18. Gulwani, S., Lev-Ami, T., Sagiv, M.: A combination framework for tracking partition sizes. In: POPL 2009, pp. 239–251. ACM Press, New York (2009)
19. Gulwani, S., Tiwari, A.: An abstract domain for analyzing heap-manipulating low-level software. In: Damm, W., Hermanns, H. (eds.) CAV 2007. LNCS, vol. 4590, pp. 379–392. Springer, Heidelberg (2007)
20. Jonkers, H.B.M.: Abstract storage structures. In: Algorithmic Languages, pp. 321–343. IFIP (1981)
21. Kassios, I.: Dynamic frames: Support for framing, dependencies and sharing without restrictions. In: Misra, J., Nipkow, T., Sekerinski, E. (eds.) FM 2006. LNCS, vol. 4085, pp. 268–283. Springer, Heidelberg (2006)
22. Manevich, R., Lev-Ami, T., Sagiv, M., Ramalingam, G., Berdine, J.: Heap decomposition for concurrent shape analysis. In: Alpuente, M., Vidal, G. (eds.) SAS 2008. LNCS, vol. 5079, pp. 363–377. Springer, Heidelberg (2008)
23. Naik, M., Aiken, A.: Conditional must not aliasing for static race detection. In: POPL 2007, pp. 327–338. ACM Press, New York (2007)

24. Pratikakis, P., Foster, J.S., Hicks, M.: Existential label flow inference via CFL reachability. In: Yi, K. (ed.) SAS 2006. LNCS, vol. 4134, pp. 88–106. Springer, Heidelberg (2006)
25. Reps, T.W., Sagiv, S., Loginov, A.: Finite differencing of logical formulas for static analysis. In: Degano, P. (ed.) ESOP 2003. LNCS, vol. 2618, pp. 380–398. Springer, Heidelberg (2003)
26. Reynolds, J.C.: Separation logic: A logic for shared mutable data structures. In: LICS 2002, pp. 55–74. IEEE Press, Los Alamitos (2002)
27. Sagiv, M., Reps, T., Wilhelm, R.: Parametric shape analysis via 3-valued logic. TOPLAS 24(3), 217–298 (2002)
28. Seidl, H., Vojdani, V.: Region analysis for race detection. In: SAS 2009. LNCS, vol. 5673, pp. 171–187. Springer, Heidelberg (2009)
29. Smans, J., Jacobs, B., Piessens, F.: VeriCool: an automatic verifier for a concurrent Object-Oriented language. In: Barthe, G., de Boer, F.S. (eds.) FMOODS 2008. LNCS, vol. 5051, pp. 220–239. Springer, Heidelberg (2008)
30. Smans, J., Jacobs, B., Piessens, F.: Implicit dynamic frames: Combining dynamic frames and separation logic. In: Drossopoulu, S. (ed.) ECOOP 2009. LNCS, vol. 5653, pp. 148–172. Springer, Heidelberg (2009)
31. Yang, H., Lee, O., Berdine, J., Calcagno, C., Cook, B., Distefano, D., O'Hearn, P.: Scalable shape analysis for systems code. In: Gupta, A., Malik, S. (eds.) CAV 2008. LNCS, vol. 5123, pp. 385–398. Springer, Heidelberg (2008)

Abstract Threads

Shuvendu K. Lahiri[1], Alexander Malkis[2], and Shaz Qadeer[1]

[1] MSR Redmond
[2] University of Freiburg

Abstract. Verification of large multithreaded programs is challenging. Automatic approaches cannot overcome the state explosion in the number of threads; semi-automatic methods require expensive human time for finding global inductive invariants. Ideally, automatic methods should not deal with the composition of the original threads and a human should not supply a global invariant. We provide such an approach. In our approach, a human supplies a specification of each thread in the program. Here he has the freedom to ignore or to use the knowledge about the other threads. The checks whether specifications of threads are sound as well as whether the composition of the specifications is error-free are handed over to the off-the-shelf verifiers. We show how to apply this divide-and-conquer approach for the interleaving semantics with shared variables communication where specifications are targeted to real-world programmers: a specification of a thread is simply another thread. The new approach extends thread-modular reasoning by relaxing the structure of the transition relation of a specification. We demonstrate the feasibility of our approach by verifying two protocols governing the teardown of important data structures in Windows device drivers.

1 Introduction

The motivation of our work is to verify the correctness of protocols embedded in large multithreaded programs. These programs typically access a variety of objects, including kernel resources and in-memory data structures; the protocols govern the policy for allocating, accessing, and freeing these objects. These protocols are hard to verify not only because of concurrency but also because the code implementing these protocols is typically spread over a large part of the program spanning multiple procedures and deep call chains. Invariably, there is no abstract formal model of these protocols; the code is the only artifact available for analysis.

A substantial amount of work has been done in formally verifying abstract protocol descriptions. However, all this work assumes that the protocol has somehow been extracted from the code implementing it. The extraction process is usually manual and hence error-prone. A bug in the manually-extracted model may not be a bug in the code; conversely, a proof of the manually-extracted model may not be a proof of the code.

Our paper contributes towards formalizing the model extraction problem, bringing much-needed rigor and automation to the process. We provide a simple

G. Barthe and M. Hermenegildo (Eds.): VMCAI 2010, LNCS 5944, pp. 231–246, 2010.

compositional approach where the user provides an abstraction of each thread in the program. The abstraction of each thread is simply another thread, albeit one that may be significantly simpler due to the elimination of details irrelevant to the property of interest. Our notion of abstraction also allows an abstract thread to fail more often than its concrete counterpart, which is often useful for making the abstractions concise; in particular by avoiding the need to expose some local state of a thread that may indeed be relevant to the property of interest.

Given these abstract threads, the verification of an n-threaded concurrent program is decomposed into $n + 1$ pieces – n local sequential checks that each thread conforms to its abstract thread, and the verification of the abstract multithreaded program obtained by composing the n abstract threads. We provide a method for checking that a concrete thread conforms to its abstract thread. The conformance check is reduced to checking the correctness of a sequential program, whose size is linear in the textual size of the concrete thread and quadratic in the number of local states of the abstract thread. In addition, the control structure of the sequential program is inherited from the thread; in particular it does not have any more loops than the underlying concrete thread. The sequential program can be automatically produced from the concrete and abstract threads.

Our method assists the model extraction process by telling whether the constructed models are sound and reporting an error when they are not; at the same time, the conformance checker uses powerful path-sensitive analysis and automated theorem provers, providing a precise way to check if a model abstracts the code, even in the presence of arithmetic and unbounded heap-allocated data structures. To the best of our knowledge, we present the first formal thread-by-thread modeling scheme.

The abstract threads serve as valuable contracts and documentation for the underlying code, and avoid performing a global analysis across the evolution of the underlying code of individual threads. The abstract multithreaded program can be considerably simpler compared to the original program and can be subjected to formal and rigorous analysis using existing techniques based on model checking [7], rely-guarantee reasoning [17] or thread-modular methods [12].

Proving correctness of a multithreaded program is much more efficient after model extraction. In general, model extraction can lead to exponential cost savings due to considering a simpler code. Even if a correctness proof unavoidably involves state explosion in the number of threads, model extraction can reduce the base by eliminating irrelevant local states, thus reducing the asymptotic verification time by an exponential factor.

In practice, the approach enables applying automatic verifiers and thus diminishes the total verification time. Since automatic verifiers cannot handle composition of large real-life threads, a user is doomed to fall back to manual global invariant specification; while creating small threads from large ones makes automatic tools usable. The price paid is identification of the relevant parts of a thread – and those parts may be taken without further inspection (of course, the user may wish to inspect them for further model reduction). This process requires less manual investment than manual specification of the whole global invariant, which would require both identification and inevitable thorough inspection of the relevant parts of a thread as a subtask.

To demonstrate the feasibility of our approach, we have applied it to the verification of two protocols governing the teardown of important data structures in Windows device drivers `battery` and `bluetooth`. The conformance check for each thread is implemented using the Boogie [2] verifier and the abstract multithreaded programs are checked using Boogie and SPIN [15].

2 Programs, Executions and Specifications

A *thread* T is a tuple $(\mathit{Global}, \mathit{Local}, \rightarrow, \mathit{Init}, \mathit{Wrong})$ where

- *Global* is a set of global states;
- *Local* is a set of local states;
- $\rightarrow \subseteq (\mathit{Global} \times \mathit{Local})^2$ is the transition relation;
- $\mathit{Init} \subseteq \mathit{Local}$ is the set of initial local states;
- $\mathit{Wrong} \subseteq \mathit{Global} \times \mathit{Local}$ is the set of error states;

This "local" error state definition is targeted towards the naturally given specifications: `assert` statements in the program code and implicit language constraints like absence of NULL-pointer dereferences. Checking general safety properties is reducible to local error checks.

We use letters g and h to denote global states and symbols $\overline{g}$ and $\overline{h}$ to denote sequences of global states. Similarly, we use letters l and m to denote local states and symbols $\overline{l}$ and $\overline{m}$ to denote sequences of local states.

A phased execution of a thread comprises an alternating sequence of transitions of this thread and transitions of the environment of this thread. The number of thread transitions, which is equal to the number of environment transitions, is the length of the execution. A phased execution of length three is shown in Figure 1; thread transitions are depicted by solid arrows going horizontally and environment transitions are depicted by dashed arrows going vertically.

Formally, a *phased execution* of T of length p is a triple $(\overline{g}, \overline{g'}, \overline{l})$, where $\overline{g}$ and $\overline{l}$ are sequences of length $p+1$ and $\overline{g'}$ is a sequence of length p, such that $\overline{l}(0) \in \mathit{Init}$, $(\overline{g}(j), \overline{l}(j)) \notin \mathit{Wrong}$, and $(\overline{g}(j), \overline{l}(j)) \rightarrow (\overline{g'}(j), \overline{l}(j+1))$ for all j such that $0 \leq j < p$.

Let $T = (\mathit{Global}, \mathit{Local}, \rightarrow, \mathit{Init}, \mathit{Wrong})$ and $T^{\#} = (\mathit{Global}, \mathit{Local}^{\#}, \rightarrow^{\#}, \mathit{Init}^{\#}, \mathit{Wrong}^{\#})$ be some threads over the same set of shared states. Let $e = (\overline{g}, \overline{g'}, \overline{l})$

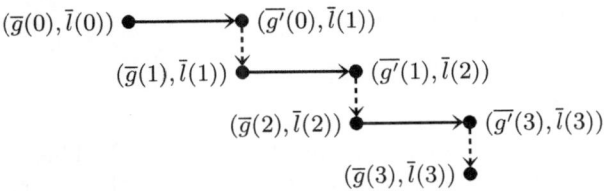

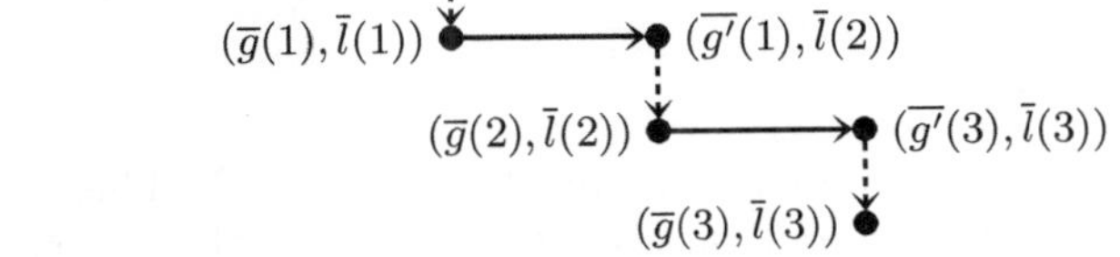

Fig. 1. A phased execution of length three

be a phased execution of T of length p and $e^\# = (\overline{h}, \overline{h'}, \overline{m})$ a phased execution of $T^\#$ of length q. Then $e^\#$ *abstracts* e if $q \le p$ and all of the following conditions hold:

- $\overline{g}|_{q+1} = \overline{h}$ and $\overline{g'}|_q = \overline{h'}$;
- if $(\overline{g}(p), \overline{l}(p)) \in \mathit{Wrong}$ or $q < p$, then $(\overline{h}(q), \overline{m}(q)) \in \mathit{Wrong}^\#$.

(Here, $\overline{x}|_y$ is the prefix of $\overline{x}$ of length y. For presentation purposes the conditions are kept simple; however, it is possible to relax them by allowing e or $e^\#$ to do some internal actions.) Intuitively, the execution $e^\#$ must be a prefix of e and must end in an error if either e ends in an error or $e^\#$ is shorter than e. An interesting aspect of our definition is that $e^\#$ is allowed to go wrong earlier than e. We show below using an example how this feature of our definition allows concise abstractions. Thread $T^\#$ is an *abstraction* of thread T if every phased execution of T is abstracted by some phased execution of $T^\#$.

A *multithreaded program* P is a tuple $(T_i)_{i \in \mathit{Tid}}$, where Tid is a set of thread identifiers and $T_i = (\mathit{Global}, \mathit{Local}, \rightarrow_i, \mathit{Init}_i, \mathit{Wrong}_i)$ is a thread. Let $\mathit{Locals} = \mathit{Tid} \rightarrow \mathit{Local}$ be the set of all tuples of local states of threads in Tid. A state s of P is a tuple $(g, \mathit{ls}) \in (\mathit{Global} \times \mathit{Locals})$. The state (g, ls) is an *initial* state if $\mathit{ls}[i] \in \mathit{Init}_i$ for all $i \in \mathit{Tid}$. The *transition relation* of P is $\longrightarrow \subseteq (\mathit{Global} \times \mathit{Locals})^2$, defined by

$$\begin{aligned} &(g, \mathit{ls}) \longrightarrow (g', \mathit{ls}') \quad :\Leftrightarrow \\ &\exists\, i \in \mathit{Tid} : (g, \mathit{ls}[i]) \rightarrow_i (g', \mathit{ls}'[i]) \wedge \forall\, j \in \mathit{Tid} \setminus \{i\} : \mathit{ls}[j] = \mathit{ls}'[j]\,. \end{aligned}$$

An *execution* of P is a sequence $\overline{s}$ of length $k > 0$ such that $\overline{s}(0)$ is an initial state and $\overline{s}(j) \longrightarrow \overline{s}(j+1)$ for all j such that $0 \le j$ and $j + 1 < k$. The program P *goes wrong* from a global state g if there exist $\mathit{ls}, \mathit{ls}' \in \mathit{Locals}$ and $g' \in \mathit{Global}$ such that all of the following conditions hold:

- (g, ls) is an initial state of P;
- there is an execution of P from (g, ls) to (g', ls');
- $(g', \mathit{ls}'[i]) \in \mathit{Wrong}_i$ for some $i \in \mathit{Tid}$.

Our definition of abstraction is sound for modular reasoning. If each thread in a multithreaded program P is abstracted by a corresponding thread in a program $P^\#$, then it suffices to prove $P^\#$ correct in order to prove P correct. This claim is captured by the following theorem.

Theorem 1 (Soundness). *Let $P = (T_i)_{i \in \mathit{Tid}}$ and $P^\# = (T_i^\#)_{i \in \mathit{Tid}}$ be multithreaded programs over the set Global of shared states such that $T_i^\#$ is an abstraction of T_i for all $i \in \mathit{Tid}$. Then, for all $g \in \mathit{Global}$, if P goes wrong from g, then $P^\#$ also goes wrong from g.*

2.1 Example

Consider the multithreaded program P in Figure 2. This program has two threads and a single shared variable `g`. We assume that every line in the program is executed atomically. Suppose we wish to prove that the assertion in the program does not fail whenever we execute P from a global state satisfying `g>0`.

Thread A

```
int x;
x := 1;
while (*) {
    if (*) {
      x := g;
    } else {
      x := x+1;
    }
}
g := x;
```

Thread B

```
int y;
y := 1;
while (*) {
    y := y+1;
}
g := y;
assert g>0;
```

Fig. 2. Multithreaded program P

Thread $A^{\#}$

Thread $B^{\#}$

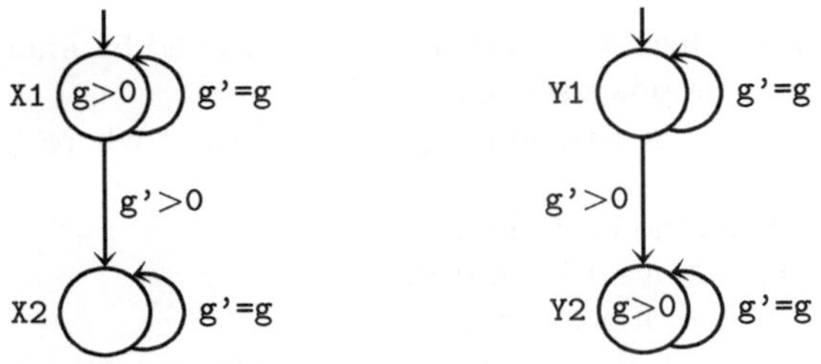

Fig. 3. Multithreaded program $P^{\#}$

Instead of proving this property directly on P, we would instead like to prove it on the simpler program $P^{\#}$ in Figure 3. Since $P^{\#}$ is intended to be a specification, it is written in the style of a state machine. The labels `X1, X2, Y1, Y2` are local states of $A^{\#}$ and $B^{\#}$, the predicate drawn in a local state is an assertion (defaults to `true` if none given) and the predicate on an edge indicates the transition relation for that edge. For example, an execution beginning at `X1` goes wrong if `g>0` is false; otherwise, either the program location and the value of `g` remain unchanged or the program location changes to `X2` and the value of `g` is updated to some number greater than zero. The initial local states of the threads are `X1` for $A^{\#}$ and `Y1` for $B^{\#}$. Note that the local state of threads in $P^{\#}$ are finite, while each thread in P has a local integer variable in addition to the set of program locations.

Each phased execution of thread A is abstracted by a phased execution of thread $A^{\#}$. Every transition of A before the update `g := x` is "simulated" by the transition of $A^{\#}$ that goes from `X1` to `X1`. The update `g := x` is "simulated" by the transition $g' > 0$ from `X1` to `X2`. The correspondence between B and $B^{\#}$ is similar. The assertion at the end of B carries over to the assertion in state `Y2`. The next section will present our conformance checking algorithm for formally proving that A is abstracted by $A^{\#}$ and B is abstracted by $B^{\#}$.

Note that while there is no assertion in A, we have introduced an assertion in $A^\#$ in the state `X1`. This assertion is essential for conformance checking to work, since otherwise thread A would have no assumption about the values read from g and could assign also negative values to g, which is in turn not modeled by $A^\#$.

Note that even though A is a small program, $A^\#$ is considerably simpler than A. Although it has more assertions, its local state has become finite by the elimination of the variable `x`. In fact, the introduced assertion is the key reason for being able to eliminate the variable `x`.

For demonstration purposes, consider a variant $\tilde{A}$ of A in which `x:=1` is replaced by `x:=-1`. Then $\tilde{A}$ could update g to a negative value, and since $A^\#$ can update g only to a positive value, $A^\#$ would not be an abstraction of $\tilde{A}$.

3 Conformance Checker

Now we show how to check that a thread is abstracted by another thread.

Let $\mathcal{P}(X)$ denote the powerset of a set X.

A *sequential program* is a tuple $(Z, \rightsquigarrow, Start, Error)$ where

- Z is a set of states;
- $\rightsquigarrow \subseteq Z^2$ is the transition relation;
- $Start \subseteq Z$ is the set of initial states;
- $Error \subseteq Z$ is the set of error states.

An *execution* of a sequential program is a nonempty sequence $\overline{z}$ of states of finite length k such that $\overline{z}(0) \in Start$ and $\overline{z}(j) \rightsquigarrow \overline{z}(j+1)$ for all j such that $0 \le j$ and $j+1 < k$. An execution is called *failing* if any of its states is in $Error$. A sequential program is *correct* if it has no failing execution.

Let $T = (Global, Local, \rightarrow, Init, Wrong)$ and $T^\# = (Global, Local^\#, \rightarrow^\#, Init^\#, Wrong^\#)$ be two threads. Our solution to the problem of checking that T is abstracted by $T^\#$ is encoded as a sequential program $C(T, T^\#)$. This program simultaneously runs both T and $T^\#$ checking that each step of T is "simulated" by the corresponding step of $T^\#$. Since $T^\#$ is potentially nondeterministic, a partial execution of T can be "simulated" by multiple executions of $T^\#$. Consequently, a state of $C(T, T^\#)$ is a pair (l, F) from the set $Local \times \mathcal{P}(Local^\#)$. The first component l is the state of T. The second component F is the set of states of $T^\#$ that are candidates for "simulating" future behaviors of T from l. Our construction provides the guarantee that $C(T, T^\#)$ goes wrong iff T is not abstracted by $T^\#$.

We now provide a formal definition of $C(T, T^\#)$. For each $l \in Local$, let $W(l) = \{g \in Global \mid (g, l) \in Wrong\}$. Similarly, for each $m \in Local^\#$, let $W^\#(m) = \{g \in Global \mid (g, m) \in Wrong^\#\}$. For each $F \in \mathcal{P}(Local^\#)$, let $W^\#(F) = \bigcup_{m \in F} W^\#(m)$. A *conformance checker* $C(T, T^\#)$ is a sequential program $(Z, \rightsquigarrow, Start, Error)$ where

- $Z = Local \times \mathcal{P}(Local^\#)$;
- $Start = Init \times \{Init^\#\}$;
- $Error = (Local \times \{\emptyset\}) \cup \{(l, F) \in Local \times \mathcal{P}(Local^\#) \mid W(l) \not\subseteq W^\#(F)\}$;
- $\rightsquigarrow$ is defined by

$$\frac{\begin{array}{c} l, l' \in \mathit{Local} \quad F, F' \subseteq \mathit{Local}^{\#} \\ \exists\, g, g' \in \mathit{Global} : g \notin W^{\#}(F) \text{ and } (g, l) \rightarrow (g', l') \text{ and} \\ F' = \{m' \mid \exists\, m \in F : (g, m) \rightarrow^{\#} (g', m')\} \end{array}}{(l, F) \rightsquigarrow (l', F')}$$

The definition of *Error* and $\rightsquigarrow$ are the most interesting and subtle parts of the definition of $C(T, T^{\#})$. The set *Error* is the union of two parts, each corresponding to a different reason why T might not be abstracted by $T^{\#}$. Consider an element $(l, \emptyset)$ of the first part. The conformance checker makes a transition to this state if it arrives in a state (x, F) and there is some transition of T out of the local state x that cannot be "simulated" by any transition of $T^{\#}$ out of any local state in F. Now, consider an element (l, F) of the second part satisfying $W(l) \not\subseteq W^{\#}(F)$. If the conformance checker arrives in this state, then T can go wrong from l but $T^{\#}$ cannot go wrong from any candidate state in F, again violating a requirement for abstraction.

Having understood the definition of *Error*, it is simple to understand the definition of $\rightsquigarrow$. We create a transition $(l, F) \rightsquigarrow (l', F')$ only when there exist g, g' such that T can make a transition from (g, l) to (g', l'). Here, we only need to pick those states g from which it is not possible for $T^{\#}$ to go wrong from a local state in F. The reason is that if $T^{\#}$ can go wrong from g, the "simulation" process can stop because we have discovered an erroneous execution in the abstraction. We collect in F' all those local states transitions to which can "simulate" the transition (g, l) to (g', l') of T.

There are two important observations about our conformance checker. First, its control structure is inherited from the thread T. Any loops in T get carried over to $C(T, T^{\#})$; moreover, if T is loop-free then so is $C(T, T^{\#})$. Second, the state of $C(T, T^{\#})$ is independent of the global state set *Global*. Essentially, the global state gets existentially quantified at each step of the conformance checking computation. This property allows us to write loop invariants for $C(T, T^{\#})$ without worrying about the behavior with respect to the global state.

There are a few special cases for which the conformance checker becomes simpler. First, if the set $\mathit{Local}^{\#}$ of abstract local states is finite, then the (in general, unbounded) quantification implicit in the definition of *Error* and the calculation of F' in the definition of $\rightsquigarrow$ become finite. The conformance checker can simply enumerate the set of abstract local states allowing the assertion logic of the sequential program to become simpler. In addition, if the concrete thread T is either finite-state or loop-free, then the correctness of the conformance checker can be verified fully automatically, using a finite-state model checker or an automated theorem prover, respectively.

The correctness of our conformance checker is captured by the following theorem.

Theorem 2. *Let* $T = (\mathit{Global}, \mathit{Local}, \rightarrow, \mathit{Init}, \mathit{Wrong})$ *and* $T^{\#} = (\mathit{Global}, \mathit{Local}^{\#}, \rightarrow^{\#}, \mathit{Init}^{\#}, \mathit{Wrong}^{\#})$ *be threads over a nonempty set of shared states Global. Then* $T^{\#}$ *is an abstraction of* T *if and only if the conformance checker* $C(T, T^{\#})$ *is correct.*

3.1 Instrumentation

Now we show how to check abstraction when threads are given in a textual form rather than as transition systems.

The conformance checker is implemented by instrumenting the source code of the concrete thread. We now describe this instrumentation for the case when the local state of the abstract thread is finite. We make the following simplifying assumptions about the code of the concrete thread. First, we assume that every statement is executed atomically: all statements have been split into atomic substatements in a standard way which depends on the platform on which the code is executed. Second, we assume that all conditionals have been eliminated using assume statements and standard control-flow-graph transformations. Thus, apart from the usual control flow, we only have assume, assert, and assignment statements in the code. Third, we assume that the program has a single global variable named v; the extension for multiple variables is straightforward.

Finally, we assume that the abstract thread is provided as a state machine (as in Figure 3) comprising a finite set of nodes N with edges among them. Each node x is labeled with a predicate $A(x)$ over the variable v capturing the assertion in that state. An edge from node x to node y is labeled with a predicate $T(x, y)$ over variables v and v' capturing the transition from local state x to local state y. The set $I \subseteq N$ is the set of initial states.

We are now ready to describe the instrumentation. We introduce a bookkeeping variable u for keeping a temporary copy of v. We also introduce a map variable $F : N \to \mathit{Boolean}$ to model the set of locations of the abstract thread. We insert the following initialization code at the beginning of the concrete thread.

$\mathit{havoc}\ v;$ // assign any value to v nondeterministically
$u := v;$
$F := \lambda y \in N.\ y \in I;$

Next, we replace each non-assert statement *st* in the program with the following code fragment.

(1) $\mathit{assert}\ \bigvee_{x \in N} F[x];$
(2) $\mathit{assume}\ \bigwedge_{x \in N} F[x] \Rightarrow A(x);$
(3) $\mathit{st};$
(4) $F := \lambda y \in N.\ \bigvee_{x \in N} F[x] \wedge T(x, y)[u/v, v/v'];$
(5) $\mathit{havoc}\ v;$
(6) $u := v;$

This instrumentation preserves the invariant that upon entry to each instrumentation code block, variables u and v are identical and unconstrained. Clearly, this property is true initially; lines 5 and 6 ensure this property upon exit from the code block. Line 1 asserts that the set F is nonempty. Line 2 assumes the assertions at each location in F. If any of these facts do not hold then the abstract execution can go wrong and the "simulation" check has succeeded. Line 3 simply executes the statement *st* and line 4 computes the new value of the set F by enumerating over all pairs of abstract nodes.

Finally, each original-code assertion *assert(ϕ)* (which specifies a property to be proven) is replaced by the check

$$assert\ \neg\phi \Rightarrow \bigvee_{x \in N} F[x] \wedge \neg A(x);$$

The check asserts that when a concrete execution goes wrong, at least one abstract execution should also go wrong.

From this instrumentation technique, it is clear that the conformance checker inherits the control structure of the concrete thread. Furthermore, the textual size of the checker is linear in the size of the concrete thread and quadratic in the size of the abstract thread. The instrumentation is a simple syntactical operation and can be performed fully automatically. If the local state of the abstract thread is finite, the analysis of the conformance checker can be automatized to the same level as that of the concrete thread, viewed as a sequential program.

4 Experiments

We demonstrate our approach on two drivers from the Windows operating system.

4.1 Bluetooth Driver

The concrete multithreaded program in Figure 4 consists of a thread PnpStop which unloads the driver and n threads PnpAdd which process data. The shared

```
// ''Unload'' thread
void PnpStop() {
     stoppingFlag=1;
     IoDecrement();
     assume(stoppingEvent);
     // release allocated resources;
     stopped=1;
}
```

```
// ''Worker'' thread
void PnpAdd() {
     int status;
     status = IoIncrement();
     if(status>0) {
         // do work here
         assert(!stopped);
     }
     IoDecrement();
}
```

```
int IoIncrement() {
     int status;
     pendingIO++;
     if(stoppingFlag)
         status=-1;
     else
         status=1;
     return status;
}
```

```
void IoDecrement() {
     pendingIO--;
     if(!pendingIO)
         stoppingEvent=1;
}
```

Fig. 4. Bluetooth driver model consisting of a single "unload" thread PnpStop and n "worker" threads PnpAdd

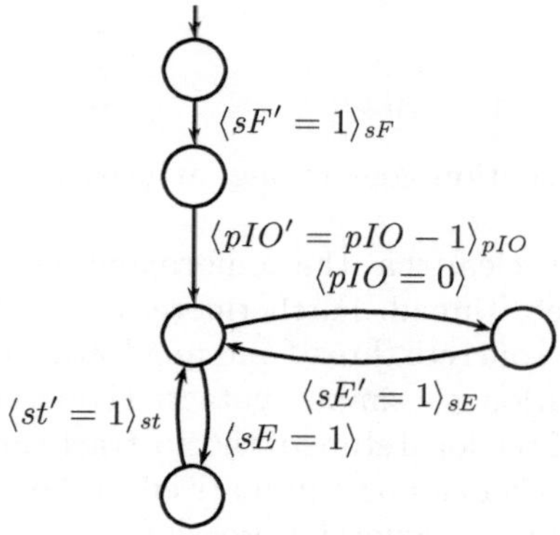

(a) Abstract "unload" thread

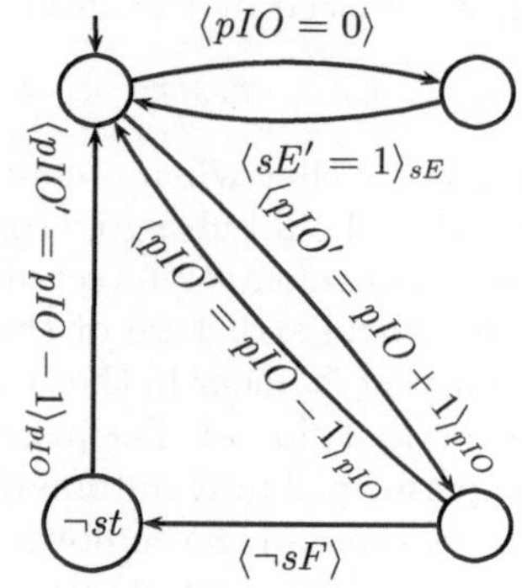

(b) Abstract "worker" thread

Fig. 5. Abstract bluetooth driver model

variables together with their initial values are `pendingIO = 1`, `stoppingFlag = stoppingEvent = stopped = 0`.

The property to be proven is the correct teardown, i.e. that in no execution a "worker" thread should try to access data after `stopped` flag has been raised by the "unload" thread.

SPIN cannot check the composition of 9 threads executing Fig. 4, as we will see. To increase the number of verifiable threads, it is reasonable to simplify the Bluetooth code. We simplified the code by eliminating the local variable `status` and merging some local states to reduce their number. A possible resulting abstract program is given in Figure 5.

We use the following shorthands: sF = `stoppingFlag`, pIO = `pendingIO`, sE = `stoppingEvent`, st = `stopped`. Further, there is a hidden idle transition associated with each node, labeled with $pIO = pIO' \wedge sF = sF' \wedge sE = sE' \wedge st = st'$. The notation $\langle \phi \rangle_{X,Y}$ is a shorthand for $\phi \wedge \bigwedge_{v \in \text{Var} \setminus \{X,Y\}} v = v'$, i.e., that all variables except X and Y remain unchanged. The formulas in the nodes denote assertions. If a formula is missing, it defaults to *true*.

Such simplification looks easy but is error-prone: without a correctness proof one never knows whether the party (a human or a tool) that did the simplification has really produced sound abstractions. Our approach automatically creates a formal proof of abstraction soundness.

To encode the driver model and its abstraction, we used the Boogie modeling language equipped with the Boogie verifier and Z3 theorem prover [10]. The conformance check succeeded fully automatically. Boogie also allowed automatic bounded verification of the composition of thread abstractions for one "unload" and two "worker" threads. All the mentioned checks together succeeded within 33 seconds. The concrete multithreaded program in Figure 4 and, separately, the abstract multithreaded program in Figure 5 were fed to the SPIN tool. Proofs by exhaustive search needed following times in seconds:

Threads	1	2	3	4	5	6	7	8	9	10	11
Concrete program	0	0	0	0.0225	0.1833	1.56	19.26	158.66	n/a	n/a	n/a
Abstract program	0	0	0	0	0.018	0.12	0.314	1.246	5.812	39.04	190.6

Zero means that the time was so small that it was below the measurement precision, "n/a" means that SPIN exceeds the 2GB memory limit. The asymptotic verification times for the concrete program and abstract programs are exponential, as expected for the general-purpose uninformed tool, with experimentally determined bases ≈ 9.3 and ≈ 4.9. Abstraction allowed verification of more threads in less time. The exponential speedup is $\approx 1.9^n$.

4.2 Battery Driver

The property to verify is correct teardown, i.e. once the dispatch routines have started the "worker" threads, and the "unload" thread has freed the data structures of the driver, no "worker" thread should try to access these data structures any more. We examine a simple version of the driver by inlining procedures and modeling the fields of the heap allocated data structure as scalar variables.

Figure 6 shows the simplified code of the "unload" and "worker" threads. A star ($*$) represents a nondeterministic value, and the variable `stopped` indicates that the object has been freed.

To ensure correct teardown, we put an implicit assertion $\neg$`stopped` before each access to a shared variable (except `NumQueuedWorkers`).

Initially, `WorkerActive` = 0, `WantToRemove` = FALSE, `ReadyToRemove` = FALSE, `InUseCount` = 2, `NumQueuedWorkers` = 0. When a worker thread is scheduled for execution by a dispatch routine (which is not depicted here), the routine increments the `WorkerActive` counter. When a copy of the worker thread is about to quit, the worker thread decrements `WorkerActive`. The variable `InUseCount` models a reference count of the number of threads accessing a shared object, and is incremented by a thread before accessing the object and decremented later. Furthermore, if the removal is signaled by `ReadyToRemove`, threads decrement `InUseCount` and try to quit themselves. We made one simplifying assumption that the decrement of `InUseCount` to 0 and the signaling of `ReadyToRemove` happens atomically. This simplification is justified because the action that sets `ReadyToRemove` to true commutes to the left of all concurrent actions of other threads.

The abstract worker thread is shown in Figure 7. We introduce shorthands: R(eadyToRemove), I(nUseCount), N(umQueuedWorkers), W(orkersActive) and S(topped). In the following pictorial representation, each assertion is implicitly conjoined with the common part: $I \geq 0 \wedge W \geq 0 \wedge N \geq 0 \wedge (R \Rightarrow I = 0) \wedge (N > 0 \Rightarrow \neg S \wedge W > 0)$. Further, there is a hidden idle transition associated with each node, labeled with $R = R' \wedge I = I' \wedge N = N' \wedge W = W' \wedge S = S'$. One interesting thing to observe is that the local variable `i` is not present in the abstract specification for the worker thread. This is important to make the set of local states of the worker thread specification finite, thus enabling us to leverage the instrumentation provided in Section 3.1.

"Unload" thread

```
WantToRemove=TRUE;
if(1 == ++WorkerActive) {
  if(*) {
    if(0 == --InUseCount)
      ReadyToRemove=TRUE;
  } else {
    ++NumQueuedWorkers;
    // Work to do,
    // start working thread.
  }
}
if(0 < --InUseCount)
  await(&ReadyToRemove);
stopped=TRUE;
```

"Worker" thread

```
atomic {
   await(NumQueuedWorkers>0);
   NumQueuedWorkers--;
}
unsigned long i;
while(TRUE) {
  if(WantToRemove) {
    if(0 == --InUseCount)
      ReadyToRemove=TRUE;
    break;
  }
  if(*) {
    ++InUseCount;
    if(WantToRemove)
      --InUseCount;
    else
      --InUseCount;
  }
  i = --WorkerActive;
  if(0==i) break;
  if(1!=i) WorkerActive=1;
}
```

Fig. 6. Battery driver: "unload" and "worker" threads

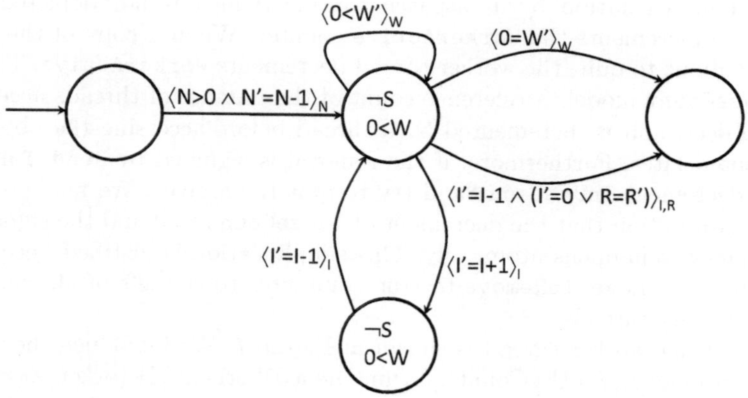

Fig. 7. Specification of worker thread

We encoded the concrete and the abstract threads into the Boogie modeling language. We supplied loop invariants for the loops in the conformance checker manually. The corresponding conformance checkers were proven correct using the Z3 theorem prover in around two minutes for all the threads.

The abstract and concrete programs were also written in the Promela modeling language after manual abstraction of the unbounded `WorkerActive` variable (one can replace it by the predicate `WorkerActive` > 0). The resulting code was fed into SPIN, which created proofs by exhaustive search in the following time in seconds:

Threads	1	2	3	4	5	6	7	8	9	10
Concrete program	0	0	0.08	1.042	7.564	54.28	242.4	929	t/o	t/o
Abstract program	0	0	0	0	0.11	0.51	1.3	3.29	7.49	19.2

The symbol "t/o" means SPIN has exceeded the time bound of 20 minutes. The empirical asymptotic runtimes are $\approx 3.832^n$ and $\approx 2.227^n$. Abstraction thus allowed an exponential speedup of $\approx 1.72^n$.

5 Related Work

In this work, we presented a compositional approach for analyzing real-world multithreaded programs based on abstract threads. Our main contribution is in providing a framework that allows the user to construct and check abstractions of each thread and verify the composition of the abstract multithreaded program. The approach can be seen as a semantic method for simplifying each thread before performing an analysis of the multithreaded program. We also believe that the abstract threads are intuitive specifications of each thread for a developer, because they allow the user to express complex control flow required to capture many real-life protocols.

We can view existing work on verifying multithreaded programs as complementary to our work — we can use any one of them for verifying our abstract multithreaded program and these techniques can use our formalism to simplify the input programs. Existing approaches to verifying multithreaded programs use methods based on inductive invariants [21,9], induction [20], rely-guarantee reasoning [17], partial invariants [24], thread-modular reasoning [12,19,8], model-checking [7], concurrent data-flow analysis [26,13,6] or even bounded analysis [22]. The analysis methods differ in the level of automation and completeness of checking the underlying system. Model-checking based methods are automatic for finite state models extracted manually or as a result of abstraction [14,4], but suffer from state explosion or imprecision in the presence of complex data types. Concurrent data-flow analysis engines extend sequential data-flow analysis in the presence of concurrency, but are restricted to particular analysis domains.

Our method is closest to the class of works based on rely-guarantee mechanism; these approaches allow the user to specify rely-guarantee contracts for each thread; however the annotation can be complex for real-life programs.

We are the first, to the best of our knowledge, to introduce our abstraction relation between threads. Classical simulation of [1] doesn't separate shared and local states, [23] uses bisimulation. Closer simulation relations can be found in process algebras [16,5,18], where a type, which is written in π-calculus or CCS, represents an abstraction of a process, which is written in π-calculus.

Two-level verification occurs in [4], where message-passing communicating processes get abstracted to pushdown automata via boolean abstraction. Apart from the difference in the communication model, we allow richer abstraction, since it is possible to encode boolean programs as abstract threads, but not every thread can be encoded as a boolean program due to the possible presence of unbounded data.

The use of ownership methodology in Spec# [3] and separation logic [25] have the potential to make the specifications more manageable by restricting annotations to the local heap. Flanagan et al. [11] allow linearly ordered control states in the specification of a thread, but do not allow rich control structure of abstract threads. Their "method may be extended to more general abstractions ... at the cost of additional complexity" (p. 166). Our method is such an extension in the call-free case.

6 Conclusion

In this work, we presented a compositional framework to check the correctness of a multithreaded program. We believe that the notion of abstract threads provides an intuitive as well as an expressive formalism for describing models of real-life multithreaded programs. We have illustrated the feasibility of our approach by studying two protocols present in real-life device drivers.

There are several directions in which we are extending the current work. Currently, procedures are treated only as control flow structures; we believe that our method can deal with procedure specifications naturally. Second, we are working on overcoming the restrictions of the real-world model-checkers, e.g. assist the tool in handling loops (as in Boogie) or unbounded variables (as in SPIN). Third, we are exploring techniques that assist a human in creating abstract threads. Finally, we are targeting more real-world examples to evaluate our method.

References

1. Baier, C., Katoen, J.-P.: Principles of Model Checking. MIT Press, Cambridge (2008)
2. Barnett, M., Chang, B.E., DeLine, R., Jacobs, B., Leino, K.R.M.: Boogie: A modular reusable verifier for object-oriented programs. In: de Boer, F.S., Bonsangue, M.M., Graf, S., de Roever, W.-P. (eds.) FMCO 2005. LNCS, vol. 4111, pp. 364–387. Springer, Heidelberg (2006)
3. Barnett, M., Leino, K.R.M., Schulte, W.: The Spec# programming system: An overview. In: Barthe, G., Burdy, L., Huisman, M., Lanet, J.-L., Muntean, T. (eds.) CASSIS 2004. LNCS, vol. 3362, pp. 49–69. Springer, Heidelberg (2005)
4. Chaki, S., Clarke, E.M., Kidd, N., Reps, T.W., Touili, T.: Verifying concurrent message-passing C programs with recursive calls. In: Hermanns, H., Palsberg, J. (eds.) TACAS 2006. LNCS, vol. 3920, pp. 334–349. Springer, Heidelberg (2006)
5. Chaki, S., Rajamani, S.K., Rehof, J.: Types as models: model checking message-passing programs. In: POPL, pp. 45–57 (2002)

6. Chugh, R., Voung, J.W., Jhala, R., Lerner, S.: Dataflow analysis for concurrent programs using datarace detection. In: Programming Language Design and Implementation (PLDI), pp. 316–326. ACM, New York (2008)
7. Clarke, E.M., Grumberg, O., Peled, D.A.: Model Checking. MIT Press, Cambridge (2000)
8. Cohen, A., Namjoshi, K.S.: Local proofs for global safety properties. In: Damm, W., Hermanns, H. (eds.) CAV 2007. LNCS, vol. 4590, pp. 55–67. Springer, Heidelberg (2007)
9. Cousot, P., Cousot, R.: Invariance proof methods and analysis techniques for parallel programs. In: Automatic Program Construction Techniques, pp. 243–271. Macmillan, Basingstoke (1984)
10. de Moura, L., Bjørner, N.: Efficient E-Matching for SMT Solvers. In: Pfenning, F. (ed.) CADE 2007. LNCS (LNAI), vol. 4603, pp. 183–198. Springer, Heidelberg (2007)
11. Flanagan, C., Freund, S.N., Qadeer, S., Seshia, S.A.: Modular verification of multithreaded programs. Theor. Comput. Sci. 338(1-3), 153–183 (2005)
12. Flanagan, C., Qadeer, S.: Thread-modular model checking. In: Ball, T., Rajamani, S.K. (eds.) SPIN 2003. LNCS, vol. 2648, pp. 213–224. Springer, Heidelberg (2003)
13. Gotsman, A., Berdine, H., Cook, B., Sagiv, M.: Thread-modular shape analysis. In: Programming Language Design and Implementation (PLDI), pp. 266–277. ACM, New York (2007)
14. Henzinger, T.A., Jhala, R., Majumdar, R.: Race checking by context inference. In: Pugh, W., Chambers, C. (eds.) PLDI, pp. 1–13. ACM, New York (2004)
15. Holzmann, G.: The SPIN model checker: Primer and reference manual. Addison-Wesley, Reading, `http://www.spinroot.com`
16. Igarashi, A., Kobayashi, N.: A generic type system for the pi-calculus. In: POPL, pp. 128–141 (2001)
17. Jones, C.B.: Tentative steps toward a development method for interfering programs. ACM Trans. Program. Lang. Syst. 5(4), 596–619 (1983)
18. Kobayashi, N., Suenaga, K., Wischik, L.: Resource usage analysis for the pi-calculus. Logical Methods in Computer Science 2(3) (2006)
19. Malkis, A., Podelski, A., Rybalchenko, A.: Precise thread-modular verification. In: Riis Nielson, H., Filé, G. (eds.) SAS 2007. LNCS, vol. 4634, pp. 218–232. Springer, Heidelberg (2007)
20. McMillan, K.L., Qadeer, S., Saxe, J.B.: Induction in compositional model checking. In: Emerson, E.A., Sistla, A.P. (eds.) CAV 2000. LNCS, vol. 1855, pp. 312–327. Springer, Heidelberg (2000)
21. Owicki, S., Gries, D.: An axiomatic proof technique for parallel programs I. Acta Inf. 6, 319–340 (1976)
22. Rabinovitz, I., Grumberg, O.: Bounded model checking of concurrent programs. In: Etessami, K., Rajamani, S.K. (eds.) CAV 2005. LNCS, vol. 3576, pp. 82–97. Springer, Heidelberg (2005)
23. Röckl, C., Esparza, J.: On the mechanized verification of infinite systems, SFB 342 Final Colloquium (2000)
24. Seidl, H., Vene, V., Müller-Olm, M.: Global invariants for analyzing multi-threaded applications. In: Proc. of Estonian Academy of Sciences: Phys., Math., pp. 413–436 (2003)
25. Vafeiadis, V., Parkinson, M.J.: A marriage of rely/guarantee and separation logic. In: Caires, L., Vasconcelos, V.T. (eds.) CONCUR 2007. LNCS, vol. 4703, pp. 256–271. Springer, Heidelberg (2007)
26. Yahav, E.: Verifying safety properties of concurrent java programs using 3-valued logic. In: POPL, pp. 27–40 (2001)

A Embedding Thread-Modular Reasoning

Now we show that any call-free finite-state program with thread-modular proof in the sense of [11] also admits abstract threads which suffice to prove the property such that the size of the abstract threads is linear in the size of the thread-modular specification and quadratic in the number of shared states.

Simplifying [11], assume a single procedure. Its control location set is *Local* and the transition relation of the procedure for each $t \in \mathit{Tid}$ is $\rightarrow_t \subseteq (\mathit{Global} \times \mathit{Local})^2$. Let $0 \in \mathit{Local}$ be the initial control location, $\mathit{pre}, \mathit{post} \subseteq \mathit{Global}$ the pre- and postconditions of the procedure. One has to prove that the concurrent execution of all $\rightarrow_t$ ($t \in \mathit{Tid}$) starting from *pre* respects an invariant $I \subseteq \mathit{Global}$ and that each thread satisfies *post* when it terminates. A thread-modular proof of this fact requires the human to write a specification $(A, E) \in (\mathcal{P}(\mathit{Global}^2))^{\mathit{Tid}} \times ((\mathcal{P}(\mathit{Global}^2))^*)^{\mathit{Tid}}$, where E denotes the environment assumptions as transition predicates and A denotes the abstractions of the threads. The abstraction is a statement sequence interleaved with the stuttering steps: $A_t = \mathit{pre}?\langle \mathtt{true} \rangle; (I?K^*; I?Y_1); \ldots; (I?K^*; I?Y_m); I?K^*; \mathtt{true}?\langle \mathit{post} \rangle$ where K is the stuttering relation and $p?X$ means a state assertion p together with a transition relation X ($t \in \mathit{Tid}$). If for each $t \in \mathit{Tid}$, the program in which the tth thread is $\rightarrow_t$ and all the other threads are E_t^* is simulated by the program in which the tth thread is A_t and all the other threads are E_t^*, then the original program is correct.

Now we transform the threads and specifications to our setting. The concrete threads are modeled straightforwardly as $T_t = (\mathit{Global}, \mathit{Local}, \rightarrow_t, \{0\}, \mathit{Wrong})$ where $\mathit{Wrong} = \{(g, l) \in \mathit{Global} \times \mathit{Local} \mid g \notin I \text{ or } (l = 0 \text{ and } g \notin \mathit{pre})\}$ ($t \in \mathit{Tid}$). The abstract threads are $T_t^\# = (\mathit{Global}, \mathit{Local}^\#, \rightarrow_t^\#, \mathit{Init}^\#, \mathit{Wrong}_t^\#)$ ($t \in \mathit{Tid}$) where

- $\mathit{Local}^\# = \{0, 1, 2, \ldots, m+1\} \times \mathit{Global}$
- $(g, (l, h)) \rightarrow_t^\# (g', (l', h'))$ iff $g' = h'$ and $((l = l'$ and $g = g')$ or $(l = l + 1 \leq m$ and $(g, g') \in Y_{l+1})$ or $(l = m$ and $l' = m + 1$ and $g' \in \mathit{post}))$
- $\mathit{Init}^\# = \{0\} \times \mathit{pre}$
- $\mathit{Wrong}_t^\# = \{(g, (l, h)) \in \mathit{Global} \times (\mathit{Local} \times \mathit{Global}) \mid g \notin I \text{ or } (l = 0 \text{ and } g \notin \mathit{pre}) \text{ or } (h, g) \notin E_t^*\}$.

For each $t \in \mathit{Tid}$, the abstract thread $T_t^\#$ should mimic the transitions and specifications given by A_t and E_t. For that, $T_t^\#$ must fail at least when A_t fails. Moreover, the abstract thread has to fail when the environment violates its specification. To track the change of the shared state by the environment, the abstract thread keeps a copy of the shared state in its own local state. A state of the abstract thread is thus $(g, (l, h))$ where g is a shared state, l the local abstract program counter and h locally stores some shared state.

The environment of the abstract thread may change g, but keeps the copy h in the local part unchanged. The abstract thread compares the shared state h before the environment transitions with the current state g and fails if the environment doesn't behave according to E_t. This is taken care of by the definition of $\mathit{Wrong}_t^\#$.

The transition relation $\rightarrow_t^\#$ mimics all the transition of $A_t^\#$ and additionally saves the current shared state at each step.

Shape Analysis with Reference Set Relations

Mark Marron[1], Rupak Majumdar[2], Darko Stefanovic[3], and Deepak Kapur[3]

[1] IMDEA-Software
mark.marron@software.imdea.org
[2] University of California Los Angeles
rupak@cs.ucla.edu
[3] University of New Mexico
{darko,kapur}@cs.unm.edu

Abstract. Tracking subset relations between the contents containers on the heap is fundamental to modeling the semantics of many common programing idioms such as applying a function to a subset of objects and maintaining multiple views of the same set of objects. We introduce a relation, *must reference sets*, which subsumes the concept of *must-aliasing* and enables existing shape analysis techniques to efficiently and accurately model many types of containment properties without the use of explicit quantification or specialized logics for containers/sets. We extend an existing shape analysis to model the concept of *reference sets*. Reference sets allow the analysis to efficiently track a number of important relations (*must*-$=$, and *must*-$\subseteq$) between objects that are the targets of sets of references (variables or pointers). We show that shape analysis augmented with reference set information is able to precisely model sharing for a range of data structures in real programs that cannot be expressed using simple must-alias information. In contrast to more expressive proposals based on logic languages (e.g., extensions of first-order predicate logic with transitive closure or the use of a decision procedure for sets), reference sets can be efficiently tracked in a shape analyzer.

1 Introduction

Precise reasoning about the structure of the program heap is crucial to understanding the behavior of a given program, particularly for object-oriented languages. Traditional *points-to* analyses, which calculate sharing properties based on coarse aggregations of the heap (for example by coalescing all cells from the same allocation site and ignoring program flow [15]), are known to be too imprecise for many applications. More precise *shape analysis* techniques [16, 5, 13, 17, 1, 9, 6, 18, 19] have been proposed when more accurate information is desired. These analyses recover precise information by distinguishing heap cells based on additional reachability, allocation site, or type information. Using this additional information, these analyses can precisely model recursive data structures [5, 19] and composite structures [1, 18, 6].

Most work on shape analysis has focused on existential (*may*) sharing properties (and by negation, separation properties) of pointers or variables—the fundamental question asked of the abstract heap representations is whether two abstract references *may* represent pointers that *alias* each other. While this is often enough to prove many sophisticated properties of data structures that have limited amounts of sharing or where the

G. Barthe and M. Hermenegildo (Eds.): VMCAI 2010, LNCS 5944, pp. 247–262, 2010.

```
01 Vector V = new Vector();
02 Data[] A = new Data[N];
03 for(int i = 0; i < N; ++i)
04   A[i] = new Data(abs(randInt()));
05 for(int i = 0; i < A.length; ++i) {
06   Data d = A[i];
07   if(d.f > 0) V.add(d);
08 }
09 for(int i = 0; i < V.size(); ++i) {
10   Data d = V.get(i);
11   d.f = 0;
12 }
```

Fig. 1. Initialize array (lines 3-4), Filter values (lines 5-7), and Update `f` fields (lines 9-11)

sharing is simple (e.g., variable aliasing), the reasoning becomes overly restrictive (and imprecise) for more complex subset relationships among sets of shared objects. Such relationships arise in programs that use multiple views of the same collection of objects (for efficiency, a class might keep the same set of objects in a *Vector* and in a *Hashtable*) or when performing updates on a set of shared elements (filter-map and subset-remove loops, where a sub-collection is first computed then operated on).

We introduce *reference set* relations that track set relations (*must*-$=$, and *must*-$\subseteq$) between the targets of sets of variables/pointers in the concrete program. Thus, *must reference set* information is stronger than, and subsumes *must-aliasing* (which only tracks *must*-$=$ between pairs of variables/pointers). We show that when an existing shape analysis is extended with two simple relations to track the most commonly occurring reference set relations it can efficiently and precisely model many sharing properties in the program, and also model how these properties affect the behavior of the program.

Sharing relations between sets of objects, including reference set relations, can be modeled by extending the analysis with a theory for sets [8] or by quantification with a "forall-exists" quantifier structure (i.e., for all objects pointed to by a reference in array *A*, does there exist a reference in array *B* pointing to the same object?). However, the introduction of additional theories or using more general logics (with quantification and disjunction) makes reasoning computationally expensive. Instead, as demonstrated in this paper, many sharing properties can be efficiently tracked on top of an existing shape analysis with enough accuracy to prove many important sharing relationships.

2 Example and Motivation

Consider the three loops in Figure 1: array initialization, filtering elements into a sub-collection, and updating the contents of the sub-collection. For simplicity the example uses a dummy class `Data` with a single integer field `f`.

The first code fragment allocates an array `A` and then fills it with `Data` objects with random non-negative values stored in their `f` fields. The second loop scans the array for elements that have strictly positive values in the `f` fields and constructs a new vector `V` of these elements. The third loop sets the `f` field of every element in the vector `V` to zero. If these loops are analyzed using one of the existing shape analysis that can model collections, such as [12], we get the abstract heap graph shown in Figure 2(a) at the end of the second loop. In this figure we have simplified the edge/node labels to focus on the concept of how *must* sharing relations between sets of objects can be used to precisely model the behavior of a program.

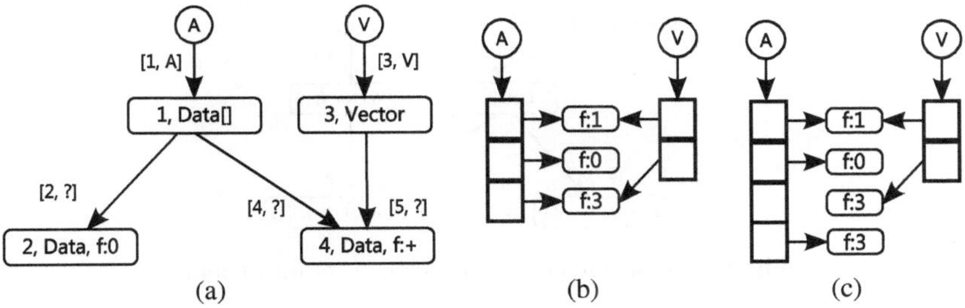

Fig. 2. Abstract model and two possible concrete heaps

The simplified model shows the variable A referring to a node with an *id* tag of 1 (a unique identifier given to each node/edge to simplify the discussions of the figures) which abstracts an object of type `Data[]`. There may be many pointers stored in this array (these pointers are abstracted by the edges with the *id*'s 2, 4); since these pointers are stored in an array we give them the special storage *offset* ? (indicating that they are stored at an indeterminate index in the array/container). The two outgoing edges indicate that the pointers stored in the array may either refer to objects abstracted by node 2 or to objects abstracted by node 4. The notation f : 0, f : +, and f : 0+ indicates the values of the integer fields using a simple *sign* domain [4], where f : 0 in node 2 indicates that all the objects that are abstracted by this node have the value 0 stored in the f field while the f : + entry in node 4 indicates that all the objects abstracted by that node have values in the range $[1,\infty)$ in their f fields (and f : 0+, used later, indicates f values in the range $[0,\infty)$). Figure 2(a) also shows the variable V which has an edge to a node abstracting a `Vector` object. The pointers stored in this vector are abstracted by edge 5 and they refer to objects abstracted by node 4.

Based on this information both of the concrete heaps shown in Figure 2(b) and 2(c) are consistent with this model (i.e., they are valid concretizations). In Figure 2(b) we see that array A contains three `Data` objects (some of which have 0 field values and some of which have positive values), the first and third of which are also stored in the `Vector` V (which only contains objects with positive values). This heap is clearly a possible result of the construction and filter loops in our example. If we look at the concrete heap shown in Figure 2(c) it is apparent that this program state is infeasible since the contents of V are not a subset of A and there is a `Data` object in A with a positive field value that is not in V. However, this concrete heap is consistent with the information provided by the abstract graph model, as the fact that edges 4 and 5 end at the same node *only* means that there *may* exist an object that is referred to by both a pointer abstracted by edge 4 and a pointer abstracted by edge 5. In particular, the abstraction is too weak to prove that at the end of the third loop, every element in A has the value zero in the f field.

Thus, in order to precisely represent the desired *must* sharing relations between various sets of pointers stored in the array and vector we need to extend the graph model with additional information. The analysis presented in this paper extends a standard shape analysis by tracking two *reference set equivalence* relations on the heap. The first relation is on pairs of abstract edges, which tracks pairs of edges such that the sets of references abstracted by the two edges *must* always refer to exactly the same set of

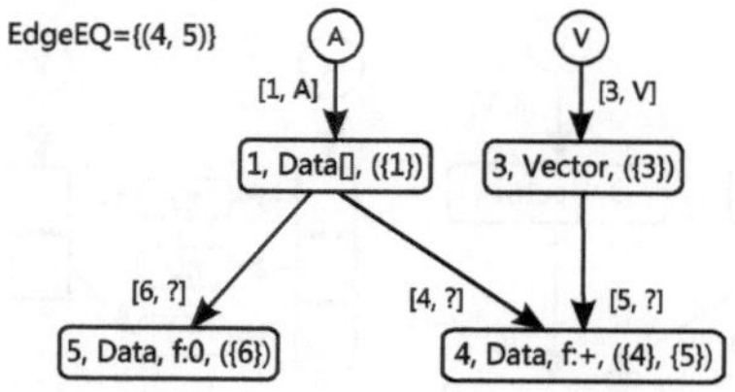

Fig. 3. Abstract Graph With Reference Set Information

objects. The second relation is on edges and nodes, and tracks edges that abstract a set of references such that all of the objects abstracted by a node are pointed to by one of the references in the set.

These reference set properties allow the analysis to precisely model the result of the construction and filter loops in our example. The model enhanced with the reference set properties is shown in Figure 3. We have made two additions to the model in Figure 2(a). First, the `EdgeEQ` relation tracks which edges abstract references that always refer to the same sets of objects. Second, for each node we add a list of sets of edges such that every object abstracted by the node is referred to by a reference represented by one of the edges in the set. Intuitively, these additional relations tell us that the set of objects referred to by references abstracted by edge 4 is equal to the set of objects referred to by references abstracted by edge 5. This information and the structure of the graph imply that every object stored in the vector `V` *must* also be stored in `A` and also that if an object is stored in `A` it must be either abstracted by node 5 (and have the value 0 stored in the `f` field) or by node 4 (and be stored in `V`, which as desired, excludes the concrete heap in Figure 2(c) from the set of feasible concretizations).

This last property then allows us to precisely model the third loop in the running example. In particular we know that since every object in `A` with a non-zero `f` field is stored in `V` we can infer that if every object in `V` has the `f` field set to 0 then after the loop every object in `A` will have 0 in the `f` field.

3 Concrete and Abstract Heaps

3.1 Concrete Heap and Reference Set Relations

The semantics of memory are defined in the usual way, using an *environment*, mapping variables into values, and a *store*, mapping addresses into values. We refer to the environment and the store together as the concrete heap, which is represented as a labeled, directed multi-graph (V, O, R) where V is a set of *variables*, O is a set of *objects* on the heap, and $R \subseteq (V \cup O) \times O \times L$ a set of *references*, where L is the set of storage location identifiers (a variable name in the environment, a field identifier for references stored in objects, or an integer offset for references stored in arrays/collections).

A *region* of memory $\mathfrak{R} = (C, P, R_{in}, R_{out})$ consists of a subset $C \subseteq O$ of the objects on the heap, all the references $P = \{(a,b,p) \in R \mid a,b \in C \wedge p \in L\}$ that connect these objects, the references that enter the region $R_{in} = \{(a,b,r) \in R \mid a \in (V \cup O) \setminus C \wedge b \in C \wedge r \in L\}$, and references exiting the region $R_{out} = \{(a,b,r) \in R \mid a \in C \wedge b \in O \setminus C \wedge r \in L\}$. Note that $\mathfrak{R}$ is determined by C, and we say a region $\mathfrak{R}$ is *induced by* a set C of objects.

Given a region $\mathfrak{R} = (C, P, R_{in}, R_{out})$ and a set of references $R_s \subseteq R_{in}$ we define the function: $Target(R_s) = \{o \in C \mid \exists a \in (V \cup O), r \in L \text{ s.t. } (a, o, r) \in R_s\}$.

Definition 1 (Reference Set Relations). *Given a region* $\mathfrak{R} = (C, P, R_{\text{in}}, R_{\text{out}})$*, reference sets* $R_s \subseteq R_{\text{in}}$ *and* $R'_s \subseteq R_{\text{in}}$*, we define the following relations:*

Reference Contains $R'_s \preceq R_s$ *if* $\text{Target}(R'_s) \subseteq \text{Target}(R_s)$.
Reference Equivalent $R'_s \sim R_s$ *if* $\text{Target}(R'_s) = \text{Target}(R_s)$.
Region Covers $R_s \triangleright \mathfrak{R}$ *if* $C \subseteq \text{Target}(R_s)$.

Aliasing of two references x, y in the concrete heap is equivalent to the reference set relation $\{x\} \sim \{y\}$, thus the *concrete reference set relations* subsume the standard notion of aliasing.

3.2 Abstract Graphs

Our abstract domain is based on the *storage shape graph* [2, 3] approach. Let $\hat{L}$ be a set of abstract storage *offsets* (variable names, field offsets, or special offsets for references stored in arrays/collections) which are related to the storage locations L by an abstraction function $\alpha_{\text{offset}} : L \mapsto \hat{L}$. A *storage shape graph (ssg)* is a tuple of the form $(\hat{V}, \hat{N}, \hat{E})$, where $\hat{V}$ is a set of nodes representing the variables, $\hat{N}$ is a set of nodes (each of which intuitively abstracts a region $\mathfrak{R}$ of the heap), and $\hat{E} \subseteq (\hat{V} \cup \hat{N}) \times \hat{N} \times \hat{L}$ are the graph edges, each of which intuitively abstracts a set of references.

Definition 2 (Valid Concretization of a ssg). *A given concrete heap* $h = (V, O, R)$ *is a* valid concretization *of a* labeled storage shape graph $g = (\hat{V}, \hat{N}, \hat{E}, \hat{U})$ *if there are functions* $\Pi_v : V \mapsto \hat{V}$, $\Pi_o : O \mapsto \hat{N}$, $\Pi_r : R \mapsto \hat{E}$ *such that* Π_v *is 1-1, and*

- *for all* $(o_1, o_2, p) \in R$ *with* $o_1, o_2 \in O$, *if* $\Pi_r(o_1, o_2, p) \equiv (n_1, n_2, l)$, *then* $n_1 = \Pi_o(o_1)$, $n_2 = \Pi_o(o_2)$, *and* $l = \alpha_{offset}(p)$.
- *for all* $(v, o, v) \in R$ *with* $v \in V$ *and* $o \in O$, *if* $\Pi_r(v, o, v) \equiv (n_1, n_2, l)$, *then* $n_1 = \Pi_v(v)$, $n_2 = \Pi_o(o)$, *and* $l = v$.

We say (Π_v, Π_o, Π_r) witness *that h is a valid concretization of g. We introduce the following notation for pre-images of nodes and edges of an ssg:*

- *We write* $h \downarrow_g e$ *for the set* $\{r \in R \mid \Pi_r(r) = e\}$ *of references in the concrete heap h that are in the pre-image of* $e \in \hat{E}$ *under* Π_r.
- *We write* $h \downarrow_g n$ *for the concrete region* $\mathfrak{R}$ *induced by the set* $\{o \in O \mid \Pi_o(o) = n\}$.

In our analysis, we extend ssg's with a set of additional instrumentation predicates that restrict the set of valid concretizations of an ssg. Let U denote a set of relations (called *instrumentation predicates*) on concrete objects and references, and let $\hat{U}$ denote instrumentation relations on the nodes and edges of an ssg, with $u : U \to \hat{U}$ a 1-1 map between them. A *labeled storage shape graphs (lssg)* is a tuple $(\hat{V}, \hat{N}, \hat{E}, \hat{U})$ where $(\hat{V}, \hat{N}, \hat{E})$ is a ssg and $\hat{U}$ is a set of relations over $\hat{N}$ and $\hat{E}$. In the following, we refer to lssg's simply as *abstract graphs*. A concrete heap h is a valid concretization of an lssg $(\hat{V}, \hat{N}, \hat{E}, \hat{U})$ if h is a valid concretization of the ssg $(\hat{V}, \hat{N}, \hat{E})$ through the functions Π_v,

Π_o, Π_r, and additionally, for each $p \in \hat{U}$, nodes $n_1, \ldots, n_k \in \hat{N}$, and edges $e_1, \ldots, e_l \in \hat{E}$, if $(n_1, \ldots, n_k, e_1, \ldots, e_l) \in p$ holds, then each tuple in $\{(o_1, \ldots, o_k, r_1, \ldots, r_l) \mid o_i \in h \downarrow_g n_i, i \in \{1, \ldots, k\}, r_j \in h \downarrow_g e_j, j \in \{1, \ldots, l\}\}$ is in $u^{-1}(p)$.

For example, in Section 2 we introduced two instrumentation relations *type* and *sign*. Formally, for a set $\{\tau_1, \ldots, \tau_k\}$ of object types, we add an instrumentation relation $\texttt{Type}[\{\tau_1, \ldots, \tau_k\}] \subseteq \hat{N}$ to $\hat{U}$ corresponding to the relation $\lambda o.\texttt{typeof}(o) \in \{\tau_1, \ldots, \tau_k\}$ on objects, and require that for each $n \in \texttt{Type}[\{\tau_1, \ldots, \tau_k\}]$ we have that each object $o \in h \downarrow_g n$ satisfies $\texttt{typeof}(o) \in \{\tau_1, \ldots, \tau_k\}$. The *sign* relation can be similarly defined.

4 Instrumentation Predicates

4.1 Abstract Reference Sets

We introduce two instrumentation relations that allow us to track many useful properties of the heap: *abstract edge equivalence*, which relates two abstract edges, and *abstract node coverage*, which relates a set of abstract edges to an abstract node.

Abstract Edge Equivalence Given two edges $e, e' \in \hat{E}$, we say e is *edge equivalent* to e', written $e \hat{\sim} e'$, iff every valid concretization h of the abstract graph g must satisfy $(h \downarrow_g e) \sim (h \downarrow_g e')$.

Abstract Node Coverage Given a set of edges $E_c \subseteq \hat{E}$ and an abstract node $n \in \hat{N}$ we say E_c *node covers* n, written $E_c \hat{\triangleright} n$, iff every valid concretization h of the abstract graph g must satisfy $\bigcup\{h \downarrow_g e' \mid e' \in E_c\} \triangleright (h \downarrow_g n)$.

Proposition 1. *Given lssg $g = (\hat{V}, \hat{N}, \hat{E}, \hat{U})$, a valid concretization h of g, $n, n' \in \hat{N}$, and $e, e' \in \hat{E}$.*

1. *If $\{e\} \hat{\triangleright} n$ and $h \downarrow_g e = \emptyset$ then $h \downarrow_g n = \emptyset$ and $h \downarrow_g e' = \emptyset$ for all e' ending at n.*
2. *If $e \hat{\sim} e'$ and $h \downarrow_g e = \emptyset$ then $h \downarrow_g e' = \emptyset$.*
3. *If $\{e\} \hat{\triangleright} n$ and $\{e'\} \hat{\triangleright} n$ then $e \hat{\sim} e'$.*
4. *If $E_c \hat{\triangleright} n$, $E_s \subseteq \{e_s \mid e_s$ ends at $n\}$ then $\bigcup\{h \downarrow_g e_s \mid e_s \in E_s\} \preceq \bigcup\{h \downarrow_g e_c \mid e_c \in E_c\}$.*

Given the definition for *abstract edge equivalence* we can express the standard concept of *must-aliasing* of edges e_1 and e_2 as a special case of the *abstract edge equivalence relation*: e_1 and e_2 *must alias* iff e_1, e_2 each represent a single reference and $e_1 \hat{\sim} e_2$.

We restricted the definition of the *abstract reference* relations to equivalence of edges plus a special relation on nodes. This allows us to track the most common occurrences of reference equivalence (the edge $\hat{\sim}$ relation) and subset relations (the $\hat{\triangleright}$ relation and Proposition 1). We could define a more general relation, where subset relations between sets of edges are tracked. However, this formulation requires tracking a binary relation on the power set of $\hat{E}$, which is undesirable from a computational standpoint.

4.2 Additional Instrumentation Predicates

In addition to tracking type properties of the nodes, and the edge/node abstract reference set relations defined above, the nodes and edges of storage graphs are augmented with the following instrumentation relations introduced in previous work [11].

Linearity. The *linearity* relation is used to track the maximum number of objects in the region abstracted by a given node or the maximum number of references abstracted by a given edge. The *linearity* property has two values: 1, indicating a cardinality of $[0,1]$, or ω, indicating any cardinality in the range $[0,\infty)$.

Connectivity and Interference. We use two instrumentation relations to track the potential that two references can reach the same heap object in the region that a particular node represents. For this paper we use simplified versions and refer the reader to [11] for a more extensive description of these relations.

Given a concrete region $\Re = (C, P, R_{in}, R_{out})$ and we say objects $o, o' \in C$, are *related* in $\Re$ if they are in the same *weakly-connected*[1] component of the graph (C, P).

To track the possibility that two incoming edges e, e' to the node n abstract references that reach *related* objects in the region abstracted by n we introduce the *connectivity* relation. We say e, e' are *connected* with respect to n if there *may* $\exists(a,o,r) \in (h \downarrow_g e), (a',o',r') \in (h \downarrow_g e')$ s.t. $o, o' \in (h \downarrow_g n) \wedge (o, o'$ are *related*). Otherwise we say the edges are *disjoint*.

To track the possibility that a single incoming edge e to the node n abstracts multiple references that reach the same object in the region abstracted by n we introduce the *interfere* relation. An edge e represents *interfering* pointers (*ip*) if there *may* $\exists(a,o,r), (a',o',r') \in (h \downarrow_g e)$ s.t. $(a,o,r) \neq (a',o',r') \wedge (o, o'$ are *related*). Otherwise we say the edge represents all *non-interfering* pointers (*np*).

Pictorial Representation. We represent abstract graphs pictorially as labeled, directed multi-graphs. Each node in the graph either represents a region of the heap or a variable. The variable nodes are labeled with the variable that they represent. The nodes representing the regions are represented as a record `[id type scalar linearity nodeCover]` that tracks the instrumentation relations for the object types (*type*), the simple scalar domain (*scalar*), the number of objects represented by the node (*linearity*, omitted when it is the default value 1), and the edge sets that cover the node (*nodeCover*).

Each edge contains a record that tracks additional information about the edge. The edges in the figures are represented as records `{id offset linearity interfere connto}`. The *offset* component indicates the offsets (abstract storage location) of the references that are abstracted by the edge. The number of references that this edge may represent is tracked with the *linearity* relation. The *interfere* relation tracks the possibility that the edge represents references that interfere. Finally, we have a field *connto* which is a list of all the other edges/variables that the edge may be connected to according to the *connected* relation. Again to simplify the figures we omit fields that are the default domain value (*linearity* = 1, *interfere* = *np*, *connto* = $\emptyset$).

Finally, we use a global equivalence relation on the edges which tracks the abstract edge equivalence relations (`EdgeEQ` in the figures).

[1] Two objects are weakly-connected if there is a (possibly non-empty) path between them (treating all edges as undirected).

5 Abstract Operations

We now define the most important and interesting dataflow transfer functions for the abstract graph domain, including how the reference set relations are updated. The domain operations are *safe* approximations of the concrete program operations. For brevity we omit proofs of these safety properties (which rely on simple case-wise reasoning about the graph structure and the instrumentation relations). For these algorithms we also assume that all the variables have unique targets (in practice this is done by creating one new abstract graph for each possible variable target, where in each new graph the variable of interest has a unique target).

5.1 Operations

Variable Nullity. When performing tests we generate one version of the abstract graph for each possible outcome. For the nullity test of a variable we create one abstract graph in which the variable *must* be *null* and one abstract graph in which the variable *must* be *non-null*. In the case where the variable is assumed to be *null* we are asserting that the concretization of the edge that represents the variable target is empty. Thus, if the variable edge covers ($\hat{\triangleright}$) a node we infer that the node does not represent any objects and all the other incoming edges must also have empty concretizations. Similarly any edge that is $\hat{\sim}$ to the edge representing the variable target must also have an empty concretization (and can be removed from the graph).

Algorithm 1. Assume Var Null (`v == null` is *true*)

input : graph g, var v
$e_v \leftarrow$ the edge representing the target of v;
$n \leftarrow$ the target node of e_v;
if $e_v \hat{\triangleright} n$ **then** $E_{\text{null}} \leftarrow$ {all incoming edges to n};
else $E_{\text{null}} \leftarrow \{e' | e' \hat{\sim} e_v\}$;
for *edge* $e \in E_{null}$ **do**
  g.removeEdge(e);

Indexing Bounds. In order to analyze nontrivial programs that manipulate arrays and collections we must be able to accurately model the effects of programs that use integer indexed loops to traverse them. To do this we use several special names for the edges that represent the pointers stored in arrays/collections. The name *?* indicates elements at arbitrary indices in an array when it is not being indexed through, *at* represents the distinct element at the index given by the indexing variable, *bi* represents all the elements stored at indices less than the indexing variable, and *ai* represents all the elements stored at indices greater than the indexing variable.

In order to simulate the effect of the test, `i < A.Length`, we again create two new abstract graphs, one where the test result is *true* and one where the test result is *false*. The true result does not provide any additional information that is applicable in our heap domain so we do not need to do anything. The false result indicates that the indexing variable now refers to an index larger than the array size. This implies that there are no elements stored at indices equal to or greater than the current value of the indexing variable, which means that the edges with *offsets at* and *ai* must have empty concretizations and can be eliminated from the abstract graph. Further, as with the variable nullity test we can use the reference set relation information to eliminate other edges and nodes that must also have empty concretizations.

Figure 4(a) shows the most general abstract heap that arises when using simple integer indexing in a loop (to focus on the loop indexing we assume the body is empty) to traverse an array as initialized in lines 3-4. In this figure we have three outgoing edges from node 1, the edge with offset *bi* (edge 6) which represents all the elements at indices less than `i` (elements that have been processed), the edge with the offset *at* (edge 7) which represents the single element stored at index `i` (the element currently being processed), and the edge with offset *ai* (edge 2) which represents all of the elements at indices greater than `i` (elements not yet processed).

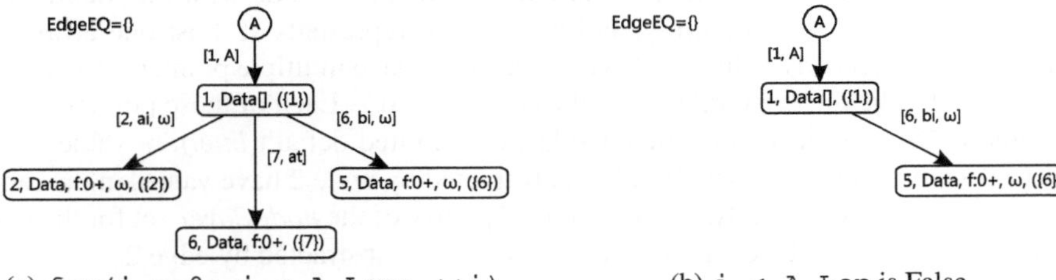

(a) `for(i = 0; i < A.Len; ++i)` (b) `i < A.Len` is False

Fig. 4. Integer Indexing and Test

Figure 4(b) shows the abstract graph that results from assuming the test, `i < A.Length`, is false. In this figure the analysis has determined that since the indexing variable (`i`) is off the end of the array all of the elements in the array must be stored at indices less than `i` and that edges 2, 7 have empty concretizations. This allows the analysis to remove them and since these edges *cover* ($\trianglerighteq$) nodes 2, 6 respectively we can infer that these nodes have empty concretizations and can be removed as well.

Load. The field load operation (`x = y.f`) first computes which node is the target of the expression `y.f`, creating a more explicit representation as needed (Subsection 5.2). Then it adds an edge from `x` to this node and if the storage location of `y.f` is unique then we know the target of `x` must be equal to the target of `y.f` (and the edges representing them are $\hat{\sim}$ and have the same $\trianglerighteq$ properties).

5.2 Materialization

The materialization operation [13] is used to transform single summary nodes into more explicit subgraph representations. For the example in this paper we only need a simple version of *Singleton* materialization which is restricted to handle the following case and otherwise conservatively leave the summary region as it is: if the incoming edges can be partitioned into two or more equivalence classes based on the *connected* instrumentation relation. Once we have identified a node and the edge partitions we create a new node for each partition.

Algorithm 2. Load (`x = y.f`)

input : graph g, var x, var y, field f
nullify x;
if $y.f \neq$ null **then**
  g.materialize(the unique target of $y.f$);
  $n \leftarrow$ target node of y;
  $e \leftarrow$ the unique edge at $y.f$;
  assign x to refer to the target of e;
  if $n.linearity = 1$ **then**
    $n' \leftarrow$ the target node of e;
    set edge representing $x \hat{\sim}$ to e;
    if $e \hat{\rhd} n'$ **then** set edge representing $x \hat{\rhd} n'$;

Figure 5(a) shows the heap abstract graph that captures all of the possible states at line 4 of the example program. The variable `A` refers to a node with the identifier 1, which represents a `Data[]` array, and we know it represents at most one array (the default omitted *linearity* value of 1). This array may have multiple pointers stored in it, represented by the *linearity* value ω in the edge with id 2. Each of these pointers refers to a unique `Data` object since the edge has the omitted default *interfere* value of *np*. The `f:0+` entry indicates that all objects abstracted by node 2 have values in the range $[0,\infty)$ in their `f` fields. Finally, based on the $\{2\}$ entry of the *nodeCover* set for the node 2, we know that each object is referred to by a pointer abstracted by edge 2.

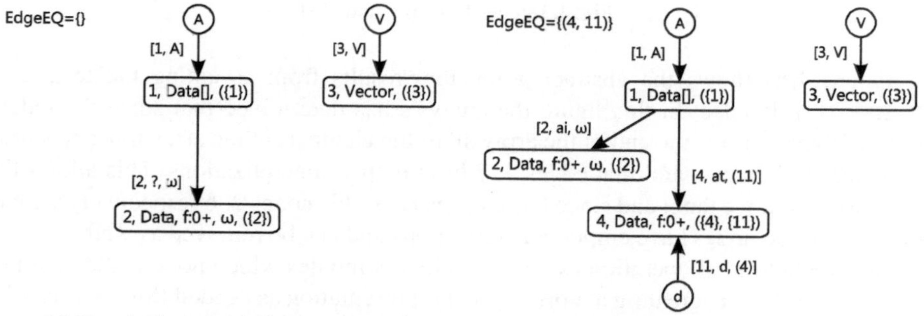

(a) Result From Initialization Loop (b) Load of $A[i]$ (when i = 0)

Fig. 5. Load of $A[0]$ on result of first loop

The result of the load, `d = A[i]` when $i = 0$ during the analysis of the first iteration of the filter loop (line 6), is shown in Figure 5(b). In this figure we have split edge 2 from Figure 5(a) into two edges, one representing the pointer stored at index 0 (edge 4, with offset `at`) and one representing all the pointers stored at indices $[1,\infty)$ (edge 2, with offset `ai`). We have also split the node which represents the `Data` objects into node 4 representing the object targeted by the pointer in `A[0]` and node 2 representing the objects targeted by the pointers stored at the other indices in the array.

Since we know that the edge that was split (edge 2) $\hat{\rhd}$ the node that was split (node 2) we know that the resulting edges in Figure 5(b) must $\hat{\rhd}$ the resulting nodes (edge 2

$\hat{\triangleright}$ node 2 and edge 4 $\hat{\triangleright}$ the node 4). Further we know that edge 4 represents a single pointer (it represents the single pointer at `A[0]`) and, since it $\hat{\triangleright}$ node 4, that node must represent at most one object (the default omitted *linearity* value of 1).

Finally, we have set the target of the variable `d` to be the same as the target of the edge that represents the pointers stored in `A[0]`. Based on the load algorithm we set the new edge (edge 11) to be $\hat{\sim}$ to edge 4 and since edge 4 $\hat{\triangleright}$ node 4, we know that edge 11 $\hat{\triangleright}$ node 4 as well.

6 Examples

Filter Loop Example. The filter loop (lines 5-7) demonstrates how the analysis uses reference set information and the control flow predicate (`d.f > 0`) to infer additional information about the heap, in particular that the set of objects stored in `V` *must* equal the set of objects with positive `f` fields in `A`. To simulate the effect of the test (`d.f > 0`) on the state of the program we create two abstract graphs, one for the result when test result is true and one when the test result is false.

Figure 6(a) shows the abstract graph that results from assuming that the test `d.f > 0` is *true* (on the first iteration of the loop, $i = 0$) and the entry is added to the `Vector V`. Since the test succeeds and we know `d` must refer to the single object abstracted by node 11 (default omitted *linearity* value of 1) we can update the scalar information to show that the `f` field must be greater than 0 (the `f:+` label). We have updated the graph

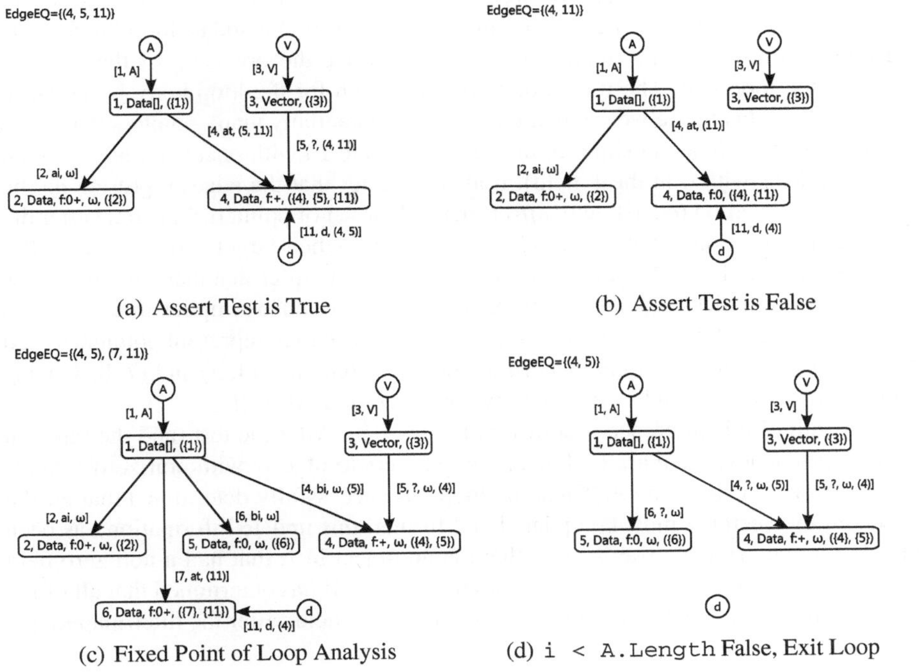

(a) Assert Test is True (b) Assert Test is False

(c) Fixed Point of Loop Analysis (d) `i < A.Length` False, Exit Loop

Fig. 6. Filter Loop Analysis

structure by adding the edge 5 to represent the pointer that is stored into the vector object. Since we know this pointer refers to the same object as `d`, which is represented by edge 4, we add the entry (4, 5) to the *EdgeEQ* relation and since edge 4 $\hat{\triangleright}$ node 4 we know that edge 5 also $\hat{\triangleright}$ node 4.

Figure 6(b) shows the abstract graph that results from assuming that the test `d.f > 0` is *false* (on the first iteration of the loop, $i = 0$) and the entry is not added to `V`. Since the test fails and again we know `A[i]` refers to a single object we update the scalar information to show that the `f` field must equal to 0 (the `f:0` label).

Figure 6(c) shows the fixed point abstract graph which represents all the states that are generated in the loop. We see that there may be many elements in the vector `V` and many elements that are not added to the vector (represented by the edges with the `bi` labels, 4 and 6 respectively). Since we tracked the $\hat{\triangleright}$ relation of each individual object as it was processed we know that every object referred to by a pointer represented by edge 4 must have been added to the vector `V` and thus is also referred to by a pointer represented by edge 5. This implies that edge 5 $\hat{\sim}$ edge 4 and both edge 4 $\hat{\triangleright}$ node 4 and edge 5 $\hat{\triangleright}$ node 4.

Figure 6(d) shows the result of assuming that `i < A.Length` returns *false*. The `at` and `ai` edges (edges 7, 2) must have empty concretizations and can be eliminated (as they abstract the pointer stored at index `i` and pointers stored at indices larger than `i`). As desired the analysis has determined that all the objects with a non-zero `f` field have been stored in the vector `V` (since node 5 only abstracts objects with 0 in the `f` field and edge 4 $\hat{\sim}$ edge 5).

Update Loop Example. For brevity we omit descriptions of how the reference set information is propagated during the individual operations of the update loop (lines 9-11) and focus on how this information is used to improve the precision of the analysis results at the loop exit. The fixed point abstract graph for the loop body is shown in Figure 7(a). In this figure we see that the there are potentially many pointers that come before the current index position in the vector `V` (edge 10 with *offset* `bi`, all of which point to objects with 0 in the `f` field). It also indicates that the edges representing the current index location (edge 8 with *offset* `at`) and the set of pointers that come after the current index position (edge 5 with *offset* `ai`) cover ($\hat{\triangleright}$) their target nodes (nodes 4, 8).

If the exit test (`i < V.size()`) is *false* then we can infer that there are no entries in the vector at indices that are greater than or equal to `i`. This implies that the edges `at` and `ai` (edges 8, 5) have empty concretizations since they represent pointers stored at indices greater than or equal to `i`. Based on the $\hat{\sim}$ relations (4, 5) and (7, 8, 11) this implies that edges 4, 7 and 11 have empty concretizations as well.

The result of this inference is shown in Figure 7(b). After the test (and the removal of the edges/nodes) there are no longer any pointers to objects with non-zero `f` fields in the vector `V` or the array `A`. Thus, the loop has successfully determined that all the objects in the vector `V` must be updated and further, this update information has been reflected in the original array `A` (i.e., there is no object in `A` that had a non-zero field that was not updated in the loop). As desired the analysis has determined that all of the objects in the array `A` have the value 0 stored in their `f` fields after the filter/map loops.

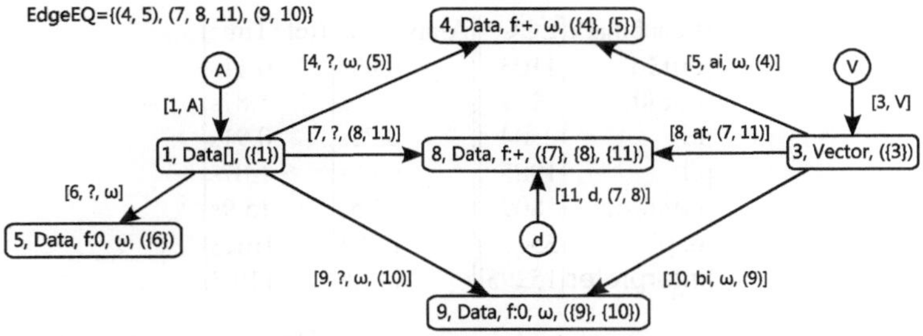

(a) Fixed Point Update of Loop

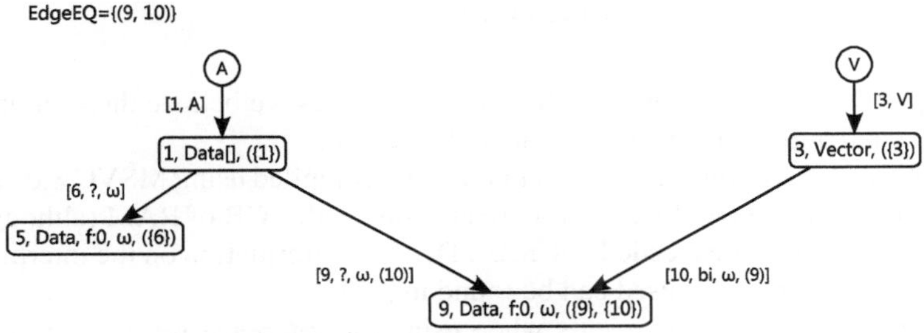

(b) After Loop Exit

Fig. 7. Fixpoint and Exit of Map Loop

7 Experimental Evaluation

We have implemented a shape analyzer based on the instrumentation relations and reference set information presented in this paper. We use a number of benchmarks[2] from our version of the Jolden suite [7], two programs from SPECjvm98 [14], and two programs (exp and interpreter) written as challenge problems. The JOlden suite contains pointer-intensive kernels (taken from high performance computing applications). We have modified the suite to use modern Java programming idioms. The benchmarks raytrace and db are taken from SPECjvm98 (with minor modifications to remove test harness code and threading).

Benchmarks *exp* and *interpreter*, our two internally developed benchmarks, are a basic arithmetic expression evaluator and an interpreter for the computational core of Java. The exp program contains a variety of heap analysis challenges (non-trivial heap structures with and without sharing, copy traversals of the structures and destructive traversals of the structures), and is still small enough to understand. The interpreter program is a large program with varied heap structures, from a large well defined tree structure in the AST, symbol and local variable tables, a call stack of pending call frames, and a very poorly defined cyclic structure in the internal model of the heap built by the interpreter (thus the heap analysis must be both precise and able to deal with ambiguity efficiently). It also has substantial amounts of sharing (variables, method signatures and objects on the interpreters internal representation of the heap are shared

[2] Benchmark/Analysis code is available at `www.software.imdea.org/~marron/`.

Benchmark	LOC	Alias Time	Ref. Time
em3d	1103	0.09s	0.11s
health	1269	1.55s	1.87s
bh	2304	0.72s	0.91s
db	1985	0.68s	1.07s
raytrace	5809	15.5s	15.9s
exp	3567	152.3	161.8
interpreter	15293	114.8	119.3

Fig. 8. Alias Time reports the analysis time with basic *must-alias* tracking while Ref. Time reports the analysis time using *reference set relations*. LOC is for the normalized program representation including library stubs required by the analysis.

in multiple structures). Because of these characteristics we believe these programs are excellent challenge problems for this area of research.

The analysis algorithm was written in C++ and compiled using MSVC 8.0. The analysis was run on a 2.6 GHz Intel quad-core machine with 2 GB of RAM (although memory consumption never exceeded 150 MB). Detailed information on the interprocedural dataflow analysis methods used can be found in [10].

We compare the analysis results when using the *reference set relations* described in this paper and when using a basic equivalence-based field-sensitive must points to relation on the abstract graph edges. In each of these benchmarks when using the reference set relations we see a moderate increase in runtime which varies based on the quantity of subset relations generated by the program (with the largest increase in db, which represents an in-memory database and views of this database via arrays). Each of these benchmarks possess some instances of data structures where the use of reference set relations allows the analysis to extract information that was not possible with simple aliasing information. In some cases this information is not particularly useful (in em3d the analysis discovers that the there are 2 vectors each of which refers to every element in one of the halves of a bipartite graph). However, in most of the programs the reference set information provides potentially valuable information. For example, in bh the analysis discovers that the leaves of the space decomposition trees are always a subset of a given vector, in db we know the set of entries in each view is a subset of the entire database, and in interpreter the analysis determines that each variable symbol is interned in a special table and that all live stack frame objects must be stored in a single list container. In addition the analysis is able to precisely model (as in the running example) most of the filter-map and subset-remove type loops that occur.

8 Conclusion

In this paper we introduced reference set relations, a novel concrete heap property that subsumes the concept of must-aliasing and allows us to compactly express a wide range of must-sharing relations (*must*-$=$ and *must*-$\subseteq$) between arrays, collections, and heap data structures. By extending an existing shape analysis with two simple relations to track the most commonly occurring reference set relations (equality via the *abstract edge equivalence* property, $\hat{\sim}$, and subset relations, indirectly, via the *abstract node cover* property and $\hat{\triangleright}$) we can model many useful sharing properties. As demonstrated by the experimental evaluation, this approach has a small impact on computational costs when compared with classic *must-aliasing* and allows the tracking of a much richer set of heap sharing properties. This work also highlights the strength of the labeled storage shape graph approach, which partitions the heap into conceptually homogeneous regions. This partitioning enables even relatively simple concepts such as the *reference set relations* presented in this work to extract rich information from the program (and conversely may enable the efficient use of strong decision procedures by limiting the complexity of the verification conditions encountered during program analysis).

Acknowledgments. He first author was supported by EU FP7 NoE S-Cube 215483 and FET IST-231620 *HATS*, Spanish MICINN project 2008-05624/TIN *DOVES* and Madrid Regional project S-0505/TIC/0407 *PROMESAS*. The second author was supported in part by the NSF grants CCF-0546170 and CCF-0702743. This material is based upon work supported by the National Science Foundation under grant CCF-0540600. This research is supported in part by the National Science Foundation under grants CCF-0540600, CCF-0546170, and CCF-0702743. The authors thank Mooly Sagiv and Roman Manevich for their useful comments on a preliminary version of this work.

References

1. Berdine, J., Calcagno, C., Cook, B., Distefano, D., O'Hearn, P., Wies, T., Yang, H.: Shape analysis for composite data structures. In: Damm, W., Hermanns, H. (eds.) CAV 2007. LNCS, vol. 4590, pp. 178–192. Springer, Heidelberg (2007)
2. Chase, D.R., Wegman, M.N., Zadeck, F.K.: Analysis of pointers and structures. In: PLDI (1990)
3. Chong, S., Rugina, R.: Static analysis of accessed regions in recursive data structures. In: SAS (2003)
4. Cousot, P., Cousot, R.: Systematic design of program analysis frameworks. In: POPL (1979)
5. Gotsman, A., Berdine, J., Cook, B.: Interprocedural shape analysis with separated heap abstractions. In: Yi, K. (ed.) SAS 2006. LNCS, vol. 4134, pp. 240–260. Springer, Heidelberg (2006)
6. Gulwani, S., Tiwari, A.: An abstract domain for analyzing heap-manipulating low-level software. In: Damm, W., Hermanns, H. (eds.) CAV 2007. LNCS, vol. 4590, pp. 379–392. Springer, Heidelberg (2007)
7. Jolden Suite, `http://www-ali.cs.umass.edu/DaCapo/benchmarks.html`
8. Kuncak, V., Rinard, M.C.: Decision procedures for set-valued fields. In: Proc. Abstract Interpretation of Object-Oriented Languages (2005)
9. Lev-Ami, T., Immerman, N., Sagiv, S.: Abstraction for shape analysis with fast and precise transformers. In: Ball, T., Jones, R.B. (eds.) CAV 2006. LNCS, vol. 4144, pp. 547–561. Springer, Heidelberg (2006)
10. Marron, M., Lhotak, O., Banerjee, A.: Call-site heuristics for scalable context-sensitive interprocedural analysis (July 2009), Report at: `www.software.imdea.org/~marron/`
11. Marron, M., Méndez-Lojo, M., Hermenegildo, M., Stefanovic, D., Kapur, D.: Sharing analysis of arrays, collections, and recursive structures. In: PASTE (2008)
12. Marron, M., Stefanovic, D., Hermenegildo, M., Kapur, D.: Heap analysis in the presence of collection libraries. In: PASTE (2007)

13. Sagiv, S., Reps, T.W., Wilhelm, R.: Solving shape-analysis problems in languages with destructive updating. In: POPL (1996)
14. Standard Performance Evaluation Corporation. JVM98 Version 1.04 (August 1998), `http://www.spec.org/jvm98`
15. Steensgaard, B.: Points-to analysis in almost linear time. In: POPL (1996)
16. Wies, T., Kuncak, V., Lam, P., Podelski, A., Rinard, M.C.: Field constraint analysis. In: Emerson, E.A., Namjoshi, K.S. (eds.) VMCAI 2006. LNCS, vol. 3855, pp. 157–173. Springer, Heidelberg (2005)
17. Wilhelm, R., Sagiv, S., Reps, T.W.: Shape analysis. In: Watt, D.A. (ed.) CC 2000. LNCS, vol. 1781, p. 1. Springer, Heidelberg (2000)
18. Yang, H., Lee, O., Berdine, J., Calcagno, C., Cook, B., Distefano, D., O'Hearn, P.W.: Scalable shape analysis for systems code. In: Gupta, A., Malik, S. (eds.) CAV 2008. LNCS, vol. 5123, pp. 385–398. Springer, Heidelberg (2008)
19. Zee, K., Kuncak, V., Rinard, M.: Full functional verification of linked data structures. In: PLDI (2008)

Shape Analysis in the Absence of Pointers and Structure

Matthew Might

University of Utah, Salt Lake City, Utah, USA
might@cs.utah.edu
http://matt.might.net/

Abstract. Shape analyses (Chase et al. 1990, Sagiv et al. 2002) discover properties of dynamic and/or mutable structures. We ask, "Is there an equivalent to shape analysis for purely functional programs, and if so, what 'shapes' does it discover?" By treating binding environments as dynamically allocated structures, by treating bindings as addresses, and by treating value environments as heaps, we argue that we can analyze the "shape" of higher-order functions. To demonstrate this, we enrich an abstract-interpretive control-flow analysis with principles from shape analysis. In particular, we promote "anodization" as a way to generalize both singleton abstraction and the notion of focusing, and we promote "binding invariants" as the analog of shape predicates. Our analysis enables two optimizations known to be beyond the reach of control-flow analysis (globalization and super-β inlining) and one previously unknown optimization (higher-order rematerialization).

1 Introduction

Control-flow analysis is not enough. In higher-order programs, the three facets of control, environment and data meet and intertwine in a single construct: λ. Deep static analysis of higher-order programs requires that all three facets be co-analyzed with one another. Yet, to date, static analysis of higher-order programs has focused largely on bounding the control facet [1,12,22,26,27,29].[1] Limited excursions have tamed parts of the environment facet [16,18,20,28], and little work even approaches the data facet [17]. These deficits in reasoning leave higher-order languages at a disadvantage with respect to optimization. Our goal in this work is to address these deficits with a holistic approach to the abstract interpretation [5,6] of higher-order programs.

1.1 Limitations of Control-Flow Analysis

To motivate the kind of analysis we need, we will consider specific problems beyond the reach of the control-flow analysis; we will identify the common thread

[1] Control-flow analyses (CFA) answer the higher-order control-flow question: Given a call site $[\![(f\ e_1 \ldots e_n)]\!]$, which procedures may be invoked here? 0CFA, for instance, answers which λ-terms may have closures invoked at the call site.

G. Barthe and M. Hermenegildo (Eds.): VMCAI 2010, LNCS 5944, pp. 263–278, 2010.

as the "generalized environment problem"; and we will then argue that the higher-order analog of shape analysis is what we need to solve it.

CFA Limitation: Super-β inlining. Inlining a function based on flow information is blocked by the lack of environmental precision in control-flow analysis. Shivers termed the inlining of a function based on flow information *super-β* inlining [27], because it is beyond the reach of ordinary β-reduction. Consider:

```
(let ((f (lambda (x h)
           (if x
               (h)
               (lambda () x)))))
  (f #t (f #f nil)))
```

Nearly any CFA will find that at the call site `(h)`, the only procedure ever invoked is a closure over the lambda term `(lambda () x)`. The lambda term's only free variable, `x`, is in scope at the invocation site. It *feels* safe to inline. Yet, if the compiler replaces the reference to `h` with the lambda term `(lambda () x)`, the meaning of the program will change from `#f` to `#t`. This happens because the closure that gets invoked was closed over an earlier binding of `x` (to `#f`), whereas the inlined lambda term closes over the binding of `x` currently in scope (which is to `#t`). Programs like this mean that functional compilers must be conservative when they inline based on information obtained from a CFA. If the inlined lambda term has a free variable, the inlining could be unsafe.

Specific problem. To determine the safety of inlining the lambda term *lam* at the call site $[\![$`(f ...)`$]\!]$, we need to know that for every environment ρ in which this call is evaluated, that $\rho[\![\texttt{f}]\!] = (\mathit{lam}, \rho')$ and $\rho(v) = \rho'(v)$ for each free variable v in the term *lam*.[2]

CFA Limitation: Globalization. Sestoft identified globalization as a second blindspot of control-flow analysis [25]. Globalization is an optimization that converts a procedure parameter into a global variable when it is safe to do so. Though not obvious, globalization can also be cast as a problem of reasoning about environments: if, for every state of execution, all *reachable* environments which contain a variable are equivalent for that variable, then it is safe to turn that variable into a global.

Specific problem. To determine the safety of globalizing the variable v, we need to know that for each reachable state, for any two environments ρ and ρ' reachable inside that state, it must be that $\rho(v) = \rho'(v)$ if $v \in \mathit{dom}(\rho)$ and $v \in \mathit{dom}(\rho')$.

CFA Limitation: Rematerialization. Compilers for imperative languages have found that it can be beneficial to rematerialize (to recompute) a value at its point of use if the values on which it depends are still available. On modern hardware, rematerialization can decrease register pressure and improve cache

[2] The symbol ρ denotes a conventional variable-to-value environment map.

performance. Functional languages currently lack analyses to drive rematerialization. Consider a trivial example:

```
((let ((z y))
  (lambda () z)))
```

At the top-level call site in this program, only a closure over the lambda term `(lambda () z)` is invoked. Yet, we cannot inline the lambda term, changing the program into `((lambda () z))`, because at the very least, the variable `z` isn't even in scope at the call site. We could, however, rematerialize the lambda term `(lambda () y)` instead. Of course, justifying this transformation goes beyond reasoning about the equivalence of environments. What we need is an analysis that can reason about the equivalence of individual *bindings* between environments, *e.g.*, the equality of the binding to the variable `z` within the closure and the binding to the variable `y` at the call site. At the moment, no such analysis exists for higher-order programs.

Specific problem To rematerialize the expression e' in place of expression e, it must be the case that for every environment ρ that evaluates the expression e into a closure (lam, ρ'), that the environment ρ evaluates the expression e' into a closure (lam', ρ'') such that the terms lam and lam' are equal under a substitution $\sigma \subseteq \mathsf{Var} \times \mathsf{Var}$ and for each $(v, v') \in \sigma$, it must be that $\rho'(v) = \rho''(v')$.

1.2 The Generalized Environment Problem

The brief survey of optimizations beyond the reach of higher-order control-flow analysis highlighted the importance of reasoning precisely about environments, and more atomically, about individual bindings. In fact, Shivers's work on k-CFA [27] classified optimizations beyond the reach of CFA as those which must solve "the environment problem."

The term *environment problem* connotes the fact that control-flow analyses excel at reasoning about the λ-term half of closures, but determine little (useful) information about the environment half. Might refined Shivers's definition of the **environment problem** to be determining the equivalence of a pair of environments, for every pair in a given set of environment pairs [16].[3] Equivalence in this case means showing that the environments agree on some specified subset of their domains. This narrow definition is suitable for enabling super-β inlining and globalization, but it is too limited for higher-order rematerialization.

For example, we could not declare the closures $(\llbracket\texttt{(lambda (z) (f z))}\rrbracket, \rho)$ and $(\llbracket\texttt{(lambda (x) (g x))}\rrbracket, \rho')$ to be equivalent unless we knew that $\rho\llbracket\texttt{f}\rrbracket \equiv \rho'\llbracket\texttt{g}\rrbracket$ as well. In this case, the analysis cares about the equality of bindings to two *different* variables in two *different* environments. Thus, the **generalized environment problem** asks whether two *bindings* are equivalent to one another,

[3] The set of pairs comes from concretizing abstract environments, *i.e.*, $\gamma(\hat{\rho}) \times \gamma(\hat{\rho}')$.

where a binding is a variable *plus* the environment in which it was bound, *e.g.*, "Is $[\![\mathtt{x}]\!]$ in environment ρ equivalent to $[\![\mathtt{y}]\!]$ in environment ρ'?"

1.3 Insight: Environments as Data Structures; Bindings as Addresses

Under the hood, environments are *dynamically allocated data structures* that determine the value of a λ-term's free variables, and as a consequence, the meaning of the function represented by a closure. When we adapt and extend the principles of shape analysis (specifically, singleton abstractions [2,4] and shape predicates [23]) to these environments, we can reason about the meaning of and relationships between higher-order functions. As we adapt, we find that, in a higher-order control-flow analysis, bindings are the proper analog of addresses. More importantly, we will be able to solve the aforementioned problems beyond the reach of traditional CFA.

1.4 Contributions

We define the generalized environment problem. We define higher-order rematerialization as a novel client of the generalized environment problem, and we note that super-β inlining and globalization—both known to be beyond the reach CFA—are also clients of the generalized environment problem. We find the philosophical analog of shape analysis for higher-order programs; specifically, we find that we can view binding environments as data structures, bindings as addresses and value environments as heaps. Under this correspondence, we discover *anodization*, a means for achieving both singleton abstraction and focusing; and we discover *binding invariants* as an analog of shape predicates. We use this analysis to solve the generalized environment problem.

2 Platform: Small-Step Semantics, Concrete and Abstract

For our investigation into higher-order shape analysis, our platform is a small-step framework for the multi-argument continuation-passing-style λ-calculus:

$$f, e \in \mathsf{Exp} = \mathsf{Var} + \mathsf{Lam} \qquad v \in \mathsf{Var} ::= id^{\ell}$$

$$\ell \in \mathsf{Lab} \text{ is a set of labels} \qquad lam \in \mathsf{Lam} ::= (\lambda^{\ell}\ (v_1 \ldots v_n)\ call)$$

$$call \in \mathsf{Call} ::= (f\ e_1 \ldots e_n)^{\ell}.$$

2.1 State-Spaces

The concrete state-space (Σ in Figure 1) for the small-step machine has four components: (1) a call site *call*, (2) a binding environment β to determine the bindings of free variables, (3) a value environment *ve* to determine the value of bindings, and (4) a time-stamp t to encode the current context/history.

The abstract state-space ($\hat{\Sigma}$ in Figure 1) parallels the structure of the concrete state-spaces. For these domains, we assume the natural partial orders; for example, $\widehat{ve} \sqcup \widehat{ve}' = \lambda\hat{b}.\widehat{ve}(\hat{b}) \cup \widehat{ve}'(\hat{b})$.

Binding environments (*BEnv*), as a component of both machine states and closures, are the environments to which the environment problem refers. In our semantics, binding environments map variables to bindings. A binding b is a commemorative token minted for each instance of a variable receiving a value; for example, in k-CFA, a binding is a variable name paired with the time-stamp at which it was bound. The value environment ve tracks the denotable values (D) associated with every binding. A denotable value d is a closure.

In CFAs, bindings—the atomic components of environments—play the role that addresses do in pointer analysis. Our ultimate goal is to infer relationships between the concrete values behind abstract bindings. For example, we want to be able to show that bindings to the variable v at some set of times are equal, under the value environment, to the bindings to the variable x at some other set of times. (In the pure λ-calculus, the only obvious relationships between bindings are equality and inequality.)

In CFA theory, time-stamps also go by the less-intuitive name of *contours*. Both the concrete and the abstract state-spaces leave the exact structure of time-stamps and bindings undefined. The choices for bindings determine the polyvariance of the analysis. Time-stamps encode the history of execution in some fashion, so that under abstraction, their structure determines the context in context-sensitivity.

The concrete and abstract state-spaces are linked by a parameterized second-order abstraction map, $\alpha^\eta : \Sigma \to \hat{\Sigma}$, where the parameter $\eta : (Addr \to \widehat{Addr}) \cup (Time \to \widehat{Time})$ abstracts both bindings and times:

$$\begin{aligned}
\alpha^\eta(call, \beta, ve, t) &= (\alpha^\eta(V), \alpha^\eta(\beta), \alpha^\eta(ve), \eta(t)) \\
\alpha^\eta_{BEnv}(\beta) &= \lambda v.\eta(\beta(v)) \\
\alpha^\eta_{VEnv}(ve) &= \lambda\hat{b}. \bigsqcup_{\eta(b)=\hat{b}} \alpha^\eta(ve(b)) \\
\alpha^\eta_D(d) &= \{\alpha^\eta_{Val}(d)\} \\
\alpha^\eta_{Val}(lam, \beta) &= (lam, \alpha^\eta(\beta)).
\end{aligned}$$

2.2 Transition Rules

With state-spaces defined, we can specify the concrete transition relation for CPS, $(\Rightarrow) \subseteq \Sigma \times \Sigma$; then we can define its corresponding abstraction under the map α^η, $(\leadsto) \subseteq \hat{\Sigma} \times \hat{\Sigma}$. With the help of an argument-expression evaluator, $\mathcal{E} : \mathsf{Exp} \times BEnv \times VEnv \rightharpoonup D$:

$$\begin{aligned}
\mathcal{E}\ (v, \beta, ve) &= ve(\beta(v)) \\
\mathcal{E}\ (lam, \beta, ve) &= (lam, \beta),
\end{aligned}$$

$$\varsigma \in \Sigma = \mathsf{Call} \times \mathit{BEnv} \times \mathit{VEnv} \times \mathit{Time}$$
$$\beta \in \mathit{BEnv} = \mathsf{Var} \rightharpoonup \mathit{Bind}$$
$$\mathit{ve} \in \mathit{VEnv} = \mathit{Bind} \rightharpoonup D$$
$$d \in D = \mathit{Val}$$
$$\mathit{val} \in \mathit{Val} = \mathit{Clo}$$
$$\mathit{clo} \in \mathit{Clo} = \mathsf{Lam} \times \mathit{BEnv}$$
$b \in \mathit{Bind}$ is an **infinite** set of bindings

$t \in \mathit{Time}$ is an **infinite** set of times

$$\hat{\varsigma} \in \hat{\Sigma} = \mathsf{Call} \times \widehat{\mathit{BEnv}} \times \widehat{\mathit{VEnv}} \times \widehat{\mathit{Time}}$$
$$\hat{\beta} \in \widehat{\mathit{BEnv}} = \mathsf{Var} \rightharpoonup \widehat{\mathit{Bind}}$$
$$\widehat{\mathit{ve}} \in \widehat{\mathit{VEnv}} = \widehat{\mathit{Bind}} \to \hat{D}$$
$$\hat{d} \in \hat{D} = \mathcal{P}(\widehat{\mathit{Val}})$$
$$\widehat{\mathit{val}} \in \widehat{\mathit{Val}} = \widehat{\mathit{Clo}}$$
$$\widehat{\mathit{clo}} \in \widehat{\mathit{Clo}} = \mathsf{Lam} \times \widehat{\mathit{BEnv}}$$
$\hat{b} \in \widehat{\mathit{Bind}}$ is a **finite** set of bindings

$\hat{t} \in \widehat{\mathit{Time}}$ is a **finite** set of times

Fig. 1. State-space for the lambda calculus: Concrete (left) and abstract (right)

we can define the single concrete transition rule for CPS:

$$
\begin{aligned}
([\![(f\ e_1 \ldots e_n)^{\ell}]\!], \beta, \mathit{ve}, t) \Rightarrow (\mathit{call}, \beta'', \mathit{ve}', t')&, \text{ where:}\\
d_i &= \mathcal{E}(e_i, \beta, \mathit{ve})\\
d_0 &= ([\![(\lambda^{\ell'}\ (v_1 \ldots v_n)\ \mathit{call})]\!], \beta')\\
t' &= \mathit{tick}(\mathit{call}, t)\\
b_i &= \mathit{alloc}(v_i, t')\\
\beta'' &= \beta'[v_i \mapsto b_i]\\
\mathit{ve}' &= \mathit{ve}[b_i \mapsto d_i].
\end{aligned}
$$

With the help of an abstract evaluator, $\hat{\mathcal{E}} : \mathsf{Exp} \times \widehat{\mathit{BEnv}} \times \widehat{\mathit{VEnv}} \to \hat{D}$:

$$
\begin{aligned}
\hat{\mathcal{E}}\ (v, \hat{\beta}, \widehat{\mathit{ve}}) &= \widehat{\mathit{ve}}(\hat{\beta}(v))\\
\hat{\mathcal{E}}\ (\mathit{lam}, \hat{\beta}, \widehat{\mathit{ve}}) &= \left\{(\mathit{lam}, \hat{\beta})\right\},
\end{aligned}
$$

we can define an analogous transition rule for the abstract semantics:

$$
\begin{aligned}
([\![(f\ e_1 \ldots e_n)^{\ell}]\!], \hat{\beta}, \widehat{\mathit{ve}}, \hat{t}) \leadsto (\mathit{call}, \hat{\beta}'', \widehat{\mathit{ve}}', \hat{t}')&, \text{ where:}\\
\hat{d}_i &= \hat{\mathcal{E}}(e_i, \hat{\beta}, \widehat{\mathit{ve}})\\
\hat{d}_0 &\ni ([\![(\lambda^{\ell'}\ (v_1 \ldots v_n)\ \mathit{call})]\!], \hat{\beta}')\\
\hat{t}' &= \widehat{\mathit{tick}}(\mathit{call}, \hat{t})\\
\hat{b}_i &= \widehat{\mathit{alloc}}(v_i, \hat{t}')\\
\hat{\beta}'' &= \hat{\beta}'[v_i \mapsto \hat{b}_i]\\
\widehat{\mathit{ve}}' &= \widehat{\mathit{ve}} \sqcup [\hat{b}_i \mapsto \hat{d}_i].
\end{aligned}
$$

2.3 Concrete and Abstract Interpretation

To evaluate a program *call* in the concrete semantics, its meaning is the set of states reachable from the initial state $\varsigma_0 = (call, [], [], t_0)$:

$$\{\varsigma : \varsigma_0 \Rightarrow^* \varsigma\}.$$

A naïve abstract interpreter could behave similarly, exploring the states reachable from the initial state $\hat{\varsigma} = (call, [], \bot, \hat{t}_0)$:

$$\{\hat{\varsigma} : \hat{\varsigma}_0 \leadsto^* \hat{\varsigma}\}.$$

In practice, widening on value environments [5] accelerates convergence [16,27].

2.4 Parameters for the Analysis Framework

Time-stamp incrementers and binding allocators serve as parameters:

$$alloc : \mathsf{Var} \times Time \to Bind \qquad \widehat{alloc} : \mathsf{Var} \times \widehat{Time} \to \widehat{Bind}$$

$$tick : \mathsf{Call} \times Time \to Time \qquad \widehat{tick} : \mathsf{Call} \times \widehat{Time} \to \widehat{Time}.$$

Time-stamps are designed to encode context/history. Thus, the abstract time-stamp incrementer $\widehat{tick}$ and the abstraction map α^η decide how much history to retain in the abstraction. As a result, the function $\widehat{tick}$ determines the context-sensitivity of the analysis. Similarly, the abstract binding allocator chooses how to allocate abstract bindings to variables, and in doing so, it fixes the polyvariance of the analysis. Once the parameters are fixed, the semantics must obey a straightforward soundness theorem:

Theorem 1. *If $\alpha^\eta(\varsigma) \sqsubseteq \hat{\varsigma}$ and $\varsigma \Rightarrow \varsigma'$, then there exists a state $\hat{\varsigma}'$ such that $\hat{\varsigma} \leadsto \hat{\varsigma}'$ and $\alpha^\eta(\varsigma') \sqsubseteq \hat{\varsigma}'$.*

3 Analogy: Singleton Abstraction to Binding Anodization

Focusing on our goal of solving the generalized environment problem—reasoning about the equality of individual bindings—we turn to singleton abstraction [4]. Singleton abstraction has been used in pointer and shape analyses to drive must-alias analysis; we extend singleton abstraction, and the framework of anodization, to determine the equivalence of bindings to the *same* variable. That is, we will be able to solve the environment problem with our singleton abstraction, but not the *generalized* environment problem. In Section 4, we will solve the generalized problem by bootstrapping binding invariants on top of anodization.

A Galois connection [6] $X \underset{\alpha}{\overset{\gamma}{\leftrightarrows}} \hat{X}$ has a singleton abstraction iff there exists a subset $\hat{X}_1 \subseteq \hat{X}$ such that for all $\hat{x} \in \hat{X}_1$, $size(\gamma(\hat{x})) = 1$. The critical property of singleton abstractions is that equality of abstract representatives implies equality of their concrete constituents. Hence, when the set X contains addresses, singleton abstractions enable must-alias analysis. Analogously, when the set X contains bindings, singleton abstraction enables binding-equality testing.

Example 1. Suppose we have a concrete machine with three memory addresses: `0x01`, `0x02` and `0x03`. Suppose the addresses abstract so that $\alpha(\texttt{0x01}) = \hat{a}_1$ and $\alpha(\texttt{0x02}) = \alpha(\texttt{0x03}) = \hat{a}_*$. The address $\hat{a}_1$ is a singleton abstraction, because it has only one concrete constituent—`0x01`. After a pointer analysis, if some pointer variable `p1` points only to address $\hat{a}'$ and another pointer variable `p2` points only to address $\hat{a}''$ and $\hat{a}' = \hat{a}_1 = \hat{a}''$ then `p1` must alias `p2`.

In order to solve the super-β inlining problem, Shivers informally proposed a singleton abstraction for k-CFA which he termed "re-flow analysis" [27]. In re-flow analysis, the CFA is re-run, but with a "golden" contour inserted at a point of interest. The golden contour—allocated only once—is a singleton abstraction by definition. While sound in theory, re-flow analysis does not work in practice: the golden contour flows everywhere the non-golden contours flow, and inevitably, golden and non-golden contours are compared for equality. Nevertheless, we can salvage the spirit of Shivers's golden contours through *anodization.* Under anodization, bindings are not golden, but may be temporarily gold-plated.

In anodization, the concrete and abstract bindings are split into two halves:

$$\mathit{Bind} = \mathit{Bind}_\infty + \mathit{Bind}_1 \qquad\qquad \widehat{\mathit{Bind}} = \widehat{\mathit{Bind}}_\infty + \widehat{\mathit{Bind}}_1,$$

and we assert "anodizing" bijections between these halves:

$$g : \mathit{Bind}_\infty \to \mathit{Bind}_1 \qquad\qquad \hat{g} : \widehat{\mathit{Bind}}_\infty \to \widehat{\mathit{Bind}}_1,$$

such that:

$$\eta(b) = \hat{b} \text{ iff } \eta(g(b)) = \hat{g}(\hat{b}).$$

Every abstract binding has two variants, a summary variant, $\hat{b}$, and an anodized variant, $\hat{g}(\hat{b})$. We will craft the concrete and abstract semantics so that the anodized variant will be a singleton abstraction. We must anodize concrete bindings as well because the concrete semantics have to employ the same anodization strategy as the abstract semantics in order to prove soundness.

The concrete semantics must also obey an abstraction-uniqueness constraint over anodized bindings, so that for any reachable state $(\mathit{call}, \beta, \mathit{ve}, t)$:

$$\text{If } g(b) \in \mathit{dom}(\mathit{ve}) \text{ and } g(b') \in \mathit{dom}(\mathit{ve}) \text{ and } \eta(b) = \eta(b') \text{ then } b = b'. \qquad (1)$$

In other words, once the concrete semantics decides to allocate an anodized binding, it must de-anodize existing concrete bindings which abstract to the same abstract binding. Anodization by itself does not dictate *when* a concrete semantics should allocate an anodized binding; this is a *policy* decision; anodization is a *mechanism.* For simple policies, the parameters *alloc* and $\widehat{\mathit{alloc}}$, by selecting anodized or summary bindings, jointly encode the policy.

As an example of the simplest anodization policy, we describe the higher-order analog of Balakrishnan and Reps's recency abstraction in Section 3.3. An example of a more complicated policy is closure-focusing (Section 3.4).

Formally, the concrete transition rule must rebuild the value environment with every transition:

$$
\begin{aligned}
([\![(f\ e_1 \ldots e_n)^{\ell}]\!], \beta, ve, t) \Rightarrow (call, \beta'', ve', t'), \text{ where:}&\\
d_i &= \mathcal{E}(e_i, \beta, ve)\\
d_0 &= ([\![(\lambda^{\ell'}\ (v_1 \ldots v_n)\ call)]\!], \beta')\\
t' &= tick(call, t)\\
b_i &= alloc(v_i, t')\\
B &= \{b_i : b_i \in Bind_1\}\\
\beta'' &= (g_B^{-1}\beta')[v_i \mapsto b_i]\\
ve' &= (g_B^{-1} ve)[b_i \mapsto (g_B^{-1} d_i)],
\end{aligned}
$$

where the de-anodization function $g_B^{-1} : (BEnv \to BEnv) \cup (VEnv \to VEnv) \cup (D \to D) \cup (Bind \to Bind)$ strips the anodization off bindings that abstract to any binding in the set B:

$$
\begin{aligned}
g_B^{-1}(b) &= b\\
g_B^{-1}(g(b)) &= \begin{cases} b & \eta(b) = \eta(b') \text{ for some } g(b') \in B\\ g(b) & \text{otherwise}\end{cases}\\
g_B^{-1}(lam, \beta) &= (lam, g_B^{-1}(\beta))\\
g_B^{-1}(\beta) &= \lambda v. g_B^{-1}(\beta(v))\\
g_B^{-1}(ve) &= \lambda b. g_B^{-1}(ve(b)).
\end{aligned}
$$

The corresponding abstract transition rule must also rebuild the value environment with every transition:

$$
\begin{aligned}
([\![(f\ e_1 \ldots e_n)^{\ell}]\!], \hat{\beta}, \widehat{ve}, \hat{t}) \leadsto (call, \hat{\beta}'', \widehat{ve}', \hat{t}'), \text{ where:}&\\
\hat{d}_i &= \hat{\mathcal{E}}(e_i, \hat{\beta}, \widehat{ve})\\
\hat{d}_0 &\ni ([\![(\lambda^{\ell'}\ (v_1 \ldots v_n)\ call)]\!], \hat{\beta}')\\
\hat{t}' &= \widehat{tick}(call, \hat{t})\\
\hat{b}_i &= \widehat{alloc}(v_i, \hat{t}')\\
\hat{B} &= \left\{\hat{b}_i : \hat{b}_i \in Bind_1\right\}\\
\hat{\beta}'' &= (\hat{g}_{\hat{B}}^{-1}\hat{\beta}')[v_i \mapsto \hat{b}_i]\\
\widehat{ve}' &= (\hat{g}_{\hat{B}}^{-1}\widehat{ve}) \sqcup [\hat{b}_i \mapsto (\hat{g}_{\hat{B}}^{-1}\hat{d}_i)],
\end{aligned}
$$

where the de-anodization function $\hat{g}_{\hat{B}}^{-1} : (\widehat{BEnv} \to \widehat{BEnv}) \cup (\widehat{VEnv} \to \widehat{VEnv}) \cup (\widehat{D} \to \widehat{D}) \cup (\widehat{Val} \to \widehat{Val}) \cup (\widehat{Bind} \to \widehat{Bind})$ strips the anodization off abstract bindings in the set $\hat{B}$:

$$\hat{g}_{\hat{B}}^{-1}(\hat{b}) = \begin{cases} \hat{b}' & \hat{b} \in \hat{B} \text{ and } \hat{b} = \hat{g}(\hat{b}') \\ \hat{b} & \text{otherwise} \end{cases}$$

$$\hat{g}_{\hat{B}}^{-1}\left\{\hat{d}_1, \ldots, \hat{d}_n\right\} = \left\{\hat{g}_{\hat{B}}^{-1}(\hat{d}_1), \ldots, \hat{g}_{\hat{B}}^{-1}(\hat{d}_n)\right\}$$

$$\hat{g}_{\hat{B}}^{-1}(lam, \hat{\beta}) = (lam, \hat{g}_{\hat{B}}^{-1}(\hat{\beta}))$$

$$\hat{g}_{\hat{B}}^{-1}(\hat{\beta}) = \lambda v.\hat{g}_{\hat{B}}^{-1}(\hat{\beta}(v))$$

$$\hat{g}_{\hat{B}}^{-1}(\widehat{ve}) = \lambda \hat{b}.\hat{g}_{\hat{B}}^{-1}(\widehat{ve}(\hat{b})).$$

Because the concrete semantics obey the uniqueness constraint (Equation 1), the abstract interpretation may treat the set $\widehat{Bind}_1$ as a set of singleton abstractions for the purpose of testing binding equality.

3.1 Solving the Environment Problem with Anodization

Given two abstract environments $\hat{\beta}_1$ and $\hat{\beta}_2$, it is easy to determine whether the concrete constituents of these environments agree on the value of some subset of their domains, $\{v_1, \ldots, v_n\}$:

Theorem 2. *If* $\alpha^\eta(\beta_1) = \hat{\beta}_1$ *and* $\alpha^\eta(\beta_2) = \hat{\beta}_2$*, and* $\hat{\beta}_1(v) = \hat{\beta}_2(v)$ *and* $\hat{\beta}_1(v) \in \widehat{Bind}_1$*, then* $\beta_1(v) = \beta_2(v)$*.*

Proof. By the abstraction-uniqueness constraint.

3.2 Implementing Anodization Efficiently

The naïve implementation of the abstract transition rule is inefficient: the de-anodizing function $\hat{g}_{\hat{B}}^{-1}$ must walk the abstract value environment with *every* transition. Even in 0CFA, this walk adds a quadratic penalty to every transition. To avoid this walk, the analysis should use serial numbers on bindings "under the hood," so that:

$$\widehat{Bind} \approx \widehat{Bind}_\infty \times \mathbb{N}.$$

That is, the value environment should be implemented as two maps:

$$\widehat{VEnv} \approx (\widehat{Bind}_\infty \rightarrow \mathbb{N} \rightarrow \hat{D}) \times (\widehat{Bind}_\infty \rightarrow \mathbb{N}).$$

Given a split value environment $\widehat{ve} = (\hat{f}, \hat{h})$, a binding $(\hat{b}, n)$ is anodized only if $n = \hat{h}(\hat{b})$, and it is not anodized if $n < \hat{h}(\hat{b})$. Thus, when the allocator chooses to anodize a binding, it does need to walk the value environment with the function $\hat{g}_{\hat{B}}^{-1}$ to strip away existing anodization; it merely needs to increment the serial number associated with that binding.

3.3 Instantiating Anodization: Recency Abstraction

In recency abstraction [2], the most-recently allocated abstract variant of a resource is tracked distinctly from previously allocated variants. Anodization makes it straightforward to model recency in a higher-order setting. In a language with mutation, recency abstraction solves the initialization problem, whereby addresses are allocated with a default value, but then set to another shortly thereafter. Recency abstraction prevents the default value from appearing as a possibility for every address, which is directly useful in eliminating null-pointer checks. In a higher-order setting, recency permits precise computation of binding equivalence for variables that are bound in non-recursive and tail-recursive procedures or that die before the recursive call.

3.4 Instantiating Anodization: Closure-Focusing

Anodization enables another shape-analytic technique known as focusing [15,23]. In focusing, a specific, previously-allocated variant is split into the singleton variant under focus—and all other variants. In a higher-order language, there is a natural opportunity to focus on all of the bindings of a closure when it is created. Focusing provides a way to solve the environment problem for closures which capture variables which have been re-bound since closure-creation.

4 Analogy: Binding Invariants as Shape Predicates

Anodization can solve the environment problem, but it cannot solve the generalized environment problem, where we need to be able to reason about the equality of bindings to *different* variables in *different* environments. To solve this problem, we cast shape predicates as *binding invariants*. A binding invariant is an equivalence relation over abstract bindings, and it can be considered as a separate, relational abstraction of program state, $\alpha^{\eta}_{\equiv} : \Sigma \to \hat{\Sigma}_{\equiv}$, where:

$$\hat{\Sigma}_{\equiv} = \mathcal{P}\left(\widehat{Bind} \times \widehat{Bind}\right),$$

such that:

$$\alpha^{\eta}_{\equiv}(call, \beta, ve, t) = \left\{(\hat{b}, \hat{b}') : ve(b) = ve(b') \text{ if } \eta(b) = \hat{b} \text{ and } \eta(b') = \hat{b}'\right\}.$$

In contrast with earlier work, binding-invariant abstraction is a relational abstract domain over *abstract bindings* rather than *program variables* [7,8].

Informally, if $(\hat{b}, \hat{b}') \in \alpha^{\eta}_{\equiv}(\varsigma)$, it means that all of the concrete constituents of the bindings $\hat{b}$ and $\hat{b}'$ agree in value. To create the analysis, we can formulate a new abstraction as the direct product of the abstractions α^{η} and $\alpha^{\eta}_{\equiv}$:

$$\dot{\alpha}^{\eta} : \Sigma \to \hat{\Sigma} \times \hat{\Sigma}_{\equiv}$$
$$\dot{\alpha}^{\eta}(\varsigma) = (\alpha^{\eta}(\varsigma), \alpha^{\eta}_{\equiv}(\varsigma)).$$

The constraints of a straightforward soundness theorem (Theorem 1) lead to an abstract transition relation over this space:

$$((\llbracket (f\ e_1 \ldots e_n)^{\ell} \rrbracket, \hat{\beta}, \widehat{ve}, \hat{t}), \equiv) \leadsto ((call, \hat{\beta}'', \widehat{ve}', \hat{t}'), \equiv'), \text{ where:}$$

$$\begin{aligned}
\hat{d}_i &= \hat{\mathcal{E}}(e_i, \hat{\beta}, \widehat{ve}) \\
\hat{d}_0 &\ni (\llbracket (\lambda^{\ell'}\ (v_1 \ldots v_n)\ call) \rrbracket, \hat{\beta}') \\
\hat{t}' &= \widehat{tick}(call, \hat{t}) \\
\hat{b}_i &= \widehat{alloc}(v_i, \hat{t}') \\
\hat{B} &= \left\{ \hat{b}_i : \hat{b}_i \in \widehat{Bind}_1 \right\} \\
\hat{\beta}'' &= (\hat{g}_{\hat{B}}^{-1} \hat{\beta}')[v_i \mapsto \hat{b}_i] \\
\widehat{ve}' &= (\hat{g}_{\hat{B}}^{-1} \widehat{ve}) \sqcup [\hat{b}_i \mapsto (\hat{g}_{\hat{B}}^{-1} \hat{d}_i)],
\end{aligned}$$

and singleton bindings are reflexively equivalent:

$$\frac{\hat{b} \in \widehat{Bind}_1}{\hat{b} \equiv' \hat{b},}$$

and bindings between singletons are trivially equivalent:

$$\frac{\hat{\beta}(e_i) \in \widehat{Bind}_1 \qquad \hat{b}_i \in \widehat{Bind}_1}{\hat{\beta}(e_i) \equiv' \hat{b}_i,}$$

and untouched bindings retain their equivalence:

$$\frac{\hat{b} \equiv \hat{b}' \qquad \hat{b} \notin \hat{B} \qquad \hat{b}' \notin \hat{B}}{\hat{b} \equiv' \hat{b}',}$$

and bindings re-bound to themselves also retain their equivalence:

$$\frac{\hat{\beta}(e_i) \equiv \hat{b}_i}{\hat{\beta}(e_i) \equiv' \hat{b}_i.}$$

4.1 Solving the Generalized Environment Problem

Under the direct product abstraction, the generalized environment theorem, which rules on the equality of individual bindings, follows naturally:

Theorem 3. *Given a compound abstract state* $((call, \hat{\beta}, \widehat{ve}, \hat{t}), \equiv)$ *and two abstract bindings* $\hat{b}$ *and* $\hat{b}'$, *if* $\dot{\alpha}^{\eta}(call, \beta, ve, t) \sqsubseteq ((call, \hat{\beta}, \widehat{ve}, \hat{t}), \equiv)$ *and* $\eta(b) = \hat{b}$ *and* $\eta(b') = \hat{b}'$ *and* $\hat{b} \equiv \hat{b}'$, *then* $ve(b) = ve(b')$.

Proof. By the structure of the direct product abstraction $\dot{\alpha}^{\eta}$.

5 Application: Higher-Order Rematerialization

Now that we have a generalized environment analysis, we can precisely state the condition under which higher-order rematerialization is safe. Might's work on the correctness of super-β inlining formally defined *safe* to mean that the transformed program and the untransformed program maintain a bisimulation in their concrete executions [16].

Theorem 4. *It is safe to rematerialize the expression e' in place of the expression e in the call site call iff for every reachable compound abstract state of the form $((call, \hat{\beta}'', \widehat{ve}, \hat{t}), \equiv)$, it is the case that $\hat{\mathcal{E}}(e', \hat{\beta}'', \widehat{ve}) = (lam', \hat{\beta}')$ and $\hat{\mathcal{E}}(e, \hat{\beta}'', \widehat{ve}) = (lam, \hat{\beta})$ and the relation $\sigma \subseteq \mathsf{Var} \times \mathsf{Var}$ is a substitution that unifies the free variables of lam′ with lam and for each $(v', v) \in \sigma$, $\hat{\beta}'(v') \equiv \hat{\beta}(v)$.*

Proof. The proof of bisimulation has a structure identical to that of the proof correctness for super-β inlining in [16].

6 Related Work

Clearly, this work draws on the Cousots' abstract interpretation [5,6]. Binding invariants succeed the Cousots' work as a relational abstraction of higher-order programs [7,8], with the distinction that binding invariants range over abstract bindings instead of formal parameters. Binding invariants were also inspired by Gulwani *et al.*'s quantified abstract domains [9]; there is an implicit universal quantification ranging over concrete constituents in the definition of the abstraction map $\alpha^{\eta}_{\equiv}$. This work also falls within and retains the advantages of Schmidt's small-step abstract interpretive framework [24]. As a generalization of control-flow analysis, the platform of Section 2 is a small-step reformulation of Shivers's denotational CFA [27], which itself was a extension of Jones's original CFA [13]. Like the Nielsons' unifying work on CFA [22], this work is an implicit argument in favor of the inherent flexibility of abstract interpretation for the static analysis of higher-order programs. In contrast with constraint-based, type-based and model-checking CFAs, small-step abstract interpretive CFAs are easy to extend via direct products and parameterization.

From shape analysis, anodized bindings draw on singleton abstraction while binding invariants are inspired by both predicate-based abstractions [3] and three-valued logic analysis [23]. Chase *et. al* had early work on counting-based singleton abstractions [4], while Hudak's work on analysis of first-order functional programs employed a precursor to counting-based singleton abstraction [10]. Anodization, using factored sets of singleton and non-singleton bindings, is most closely related to the Balakrishnan and Reps's recency abstraction [2], except that anodization works on bindings instead of addresses, and anodization is not restricted to a most-recent allocation policy. Superficially, one might also term Jones and Bohr's work on termination analysis of the untyped λ-calculus via size-change as another kind of shape analysis for higher-order programs [14].

Given the importance of inlining and globalization, the functional community has responded with *ad hoc* extensions to control-flow analyses to support these optimizations. Shivers's re-flow analysis developed the concept of singleton abstraction independently to determine equivalence over environments [27]. Wand and Steckler approached the environment problem by layering a constraint-based environment-equivalence analysis on top of 0CFA [28]. Jagannathan *et al.* developed a counting-based constraint analysis to drive lightweight closure conversion [11]. More recently, Might and Shivers attacked the problem with stack-driven environment-analysis (ΔCFA), but this analysis also proved too brittle for many programs [18]. Might and Shivers' reachability- and counting-driven environment analysis (ΓCFA) provides a scalable analysis which can reason about environment equivalence [19,21]. All of these extensions are capable of solving the environment problem in limited cases; none of them can solve the generalized environment problem, and none take the principled, flexible approach provided by anodization and binding invariants.

7 Conclusion

We motivated the need to reason about the equivalence of environments in higher-order programs by finding optimizations beyond the reach of ordinary control-flow analysis: super-β inlining, globalization and higher-order rematerialization. We distilled the core problem which must be solved in order to enable these optimizations—the generalized environment problem. The generalized environment problem asks whether two variables bound in different environments are equivalent, *e.g.*, "Is $[\![x]\!]$ in bound in ρ equivalent to $[\![y]\!]$ bound in ρ'?" We then created an analysis framework for solving the generalized environment problem by considering the analog of shape analysis in terms of control-flow analysis. We rendered the principle of singleton abstraction as anodization, and we rendered the principle of shape predicates as binding invariants. By composing anodization and binding invariants, we arrived at an extended higher-order flow-analysis framework that can solve the generalized environment problem.

8 Future Work

Next steps for this work include folding more language features into the framework, considering the impact of these features on both anodization and binding invariants and integrating Gulwani's techniques for bounding of numeric variables [9]. For instance, once numbers are introduced, we could enrich binding invariants to reason about both equality and inequality among the concrete constituents of abstract bindings. We also expect that when we introduce dynamic allocation, that anodization and binding invariants will naturally morph back into the must-alias analysis and shape predicates from whence they came. This technology is also being introduced into the U Combinator higher-order flow analysis toolkit; the latest beta version of this toolkit is always available from `http://www.ucombinator.org/`.

References

1. Agesen, O.: The cartesian product algorithm: Simple and precise type inference of parametric polymorphism. In: Olthoff, W. (ed.) ECOOP 1995. LNCS, vol. 952, pp. 2–26. Springer, Heidelberg (1995)
2. Balakrishnan, G., Reps, T.: Recency-abstraction for heap-allocated storage. In: Yi, K. (ed.) SAS 2006. LNCS, vol. 4134, pp. 221–239. Springer, Heidelberg (2006)
3. Ball, T., Majumdar, R., Millstein, T., Rajamani, S.K.: Automatic predicate abstraction of c programs. In: PLDI 2001: Proceedings of the ACM SIGPLAN 2001 Conference on Programming Language Design and Implementation, pp. 203–213. ACM Press, New York (2001)
4. Chase, D.R., Wegman, M., Zadeck, F.K.: Analysis of pointers and structures. In: PLDI 1990: Proceedings of the ACM SIGPLAN 1990 Conference on Programming Language Design and Implementation, pp. 296–310. ACM Press, New York (1990)
5. Cousot, P., Cousot, R.: Abstract interpretation: A unified lattice model for static analysis of programs by construction or approximation of fixpoints. In: Conference Record of the Fourth ACM Symposium on Principles of Programming Languages, pp. 238–252. ACM Press, New York (1977)
6. Cousot, P., Cousot, R.: Systematic design of program analysis frameworks. In: POPL 1979: Proceedings of the 6th ACM SIGACT-SIGPLAN Symposium on Principles of Programming Languages, pp. 269–282. ACM Press, New York (1979)
7. Cousot, P., Cousot, R.: Relational abstract interpretation of higher-order functional programs. In: JTASPEFL 1991, Bordeaux. BIGRE 74, pp. 33–36 (1991)
8. Cousot, P., Cousot, R.: Higher-order abstract interpretation (and application to comportment analysis generalizing strictness, termination, projection and per analysis of functional languages). In: Proceedings of the 1994 International Conference on Computer Languages, pp. 95–112. IEEE Computer Society Press, Los Alamitos (1994)
9. Gulwani, S., Mccloskey, B., Tiwari, A.: Lifting abstract interpreters to quantified logical domains. In: POPL 2008: Proceedings of the 35th annual ACM SIGPLAN-SIGACT Symposium on Principles of Programming Languages, pp. 235–246. ACM, New York (2008)
10. Hudak, P.: A semantic model of reference counting and its abstraction. In: LFP 1986: Proceedings of the 1986 ACM Conference on LISP and Functional Programming, pp. 351–363. ACM, New York (1986)
11. Jagannathan, S., Thiemann, P., Weeks, S., Wright, A.: Single and loving it: must-alias analysis for higher-order languages. In: POPL 1998: Proceedings of the 25th ACM SIGPLAN-SIGACT Symposium on Principles of Programming Languages, pp. 329–341. ACM, New York (1998)
12. Jagannathan, S., Weeks, S.: A unified treatment of flow analysis in higher-order languages. In: POPL 1995: Proceedings of the 22nd ACM SIGPLAN-SIGACT Symposium on Principles of Programming Languages, pp. 393–407. ACM, New York (1995)
13. Jones, N.D.: Flow analysis of lambda expressions (preliminary version). In: Even, S., Kariv, O. (eds.) ICALP 1981. LNCS, vol. 115, pp. 114–128. Springer, Heidelberg (1981)
14. Jones, N.D., Bohr, N.: Call-by-value termination in the untyped lambda-calculus. Logical Methods in Computer Science 4(1), 1–39 (2008)
15. Kidd, N., Reps, T., Dolby, J., Vaziri, M.: Finding concurrency-related bugs using random isolation. In: Jones, N.D., Müller-Olm, M. (eds.) VMCAI 2009. LNCS, vol. 5403, pp. 198–213. Springer, Heidelberg (2009)

16. Might, M.: Environment Analysis of Higher-Order Languages. PhD thesis, Georgia Institute of Technology (June 2007)
17. Might, M.: Logic-flow analysis of higher-order programs. In: POPL 2007: Proceedings of the 34th annual ACM SIGPLAN-SIGACT symposium on Principles of programming languages, pp. 185–198. ACM Press, New York (2007)
18. Might, M., Shivers, O.: Environment analysis via delta-cfa. In: POPL 2006: Conference record of the 33rd ACM SIGPLAN-SIGACT symposium on Principles of programming languages, pp. 127–140. ACM, New York (2006)
19. Might, M., Shivers, O.: Improving flow analyses via gamma-cfa: Abstract garbage collection and counting. In: ICFP 2006: Proceedings of the Eleventh ACM SIGPLAN International Conference on Functional Programming, pp. 13–25. ACM, New York (2006)
20. Might, M., Shivers, O.: Analyzing the environment structure of higher-order languages using frame strings. Theoretical Computer Science 375(1-3), 137–168 (2007)
21. Might, M., Shivers, O.: Exploiting reachability and cardinality in higher-order flow analysis. Journal of Functional Programming 18(special double issue 5-6), 821–864 (2008)
22. Nielson, F., Nielson, H.R.: Infinitary control flow analysis: a collecting semantics for closure analysis. In: POPL 1997: Proceedings of the 24th ACM SIGPLAN-SIGACT Symposium on Principles of Programming Languages, pp. 332–345. ACM, New York (1997)
23. Sagiv, M., Reps, T., Wilhelm, R.: Parametric shape analysis via 3-valued logic. ACM Transactions on Programming Languages and Systems 24(3), 217–298 (2002)
24. Schmidt, D.A.: Abstract interpretation of small-step semantics. In: Dam, M. (ed.) LOMAPS-WS 1996. LNCS, vol. 1192, pp. 76–99. Springer, Heidelberg (1997)
25. Sestoft, P.: Analysis and efficient implementation of functional programs. PhD thesis, University of Copenhagen, Denmark (October 1991)
26. Shivers, O.: Control flow analysis in Scheme. In: Proceedings of the ACM SIGPLAN 1988 Conference on Programming Language Design and Implementation, vol. 23, pp. 164–174. ACM, New York (1988)
27. Shivers, O.G.: Control-Flow Analysis of Higher-Order Languages. PhD thesis, Carnegie Mellon University (1991)
28. Wand, M., Steckler, P.: Selective and lightweight closure conversion. In: POPL 1994: Proceedings of the 21st ACM SIGPLAN-SIGACT Symposium on Principles of Programming Languages, pp. 435–445. ACM, New York (1994)
29. Wright, A.K., Jagannathan, S.: Polymorphic splitting: An effective polyvariant flow analysis. ACM Transactions on Programming Languages and Systems 20(1), 166–207 (1998)

An Analysis of Permutations in Arrays*

Valentin Perrelle and Nicolas Halbwachs

Vérimag**, Grenoble University – France
{Valentin.Perrelle,Nicolas.Halbwachs}@imag.fr

Abstract. This paper is concerned with the synthesis of invariants in programs with arrays. More specifically, we consider properties concerning array contents *up to a permutation.* For instance, to prove a sorting procedure, one has to show that the result is sorted, but also that *it is a permutation of the initial array.* In order to analyze this kind of properties, we define an abstract interpretation working on multisets of values, and able to discover invariant equations about such multisets.

1 Introduction

The analysis of properties of data structures is a challenging goal. It has been widely studied, but still strongly needs to be improved, concerning the efficiency and precision of analyzes, but also the class of properties that can be handled. Roughly speaking, data structure properties can be divided into three classes: (1) The most widely studied properties are *structural properties*: they concern the shape of data structures and the correctness of their accesses, independently of their contents. Array bound checking (e.g., [CC76, LS79]), and shape analysis (e.g., [WSR00, SRW02, DRS03]) address this class of properties. (2) More recently, several methods were proposed for analyzing *positional properties* of data structure contents, i.e., properties relating the value of a cell with its position in the structure [BMS06, IHV08, FQ02, LB04, JM07, GMT08, Cou03, GRS05, HP08]. The fact that two arrays are pointwise equal, or that a list is sorted, are examples of such properties. (3) In this paper, we will consider an instance of *non positional* properties, which concern the whole content of a data structure, independently of the structure itself. A typical example is the fact that an array is a permutation of another array. Showing that the result of a sorting procedure is indeed sorted is not enough to prove the procedure; one has to show also that the result is a permutation of the initial structure. There are many examples of such algorithms which are intended to reorganize a data structure without changing its global content. Showing that the global content is not changed is therefore an issue. Such non positional properties are not easily expressible with usual formalisms: they cannot be expressed as "$\forall \ldots \exists \ldots$" formulas as those considered in [SG09], and [SJ80] remarks that the fact that two arrays are equal *up*

* This work has been partially supported by the ASOPT project of the "Agence Nationale de la Recherche" of the French Ministry of Research.

** Verimag is a joint laboratory of Université Joseph Fourier, CNRS and Grenoble-INP.

G. Barthe and M. Hermenegildo (Eds.): VMCAI 2010, LNCS 5944, pp. 279–294, 2010.

to a permutation cannot be expressed by a first order formula. This may explain that these properties have been more or less ignored in the literature on program analysis.

In this paper, we describe an analysis technique able to discover equations about global contents of arrays. Such a global content is a multiset, since several cells may contain the same value. For simplicity, the paper is specialized on (one-dimensional) array analysis, but the approach could be extended to other data structures. For instance, our method is able to discover that if, at the beginning of an insertion sort procedure, the array A to be sorted contains a multiset $\mathcal{M}$ of values, it contains the same multiset at the end of the procedure. Combined with an analysis of positional properties such as [HP08], it provides an automatic method for *discovering* the exact input/output behavior of the procedure.

Basically, our analysis is an abstract interpretation propagating multiset equations. It is helped by other, more classical analyzes, discovering equalities and disequalities between indexes — which are, of course, very important to deal with aliases[1] — and equalities between variables and array cells. After giving the basic notations and definitions (Section 2), we introduce the analysis by an example (Section 3). Section 4 presents the principles of the analysis, before addressing the main problem, which concerns the computation of an upper bound of two abstract values.

Section 5 presents a first version of our abstract lattice, together with an algorithm for the upper bound. This operation is reduced to a classical problem of maximum flow in a network. However, we show that the result is sometimes not the most precise we could get, mainly because of the separation between variable equalities and multiset equations. So, this solution is not completely satisfactory, but still deserves to be presented as an unexpected application of max-flow algorithms in this context.

Another solution is presented in Section 6, where variables equalities are considered as (singleton-) multiset equalities, and merged with multiset equations. Now, we have to deal with systems of multiset equations, which are all linear equations. The new idea is to use the classical lattice proposed by Karr as early as 1976 [Kar76], to deal with affine equalities among numerical variables. Since this lattice only uses the affine structure of the space, its operations can be straightforwardly applied to our problem, and provide a well-defined and precise upper bound operator. This solution has been implemented, and some experimental results are given in Section 7.

2 Definitions and Notations

For simplicity, we consider a unique set X of *contents values*. As said before, the content of an array should be considered as a multiset of values of X. Since a multiset may contain several instances of the same value, it can be formalized as a function from X to the set of naturals $\mathbb{N}$: if $\mathcal{M}$ is a multiset, $\mathcal{M}(x)$ is

[1] knowing that $i = j$ or $i \neq j$ is essential to know whether an assignment to $A[i]$ may or must affect the value of $A[j]$.

the number of instances of the value x in $\mathcal{M}$. $\mathcal{M}$ is included in $\mathcal{M}'$ (noted $\mathcal{M} \subseteq \mathcal{M}'$ as usual) iff $\forall x \in X, \mathcal{M}(x) \leq \mathcal{M}'(x)$. We use the generalized notion, sometimes called *hybrid multiset* [Syr01, SIYJ07], of multiset with positive or negative multiplicities, i.e., functions from X to the set $\mathbb{Z}$ of integers. $\oplus$ and $\ominus$ denote the sum (disjoint union) and difference of (hybrid) multisets:

$$\mathcal{M} \oplus \mathcal{M}' = \lambda x.\mathcal{M}(x) + \mathcal{M}'(x) \ , \quad \mathcal{M} \ominus \mathcal{M}' = \lambda x.\mathcal{M}(x) - \mathcal{M}'(x)$$

A sum of k instances of $\mathcal{M}$ can be noted $k \otimes \mathcal{M}$.

For simplicity, we restrict ourselves to programs containing integer variables (noted i, j), variables with values in X (noted v, w), and one-dimensional arrays with values in X (noted A, B).

Let A be a one-dimensional array, indexed from 1 to $|A|$ (the size of A). Then $\hat{A}$ denotes the multiset of contents of A, i.e.,

$$\hat{A} = \lambda x. \sum_{i=1}^{|A|} \delta_{x,A[i]} \ , \qquad \text{where } \delta_{x,y} = (\textit{if } x = y \textit{ then } 1 \textit{ else } 0)$$

An *atom* is either a value in X, or a variable valued in X, or an array cell. If a is an atom, a will also denote the singleton multiset $\lambda x.\delta_{x,a}$.

Our analysis relies on (approximate but conservative) results obtained by two other standard analyzes:

- We use equalities and disequalities about variables and constants used as array indices, to simplify the treatment of aliases: the knowledge that $i = j$ (resp., $i \neq j$) involves that $A[i]$ and $A[j]$ are (resp., are not) aliased. So, we assume the availability of a standard analysis (e.g., based on potentials [Dil89, ACD93], octagons [Min01], or dDBMs [PH07]) giving this kind of informations at each control point. We call it *index analysis.*
- We also use equalities among content variables and array cells. Some of these relations result from the index analysis, others come from assignments and conditional statements. This analysis is called *content analysis.*

So, our abstract values are triples made of

- a system of equations and disequations between integer variables and constants used as array indices, provided by the index analysis;
- a system of equations between atoms, provided by the content analysis;
- a system of equations between multiset expressions, which is computed by our specific *multiset analysis.*

3 An Example of Analysis

Let's consider the program fragment of Fig. 1.a, which switches the values of two array cells. An analysis could run as follows:

- *At control point 1,* the analysis starts with the multiset equation $(\hat{A} = \mathcal{M})$ — i.e., naming $\mathcal{M}$ the initial content of the array.
- *At point 2,* the content analysis provides the equation $(v = A[i])$, while the previous multiset equation $(\hat{A} = \mathcal{M})$ is preserved.
- *At point 3,* we have to compute the effect of the assignment A[i] := A[j]; two cases may occur:

1. either $i = j$, in which case $A[i]$ and $A[j]$ are aliased, the assignment does nothing, and we get the postcondition $(i = j) \wedge (v = A[i] = A[j]) \wedge (\hat{A} = \mathcal{M})$;
2. or $i \neq j$, and the usual semantics of the assignment provides $(i \neq j) \wedge (A[i] = A[j]) \wedge (\exists x_0, (v = x_0), (\hat{A} = \mathcal{M} \ominus x_0 \oplus A[j]))$ (x_0 is the previous value of $A[i]$, which is overwritten and disappears from the array content, while the value of $A[j]$ is duplicated). So, after simplification, we get $(i \neq j) \wedge (A[i] = A[j]) \wedge (\hat{A} = \mathcal{M} \ominus v \oplus A[j])$

(a) Program	(b) Results
	.........$\{(\hat{A} = \mathcal{M})\}$
1 v := A[i] ;	.........$\{(v = A[i]) \wedge (\hat{A} = \mathcal{M})\}$
2 A[i] := A[j] ;	.........$\{(A[i] = A[j]) \wedge (\hat{A} = \mathcal{M} \ominus v \oplus A[j])\}$
3 A[j] := v ;	.........$\{(\hat{A} = \mathcal{M})\}$
4	

(a) Program (b) Results

Fig. 1. Switch example

Now, as a postcondition of the assignment, we want to compute an upper approximation of the disjunction

$$\Big((i = j) \wedge (v = A[i] = A[j]) \wedge (\hat{A} = \mathcal{M})\Big) \vee \Big((i \neq j) \wedge (A[i] = A[j]) \wedge (\hat{A} = \mathcal{M} \ominus v \oplus A[j])\Big)$$

This (least) upper bound computation will be the main topic of the paper. Obviously, since the first term of the disjunction contains the equation $(v = A[j])$, it can be rewritten into $(i = j) \wedge (v = A[i] = A[j]) \wedge (\hat{A} = \mathcal{M} \ominus v \oplus A[j])$. Now, both terms contain the same multiset equation and can be unified into $(A[i] = A[j]) \wedge (\hat{A} = \mathcal{M} \ominus v \oplus A[j])$, which is a correct (and precise) postcondition.

– *At point 4*, the computation of the effect of the assignment A[j] := v is similar:
  1. either $i = j$, and we get $(i = j) \wedge (A[i] = A[j]) \wedge (\exists x_0, \hat{A} = \mathcal{M} \ominus v \oplus x_0 \ominus x_0 \oplus v)$, i.e., $(i = j) \wedge (A[i] = A[j]) \wedge (\hat{A} = \mathcal{M})$;
  2. or $i \neq j$, and we get $(i \neq j) \wedge (\exists x_0, (A[i] = x_0) \wedge (\hat{A} = \mathcal{M} \ominus v \oplus x_0 \ominus x_0 \oplus v)$, i.e., $(i \neq j) \wedge (\hat{A} = \mathcal{M})$.

  So, the two cases unify into $(\hat{A} = \mathcal{M})$, as expected.

4 Principles of the Analysis

As said before, our abstract values are triples $(\varphi_I, \varphi_X, \varphi_{\mathcal{M}})$, where

- φ_I is a system of equations, and possibly disequations, between indices; it belongs to an abstract lattice $(L_I, \sqsubseteq_I, \sqcup_I, \sqcap_I, \top_I, \bot_I)$.
- φ_X is a system of equations between atoms; it belongs to an abstract lattice $(L_X, \sqsubseteq_X, \sqcup_X, \sqcap_X, \top_X, \bot_X)$.
- $\varphi_{\mathcal{M}}$ is a system of equations between multiset expressions.

All array cells appearing in φ_X or (as singletons) in $\varphi_{\mathcal{M}}$ are of the form $A[i]$, meaning that, e.g., $A[i+1]$ is rewritten as $A[k]$ where k is a fresh variable and the equation $(k = i+1)$ is expressed in φ_I.

We assume that we analyze a procedure taking arrays $A_1, \ldots, A_p$ as reference parameters, and whose body is made of assignments, conditional statements and loops.

At the entry point of the procedure, a multiset equation is generated for each array, to record its initial content. So the abstract value at the entry point is $\varphi_I = \top_I$, $\varphi_X = \top_X$, $\varphi_{\mathcal{M}} = (\hat{A}_1 = \mathcal{A}_1, \ldots, \hat{A}_p = \mathcal{A}_p)$. Of course, initial knowledge about indices and contents could be taken into account in φ_I and φ_X, instead of taking $\top_I$ and $\top_X$.

We assume that operations are available to propagate abstract values in L_I and L_X among statements, together with widening or acceleration operators to avoid infinite iterations around loops. So, we concentrate on the propagation of multiset equations. Apart from the upper bound — that will be addressed in next sections —, the only non-trivial operation is the assignment to an array cell: let $\boxed{\text{A[i]:=e}}(\varphi_I, \varphi_X, \varphi_{\mathcal{M}})$ denote the effect of the assignment $A[i] := e$ to the abstract value $(\varphi_I, \varphi_X, \varphi_{\mathcal{M}})$. Let J be the set of index variables such that $A[j]$ appears in φ_X or $\varphi_{\mathcal{M}}$. To get the correct and most precise result, we have to consider all the alias cases that should be taken into account, i.e., all the cases where i is equal to some variables $j \in J$. An alias case is subsumed by a subset K of J, interpreted as the index formula $(\forall j \in K, i = j) \wedge (\forall j \in J \setminus K, i \neq j)$. We note $E[\![x/y]\!]$ the substitution of x in place of all occurrences of y in E, and $E[\![x/A[i,K]]\!]$ the substitution in E of x in place of $A[i]$ and all occurrences of $A[j]$, for all $j \in K$. With these notations, the rule of array assignment is the following:

$$\boxed{\text{A[i]:= e}}(\varphi_I, \varphi_X, \varphi_{\mathcal{M}}) = \bigsqcup_{K \subseteq J} \Phi_K$$

where $\Phi_K =$

(1) $\Big(\varphi_I \sqcap_I (\bigwedge_{j \in K} j = i) \sqcap_I (\bigwedge_{j \in J \setminus K} j \neq i),$

$\exists x_0,$

(2) $\varphi_X[\![x_0/A[i,K]]\!] \sqcap_X (A[i] = e[\![x_0/A[i,K]]\!] \wedge \bigwedge_{\substack{j \in K \\ \ell=1..p}} A_\ell[j] = A_\ell[i]),$

(3) $\varphi_{\mathcal{M}}[\![x_0/A[i,K]]\!][\![\hat{A} \oplus x_0 \ominus A[i]/\hat{A}]\!]\Big)$

Each Φ_K is a triple $(\varphi_{I,K}, \varphi_{X,K}, \varphi_{\mathcal{M},K})$ corresponding to an alias case K. In the formula above, line (1) defines $\varphi_{I,K}$ and expresses that K is an alias case (notice that it is $\bot_I$ if φ_I makes it unfeasible), lines (2) and (3) classically involve a common quantified variable x_0 representing the previous value of $A[i]$: line (2) defines $\varphi_{X,K}$ and expresses the changes in φ_X, taking into account the aliases, and line (3) reflects in $\phi_{\mathcal{M}}$ that x_0 represents the common previous value of all the array elements aliased with $A[i]$ and that, in the multiset $\hat{A}$, the previous value of $A[i]$ has been replaced by its new value. Once again, the only non-trivial operation is the upper bound $\sqcup$ that we consider now.

5 Upper Bound: A Solution Based on Flows

While the least upper bound operators for systems of index and atom equations are provided by the corresponding lattices, we have to define it for multiset equations, i.e., to unify two multiset equations, each of which being considered together with a system of atom equations.

Coming back to the computation made at point 3 in the example of §3, we had to unify the multiset equation $\hat{A} \ominus \mathcal{M} = \emptyset$, knowing that $(v = A[i] = A[j])$, with the equation $\hat{A} \ominus \mathcal{M} = A[j] \ominus v$, knowing that $(A[i] = A[j])$.

Formally, given two multiset expressions E_1 and E_2 ($\emptyset$ and $A[j] \ominus v$ in our example), and two equivalence relations $\equiv_1$ and $\equiv_2$ over atoms involved in E_1 and E_2 ($(v \equiv_1 A[i] \equiv_1 A[j])$ and $(A[i] \equiv_2 A[j])$ in our example), we want to rewrite each E_i into a common multiset expression E, such that $E_i \equiv_i E, i = 1, 2$.

Basically, the rewriting of an expression E_i into an expression E'_i can be done by adding to E_i a term $a \ominus b$ such that $a \equiv_i b$. In our example, such a rewriting is immediate, since $E_1 = \emptyset \equiv_1 (A[j] \ominus v)$ and $(A[j] \ominus v) = E_2$.

5.1 Rewriting Atoms

As said before, when an atom a appears only in E_1, one it can be introduced in E_2 by adding $a \ominus b$ to E_2, for some b such that $a \equiv_2 b$. This rewriting introduces b in E_2, so it may have to be introduced in E_1 in turn, and so on. The process of finding a common rewriting for atoms can be seen as a travel in a graph: consider equivalence classes of $\equiv_1$ and $\equiv_2$ as vertices, and connect two vertices V, V' with an edge labelled by x if $x \in V \cap V'$. The obtained graph is obviously bipartite: each edge connects classes of $\equiv_1$ and $\equiv_2$. The graph drawn below corresponds to an example where we have to unify $E_1 = a$ with $E_2 = e$, knowing $(b \equiv_1 c \equiv_1 d)$ and $(a \equiv_2 b, d \equiv_2 e)$. Now, finding a rewriting from $E_1 = x$ into $E_2 = y$ boils down to finding a path from $[x]_1$ (the vertex corresponding to the class of x according to $\equiv_1$) to $[y]_2$ in the graph: each succession of two edges $\xrightarrow{z}[.]_1\xrightarrow{w}$ around a vertex of class 1 in such a path, corresponds to a rewriting of E_1 into $E_1 \oplus w \ominus z$; conversely, each succession of edges $\xrightarrow{z}[.]_2\xrightarrow{w}$ corresponds to a rewriting of E_2 into $E_2 \oplus z \ominus w$.

For our example (see the opposite figure) the solution is the path $[a]_1\xrightarrow{a}[a,b]_2\xrightarrow{b}[b,c,d]_1\xrightarrow{d}[d,e]_2$: traversing the vertex $[a,b]_2$ corresponds to the rewriting $E_2 = e \equiv_2 a \ominus b \oplus e$, then traversing the vertex $[b,c,d]_1$ corresponds to $E_1 = a \equiv_1 a \ominus b \oplus d$, and finally reaching $[d,e]_2$ allows to deduce $E_2 \equiv_2 a \ominus b \oplus d$, the common rewriting.

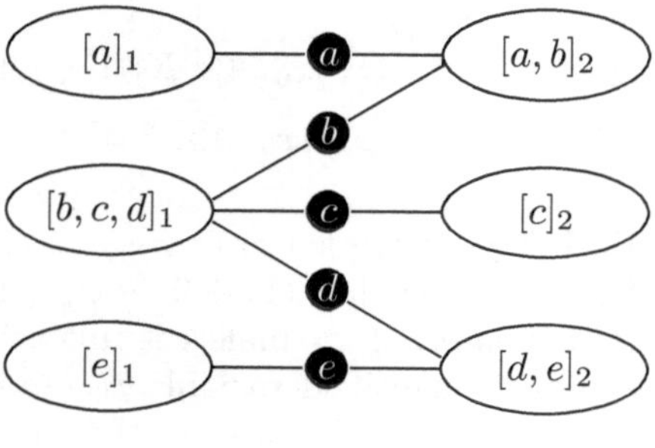

5.2 General Case

In general, we want to find, if it exists, a common rewriting of multiset expressions E_1 and E_2, which are sums and differences of atoms, possibly with positive coefficients (e.g., $E_1 = a \ominus (2 \otimes b) \oplus (3 \otimes c)$). We could use the previous procedure to find a common rewriting between each atom in E_1 and an atom of E_2. Instead, we can directly convert our problem into the classical problem of finding a maximal flow in a graph with capacities: we split each expression E_i into a difference $F_i \ominus G_i$ where F_i and G_i are sums of atoms with positive coefficients. Now, we consider again the graph of equivalence classes, as before, where all edges are assigned an infinite capacity, and we extend it with

- a source vertex, labelled with $F_1 \oplus G_2$; for each term $k \otimes a$ in F_1 (resp., in G_2), we create an edge of capacity k from the source vertex to the vertex $[a]_1$ (resp., $[a]_2$);
- and a target vertex, labelled with $F_2 \oplus G_1$; for each term $k \otimes a$ in F_2 (resp., in G_1), we create an edge of capacity k from the vertex $[a]_2$ (resp., $[a]_1$) to the target vertex.

Let's recall that a flow in such a graph with capacities consists of an orientation of the graph (from the source to the target), together with a function ϕ associating with each edge $e = (V_1, V_2)$ of the graph a natural $\phi(e)$, such that (1) for each edge e, $\phi(e)$ does not exceed the capacity $\kappa(e)$ of e, and (2) for each vertex V which is neither the source nor the target, the sum of the values of the flow over all incoming edges to V is equal to the sum of the flow over all outgoing edges. We compute a maximal flow $\phi_{\max}$ from the source to the target (using, e.g, Ford-Fulkerson [FF56] or Edmonds-Karp [EK72] algorithms); if this maximal flow saturates the capacity of edges from the source and to the target, it corresponds to a solution to the initial problem. The common rewriting of E_1 and E_2 is

$$E = \bigoplus_{\substack{V_1 \in \equiv_1 \\ e = V_1 \xrightarrow{a} V_2}} \phi_{\max}(e) \otimes a \ominus \bigoplus_{\substack{V_2 \in \equiv_2 \\ e = V_2 \xrightarrow{a} V_1}} \phi_{\max}(e) \otimes a$$

Example: Let $E_1 = a \ominus (2 \otimes b)$, $E_2 = (2 \otimes c) \ominus (3 \otimes d)$, and $(a \equiv_1 c, b \equiv_1 d), (a \equiv_2 d, c \equiv_2 b)$. The corresponding graph is represented by Fig. 2, together with a maximum flow (each edge e is associated with $\kappa(e)/\phi_{\max}(e)$). The common rewriting is then $E = (2 \otimes c) \ominus a \ominus (2 \otimes d)$

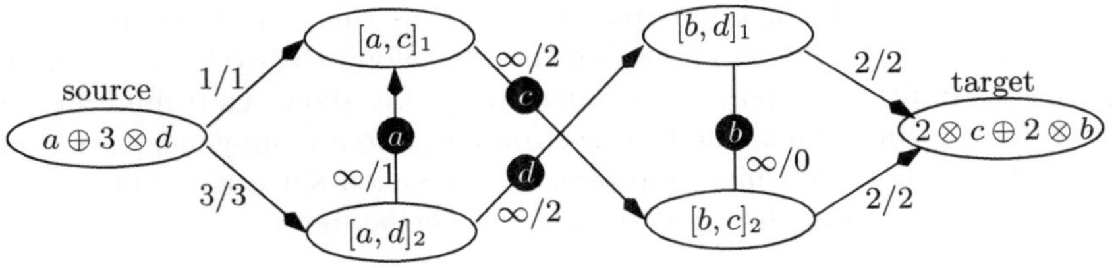

Fig. 2. Max-flow example

Conversely if there is a solution E to the initial problem, it corresponds to a flow : for each atom e in E add one flow unit to the vertex labeled by e, saturate the edges from the source and to the target and the flow conservation will follow from the equation $E_1 \equiv_1 E \equiv_2 E_2$. The reduction is hence sound and complete.

5.3 The Canonicity Problem

Unfortunately, there can be several maximum flows in the graph, which provide several, non-equivalent solutions for the unified multiset equation. Let's consider the following program fragment:

```
1  d:= A[i]; A[i]:= c;
2  if cond then a:= c; b :=d;
3  else a:= d; b:= c;
4  endif
5  c:= x;
```

Starting with $\hat{A} \ominus \mathcal{M} = \emptyset$ as before, at point 2 we get $\hat{A} \ominus \mathcal{M} = c \ominus d$, then, after the "then" branch, $(a = c \wedge b = d) \wedge (\hat{A} \ominus \mathcal{M} = c \ominus d)$, and after the "else" branch, $(a = d \wedge b = c) \wedge (\hat{A} \ominus \mathcal{M} = c \ominus d)$. After line 4, we have to compute the unification of the previous two values. The max-flow algorithm provides two solutions:

1. $(\hat{A} \ominus \mathcal{M} = c \ominus d)$
2. $(\hat{A} \ominus \mathcal{M} = a \oplus b \ominus (2 \otimes d))$

If we choose the solution (1), after line 5 we lose all information since the value of c is lost; however, if we choose the solution (2) which does not involve c, the equation $(\hat{A} \ominus \mathcal{M} = a \oplus b \ominus (2 \otimes d))$ is preserved after line 5.

So, the max-flow method provides a correct upper bound which is not always the most precise. However, it suggests another approach: notice that the multiplicity of solutions comes from the presence of cycles in the graph. Since the capacities of the edges in a cycle are infinite, we can add or remove flow along a cycle and still get a solution. So, as soon as there is a cycle in the graph, we get an infinite set of solutions. Conversely if there are several solutions, one can be found from another by adding or removing flow along a cycle. An idea is to keep track of the informations given by these cycles. In the previous example before the final assignment, we have the property $a \oplus b = c \oplus d$ (which means $(a = c \wedge b = d) \vee (a = d \wedge b = c)$. It is true since the only difference between the two branches is that c and d are swapped which does not alter the equation. Moreover, this equation corresponds to the cycle found in the graph (which is the same as Fig 2 with different capacities). Adding this equation to one solution is exactly the same thing as increasing the flow along the cycle a, c, b, d. Thus keeping this additional equation between singletons allows us to find any other solution from a single one. The next section describe a more general solution to compute upper bounds which improves the precision since it is able to retain singleton equations and then find the least upper bound.

6 A Solution Based on Linear Algebra

Another solution is to consider the atom equations as (singleton) multiset equations, and to handle them together with other multiset equations: then, we get the conjunction of two systems of multiset equations, which are all *linear*. The next idea is to use classical operators in linear algebra, and in particular those proposed by Karr [Kar76] for propagating affine equations between numerical variables. The key operator is the least upper bound, which computes the system of equations of the least affine space containing two given affine spaces. Of course, we don't consider numerical affine spaces, but the only operations used are those of a vectorial space. Notice also that our equations are always linear (with a null constant term).

The lattice of linear equations: Let us briefly recall the principles of Karr's analysis. Karr's domain is the lattice of linear varieties of an n-dimensional vectorial space. Such a linear variety is defined by a vectorial equation $MX = C$, where M is an $(m \times n)$-matrix, and C is a constant vector. In our special case, the coefficients in M are integers, and C is the null vector (all its components are the empty multiset). There is a classical normal form to this kind of equations, by putting M in *row-echelon form*, using Gauss procedure. The propagation of system of equations through linear assignments is straightforward. The least upper bound operator provides the least linear variety containing its arguments; it is therefore well-defined, geometrically. The procedure proposed by M. Karr is recalled in the appendix: taking 2 matrices M_1 and M_2 in canonical form, it returns a matrix M, also in canonical form, such that the variety $MX = 0$ is the least variety containing both $M_1X = 0$ and $M_2X = 0$.

Coming back to the example of §5.3, we have to compute the least upper bound $\left(a = c \wedge b = d \wedge \hat{A} \ominus \mathcal{M} = c \ominus d\right) \sqcup \left(a = d \wedge b = c \wedge \hat{A} \ominus \mathcal{M} = c \ominus d\right)$ Karr's operator provides the result $a \oplus b = c \oplus d \wedge \hat{A} \ominus \mathcal{M} = c \ominus d$. Eliminating c to compute the result after line 5, we get the precise result $\hat{A} \ominus \mathcal{M} = a \oplus b \ominus (2 \otimes d)$.

Taking into account that the theoretical complexity of the max-flow algorithm (n^2) is better than the complexity of Karr's affine hull (n^3), we could use the max-flow solution to deal with the multiset equations, and apply the affine hull to unify atom equations. However, it is not likely that, in practice, the considered systems of equation become very large, so the complexity is not really an issue.

Let's recall that Karr's lattice is of finite depth: the size of strictly increasing chains is bounded by the number of variables (the dimension of the space), so there is no need for widening to ensure the termination.

Atoms are not numbers

The fact that, in contrast with [Kar76], we are not working in a numerical vectorial space may raise some questions, concerning the existence of solutions, and some implicit consequences of atom equations.

The emptiness problem: some systems of equations have solutions in the usual numerical space, but not in our multiset space. For instance, the equation $a \oplus b = c$, where a, b, c are atoms, has no solution. It is the case of all atom equations which are not balanced (i.e., where the sum of coefficients of both members are not equal). However, this question is not relevant for our analysis, since all the equations considered in the analysis are well-balanced.

Implicit equations: on the other hand, some systems of equations have implicit consequences in our multiset space, which would not occur in the numerical space. For instance, the equation $a \oplus b = 2 \otimes c$, where a, b, c are atoms, implies $a = b = c$. Detecting all such implicit equations is NP-hard (see, e.g., [DV99, DPR08]). However, we don't have any example of program where this kind of implicit equations would appear and be useful. Moreover, finding equalities between atoms is not the goal of the multiset analysis.

So, while algorithms exist for discovering such implicit equations, they were not implemented in our analyzer, because of their excessive cost and the debatable interest of such additional properties. However, notice that this does not change the correctness of our analysis.

7 Experimental Results

This analysis has been implemented within the analyzer developed by M. Péron [HP08], taking as input the same language restricted to simple loops and one-dimensional arrays. However, many language restrictions could be easily released for our analysis.

In this section, we show some examples of analyzes. Notice that, for all the examples presented below, the analysis based on flows gives the same results as Karr's lattice. The reported execution times are those with Karr's lattice.

7.1 Insertion Sort

We detail below the analysis of the "insertion sort" procedure. We indicate at each line the three properties, respectively concerning indices, contents, and multisets. We assume that the lattice of index properties is the lattice of potentials, with a reasonable widening. The analysis terminates after 3 iterations.

First iteration

for i:= 1 to n do $\ldots \{(i = 1), (\hat{A} = \mathcal{M})\}$
  x:=A[i]; j:=i-1; $\ldots \{(i = 1, j = i - 1), (x = A[i]), (\hat{A} = \mathcal{M})\}$
  while j>=1 and A[j]>k do $\ldots \{(i = 1, j = i - 1), (x = A[i]), (\hat{A} = \mathcal{M})\}$
    A[j+1]:= A[j];$\ldots \{(i = 1, j = i - 1), (x = A[i]), (\hat{A} = \mathcal{M} \ominus x \oplus A[j])\}$
    j:=j-1; $\ldots \{(i = 1, j = i - 2), (x = A[i]), (\hat{A} = \mathcal{M} \ominus x \oplus A[j+1])\}$
  end
  A[j+1] := x;
end

Second iteration

for i:= 1 to n do $\ldots \{(i = 1), (\hat{A} = \mathcal{M})\}$
  x:=A[i]; j:=i-1; $\ldots \{(i = 1, j = i - 1), (x = A[i]), (\hat{A} = \mathcal{M})\}$
  while j>=1 and A[j]>k do $..(i = 1, 1 \leq j < i), (x = A[i]), (\hat{A} = \mathcal{M} \ominus x \oplus A[j+1])$
    A[j+1]:= A[j]; $\ldots \{(i = 1, 0 \leq j < i), (x = A[i]), (\hat{A} = \mathcal{M} \ominus x \oplus A[j])\}$
    j:=j-1; $\ldots \{(i = 1, 0 \leq j < i - 1), (x = A[i]), (\hat{A} = \mathcal{M} \ominus x \oplus A[j+1])\}$
  end $\ldots \{(i = 1, 0 \leq j < i), (x = A[i]), (\hat{A} = \mathcal{M} \ominus x \oplus A[j+1])\}$
  A[j+1] := x;$\ldots \{(i = 1, 0 \leq j < i), (x = A[i]), (\hat{A} = \mathcal{M})\}$
end

Third iteration

for i:= 1 to n do $\ldots\{(1 \le i \le n), (\hat{A} = \mathcal{M})\}$
  x:=A[i]; j:=i-1; $\ldots\{(1 \le i \le n, j = i-1), (x = A[i]), (\hat{A} = \mathcal{M})\}$
  while j>=1 and A[j]>k do..$(1 \le i \le n, 1 \le j < i), (x = A[i]), (\hat{A} = \mathcal{M} \ominus x \oplus A[j+1])$
    A[j+1]:= A[j]; $\ldots\{(1 \le i \le n, 1 \le j < i), (x = A[i]), (\hat{A} = \mathcal{M} \ominus x \oplus A[j])\}$
    j:=j-1; $\ldots\{(1 \le i \le n, 0 \le j < i-1), (x = A[i]), (\hat{A} = \mathcal{M} \ominus x \oplus A[j+1])\}$
  end $\ldots\{(1 \le i \le n, 0 \le j < i), (x = A[i]), (\hat{A} = \mathcal{M} \ominus x \oplus A[j+1])\}$
  A[j+1] := x;$\ldots\{(1 \le i \le n, 0 \le j < i), (x = A[i]), (\hat{A} = \mathcal{M})\}$
end $\ldots\{(\hat{A} = \mathcal{M})\}$

7.2 An Aliasing Surprise

As another simple example, consider two versions of a procedure, intended to perform a circular permutation of the contents of three array cells:

$\ldots\{\hat{A} = \mathcal{M}\}$
x:=A[i]; $\ldots\{x = A[i], \hat{A} = \mathcal{M}\}$
A[i]:=A[j];
$\ldots\{A[i] = A[j], \hat{A} = \mathcal{M} \ominus x \oplus A[j]\}$
A[j]:=A[k];
$\ldots\{A[j] = A[k], \hat{A} = \mathcal{M} \ominus x \oplus A[k]\}$
A[k]:=x; $\ldots\{A[k] = x, \hat{A} = \mathcal{M}\}$

(a) rotation

$\ldots\{\hat{A} = \mathcal{M}\}$
x:=A[i];$\ldots\{x = A[i], \hat{A} = \mathcal{M}\}$
y:=A[j];$\ldots\{x = A[i], y = A[j], \hat{A} = \mathcal{M}\}$
z:=A[k];
$\ldots\{x = A[i], y = A[j], z = A[k], \hat{A} = \mathcal{M}\}$
A[i]:=y;$\ldots\{y = A[j] = A[i], \hat{A} = \mathcal{M} \ominus x \oplus y\}$
A[j]:=z;$\ldots\{A[j] = z, \hat{A} = \mathcal{M} \ominus x \oplus z\}$
A[k]:=x; $\ldots\{A[k] = x\}$

(b) copy-store

Fig. 3. Permuting 3 values

- The first version (Fig. 3.a) performs a simple rotation, using a buffer x. The analysis proves that the final content of the array is a permutation of the initial one.
- In the second version (Fig. 3.b), the three values are first copied in buffers, and then stored back at their respective places. On that program, the analysis is not able to show anything interesting about the final content. Of course, this could result from some imprecision; but if we look closer at the cause of the failure, it appears that there is a case where the content of the array is not preserved: if $i = k \neq j$, the initial value of $A[i]$ is copied twice in the final array, and the initial value of $A[j]$ is lost. So, our analysis is precise and detects a bug in the program.

7.3 Combining the Analysis with Array Partitioning

Our analysis can be easily combined with the methods [GRS05, HP08] which partition the arrays into symbolic slices, and associate a *summary variable* with each such slice.

For instance, we used the method of [HP08] to partition arrays into relevant slices, and used our abstract domain to analyze the properties of these slices.

Table 1. Some experimental results

Program	exp. res.	results	time	nb.iter.
switch 2 cells by rotation	$\hat{A} = \mathcal{A}$	ok	<4ms	1
switch 2 cells by copy-store	$\hat{A} = \mathcal{A}$	ok	<4ms	1
switch 3 cells by rotation	$\hat{A} = \mathcal{A}$	ok	<4ms	1
switch 3 cells by copy-store	$\hat{A} \neq \mathcal{A}$	ok	<4ms	1
Dutch national flag [Dij76]	$\hat{A} = \mathcal{A}$	ok	<4ms	2
Insertion sort	$\hat{A} = \mathcal{A}$	ok	<4ms	3
Selection sort	$\hat{A} = \mathcal{A}$	ok	<4ms	2
Bubble sort	$\hat{A} = \mathcal{A}$	ok	<4ms	3
With array partitioning				
Array copy	$A\widehat{[0..n-1]}=B\widehat{[0..n-1]}$	ok	< 4ms	2
Split on sign [KV09]	$A\widehat{[0..a-1]}=B\widehat{[0..b-1]}\oplus C\widehat{[0..c-1]}$	ok	12ms	2

In [HP08], array accesses and loop indices are used to separate array cells that should be considered separately (as singleton slices). Then an array is partitioned into these singleton slices, and contiguous slices separating these singletons.

Only a small amount of work is needed to adapt the abstract domain to this slicing technique. When an index is progressing, a slice may be growing and then we have to perform a substitution in the equation system to reflect that the new slice is the union of old slice with some singleton.

This combination of techniques can now be used to find some other interesting properties. For instance in a program which copies an array A to an array B we are now able to state at each step of the loop indexed by i that the multisets of values of cells with index greater than 0 but less than i are equals in the array A and in the array B. Then this intermediate property allows us to discover the multiset equality of A and B and finally use it to prove more specific properties.

The opposite program is another interesting example considered in [KV09]: it splits an array A into B and C according to the signs of the elements. Using our combined analysis we get respectively for each array A, B and C the partitions $\{A[0..a-1], A[a], A[a+1..n-1]\}$, $\{B[0..b-1], B[b], B[b+1..n-1]\}$ and $\{C[0..c-1], C[c], B[c+1..n-1]\}$. Propagating the multiset properties between these slices, we find the expected loop invariant:

```
a := 0, b := 0, c := 0 ;
while a < n do
    if A[a] ≥ 0 then
        B[b] := A[a] ;
        b++ ;
    else
        C[c] := A[a] ;
        c++ ;
    a++ ;
```

$$A\widehat{[0..a-1]} = B\widehat{[0..b-1]} \oplus C\widehat{[0..c-1]}$$

which, once again, could not be expressed as a first-order formula.

7.4 Other Examples

Table 1 shows the analysis time for several small programs. All the results are as expected.

7.5 An Example with Linked Data Structures

Our lattice of multiset equations can be used for other data structures than arrays. As an example of possible application, we have analyzed (by hand) the Deutsch-Schorr-Waite data structure traversal algorithm [SW67]. In fact, we consider the version of [Lin73], dedicated to data structures without cycles, and which does not involve any auxiliary marking. A slightly different version of this algorithm has been completely proven with TVLA [LRS06]. We recall that this algorithm traverses a binary structure (a dag or a tree), without using a stack, by redirecting pointers in the structure to store the return path. We note $\hat{T}$ the multiset of pointers contained in the structure, i.e., contained in a node initially reachable from the root of the structure. The goal would be to show that this multiset is restored at the end of the traversal (of course, this does not show that the structure has been restored). The results are shown in Fig. 4. The goal is not reached, because it needs the additional fact that, at the end of the program, **root = prev**, a fact that would need another kind of analysis, and the knowledge that "**-1**" does not appear in the initial structure. However, the computed invariants are precise.

prev:=-1; cur:=root; $\ldots\{prev = -1, cur = root, \hat{T} = \mathcal{M}\}$
while cur<>-1 $\ldots\{\hat{T} = \mathcal{M} \oplus root \oplus -1 \ominus cur \ominus prev\}$
  next:=cur->left; cur->left:=cur->right;
  cur->right:=prev; $\ldots\{\hat{T} = \mathcal{M} \oplus root \oplus -1 \ominus cur \ominus next\}$
  prev:=cur; cur:=next; $\ldots\{cur = next, \hat{T} = \mathcal{M} \oplus root \oplus -1 \ominus prev \ominus next\}$
  if cur=NULL $\ldots\{cur = next = NULL, \hat{T} = \mathcal{M} \oplus root \oplus -1 \ominus prev \ominus next\}$
    cur:=prev; prev=NULL;
    $\ldots\{prev = next = NULL, \hat{T} = \mathcal{M} \oplus root \oplus -1 \ominus cur \ominus next\}$
  end $\ldots\{\hat{T} = \mathcal{M} \oplus root \oplus -1 \ominus cur \ominus prev\}$
end $\ldots\{\hat{T} = \mathcal{M} \oplus root \ominus prev\}$

Fig. 4. Results for the Deutsch-Schorr-Waite algorithm

8 Conclusion

To our knowledge, it is the first automatic analysis for handling permutation-invariant properties of data-structures. Basically, our abstract values are equations between multiset expressions, together with equations, gathered by other analyzes, between locations (indices, pointers) and structure contents. Two ways for computing least upper bounds of multiset equations have been proposed: the solution based on flows is theoretically more efficient, but may be less precise in general; the other solution makes use of the standard lattice of linear equations, and deals jointly with multiset and content equations.

The paper is specialized to the analysis of arrays, but our lattice could be used for any kind of data structures, as shown by the Deutsch-Schorr-Waite example, provided a suitable interpretation of statements on these data-structures is available. This would give a relevant abstraction for every collection data structure and thus could be used in a shape-value abstraction [Vaf09] in conjunction with a shape analysis to derive properties of these structures or to use these properties in programs manipulating collections. It would be also useful to consider more general programs (e.g., recursive programs) and statements (e.g., indirect indexing), but this would not interfere with the definition of the lattice and its operations. Another perspective is to consider multiset inclusions, in order to be able to show that some data structure is included, up to some permutation, inside another one.

References

[ACD93] Alur, R., Courcoubetis, C., Dill, D.L.: Model-checking in dense real-time. Information and Computation 104(1), 2–34 (1993); Preliminary version appears in the Proc. of 5th LICS (1990)

[BMS06] Bradley, A.R., Manna, Z., Sipma, H.B.: What's decidable about arrays? In: Emerson, E.A., Namjoshi, K.S. (eds.) VMCAI 2006. LNCS, vol. 3855, pp. 427–442. Springer, Heidelberg (2006)

[CC76] Cousot, P., Cousot, R.: Static determination of dynamic properties of programs. In: 2nd Int. Symp. on Programming, Dunod, Paris (1976)

[Cou03] Cousot, P.: Verification by abstract interpretation. In: Dershowitz, N. (ed.) Proc. Int. Symp. on Verification – Theory & Practice – Honoring Zohar Manna's 64th Birthday, Taormina, Italy, June 29-July 4, pp. 243–268. Springer, Berlin (2003)

[Dij76] Dijkstra, E.W.: A Discipline of Programming. Prentice-Hall Series in Automatic Computation (1976)

[Dil89] Dill, D.L.: Timing assumptions and verification of finite state concurrent systems. In: Sifakis, J. (ed.) CAV 1989. LNCS, vol. 407. Springer, Heidelberg (1990)

[DPR08] Dovier, A., Piazza, C., Rossi, G.: A uniform approach to constraint-solving for lists, multisets, compact lists, and sets. ACM TOCL 9(3) (May 2008)

[DRS03] Dor, N., Rodeh, M., Sagiv, M.: CCSV: towards a realistic tool for statically detecting all buffer overflows in C. In: ACM Conference on Programming Language Design and Implementation, PLDI 2003, San Diego, June 2003, pp. 155–167 (2003)

[DV99] Dantsin, E., Voronkov, A.: A nondeterministic polynomial-time unification algorithm for bags, sets and trees. In: Thomas, W. (ed.) FOSSACS 1999. LNCS, vol. 1578, pp. 180–196. Springer, Heidelberg (1999)

[EK72] Edmonds, J., Karp, R.M.: Theoretical improvements in algorithmic efficiency for network flow problems. J. ACM 19(2), 248–264 (1972)

[FF56] Ford, L.R., Fulkerson, D.R.: Maximal flow through a network. Canadian Journal of Mathematics 8, 399–404 (1956)

[FQ02] Flanagan, C., Qadeer, S.: Predicate abstraction for software verification. In: POPL 2002, pp. 191–202. ACM, New York (2002)

[GMT08] Gulwani, S., McCloskey, B., Tiwari, A.: Lifting abstract interpreters to quantified logical domains. In: Necula, G.C., Wadler, P. (eds.) POPL 2008, pp. 235–246. ACM, New York (2008)

[GRS05] Gopan, D., Reps, T., Sagiv, M.: A framework for numeric analysis of array operations. In: Proc. of POPL 2005, Long Beach, CA, pp. 338–350 (2005)

[HP08] Halbwachs, N., Péron, M.: Discovering properties about arrays in simple programs. In: ACM Conference on Programming Language Design and Implementation, PLDI 2008, Tucson (Az.), June 2008, pp. 339–348 (2008)

[IHV08] Habermehl, P., Iosif, R., Vojnar, T.: What else is decidable about integer arrays? In: Amadio, R.M. (ed.) FOSSACS 2008. LNCS, vol. 4962, pp. 474–489. Springer, Heidelberg (2008)

[JM07] Jhala, R., McMillan, K.L.: Array abstractions from proofs. In: Damm, W., Hermanns, H. (eds.) CAV 2007. LNCS, vol. 4590, pp. 193–206. Springer, Heidelberg (2007)

[Kar76] Karr, M.: Affine relationships among variables of a program. Acta Informatica 6, 133–151 (1976)

[KV09] Kovács, L., Voronkov, A.: Finding loop invariants for programs over arrays using a theorem prover. In: FASE 2009. LNCS, vol. 5503, pp. 470–485. Springer, Heidelberg (2009)

[LB04] Lahiri, S.K., Bryant, R.E.: Indexed predicate discovery for unbounded system verification. In: Alur, R., Peled, D.A. (eds.) CAV 2004. LNCS, vol. 3114, pp. 135–147. Springer, Heidelberg (2004)

[Lin73] Lindstrom, G.: Scanning list structures without stacks or tag bits. Information Processing Letters 2(2), 47–51 (1973)

[LRS06] Loginov, A., Reps, T.W., Sagiv, M.: Automated verification of the Deutsch-Schorr-Waite tree-traversal algorithm. In: Yi, K. (ed.) SAS 2006. LNCS, vol. 4134, pp. 261–279. Springer, Heidelberg (2006)

[LS79] Luckham, D.C., Suzuki, N.: Verification of array, record, and pointer operations in Pascal. ACM Trans. Program. Lang. Syst. 1(2), 226–244 (1979)

[Min01] Miné, A.: The octagon abstract domain. In: AST 2001 in WCRE 2001, pp. 310–319. IEEE CS Press, Los Alamitos (2001)

[PH07] Péron, M., Halbwachs, N.: An abstract domain extending Difference-Bound Matrices with disequality constraints. In: Cook, B., Podelski, A. (eds.) VMCAI 2007. LNCS, vol. 4349, pp. 268–282. Springer, Heidelberg (2007)

[SG09] Srivastava, S., Gulwani, S.: Program verification using templates over predicate abstraction. In: ACM Conference on Programming Language Design and Implementation, PLDI 2009, pp. 223–234 (2009)

[SIYJ07] Singh, D., Ibrahim, A.M., Yohanna, T., Singh, J.N.: An overview of the applications of multisets. Novi. Sad J. Math. 37(2), 73–92 (2007)

[SJ80] Suzuki, N., Jefferson, D.: Verification decidability of Presburger array programs. J. ACM 27(1) (January 1980)

[SRW02] Sagiv, S., Reps, T.W., Wilhelm, R.: Parametric shape analysis via 3-valued logic. ACM Trans. Program. Lang. Syst. 24(3), 217–298 (2002)

[SW67] Schorr, H., Waite, W.: An efficient machine independent procedure for garbage collection in various list structures. Communications of the ACM 10(8), 501–506 (1967)

[Syr01] Syropoulos, A.: Mathematics of multisets. In: Calude, C.S., Pun, G., Rozenberg, G., Salomaa, A. (eds.) Multiset Processing. LNCS, vol. 2235, pp. 347–358. Springer, Heidelberg (2001)

[Vaf09] Vafeiadis, V.: Shape-value abstraction for verifying linearizability. In: Jones, N.D., Müller-Olm, M. (eds.) VMCAI 2009. LNCS, vol. 5403, pp. 335–348. Springer, Heidelberg (2009)

[WSR00] Wilhelm, R., Sagiv, S., Reps, T.W.: Shape analysis. In: Watt, D.A. (ed.) CC 2000. LNCS, vol. 1781, pp. 1–17. Springer, Heidelberg (2000)

Appendix: Karr's Algorithm for Linear Hull

Let's recall the algorithm proposed in [Kar76] for computing the linear hull: given two linear subspaces, defined by their matrices M and M' in reduced row-echelon form (i.e., (1) each row has at least one non-zero entry, and for any row i_0, if j_0 is the first column with a non zero entry of the row, then (2) for all $i > i_0, j <= j_0$, $M_{ij} = 0$ and (3) forall $i \neq i_0, M_{i,j_0} = 0$), the algorithm returns the matrix (in reduced echelon form) of the least linear subspace containing the two given subspaces. The algorithm progressively modifies M and M' so that, at the end of step s, the first s columns of M and M' are equal. After n steps, M and M' are equal, and it is the solution. The two matrices are maintained in the following form:

$$M = \left(\begin{array}{c|c} \frac{C}{0} & N \end{array}\right) \;,\; M' = \left(\begin{array}{c|c} \frac{C}{0} & N' \end{array}\right)$$

where the common part C has s columns at step s.

At the beginning of step s, let r be the number of rows of C plus 1. There are 3 cases according to the values of N_{rs} and N'_{rs}:

1. either $N_{rs} = N'_{rs} = 1$, then, from the hypotheses on M and M', we have:

$$M = \left(\begin{array}{cc|c} C & \vdots & \\ & 0 & N \\ \hline & \boxed{1} & \\ & & \end{array}\right) \;,\; M' = \left(\begin{array}{cc|c} C & \vdots & \\ & 0 & N' \\ \hline & \boxed{1} & \\ & & \end{array}\right)$$

   and we just increment r and s;

2. or $N_{rs} = 1$ and $N'_{rs} = 0$ (or conversely), and the matrices are in the form:

$$M = \left(\begin{array}{cc|c} C & \vdots & \\ & 0 & N \\ \hline & \boxed{1} & \\ & & \end{array}\right) \;,\; M' = \left(\begin{array}{c|c} \frac{C|\beta}{} & N' \end{array}\right)$$

   then, M is modified by obtaining the column β in the $r-1$ positions of column s (previously 0), by performing suitable linear combinations of there $r-1$ rows with row s. Row s of M is then suppressed.

3. or $N_{rs} = N'_{rs} = 0$, and the matrices are in the form:

$$M = \left(\begin{array}{c|c} \frac{C|\alpha}{} & N \end{array}\right) \;,\; M' = \left(\begin{array}{c|c} \frac{C|\beta}{} & N' \end{array}\right)$$

   If columns α and β are the same, s is just incremented. Otherwise, let ℓ be the greatest row index such that $\alpha_\ell \neq \beta_\ell$. Then, in each matrix, let R_ℓ be the row ℓ and R_i be a row on index $< \ell$; replace each R_i by $R_i - (\alpha_i - \beta_i)/(\alpha_\ell - \beta_\ell)R_\ell$; finally, delete row ℓ in both matrices: columns s are the same in both matrices, and s can be incremented.

Regular Linear Temporal Logic with Past

César Sánchez[1,2] and Martin Leucker[3]

[1] Madrid Institute for Advanced Studies (IMDEA Software), Spain
[2] Spanish Council for Scientific Research (CSIC), Spain
[3] Technische Universität München, Germany

Abstract. This paper upgrades Regular Linear Temporal Logic (RLTL) with past operators and complementation. RLTL is a temporal logic that extends the expressive power of linear temporal logic (LTL) to all ω-regular languages. The syntax of RLTL consists of an algebraic signature from which expressions are built. In particular, RLTL does not need or expose fix-point binders (like linear time μ-calculus), or automata to build and instantiate operators (like ETL_*).

Past operators are easily introduced in RLTL via a single previous-step operator for basic state formulas. The satisfiability and model checking problems for RLTL are PSPACE-complete, which is optimal for extensions of LTL. This result is shown using a novel linear size translation of RLTL expressions into 2-way alternating parity automata on words. Unlike previous automata-theoretic approaches to LTL, this construction is compositional (bottom-up). As alternating parity automata can easily be complemented, the treatment of negation is simple and does not require an upfront transformation of formulas into any normal form.

1 Introduction

In his seminal paper [23], Pnueli proposed Linear temporal logic (LTL) [20] as a specification language for reactive systems. LTL is a modal logic over a linear frame, whose formulas express properties of infinite traces using two *future* modalities: *nexttime* and *until*. Although extending LTL with past operators (e.g., [12]), does *not* increase its expressive power [8], it has been widely noticed that it caters for specifications that are shorter, easier and more intuitive [19]. For example,[17] shows that there is a family of LTL formulas with past operators whose equivalent future only formulas are exponentially larger. Likewise, recalling the classical example from [27], the specification that *Every alarm is due to a fault* can easily be expressed by $\Box(\mathit{alarm} \rightarrow \diamondminus \mathit{fault})$, where $\Box$ means *globally/always* and $\diamondminus$ means *once in the past*. An equivalent formulation using only future operators is $\neg(\neg \mathit{fault}\ \mathcal{U}\ (\mathit{alarm} \wedge \neg \mathit{fault}))$, which is, however, less intuitive. The problems of satisfiability and model checking are PSPACE-complete [17] for LTL with and without past operators, so the past does not seem to harm in terms of complexity.

With regards to expressivity, Wolper [32] showed that LTL cannot express all ω-regular properties. In particular, it cannot express the property "p holds only at even moments". In spite of being a useful specification language, this lack of expressivity seems to surface in practice [25]. To alleviate the expressivity

G. Barthe and M. Hermenegildo (Eds.): VMCAI 2010, LNCS 5944, pp. 295–311, 2010.

problem, Wolper suggested *extended temporal logic* (ETL) in which new operators are defined using automata, and instantiated using language composition. ETL was later extended [31,14] to different kinds of automata. The main drawback of these logics is that, in order to obtain the full expressivity, an infinite number of operators is needed. Among other consequences for its practical usage, this implies that ETL is not algebraic. An alternative approach consists of adapting the modal μ-calculus [6,13] to the linear setting (νTL) [1]. Here, the full expressivity is obtained by the use of fix point operators. In νTL one needs to specify recursive equations to describe temporal properties, since the only modality is *nexttime*, which tends to make typical specifications cumbersome.

At the same time, some studies [3] point out that regular expressions are very convenient in addition to LTL in formal specifications, partly because practitioners are familiar with regular expressions, partly because specifications are more natural. Even though every ground regular expression can be translated into a νTL expression [15], the concatenation operator cannot be directly represented in νTL. No context of νTL can capture concatenation. Extending νTL with concatenation leads to *fix point logic with chop* (FLC) [22] that allows expressing non-regular languages, but at the price of undecidable satisfiability and equivalence problems.

Some dynamic logics also try to merge regular expressions (for the program part) with LTL (for the action part), for example, Regular Process Logic [9]. However, the satisfiability problem is non-elementary because one can combine arbitrarily negations and regular operators. Dynamic linear-temporal logic DLTL [10] (see also [16]) keeps the satisfiability problem in PSPACE, but restricts the use of regular expressions only as a generalization of the until operator. The until operator $p\mathcal{U}^{\alpha}q$ in DLTL is equipped with a regular expression (α) and establishes that the until part (q) must be fulfilled at some position in which α matches, while the first argument p must hold at all positions in between. It is unclear then how to extend DLTL with past operators. The approach of defining past operators using past regular expressions, presented in Section 2 for RLTL cannot be used for DLTL since the notion of "in-between" is not clear anymore. Another extension of LTL to regular expressions is the logic RELTL from [4]. However, this logic does not include past operators or negation. Moreover, it requires a translation into positive normal form for the LTL part that makes this translation not compositional. Also, the interaction of regular expressions and linear temporal logic in RELTL is restricted to prefixes, while in RLTL we consider more sophisticated combinations.

The popularity of regular expressions led also to their inclusion in the industry standard specification language PSL [7]. While decision procedures and their complexities for full PSL are still an area of active research, [16] shows that the fragment of PSL that contains LTL and semi-extended regular expressions, even though it allows more succinct specifications, leads to EXPSPACE-complete satisfiability and model checking problems, which may limit its practical applicability.

In this paper, we upgrade *Regular Linear Temporal Logic* (RLTL) [18] with past operators. RLTL is a temporal logic that extends the expressive power of

LTL to all ω-regular languages. It has an algebraic signature and fuses LTL and regular expressions. To enrich RLTL by past operators, it suffices, as we show here, to simply add *basic past expressions*, which allow the formulation of past regular expressions. Intuitively, regular expressions with past expressions can define finite segments of infinite strings in an arbitrary forward and backward manner. The main contribution of RLTL comes perhaps from the simplicity of the novel power operators, which allow the definition of most other temporal operators and, as we show here, the treatment of past and negation while avoiding non-algebraic constructs like fix-points bindings or automata instantiations. The power operators are the key to obtain compositionality without requiring an upfront translation to positive normal forms.

To address satisfiability and model checking for RLTL, we follow the automata theoretic approach, but need a more sophisticated translation than in [18] to cope with the new operators. This novel linear size translation uses 2-way alternating parity automata on words. Besides being useful for RLTL, this translation is also interesting for plain LTL, as it is compositional (bottom-up) unlike previous automata-theoretic approaches to LTL. As alternating parity automata can easily be complemented, the treatment of negation is simple and does not require an upfront transformation of formulas into positive or other normal form. A notable exception is [26], which presents another compositional translation from LTL, but this translation generates testers instead of automata.

Building on recent automata results [5], we show here that the satisfiability and model checking problems for RLTL (with past) are PSPACE-complete, which is optimal for extensions of LTL.

This paper is structured as follows. Section 2 introduces RLTL. Section 3 recalls the basic definitions of LTL with past, and presents the translation into RLTL. Section 4 describes the translation from RLTL into automata. Finally, Section 5 contains the conclusions. Due to space limitations some proofs are missing, but they can be easily reconstructed.

2 Regular Linear Temporal Logic

We define *regular linear temporal logic* (RLTL) in two stages, similarly to PSL or ForSpec. First, we present a variation of regular expressions enriched with a simple past operator. Then we use these regular expressions to define regular linear temporal logic as a language that describes sets of infinite words. The syntax of each of these two formalisms consists of an algebraic signature containing a finite collection of constructor symbols. The semantics is given by interpreting these constructors. In particular, the language of RLTL contains no fix-point operators.

2.1 Regular Expressions with Past

We first introduce a variation of regular expressions with a past operator to describe finite segments of infinite words. The basic elements are *basic expressions*, which are Boolean combinations of a finite set of elementary propositions, interpreted in a single state (or in a single action between two states). Each set of propositions (or equivalently, each basic expression) can also be interpreted as a symbol from a discrete alphabet Σ that includes **true** (for all propositions) and **false** for the empty set or propositions.

Syntax. The language of regular expressions for finite words is given by the following grammar:

$$\alpha ::= \alpha + \alpha \;\mid\; \alpha \,;\, \alpha \;\mid\; \alpha * \alpha \;\mid\; p \;\mid\; {}^{-}p$$

where p ranges over basic expressions. The intended interpretation of the operators $+$, ; and $*$ are the standard union, concatenation and binary Kleene-star. There is one expression of the form ${}^{-}p$ for each basic expression p. Informally, p indicates that the next "action", or input symbol, satisfies the basic expression p; similarly, ${}^{-}p$ establishes that the previous action or symbol satisfies p. Expressions of the form ${}^{-}p$ are called *basic past expressions.* Regular expressions are defined using an algebraic signature (symbols like p and ${}^{-}p$ are constants, and $+$, ; and $*$ are binary symbols).

Semantics. Our version of regular expressions describe *segments* of infinite words. An infinite word w is a map from ω into Σ (i.e., an element of Σ^{ω}). A *position* is a natural number. We use $w[i]$ for the symbol at position i in word w. If $w[i]$ satisfies the basic expression p, we write $w[i] \vDash p$, which is defined in the standard manner. Given an infinite word w and two positions i and j, the tuple (w, i, j) is called the *segment* of the word w between positions i and j. It is not necessarily the case that $i < j$ or even that $i \leq j$. Note that a segment consists of the whole word w with two tags, not just the sequence of symbols that occur between two positions. A *pointed word* is a pair (w, i) formed by a word w and a position i. The semantics of regular expressions is formally defined as a binary relation $\vDash_{\text{RE}}$ between segments and regular expressions. This semantics is defined inductively as follows. Given a basic expression p, regular expressions x, y and z, and a word w:

- $(w, i, j) \vDash_{\text{RE}} p$ whenever $w[i]$ satisfies p and $j = i + 1$.
- $(w, i, j) \vDash_{\text{RE}} x + y$ whenever either $(w, i, j) \vDash_{\text{RE}} x$ or $(w, i, j) \vDash_{\text{RE}} y$, or both.
- $(w, i, j) \vDash_{\text{RE}} x \,;\, y$ whenever for some k, $(w, i, k) \vDash_{\text{RE}} x$ and $(w, k, j) \vDash_{\text{RE}} y$.
- $(w, i, j) \vDash_{\text{RE}} x * y$ whenever either $(w, i, j) \vDash_{\text{RE}} y$, or for some sequence $(i_0 = i, i_1, \ldots i_m)$ and all $k \in \{0, .., m-1\}$ $(w, i_k, i_{k+1}) \vDash_{\text{RE}} x$ and $(w, i_m, j) \vDash_{\text{RE}} y$.
- $(w, i, j) \vDash_{\text{RE}} {}^{-}p$ whenever $w[j]$ satisfies p and $j = i - 1$.

One interesting expression using past is:

$$\mathit{notfirst} \stackrel{\text{def}}{=} {}^{-}\mathbf{true} \,;\, \mathbf{true}$$

which matches all segments of the form (w, i, i) that are not initial prefixes (i.e., $i \neq 0$). The semantics style used here is more conventional in logic than in automata theory, where regular expressions define sets of finite words. If one omits the basic past expressions, then a given regular expression x can be associated with a set of words $\mathcal{L}(x) \subseteq \Sigma^+$, by $v \in \mathcal{L}(x)$ precisely when for some $w \in \Sigma^\omega$, $(vw, 0, |v|) \vDash_{\text{RE}} x$. Following this alternative interpretation, our operators correspond to the classical ones and regular expressions define precisely regular sets of non-empty words.

The following theorem shows that only a finite bounded amount of information is needed to determine whether a segment satisfies a regular expression. All modified words that preserve all symbols within these bounds will contain a corresponding matching segment.

Theorem 1 (Relevant segment). *Let x be a regular expression and (w, i, j) a segment of an infinite word for which $(w, i, j) \vDash_{\text{RE}} x$. There exists bounds $A \leq i, j \leq B$ such that for every word prefix $v \in \Sigma^*$ and suffix $u \in \Sigma^\omega$, the infinite word $w' = vw[A, B]u$ satisfies:*

$$(w', |v| + (i - A), |v| + (j - A)) \vDash_{\text{RE}} x$$

Here, $w[A, B]$ is the finite word $w[A]w[A+1] \cdots w[B]$.

Expressions that do not include basic past expressions ^{-}p are called future-only regular expressions and satisfy strict bounds: $A = i \leq j = B$.

Past Expressions In order to justify that basic past expressions allow to express conditions on the input symbols previously seen we introduce a new operator for regular expressions, by lifting basic past expressions into a past operator $(\cdot)^{-1}$:

$$\begin{array}{ll} (p)^{-1} \stackrel{\text{def}}{=} {}^{-}p & (x + y)^{-1} \stackrel{\text{def}}{=} x^{-1} + y^{-1} \\ ({}^{-}p)^{-1} \stackrel{\text{def}}{=} p & (x \,;\, y)^{-1} \stackrel{\text{def}}{=} y^{-1} \,;\, x^{-1} \\ & (x * y)^{-1} \stackrel{\text{def}}{=} y^{-1} + y^{-1} \,;\, (x^{-1} * x^{-1}) \end{array}$$

This definition is inductive, so every past expression can be transformed into an equivalent expression without $(\cdot)^{-1}$ (but perhaps with one or more ^{-}p).

We now study some properties of past expressions, justifying that $(\cdot)^{-1}$ is a good definition for a past construct. First, $(\cdot)^{-1}$ is its own self-inverse:

Lemma 1. *Every regular expression x is semantically equivalent to $(x^{-1})^{-1}$.*

Semantic equivalence means that both expressions define precisely the same set of segments. Intuitively, matching an expression x with a sequence of events should correspond to matching the past expression x^{-1} with the *reversed* sequence of events. Since input words are infinite only on one end, this intuition is not justified simply by reversing the linear order of symbols in an infinite word. The following theorem formalizes this intuition of reverse by providing an evidence of a finite portion of input that can be chopped and reversed to match the inverse expression.

Theorem 2 (Inverse and reverse). *Let x be a regular expression and (w, i, j) a segment of an infinite word for which $(w, i, j) \vDash_{\text{RE}} x$. There exists bounds*

$A \leq i, j \leq B$ for which for all prefix $v \in \Sigma^*$ and suffix $u \in \Sigma^\omega$, the infinite word $w' = vw[A,B]^{rev}u$ satisfies:

$$(w', |v| + (B - j), |v| + (B - i)) \vDash_{\text{RE}} x^{-1}$$

Here, $w[A,B]^{rev}$ is the finite word $w[B]w[B-1] \cdots w[A]$, the reverse of $w[A,B]$.

Finally, the following theorem justifies that if an expression x matches some input, then the concatenation of x with its inverse x^{-1} must match the segment that goes back to the initial position.

Theorem 3 (Inverse and sequential). *Let x be a regular expression and (w, i, j) a segment for which $(w, i, j) \vDash_{\text{RE}} x$. Then $(w, i, i) \vDash_{\text{RE}} x \,;\, x^{-1}$*

2.2 Regular Linear Temporal Logic over Infinite Words

Regular Linear Temporal Logic expressions denote languages over infinite words. The key elements of RLTL are the two *power* operators that generalize many constructs from different linear-time logics and calculi.

Syntax The syntax of RLTL expressions is defined by the following grammar:

$$\varphi ::= \varnothing \;\big|\; \varphi \vee \varphi \;\big|\; \neg\varphi \;\big|\; \alpha \,;\, \varphi \;\big|\; \varphi|\alpha\rangle\!\rangle\varphi \;\big|\; \varphi\,|\alpha\rangle\varphi$$

where α ranges over regular expressions. Informally, $\vee$ stands for union of languages (disjunction in a logical interpretation), and $\neg$ represents language complement (or negation in a logical framework). The symbol ; stands for the conventional concatenation of an expression over finite words followed by an expression over infinite words. The operator $\varnothing$ represents the empty language (or *false* in a logical interpretation).

The operators $\varphi|\alpha\rangle\!\rangle\varphi$ and its weak version $\varphi\,|\alpha\rangle\varphi$ are the power operators. The power expressions $x|z\rangle\!\rangle y$ and $x\,|z\rangle y$ (read *x at z until y*, and, respectively, *x at z weak-until y*) are built from three elements: y (the *attempt*), x (the *obligation*) and z (the *delay*). Informally, for $x|z\rangle\!\rangle y$ to hold, either the attempt holds, or the obligation is met and the whole expression evaluates successfully after the delay; in particular, for a power expression to hold the obligation must be met after a finite number of delays. On the contrary, $x\,|z\rangle y$ does not require the obligation to be met after a finite number of delays. These two simple operators allow the construction of many conventional recursive definitions. For example, the strong until operator of LTL $x\,\mathcal{U}\,y$ can be seen as an attempt for y to hold, and otherwise an obligation for x to be met and a delay of a single step. Similarly, the ω-regular expression x^ω can be interpreted as a weak power operator having no possible escape and a trivially fulfilled obligation, with a delay indicated by x. Conventional ω-regular expressions can describe sophisticated delays with trivial obligations and escapes, while conventional LTL constructs allow complex obligations and escapes, but trivial one-step delays. Power operators can be seen as a generalization of both types of constructs. The completeness of RLTL with respect to ω-regular languages is easily derived from the expressibility of ω-regular expressions. In particular, Wolper's example is captured by $p|\textbf{true} \,;\, \textbf{true}\rangle\textbf{false}$.

Note that the signature of RLTL is, like that of RE, purely algebraic: the constructors $\vee$ and $;$ are binary, $\neg$ is unary, the power operators are ternary, and $\varnothing$ is a constant. Even though the symbol $;$ is overloaded we consider the signatures of RE and RLTL to be disjoint (the disambiguation is clear from the context). The *size* of an RLTL formula is defined as the total number of its symbols.

Semantics. The semantics of RLTL expressions is introduced as a binary relation $\models$ between expressions and pointed words, defined inductively. Given two RLTL expressions x and y, a regular expression z, and a word w:

- $(w, i) \models \varnothing$ never holds.
- $(w, i) \models x \vee y$ whenever either $(w, i) \models x$ or $(w, i) \models y$, or both.
- $(w, i) \models \neg x$ whenever $(w, i) \not\models x$, i.e., $(w, i) \models x$ does not hold.
- $(w, i) \models z \,;\, y$ whenever for some position k, $(w, i, k) \models_{\text{RE}} z$ and $(w, k) \models y$.
- $(w, i) \models x|z\rangle\!\rangle y$ whenever $(w, i) \models y$ or for some sequence $(i_0 = i, i_1, \ldots i_m)$ $(w, i_k, i_{k+1}) \models_{\text{RE}} z$ and $(w, i_k) \models x$, and $(w, i_m) \models y$
- $(w, i) \models x\,|z\rangle y$ whenever one of:
  (*i*) $(w, i) \models y$.
  (*ii*) for some sequence $(i_0 = i, i_1, \ldots i_m)$ $(w, i_k, i_{k+1}) \models_{\text{RE}} z$ and $(w, i_k) \models x$, and $(w, i_m) \models y$
  (*iii*) for some infinite sequence $(i_0 = i, i_1, \ldots)$ $(w, i_k, i_{k+1}) \models_{\text{RE}} z$ and $(w, i_k) \models x$

The semantics of $x|z\rangle\!\rangle y$ establishes that either the obligation y is satisfied at the point i of the evaluation, or there is a sequence of delays—each determined by z—after which y holds, and x holds after each individual delay. The semantics of $x\,|z\rangle y$ also allow the case where y never holds, but x always holds after any number of evaluations of z. As with regular expressions, languages can also be associated with RLTL expressions in the standard form: a word $w \in \Sigma^\omega$ is in the language of an expression x, denoted by $w \in \mathcal{L}(x)$, whenever $(w, 0) \models x$. The following lemma follows easily from the definitions:

Lemma 2. *For every RLTL expressions x and y and* RE *expression z:*
- *$x|z\rangle\!\rangle y$ is semantically equivalent to $y \vee (x \wedge z \,;\, x|z\rangle\!\rangle y)$.*
- *$x\,|z\rangle y$ is semantically equivalent to $y \vee (x \wedge z \,;\, x\,|z\rangle y)$.*

Again, semantic equivalence establishes that both expressions capture the same set of pointed words. Although the semantics of the power operators is not defined using fix point equations, it can be characterized by such equations, similar to the until operator in LTL. A power expression $x|z\rangle\!\rangle y$ is then characterized to a least fix point, while $x\,|z\rangle y$ is characterized by a greatest fix-point.

Remark 1. It should be noted that although RLTL includes complementation it does not allow the use of complementation within regular expressions. It is well-known [29] that emptiness of extended regular expressions (regular expressions with complementation) is not elementary decidable, so this separation is crucial to meet the desired complexity bounds. Similarly, adding intersection to regular expressions—the so-called semi-extended regular expresions—makes the satisfiability problem of similar logics EXPSPACE-complete [16].

The expression $\varnothing$ is needed in RLTL for technical purposes, as a basic case of induction; all other RLTL constructs need some preexisting RLTL expression. The expression $x \,;\, \neg\varnothing$ that appends sequentially the negation of empty (which corresponds to all pointed words) to a finite expression x serves as a *pump* of the finite models (segments) denoted by x to all infinite words that extend it. Pumping was a primitive operator in [18], for a simpler logic without negation. To ease the translation from LTL into RLTL presented in the next section we introduce some RLTL syntactic sugar:

$$\top \stackrel{\text{def}}{=} \neg\varnothing \qquad\qquad \mathit{first} \stackrel{\text{def}}{=} \neg(\mathit{notfirst} \,;\, \top)$$

3 LTL with Past

In this section we show how to translate LTL (past and future) into RLTL. Unlike in [18], the translation presented here does not require a previous transformation of LTL expressions into their negation normal form. The translation is purely linear: every LTL operator corresponds to an RLTL context with the same number of "holes".

We consider the following minimal definition of LTL, with an interpretation of atomic propositions as actions. Given a finite set of propositions *Prop* (with p a representative) called basic action expressions, the language of LTL expressions given by the following grammar:

$$\psi ::= p \;\big|\; \psi \vee \psi \;\big|\; \neg\psi \;\big|\; \bigcirc\psi \;\big|\; \psi\,\mathcal{U}\,\psi \;\big|\; \ominus\psi \;\big|\; \psi\,\mathcal{B}\,\psi$$

Here, $\neg$ and $\vee$ are the conventional Boolean expressions. The operators $\bigcirc$, and $\mathcal{U}$ are the future operators. Finally, $\ominus$ and $\mathcal{B}$ are called past operators.

Informal semantics LTL expressions define sets of pointed words. A pointed word (w, i) satisfies a basic action expression p if action p is taken from $w[i]$. Boolean operators are interpreted in the conventional way. An expression $\bigcirc x$ (read *next* x) indicates that in order for a pointed word (w, i) to satisfy $\bigcirc x$ its sub-expression x must hold when interpreted at the next position: $(w, i + 1)$. Similarly, $\ominus x$ (read *previous* x) holds at (w, i) if x holds at $(w, i - 1)$ or i is the initial position $(w, 0)$. The operator $x\,\mathcal{U}\,y$ (read x *until* y) holds at (w, i) whenever y holds at some future position and x holds in all positions in between. Similarly, $x\,\mathcal{B}\,y$ (read x *back-to* y) states that x holds in all previous positions (including the present) starting at the last position y held (or from the initial position 0 if y does not hold in any past position).

Semantics. The semantics of LTL expressions is defined inductively. Let p be a basic expression, and x and y be arbitrary LTL expressions.

- $(w,i) \vDash_{\mathrm{LTL}} p$ whenever $w[i]$ satisfies p.
- $(w,i) \vDash_{\mathrm{LTL}} x \vee y$ whenever $(w,i) \vDash_{\mathrm{LTL}} x$ or $(w,i) \vDash_{\mathrm{LTL}} y$.
- $(w,i) \vDash_{\mathrm{LTL}} \bigcirc x$ whenever $(w,i+1) \vDash_{\mathrm{LTL}} x$.
- $(w,i) \vDash_{\mathrm{LTL}} x\,\mathcal{U}\,y$ whenever for some $j \geq i$, $(w,j) \vDash_{\mathrm{LTL}} y$, and $(w,k) \vDash_{\mathrm{LTL}} x$ for all $i \leq k < j$.
- $(w,i) \vDash_{\mathrm{LTL}} \ominus x$ whenever either $i = 0$ or $(w,i-1) \vDash_{\mathrm{LTL}} x$.
- $(w,i) \vDash_{\mathrm{LTL}} x\,\mathcal{B}\,y$ whenever $(w,j) \vDash_{\mathrm{LTL}} x$ for all $j \leq i$, or for some $k \leq i$, $(w,k) \vDash_{\mathrm{LTL}} y$ and for all l within $k < l \leq i$, $(w,l) \vDash_{\mathrm{LTL}} x$.

We now show how to translate LTL expressions into RLTL. First, we define recursively a map between LTL expressions and RLTL expressions and then prove that each LTL expression is equivalent to its image.

$$\begin{aligned} f(p) &= p & f(\bigcirc x) &= \mathbf{true} \,;\, f(x)\\ f(x \vee y) &= f(x) \vee f(y) & f(x\,\mathcal{U}\,y) &= f(x)|\mathbf{true}\rangle\!\rangle f(y)\\ f(\neg x) &= \neg f(x) & f(\ominus x) &= \mathit{first} \vee {}^{-}\mathbf{true} \,;\, f(x)\\ & & f(x\,\mathcal{B}\,y) &= f(x)\,|{}^{-}\mathbf{true}\rangle f(y) \end{aligned}$$

The function $f(\cdot)$ is well-defined by construction. Since both LTL and RLTL expressions define sets of pointed words equivalence $\equiv$ is simply equality between two sets of pointed words.

Theorem 4. *Every LTL expression is equivalent to its RLTL translation.*

A practical specification language based on LTL offers more operators than the minimal set presented above, including other Boolean connectives and additional future operators like $\Box x$ (*always* x or *henceforth* x), $\Diamond x$ (read *eventually* x), $y\mathcal{R}x$ (y *release* x), etc. Additional past operators include $\circleddash x$ (a strong version of $\ominus x$), $\boxminus x$ (*has always been* x), $\diamondminus x$ (*once* x), $x\,\mathcal{S}\,y$ (read x *since* y), etc. All these can be defined in terms of the minimal set using the following LTL equivalences [20]:

$$\begin{aligned} \Diamond x &\equiv \mathbf{true}\,\mathcal{U}\,x & x\,\mathcal{R}\,y &\equiv \neg(\neg y\mathcal{U}\neg x)\\ \Box x &\equiv \neg\Diamond\neg x & x\,\mathcal{W}\,y &\equiv (x\,\mathcal{U}\,y) \vee \Box x\\ \boxminus x &\equiv x\,\mathcal{B}\,\mathbf{false} & \circleddash x &\equiv \neg\ominus\neg x\\ \diamondminus x &\equiv \neg\boxminus\neg x & x\,\mathcal{S}\,y &\equiv (x\,\mathcal{B}\,y) \wedge \diamondminus y \end{aligned}$$

Proceeding with these equivalences, however, does not generate an LTL expression (and consequently a RLTL expression) of linear size. In particular $\mathcal{W}$ and $\mathcal{S}$ duplicate one of their parameters. A formula with a stack of nested $\mathcal{W}$ or $\mathcal{S}$ symbols will generate an exponentially larger formula. On the contrary, the following direct translations into RLTL are linear:

$$f(x\,\mathcal{W}\,y) = f(x)\,|\mathbf{true}\rangle f(y) \qquad f(x\,\mathcal{S}\,y) = f(x)|{}^{-}\mathbf{true}\rangle\!\rangle f(y)$$

The translation function f only involves a linear expansion in the size of the original formula. Since checking satisfiability of linear temporal logic is PSPACE-hard [28] this translation implies a lower bound on the complexity of RLTL.

Proposition 1. *The problems of satisfiability and equivalence for regular linear temporal logic are PSPACE-hard.*

4 From RLTL to Automata

We now show how to translate an RLTL expression into a 2-way Alternating Parity Automaton of linear size that accepts precisely the same set of pointed words. As we justify below this implies that the problems of emptiness and model checking for RLTL are in PSPACE.

Preliminaries Let us first present the necessary definitions of non-deterministic automata on finite words and alternating automata on infinite words.

A 2-*way nondeterministic finite automaton* (2NFA) is a tuple $\mathcal{A}: \langle \Sigma, Q, q_0, \delta, F\rangle$ where Σ is the alphabet, Q a finite set of *states*, $q_0 \in Q$ the *initial state*, $\delta : Q \times \Sigma \to 2^{Q\times\{-1,0,1\}}$ the *transition function*, and $F \subseteq Q$ is the set of *final states*. Intuitively, the automaton works by reading an input tape. The transition function indicates the legal moves from a given state and character in the tape. A transition is a successor state and the direction of the head of the tape. Our version of 2NFA operates on segments of infinite words. A *run* of $\mathcal{A}$ on a word $w \in \Sigma^\omega$, starting at position i_0 and finishing at position i_n is a sequence of states and positions $i_0 q_0 i_1 q_1 i_1 \ldots i_n q_n$, where q_0 is the initial state of $\mathcal{A}$, and for all $k \in \{1, \ldots n\}$ we have that $(q_k, i_k - i_{k-1}) \in \delta(q_{k-1}, w[i_{k-1}])$. The run is called *accepting* if $q_n \in F$. A 2NFA accepts a segment (w, i, j) whenever there is an accepting run starting at i and finishing at j. There is an immediate correspondence to regular expressions:

Lemma 3. *Each regular expression can be translated into an equivalent* 2NFA.

In the proof of Lemma 3 the translation from regular expressions into 2NFA follows the standard bottom-up construction used for conventional regular expressions into NFA [11] for the operators ;, $*$ and $+$, and the basic expressions p. The translation of basic past expression ${}^-p$ is the automaton: $\langle \Sigma, \{q_0, q_1, q_2\}, q_0, \delta, \{q_2\}\rangle$ with

$$\delta(q_0, \mathbf{true}) = \{(q_1, -1)\}, \qquad \delta(q_1, p) = \{(q_2, 0)\}, \qquad \delta(q_2, true) = \{\},$$

depicted graphically:

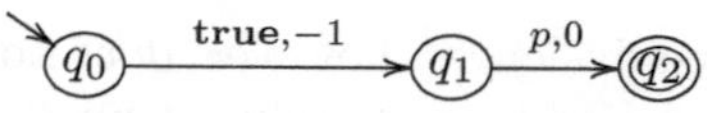

This translation clearly coincides with the semantics of ${}^-p$. The number of states of the 2NFA obtained is linear in the size of the regular expression.

We define now alternating automata on infinite-words. For a finite set $\mathcal{X}$ of variables, let $\mathcal{B}^+(\mathcal{X})$ be the set of *positive Boolean formulas* over $\mathcal{X}$, i.e., the smallest set such that $\mathcal{X} \subseteq \mathcal{B}^+(\mathcal{X})$, $\mathbf{true}, \mathbf{false} \in \mathcal{B}^+(\mathcal{X})$, and $\varphi, \psi \in \mathcal{B}^+(\mathcal{X})$ implies $\varphi \wedge \psi \in \mathcal{B}^+(\mathcal{X})$ and $\varphi \vee \psi \in \mathcal{B}^+(\mathcal{X})$. We say that a set $Y \subseteq \mathcal{X}$ *satisfies* (or is a *model* of) a formula $\varphi \in \mathcal{B}^+(\mathcal{X})$ iff φ evaluates to **true** when the variables in Y are assigned to **true** and the members of $\mathcal{X} \backslash Y$ are assigned to **false**. A model is called *minimal* if none of its proper subsets is a model. For example, $\{q_1, q_3\}$ as well as $\{q_2, q_3\}$ are minimal models of the formula $(q_1 \vee q_2) \wedge q_3$. The dual of a formula $\theta \in \mathcal{B}^+(\mathcal{X})$ is the formula $\overline{\theta} \in \mathcal{B}^+(\mathcal{X})$ obtained by exchanging **true** and **false**, and $\wedge$ and $\vee$.

A *2-way Alternating Parity Automaton on Words* (2APW) is a tuple $\mathcal{A}$: $\langle \Sigma, Q, q_0, \delta, F \rangle$ where Σ, Q are as for 2NFA. The transition function δ yields a positive Boolean combination of successor states, together with a direction: $\delta : Q \times \Sigma \rightarrow \mathcal{B}^+(Q \times \{-1, 0, 1\})$. The acceptance condition F that we use here is the *parity* acceptance condition:

$$F : Q \rightarrow \{0 \ldots k\}.$$

The set $\{0 \ldots k\}$ is called the set of colors. A 2APW operates on infinite words: a *run* over an infinite word $w \in \Sigma^\omega$ is a directed graph (V, E) such that $V \subseteq Q \times \mathbb{N}$ satisfying the following properties:

1. $(q_0, 0)$ is in V, and it is called the initial vertex. It may have no predecessor.
2. every non-initial vertex has a predecessor. For every (q, l) distinct from $(q_0, 0)$

$$\{(q', l') \in V \mid (q', l') \rightarrow_E (q, l)\} \neq \emptyset$$

3. the successors of every node form a minimal model for δ, i.e., for every vertex (q, l), the set $\{(q', l' - l) \mid (q, l) \rightarrow_E (q', l')\}$ is a minimal model of $\delta(q, w[l])$.

The set of vertices that occurs infinitely often in an infinite path π is denoted $\mathit{inf}(\pi)$. A run (V, E) is *accepting* according to F if every maximal finite path ends in a vertex (q, l) with $\delta(q, w[l]) = \textbf{true}$ and every infinite path π accepts the parity condition:

$$\mathit{max}\{i \mid i = F(q) \text{ for some } q \text{ in } \mathit{inf}(\pi)\} \text{ is even.}$$

The language $\mathcal{L}(\mathcal{A})$ of a 2APW $\mathcal{A}$ is determined by all strings for which an accepting run of $\mathcal{A}$ exists. We measure the *size* of a 2APW in terms of its number of states and its number of colors.

4.1 Complementing 2APW

Every 2APW $\mathcal{A}$ can be easily complemented into another 2APW $\overline{\mathcal{A}}$ of the same size. Let n be the number of states of $\mathcal{A}$. The key observation is that $\mathcal{A}$ can be transformed into an equivalent automaton with a color set $\{0 \ldots k\}$ satisfying $k \leq n + 1$, by only changing the acceptance condition.

Let F be the acceptance condition for $\mathcal{A}$, and let F' be another acceptance condition such that,

Acc1. for every two nodes p and q, if $F(p) \leq F(q)$ then $F'(p) \leq F'(q)$.
Acc2. for every node p, $F(p)$ is even if and only if $F'(p)$ is even.

Then, given a path π of a run of $\mathcal{A}$, if q is a node occurring infinitely often with maximum color according to F, then q is also maximum according to F'.

Moreover, $F(q)$ is even if and only if $F'(q)$ is even. Therefore, every run of $\mathcal{A}$ is accepting according to F if and only if it is also accepting according to F'.

Consequently, the following *gap reduction* procedure can be applied. Assume for some color i there is no node q with $F(q) = i$, but for some $j < i$ and for some $k > i$, there are such nodes $F(q_j) = j$ and $F(q_k) = k$. Color i is called a gap in F. The following F' is equivalent to F according to the conditions (Acc1) and (Acc2) described above:

$$F'(q) = \begin{cases} F(q) & \text{if } F(q) < i \\ F(q) - 2 & \text{if } F(q) > i \end{cases}$$

Similarly, if for no node q, $F(q) = 0$ or $F(q) = 1$, then an equivalent F' can be defined as $F'(q) = F(q) - 2$ for all q. By applying these transformations until no gap exists we ensure that all assigned colors are consecutive, and starting either at 0 or at 1. We use F^* to denote the accepting condition obtained after repeatedly applying the gap reduction procedure. It follows that the maximum color assigned by F^* can be at most $n + 1$. This property ensures the following lemma.

Lemma 4. *Every* 2APW *can be complemented into another* 2APW *of the same number of states and with highest color at most* $n + 1$.

Proof (Sketch). Let $\mathcal{A}$ be a 2APW. The following 2APW accepts the complement language:

$$\overline{\mathcal{A}} : \langle \Sigma, Q, q_0, \overline{\delta}, \overline{F}^* \rangle$$

where $\overline{\delta}(q, a)$ is the dual of the transition $\delta(q, a)$ and $\overline{F}(q) = F(q)+1$, with $\overline{F}^*$ be the gap reduced version of $\overline{F}$. The maximum color in $\overline{F}^*$ is guaranteed to be at most $n+1$ (also at most 1 plus the number of colors in F^*). It is well-known [21] that the dualization of the transition function and acceptance condition satisfies that $\mathcal{L}(\mathcal{A}) = \Sigma^\omega \setminus \mathcal{L}(\overline{\mathcal{A}})$. □

4.2 Translating from RLTL to 2APW

We are now ready to formulate the main theorem of this section:

Theorem 5. *For every RLTL formula* φ*, there is a* 2APW *with size linear in the size of* φ *that accepts precisely the same set of* ω*-words.*

The proof proceeds according to the following translation from RLTL into 2APW. The procedure works bottom-up the parse tree of the RLTL expression φ, building the resulting automaton using the subexpressions' automata as components. Our translation does not require an upfront transformation into negation normal form. On the contrary, it is truly compositional in a bottom-up fashion. The automaton for an expression is built from the automata of its subexpressions with all the structure preserved.

For RLTL expressions x, y and a regular expression z let $\mathcal{A}_x : \langle \Sigma, Q^x, q^x_o, \delta^x, F^x \rangle$ and $\mathcal{A}_y : \langle \Sigma, Q^y, q^y_o, \delta^y, F^y \rangle$ be two 2APW automata equivalent to x and y, and let $\mathcal{A}_z : \langle \Sigma, Q^z, q_o^z, \delta^z, F^z \rangle$ be a 2NFA for z. Without loss of generality, we assume that their state spaces are disjoint, and that the coloring is minimal ($F^x = (F^x)^*$ and $F^y = (F^y)^*$) . We consider the different operators of RLTL:

- **Empty**: The automaton for $\varnothing$ is $\mathcal{A}_\varnothing : \langle \Sigma, \{q_0\}, q_0, \delta, F \rangle$ with $\delta(q_0, a) =$ **false** for every a, and $F(q_0) = 0$ (any number works here). Clearly, the language of $\mathcal{A}_\varnothing$ is empty.
- **Disjunction**: The automaton for $x \vee y$ is:

$$\mathcal{A}_{x \vee y} \; : \; \langle \Sigma, Q^x \cup Q^y, q_0, \delta, F \rangle$$

where q_0 is a fresh new state. The transition function is defined as

$$\delta(q, a) = \begin{cases} \delta^x(q, a) & \text{if } q \in Q^x \\ \delta^y(q, a) & \text{if } q \in Q^y \end{cases} \qquad \delta(q_0, a) = \delta^x(q_0^x, a) \vee \delta^y(q_0^y, a).$$

For F, we consider the union of the characteristic graph of the function:

$$F(q) = \begin{cases} F^x(q) & \text{if } q \text{ is in } Q^x \\ F^y(q) & \text{if } q \text{ is in } Q^y \\ min\{F^x(\cdot), F^y(\cdot)\} & \text{if } q = q_0 \end{cases}$$

Thus, from the fresh initial state q_0, $\mathcal{A}_{x \vee y}$ chooses non-deterministically one of the successor states of $\mathcal{A}_x$'s or $\mathcal{A}_y$'s initial state. Clearly, the accepted language is the union of the languages of x and y.
- **Complementation**: The automaton for $\neg x$ is:

$$\mathcal{A}_{\neg x} \; : \; \langle \Sigma, Q^x, q_0^x, \overline{\delta}, \overline{F^x}^* \rangle$$

where $\overline{\delta}$ and $\overline{F^x}^*$ is as defined in Lemma 4, which guarantees that the language for $\mathcal{A}_{\neg x}$ is the complement of that of $\mathcal{A}_x$.
- **Concatenation**: The automaton for $z \,;\, x$ is:

$$\mathcal{A}_{z;x} \; : \; \langle \Sigma, Q^z \cup Q^x, q_0^z, \delta, F^x \rangle$$

where δ is defined, for $q \in Q^z$ as:

$$\delta(q, a) = \begin{cases} \bigvee\{\delta^z(q, a)\} & \text{if } \delta^z(q, a) \cap F^z = \emptyset \\ \bigvee\{\delta^z(q, a)\} \vee q_0^x & \text{if } \delta^z(q, a) \cap F^z \neq \emptyset \end{cases}$$

and, for $q \in Q^x$ as $\delta(q, a) = \delta^x(q, a)$. Recall that $\mathcal{A}_z$ is a 2NFA automaton. The accepting condition is $F(q) = F^x(q)$ for q in Q^x, and $F(q) = 1$ for q in Q^z ensuring that looping forever in z is not a satisfying path. Whenever $\mathcal{A}_z$ can non-deterministically choose a successor that is a final state, it can also move to the initial state of $\mathcal{A}_x$. Thus, the accepted language is indeed the concatenation.

- **Power**: The automaton for $x\,|\,z\rangle\!\rangle y$ is:

$$\mathcal{A}_{x|z\rangle\!\rangle y} \;:\; \langle \Sigma, Q^z \cup Q^x \cup Q^y \cup \{q_0\}, q_0, \delta, F\rangle$$

  where the initial state q_0 is a fresh state. The transition function δ is defined as follows. The a successor of q_0 is:

$$\delta(q_0, a) = \delta^y(q_0^y, a) \vee (\delta^x(q_0^x, a) \wedge \bigvee\{\delta^z(q_0^z, a)\})$$

  The successor of Q^x and Q^y are defined as in $\mathcal{A}_x$ and $\mathcal{A}_y$, i.e., $\delta^x(q,a)$ for $q \in Q^x$, $\delta^y(q,a)$ for $q \in Q^y$. For $q \in Q_z$

$$\delta(q,a) = \begin{cases} \bigvee\{\delta^z(q,a)\} & \text{if } \delta^z(q,a) \cap F^z = \emptyset \\ \bigvee\{\delta^z(q,a)\} \vee q_0 & \text{if } \delta^z(q,a) \cap F^z \neq \emptyset \end{cases}$$

  The construction follows precisely the equivalence $x|z\rangle\!\rangle y \equiv y \vee (x \wedge z; x|z\rangle\!\rangle y)$ established in Lemma 2 and the construction for disjunction, conjunction, and concatenation. Finally, the looping in z is prevented by assigning $F(q) = 1$ whenever q is in Q^z, and otherwise $F(q) = F^x(q)$ or $F(q) = F^y(q)$ whenever q is in Q^x (resp. Q^y). Finally, $F(q_0) = 1$ to ensure that an infinite path that traverses only states from Q^z and q_0 is not accepting.
- **Weak power**: The automaton for $x\,|z\rangle y$ is:

$$\mathcal{A}_{x|z\rangle y} \;:\; \langle \Sigma, Q^z \cup Q^x \cup Q^y \cup \{q_0\}, q_0, \delta, F\rangle$$

  where q_0 and δ are like for Power. The states in Q^y and Q^x are mapped to the same colors, as before. Now, $F(q_0) = 2$, and $F(q) = 1$ for all q in Q^z. Then, a path that accepts z and visits q_0 infinitely often is accepting.

Complexity. From Lemma 3 every regular expression can be translated into a 2NFA with only a linear blow-up in size. Each of the steps in the procedure for translating RLTL expressions into a 2APW add at most one extra state. Therefore, the number of states in the produced automaton is at most the number of symbols in the original expression. For the colors, the only construct that increases the number of colors is complementation. The rest of the constructs use constant colors (1 and 2), or the union of sets of colors. Therefore, the highest color in a generated automaton corresponds to the largest number of nested negations $\neg$ in the starting expression.

Second, the structure of the sub-automata is preserved in all stages. We do not use automata constructions like product or subset constructions; instead only new states and transitions are added. For the accepting condition, all operations preserve the accepting condition of the automata corresponding to the sub-expression, except for complementation. Observe also how the automaton for $\neg\neg x$ is exactly the same automaton as for x.

Given a 2APW with n states and k colors one can generate on-the-fly successor states and final states of an equivalent 1-way nondeterministic Büchi automaton on words (NBW) with $2^{O((nk)^2)}$ states [5]. Since emptiness of NBW can be checked in NLOGSPACE via reachability [30], it follows that emptiness of 2APW is in PSPACE. Hence, the satisfiability, equivalence and model checking problems for RLTL are in PSPACE. Together with Proposition 1:

Corollary 1. *Checking satisfiability of an RLTL formula is PSPACE-complete.*

Using clever manipulation of the automata during the bottom-up construction one can show that only 3 colors are needed, leading to a better translation into NBW than the one presented in this paper, using only $2^{O(n^2)}$ states. The detailed explanation of this advanced translation is out of the scope of this paper.

5 Conclusion and Future Work

Amir Pnueli postulated in [24]: *"In order to perform compositional specification and verification, it is convenient to use the past operators but necessary to have the full power of ETL"*. In this paper, we have introduced *regular linear temporal logic* (RLTL) with past operators that exactly fulfills Pnueli's requirements, while at the same time keeping satisfiability and model checking in the same complexity class as for LTL (PSPACE). RLTL (with past) has a finite set of temporal operators giving it a temporal logic flavor and allows the integration of regular expressions. Moreover, we have introduced a novel translation of RLTL formulas into corresponding automata, which may be of its own interest, as it is truly compositional (bottom-up).

It should be stressed that a practically relevant specification language needs a variety of different operators as well as macros to support engineers in the complex job of specifying requirements. In fact, together with industrial partners, the second author was involved in the development of the language SALT [2] which acts as a high-level specification language offering a variety of different constructs while at the same time allowing a translation to LTL. However, the lack of regular expressions and past operators makes such a translation difficult, error prone, and leads to automata that do not reflect the structure of the original formula and might be larger than necessary. It is therefore essential to have a core logic that is expressive and allows a simple, verifiable translation to automata and allows a simple translation from high-level languages like SALT. We consider RLTL to exactly meet this goal. As future work, it remains to build corresponding satisfiability and model checking tools to push RLTL into industrial applications. Also, some of the operators in PSL can already be mapped into RLTL. For example, "*whenever α is matched p must be true*" can be expressed as $\neg(\alpha\ ;\neg p)$. The blow-up in complexity in PSL (EXPSPACE) with respect to RLTL (PSPACE) can then fully blamed to the availability of semi-extended regular expressions. Moreover, the sequential connective in PSL that connects a temporal operator with a regular expression requiring the overlap of the last symbol can be easily expressed in RLTL as $(z\ ;\ \mathbf{true}^{-1}\ ;\ x)$, which coincides with the PSL semantics, for future regular expressions. Future study include other PSL operators like bounded iteration and abort.

Another interesting line of future research is to study symbolic model-checking algorithms for RLTL.

Acknowledgements. We wish to thank the anonymous reviewers for their helpful comments and suggestions.

References

1. Barringer, H., Kuiper, R., Pnueli, A.: A really abstract concurrent model and its temporal logic. In: POPL 1986 (1986)
2. Bauer, A., Leucker, M., Streit, J.: SALT—structured assertion language for temporal logic. In: Liu, Z., He, J. (eds.) ICFEM 2006. LNCS, vol. 4260, pp. 757–775. Springer, Heidelberg (2006)
3. Beer, I., Ben-David, S., Eisner, C., Fisman, D., Gringauze, A., Rodeh, Y.: The temporal logic Sugar. In: Berry, G., Comon, H., Finkel, A. (eds.) CAV 2001. LNCS, vol. 2102, p. 363. Springer, Heidelberg (2001)
4. Bustan, D., Flaisher, A., Grumberg, O., Kupferman, O., Vardi, M.Y.: Regular vacuity. In: Borrione, D., Paul, W. (eds.) CHARME 2005. LNCS, vol. 3725, pp. 191–206. Springer, Heidelberg (2005)
5. Dax, C., Klaedtke, F.: Alternation elimination by complementation. In: Cervesato, I., Veith, H., Voronkov, A. (eds.) LPAR 2008. LNCS (LNAI), vol. 5330, pp. 214–229. Springer, Heidelberg (2008)
6. Emerson, A., Clarke, E.: Characterizing correctness properties of parallel programs using fixpoints. In: de Bakker, J.W., van Leeuwen, J. (eds.) ICALP 1980. LNCS, vol. 85. Springer, Heidelberg (1980)
7. Fisman, D., Eisner, C., Havlicek, J.: Formal syntax and Semantics of PSL: Appendix B of Accellera Property Language Reference Manual, Version 1.1. (2004)
8. Gabbay, D., Pnueli, A., Shelah, S., Stavi, J.: On the temporal basis of fairness. In: POPL 1980 (1980)
9. Harel, D., Peleg, D.: Process logic with regular formulas. TCS 38, 307–322 (1985)
10. Henriksen, J., Thiagarajan, P.S.: Dynamic linear time temporal logic. Annals of Pure and Applied Logic 96(1-3), 187–207 (1999)
11. Hopcroft, J., Ullman, J.: Introduction to automata theory, languages and computation. Addison-Wesley, Reading (1979)
12. Kamp, H.: Tense Logic and the Theory of Linear Order. PhD thesis, UCLA (1968)
13. Kozen, D.: Results on the propositional μ-calculus. In: Nielsen, M., Schmidt, E.M. (eds.) ICALP 1982. LNCS, vol. 140. Springer, Heidelberg (1982)
14. Kupferman, O., Piterman, N., Vardi, M.: Extended temporal logic revisited. In: Larsen, K.G., Nielsen, M. (eds.) CONCUR 2001. LNCS, vol. 2154, p. 519. Springer, Heidelberg (2001)
15. Lange, M.: Weak automata for the linear time μ-calculus. In: Cousot, R. (ed.) VMCAI 2005. LNCS, vol. 3385, pp. 267–281. Springer, Heidelberg (2005)
16. Lange, M.: Linear time logics around PSL: Complexity, expressiveness, and a little bit of succinctness. In: Caires, L., Vasconcelos, V.T. (eds.) CONCUR 2007. LNCS, vol. 4703, pp. 90–104. Springer, Heidelberg (2007)
17. Laroussinie, F., Markey, N., Schnoebelen, Ph.: Temporal logic with forgettable past. In: LICS 2002 (2002)
18. Leucker, M., Sánchez, C.: Regular linear temporal logic. In: Jones, C.B., Liu, Z., Woodcock, J. (eds.) ICTAC 2007. LNCS, vol. 4711, pp. 291–305. Springer, Heidelberg (2007)

19. Lichtenstein, O., Pnueli, A., Zuck, L.: The glory of the past. In: Parikh, R. (ed.) Logic of Programs 1985. LNCS, vol. 193. Springer, Heidelberg (1985)
20. Manna, Z., Pnueli, A.: Temporal Verif. of Reactive Systems. Springer, Heidelberg (1995)
21. Muller, D., Schupp, P.: Altenating automata on infinite trees. TCS 54, 267–276 (1987)
22. Müller-Olm, M.: A modal fixpoint logic with chop. In: Meinel, C., Tison, S. (eds.) STACS 1999. LNCS, vol. 1563, pp. 510–520. Springer, Heidelberg (1999)
23. Pnueli, A.: The temporal logic of programs. In: FOCS 1977 (1977)
24. Pnueli, A.: In transition from global to modular temporal reasoning about programs. In: Logics and models of concurrent systems, NATO ASI F-13. Springer, Heidelberg (1985)
25. Pnueli, A.: Applications of temporal logic to the specification and verification of reactive systems–a survey of current trends. In: Current Trends in Concurrency. LNCS, vol. 224. Springer, Heidelberg (1986)
26. Pnueli, A., Zaks, A.: PSL model checking and run-time verification via testers. In: Misra, J., Nipkow, T., Sekerinski, E. (eds.) FM 2006. LNCS, vol. 4085, pp. 573–586. Springer, Heidelberg (2006)
27. Schnoebelen, Ph.: The complexity of temporal logic model checking. In: AiML 2002 (2002)
28. Sistla, A.P., Clarke, E.: The complexity of propositional linear termporal logics. JACM 32(3), 733–749 (1985)
29. Stockmeyer, L.: The Computational Complexity of Word Problems. PhD thesis. MIT (1974)
30. Vardi, M.: An automata-theoretic approach to linear temporal logic. In: Moller, F., Birtwistle, G. (eds.) Logics for Concurrency. LNCS, vol. 1043. Springer, Heidelberg (1996)
31. Vardi, M., Wolper, P.: Reasoning about infinite computations. Inf. Comp. 115, 1–37 (1994)
32. Wolper, P.: Temporal logic can be more expressive. Info.& Control 56, 72–99 (1983)

Model-Checking In-Lined Reference Monitors*

Meera Sridhar and Kevin W. Hamlen

The University of Texas at Dallas
800 W. Campbell Rd., Richardson, TX 75080, USA
meera.sridhar@student.utdallas.edu, hamlen@utdallas.edu
http://www.cs.utdallas.edu

Abstract. A technique for elegantly expressing In-lined Reference Monitor (IRM) certification as model-checking is presented and implemented. In-lined Reference Monitors (IRM's) enforce software security policies by in-lining dynamic security guards into untrusted binary code. Certifying IRM systems provide strong formal guarantees for such systems by verifying that the instrumented code produced by the IRM system satisfies the original policy. Expressing this certification step as model-checking allows well-established model-checking technologies to be applied to this often difficult certification task. The technique is demonstrated through the enforcement and certification of a URL anti-redirection policy for ActionScript web applets.

1 Introduction

In-Lined Reference Monitors (IRM's) [17] enforce safety policies by injecting runtime security guards directly into untrusted binaries. The guards test whether an impending operation constitutes a policy violation. If so, corrective action is taken to prevent the violation, such as premature termination. The result is *self-monitoring* code that can be safely executed without external monitoring.

IRM's dynamically observe security-relevant events exhibited by the untrusted code they monitor and maintain persistent internal state between these observations, enabling them to accept or reject based on the *history* of events observed. This allows them to enforce powerful security policies, such as safety policies, that are not precisely enforceable by any purely static analysis [14]. Additionally, IRM's afford code consumers the flexibility of specifying or modifying the security policy after receiving the code, whereas purely static analyses typically require the security policy to be known by the code producer.

Certifying IRM systems [1,13] verify that IRM's generated by a binary *rewriter* are policy-adherent. Since the binary rewriters that in-line security guards into untrusted code can be large and complex, a separate verifier is useful for shifting this complexity out of the trusted computing base. Since the verifier does not perform any code generation, it is typically smaller and less subject to change than a rewriter, and therefore constitutes a more acceptable trusted component. Past work has implemented IRM certifiers using type-checking [13] and contracts [1].

* This research was supported by AFOSR YIP award number FA9550-08-1-0044.

G. Barthe and M. Hermenegildo (Eds.): VMCAI 2010, LNCS 5944, pp. 312–327, 2010.

Model-checking is an extremely powerful software verification paradigm that is useful for verifying properties that are more complex than those typically expressible by type-systems and more semantically flexible and abstract than those typically encoded by contracts. Yet to our knowledge, model-checking has not yet been applied to verify IRM's. In this paper we describe and implement a technique for doing so. The work's main contributions are as follows:

- We present the design and implementation of a prototype IRM model-checking framework for ActionScript bytecode.
- Our design centers around a novel approach for constructing a *state abstraction lattice* from a *security automaton* [2], for precise yet tractable abstract interpretation of IRM code.
- Rigorous proofs of soundness and convergence are formulated for our system using Cousot's abstract interpretation framework [6].
- The feasibility of our technique is demonstrated by enforcing a URL anti-redirection policy for ActionScript bytecode programs.

The rest of the paper is organized as follows. Section 2 discusses related work. Section 3 gives an overview of our IRM framework, including an operational semantics and the abstract interpretation algorithm. Section 4 provides a formal soundness proof for our algorithm and a proof of fixed point convergence for the abstract machine. Section 5 discusses the details of our implementation of the system for ActionScript bytecode. Finally, Sect. 6 suggests future work.

2 Related Work

In-lined Reference Monitors were first formalized by Erlingsson and Schneider in the development of the PoET/PSLang/SASI systems [10,17], which implement IRM's for Java bytecode and GNU assembly code. Subsequently, a variety of IRM implementations have been developed. The Java-MOP system [5] allows policy-writers to choose from a sizable collection of formal policy specification languages, including LTL. Mobile [13] targets Microsoft .NET bytecode by transforming untrusted CIL binaries into well-typed Mobile code (a subset of CIL). ConSpec [1] restricts IRM-injected code to effect-free operations, which allows a static analysis to verify that a rewritten program does not violate the intended policy. Finally, SPoX [12] rewrites Java bytecode programs to satisfy declarative, Aspect-Oriented security policies.

To our knowledge, ConSpec [1] and Mobile [13] are the only IRM systems to yet implement automatic certification. The ConSpec verifier performs a static analysis to verify that pre-specified guard code appears at each security-relevant code point; the guard code itself is trusted. Mobile implements a more general certification algorithm by type-checking the resulting Mobile code. While type-checking has the advantage of being light-weight, it comes at the expense of limited computational power. For instance, Mobile cannot enforce certain dataflow-sensitive security policies since its type-checking algorithm is strictly control-flow based. While the security policies described by these systems are declarative and therefore amenable to a more general verifier, both use a verifier tailored to a specific rewriting strategy.

Related research on general model-checking is vast, but to our knowledge no past work has applied model-checking to the IRM verification problem. A majority of model-checking research has focused on detecting deadlock and assertion violation properties of source code. For example, Java PathFinder (JPF) [15] and Moonwalker [16] verify properties of Java and .NET source programs, respectively. Model-checking of binary code is useful in situations where the code consumer may not have access to source code. For example, CodeSurfer/x86 and WPDS++ have been used to extract and check models for x86 binary programs [3]. In prior work [9], we have presented a general model-checking system for ActionScript bytecode implemented using co-logic programming [19]. This paper extends that work by introducing new formalisms specific to the verification of safety policies enforced by IRM's.

ActionScript is a binary virtual machine language by Adobe Systems similar to Java bytecode. It is important as a general web scripting language and is widely used in portable web ads, online games, streaming media, and interactive webpage animations. The ActionScript VM includes standard object-level encapsulation as well as a sandboxing model. While useful, these protections are limited to enforcing a restricted class of low-level, coarse-grained security policies. Several past malware attacks have used ActionScript as a vehicle within the past few years, including several virus families [11], as well as an emerging class of malicious URL-redirection attacks. URL-redirection attacks allow an embedded webpage widget (possibly served by a third party) to redirect the user's browser to a different website. These attacks are particularly problematic in the context of web advertising, since in these scenarios the security policy is typically a fusion of constraints prescribed by multiple independent parties, such as ad distributors and web hosts, who lack access to the applet source code. We apply our certified IRM framework to protect against such attacks in Sect. 5.

3 System Overview

3.1 IRM Framework

Figure 1 depicts the core of our IRM framework, consisting of a collection of rewriters that automatically transform untrusted ActionScript bytecode into self-monitoring ActionScript bytecode, along with a model-checking verifier that certifies the resulting IRM against the original security policy.[1] The untrusted code is obtained from *ShockWave Flash* (SWF) binary archives, which package ActionScript code with related data such as images and sound. Once the raw bytecode is extracted, a Definite Clause Grammar (DCG) [18] parser converts it to an annotated abstract syntax tree (AST) for easy analysis and manipulation. We implemented this parser in Prolog so that the same code functions as a code generator due to the reversible nature of Prolog predicates [9]. Modified AST's

[1] The IRM framework includes a rewriter per security policy class.

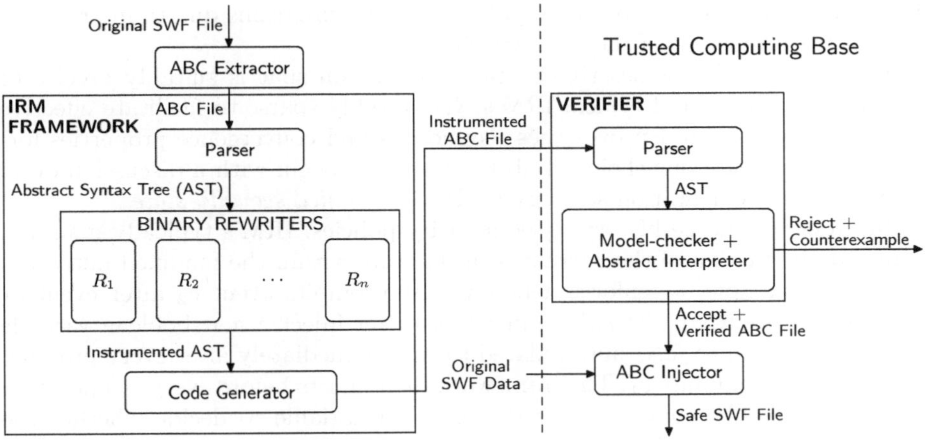

Fig. 1. Certifying ActionScript IRM architecture

produced by the rewriter are thereby transformed back into bytecode, and the ABC Injector reconstructs a modified SWF file by packaging the new code with the original data.

In practice it is usually infeasible to develop only one binary rewriter that can efficiently enforce all desired policies for all untrusted applications. Our IRM framework therefore actually consists of a collection of rewriters that have been tailored to different policy classes and rewriting strategies, and that are subject to change as new policies and runtime efficiency constraints arise. All rewriters remain untrusted since their output is certified by a single, trusted verifier. The verifier is more general than the rewriters, and therefore less subject to change. This results in a significantly smaller trusted computing base than if all rewriters were trusted.

The rewriter implementation is discussed in Sect. 5; the remainder of this section discusses the verifier.

3.2 Verifier Overview

The verifier is an abstract machine that non-deterministically explores all control-flow paths of untrusted code, inferring an abstract state for each code point. This process continues, bottom-up, until it converges to a (least) fixed point. The model-checker then verifies that each inferred abstract state is policy-satisfying.

A standard challenge in implementing such an abstract interpreter is to choose an expressive yet tractable language of state abstractions for the abstract machine to consider. A highly expressive state abstraction language allows very precise reasoning about untrusted code, but might cause the iteration process to converge slowly or not at all, making verification infeasible in practice. In contrast, a less expressive language affords faster convergence, but might result in conservative rejection of many policy-adherent programs due to information lost by the coarseness of the abstraction.

In what follows, we describe a state abstraction that is suitably precise to facilitate verification of typical IRM's, yet suitably sparse to facilitate effective convergence. Section 4 proves these soundness and convergence properties formally. To motivate our choice of abstractions, we begin with a discussion of an important implementation strategy for IRM's—*reified security state.*

In order to enforce history-based security policies, IRM's typically maintain a reified abstraction of the current security state within the modified untrusted code. For example, to enforce a policy that prohibits event e_2 after event e_1 has already occurred, the IRM framework might inject a new boolean variable that is initialized to *false* and updated to *true* immediately after every program operation that exhibits e_1. The framework then injects before every e_2 operation new code that dynamically tests this injected variable to decide whether the impending operation should be permitted.

When security policies are expressed as security automata [2], this reification strategy can be generalized as an integer variable that tracks the current state of the automaton. Security automata encode security policies as Büchi automata that accept the language of policy-satisfying event sequences. Formally, a deterministic security automaton $A = (Q, \Sigma, q_0, \delta)$ can be expressed as a set of states Q, an alphabet of security-relevant events Σ, a start state $q_0 \in Q$, and a transition relation $\delta : Q \times \Sigma \to Q$. For the purpose of this paper, we assume that Q is finite.[2] The automaton accepts all finite or infinite sequences for which δ has transitions. Security automata therefore accept policies that are prefix-closed. That is, to prove that infinite executions of an untrusted program satisfy such a policy, it suffices to prove that every finite execution prefix satisfies the policy. We therefore define the set of finite prefixes $\mathcal{P}$ of the security policy denoted by a deterministic security automaton as follows.

Definition 1 (Security Policy). *Let $A = (Q, \Sigma, q_0, \delta)$ be a deterministic security automaton. The* security policy *$\mathcal{P}_A$ for automaton A is defined by $\mathcal{P}_A = Res_A(Q)$, where notation $Res_A(q)$ denotes the* residual *[8] of state q in automaton A—that is, the set of finite sequences that cause the automaton to arrive in state q—and we lift Res_A to sets of states via $Res_A(Q) = \cup_{q \in Q} Res_A(q)$. When automaton A is unambiguous, we will omit subscript A, writing $\mathcal{P} = Res(Q)$.*

Our verifier accepts as input security policies expressed as security automata and IRM's that implement reified security state as integer automaton states. To verify that the untrusted code accurately maintains these state variables to track the runtime security state, our abstract states include an *abstract trace* and *abstract program variable values* defined in terms of this automaton.

Definition 2 (Abstract Traces). *The language SS of* abstract traces *is $SS = \{(Res(Q_0), \tau) \mid Q_0 \subseteq Q, \tau \in \Sigma^*, |\tau| \leq k\} \cup \{\top_{SS}\}$ where $\top_{SS} = \Sigma^*$. Abstract traces are ordered by subset relation $\subseteq$, forming the lattice $(SS, \subseteq)$.*

[2] Any actual implementation of an IRM must have a finite Q since otherwise the IRM would require infinite memory to represent the current security state.

Intuitively, Definition 2 captures the idea that an IRM verifier must track abstract security states as two components: a union of residuals $Res(Q_0)$ and a finite sequence τ of literal events. Set $Res(Q_0)$ encodes the set of possible security states that the untrusted program might have been in when the reified state variable was last updated by the IRM to reflect the current security state. The actual current security state of the program can potentially be out of sync with the reified state value at any given program point because IRM's typically cannot update the state value in the same operation that exhibits a security-relevant event. Thus, trace τ models the sequence of events that have been exhibited since the last update of the state value. In general, an IRM may delay updates to its reified state variables for performance reasons until after numerous security-relevant events have occurred. Dynamic tests of reified state variables therefore reveal information about an earlier security state that existed before τ occurred, rather than the current security state. This distinction is critical for accurately reasoning about real IRM code.

We limit the length of τ in our definition to a fixed constant k to keep our abstract interpretation tractable. This means that when an IRM performs more than k security-relevant operations between state variable updates, our verifier will conservatively approximate traces at some program points, and might therefore conservatively reject some policy-adherent programs. The choice of constant k dictates a trade-off between IRM performance and verification efficiency. A low k forces IRM's to update security state variables more frequently in order to pass verification, potentially increasing runtime overhead. A high k relaxes this burden but yields a larger language of abstract states, potentially increasing verification overhead. For our implementation, $k = 1$ suffices.

Reified state values themselves are abstracted as integers or $\top_{VS}$ (denoting an unknown value). For simplicity, our formal presentation treats all program values as integers and abstracts them in the same way.

Definition 3 (Abstract Values). *Define $VS = \mathbb{Z} \cup \{\top_{VS}\}$ to be the set of* abstract program values, *and define* value order *relation $\leq_{VS}$ by $(n \leq_{VS} n)$ and $(n \leq_{VS} \top_{VS})$ $\forall n \in VS$. Observe that $(VS, \leq_{VS})$ forms a height-2 lattice.*

3.3 Concrete Machine

The abstract states described above abstract the behavior of a concrete machine that models the actual behavior of ActionScript bytecode programs as interpreted by the ActionScript virtual machine. We define the concrete machine to be a tuple $(\mathcal{C}, \chi_0, \mapsto)$, where $\mathcal{C}$ is the set of concrete *configurations*, χ_0 is the initial configuration, and $\mapsto$ is the transition relation in the concrete domain. Figure 2 defines a configuration $\chi = \langle L : i, \sigma, \nu, m, \tau \rangle$ as a *labeled instruction* $L : i$, an *operand stack* σ, a *local variable store* ν, a reified security state value m, and a trace τ of security-relevant events that have been exhibited so far during the current run. A *program* $P = (L, p, s)$ consists of a program entrypoint label L, a mapping p from code labels to program instructions, and a label successor function s that defines the destinations of non-branching instructions.

$\chi ::= \langle L : i, \sigma, \nu, m, \tau \rangle$	(configurations)
L	(code labels)
$i ::= \textbf{ifle}\ L \mid \textbf{getlocal}\ n \mid \textbf{setlocal}\ n \mid \textbf{jmp}\ L \mid$ $\textbf{event}\ e \mid \textbf{setstate}\ n \mid \textbf{ifstate}\ n\ L$	(instructions)
$\sigma ::= \cdot \mid v :: \sigma$	(concrete stacks)
$v \in \mathbb{Z}$	(concrete values)
$\nu : \mathbb{Z} \to v$	(concrete stores)
$m \in \mathbb{Z}$	(concrete reified state)
$e \in \Sigma$	(events)
$\tau \in \Sigma^*$	(concrete traces)
$\chi_0 = \langle L_0 : p(L_0), \cdot, \nu_0, 0, \epsilon \rangle$	(initial configurations)
$\nu_0 = \mathbb{Z} \times \{0\}$	(initial stores)
$P ::= (L, p, s)$	(programs)
$p : L \to i$	(instruction labels)
$s : L \to L$	(label successors)

Fig. 2. Concrete machine configurations and programs

To simplify the discussion, we here consider only a core language of ActionScript bytecode instructions. Instructions **ifle** L and **jmp** n implement conditional and unconditional jumps, respectively, and instructions **getlocal** n and **setlocal** n read and set local variable values, respectively. Instruction **event** e models a security-relevant operation that exhibits event e.

The **setstate** n and **ifstate** n L instructions set the reified security state and perform a conditional jump based upon its current value, respectively. While the real ActionScript instruction set does not include these last three operations, in practice they are implemented as fixed instruction sequences that perform security-relevant operations (e.g., system calls), store an integer constant in a safe place (e.g., a reserved private field member), and conditionally branch based on that stored value, respectively. The bytecode language's existing object encapsulation and type-safety features are leveraged to prevent untrusted code from corrupting reified security state.

Figure 3 provides a complete small-step operational semantics for the concrete machine. Observe that in Rule (CEvent), policy-violating events cause the concrete machine to enter a stuck state. Thus, security violations are modeled in the concrete domain as stuck states. The concrete semantics have no explicit operation for normal program termination; we model termination as an infinite stutter state. The soundness proof in Sect. 4 shows that any program that is accepted by the abstract machine will never enter a stuck state during any concrete run; thus, verification is sufficient to prevent policy violations.

$$\frac{n_1 \le n_2}{\langle L_1 : \textbf{ifle}\ L_2, n_1{::}n_2{::}\sigma, \nu, m, \tau\rangle \mapsto \langle L_2 : p(L_2), \sigma, \nu, m, \tau\rangle}\ (\textsc{CIflePos})$$

$$\frac{n_1 > n_2}{\langle L_1 : \textbf{ifle}\ L_2, n_1{::}n_2{::}\sigma, \nu, m, \tau\rangle \mapsto \langle s(L_1) : p(s(L_1)), \sigma, \nu, m, \tau\rangle}\ (\textsc{CIfleNeg})$$

$$\overline{\langle L : \textbf{getlocal}\ n, \sigma, \nu, m, \tau\rangle \mapsto \langle s(L) : p(s(L)), \nu(n){::}\sigma, \nu, m, \tau\rangle}\ (\textsc{CGetlocal})$$

$$\overline{\langle L : \textbf{setlocal}\ n, n_1{::}\sigma, \nu, m, \tau\rangle \mapsto \langle s(L) : p(s(L)), \sigma, \nu[n := n_1], m, \tau\rangle}\ (\textsc{CSetlocal})$$

$$\overline{\langle L_1 : \textbf{jmp}\ L_2, \sigma, \nu, m, \tau\rangle \mapsto \langle L_2 : p(L_2), \sigma, \nu, m, \tau\rangle}\ (\textsc{CJmp})$$

$$\frac{\tau e \in \mathcal{P}}{\langle L : \textbf{event}\ e, \sigma, \nu, m, \tau\rangle \mapsto \langle s(L) : p(s(L)), \sigma, \nu, m, \tau e\rangle}\ (\textsc{CEvent})$$

$$\overline{\langle L : \textbf{setstate}\ n, \sigma, \nu, m, \tau\rangle \mapsto \langle s(L) : p(s(L)), \sigma, \nu, n, \tau\rangle}\ (\textsc{CSetstate})$$

$$\overline{\langle L_1 : \textbf{ifstate}\ n\ L_2, \sigma, \nu, n, \tau\rangle \mapsto \langle L_2 : p(L_2), \sigma, \nu, n, \tau\rangle}\ (\textsc{CIfstatePos})$$

$$\frac{m \ne n}{\langle L_1 : \textbf{ifstate}\ n\ L_2, \sigma, \nu, m, \tau\rangle \mapsto \langle s(L_1) : p(s(L_1)), \sigma, \nu, m, \tau\rangle}\ (\textsc{CIfstateNeg})$$

Fig. 3. Small-step operational semantics for the concrete machine

3.4 Abstract Machine

We define our abstract machine as a tuple $(\mathcal{A}, \chi_0, \rightsquigarrow)$, where $\mathcal{A}$ is the set of configurations of the abstract machine, χ_0 is the same initial configuration as the concrete machine, and $\rightsquigarrow$ is the transition relation in the abstract domain. Abstract configurations are formally defined in Fig. 4. Figure 5 lifts the $\le_{VS}$ relation to operand stacks and stores to form a lattice $(\mathcal{A}, \le_{\hat{\chi}})$ of abstract states. That is, stacks (stores) are related if their sizes (domains) are identical and their corresponding members are related.

The small-step operational semantics of the abstract machine are given in Fig. 6. When the abstract machine can infer concrete values for operands, as in Rule (AIflePos), it performs a transition resembling the corresponding concrete transition. However, when operand values are unknown, as in Rule (AIfleTop), the abstract machine non-deterministically explores all possible control flows resulting from the operation.

The premises of rules (AEvent), (ASetstate), and (AIfstateNeg) appeal to a model-checker that decides subset relations for abstract states according to Definition 2. Thus, the abstract machine enters a stuck state when it encounters a potential policy violation (see Rule (AEvent)). Abstract stuck states correspond to rejection by the verifier.

Rule (ASetstate) requires that acceptable programs must maintain a reified security state that is consistent with the actual security state of the program during any given concrete execution. This allows the (AIfstatePos) and (AIfstateNeg) rules of the abstract machine to infer useful security information in the positive and negative branches of program operations that dynamically

$$
\begin{array}{lr}
\hat{\chi} ::= \bot \mid \langle L : i, \hat{\sigma}, \hat{\nu}, m, (Res(q_m), \bar{\tau})\rangle \mid \langle L : i, \hat{\sigma}, \hat{\nu}, \top_{VS}, \hat{\tau}\rangle & \text{(abstract configs)} \\
\hat{\sigma} ::= \cdot \mid \hat{v} :: \hat{\sigma} & \text{(evaluation stacks)} \\
\hat{v} \in VS & \text{(abstract values)} \\
\hat{\nu} : \mathbb{Z} \rightarrow \hat{v} & \text{(abstract stores)} \\
\hat{m} \in \mathbb{Z} \cup \top_{VS} & \text{(abstract reified state)} \\
\bar{\tau} \in \cup_{n \leq k} \Sigma^n & \text{(bounded traces)} \\
\hat{\tau} \in SS & \text{(abstract traces)}
\end{array}
$$

Fig. 4. Abstract machine configurations

$$\frac{}{\bot \leq_{\hat{\chi}} \hat{\chi}} \qquad \frac{}{\cdot \leq_{VS} \cdot}$$

$$\frac{\hat{\sigma} \leq_{VS} \hat{\sigma}' \qquad \hat{\nu} \leq_{VS} \hat{\nu}' \qquad R_m\tau \subseteq R_m\tau'}{\langle L : i, \hat{\sigma}, \hat{\nu}, m, (R_m, \tau)\rangle \leq_{\hat{\chi}} \langle L : i, \hat{\sigma}', \hat{\nu}', m, (R_m, \tau')\rangle} \qquad \frac{\hat{\sigma}_1 \leq_{VS} \hat{\sigma}_2 \qquad va_1 \leq_{VS} va_2}{va_1 :: \hat{\sigma}_1 \leq_{VS} va_2 :: \hat{\sigma}_2}$$

$$\frac{\hat{\sigma} \leq_{VS} \hat{\sigma}' \qquad \hat{\nu} \leq_{VS} \hat{\nu}' \qquad \hat{\tau} \subseteq \hat{\tau}'}{\langle L : i, \hat{\sigma}, \hat{\nu}, \hat{m}, \hat{\tau}\rangle \leq_{\hat{\chi}} \langle L : i, \hat{\sigma}', \hat{\nu}', \top, \hat{\tau}'\rangle} \qquad \frac{\hat{\nu}_1(n) \leq_{VS} \hat{\nu}_2(n) \quad \forall n \in \mathbb{Z}}{\hat{\nu}_1 \leq_{VS} \hat{\nu}_2}$$

Fig. 5. State-ordering relation $\leq_{\hat{\chi}}$

$$\frac{n_1 \leq n_2}{\langle L_1 : \textbf{ifle}\ L_2, n_1{::}n_2{::}\hat{\sigma}, \hat{\nu}, \hat{m}, \hat{\tau}\rangle \rightsquigarrow \langle L_2 : p(L_2), \hat{\sigma}, \hat{\nu}, \hat{m}, \hat{\tau}\rangle}\ (\text{AIfLEPos})$$

$$\frac{n_1 > n_2}{\langle L_1 : \textbf{ifle}\ L_2, n_1{::}n_2{::}\hat{\sigma}, \hat{\nu}, \hat{m}, \hat{\tau}\rangle \rightsquigarrow \langle s(L_1) : p(s(L_1)), \hat{\sigma}, \hat{\nu}, \hat{m}, \hat{\tau}\rangle}\ (\text{AIfLENeg})$$

$$\frac{\top_{VS} \in \{va_1, va_2\} \qquad L' \in \{L_2, s(L_1)\}}{\langle L_1 : \textbf{ifle}\ L_2, va_1{::}va_2{::}\hat{\sigma}, \hat{\nu}, \hat{m}, \hat{\tau}\rangle \rightsquigarrow \langle L' : p(L'), \hat{\sigma}, \hat{\nu}, \hat{m}, \hat{\tau}\rangle}\ (\text{AIfLETop})$$

$$\overline{\langle L : \textbf{getlocal}\ n, \hat{\sigma}, \hat{\nu}, \hat{m}, \hat{\tau}\rangle \rightsquigarrow \langle s(L) : p(s(L)), \hat{\nu}(n){::}\hat{\sigma}, \hat{\nu}, \hat{m}, \hat{\tau}\rangle}\ (\text{AGetlocal})$$

$$\overline{\langle L : \textbf{setlocal}\ n, va_1{::}\hat{\sigma}, \hat{\nu}, \hat{m}, \hat{\tau}\rangle \rightsquigarrow \langle s(L) : p(s(L)), \hat{\sigma}, \hat{\nu}[n := va_1], \hat{m}, \hat{\tau}\rangle}\ (\text{ASetlocal})$$

$$\overline{\langle L_1 : \textbf{jmp}\ L_2, \hat{\sigma}, \hat{\nu}, \hat{m}, \hat{\tau}\rangle \rightsquigarrow \langle L_2 : p(L_2), \hat{\sigma}, \hat{\nu}, \hat{m}, \hat{\tau}\rangle}\ (\text{AJmp})$$

$$\frac{\hat{\tau}e \subseteq \hat{\tau}' \subseteq \mathcal{P}}{\langle L : \textbf{event}\ e, \hat{\sigma}, \hat{\nu}, \hat{m}, \hat{\tau}\rangle \rightsquigarrow \langle s(L) : p(s(L)), \hat{\sigma}, \hat{\nu}, \hat{m}, \hat{\tau}'\rangle}\ (\text{AEvent})$$

$$\frac{\hat{\tau} \subseteq Res(q_n)}{\langle L : \textbf{setstate}\ n, \hat{\sigma}, \hat{\nu}, \hat{m}, \hat{\tau}\rangle \rightsquigarrow \langle s(L) : p(s(L)), \hat{\sigma}, \hat{\nu}, n, (Res(q_n), \epsilon)\rangle}\ (\text{ASetstate})$$

$$\frac{\hat{m} \in \{n, \top\}}{\langle L_1 : \textbf{ifstate}\ n\ L_2, \hat{\sigma}, \hat{\nu}, \hat{m}, (S, \tau)\rangle \rightsquigarrow \langle L_2 : p(L_2), \hat{\sigma}, \hat{\nu}, n, (Res(q_n), \tau)\rangle}\ (\text{AIfstatePos})$$

$$\frac{\hat{m} \neq n \qquad (S - Res(q_n))\tau \subseteq \hat{\tau}}{\langle L_1 : \textbf{ifstate}\ n\ L_2, \hat{\sigma}, \hat{\nu}, \hat{m}, (S, \tau)\rangle \rightsquigarrow \langle s(L_1) : p(s(L_1)), \hat{\sigma}, \hat{\nu}, \hat{m}, \hat{\tau}\rangle}\ (\text{AIfstateNeg})$$

Fig. 6. Small-step operational semantics for the abstract machine

test this state. The verifier can therefore reason that dynamic security guards implemented by an IRM suffice to prevent runtime policy violations.

3.5 An Abstract Interpretation Example

Abstract interpretation involves iteratively computing an abstract state for each code point. Multiple abstract states obtained for the same code point are combined by computing their join in lattice $(\mathcal{A}, \leq_{\hat{\chi}})$. This process continues until a fixed point is reached.

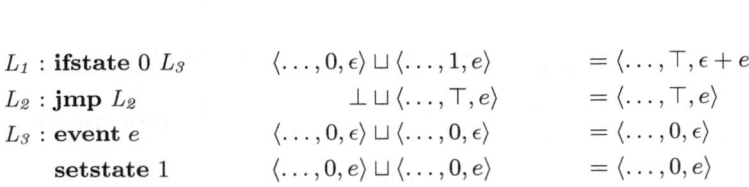

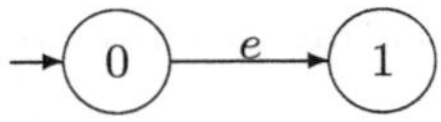

L_1 : **ifstate** 0 L_3	$\langle \ldots, 0, \epsilon \rangle \sqcup \langle \ldots, 1, e \rangle$	$= \langle \ldots, \top, \epsilon + e \rangle$
L_2 : **jmp** L_2	$\bot \sqcup \langle \ldots, \top, e \rangle$	$= \langle \ldots, \top, e \rangle$
L_3 : **event** e	$\langle \ldots, 0, \epsilon \rangle \sqcup \langle \ldots, 0, \epsilon \rangle$	$= \langle \ldots, 0, \epsilon \rangle$
setstate 1	$\langle \ldots, 0, e \rangle \sqcup \langle \ldots, 0, e \rangle$	$= \langle \ldots, 0, e \rangle$
jmp L_1	$\langle \ldots, 1, e \rangle \sqcup \langle \ldots, 1, e \rangle$	$= \langle \ldots, 1, e \rangle$

Fig. 7. An abstract interpretation example

To illustrate this, we here walk the abstract interpreter through the simple example program shown in the first column of Fig. 7, enforcing the policy $\epsilon + e$ whose security automaton is depicted at the top of the figure. Abstract states inferred on *first entry* to each code point are written to the left of the $\sqcup$ in the second column. (All but the reified state value 0 and trace ϵ are omitted from each configuration since they are irrelevant to this particular example.) Abstract states inferred on *second entry* are written after the $\sqcup$, and the resulting join of these states is written in the third column. In this example a fixed point is reached after two iterations.

The abstract interpreter begins at entrypoint label L_1 in initial configuration $\chi_0 = \langle \ldots, 0, \epsilon \rangle$. Since the reified state is known, the abstract machine performs transition (AIfstatePos) and arrives at label L_3. Operation **event** e appends e to the trace, operation **setstate** 1 updates the reified state, and operation **jmp** L_1 returns to the original code point.

The join of these two states yields a new configuration in which the reified state is unknown ($\top$), so on the second iteration the abstract machine non-deterministically transitions to both L_2 and L_3. However, both transitions infer useful security state information based on the results of the dynamic test. Transition (AIfstatePos) to label L_3 refines the abstract trace from $\epsilon + e$ to $Res(q_0) = \epsilon$, and transition (AIfstateNeg) to label L_2 refines it to $\epsilon + e - Res(q_0) = e$. These refinements allow the verifier to conclude that all abstract states are policy-satisfying. In particular, the dynamic state test at L_1 suffices to prevent policy violations at L_3.

4 Analysis

4.1 Soundness

The abstract machine defined in Section 3.4 is *sound* with respect to the concrete machine defined in Section 3.3 in the sense that each inferred abstract state $\hat{\chi}$ conservatively approximates all concrete states χ that can arise at the same program point during an execution of the concrete machine on the same program. This further implies that if the abstract machine does not enter a stuck state for a given program, nor does the concrete machine. Since concrete stuck states model security violations, this implies that a verifier consistent with the abstract machine will reject all policy-violating programs.

$$\frac{\sigma \leq_{VS} \hat{\sigma} \qquad \nu \leq_{VS} \hat{\nu} \qquad \tau \in \hat{\tau}}{\langle L : i, \sigma, \nu, m, \tau\rangle \sim \langle L : i, \hat{\sigma}, \hat{\nu}, \top, \hat{\tau}\rangle} (\text{SoundTop})$$

$$\frac{\sigma \leq_{VS} \hat{\sigma} \qquad \nu \leq_{VS} \hat{\nu} \qquad \tau \in Res(q_m)\tau' \qquad \tau \in S\tau'}{\langle L : i, \sigma, \nu, m, \tau\rangle \sim \langle L : i, \hat{\sigma}, \hat{\nu}, m, (S, \tau')\rangle} (\text{SoundInt})$$

Fig. 8. Soundness relation $\sim$

We define the soundness of state abstractions in terms of a *soundness relation* [7] written $\sim \subseteq \mathcal{C} \times \mathcal{A}$ that is defined in Fig. 8. Following the approach of [4], soundness of the operational semantics given in Figs. 3 and 6 is then proved via progress and preservation lemmas. The preservation lemma proves that a bisimulation of the abstract and concrete machines preserves the soundness relation, while the progress lemma proves that as long as the soundness relation is preserved, the concrete machine does not enter a stuck state. Together, these two lemmas dovetail to form an induction over arbitrary length execution sequences, proving that programs accepted by the verifier will not commit policy violations.

We sketch interesting cases of the progress and preservation proofs below.

Lemma 1 (Progress). *For every $\chi \in \mathcal{C}$ and $\hat{\chi} \in \mathcal{A}$ such that $\chi \sim \hat{\chi}$, if there exists $\hat{\chi}' \in \mathcal{A}$ such that $\hat{\chi} \rightsquigarrow \hat{\chi}'$, then there exists $\chi' \in \mathcal{C}$ such that $\chi \mapsto \chi'$.*

Proof. Let $\chi = \langle L : i, \sigma, \nu, m, \tau\rangle \in \mathcal{C}$, $\hat{\chi} = \langle L : i, \hat{\sigma}, \hat{\nu}, \hat{m}, \hat{\tau}\rangle \in \mathcal{A}$, and $\hat{\chi}' \in \mathcal{A}$ be given, and assume $\chi \sim \hat{\chi}$ and $\hat{\chi} \rightsquigarrow \hat{\chi}'$ both hold. Proof is by a case distinction on the derivation of $\hat{\chi} \rightsquigarrow \hat{\chi}'$. The one interesting case is that for Rule (AEvent), since the corresponding (CEvent) rule in the concrete semantics is the only one with a non-trivial premise. For brevity, we show only that case below.

Case (AEvent)**:** From Rule (AEvent) we have $i = \textbf{event } e$ and $\hat{\chi}' = \langle s(L) : p(s(L)), \hat{\sigma}, \hat{\nu}, \hat{m}, \hat{\tau}'\rangle$, where $\hat{\tau}e \subseteq \hat{\tau}' \subseteq \mathcal{P}$ holds. Choose configuration $\chi' = \langle s(L) : p(s(L)), \sigma, \nu, m, (\tau, e)\rangle$. From $\chi \sim \hat{\chi}$ we have $\tau \in \hat{\tau}$. It follows that $\hat{\tau}e \subseteq \mathcal{P}$ holds. By Rule (CEvent), we conclude that $\chi \mapsto \chi'$ is derivable.

The remaining cases are straightforward, and are therefore omitted. □

Lemma 2 (Preservation). *For every $\chi \in \mathcal{C}$ and $\hat{\chi} \in \mathcal{A}$ such that $\chi \sim \hat{\chi}$, if there exists a non-empty $\mathcal{A}' \subseteq \mathcal{A}$ such that $\hat{\chi} \rightsquigarrow \mathcal{A}'$, then for every $\chi' \in \mathcal{C}$ such that $\chi \mapsto \chi'$ there exists $\hat{\chi}' \in \mathcal{A}'$ such that $\chi' \sim \hat{\chi}'$.*

Proof. Let $\chi = \langle L : i, \sigma, \nu, m, \tau \rangle \in \mathcal{C}$, $\hat{\chi} = \langle L : i, \hat{\sigma}, \hat{\nu}, \hat{m}, \hat{\tau} \rangle \in \mathcal{A}$, and $\chi' \in \mathcal{C}$ be given such that $\chi \mapsto \chi'$. Proof is by case distinction on the derivation of $\chi \mapsto \chi'$. For brevity we sketch only the most interesting cases below.

Case (CEvent)**:** From Rule (CEvent) we have $i =$ **event** e and $\chi' = \langle s(L) : p(s(L)), \sigma, \nu, m, \tau e \rangle$. Since $\mathcal{A}'$ is non-empty, we may choose $\hat{\chi}' = \langle s(L) : p(s(L)), \hat{\sigma}, \hat{\nu}, \hat{m}, \hat{\tau}' \rangle$ such that $\hat{\tau} e \subseteq \hat{\tau}' \subseteq \mathcal{P}$ by (AEvent). We can then obtain a derivation of $\chi' \sim \hat{\chi}'$ from the derivation of $\chi \sim \hat{\chi}$ by appending event e to all of the traces in the premises of (SoundTop) or (SoundInt), and observing that the resulting premises are provable from $\hat{\tau} e \subseteq \hat{\tau}'$.

Case (CSetstate)**:** From Rule (CSetstate) we have $i =$ **setstate** n and $\chi' = \langle s(L) : p(s(L)), \sigma, \nu, n, \tau \rangle$. Since $\mathcal{A}'$ is non-empty, we may choose $\hat{\chi}' = \langle s(L) : p(s(L)), \hat{\sigma}, \hat{\nu}, n, (Res(q_n), \epsilon) \rangle$ such that $\hat{\tau} \subseteq Res(q_n)$ holds by Rule (ASetstate). From $\chi \sim \hat{\chi}$ we have $\tau \in \hat{\tau}$. Thus, $\tau \in Res(q_n)$ holds and relation $\chi' \sim \hat{\chi}'$ follows from Rule (SoundInt).

Case (CIfstatePos)**:** From Rule (CIfstatePos) we have $i =$ **ifstate** $n\ L_2$ and $\chi' = \langle L_2 : p(L_2), \sigma, \nu, n, \tau \rangle$. If $\hat{m} = n \neq \top$, then $\hat{\tau} = (S, \bar{\tau})$ by (AIfstatePos), so choose $a' = \langle L_2 : p(L_2), \hat{\sigma}, \hat{\nu}, n, (Res(q_n), \bar{\tau}) \rangle$. Relation $\chi \sim \hat{\chi}$ proves $\chi' \sim \hat{\chi}'$ by (SoundInt). Otherwise $\hat{m} = \top$, so choose $\hat{\chi}' = \langle L_2 : p(L_2), \hat{\sigma}, \hat{\nu}, \top, \hat{\tau} \rangle$. Relation $\chi \sim \hat{\chi}$ proves $\chi' \sim \hat{\chi}'$ by (SoundTop).

Case (CIfstateNeg)**:** From Rule (CIfstateNeg) we have $i =$ **ifstate** $n\ L_2$ and $\chi' = \langle s(L_1) : p(s(L_1)), \sigma, \nu, m, \tau \rangle$, where $n \neq m$. If $\hat{m} \neq \top$ then $\hat{\tau} = (S, \bar{\tau})$ by (AIfstateNeg), so choose $\hat{\chi}' = \langle s(L_1) : p(s(L_1)), \hat{\sigma}, \hat{\nu}, \hat{m}, \hat{\tau}' \rangle$ such that $(S - Res(q_n))\bar{\tau} \subseteq \hat{\tau}'$ holds by (AIfstateNeg). In any deterministic security automaton, every residual is disjoint from all others. Thus, $\hat{m} \neq n$ implies that $\hat{\tau} \notin Res(q_n)\bar{\tau}$, and therefore $\hat{\tau} \subseteq (S - Res(q_n))\bar{\tau}$. A derivation of $\chi' \sim \hat{\chi}'$ can therefore be obtained from the one for $\chi \sim \hat{\chi}$ using (SoundInt). Otherwise $\hat{m} = \top$, and the rest of the case follows using logic similar to the case for (CIfstatePos). □

Theorem 1 (Soundness). *If the abstract machine does not enter a stuck state from the initial state χ_0, then for any concrete state $\chi \in \mathcal{C}$ reachable from the initial state χ_0, the concrete machine can make progress. If state χ is a security-relevant event then this progress is derived by rule* (CEvent) *of Fig. 3, whose premise guarantees that the event does not cause a policy violation. Thus, any program accepted by the abstract machine does not commit a policy violation when executed.*

Proof. The theorem follows from the progress and preservation lemmas by an induction on the length of an arbitrary, finite execution prefix. □

4.2 Convergence

In practice, effective verification depends upon obtaining a fixed point for the abstract machine semantics in reasonable time for any given untrusted program.

The convergence rate of the algorithm described in Sect. 3.5 depends in part on the height of the lattice of abstract states. This height dictates the number of iterations required to reach a fixed point in the worst case. All components of the language of abstract states defined in Fig. 4 have height at most 2, except for the lattice SS of abstract traces. Lattice SS is finite whenever security automaton A is finite; therefore convergence is guaranteed in finite time. In the proof that follows we prove the stronger result that lattice SS has non-exponential height—in particular, it has height that is quadratic in the size of the security automaton.

Theorem 2. *Let $A = (Q, \Sigma, \delta)$ be a deterministic, finite security automaton. Lattice $(SS, \subseteq)$ from Definition 2 has height $O(|Q|^2 + k|Q|)$.*

Proof. Let $Q_1, Q_2 \subseteq Q$ and $\tau_1, \tau_2 \in \cup_{n \leq k} \Sigma^n$ be given. For all $i \in \{1, 2\}$ define $L_i = Res(Q_i)\tau_i$, and assume $\emptyset \subsetneq L_1 \subsetneq L_2 \subseteq \mathcal{P}$. Define

$$m(L) = (|Q| + 1)|suf(L)| - |Pre(L)|$$

where $suf(L) = \max\{\tau \in \Sigma^* \mid L \subseteq \Sigma^*\tau\}$ is the largest common suffix of all strings in non-empty language L and $Pre(L) = \{q \in Q \mid Res(q)suf(L) \cap L \neq \emptyset\}$ is the set of possible automaton states that an accepting path for a string in L might be in immediately prior to accepting the common suffix. We will prove that $m(L_1) > m(L_2)$. By the pumping lemma, $|suf(L_i)| = |suf(Res(Q_i)\tau_i)|$ is at most $|Q| + k$, so this proves that any chain in lattice $(SS, \subseteq)$ has length at most $O(|Q|^2 + k|Q|)$.

We first prove that $Res(Pre(L_i))suf(L_i) = L_i \ \forall i \in \{1, 2\}$. The $\supseteq$ direction of the proof is immediate from the definition of Pre; the following proves the $\subseteq$ direction. Let $\tau \in Res(Pre(L_i))suf(L_i)$ be given. There exists $q \in Pre(L_i)$ and $\tau' \in Res(q)$ such that $\tau = \tau' suf(L_i)$. Since $L_i = Res(Q_i)\tau_i$, τ_i is a suffix of $suf(L_i)$, so there exists $\tau_i' \in \Sigma^*$ such that $suf(L_i) = \tau_i'\tau_i$. From $q \in Pre(L_i)$ we obtain $Res(q)suf(L_i) \cap L_i = Res(q)\tau_i'\tau_i \cap Res(Q_i)\tau_i = (Res(q)\tau_i' \cap Res(Q_i))\tau_i \neq \emptyset$. Thus, there is an accepting path for τ_i' from q to some state in $Res(Q_i)$. It follows that $\tau'\tau_i' \in Res(Q_i)$, so $\tau = \tau'\tau_i'\tau_i \in Res(Q_i)\tau_i = L_i$. We conclude that $Res(Pre(L_i))suf(L_i) \subseteq L_i$.

From this result we prove that $m(L_1) > m(L_2)$. Since $L_1 \subsetneq L_2$, it follows that $suf(L_2)$ is a suffix of $suf(L_1)$. If it is a strict suffix then the theorem is proved. If instead $suf(L_1) = suf(L_2) = x$, then we have the following:

$$\begin{aligned} L_1 &\subsetneq L_2 \\ Res(Pre(L_1))x &\subsetneq Res(Pre(L_2))x \\ Res(Pre(L_1)) &\subsetneq Res(Pre(L_2)) \end{aligned}$$

Since A is deterministic and therefore each residual is disjoint, we conclude that $Pre(L_1) \subsetneq Pre(L_2)$ and therefore $m(L_1) > m(L_2)$. □

5 Implementation

We used our IRM framework to enforce and verify a URL anti-redirection policy for ActionScript ad applets. ActionScript bytecode performs a URL redirection using the navigateToURL system call, which accepts the URL target as its argument. To protect against malicious redirections, we enforced a policy that requires check_url(s) to be called sometime before any call to navigateToURL(s), for each string constant s. Here, check_url is a trusted implementation provided by the ad distributor and/or web host, and may therefore rely on dynamic information such as the webpage that houses the current ad instance, the current user's identity, etc.

A naïve IRM can satisfy this policy by simply inserting a call to check_url immediately before each call to navigateToURL. Since calls to check_url are potentially expensive, our IRM takes the more efficient approach of reifying a separate security state variable into the untrusted binary for each string constant.[3] The reified state tracks whether that string has yet passed inspection and avoids duplicate calls for the same constant. In the less common case where the untrusted code must call navigateToURL with a dynamically generated string, the IRM resorts to the naïve approach described above. Maintaining persistent internal state for dynamically generated strings is left for future work.

Program Tested	Size Before	Size After	Rewriting Time	Verification Time
countdownBadge.abc	1.80 KB	1.95 KB	1.429s	0.532s
NavToURL.abc	0.93 KB	1.03 KB	0.863s	0.233s

Fig. 9. Experimental Results

The resulting instrumented binaries are independently certified by the model-checking verifier using the original security policy expressed as a security automaton. Figure 9 shows the results of rewriting and verifying binaries extracted from two real-world SWF ads that perform redirections. All tests were performed on an Intel Pentium Core 2 Duo machine running Yap Prolog v5.1.4. In both cases the IRM passed verification and prevented malicious URL redirections.

6 Conclusion

We have presented a technique for certifying IRM's through model-checking. Our technique derives a state abstraction lattice from a security automaton to facilitate precise abstract interpretation of IRM code. Formal proofs of soundness and convergence guarantee reliability and tractability of the verification process. Finally, we demonstrate the feasibility of our technique by enforcing a URL anti-redirection policy for ActionScript bytecode programs.

While our algorithm successfully verifies an important class of IRM implementations involving reified security state, it does not support all IRM rewriting strategies. Reified security state that is per-object [13] instead of global, or that is updated by the IRM before the actual security state changes at runtime rather

[3] The number of string constants is known at rewriting time based on the size of the constant pool in the ActionScript binary.

than after, are two examples of IRM strategies not supported by our model. In future work we intend to investigate ways of generalizing our approach to cover these cases.

We also plan to augment our system with support for recursion and mutual recursion, which is currently not handled by our implementation. Finally, we also plan to extend our technique to other binary languages and the IRM systems that have been implemented for them.

Acknowledgments

The authors thank Peleus Uhley at Adobe Research for providing real-world SWF applets of interest for testing and certification, and R. Chandrasekaran and Feliks Kluzniak for various helpful discussions.

References

1. Aktug, I., Naliuka, K.: ConSpec - a formal language for policy specification. Science of Computer Programming 74, 2–12 (2008)
2. Alpern, B., Schneider, F.B.: Recognizing safety and liveness. Distributed Computing 2, 117–126 (1986)
3. Balakrishnan, G., Reps, T.W., Kidd, N., Lal, A., Lim, J., Melski, D., Gruian, R., Yong, S.H., Chen, C.-H., Teitelbaum, T.: Model checking x86 executables with CodeSurfer/x86 and WPDS++. In: Etessami, K., Rajamani, S.K. (eds.) CAV 2005. LNCS, vol. 3576, pp. 158–163. Springer, Heidelberg (2005)
4. Chang, B.-Y.E., Chlipala, A., Necula, G.C.: A framework for certified program analysis and its applications to mobile-code safety. In: Emerson, E.A., Namjoshi, K.S. (eds.) VMCAI 2006. LNCS, vol. 3855, pp. 174–189. Springer, Heidelberg (2005)
5. Chen, F.: Java-MOP: A monitoring oriented programming environment for Java. In: Halbwachs, N., Zuck, L.D. (eds.) TACAS 2005. LNCS, vol. 3440, pp. 546–550. Springer, Heidelberg (2005)
6. Cousot, P., Cousot, R.: Abstract interpretation: A unified lattice model for static analysis of programs by construction or approximation of fixpoints. In: Proc. Symposium on Principles of Prog. Languages, pp. 234–252 (1977)
7. Cousot, P., Cousot, R.: Abstract interpretation frameworks. J. Log. Comput. 2(4), 511–547 (1992)
8. Denis, F., Lemay, A., Terlutte, A.: Residual finite state automata. In: Ferreira, A., Reichel, H. (eds.) STACS 2001. LNCS, vol. 2010, pp. 144–157. Springer, Heidelberg (2001)
9. DeVries, B.W., Gupta, G., Hamlen, K.W., Moore, S., Sridhar, M.: ActionScript bytecode verification with co-logic programming. In: Proc. ACM Workshop on Prog. Languages and Analysis for Security (PLAS) (2009)
10. Erlingsson, Ú., Schneider, F.B.: SASI enforcement of security policies: A retrospective. In: Proc. New Security Paradigms Workshop (1999)
11. fukami, Fuhrmannek, B.: SWF and the malware tragedy. In: Proc. OWASP Application Security Conference (2008)
12. Hamlen, K.W., Jones, M.: Aspect-oriented in-lined reference monitors. In: Proc. ACM Workshop on Prog. Languages and Analysis for Security (PLAS) (2008)

13. Hamlen, K.W., Morrisett, G., Schneider, F.B.: Certified in-lined reference monitoring on.NET. In: Proc. ACM Workshop on Prog. Languages and Analysis for Security (PLAS) (2006)
14. Hamlen, K.W., Morrisett, G., Schneider, F.B.: Computability classes for enforcement mechanisms. In: ACM Trans. Prog. Languages and Systems (2006)
15. Kisser, W., Havelund, K., Brat, G., Park, S., Lerda, F.: Model checking programs. Automated Software Engineering Journal 10(2) (April 2003)
16. Ruys, T.C., de Brugh, N.H.M.A.: MMC: the Mono Model Checker. Electron. Notes Theor. Comput. Sci. 190(1), 149–160 (2007)
17. Schneider, F.B.: Enforceable security policies. ACM Trans. Information and System Security 3, 30–50 (2000)
18. Shapiro, L., Sterling, E.Y.: The Art of PROLOG: Advanced Programming Techniques. MIT Press, Cambridge (1994)
19. Simon, L., Mallya, A., Bansal, A., Gupta, G.: Coinductive logic programming. In: Etalle, S., Truszczyński, M. (eds.) ICLP 2006. LNCS, vol. 4079, pp. 330–345. Springer, Heidelberg (2006)

Considerate Reasoning and the Composite Design Pattern

Alexander J. Summers[1,2] and Sophia Drossopoulou[1]

[1] Imperial College London
[2] ETH Zürich

Abstract. We propose *Considerate Reasoning*, a novel specification and verification technique based on object invariants. This technique supports succinct specifications of implementations which follow the pattern of breaking properties of other objects and then notifying them appropriately. It allows the specification to be concerned only with the properties directly relevant to the current method call, with no need to explicitly mention the concerns of subcalls. In this way, the specification reflects the division of responsibility present in the implementation, and reflects what we regard as the natural argument behind the design.

We specify and prove the well-known Composite design pattern using Considerate Reasoning. We show how to encode our approach in Boogie2. The resulting specification verifies automatically within a few seconds; no manual guidance is required beyond the careful representation of the invariants themselves.

1 Introduction

Verification for imperative object-oriented languages is challenging. The arbitrarily complicated heap structures which can arise out of even quite short programs, and the potential for *aliasing* make it difficult to structure the verification argument in an organised fashion, or to predict the effects of code fragments.

Some approaches to these challenges use specification languages which reflect the heap structure explicitly, describing the intended topology of objects and references in a logic which includes customised assertions for the purpose. Such approaches include separation logic [18,20], dynamic frames [10], implicit dynamic frames [23] and regional logic [2].

Other approaches build on the concept of *object invariant*, and usually support some variation of *visible states semantics* (with the notable exception of the Boogie methodology [3]). In visible states semantics, object invariants should hold at the pre- and post-states of method calls, but may be temporarily broken during method execution. Various refinements have been proposed, usually based on some notion of *ownership* - a way of imposing structure on the heap by requiring that one object is encapsulated within another. This idea neatly supports client-provider implementations in which the encapsulated object is only modified via its owner; but it cannot support another programming pattern, whereby methods may break other objects' invariants and then notify them, ie

G. Barthe and M. Hermenegildo (Eds.): VMCAI 2010, LNCS 5944, pp. 328–344, 2010.

```
class Composite {
  private Composite parent;
  private Composite[] comps;
  private int count = 0;
  private int total = 1;

  // Inv1: 1 ≤ total ∧ 0 ≤ count
  // Inv2: total = 1 + Σ_{0≤i<count} comps[i].total

  // requires : c ≠ null && c.parent = null;
  public void add(Composite c) {
    // resize array if necessary
    comps[count] = c;
    count++;
    c.parent = this;
    addToTotal(c.total);
  }

  private void addToTotal(int p) {
    total += p;
    if(parent != null) parent.addToTotal(p);
  }
}
```

Fig. 1. A single-class variant of the Composite pattern

call other methods to fix them. This kind of pattern is prevalent, e.g., in the Marriage example, the Subject-Observer and Composite patterns [7], and the Priority Inheritance Protocol [22].

The Composite pattern, recently proposed as a verification challenge in [11], was the 2008 challenge problem at the SAVCBS workshop. It describes a tree-structure, and allows addition of subtrees in any part of the tree. Figure 1 contains a simplified version of the code from [11]. A Composite node has fields comps which contain all its direct descendants, parent which points to its parent, and integer total. The code has to preserve the invariant that the total field of an object is equal to the size of the subtree rooted at that object.

The major difficulty in verifying this invariant is that the data structure can be directly modified at any point, by calling add on any Composite object. This is problematic for, e.g., ownership-based approaches, since these typically require modification of owned objects to be controlled by the owning object (thus modification would be preceeded by a top-down traversal of the tree-structure). Similarly, separation logic specifications of such patterns typically require recursive predicates describing properties over the data structure [17,18]; such predicates are easier to fold/unfold from the root of the structure downwards.

In this paper we propose *Considerate Reasoning*, a novel approach to verification, and apply it to the Composite problem. Considerate Reasoning was briefly outlined in [24]; it extends the work of Middelkoop et. al. [15], and is related to [4,12]. It is based on visible states semantics; in order to support methods meant to fix invariants, it introduces the specification construct broken. Invariants declared "broken"in a method specification are *not* expected to hold before calls to the corresponding methods, but are expected to be re-established by these methods. All invariants are expected to hold at the end of a method execution. Thus, the specification of method addToTotal contains broken : Inv2(this), cf. Fig. 2.

In Fig. 2 we give a specification of the Composite in Considerate Reasoning. This specification is concerned only with properties directly relevant to the current method call, without needing to explicitly mention the concerns of subcalls. In this way, the specification reflects the division of responsibility present in the implementation, and reflects what we regard as the natural argument behind the design.[1] This is the specification we ultimately expect the user to have to write (up to a couple of additional keywords whose use will become apparent).

Considerate Reasoning also introduces *concerns-descriptions*, which describe which invariants may be broken by a field update. These are used to determine which invariants may be broken (ie are *vulnerable*) at each code point, and therefore must be re-established at the end of a method body. Because no tool directly supports Considerate Reasoning, we have encoded our approach in Boogie2 [13], using explicit assume and assert statements to describe our handling of invariants. We developed refinements which allow for simplifications of the required proof obligations. The resulting specification is natural and succinct, and verifies automatically in approximately six seconds. In section 3.5 we outline how a tool could infer concerns-descriptions and other internal concepts.

Conventions. To simplify the presentation, we make the following simplifying assumptions: The names of fields declared in different classes should be distinct. The names of invariants declared in different classes should be distinct. Type-incorrect expressions in the specifications are considered false. The predicate describing the meaning of an invariant I is called P_I. Invariants only depend on path expressions containing field accesses, and in particular do not feature predicates. [2]

2 A Considerate Specification of the Composite

We first identify what we believe to be the intuitive argument underlying the implementation. By making this argument precise, we are able to identify and

[1] Our specification does not express framing, which we left to further work. Note however, that in the Composite example, we believe that the client naturally should not depend on the value of total remaining unmodified.

[2] The last assumption is the only one to represent a true restriction. Note, however, that all invariants we require for the Composite pattern have definitions we permit, even though other specifications of the Composite used recursive predicates. We expect recursively defined predicates to be expressible through explicit invariants in a semantics where the invariants of all objects are expected to hold by default.

incorporate invariants and conditions which are necessary for soundness but missing from the original code.

Had we only been interested in the preservation of $Inv2$(this), then the following would have been an adequate implementation for adding a component:

```
public void addWeak(Composite c) {
  // resize array if necessary
  comps[count] = c;
  count++; // breaks Inv2(this)
  c.parent = this;
  total += c.total; // fixes Inv2(this),
                    // breaks Inv2(o), where this ∈ o.comps
}
```

This simpler implementation does preserve the invariant of the receiver, but in turn it breaks Inv2 of any object with the receiver in its comps. The real

```
class Composite {
  private Composite parent;
  private Composite[] comps;
  private int count = 0;
  private int total = 1;

  // Inv1(o): 1 ≤ o.total ∧ 0 ≤ o.count
  // Inv2(o): o.total = 1 + Σ_{0≤i<o.count} o.comps[i].total
  // Inv3(o): ∀0≤i<o.count : o.comps[i].parent = o
  // Inv4(o): o.parent ≠ null ⇒ ∃0≤i<o.parent.count : o.parent.comps[i] = o
  // Inv5(o): ∀0≤i≠j<o.count : o.comps[i] ≠ o.comps[j]

  // requires : c ≠ null;
  // requires : c.parent = null;
  public void add(Composite c) {
     comps[count] = c;
     count++;
     c.parent = this;
     addToTotal(c.total);
  }

  // broken: Inv2(this)
  // requires : this.total + p = 1 + Σ_{0≤i<count} comps[i].total
  private void addToTotal(int p) {
     total += p;
     if (parent != null) parent.addToTotal(p);
  }
}
```

Fig. 2. A considerate-style specification in Java

implementation takes account of this fact: the method addToTotal performs the role not only of fixing the invariant of the receiver, but also of being *considerate* of the invariants of other objects. In particular, after the total field of the receiver is updated, the parent of the receiver is notified of the change by another call to addToTotal, in order to ensure that their invariant can also be maintained.

How do we know that this implementation is indeed correctly considering *exactly the* concerned invariants? In particular, why is it correct for the addToTotal method to recursively call the parent of the current receiver? The intuitive argument here depends on the assumption that the comps of any object are exactly those objects which point to it via parent fields. This assumption is *implicit* in the design pattern, but was missing in [11]. We add two further invariants:

Inv3(o): $\forall 0 \leq i < \mathsf{o.count} : \mathsf{o.comps[i].parent} = \mathsf{o}$

Inv4(o): $\mathsf{o.parent} \neq \mathsf{null} \Rightarrow \exists 0 \leq i < \mathsf{o.parent.count} : \mathsf{o.parent.comps[i]} = \mathsf{o}$

A further subtle problem arises if the comps of an object are not distinct. If an object is in the comps of another object *twice*, then the implementation of addToTotal would be incorrect. We add a further invariant:

Inv5(o): $\forall 0 \leq i \neq j < \mathsf{count} : \mathsf{o.comps[i]} \neq \mathsf{comps[j]}$

This invariant may seem redundant, since it is *preserved* by the methods of the class Composite; however there is no guarantee that the heap structure is *already* a tree; this is indispensable in the proof that the information propagated upwards through addToTotal is correct. Note that the *combination* of the invariants Inv3, Inv4 and Inv5 guarantee that the whole Composite structure is a tree.

We now give a specification of the Composite in Figure 2. We include in the specification of addToTotal the declaration broken : Inv2(this), reflecting that this method fixes a broken invariant. The precise semantics of this construct will be made clear in the following section. In order to make it possible for addToTotal to guarantee to fix the declared invariant, we add a pre-condition requiring that the value of total is "out" by exactly the value passed as argument to the method.

3 Considerate Reasoning

Our proposed methodology, once fully supported by tools, requires the user to:

1. Define the invariants.
2. Declare certain invariants as *structural* (Definition 5 below).
3. Define the broken declarations along with method specifications.

We will now explain the workings of our methodology, and then in Section 3.5 we will outline how it can be automated. Our methodology consists of the following:

1. An *invariant semantics*, specifying which invariants must hold at which points in execution.
2. The concept of a *concerns-description*, which describes which objects' invariants are concerned with field updates in a program.
3. The derivation of *vulnerable invariants* at all intermediate program points, computed from the code and concerns-description.
4. A *verification technique*, defining sufficient proof obligations to guarantee soundness with respect to the invariant semantics.

3.1 Invariant Semantics

Visible states semantics [19,16] requires all invariants of all objects to hold immediately before and immediately after any method calls. For simplicity of the presentation, we base the work in this paper on this simple visible states semantics, but our work could be applied to weaker variants of the semantics, in which only the invariants of certain objects need hold in the visible states. programming patterns which involve calling certain methods to *fix* broken invariants (e.g method addToTotal in our example), the visible states semantics requirement is too restrictive. In the Considerate Reasoning methodology we add the necessary flexibility with the extra specification construct broken : to explicitly declare exceptions to the visible states semantics. Invariants declared "broken" in a method specification are *not* required to hold before calls to the corresponding methods, but are expected to be fixed by these methods.

Definition 1 (Broken Declarations and Invariant Semantics). *A method specification may contain a declaration* broken : $\mathsf{I}_1(\mathsf{e}_1), \mathsf{I}_2(\mathsf{e}_2), .., \mathsf{I}_n(\mathsf{e}_n)$.
A verification methodology is sound *if for any method* m *whose specification contains* broken : $\mathsf{I}_1(\mathsf{e}_1), \mathsf{I}_2(\mathsf{e}_2), .., \mathsf{I}_n(\mathsf{e}_n)$, *it guarantees that:*

1. *At the beginning of execution of* m, *all invariants of all objects must hold, except for* I_i *for those objects denoted by an expressions* e_i, *for* $i \in \{1, ..., n\}$.
2. *At the end of method execution, all invariants of all objects must hold.*

3.2 Concerns-Descriptions

Updating objects' fields may break invariants of other objects. For example, updating total of this, may break *Inv2* of this.parent. We say that objects whose invariants may be broken when a field of another object is updated, are *concerned* with the field. Obviously, concern is naturally a dynamic notion. For a static approximation of this notion, we define *concerns-descriptions* which associate with each field name f (the field to be updated) and invariant name I (the invariant under consideration), a description of the set of concerned objects. This set usually depends on the identity of the object being updated, therefore the set description may mention a special variable mod, which denotes the object being modified. Thus, the variable mod has a special meaning for concerns-descriptions, similar to the way the variable this has a special meaning for methods. Furthermore, we allow additional flexibility to the descriptions by also including a (possibly empty) list of invariant names, which we call *supporting invariants.* Their intuitive meaning is that the set described is only guaranteed to be conservative at program points where the supporting invariants are guaranteed to hold (for all objects). This allows us to use more-refined definitions of the sets of concerned objects, which depend on the guarantees that other invariants provide - the use of this feature will become clear shortly.

Definition 2 (Concerns Descriptions). *A* concerns-description $\mathcal{D}$ *is a mapping from a field name and an invariant name to a pair consisting of a* set description, *and a (possibly-empty) set of invariant names - the* supporting invariants. [3] *A* set description *is a description of a set of references, parameterised by a special variable* mod*; it may be described using usual set-theoretical operations, including comprehensions.*

For the Composite pattern, a possible concerns-description would determine $\mathcal{D}(\mathsf{count}, \mathsf{Inv1}) = (\{\mathsf{mod}\}, \emptyset)$, specifying that when the field count of any object mod is modified, at most the single object mod has invariant Inv1 broken. To obtain a sound verification methodology, the concerns-descriptions should be "big enough", i.e., any object whose invariant could be violated by a field update should fall within the corresponding described set. In fact, we make the weaker requirement that the set must be guaranteed "big enough" so long as the supporting invariants hold for all objects.

Definition 3 (Admissible Descriptions). *A concerns-description $\mathcal{D}$ is* admissible *if, for all invariants $\mathsf{I}, \mathsf{I}_1, \mathsf{I}_2, \ldots, \mathsf{I}_\mathsf{m}$, such that $\mathcal{D}(\mathsf{f}, \mathsf{I})\!\downarrow_2 = \{\mathsf{I}_1, \mathsf{I}_2, \ldots, \mathsf{I}_\mathsf{m}\}$ and for any (sub-)expression $o.\mathsf{f}_1.\mathsf{f}_2 \ldots .\mathsf{f}_n.\mathsf{f}$ (with $n \geq 0$) occurring in $P_\mathsf{I}(o)$, we can prove for arbitrary o that:*

$$(\forall o', P_{\mathsf{I}_1}(o') \wedge P_{\mathsf{I}_2}(o') \ldots P_{\mathsf{I}_m}(o')) \wedge P_\mathsf{I}(o) \Rightarrow o \in \mathcal{D}(\mathsf{f}, \mathsf{I})\!\downarrow_1[o.\mathsf{f}_1.\mathsf{f}_2 \ldots .\mathsf{f}_n/\mathsf{mod}]$$

Consider the simple case of no supporting invariants being specified (i.e., $\mathcal{D}(\mathsf{f}, \mathsf{I}) = (S, \emptyset)$ for some set description S, and $m = 0$ in the definition above). Then admissibility guarantees that whenever we modify the field f of an object mod and the invariant I of an object o can become broken as a result, it must be the case that o$\in S$.

Note that we only need to show that o is in the described set if the invariant of o actually held - since we are trying to predict the invariants which *get* broken by a particular field update, we are only interested in the case where an invariant held prior to the update. There is a simple, mechanical way of deriving one such admissible concerns-description directly from the definitions of the invariants:

Definition 4 (Simplest Concerns-Descriptions). *For expressions* e_1 *and* e_2 *we write* $\mathrm{e}_1 \sqsubseteq \mathrm{e}_2$ *to mean* e_1 *is a syntactic subexpression of* e_2*. We then define the* simplest concerns-description $\mathcal{D}_S$ *for any field* f *and invariant* I *as follows:*

$$\mathcal{D}_S(\mathsf{f}, I) = \left(\bigcup_{n \geq 0,\ \mathsf{this}.\mathsf{f}_1.\mathsf{f}_2 \ldots .\mathsf{f}_n.\mathsf{f} \sqsubseteq P_\mathsf{I}(this)} \{o \mid o.\mathsf{f}_1.\mathsf{f}_2 \ldots .\mathsf{f}_n = \mathsf{mod}\}\ ,\ \emptyset \right)$$

We treat array accesses analogously to field accesses, except that if any quantified variables occur in an array index expression, we additionally include existential quantifiers (with the same bounds) around the equality generated in the set comprehension.

---

[3] We write $Q\!\downarrow_1$ and $Q\!\downarrow_2$ for the first and second projections of pair Q, respectively.

For the Composite, we derive the following simplest concerns-description, in which the shorthand $\mathsf{o} \in \mathsf{o}'.\mathsf{comps}$ stands for $\exists 0 \leq i < \mathsf{o}'.\mathsf{count} :: \mathsf{o}'.\mathsf{comps}[\mathsf{i}] = \mathsf{o}$:

$$\begin{array}{ll}
\mathcal{D}_S(\mathsf{parent}, \mathsf{Inv3}) = (\{o \mid \mathsf{mod} \in o.\mathsf{comps}\}, \emptyset) & \mathcal{D}_S(\mathsf{parent}, \mathsf{Inv4}) = (\{\mathsf{mod}\}, \emptyset) \\
\mathcal{D}_S(\mathsf{comps}, \mathsf{Inv2}) = (\{\mathsf{mod}\}, \emptyset) & \mathcal{D}_S(\mathsf{comps}, \mathsf{Inv3}) = (\{\mathsf{mod}\}, \emptyset) \\
\mathcal{D}_S(\mathsf{comps}, \mathsf{Inv4}) = (\{o \mid o.\mathsf{parent} = \mathsf{mod}\}, \emptyset) & \mathcal{D}_S(\mathsf{comps}, \mathsf{Inv5}) = (\{\mathsf{mod}\}, \emptyset) \\
\mathcal{D}_S(\mathsf{count}, \mathsf{Inv1}) = (\{\mathsf{mod}\}, \emptyset) & \mathcal{D}_S(\mathsf{count}, \mathsf{Inv2}) = (\{\mathsf{mod}\}, \emptyset) \\
\mathcal{D}_S(\mathsf{count}, \mathsf{Inv3}) = (\{\mathsf{mod}\}, \emptyset) & \mathcal{D}_S(\mathsf{count}, \mathsf{Inv4}) = (\{o \mid o.\mathsf{parent} = \mathsf{mod}\}, \emptyset) \\
\mathcal{D}_S(\mathsf{count}, \mathsf{Inv5}) = (\{\mathsf{mod}\}, \emptyset) & \mathcal{D}_S(\mathsf{total}, \mathsf{Inv1}) = (\{\mathsf{mod}\}, \emptyset) \\
\mathcal{D}_S(\mathsf{total}, \mathsf{Inv2}) = (\{\mathsf{mod}\} \cup \{o \mid \mathsf{mod} \in o.\mathsf{comps}\}, \emptyset) & \\
\mathcal{D}_S(\mathsf{f}, \mathsf{I}) = (\emptyset, \emptyset) \ \textit{otherwise} &
\end{array}$$

Admissibility is trivially satisfied by the simplest concerns-description:

Proposition 1. *The simplest concerns-description $\mathcal{D}_S$ is admissible.*

Observe that $\mathcal{D}_S$ given above uses sets $\{\mathsf{mod}\}$, $\{o \mid o.\mathsf{parent} = \mathsf{mod}\}$, and $\{o \mid \mathsf{mod} \in o.\mathsf{comps}\}$. We call a set description *direct*, if any field access paths start at mod, and *indirect* otherwise. Thus, the set description $\{\mathsf{mod}\}$ is direct, and the other two above are indirect. Indirect set descriptions turn out to be undesirable in practice, since they give rise to proof obligations concerning indirectly described objects, which are often too difficult for the automated theorem prover.

We shall attempt to transform the four cases of indirect sets in our example into direct ones. We start with $\mathcal{D}_S(\mathsf{parent}, \mathsf{Inv3})$, which specifies that modification of parent of an object mod may break invariant Inv3 for those objects which contain mod in their comps. Recall however that the "structural" invariant Inv3 guarantees that for any o', if $o' \in o.\mathsf{comps}$ then $o'.\mathsf{parent} = o$. Therefore, we can conclude that *if* an object o satisfies Inv3, then $o \in \{o \mid \mathsf{mod} \in o.\mathsf{comps}\} \Rightarrow o \in \{\mathsf{mod.parent}\}$; the latter set is direct. Since the definition of admissibility allows us to assume that the concerned invariant (in this case Inv3) holds, applying the invariant's definition to the set description does not affect admissibility:

Proposition 2. *Suppose $\mathcal{D}$ and $\mathcal{D}'$ are concerns-descriptions, and that for all fields* f *and invariants* I*, it holds that $\mathcal{D}(\mathsf{f}, \mathsf{I})\downarrow_2 = \mathcal{D}'(\mathsf{f}, \mathsf{I})\downarrow_2$ and we can prove for arbitrary o that if $P_{\mathsf{I}}(o)$ holds and $o \in \mathcal{D}(\mathsf{f}, \mathsf{I})\downarrow_1$ then $o \in \mathcal{D}'(\mathsf{f}, \mathsf{I})\downarrow_1$. Then, if $\mathcal{D}$ is admissible then $\mathcal{D}'$ is admissible.*

Using this proposition, we can take a set description from a concerns-description known to be admissible, and rewrite it using the definition of the invariant it is concerned with. Admissibility of the resulting concerns description is guaranteed to be preserved. In particular, for the Composite we can replace the concerns-description for parent and Inv3 as follows:

$\mathcal{D}(\mathsf{parent}, \mathsf{Inv3}) = (\{\mathsf{mod.parent}\}, \emptyset)$

Similarly, we can replace the next two indirect set descriptions with the following:

$\mathcal{D}(\mathsf{comps}, \mathsf{Inv4}) = (\{o \in \mathsf{mod.comps}\}, \emptyset)$

$\mathcal{D}(\mathsf{count}, \mathsf{Inv4}) = (\{o \in \mathsf{mod.comps}\}, \emptyset)$

This leaves us now with one remaining indirect set description:
$\mathcal{D}(\mathsf{total}, \mathsf{Inv2}) = (\{\mathsf{mod}\} \cup \{o \mid \mathsf{mod} \in o.\mathsf{comps}\}, \emptyset)$
This set comprehension is the same as for the first case, therefore if we could assume that Inv3 held for all objects in the set, we could rewrite the set into the direct form, {mod.parent} as before. In this case, Proposition 2 does not apply, because we wish to use a different invariant Inv3 to rewrite the set description for Inv2. In order to justify the desired rewriting of the set comprehension, we can instead make use of the supporting invariants, and explicitly mark that the correctness of the new set description depends on Inv3 holding, i.e., we define
$\mathcal{D}(\mathsf{total}, \mathsf{Inv2}) = (\{\mathsf{mod}\} \cup \{o \mid \mathsf{mod.parent}\}, \{\mathsf{Inv3}\})$
This can be understood at an intuitive level also: We can be sure that the objects whose invariants Inv2 are affected by modifying the total of mod are (at most) the objects mod and mod.parent *only if* we can be sure that mod cannot be in the comps of any other object. This is what invariant Inv3 guarantees. We can generalise the process we applied above with the following result:

Proposition 3. *Suppose $\mathcal{D}$ is an admissible concerns-description, and $\mathcal{D}'$ is a concerns-description identical to $\mathcal{D}$ except for the definition of $\mathcal{D}(\mathsf{f}, \mathsf{I})$ for some particular* f *and* I. *Suppose further that for some invariant* J *we have $\mathcal{D}'(\mathsf{f}, \mathsf{I})\downarrow_2 = \mathcal{D}(\mathsf{f}, \mathsf{I})\downarrow_2 \cup \{\mathsf{J}\}$. Then, if by assuming that $\forall o, P_{\mathsf{J}}(o)$ holds, we can prove that $\mathcal{D}(\mathsf{f}, \mathsf{I})\downarrow_1 \subseteq \mathcal{D}'(\mathsf{f}, \mathsf{I})\downarrow_1$, then $\mathcal{D}'$ is admissible.*

Using this proposition, we can take a set description from a concerns description known to be admissible, and rewrite it using the definition of any invariant we like (adding the invariant to the supporting invariants). Admissibility of the resulting concerns-description is guaranteed to be preserved. However, in order for a verification technique based on the resulting concerns-description to be sound, we require a mechanism for guaranteeing that supporting invariants will hold when required. For example, in case of the Composite, we require some way of ensuring that whenever we wish to use $\mathcal{D}_S(\mathsf{total}, \mathsf{Inv2})\downarrow_1$, the condition $\forall o :: P_{\mathsf{Inv3}}(o)$ holds. For this reason, we need a way of treating the invariant Inv3 in some special fashion. We recall that the invariants Inv3 and Inv4 were introduced to make explicit the inverse relationship between components and parent, which is implicitly intended in the implementation. As such, we expect these invariants to hold *almost* all of the time. The only reason the invariants ever need to be broken is that it is impossible to simultaneously update the necessary fields to keep the implementation of this relationship consistent. For this reason, the invariant semantics of Definition 1 seems too coarse-grained for these invariants, since it allows them to be broken for arbitrarily long code fragments (so long as no method boundaries are reached), whereas in fact they are only required to be broken for a handful of consecutive statements at a time.

Using this observation, we introduce a refinement of our treatment of invariants. The idea is to allow some invariants to be declared as more fundamental, and to only allow these invariants to be broken for short and prescribed sections of the code. A scoped declaration unreliable is used to specify that certain named invariants may possibly be violated for the duration of the scope (which is expected to enclose only a brief fragment of the code). This follows the intuition behind why these "structural invariants" are broken at all - it is just while the necessary field updates can all be made, to modify the intended parent-components relation.

Definition 5 (Structural Invariants and Unreliable Declarations). *The keyword* structural *may be placed before an invariant declaration, to mark the invariant as a* structural invariant. *By default, invariants are not structural.*

1. *Concerns-descriptions $\mathcal{D}$ are restricted to only allow structural invariants to be mentioned in the supporting invariants.*
2. *A scoped construct* unreliable: $\mathsf{I}_1, \mathsf{I}_2, \ldots, \mathsf{I}_n\{..\}$, *may be placed around any sequence of statements which do not contain any method calls (specifying which structural invariants may possibly be broken within the scope).*
3. *Programs are restricted as follows: for any field update* $\mathsf{e.f} = \mathsf{e}'$, *and for any invariant* I, *if* $\mathcal{D}(\mathsf{f}, \mathsf{I})\!\downarrow_1\![\mathsf{e}/\mathsf{mod}]$ *is non-empty, then the field update* must not *occur within an* unreliable *declaration which names any (structural) invariants* I' *in* $\mathcal{D}(\mathsf{f}, \mathsf{I})\!\downarrow_2$. *Additionally, if* I *is itself a* structural *invariant, then the field update* must *occur within an* unreliable *block declaring* I.
4. *Structural invariants may not be mentioned in* broken *declarations.*

Note that the restrictions in the latter two points above do not introduce extra proof obligations for the verification process, since they can be guaranteed by syntactic checks on the program code.

Intuitively, this approach guarantees that structural invariants can only be violated within unreliable blocks which explicitly declare that they might be, while structural invariants may be *depended* on to accurately predict the concerns of a field update only outside the scope of such blocks. Furthermore, any structural invariants violated within an unreliable block should be re-established by the end of the block[4]. From a practical perspective, the burden of determining which objects' invariants are "concerned" with a field update can be completely lifted from the prover - not only are supporting invariants used to precisely identify which objects should be considered, but the validity of the supporting invariants is guaranteed by purely syntactic means.

3.3 Verification Technique

We say that an object's invariant is *vulnerable* at some point in the code, if we have no guarantee that it holds at that point. We calculate vulnerable invariants based on the concerns-descriptions $\mathcal{D}$. Namely, for an update to r.f, and invariant I, the set $\mathcal{D}(\mathsf{f}, \mathsf{I})\!\downarrow_1\![r/\mathsf{mod}]$ gives a conservative approximation of the vulnerable invariants. For sequences of statements we accumulate the vulnerable invariants

[4] Our unreliable blocks described are similar to the expose blocks used in the Spec♯ methodology [3], but are simpler since they only mention invariants by name, rather than distinguishing them for particular objects.

for each statement, in a similar fashion to standard static code analysis techniques. [5] For conditional branches we accumulate the effects of each branch.[6] Finally, according to the invariant semantics, after a method finishes executing all invariants must hold, and so it is justified after a call to "reset" the vulnerable set to empty.

Definition 6 (Vulnerable Invariants). *At any program point, the* vulnerable invariants *are represented by a map $\mathcal{V}$ from invariant names to descriptions of sets of references (denoting which objects may possibly not satisfy the invariant). It is computed as follows.*

1. *At the start of a method body, the vulnerable invariants are exactly those declared by the method's* broken *constructs (if any).*
2. *After a field assignment* $\mathsf{e.f} = \mathsf{e}'$, *if $\mathcal{V}$ describes the vulnerable invariants* before *the assignment, then the vulnerable invariants* after *the assignment, $\mathcal{V}'$ are defined for each invariant* I, *by:* $\mathcal{V}'(\mathsf{I}) = \mathcal{V}(\mathsf{I}) \cup \mathcal{D}(\mathsf{f},\mathsf{I})\downarrow_1[\mathsf{e}/\mathsf{mod}]$.[7]
3. *After a conditional statement, the vulnerable invariants for each invariant is the union of those at the end of each branch.*
4. *After the end of an* unreliable *block, for each (structural) invariant* I *named by the block and not named by a further enclosing* unreliable *block, $\mathcal{V}(\mathsf{I})$ is empty. For all other invariants, $\mathcal{V}(\mathsf{I})$ is as it was at the end of the block.*
5. *After a method call, $\mathcal{V}(\mathsf{I})$ is empty for all invariants* I.

Note that we allow for the possibility of nesting unreliable blocks within each other. While we don't require this feature for our specification of the Composite, it could add extra flexibility in a setting where several structural invariants are mutually dependent - in this case it may be useful to accurately reflect the situation when some structural invariants are re-established before others by closing one block and leaving another open.

Our verification technique allows us to make assumptions about the validity of invariants and imposes proof obligations for invariants as follows:

Definition 7 (Considerate Verification Technique). *Given a program annotated with specifications, invariants, an (admissible) concern-description $\mathcal{D}$ and* unreliable *blocks, our methodology handles invariants as follows:*

1. *At the start of a method body, all invariants of all objects may be assumed to hold, except those explicitly declared as* broken *in the method specification.*
2. *Before call to a method* m, *for every invariant* I, *if S is the set of expressions e for which $\mathsf{I}(e)$ is mentioned in a* broken *declaration of* m, *then $\forall o, o \in \mathcal{V}(\mathsf{I}) \wedge o \notin S \Rightarrow P_{\mathsf{I}}(o)$ must be proven.*

[5] In fact, the meaning of the set descriptions may be affected by subsequent field updates. We cater for this by recording copies of the symbolic heap, and writing assert and assume statements in terms of these copies, cf. [1]

[6] For simplicity we do not handle loops here, but believe that they can be handled by suitably extending the usual loop-invariant-based approach from Hoare Logic.

[7] Recall that we are eliding details of how to handle field updates which change the meaning of the vulnerable invariants recorded so far.

3. After a method call, all the invariants of all objects may be assumed to hold.
4. At the end-point of an unreliable *block, for every invariant* I *declared in the block but not in an enclosing such block,* $\forall o, o \in \mathcal{V}(\mathsf{I}) \Rightarrow P_{\mathsf{I}}(o)$ *must be proved.*
5. At the end of a method body, for every invariant I, $\forall o, o \in \mathcal{V}(\mathsf{I}) \Rightarrow P_{\mathsf{I}}(o)$ *must be proven.*

Proposition 4. *The Considerate Verification Technique is sound.*

Proof sketch. We first show as an easy lemma that the vulnerable set for a structural invariant I is empty at all program points which are not inside an unreliable block declaring I.

This allows us to prove that any invariants which are broken by any field assignment fall within the described vulnerable set, as follows. Because we assume invariants only depend on the heap via field accesses, we know that if $\mathsf{I}(o)$ holds in heap h, but does not hold in heap h', and h' differs from h only in the value of $o'.f$, then there exist fields f_1, ... f_n, such that $o.\mathsf{f}_1...\mathsf{f}_n.\mathsf{f}$ appears in $P_I(o)$, and $o.\mathsf{f}_1...\mathsf{f}_n = o'$ in h. By the previous lemma, we know that for any structural invariant $\mathsf{I}' \in \mathcal{D}(\mathsf{f}, I)\downarrow_2$, it is safe to assume $\forall o', P_{\mathsf{I}'} o'$ holds. By definition 3, we obtain that $o \in \mathcal{D}(\mathsf{f}, I)\downarrow_1[o.\mathsf{f}_1...\mathsf{f}_n/\mathsf{mod}]$. The latter set corresponds in h to $\mathcal{D}(\mathsf{f}, I)[o'/\mathsf{mod}]$, which is the set added to the vulnerable invariants.

We can now show that assuming that all methods have been checked according to Def. 7, then execution preserves the property that any invariants which do not hold are within those calculated to be vulnerable according to Def. 6. This can be shown by induction on the execution.

At all point where our invariant semantics (Def. 1) specifies that invariants must hold, our technique imposes proof obligations to show that all required invariants which are also vulnerable, are shown to hold. Therefore, by the above, no required invariants can be false at these points.

3.4 Verification of the Composite Pattern

For the Composite code, we use the improved concerns-description developed earlier in the paper, which we recall here in full, for reference:

$$
\begin{array}{llll}
\mathcal{D}(\mathsf{parent}, \mathsf{Inv3}) = (\{\mathsf{mod.parent}\}, \emptyset) & & \mathcal{D}(\mathsf{parent}, \mathsf{Inv4}) = (\{\mathsf{mod}\}, \emptyset) \\
\mathcal{D}(\mathsf{comps}, \mathsf{Inv2}) = (\{\mathsf{mod}\}, \emptyset) & & \mathcal{D}(\mathsf{comps}, \mathsf{Inv3}) = (\{\mathsf{mod}\}, \emptyset) \\
\mathcal{D}(\mathsf{comps}, \mathsf{Inv4}) = (\{o \mid o \in \mathsf{mod.comps}\}, \emptyset) & & \mathcal{D}(\mathsf{comps}, \mathsf{Inv5}) = (\{\mathsf{mod}\}, \emptyset) \\
\mathcal{D}(\mathsf{count}, \mathsf{Inv1}) = (\{\mathsf{mod}\}, \emptyset) & & \mathcal{D}(\mathsf{count}, \mathsf{Inv2}) = (\{\mathsf{mod}\}, \emptyset) \\
\mathcal{D}(\mathsf{count}, \mathsf{Inv3}) = (\{\mathsf{mod}\}, \emptyset) & & \mathcal{D}(\mathsf{count}, \mathsf{Inv4}) = (\{o \mid o \in \mathsf{mod.comps}\}, \emptyset) \\
\mathcal{D}(\mathsf{count}, \mathsf{Inv5}) = (\{\mathsf{mod}\}, \emptyset) & & \mathcal{D}(\mathsf{total}, \mathsf{Inv1}) = (\{\mathsf{mod}\}, \emptyset) \\
\mathcal{D}(\mathsf{total}, \mathsf{Inv2}) = (\{\mathsf{mod}, \mathsf{mod.parent}\}, \{\mathsf{Inv3}\}) & & \\
\mathcal{D}(\mathsf{f}, \mathsf{I}) = (\emptyset, \emptyset) \ \textit{otherwise} & &
\end{array}
$$

We consider the invariants Inv3, Inv4 and Inv5 to be structural, and place an unreliable block around the three assignment statements in the add method which temporarily violate these invariants. Def. 5 requires that a total field is not modified within such a block - this is indeed the case. Using the concerns-description, we analyse the code to predict vulnerable invariants at each point, and generate proof obligations according to Def. 7. Figure 3 shows the complete code, including assume/assert statements which encode the proof obligations. Note that these statements are exactly as specified by Def. 7 - no additional manual assertions are required, and no further assert/assume statements need to be provided. We map this specification to Boogie2, which then passes the proof obligations to the Z3 automatic theorem prover for verification.

Verification of the Boogie2 code opens up a low-level problem concerning the prover's treatment of quantifiers. In particular, some control needs to be imposed to stop the prover from taking arbitrarily many (mostly irrelevant) instances of a quantifier formula it "knows", and thus looping forever. The very strong assumptions made by our methodology at the beginning of a method body and after a method call, can actually *negatively* impact the performance of the prover, if not controlled. This problem is generic to the use of quantifiers with the Z3 prover, and can be tackled by using *triggers* [6,13,14], a mechanism which restricts the situations under which the prover instantiates quantified formulae. We do not go into detail here; however, we have developed a methodology for defining triggers for the formulae concerned with our methodology, which we will describe in future work. Our Boogie2 code [1] uses triggers.

Verification of the Boogie2 code succeeds, in approximately six seconds. Interestingly, if one takes the simplest concerns-description instead (which still employs indirect set comprehensions), the resulting specification does not verify. Therefore, the improvements introduced by Propositions 2 and 3 are essential for our approach to be practical. However, the current need to annotate the code with unreliable declarations and concerns-descriptions seems to place an extra burden to the user; we next consider how to alleviate it.

3.5 Automation of Our Technique

We now explain how the various aspects of our methodology could be supported by automatic tools.

Determine Concerns-Description: A tool can straightforwardly derive the simplest concerns-description $\mathcal{D}'$ (Def. 4). Next, any declared structural invariants expressing "inverse" relationships (e.g., $\mathsf{o.components[i].parent} = \mathsf{o}$) can be used to rewrite any indirect set descriptions. Given a set description of the form $\{o \mid o.\mathsf{f}_1 \ldots .\mathsf{f}_{m-1}.\mathsf{f}_\mathsf{m} = \mathsf{mod.g}_1 \ldots .\mathsf{g}_\mathsf{n}\}$ a structural invariant of the form $\mathsf{o}'.\mathsf{f}_\mathsf{m}.\mathsf{h} = o'$ (i.e., declaring an inverse relationship for the field f_m) should be sought. The set description can then be rewritten to $\{o \mid o.\mathsf{f}_1 \ldots .\mathsf{f}_{m-1} = \mathsf{mod.g}_1 \ldots .\mathsf{g}_\mathsf{n}.\mathsf{h}\}$ in which the length of the "indirect" field access from o has been reduced. To preserve admissibility, a structural invariant used to rewrite the set must be recorded in the supporting invariants (cf. Prop. 3), unless it is the same invariant as the one being described by $\mathcal{D}$ (c.f. Prop. 2). This process of rewriting the set can be repeated until the length of the indirect field access is zero, at which point the set comprehension describes precisely one object, and the set can be made direct. In practice, invariants of the desired kind tend to exist in

```
// requires : c ≠ null;
// requires : c.parent = null;
public void add(Composite c) {
  assume ∀ o :: Inv1(o) ∧ Inv2(o) ∧ Inv3(o) ∧ Inv4(o) ∧ Inv5(o);

  // unreliable : Inv3, Inv4, Inv5 {
  this.comps[this.count] = c;
  this.count = this.count + 1;
  c.parent = this;
  assert Inv3(this) ∧ Inv3(c.parent);
  assert ∀ o :: o=c ∨ (∃0≤i≤this.count i:int :: this.comps[i] = o) ⇒ Inv4(o);
  assert Inv5(this);
  //}

  assert Inv1(this);
  assert this ≠ this ⇒ Inv2(this); // trivial — by "broken" declaration
  addToTotal(this,c.total);
  assume ∀ o :: Inv1(o)∧Inv2(o)∧Inv3(o)∧Inv4(o)∧Inv5(o);

}

// broken: Inv2(this)
// requires : this.total + p = 1 + Σ_{0≤i<count} comps[i].total
private void addToTotal(int p) {
{
  assume ∀ o :: Inv1(o)∧Inv3(o)∧Inv4(o)∧Inv5(o);
  assume ∀ o :: o≠ this ⇒ Inv2(o);

  this.total = this.total + p;
  if(parent != null) {

    assert Inv1(this);
    assert ∀ o :: (o=this ∨ o=this.parent) ∧ o≠ this.parent ⇒ Inv2(o);
    parent.addToTotal(p);
    assume ∀ o :: Inv1(o)∧Inv2(o)∧Inv3(o)∧Inv4(o)∧Inv5(o);
  }

  assert Inv1(this);
  assert ∀ o :: (o=this ∨ o=this.parent) ⇒ Inv2(o);
}
```

Fig. 3. Proof Obligations for the Composite

"considerate" implementations, since the inverse field references are required for the implementation to be able to notify objects appropriately (e.g., the parent field in the Composite). However, if at any point a suitable structural invariant cannot be found, either an error can be reported to the user (suggesting that further structural invariants may need to be specified), or a warning could be given, and the verification optimistically continued using the indirect description.

Introduce unreliable blocks: One can automatically infer when an unreliable block needs to begin, and which invariants need to be named, by using $\mathcal{D}$ to identify the points in the code at which structural invariants may be invalidated. Inferring where to *end* the unreliable blocks is more challenging, since we need to "guess" how soon we re-establish these invariants. The simplest solution is to be lazy, and leave the block open until these invariants are required to hold again, either because a method call, end of method or conditional block is reached, or because they appear in the supporting invariants of a concerns-description for a field update. In practice, this typically doesn't leave much scope for "laziness", and showing that the structural invariants are re-established at the derived point is not problematic. For example, in the Composite add method, the structural invariants must be re-established before addToTotal can be called.
Calculate proof obligations: The vulnerable invariants can be calculated (Def. 6) and corresponding assume/assert statements derived (Defs. 7 and 5).

4 Conclusions, Related and Future Work

We have proposed Considerate Reasoning, a specification/verification methodology based on object invariants, which, we claim, neatly reflects the natural argument of the implementation, and leads to succinct specifications. We have outlined soundness of the technique, described how its support could be automated, and applied it to specify the Composite pattern.

Our work is based on, and extends, that of Middelkoop et. al. [15]. Our concerns-descriptions add to their "coop-sets" the concept of supporting invariants; we introduced inference of admissible concerns-descriptions, structural invariants, unreliable blocks, and the application to Boogie2.

Several specifications of the Composite were proposed for SAVCBS 2008. For example, Jacobs et. al. [9] give a specification in separation logic, which expresses the decomposition of a tree-structure into different context-tree views from the viewpoint of the current receiver. The specification is not able to enforce invariants for all objects, and thus cannot guarantee preservation of the main invariant, Inv2, for *all* objects in the heap. It was machine-verified using VeriFast [8]. The verification was interactive, and required the manual addition of lemmas, and open/close and assert statements.

Bierhoff and Aldrich [5] present a specification using data groups, fractional permissions, type states, and explicitly marking the violation/re-establishing of invariants through unpack/pack statements. Permissions control state dependencies in invariants - essentially each object depending on certain state for its invariant must carry some permission to that state. The authors outline a manual verification, and discuss how a tool could infer unpack/pack statements.

More recently, Rosenberg et. al. [21] give a specification of the Composite using regional logic [2]. They express an invariant semantics similar to ours, whereby they explicitly quantify over the set of all allocated objects, and require in the pre- and post- conditions of the methods the invariants of all objects to hold, except for those objects belonging to a further region (this corresponds to our broken declarations). They mapped the specification into Boogie2 and verified it in approx 6 secs. However, because their handling of invariants is explicit, rather than with a prescribed methodology, some guidance is needed for the verified, which takes the form of several lemmas, and manually annotating the Boogie code with several assume/assert statements.

All these specifications required significant technical development; this is reflected in their length. Conversely, we have tried to retain in the specification only those details which are essential and intuitive from the point of view of the programmer. Furthermore, verification of these specifications requires further work from the programmer, in that he needs to provide lemmas and insert further annotations into the code. Conversely, our methodology can be automated as we discussed earlier on; with our hypothetical tool, the programmer will only need to provide the 25 lines of code and specification shown in Fig. 2. On the other hand, our methodology does not deal with framing, whereas the above approaches address this issue.

In future work we will formalise and prove soundness of Considerate Reasoning, and will combine it with other methodologies supporting complementary programming patterns, as e.g., ownership-based methodologies. We will also address the framing problem, and investigate extending our work to more-general kinds of invariants and patterns in which *collections* of objects may be broken at a time.

We have considered the extension of our approach to concurrency. We propose a locking discipline based on the calculated vulnerable invariants (calculated per thread). Any object in the vulnerable invariants should be locked by the current thread. Correspondingly, objects can only be unlocked if all of their invariants which are vulnerable, can be shown to have been re-established. When applied to the Composite, this idea allows a hand-over-hand locking discipline which can handle many threads updating the tree structure concurrently. Formalising this idea and its extensions will be interesting future work.

Acknowledgments. This work was funded in part by the Information Society Technologies program of the European Commission, Future and Emerging Technologies under the IST-2005-015905 MOBIUS project. We thank the anonymous reviewers for many insightful suggestions, and Arsenii Rudich, Claude Marché, Frank Piessens, Jan Smans, Ronald Middelkoop, Joseph Ruskiewicz and most particularly and specially Peter Müller, for many stimulating discussions.

References

1. Boogie 2 code, `http://people.inf.ethz.ch/summersa/wiki/lib/exe/fetch.php?media=papers:boogie-composite.zip`
2. Banerjee, A., Naumann, D., Rosenberg, S.: Regional logic for local reasoning about global invariants. In: Vitek, J. (ed.) ECOOP 2008. LNCS, vol. 5142, pp. 387–411. Springer, Heidelberg (2008)

3. Barnett, M., DeLine, R., Fähndrich, M., Leino, K.R.M., Schulte, W.: Verification of object-oriented programs with invariants. JOT 3(6), 27–56 (2004)
4. Barnett, M., Naumann, D.: Friends need a bit more: Maintaining invariants over shared state. In: Kozen, D. (ed.) MPC 2004. LNCS, vol. 3125, pp. 54–84. Springer, Heidelberg (2004)
5. Bierhof, K., Aldrich, J.: Permissions to specify the Composite Design Pattern. In: SAVCBS (2008)
6. Detlefs, D., Nelson, G., Saxe, J.B.: Simplify: a theorem prover for program checking. Journal of the ACM (52) (2005)
7. Gamma, E., Helm, R., Johnson, R., Vlissides, J.: Design patterns: elements of reusable object-oriented software. Addison-Wesley, Reading (1995)
8. Jacobs, B., Piessens, F.: The verifast program verifier. Technical report, Katholieke Universiteit Leuven (August 2008)
9. Jacobs, B., Smans, J., Piessens, F.: Verifying the Composite Pattern using Separation Logic. In: SAVCBS (2008)
10. Kassios, I.T.: Dynamic frames: Support for framing, dependencies and sharing without restrictions. In: Misra, J., Nipkow, T., Sekerinski, E. (eds.) FM 2006. LNCS, vol. 4085, pp. 268–283. Springer, Heidelberg (2006)
11. Leavens, G.T., Leino, K.R.M., Müller, P.: Specification and verification challenges for sequential object-oriented programs. FAC 19(2), 159–189 (2007)
12. Leino, K.R.M., Müller, P.: Object invariants in dynamic contexts. In: Odersky, M. (ed.) ECOOP 2004. LNCS, vol. 3086, pp. 491–515. Springer, Heidelberg (2004)
13. Rustan, K., Leino, M.: This is Boogie 2, `http://research.microsoft.com/en-us/um/people/leino/papers.html`
14. Leino, K.R.M., Monahan, R.: Reasoning about comprehensions with first-order smt solvers. In: SAC 2009. ACM, New York (2009)
15. Middelkoop, R., Huizing, C., Kuiper, R., Luit, E.J.: Invariants for non-hierarchical object structures. ENTCS 195, 211–229 (2008)
16. Müller, P., Poetzsch-Heffter, A., Leavens, G.T.: Modular invariants for layered object structures. Science of Computer Programming 62, 253–286 (2006)
17. O'Hearn, P.W., Yang, H., Reynolds, J.C.: Separation and information hiding. In: POPL. ACM Press, New York (2004)
18. Parkinson, M., Bierman, G.: Separation logic and abstraction. In: POPL. ACM Press, New York (2005)
19. Poetzsch-Heffter, A.: Specification and verification of object-oriented programs. Habilitation thesis, Technical University of Munich (1997)
20. Reynolds, J.C.: Separation logic: A logic for shared mutable data structures. In: LICS. IEEE Computer Society Press, Los Alamitos (2002)
21. Rosenberg, S., Banerjee, A., Naumann, D.: Local Reasoning and Dynamic Framing for the Composite Pattern and its Clients, `http://www.cs.stevens.edu/~naumann/publications/RosenbergBanerjeeNaumann09a.pdf`
22. Sha, L., Rajkumar, R., Lehoczky, J.P.: Priority inheritance protocols: An approach to real-time synchronization. IEEE Trans. Comp. 39(9), 1175–1185 (1990)
23. Smans, J., Jacobs, B., Piessens, F.: Implicit dynamic frames: Combining dynamic frames and separation logic. In: Drossopoulou, S. (ed.) ECOOP 2009. LNCS, vol. 5653, pp. 148–172. Springer, Heidelberg (2009)
24. Summers, A.J., Drossopoulou, S., Müller, P.: The need for flexible Object Invariants. In: IWACO 2009 (2009)

RGSep Action Inference

Viktor Vafeiadis

Microsoft Research Cambridge, UK

Abstract. We present an automatic verification procedure based on RGSep that is suitable for reasoning about fine-grained concurrent heap-manipulating programs. The procedure computes a set of RGSep actions overapproximating the interference that each thread causes to its concurrent environment. These inferred actions allow us to verify safety, liveness, and functional correctness properties of a collection of practical concurrent algorithms from the literature.

1 Introduction

Low level C programmers constantly rely on two very error-prone programming features: manual memory management (`malloc`/`free`) and concurrency. While there are several verification techniques for reasoning about either feature in isolation, few techniques can handle programs using both features.

One such technique is RGSep [20], a recent extension of rely-guarantee reasoning [11] that incorporates separation logic [15]. RGSep specifications describe the updates to the shared state using two binary relations: the rely and the guarantee. A thread's rely relation under-approximates the interference it can tolerate from its environment (that is, the updates that other threads are allowed to do), whereas the guarantee over-approximates the updates the thread can do, i.e. the interference that it causes to its concurrent environment. RGSep represents these binary relations as the reflexive and transitive closure of a set of *actions*, which are precondition-postcondition pairs describing the possible small updates.

On its own RGSep is just a program logic: users must prove their programs correct with pencil and paper using RGSep's proof rules. As constructing such proofs manually is quite tedious and often error-prone, there has been some work on constructing such proofs semi-automatically [5,19] by letting the programmer supply the rely and guarantee relations and doing abstract interpretation to figure out the more tedious aspects of the proof.

Here, we extend the aforementioned work to be fully automatic. We present an algorithm (Infer-Actions, §3) that calculates the rely and guarantee relations as a set of actions, each of which is extended with a special context assertion describing the part of the state that is not affected by the action. These contexts arise naturally during action inference and allow us to define a useful join on actions (§4).

In the process of inferring these actions, our algorithm also proves memory safety, discovers shape invariants, and discharges any user-supplied assertions. The output of action inference has been used to prove advanced safety properties, such as linearizability, and conditional termination [9].

G. Barthe and M. Hermenegildo (Eds.): VMCAI 2010, LNCS 5944, pp. 345–361, 2010.

2 Preliminaries

We consider programs in a first-order subset of C. Programs consist of an initialization phase followed by a top-level parallel composition of a possibly unbounded number of threads. The programs for the initialization phase and for each thread are converted to the following simpler language of commands:

$$C ::= \texttt{skip} \mid x := E \mid x := [E] \mid [E] := E' \mid x := \texttt{malloc}() \mid \texttt{assume}(E) \mid C_1; C_2 \mid C_1 \oplus C_2 \mid C^* \mid \texttt{atomic}\ C$$

where x ranges over program variables and E over arithmetic expressions. Program commands, C, include the empty command, variable assignments, memory loads and stores, memory allocation, assume statements, sequential composition, non-deterministic choice, loops, and atomic commands.

An important aspect of our intermediate language is that the atomicity of memory accesses is explicit. By default, we assume that memory accesses are non-atomic. When, however, a memory access is guaranteed to be atomic by the memory model (for example, a single-word memory access to a volatile variable or field), we make this explicit by enclosing it in an atomic block. Similarly, we also use atomic blocks to encode complex atomic instructions such as compare-and-swap. As data races on non-atomic memory accesses can lead to incoherent results, our proof system ensures that there are no races on non-atomic memory accesses, but permits races between two atomic commands.

2.1 Underlying Separation Logic Domain

Our verification is parametric with respect to an underlying separation logic abstract domain. Elements of a separation logic domain are assertions belonging to a fragment of separation logic and are ordered by logical implication. Further, we assume that this fragment of separation logic includes $\mapsto$-assertions, disjunction, $*$-conjunction and that assertions can have free logical variables. We shall use uppercase italic letters (P, Q, R) to range over such separation logic assertions. Their meaning with respect to an interpretation ($\mathcal{I}$) mapping logical variables to values is a set of heaps (partial finite maps from addresses to values):

$$\begin{aligned} [\![\mathsf{emp}]\!]_\mathcal{I} &\stackrel{\text{def}}{=} \{h \mid \mathbf{dom}\ h = \emptyset\} \\ [\![E \mapsto E']\!]_\mathcal{I} &\stackrel{\text{def}}{=} \{h \mid \mathbf{dom}\ h = \{[\![E]\!]_\mathcal{I}\} \wedge h([\![E]\!]_\mathcal{I}) = [\![E']\!]_\mathcal{I}\} \\ [\![P * Q]\!]_\mathcal{I} &\stackrel{\text{def}}{=} \{h_1 \uplus h_2 \mid h_1 \in [\![P]\!]_\mathcal{I} \wedge h_2 \in [\![Q]\!]_\mathcal{I}\} \end{aligned}$$

where $h_1 \uplus h_2$ denotes the union of the functions h_1 and h_2 if their domains are disjoint, and is undefined if their domains overlap. Finally, the abstract domain must support the following three operations:

Abstraction: $\textsc{Abstract}(P)$ over-approximates P ($[\![P]\!]_\mathcal{I} \subseteq [\![\textsc{Abstract}(P)]\!]_\mathcal{I}$) ensuring that fixpoint calculations of the form $P \leftarrow P \vee \alpha(\mathit{transform}(P))$ terminate. This is usually achieved by $\textsc{Abstract}$ having a finite range.

(Must-)Subtraction: $\textsc{Subtract}(P, Q, A)$ is an enhanced entailment checking procedure and is also known as 'frame inference' [2]. It takes two assertions (P, Q) and a set of logical variables (A) that are implicitly existentially quantified in Q. Subtraction tries to find an assertion F such that $P \implies \exists A.\ Q * F$. If such an assertion exists, it returns it; otherwise, it throws an exception (usually resulting in a verification failure). Note that the frame F may provide witnesses for the existentially quantified variables A.

May-Subtraction: $\textsc{May-Subtract}(P, Q, R)$ takes three assertions P, Q, and R and returns an assertion S denoting the left-over state if Q and R are removed from P and the R-part is added back. Formally, for all $\mathcal{I}$, h_1, and h_2, if $(h_1 \uplus h_2) \in [\![P]\!]_{\mathcal{I}}$ and $h_1 \in [\![Q]\!]_{\mathcal{I}}$ and $h_2 \in [\![R * \mathsf{true}]\!]_{\mathcal{I}}$, then $h_2 \in [\![S]\!]_{\mathcal{I}}$. May-subtraction is an overapproximation of the separation logic formula $(Q \mathbin{-\!\circledast} P) \wedge (R * \mathsf{true})$, where $\mathbin{-\!\circledast}$ is the 'septraction' operator [20,5].

The difference between $\textsc{Subtract}$ and $\textsc{May-Subtract}$ is rather important. $\textsc{Subtract}(P, Q, \emptyset)$ proves that Q can be removed from P and returns the remaining part of the state. In contrast, $\textsc{May-Subtract}(P, Q, \mathsf{emp})$ considers all the ways that Q might be removed from P and returns the remaining parts of the state. Consider the following example:

Example 1. Let $P \equiv x \mapsto 1 * y \mapsto 2$, $Q \equiv a \mapsto b$. Calling $\textsc{Subtract}(P, Q, \emptyset)$ would throw an exception because P does not imply that a is allocated. In contrast, $\textsc{May-Subtract}(P, Q, \mathsf{emp})$ would return $(a = x \wedge b = 1 \wedge y \mapsto 2) \vee (a = y \wedge b = 2 \wedge x \mapsto 1)$. Similarly, $\textsc{May-Subtract}(P, \mathsf{emp}, Q)$ would return $(a = x \wedge b = 1 \wedge x \mapsto 1 * y \mapsto 2) \vee (a = y \wedge b = 2 \wedge x \mapsto 1 * y \mapsto 2)$.

During action inference, we shall use $\textsc{Subtract}$ to calculate the effect of the atomic commands of the current thread, and $\textsc{May-Subtract}$ to calculate the effect of interference (i.e., of the commands of the other threads).

Our implementation uses the abstract domains from Distefano et al. [6] and Vafeiadis [19] as underlying separation logic domains. For $\textsc{Subtract}$, we used the entailment algorithm of Berdine et al. [2], and for $\textsc{May-Subtract}$ an improvement over the septraction elimination algorithm of Calcagno et al. [5], which is reported in Appendix A.

2.2 RGSep

RGSep [20] is the program logic on top of which our verification is based. RGSep logically partitions the state of the program into a number of (disjoint) components, which are called regions. Each thread owns one region for its local data, and there is also one region containing data that is shared among threads. RGSep assertions describe only the shared region and the current thread's region and are given by the following grammar:

$$p, q ::= P_{\mathrm{L}} * \boxed{P_{\mathrm{S}}} \mid p \vee q \mid \exists x.\ p$$

The first assertion form says that the thread's local state satisfies P_{L} and that the shared state is disjoint and satisfies P_{S}. Formally,

$$[\![P_{\mathrm{L}} * \boxed{P_{\mathrm{S}}}]\!]_{\mathcal{I}} \stackrel{\mathrm{def}}{=} \{(h_{\mathrm{L}}, h_{\mathrm{S}}) \mid h_{\mathrm{L}} \in [\![P_{\mathrm{L}}]\!]_{\mathcal{I}} \wedge h_{\mathrm{S}} \in [\![P_{\mathrm{S}}]\!]_{\mathcal{I}} \wedge \mathrm{defined}(h_{\mathrm{L}} \uplus h_{\mathrm{S}})\}$$

Note that the separation logic formulas P_L and P_S can have common variables. Such common variables keep track of the correlation between each thread's local state and the shared state. In contrast, there is no way of expressing correlations between the local states of two threads.

The concurrent behaviour of a thread is abstracted by a set of precondition-postcondition pairs, $P \leadsto Q$, known as actions. Actions summarise what modifications the atomic statements of a thread can perform on the shared state. Their semantics is formally defined as follows:

$$\mathcal{A}[\![P \leadsto Q]\!] \stackrel{\text{def}}{=} \{(s \uplus s_0, s' \uplus s_0) \mid \exists \mathcal{I}.\ \ s \in [\![P]\!]_{\mathcal{I}} \wedge s' \in [\![Q]\!]_{\mathcal{I}}\}$$

The action's precondition and postcondition describe only the part of the state that changes; the remaining part (s_0) is assumed not to change, and is not further constrained. The assertions P and Q can have some free logical variables (in the domain of $\mathcal{I}$): these are implicitly existentially quantified and their scope extends over both P and Q.

In this paper, we extend the notion of actions with a context assertion, R, restricting when the action can execute. Contexts are very useful during action inference and, in particular, for defining a good join operation (see §4). Formally, their meaning is:

$$\begin{aligned}\mathcal{A}[\![R \mid P \leadsto Q]\!] &\stackrel{\text{def}}{=} \mathcal{A}[\![P \leadsto Q]\!] \cap \mathcal{A}[\![P * R \leadsto Q * R]\!] \\ &= \{(s \uplus s_0, s' \uplus s_0) \mid \exists \mathcal{I}.\ \ s \in [\![P]\!]_{\mathcal{I}} \wedge s' \in [\![Q]\!]_{\mathcal{I}} \wedge s_0 \in [\![R * \mathsf{true}]\!]_{\mathcal{I}}\}\end{aligned}$$

The meaning of a set of actions is the reflexive and transitive closure of the union of the meanings of the individual actions:

$$[\![\{a_1, \ldots, a_n\}]\!] \stackrel{\text{def}}{=} (\mathcal{A}[\![a_1]\!] \cup \ldots \cup \mathcal{A}[\![a_n]\!])^*$$

Reflexive and transitive closure models any arbitrary interleaving of any number of repetitions of the actions a_1 to a_n.

RGSep judgments are of the form $\mathit{Rely}, \mathit{Guar} \vdash_{\mathsf{RGSep}} \{p\}\ C\ \{q\}$, where *Rely* and *Guar* are sets of actions and p and q are RGSep assertions. Informally, this specification says that if the initial state satisfies p and all environment transitions are included in *Rely*, then (a) C does not fault, (b) all of C's transitions are included in *Guar*, and (c) if C terminates, then the final state satisfies q. RGSep provides a collection of proof rules for deriving such judgments, which we omit for brevity. These can be found in [20,18].

Stabilization. An important requirement of the RGSep proof rules is that certain assertions appearing in the proof of a thread are stable under the rely condition. Stability is formally defined as follows:

Definition 1 (Stability). *An assertion P about the shared state is* stable *under the binary relation R, if and only if interference with R cannot falsify P: i.e. for all $\mathcal{I}$, s, s', if $s \in [\![P]\!]_{\mathcal{I}}$ and $(s, s') \in R$, then $s' \in [\![P]\!]_{\mathcal{I}}$.*

Algorithm 1. STABILIZE($S, Rely$)

repeat
  $S_{\text{old}} \leftarrow S$
  for all $(R \mid P \leadsto Q) \in Rely$ **do**
    $S \leftarrow S \vee \text{ABSTRACT}(\text{MAY-SUBTRACT}(S, P, R) * Q)$
until $S = S_{\text{old}}$
return S

Given a rely condition *Rely* and a possibly unstable assertion S, Alg. 1 computes a weaker assertion S' that is stable under *Rely*. It does so by taking into account interference with each action in *Rely* until a fixpoint is reached. To ensure that the fixpoint calculation converges, we apply abstraction at each loop iteration.

Theorem 1 (Stabilization Soundness). *If* STABILIZE$(S, Rely) = S'$, *then for all* $\mathcal{I}$, $[\![S]\!]_{\mathcal{I}} \subseteq [\![S']\!]_{\mathcal{I}}$ *and* S' *is stable under Rely.*

The proof of this theorem follows directly from the definitions of stability, RGSep actions, and the specification of MAY-SUBTRACT.

Note that the execution time of STABILIZE($S, Rely$) is linear in the number of actions in *Rely*. Since stabilization is the most time-consuming component of action inference, it is important that action inference infers small sets of actions. We shall return to this point in Sect. 4.

3 Action Inference Algorithm

A library consists of an initialization method, *init*, and a number of access methods, *Ms*, which can be executed concurrently after the initialization method has finished. The most general concurrent client of a library is defined as follows:

Definition 2 (Most General Client). *The* most general client *of a library executes its initialization method followed by an unbounded number of threads, each executing any number of the access methods in any order:*

$$\text{MGC}(init, \{C_1, \ldots, C_n\}) \stackrel{\text{def}}{=} init; \|(C_1 \oplus \ldots \oplus C_n)^*$$

The most general client over-approximates all legal clients of the library in that concrete clients will use the module in a more constrained way than the most general client.

Some libraries require that their methods are called in a more constrained fashion than the most general client above. For example, a lock library typically assumes that threads do not attempt to acquire any locks that they already hold nor to release any locks that they do not hold. These requirements can be formalized with a simple state machine per thread describing which methods the thread is allowed to call at each time. To verify the lock library, one can encode the state machine in the body of the `acquire` and `release` methods using an auxiliary thread-local variable.

Algorithm 2. INFER-ACTIONS($init, Ms$)

$G \leftarrow \emptyset$
$(-, Inv) \leftarrow$ SYMB-EXEC($\mathsf{emp}, \emptyset, init$)
repeat
  $G_{\text{old}} \leftarrow G$
  $Inv \leftarrow$ STABILIZE(Inv, G)
  for all $C \in Ms$ **do**
    $(G_{\text{new}}, -) \leftarrow$ SYMB-EXEC($\boxed{Inv}, G, C$)
    $G \leftarrow G \cup G_{\text{new}}$
until $G = G_{\text{old}}$
return (G, Inv)

Algorithm 3. Memory reads: SYMB-EXEC($\exists \boldsymbol{z}.\ P_{\text{L}} * \boxed{P_{\text{S}}}, Rely, \mathtt{x} := [E]$)

if SUBTRACT($P_{\text{L}}, E \mapsto \alpha, \{\alpha\}$) $= R_{\text{L}}$ **then**
  return $(\emptyset,\ \exists \boldsymbol{z}\, \alpha\, \beta.\ \mathtt{x} = \alpha \wedge E \mapsto \alpha * R_{\text{L}}[\beta/\mathtt{x}] * \boxed{P_{\text{S}}[\beta/\mathtt{x}]})$
else if inside an atomic block **and** SUBTRACT($P_{\text{S}}, E \mapsto \alpha, \{\alpha\}$) $= R_{\text{S}}$ **then**
  return $(\emptyset,\ \exists \boldsymbol{z}\, \alpha\, \beta.\ \mathtt{x} = \alpha \wedge P_{\text{L}}[\beta/\mathtt{x}] * \boxed{E \mapsto \alpha * R_{\text{S}}[\beta/\mathtt{x}]})$
else
  return ERROR

INFER-ACTIONS (see Alg. 2) takes a library and computes the total interference caused by its access methods (G) and its data structure invariant (Inv) by considering the library's most general client and doing a fixpoint computation. The algorithm assumes that clients of the library cannot directly access the library's internal state; thus, there is no external rely condition.

To calculate the interference produced by a command, INFER-ACTIONS calls our new symbolic execution procedure, SYMB-EXEC. This takes a precondition p, a rely R, and a command C and tries to prove memory safety returning a guarantee G and a postcondition q such that $R, G \vdash_{\text{RGSep}} \{p\}\ C\ \{q\}$. If SYMB-EXEC($p, R, C$) fails to prove memory safety, then it returns ERROR.

We consider memory safety to be the most basic property that all programs should have, and thus fail verification if this property cannot be established. In addition to memory safety, however, action inference can prove much more interesting properties, such as data structure invariants, and discharge user-supplied assertions.

Symbolic execution is defined by induction on the command, C.

Memory Reads. When symbolic execution encounters a memory read (see Alg. 3), it tries to apply the memory read axiom of separation logic. If it is a non-atomic read, the memory location must be in the local state: this is to prevent race conditions. Otherwise, if the read is inside an atomic block (e.g. because the read is atomic, or it used to implement a complex atomic instruction such as CAS), the memory location can also be in the shared state. As memory reads do not change the heap, the guarantee condition is empty. If SYMB-EXEC cannot prove that the

Algorithm 4. Memory writes: $\textsc{Symb-Exec}(\exists \boldsymbol{z}.\ P_{\mathrm{L}} * \boxed{P_{\mathrm{S}}}, \mathit{Rely}, [E] := E')$

if $\textsc{Subtract}(P_{\mathrm{L}}, E \mapsto \alpha, \{\alpha\}) = R_{\mathrm{L}}$ **then**
  return $(\emptyset,\ \exists \boldsymbol{z}.\ E \mapsto E' * R_{\mathrm{L}} * \boxed{P_{\mathrm{S}}})$
else if inside an atomic block **and** $\textsc{Subtract}(P_{\mathrm{S}}, E \mapsto \alpha, \{\alpha\}) = R_{\mathrm{S}}$ **then**
  $(P_{\mathrm{L2S}}, P'_{\mathrm{L}}) \leftarrow \textsc{Reachable-Split}(P_{\mathrm{L}}, E \mapsto E')$
  $\mathit{act} \leftarrow \textsc{A-Abs}(R_{\mathrm{S}} \mid E \mapsto \alpha \rightsquigarrow E \mapsto E' * P_{\mathrm{L2S}})$
  return $(\{\mathit{act}\},\ \exists \boldsymbol{z}.\ P'_{\mathrm{L}} * \boxed{E \mapsto E' * P_{\mathrm{L2S}} * R_{\mathrm{S}}})$
else
  return ERROR

memory cell exists, it returns ERROR. This is consistent with the standard memory model, where programs fail when they access unallocated memory.

If the precondition is disjunctive, SYMB-EXEC does the obvious case split:

$\textsc{Symb-Exec}(\bigvee_i \exists \boldsymbol{z}_i.\ P_i * \boxed{Q_i}, \mathit{Rely}, \mathtt{x} := [E]) \stackrel{\mathrm{def}}{=}$
  for each i **do**
    $(G_i, q_i) \leftarrow \textsc{Symb-Exec}(\exists \boldsymbol{z}_i.\ P_i * \boxed{Q_i}, \mathit{Rely}, \mathtt{x} := [E])$
  return $(\bigcup_i G_i,\ \bigvee_i q_i)$

Memory Writes. If the precondition is disjunctive, symbolic execution does the same case split as for memory reads above. For non-disjunctive preconditions, see Alg. 4. If the write is local, it does not affect the shared state; so $G = \emptyset$. If, however, the write is on the shared state (and hence the write is required to be within an atomic block), then its effect is an action, *act*, which might include some transfer of ownership that re-adjusts the boundary between the local and the shared states. The algorithm relies on a simple reachability heuristic to decide how to re-adjust this boundary. After the memory write, any part of the local state that is reachable from E' is accessible from the shared memory location E, and thus can be accessed by other threads. Therefore, symbolic execution splits the local assertion P_{L} into two parts: P_{L2S} that becomes shared, and P'_{L} that remains local.

As a final step, symbolic execution calls action abstraction, A-ABS, which over-approximates the inferred action. Its input an action $R \mid P \rightsquigarrow Q$ and returns a larger action $R' \mid P' \rightsquigarrow Q'$; i.e. $\mathcal{A}[\![R \mid P \rightsquigarrow Q]\!] \subseteq \mathcal{A}[\![R' \mid P' \rightsquigarrow Q']\!]$. Over-approximation is necessary in order to ensure convergence of the algorithm.

Our implementation of A-ABS consists of two steps. First, it existentially quantifies over local program variables and forgets any pure facts involving them. Second, it applies the underlying abstraction of the separation logic domain to R, P, and Q. We have also experimented with a more aggressive abstraction that removes any list segments appearing in the context. This was partly motivated by our experience: actions containing list segments are rarely needed in manual proofs. Nevertheless, they are necessary for some examples.

Other Program Constructs. Dealing with the other constructs is easy and follows directly from the corresponding RGSep proof rules (see Alg. 5).

Assignments: For simplicity, we assume that all shared variables are allocated in the heap. This is easy to achieve by a preprocessing step which allocates global variables at statically known memory addresses, converting any assignments to global variables into memory writes. Thus, the remaining assignments affect only local variables, and their guarantee condition is empty.

Allocation Commands: Allocated cells are part of the local state.

Sequencing: The guarantee condition of a sequential composition, $C_1; C_2$, is the union of the guarantee conditions of the two commands, C_1 and C_2.

Choice: Similarly, the guarantee condition of $C_1 \oplus C_2$ is the union of the guarantee conditions of the two branches, C_1 and C_2.

Loops: Calculating the loop invariant involves a standard fixpoint computation which applies widening after each iteration. The guarantee condition of the loop is the guarantee condition of the last iteration in the fixpoint computation. To ensure that the fixpoint converges, at each iteration p is abstracted by performing the abstraction of the underlying separation logic domain (ABSTRACT) to all its P_L and P_S components.

Atomic Commands: Symbolic execution runs the body of the atomic command assuming that there is no interference ($\mathit{Rely} = \emptyset$) and then does a stabilization step to take into account interference from other threads. The guarantee condition of the atomic block is just the guarantee condition of its body.

Symbolic execution and action inference are sound in the following sense:

Theorem 2 (Symbolic Execution Soundness). *If* SYMB-EXEC(p, Rely, C) *returns* (G, q), *then* $\mathit{Rely}, G \vdash_{\mathrm{RGSep}} \{p\}\ C\ \{q\}$.

Theorem 3 (Action Inference Soundness). *If* INFER-ACTIONS$(\mathit{init}, \mathit{Ms})$ *returns* (G, Inv), *then* $\emptyset, G \vdash_{\mathrm{RGSep}} \{\mathsf{emp}\}\ \mathrm{MGC}(\mathit{init}, \mathit{Ms})\ \{\boxed{\mathit{Inv}}\}$.

To prove these theorems, we first have to prove the following simpler lemma:

Lemma 1. *If* SYMB-EXEC$(p, \emptyset, C)$ *returns* (G, q), *then* $\emptyset, G \vdash_{\mathrm{RGSep}} \{p\}\ C\ \{q\}$.

This follows from the RGSep proof rule for atomic blocks and the proof rules in Section 4.2 of Vafeiadis's thesis [18]. The theorems then follow easily from the RGSep proof rules [20] and from Lemma 1.

Incompleteness. There are three sources of incompleteness to consider.

First, without auxiliary variables rely-guarantee reasoning is intentionally incomplete. This incompleteness is exactly what makes rely-guarantee reasoning tractable. In practice, auxiliary variables are rarely needed for the sort of programs we have looked at. (None of the memory safety benchmarks of Sect. 5 needed auxiliary variables, except that in the algorithms using locks we modelled locks as storing the identifier of the thread holding the lock. In the linearizability benchmarks, auxiliary variables are used as part of the specification.) Symbolic execution does not attempt to infer such auxiliary variables.

Algorithm 5. $\textsc{Symb-Exec}(p, \mathit{Rely}, C)$ where $p \equiv \bigvee_i \exists \boldsymbol{z}_i.\ P_i * \boxed{Q_i}$

if C is $\texttt{skip}$ **then**
  return $(\emptyset, p)$
else if C is $\texttt{assume}(E)$ **then**
  return $(\emptyset, \bigvee_i \exists \boldsymbol{z}_i.\, E{\neq}0 \wedge P_i * \boxed{Q_i})$
else if C is $\mathtt{x} := E$ **then**
  return $(\emptyset, \bigvee_i \exists \boldsymbol{z}_i.\, \exists \beta.\ \mathtt{x}{=}E[\beta/\mathtt{x}] \wedge P_i[\beta/\mathtt{x}] * \boxed{Q_i[\beta/\mathtt{x}]})$
else if C is $\mathtt{x} := \mathtt{malloc()}$ **then**
  return $(\emptyset, \bigvee_i \exists \boldsymbol{z}_i.\, \exists \alpha\, \beta.\ \mathtt{x}{\mapsto}\alpha * P_i[\beta/\mathtt{x}] * \boxed{Q_i[\beta/\mathtt{x}]})$
else if C is $(C_1; C_2)$ **then**
  $(G_1, q_1) \leftarrow \textsc{Symb-Exec}(p, \mathit{Rely}, C_1)$
  $(G_2, q_2) \leftarrow \textsc{Symb-Exec}(q_1, \mathit{Rely}, C_2)$
  return $(G_1 \cup G_2, q_2)$
else if C is $(C_1 \oplus C_2)$ **then**
  $(G_1, q_1) \leftarrow \textsc{Symb-Exec}(p, \mathit{Rely}, C_1)$
  $(G_2, q_2) \leftarrow \textsc{Symb-Exec}(p, \mathit{Rely}, C_2)$
  return $(G_1 \cup G_2, q_1 \vee q_2)$
else if C is $(C_0)^*$ **then**
  repeat
    $p_{\text{old}} \leftarrow p$
    $(G_{\text{new}}, p) \leftarrow \textsc{Abs-Post}(\textsc{Symb-Exec}(p, \mathit{Rely}, \texttt{skip} \oplus C_0))$
  until $p = p_{\text{old}}$
  return $(G \vee G_{\text{new}}, p)$
else if C is $\texttt{atomic}\, C_0$ **then**
  $(G, \bigvee_i \exists \boldsymbol{x}_i.\ P_i * \boxed{Q_i}) \leftarrow \textsc{Symb-Exec}(p, \emptyset, C_0)$
  return $(G, \bigvee_i \exists \boldsymbol{x}_i.\ P_i * \boxed{\textsc{Stabilize}(Q_i, \mathit{Rely})})$

Second, symbolic execution of atomic blocks is incomplete if the body of an atomic block contains an execution path with more than one memory write. For example, consider the atomic block $\texttt{atomic}$ ([a] := 10; [b] := 10). Assuming the two memory locations a and b were initialized to α and β respectively, then the atomic block does the action:

$$A \stackrel{\text{def}}{=} (\mathsf{emp} \mid \mathsf{a}{\mapsto}\alpha * \mathsf{b}{\mapsto}\beta \leadsto \mathsf{a}{\mapsto}10 * \mathsf{b}{\mapsto}10)$$

However, calling $\textsc{Symb-Exec}$ would return two actions:

$$G \stackrel{\text{def}}{=} \{(\mathsf{b}{\mapsto}\beta \mid \mathsf{a}{\mapsto}\alpha \leadsto \mathsf{a}{\mapsto}10),\ (\mathsf{a}{\mapsto}10 \mid \mathsf{b}{\mapsto}\beta \leadsto \mathsf{b}{\mapsto}10)\}$$

It is easy to show that $[\![\{A\}]\!] \subsetneq [\![G]\!]$. Action A can be simulated by doing the two actions of G in sequence. In the other direction, G allows us to change one field at a time, whereas A demands that both fields are modified in one step.

Normally this form of incompleteness is harmless because atomic commands arise from a single memory read, write or CAS and hence contain at most one memory write. More advanced atomic commands, such as those due to a DCAS or ones containing assignments to auxiliary variables, can contain more than one memory writes. To deal with such atomic commands precisely we introduce a parallel memory write command, which writes to multiple heap locations in one step. This is analogous to the parallel assignment statement present in some programming languages. Symbolic execution of parallel memory writes executes each write separately, but collects all the updates together and returns one action describing all the updates.

Third, the sub-procedures used by the analysis are often incomplete. This includes SUBTRACT, MAY-SUBTRACT, the abstraction of separation logic assertions and of RGSep actions, and the reachability heuristic for deciding ownership transfer. From all these, incompleteness arising from the abstraction of separation logic assertions is the most frequent.

Small Example. To illustrate our symbolic execution and action inference algorithms, consider a trivial shared stack which supports only a push operation:

$$\begin{aligned} \mathit{init} &\stackrel{\text{def}}{=} \mathtt{S} := \mathtt{malloc}();\ [\mathtt{S}] := \mathtt{NULL} \\ \mathit{push} &\stackrel{\text{def}}{=} \mathtt{y} := \mathtt{malloc}();\ \mathtt{b} := \mathtt{false}; \\ &\left(\begin{array}{l} \mathtt{assume}(\neg\mathtt{b});\ \mathtt{atomic}\langle \mathtt{x} := [\mathtt{S}]\rangle;\ \mathtt{atomic}\langle [\mathtt{y}] := \mathtt{x}\rangle; \\ \mathtt{atomic}\left\langle \mathtt{t} := [\mathtt{S}];\ \left(\begin{array}{l} (\mathtt{assume}(\mathtt{t} = \mathtt{x}); [\mathtt{S}] := \mathtt{y}; \mathtt{b} := \mathtt{true}) \\ \oplus\ \mathtt{assume}(\mathtt{t} \neq \mathtt{x}) \end{array}\right)\right\rangle \end{array}\right)^{*}; \\ &\mathtt{assume}(\mathtt{b}) \end{aligned}$$

The stack is implemented as a linked list starting from address S. The initialization method, *init*, creates an empty stack. The method *push* creates a new node (y) and tries to add it at the beginning of the stack using a compare&swap (CAS) instruction inside a loop. The big atomic block inside the loop results from desugaring the CAS instruction. Similarly, the variable b arises from a break statement.

Let us execute action inference on this example: SYMB-EXEC(emp, $\emptyset$, *init*) returns the postcondition $\mathtt{S} \mapsto \mathtt{NULL}$. As every assertion is stable under the empty rely, stabilization does nothing and returns the same assertion. Then, action inference calls SYMB-EXEC($\boxed{\mathtt{S} \mapsto \mathtt{NULL}}$, $\emptyset$, *push*). Symbolically executing the first two commands of *push* results in the state $\exists\alpha.\ \neg\mathtt{b} * \mathtt{y}{\mapsto}\alpha * \boxed{\mathtt{S} \mapsto \mathtt{NULL}}$.

Now consider the loop of *push*. The first memory read is from the shared state and gives us the postcondition: $\exists\alpha.\ \mathtt{x} = \mathtt{NULL} * \neg\mathtt{b} * \mathtt{y}{\mapsto}\alpha * \boxed{\mathtt{S} \mapsto \mathtt{NULL}}$. Next, there is a local write, which gives the postcondition: $\mathtt{x}{=}\mathtt{NULL} * \neg\mathtt{b} * \mathtt{y}{\mapsto}\mathtt{x} * \boxed{\mathtt{S} \mapsto \mathtt{NULL}}$. Then, there is the big atomic block representing a CAS. After the memory read, $\mathtt{t} := [\mathtt{S}]$, we get: $\mathtt{t}{=}\mathtt{x} * \mathtt{x}{=}\mathtt{NULL} * \neg\mathtt{b} * \mathtt{y}{\mapsto}\mathtt{x} * \boxed{\mathtt{S} \mapsto \mathtt{NULL}}$. Therefore, from the two conditional branches, only the first one is possible. In this branch, the memory write is shared; so symbolic execution has to compute an action. According to reachability heuristic, the memory cell $\mathtt{y}{\mapsto}\mathtt{x}$ becomes shared, as it is reachable from y. The postcondition is $\mathtt{t}{=}\mathtt{x} * \mathtt{x}{=}\mathtt{NULL} * \neg\mathtt{b} * \boxed{\mathtt{S} \mapsto \mathtt{y} * \mathtt{y}{\mapsto}\mathtt{NULL}}$ and the inferred action is

$$A_1 \stackrel{\text{def}}{=} \mathsf{emp} \mid \mathtt{S} \mapsto \mathtt{NULL} \leadsto \mathtt{S} \mapsto y * y \mapsto \mathtt{NULL}$$

Then, as b becomes true, symbolic execution exits the loop, and returns.

Therefore, in the first iteration of its fixpoint loop, action inference has computed $G = \{A_1\}$ and $Inv = \mathtt{S} \mapsto \mathtt{NULL}$. In the second iteration, Inv is no longer stable. Stabilization returns $Inv = (\mathtt{S} \mapsto \mathtt{NULL} \vee \exists y.\ \mathtt{S} \mapsto y * y \mapsto \mathtt{NULL})$, and symbolic execution also returns the action $A_2 \stackrel{\text{def}}{=} x \mapsto \mathtt{NULL} \mid \mathtt{S} \mapsto x \rightsquigarrow \mathtt{S} \mapsto y * y \mapsto x$. In the third iteration, Inv becomes $listseg(\mathtt{S}, \mathtt{NULL})$[1] and symbolic execution also returns: $A_3 \stackrel{\text{def}}{=} listseg(x, 0) \mid \mathtt{S} \mapsto x \rightsquigarrow \mathtt{S} \mapsto y * y \mapsto x$. In the fourth iteration, Inv is already stable, and symbolic execution returns no new actions. Therefore, action inference terminates after four iterations and having found three actions.

4 Non-standard Join

As presented above, the Infer-Actions and Symb-Exec algorithms use set union to combine sets of actions. Using set union, however, produces too many actions, many of which are unnecessary. For instance, in the stack example above, the actions A_1 and A_2 are both included in the action A_3, and hence are unnecessary once A_3 is discovered.

As remarked in Sect. 2, having a large set of actions makes stabilization calculations slower, which in turn slows down action inference. More importantly, however, the output of action inference becomes difficult to read and slows down any verification procedures that use action inference as their first step (e.g. [9]).

Therefore, we shall replace set union with a more aggressive join operation. The idea is to define a 'lossless' join that removes actions that are already included in other actions. Note that there is a natural inclusion order on actions: action a is semantically included in action b if and only if $\mathcal{A}[\![a]\!] \subseteq \mathcal{A}[\![b]\!]$. In general, testing whether $\mathcal{A}[\![a]\!] \subseteq \mathcal{A}[\![b]\!]$ is undecidable. We can, however, define the following decidable approximation to action inclusion:

Definition 3. $(R_1 \mid P_1 \rightsquigarrow Q_1) \sqsubseteq (R_2 \mid P_2 \rightsquigarrow Q_2)$ *if and only if there exists a substitution* σ *of the logical variables such that* $P_1 = \sigma(P_2)$, $Q_1 = \sigma(Q_2)$, *and* $R_1 \vdash \sigma(R_2) * \mathsf{true}$.

It is easy to check that if $a \sqsubseteq b$, then $\mathcal{A}[\![a]\!] \subseteq \mathcal{A}[\![b]\!]$. To calculate $(R_1 \mid P_1 \rightsquigarrow Q_1) \sqsubseteq (R_2 \mid P_2 \rightsquigarrow Q_2)$, we run first order unification to find a substitution σ such that $P_1 = \sigma(P_2)$ and $Q_1 = \sigma(Q_2)$, and then call Subtract$(R_1, \sigma(R_2), \emptyset)$ to decide whether $R_1 \vdash \sigma(R_2) * \mathsf{true}$.

Example 2. Consider the actions $A \stackrel{\text{def}}{=} (\mathtt{y} \mapsto 3 \mid \mathtt{x} \mapsto 0 \rightsquigarrow \mathtt{x} \mapsto 1)$, $A' \stackrel{\text{def}}{=} (\mathtt{x} \mapsto 0 * \mathtt{y} \mapsto 3 \rightsquigarrow \mathtt{x} \mapsto 1 * \mathtt{y} \mapsto 3)$, and $B \stackrel{\text{def}}{=} (\mathtt{x} \mapsto a \rightsquigarrow \mathtt{x} \mapsto 1)$. Clearly, $\mathcal{A}[\![A]\!] = \mathcal{A}[\![A']\!] \subseteq \mathcal{A}[\![B]\!]$, because A and A' allow us to write 1 to x only when it previously contained 0 and y contained 3, whereas B allows us to write 1 to x regardless of the original value of x and the value of y. It is also easy to check that $A \sqsubseteq B$; just take σ to be the substitution mapping a to 0. In contrast, $A' \not\sqsubseteq B$, $A \not\sqsubseteq A'$, and $A' \not\sqsubseteq A$. In principle, we could have defined a finer approximation to inclusion so that

[1] The list segment comes from applying Distefano's abstraction to the formula $\exists yz.\ \mathtt{S} \mapsto y * y \mapsto z * z \mapsto \mathtt{NULL}$, which arises during the initial stabilization.

Data structure	No join			Lossless join			Man
	#I	#A	Time	#I	#A	Time	#A
Treiber stack [17]	4	5	0.09s	4	2	0.08s	2
M&S two-lock queue [13]	5	26	0.33s	5	12	0.25s	6
M&S non-blocking queue [13]	5	10	1.69s	5	6	1.45s	3
DGLM non-blocking queue [7]	5	12	2.23s	5	8	1.97s	3
Lock-coupling list [10]	4	21	0.98s	4	10	0.81s	4
Optimistic list [10]	5	30	109.06s	5	10	52.29s	4
Lazy list [10]	5	48	59.98s	5	13	26.21s	5
CAS-based set [21]	3	9	24.74s	2	5	8.80s	3
DCAS-based set [21]	2	6	0.31s	2	4	0.27s	2

Fig. 1. Verification times for the memory safety benchmarks

Data structure	No join			Lossless join			Man
	#I	#A	Time	#I	#A	Time	#A
Treiber stack [17]	4	5	0.14s	4	2	0.09s	2
M&S two-lock queue [13]	6	39	0.70s	6	13	0.48s	6
M&S non-blocking queue [13]	6	14	4.37s	6	7	3.76s	3
DGLM non-blocking queue [7]	6	16	4.88s	6	9	4.22s	3

Fig. 2. Verification times for the linearizability benchmarks

the latter three inclusions were also true, but such a finer approximation would have been significantly slower to compute. Instead, we simply avoid generating problematic actions such as A'.

From this computable check for action inclusion, we define the following 'lossless' join operator:

$$
\begin{aligned}
A \sqcup \{b\} &\stackrel{\text{def}}{=} \textbf{if } \exists a \in A.\ b \sqsubseteq a \textbf{ then } A \textbf{ else } \{b\} \cup \{a \in A \mid a \not\sqsubseteq b\} \\
A \sqcup \{b_1, \ldots, b_n\} &\stackrel{\text{def}}{=} (\cdots (A \sqcup \{b_1\}) \sqcup \ldots) \sqcup \{b_n\}
\end{aligned}
$$

The join $A \sqcup B$ inserts the actions of B into A one at a time. For every such action, b, if it is already included in A, it is discarded; otherwise, b is added into A and every action of A that is included in b is removed.

Finally, we prove that join does not forget any information.

Lemma 2. *For all sets of actions A and B, $[\![A \sqcup B]\!] = [\![A \cup B]\!]$.*

The proof of this lemma follows from the observation that if $a \sqsubseteq b$, then $[\![\{a, b\}]\!] = [\![\{b\}]\!]$. Lemma 2 means that we can replace union by the lossless join in the INFER-ACTIONS and SYMB-EXEC algorithms without any loss in precision.

5 Evaluation

We have run action inference on a number of fine-grained concurrent algorithms from the literature. For the first set of benchmarks (Fig. 1), we have proved memory safety and inferred the expected data structure shape invariants (e.g., in all cases we can show the data structures are acyclic). For the second set of benchmarks (Fig. 2), we have taken the stack and queue algorithms from Fig. 1 and have proved linearizability using the method described in [19,1], which is to instrument the algorithms by manually inserting auxiliary code describing the linearization points of each algorithm.

We have run our tool in two modes: with no join enabled, and with lossless join enabled. For each run, we have recorded the number of iterations that INFER-ACTION takes in order to reach a fixpoint (**#I**), the number of actions inferred (**#A**), and the total verification time (**Time**). The final column reports the minimum number of actions needed for a manual proof of the algorithm. The tests were conducted on a 3.4GHz Pentium 4 processor running Windows Vista.

Enabling join significantly reduces the number of actions inferred, and hence also the verification times especially for the more difficult benchmarks. The number of actions inferred using the lossless join is still quite larger than what would have been written by hand. This is mainly due to a number of unnecessary case splits present in the set of inferred actions. Normally, enabling lossless join does not affect the number of iterations taken by INFER-ACTION. This is expected, because the action set calculated using lossless join is semantically equivalent to the set calculated using normal set union. Somewhat counter-intuitively, however, the CAS-based set example finishes in fewer iterations when lossless join is used. This is probably due to the incompleteness of entailment checking between separation logic formulas.

Trying to further reduce the number of inferred actions, we have experimented with a more aggressive action abstraction that drops all list segments from the actions' contexts. While this abstraction works well for most of the examples, the resulting actions are too weak to prove functional correctness of the linked list benchmarks. (They are sufficient for proving memory safety.)

Other Uses of Action Inference. Action inference has already been used as a subcomponent in two related verification procedures. The first use was in verifying liveness properties of non-blocking algorithms by Gotsman et al. [9]. There, one first runs action inference to prove memory safety and to compute a set of RGSep actions. Then, one does a layered proof search attempting to show that certain actions are not executed infinitely often and that certain operations terminate. This proof search is quadratic in the number of inferred actions; so inferring few actions is necessary for achieving good performance.

The second use is in a new verification procedure for linearizability that does not require linearization point annotations. This procedure constructs a list of candidate linearization point assignments, and then searches through the list checking whether any of those assignments is valid. In this case, action inference is executed both as an initial phase in order to find candidate linearization point assignments and at each step of the proof search in order to determine whether a given linearization point assignment is valid. This procedure can verify the benchmarks in Fig. 2 within 10 seconds each.

6 Related Work

Action inference extends the original work on RGSep shape analysis [5]. It is similar in spirit to the thread-local shape analysis by Gotsman et al. [8], but technically quite different. Both works attempt to verify one thread at a time and do a global fixpoint calculation to compute the interaction between threads. The major difference is that Gotsman calculates resource invariants, whereas we calculate a set of actions. The shift from invariants to sets of actions makes our method more expressive and thus able to reason about fine-grained concurrency, but also required us to introduce concepts such as stabilization. In contrast, Gotsman et al. can handle only coarse-grained concurrency.

Manevich et al. [12], Berdine et al. [3], and Segalov et al. [16] have developed a series of related shape analyses that suitably restrict the correlations between the states of different threads that are tracked. This gives them a very strong thread-modular flavour. Their main difference is that action inference does an abstract interpretation over both invariants and actions, whereas the other three analyses do abstract interpretation only over invariants. The second important difference is the underlying abstract domain: we use separation logic, whereas they use three value logic. Using action inference, we can verify roughly the same programs and properties as the other three analyses, but our verification times have so far been significantly faster.

7 Conclusion

We have presented an algorithm for computing the interference caused by a program enabling us to verify safety properties of concurrent heap-manipulating programs. Our action inference algorithm forms the basis of more advanced verification methods for proving certain liveness properties [9] and linearizability.

In the future, we would like to apply action inference to larger and more complex concurrent libraries. The main technical obstacle in achieving this is to make the sequential shape analyses expressive enough to describe the invariants of such libraries. We would also like to consider program verification in the context of relaxed memory models, and to replace the reachability heuristic for determining ownership transfer with a more robust technique possibly based on footprint analysis [14] or bi-abduction [4].

Acknowledgements. I would like to thank Alexey Gotsman, Matthew Parkinson, Mohammad Raza, Mooly Sagiv, and Hongseok Yang for useful discussions and comments, and especially the anonymous reviewers for their constructive and detailed feedback.

References

1. Amit, D., Rinetzky, N., Reps, T., Sagiv, M., Yahav, E.: Comparison under abstraction for verifying linearisability. In: Damm, W., Hermanns, H. (eds.) CAV 2007. LNCS, vol. 4590, pp. 477–490. Springer, Heidelberg (2007)

2. Berdine, J., Calcagno, C., O'Hearn, P.W.: Symbolic execution with separation logic. In: Yi, K. (ed.) APLAS 2005. LNCS, vol. 3780, pp. 52–68. Springer, Heidelberg (2005)
3. Berdine, J., Lev-Ami, T., Manevich, R., Ramalingam, G., Sagiv, S.: Thread quantification for concurrent shape analysis. In: Gupta, A., Malik, S. (eds.) CAV 2008. LNCS, vol. 5123, pp. 399–413. Springer, Heidelberg (2008)
4. Calcagno, C., Distefano, D., O'Hearn, P.W., Yang, H.: Compositional shape analysis by means of bi-abduction. In: POPL 2009, pp. 289–300. ACM, New York (2009)
5. Calcagno, C., Parkinson, M., Vafeiadis, V.: Modular safety checking for fine-grained concurrency. In: Riis Nielson, H., Filé, G. (eds.) SAS 2007. LNCS, vol. 4634, pp. 233–248. Springer, Heidelberg (2007)
6. Distefano, D., O'Hearn, P.W., Yang, H.: A local shape analysis based on separation logic. In: Hermanns, H., Palsberg, J. (eds.) TACAS 2006. LNCS, vol. 3920, pp. 287–302. Springer, Heidelberg (2006)
7. Doherty, S., Groves, L., Luchangco, V., Moir, M.: Formal verification of a practical lock-free queue algorithm. In: de Frutos-Escrig, D., Núñez, M. (eds.) FORTE 2004. LNCS, vol. 3235, pp. 97–114. Springer, Heidelberg (2004)
8. Gotsman, A., Berdine, J., Cook, B., Sagiv, M.: Thread-modular shape analysis. In: PLDI 2007. ACM, New York (2007)
9. Gotsman, A., Cook, B., Parkinson, M., Vafeiadis, V.: Proving that non-blocking algorithms don't block. In: POPL 2009, pp. 16–28. ACM, New York (2009)
10. Herlihy, M., Shavit, N.: The Art of Multiprocessor Programming. Morgan Kaufmann, San Francisco (2008)
11. Jones, C.B.: Specification and design of (parallel) programs. In: IFIP Congress, pp. 321–332 (1983)
12. Manevich, R., Lev-Ami, T., Ramalingam, G., Sagiv, M., Berdine, J.: Heap decomposition for concurrent shape analysis. In: Alpuente, M., Vidal, G. (eds.) SAS 2008. LNCS, vol. 5079, pp. 363–377. Springer, Heidelberg (2008)
13. Michael, M., Scott, M.: Simple, fast, and practical non-blocking and blocking concurrent queue algorithms. In: PODC 1996. ACM, New York (1996)
14. Raza, M., Calcagno, C., Gardner, P.: Automatic parallelization with separation logic. In: Castagna, G. (ed.) ESOP 2009. LNCS, vol. 5502, pp. 348–362. Springer, Heidelberg (2009)
15. Reynolds, J.C.: Separation logic: A logic for shared mutable data structures. In: LICS, pp. 55–74. IEEE Computer Society, Los Alamitos (2002)
16. Segalov, M., Lev-Ami, T., Manevich, R., Ramalingam, G., Sagiv, M.: Efficiently tracking thread correlations. In: APLAS 2009. LNCS. Springer, Heidelberg (2009)
17. Treiber, R.K.: Systems programming: Coping with parallelism. Technical Report RJ5118, IBM Almaden Res. Ctr. (1986)
18. Vafeiadis, V.: Fine-grained concurrency verification. PhD dissertation, University of Cambridge Computer Laboratory. Tech. report UCAM-CL-TR-726 (2007)
19. Vafeiadis, V.: Shape-value abstraction for verifying linearizability. In: Jones, N.D., Müller-Olm, M. (eds.) VMCAI 2009. LNCS, vol. 5403, pp. 335–348. Springer, Heidelberg (2009)
20. Vafeiadis, V., Parkinson, M.: A marriage of rely/guarantee and separation logic. In: Caires, L., Vasconcelos, V.T. (eds.) CONCUR 2007. LNCS, vol. 4703, pp. 256–271. Springer, Heidelberg (2007)
21. Vechev, M., Yahav, E.: Deriving linearizable fine-grained concurrent objects. In: PLDI 2008, pp. 125–135. ACM, New York (2008)

A May-Subtraction Implementation

This section describes an efficient implementation of may-subtraction for the following simple list segment domain:

$$\begin{array}{rll} P, Q, R ::= & \mathsf{false} \mid (\exists \boldsymbol{z}.\, \Pi \wedge \Sigma) \mid P \vee Q & \text{Full assertions} \\ \Pi ::= & \mathsf{true} \mid E = E' \mid E \neq E' \mid \Pi \wedge \Pi & \text{Pure part} \\ \Sigma ::= & \mathsf{emp} \mid \mathsf{true} \mid E \mapsto_A E' \mid ls_A(E, E') \mid \Sigma * \Sigma & \text{Spatial part} \end{array}$$

To implement may-subtraction efficiently, each primitive assertion is annotated with a permission set, $\emptyset \neq A \subseteq \{1, 2, 3\}$, represented as a bit-vector. These permission annotations are used only internally within the may-substraction calculation; its interface does not expose the permission annotations.

Similar to Berdine et al. [2], we represent formulas in a canonical form up to the usual properties of $*$, $\wedge$, and $\vee$ (commutativity, associativity, distribution of $*$ and $\wedge$ over disjunction, identity and nullary elements, $\mathsf{true} * \mathsf{true} = \mathsf{true}$), substitution of equated terms, and the following three new normalization rules:

$$\begin{array}{rcl} x \mapsto_A y * x \mapsto_B z & \iff & y = z \wedge x \mapsto_{A \odot B} y \\ x \mapsto_A y * ls_B(x, z) & \iff & x = z \wedge x \mapsto_A y \vee x \mapsto_{A \odot B} y * ls_B(y, z) \\ ls_A(x, y) * ls_B(x, z) & \iff & ls_{A \odot B}(x, y) * ls_B(y, z) \vee ls_{A \odot B}(x, z) * ls_A(z, y) \end{array}$$

where we take $x \mapsto_{A \odot B} y$ to mean $x \mapsto_{A \cup B} y$ if $A \cap B = \emptyset$ and false otherwise. Similarly, $ls_{A \odot B}(x, y)$ stands for $ls_{A \cup B}(x, y)$ if $A \cap B = \emptyset$, and $x = y \wedge \mathsf{emp}$ otherwise. These rules check whether there are any overlapping spatial conjuncts, and perform case splits to eliminate such conjuncts. (Repeated application of these rules terminates, because within each disjunct each rule either reduces the number of spatial conjuncts, or keeps the same number of spatial conjuncts, but increments one of their permission annotations.) Our rules are better than the normalization rules of Berdine et al. [2], as they resolve all 'spooky' disjuncts and avoid a quadratic expansion of the formula in the common case.

Our implementation of may-subtraction uses the permission annotations to exploit the above normalization rules. It is defined in terms of a helper function:

$$\textsc{May-Subtract}(P, Q, R) \stackrel{\text{def}}{=} \textsc{MaySubHelper}(P_{\{1\}} * R_{\{2\}} * Q_{\{2,3\}})$$

where P_A marks the spatial conjuncts of the (non-annotated) assertion P with A. Permission $\{1\}$ indicates that the conjunct belongs the P; permission $\{2\}$ says that it belongs to either Q or the context R (and has to be matched with something in P), whereas permission $\{3\}$ indicates the conjunct has to be matched with something in P and then removed for the result.

The helper function, MaySubHelper, is defined in Alg. 6. First, it applies the normalization rules. If all conjuncts are matched (i.e., none remain with a label not containing 1), it returns all the conjuncts that must not be removed (i.e., those whose label does not contain 3). If, there is an unmatched $\mapsto$, then MaySubHelper does a case split as to which primitive conjunct the $\mapsto$ belongs, and continues. Otherwise, if an unmatched list segment remains,

Algorithm 6. MAYSUBHELPER(P)

$Res \leftarrow \mathsf{false}$
for each disjunct $\Pi \wedge \Sigma$ in NORMALIZE(P) **do**
  if $\exists x, y, A$ such that $(x \mapsto_A y) \in \Sigma$ and $1 \notin A$ **then**
    $Res \leftarrow Res \vee \text{MAYSUBHELPER}(\bigvee_{S \in \Sigma} \Pi \wedge \text{EXPOSE}(x, y, S) * \circledast(\Sigma \setminus S))$
  else if $\exists x, y, A$ such that $(ls_A(x, y)) \in \Sigma$ and $1 \notin A$ and $3 \notin A$ **then**
    $Res \leftarrow Res \vee \text{MAYSUBHELPER}(\Pi \wedge \Sigma)$
  else if $\exists x, y, A$ such that $(ls_A(x, y)) \in \Sigma$ and $1 \notin A$ **then**
    $Res \leftarrow Res \vee (\Pi \wedge \mathsf{true})$
  else
    $Res \leftarrow Res \vee (\Pi \wedge \circledast\{S \mid S_A \in \Sigma \wedge 3 \notin A\})$
return Res

where

$\text{EXPOSE}(x, y, \mathsf{true}) \stackrel{\text{def}}{=} x \mapsto_{\{1\}} y * \mathsf{true}$ $\text{EXPOSE}(x, y, z \mapsto_B w) \stackrel{\text{def}}{=} x = z \wedge x \mapsto_B w$

$\text{EXPOSE}(x, y, ls_B(z, w)) \stackrel{\text{def}}{=} ls_B(z, x) * x \mapsto_B y * ls_B(y, w)$

MAYSUBHELPER conservatively assumes that it could match any part of the formula.

Our MAY-SUBTRACT algorithm is a significant improvement over the septraction elimination algorithm by Calcagno et al. [5], as it can handle contextual matches (i.e., the R component) and it delays the application of the expensive rule that exposes $\mapsto$-assertions. The soundness of our algorithm follows from the semantics of separation logic assertions and permissions.

Best Probabilistic Transformers

Björn Wachter[1] and Lijun Zhang[2,1]

[1] Saarland University, Saarbrücken, Germany
[2] Oxford University Computing Laboratory, UK

Abstract. This paper investigates relative precision and optimality of analyses for concurrent probabilistic systems. Aiming at the problem at the heart of probabilistic model checking – computing the probability of reaching a particular set of states – we leverage the theory of abstract interpretation. With a focus on predicate abstraction, we develop the first abstract-interpretation framework for Markov decision processes which admits to compute both lower and upper bounds on reachability probabilities. Further, we describe how to compute and approximate such abstractions using abstraction refinement and give experimental results.

1 Introduction

Markov decision processes (MDPs) play a crucial role as a semantic model in the analysis of systems with random phenomena like network protocols and randomized algorithms. MDPs feature non-determinism and probabilistic choice. Typically one is interested in computing (maximal or minimal) reachability probabilities, e.g., the probability of delivering three messages after ten transmission attempts. For finite MDPs, probabilistic reachability can be reduced to a linear optimization problem [1]. Recently predicate-abstraction techniques have evolved [2,3] that scale to realistic programs which map to very large, even infinite MDPs. However, fundamental questions remain open, e.g. for given predicates, what is the most precise abstract program that is still a valid abstraction?

The theory of abstract interpretation [4] has provided answers to such questions in the non-probabilistic case [5] and has served as a foundation and design paradigm for a wide range of other program analyses, e.g. [6,7,8]. In abstract interpretation, program analyses are expressed in terms of non-standard abstract semantics obtained by replacing the actual domain of computation (also called *concrete domain*) by an *abstract domain.* Concrete and abstract domain are partially ordered sets where ordering describes relative precision of the denotations.

A specification of the *most precise* analysis is given by the composition $f^\sharp = \alpha \circ f \circ \gamma$ of concretization function γ, the functional f characterizing the program semantics and abstraction function α, under the condition that functions α and γ form a Galois connection. Being the limit on the best achievable precision for *any* valid abstraction, functional $f^\sharp$ is called *best transformer* [9].

These concepts are the starting point of our work. Yet a key element is missing: a suitable instantiation of abstract interpretation for our setting.

G. Barthe and M. Hermenegildo (Eds.): VMCAI 2010, LNCS 5944, pp. 362–379, 2010.

Related Work. While in [10,11,12,13] ideas from abstract interpretation have been applied to probabilistic models, to the best of our knowledge, there is no preceding framework for MDP abstraction with Galois connections and best transformers. Papers [11,12,13] target deterministic models and not MDPs.

The pioneering contribution in terms of abstract interpretation for MDPs is due to Monniaux [10]. His parametric concept of abstract domains allows to plug in a wealth of base domains from static analysis. However, the resulting abstract domains contain distinct abstract values with the same denotation [14], which means that the abstract domain is not partially ordered (the order is not anti-symmetric). Thus the abstraction precludes Galois connections and is not suitable to develop best transformers.

Further, the aforementioned abstract-interpretation approaches have yet to be combined with abstraction refinement. Refinement admits to adjust the abstraction to the desired precision, which is particularly important in our quantitative setting. In this respect, abstraction refinement based on predicate abstraction has recently shown promising results. The abstraction-refinement method Probabilistic CEGAR [2] computes upper bounds on reachability probabilities for concurrent probabilistic programs, an infinite-state variation of the language of the popular probabilistic model checker `PRISM` [15]. The software model checker in [3] employs predicate abstraction and game-based abstraction [16]. Game-based abstraction maps MDPs to stochastic games. The salient and inspiring point of this influential work is that game-based abstraction yields *both* lower and upper bounds on reachability probabilities, rather than just one bound.

Contribution. Our major theoretical contribution (Sec. 3) is the first abstract-interpretation framework for MDPs which admits to compute both lower and upper bounds on reachability probabilities. This provides a solid basis to reason about the relative precision and optimality of abstract transformers. Further, we prove equivalence of game-based abstraction with best transformers in our framework. Crucial differences to the abstract-interpretation framework [10,14] are: we consider not only upper but also lower bounds, we target predicate abstraction not classical domains from static analysis, and we express our abstraction in terms of Galois connections.

Our second contribution (Sec. 4) is the first abstraction-refinement technique for concurrent probabilistic programs that yields both lower and upper bounds. Previous analysis techniques for such programs are [17,2,18], also based on predicate abstraction. While [2] comes with refinement, it employs an MDP-based abstraction [19] that gives only effective upper bounds. Whereas [18] comes without refinement and uses game-based abstraction, which yields these bounds but requires up to exponentially higher construction cost than MDP-based abstraction and tracking of complex dependencies between commands, which makes all the difference in practice. The basis of our refinement technique is parallel abstraction, a novel abstraction, computable with the same complexity as MDP-based abstraction [17,2]. Parallel abstraction yields effective lower and upper bounds and combines well with refinement. We have implemented our ideas in the `PASS` tool and report on experimental results (Sec. 5).

2 Background

Sec. 2.1 first recalls basic notions of abstract interpretation including lattices, Galois connections and best transformers. We then introduce the lattice of valuations, the domain for abstract probabilistic reachability analysis, in which probabilities can be represented and computed. In Sec. 2.2, we turn to MDPs and probabilistic reachability.

2.1 Galois Connections, Best Transformers and Valuations

The pair $(A, \leq)$ is a partially-ordered set, or poset, if A is a set and $\leq \subseteq A \times A$ a partial order, i.e. a reflexive, antisymmetric and transitive relation. Let $(A, \leq)$, $(B, \leq)$, $(C, \leq)$ be posets. For two functions $f, g : A \to B$, we write $f \leq g$ if $f(a) \leq g(a)$ for all $a \in A$. We denote the composition of two functions $f_1 : A \to B$ and $f_2 : B \to C$ by $(f_2 \circ f_1) : A \to C$ where $(f_2 \circ f_1)(a) = f_2(f_1(a))$ for all $a \in A$. Function $f : A \to B$ is monotone if for all $a, a' \in A$, $a \leq a' \implies f(a) \leq f(a')$.

A (complete) lattice is a poset $(L, \leq)$ in which each subset $M \subseteq L$ has a greatest lower bound $\bigsqcap M$ and least upper bound $\bigsqcup M$ w.r.t. $\leq$. For a monotone function $f : L \to L$ over a lattice $(L, \leq)$, Tarski's theorem [20] guarantees existence of least and greatest fixpoints, $\mathit{lfp}_{\leq}\ f$ and $\mathit{gfp}_{\leq}\ f$ respectively. They are given by: $\mathit{lfp}_{\leq}(f) = \bigsqcap\{x \in L | f(x) \leq x\}$ and $\mathit{gfp}_{\leq}(f) = \bigsqcup\{x \in L | f(x) \geq x\}$.

In abstract interpretation, the original program semantics, also called concrete semantics, is typically defined over a lattice $(L, \leq)$, called concrete domain, and the abstract semantics is defined over a lattice $(M, \leq)$, called abstract domain. The intuition behind the order $\leq$ in both lattices is that elements higher in the order represent less information. Thus an element $m \in M$ is more precise than another element $m' \in M$ if $m \leq m'$, so m' over-approximates m. For L, the analog holds. The program semantics is described by a concrete transformer, a monotone function $f : L \to L$. An abstract transformer is a monotone function $g^\sharp : M \to M$. Two monotone functions relate abstract and concrete world: the abstraction function $\alpha : L \to M$ and the concretization function $\gamma : M \to L$. The pair (α, γ) is a *Galois connection*, denoted by $(L, \leq) \underset{\alpha}{\overset{\gamma}{\leftrightarrows}} (M, \leq)$, if for all $l \in L$ and $m \in M$, we have $\alpha(l) \leq m \iff l \leq \gamma(m)$.

We call an abstract transformer $g^\sharp : M \to M$ a *valid* abstraction of f if $(f \circ \gamma) \leq (\gamma \circ g^\sharp)$. For transformer $f : L \to L$, the *best transformer* [9], is the composition of functions: $f^\sharp = \alpha \circ f \circ \gamma$. By construction, $f^\sharp$ is the most precise abstract transformer that is a valid abstraction of f, i.e. $f^\sharp \leq g^\sharp$ for any valid transformer $g^\sharp : M \to M$. This follows from properties of the Galois connection.

Lattice of Valuations. A valuation over a set S is a function $w : S \to [0, 1]$ that maps elements of S to probabilities. The valuations $W_S = \{w \mid w : S \to [0, 1]\}$ over S form a lattice $(W_S, \leq)$ with order $\leq$ where $w \leq w'$ if $w(s) \leq w'(s)$ for all $s \in S$. The figure to the right shows two valuations w_1 and w_2 over a set S with 16 elements. Each element is drawn as a circle and the corresponding value is

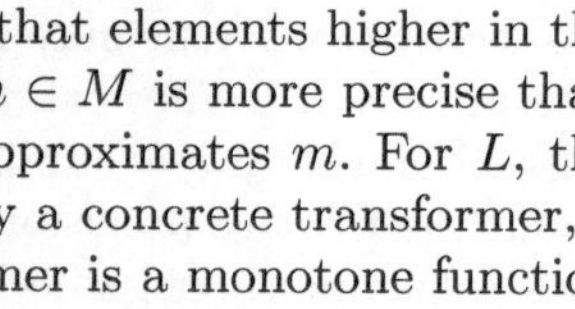

annotated above the circle. We have $w_1 \leq w_2$, i.e., w_2 is an upper bound for w_1, and w_1 a lower bound for w_2. The lattice $(W_S, \geq)$ results by inverting the order in $(W_S, \leq)$. We later use lattice $(W_S, \geq)$ for abstractions yielding lower bounds and lattice $(W_S, \leq)$ for upper bounds. Two lattices are necessary because lattice ordering represents precision, and a lower bound is the more precise the larger it is, while an upper bound is the more precise the smaller it is. To avoid confusion: symbols $\bigsqcap$ and $\bigsqcup$ always refer to the least elements and greatest elements respectively in $(W_S, \leq)$ as given above, and *not* the ones in $(W_S, \geq)$. We have $(\bigsqcap V)(s) = \inf_{w \in V} w(s)$, and $(\bigsqcup V)(s) = \sup_{w \in V} w(s)$ for $V \subseteq W_S$. A *valuation transformer* is a monotone function $f : W_S \to W_S$. Due to duality, we have $(\mathit{gfp}_{\geq}\ f) = (\mathit{lfp}_{\leq}\ f)$ and $(\mathit{lfp}_{\geq}\ f) = (\mathit{gfp}_{\leq}\ f)$.

2.2 Markov Decision Processes

A *distribution* π over S is a function $\pi : S \to [0,1]$ such that $\sum_{s \in S} \pi(s) = 1$. Let Distr_S be the set of distributions over S. For a distribution $\pi \in \mathit{Distr}_S$, we denote by $\mathit{Supp}(\pi) = \{s \in S \mid \pi(s) > 0\}$ its support and abbreviate summation over a subset $S' \subseteq S$ by $\pi(S') := \sum_{s \in S'} \pi(s)$.

A *Markov decision process* (MDP) $\mathcal{M}$ is a tuple $(S, I, \mathcal{A}, R)$ where S is a set of states, $I \subseteq S$ is a set of initial states, $\mathcal{A}$ is a finite action alphabet, and $R : S \times \mathcal{A} \rightharpoonup \mathit{Distr}_S$ the transition function. The transition function R is a partial function, as indicated by the $\rightharpoonup$ arrow: only certain actions may be enabled in a state of the MDP or even none. In the latter case, the state is called *absorbing*. For $s \in S$, we denote its enabled actions by $\mathcal{A}(s) = \{a \mid \exists \pi \in \mathit{Distr}_S.\ \pi = R(s,a)\}$, and its out-going distributions by $\mathit{Distr}(s) = \{R(s,a) \mid a \in \mathcal{A}(s)\}$. For $a \in \mathcal{A}(s)$, we define $\pi_{(s,a)} := R(s,a)$ and say that $(s, a, \pi_{(s,a)})$ is a transition of $\mathcal{M}$.

A path is a sequence $(s_0, a_0, \pi_0), (s_1, a_1, \pi_1), \ldots$ such that $s_0 \in I$, (s_i, a_i, π_i) are transitions of $\mathcal{M}$, and $s_{i+1} \in \mathit{Supp}(\pi_i)$ for all $i \in \mathbb{N}$. Let $\mathit{Path}(\mathcal{M})$ denote the set of all paths over $\mathcal{M}$. Similarly finite paths can be defined. For $\beta \in \mathit{Path}(\mathcal{M})$, let $\beta[i] = s_i$ denote the $(i+1)$-th state of β.

Markov chains are special cases of MDPs, deterministic MDPs where for every state s there is at most one enabled transition $|\mathcal{A}(s)| \leq 1$. Unlike a Markov chain, an MDP is not a fully determined stochastic process. In order to obtain a probability measure, the notion of a *strategy* is needed to resolve non-determinism. In general, a strategy σ of an MDP $\mathcal{M}$ is a function from finite paths to distributions over actions. We denote the set of strategies of $\mathcal{M}$ by $\Sigma_{\mathcal{M}}$. For a given state $s \in S$ and a strategy σ, let Pr_s^{σ} denote the corresponding probability measure [1] over $\mathit{Path}(\mathcal{M})$.

Probabilistic Reachability. Let $\mathcal{M} = (S, I, \mathcal{A}, R)$ be an MDP, and let $F \subseteq S$ be a set of goal states. Let $p_s^{\sigma}(F) := \mathit{Pr}_s^{\sigma}(\{\beta \in \mathit{Path}(\mathcal{M}) \mid \exists i \in \mathbb{N} :\ \beta[i] \in F\})$ denote the probability of reaching a goal state in F from state $s \in S$ with strategy σ. For a fixed strategy σ, this defines a valuation $p^{\sigma}(F) \in W_S$ which maps a state s to $p_s^{\sigma}(F)$. In the context of MDPs, one studies minimal $p^-(F) \in W_S$ and maximal $p^+(F) \in W_S$ reachability probabilities where $p^-(F) = \bigsqcap\{p^{\sigma}(F) \mid \sigma \in \Sigma_{\mathcal{M}}\}$

is the infimum and $p^+(F) = \bigsqcup\{p^\sigma(F) \mid \sigma \in \Sigma_{\mathcal{M}}\}$ the supremum over all strategies. Below we define two valuation transformers to characterize the minimal and maximal reachability probabilities.

Definition 1 (Valuation Transformers for MDPs). *Let $F_0 \subseteq S$ be the set of states that cannot reach states in F. The valuation transformer $pre_F^- : W_S \to W_S$ is defined by: $pre_F^-(w)(s) = 1$ if $s \in F$, $pre_F^-(w)(s) = 0$ if $s \in F_0$, and otherwise:*

$$pre_F^-(w)(s) = \min_{a \in \mathcal{A}(s)} \sum_{s' \in S} \pi_{(s,a)}(s') \cdot w(s').$$

The valuation transformer $pre_F^+ : W_S \to W_S$ is defined analogously, with the difference that it maximizes over all enabled actions.

Example 1. We illustrate the transformer pre_F^- by considering the MDP in Figure 1. Assume that the goal states are given by the set $F = \{s_2, s_3\}$ and that valuation w assigns probability 1 to s_0, s_2 and s_3 respectively and probability 0 to all other states. Inserting the values and solving for state s_0, we get $pre_F^-(w)(s_0) = \min\{w(s_0), \frac{w(s_1)+w(s_2)}{2}, \frac{w(s_2)+w(s_3)+w(s_4)}{3}\} = \min\{1, \frac{1}{2}, \frac{2}{3}\} = \frac{1}{2}$. For state s_4, we have: $pre_F^-(w)(s_4) = \frac{1}{3}w(s_0) + \frac{2}{3}w(s_4) = \frac{1}{3}$. ■

Minimal and maximal reachability probabilities are expressible as *least fixpoints* of valuation transformers pre_F^- and pre_F^+ respectively [21] or more formally $p^-(F) = lfp_{\leq}\, pre_F^-$ and $p^+(F) = lfp_{\leq}\, pre_F^+$. This fixpoint characterization together with the background on abstract interpretation allows us to express abstractions for probabilistic reachability.

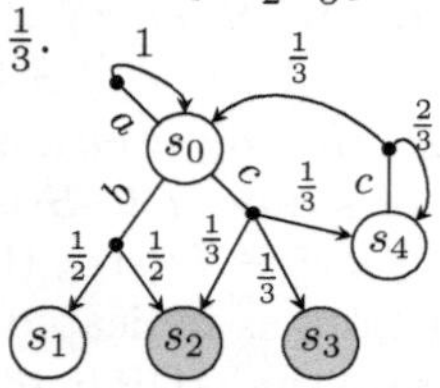

Fig. 1.

3 Abstraction

We present our novel abstract-interpretation framework for MDP abstraction. The concrete and abstract domain are given by lattices of valuations. Thereby lattice order expresses the concept of lower and upper bounds. In Sec. 3.1, we develop the abstract domain and apply the resulting abstraction framework to transformers, their fixpoints and particularly probabilistic reachability. Sect. 3.3 reveals a strong connection between the game-theoretical construction of game-based abstraction and certain best transformers.

3.1 Lower- and Upper-Bound Abstraction

Let S be a set of states. A partition Q of S is a finite set of pairwise disjoint, nonempty subsets of S such that $S = \bigcup_{B \in Q} B$. Elements of Q are called blocks. For a state $s \in S$, we denote by $\overline{s}$ the unique block B containing s, i.e., $s \in B$. Abstract valuations are valuations over blocks, elements of W_Q.

We give two abstraction functions that, given a valuation over states, yield a valuation over blocks: *lower-bound abstraction* $\alpha^{\mathfrak{l}} : W_S \to W_Q$ returns the infimum of the values $\alpha^{\mathfrak{l}}(w)(B) = \inf_{s \in B} w(s)$ within a block while *upper-bound abstraction* $\alpha^{\mathfrak{u}} : W_S \to W_Q$ returns the supremum $\alpha^{\mathfrak{u}}(w)(B) = \sup_{s \in B} w(s)$.

The *concretization* of an abstract valuation $w^\sharp \in W_Q$ is the valuation over states $\gamma(w^\sharp)$ that assigns each state the value of its block $\gamma(w^\sharp)(s) = w^\sharp(\overline{s})$. This defines the concretization function $\gamma : W_Q \to W_S$.

A lower bound is the more precise the larger it is, while the converse is true for an upper bound. This notion of precision is reflected by the lattice order: the order is $\geq$ if we compare lower bounds, and $\leq$ for upper bounds.

We obtain two Galois connections corresponding to $\alpha^{\mathfrak{l}}$ and $\alpha^{\mathfrak{u}}$ respectively:

Lemma 1 (Galois Connections). *For a given partition Q, let $\alpha^{\mathfrak{l}}$, $\alpha^{\mathfrak{u}}$, γ be the functions defined above. We have the following two Galois connections:*

(a) $(W_S, \geq) \underset{\alpha^{\mathfrak{l}}}{\overset{\gamma}{\leftrightarrows}} (W_Q, \geq)$ *(lower-bound abstraction)*

(b) $(W_S, \leq) \underset{\alpha^{\mathfrak{u}}}{\overset{\gamma}{\leftrightarrows}} (W_Q, \leq)$ *(upper-bound abstraction)*

Proof. We focus on lower-bound abstraction. Monotonicity of $\alpha^{\mathfrak{l}}$ and γ follows directly by definition. It remains to show that for all $w \in W_S$ and $w^\sharp \in W_Q$, it holds that: $w \geq \gamma(w^\sharp) \Leftrightarrow \alpha^{\mathfrak{l}}(w) \geq w^\sharp$. First assume $w \geq \gamma(w^\sharp)$. For $B \in Q$, we have $\alpha^{\mathfrak{l}}(w)(B) = \inf_{s \in B} w(s) \geq \inf_{s \in B} \gamma(w^\sharp)(s) = w^\sharp(B)$. Now assume $\alpha^{\mathfrak{l}}(w) \geq w^\sharp$. Then, for all $s \in S$, we have $w(s) \geq \alpha^{\mathfrak{l}}(w)(\overline{s}) \geq w^\sharp(\overline{s}) = \gamma(w^\sharp)(s)$. The proof for upper-bound abstraction works analogously. ■

The two Galois connections are illustrated in Figure 2. The big dashed box on the left represents valuations over states W_S (concrete domain), the one on the right represents valuations over blocks W_Q (abstract domain). The partition into blocks B_1, B_2, B_3 is depicted by rectangles surrounding states. Consider the valuation w with the thick border. Abstraction $\alpha^{\mathfrak{l}}(w)$ provides a lower bound, i.e. $\gamma(\alpha^{\mathfrak{l}}(w)) \leq w$. Taking the $\alpha^{\mathfrak{u}}$-abstraction yields an upper bound $\alpha^{\mathfrak{u}}(w)$, i.e. we get $w \leq \gamma(\alpha^{\mathfrak{u}}(w))$.

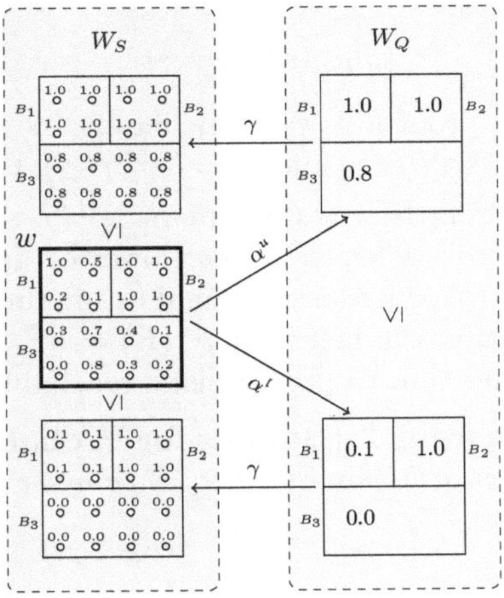

Fig. 2. Functions $\alpha^{\mathfrak{l}}$ and $\alpha^{\mathfrak{u}}$

Remark. We point out crucial differences to Monniaux's framework [10]: unlike in this paper, only upper bounds *not* lower bounds are computed, his abstract domains are in general not partially ordered, and the concrete domain consists of sets of valuations rather than valuations. Therefore, unlike in our setting, the concretization function maps an abstract valuation to a set of valuations, as opposed to a single valuation.

Lower and Upper Bounds of Fixpoints. Aiming for probabilistic reachability, we consider fixpoints of valuation transformers. If a valuation transformer is bounded from below and above by two abstract transformers which are valid abstractions w.r.t. lower-bound and upper-bound abstraction respectively, the fixpoints of these two abstract transformers enclose the fixpoint of the valuation transformer, which is formalized in Lemma 2. In the following, we fix Q as the given partition, and let α^{l}, α^{u}, γ be the functions defined above.

Lemma 2 (Bounds from Valid Transformers). *Let $f : W_S \to W_S$. Let $f_1^\sharp, f_2^\sharp : W_Q \to W_Q$ be valuation transformers such that $f_1^\sharp$ is a valid lower-bound of f and $f_2^\sharp$ a valid upper-bound abstraction of f, i.e., $\gamma \circ f_1^\sharp \leq f \circ \gamma \leq \gamma \circ f_2^\sharp$. Then the following inequality holds regarding the fixpoints of these functions:*

$$\gamma\left(gfp_{\geq}(f_1^\sharp)\right) \quad \leq \quad lfp_{\leq}(f) \quad \leq \quad \gamma\left(lfp_{\leq}(f_2^\sharp)\right) \; .$$

Proof. Let $w^* = lfp_{\leq}(f_2^\sharp)$ be the least fixpoint of $f_2^\sharp$. It holds that $f_2^\sharp(w^*) = w^*$ and hence $(\gamma \circ f_2^\sharp)(w^*) = \gamma(w^*)$. By assumption, we have $f \circ \gamma \leq \gamma \circ f_2^\sharp$, which implies $(f \circ \gamma)(w^*) \leq (\gamma \circ f_2^\sharp)(w^*) = \gamma(w^*)$ and $\gamma(w^*) \in \{x \in W_S \mid f(x) \leq x\}$. Hence $lfp_{\leq}(f) = \bigsqcap\{x \in W_S \mid f(x) \leq x\} \leq \gamma(w^*)$, as claimed. The other inequality can be shown in a dual way. ■

For any concrete valuation transformer f, the fixpoints of the best transformers w.r.t. lower- and upper-bound abstraction enclose the least fixpoint of f:

Lemma 3 (Fixpoints of Best Transformers). *Let $f : W_S \to W_S$ be a given valuation transformer. Then the following inequalities hold:*

$$\gamma\left(gfp_{\geq}(\alpha^{\mathsf{l}} \circ f \circ \gamma)\right) \quad \leq \quad lfp_{\leq}(f) \quad \leq \quad \gamma\left(lfp_{\leq}(\alpha^{\mathsf{u}} \circ f \circ \gamma)\right) \; .$$

The proof follows immediately by applying Lemma 2 to the best transformers $f_1^\sharp = (\alpha^{\mathsf{l}} \circ f \circ \gamma)$ and $f_2^\sharp = (\alpha^{\mathsf{u}} \circ f \circ \gamma)$. For probabilistic reachability, we consider four different best transformers: $\alpha^{\{\mathsf{l},\mathsf{u}\}} \circ pre_F^{\{-,+\}} \circ \gamma$ where the abstraction function controls whether we get lower or upper bounds, and the valuation transformer controls whether maximal or minimal reachability probability is considered. Exploiting the fact that $p^-(F) = lfp_{\leq}\, pre_F^-$ and $p^+(F) = lfp_{\leq}\, pre_F^+$, we have the connection to probabilistic reachability:

Theorem 1 (Bounds for Probabilistic Reachability). *Let $\mathcal{M} = (S, I, \mathcal{A}, R)$ be an MDP and let $F \subseteq S$ be a set of goal states. Then we have:*

$$\gamma(gfp_{\geq}(\alpha^{\mathsf{l}} \circ pre_F^+ \circ \gamma)) \leq p^+(F) \leq \gamma(lfp_{\leq}(\alpha^{\mathsf{u}} \circ pre_F^+ \circ \gamma))$$
$$\gamma(gfp_{\geq}(\alpha^{\mathsf{l}} \circ pre_F^- \circ \gamma)) \leq p^-(F) \leq \gamma(lfp_{\leq}(\alpha^{\mathsf{u}} \circ pre_F^- \circ \gamma))$$

The best transformer $(\alpha^{\mathsf{u}} \circ pre_F^- \circ \gamma)$ for the upper bound of minimal reachability contains an alternation between minimization, as in pre_F^-, and maximization, as in α^{u}. This suggests a connection to stochastic games where minimization and maximization are the objectives of two adversarial players. After an interlude on stochastic games in Sec. 3.2, we make the connection to game-based abstraction.

3.2 Stochastic Games

We consider turn-based stochastic games with two players [22]. A stochastic game is a tuple $\mathcal{G} = ((V, E), V_{init}, (V_1, V_2, V_p), \delta)$ where (V, E) is a *finite* directed graph with edges $E \subseteq V \times V$, $V_{init} \subseteq V_1$ is the set of initial vertices, (V_1, V_2, V_p) is a partition of the set V, and $\delta : V_p \to Distr_V$ where $\delta(v)(v') > 0$ implies that $(v, v') \in E$. The vertex sets V_1, V_2 are called player 1 vertices and player 2 vertices respectively. For $v \in V$, let $E(v) = \{w \mid (v, w) \in E\}$ be the successors of v. A *play* of the game is a sequence $\omega = v_0 v_1 \ldots$ such that $v_{i+1} \in E(v_i)$ for all $i \in \mathbb{N}$. Let $\omega[i] = v_i$ denote the $(i+1)$-th vertex of ω, and denote the last vertex by $last(\omega) = v_n$ if ω is finite.

A player 1 strategy is a function $\sigma_1 : V^* V_1 \to Distr_V$ such that for any finite play ω, $\sigma_1(\omega)(v) > 0$ implies that $(last(\omega), v) \in E$. Player 2 strategies are defined analogously. A strategy σ_i is called *pure memoryless* if it does not use randomization and is memoryless: it is a function $\sigma_i : V_i \to V$ for $i = 1, 2$. For any vertex $v \in V_{init}$, a fixed pair of strategies corresponds probability measure $Pr_v^{\sigma_1,\sigma_2}$ over infinite plays. Given a vertex v, a *reachability objective* $F \subseteq V_1$, and strategies σ_1, σ_2, $p_v^{\sigma_1,\sigma_2}(F)$ denotes the probability of reaching F starting in v: $p_v^{\sigma_1,\sigma_2}(F) = Pr_v^{\sigma_1,\sigma_2}(\{\omega \mid \exists i \in \mathbb{N} : \omega[i] \in F\})$. This defines a valuation $p^{\sigma_1,\sigma_2}(F) \in W_V$. *Optimal valuations* for player 1 and player 2 w.r.t. F are defined by: $\sup_{\sigma_1} \inf_{\sigma_2} p^{\sigma_1,\sigma_2}(F), \inf_{\sigma_1} \sup_{\sigma_2} p^{\sigma_1,\sigma_2}(F) \in W_V$ respectively. Player 1 strategy σ_1 is *optimal* for $v \in V$ if $\inf_{\sigma_2} p_v^{\sigma_1,\sigma_2}(F) = \sup_{\sigma_1} \inf_{\sigma_2} p_v^{\sigma_1,\sigma_2}(F)$. The optimal player 2 strategy can be defined similarly. We also consider the cases where both players cooperate $\inf_{\sigma_1,\sigma_2} p^{\sigma_1,\sigma_2}(F)$ and $\sup_{\sigma_1,\sigma_2} p^{\sigma_1,\sigma_2}(F)$. Below we define four valuation transformers to characterize these optimal valuations:

Definition 2 (Valuation Transformers for Games). *Given a reachability objective F, let $F_0 \subseteq V_1$ be the set of vertices that cannot reach F. The valuation transformer $pre_F^{+-} : W_{V_1} \to W_{V_1}$ is defined by: $pre_F^{+-}(d)(v)$ equals 1 if $v \in F$ and 0 if $v \in F_0$, and otherwise,*

$$pre_F^{+-}(d)(v) = \max_{v_2 \in E(v)} \min_{v_p \in E(v_2)} \sum_{v' \in E(v_p)} \delta(v_p)(v') \cdot d(v').$$

The valuation transformers $pre_F^{--}, pre_F^{-+}, pre_F^{++}$ can be defined analogously by changing the extrema in the summation accordingly, e.g. pre_F^{-+} minimizes over $E(v)$ and maximizes over $E(v_2)$.

The optimal valuations are least fixpoints of valuation transformers, e.g. $\sup_{\sigma_1} \inf_{\sigma_2} p^{\sigma_1,\sigma_2}(F) = lfp_{\leq}\ pre_F^{+-}$, and $\sup_{\sigma_1} \sup_{\sigma_2} p^{\sigma_1,\sigma_2}(F) = lfp_{\leq}\ pre_F^{++}$.

3.3 Best Transformers and Game-Based Abstraction

Given a finite partition, game-based abstraction maps an MDP to a stochastic game[1]. The blocks of the partition are the player 1 vertices and player 2 vertices

[1] In full generality, infinite stochastic games may arise through game-based abstraction. From now on, we assume finiteness. In effect, this excludes MDPs with infinitely many different transition probabilities, which are not representable in our modeling language. In subsequent proofs of this section, finiteness of the games also implies that the abstraction functions α^{u} and α^{l} are applied to valuations for which not only infima and suprema but minima and maxima exist.

are sets of abstract distributions. The abstraction of a distribution $\pi \in \mathit{Distr}_S$ is the distribution $\overline{\pi} \in \mathit{Distr}_Q$ with $\overline{\pi}(B) := \sum_{s \in B} \pi(s)$. The abstraction of a set of distributions D is the set $\overline{D} = \{\overline{\pi} \mid \pi \in D\}$ for $D \subseteq \mathit{Distr}_S$.

Definition 3 (Game-based Abstraction [16]). *Let $\mathcal{M} = (S, I, \mathcal{A}, R)$ be an MDP, and Q be a partition. The game abstraction of $\mathcal{M}$ w.r.t. Q is the stochastic game $\mathcal{G}_{\mathcal{M},Q} = ((V, E), V_{init}, (V_1, V_2, V_p), \delta)$ where the player 1 vertices $V_1 = Q$ are given by the blocks, the player 2 vertices $V_2 = \{\overline{\mathit{Distr}(s)} \mid s \in S\} \subseteq 2^{\mathit{Distr}_Q}$ are sets of distributions and the vertices $V_p = \{\overline{\pi} \mid \exists s \in S : \ \pi \in \mathit{Distr}(s)\}$ distributions. $\delta : V_p \to \mathit{Distr}_V$ is the identity function. The initial vertices are $V_{init} = \{B \in Q \mid B \cap I \neq \emptyset\}$ and the edges E are given by:*

$$E = \{(v_1, v_2) \mid v_1 \in V_1, \exists s \in v_1 : \ v_2 = \overline{\mathit{Distr}(s)}\} \\ \cup \{(v_2, v_p) \mid v_2 \in V_2, v_p \in v_2\} \cup \{(v_p, v_1) \mid v_p \in V_p, v_p(v_1) > 0\} \ .$$

Intuitively, a player 1 decision is a concretization step for a given block. The abstract distributions of a player 2 vertex correspond to the out-going distributions of a concrete state. The player 2 decision is then like the application of the concrete transformer ensued by an abstraction step. In fact, the best transformers w.r.t. lower and upper bound abstraction (see Sec. 3.1) are exactly the valuation transformers of game-based abstraction:

Theorem 2 (Game-based Abstraction and Best Transformer). *Let $\mathcal{M}$ be an MDP and $F \subseteq S$ a set of goal states. Further, consider the partition Q of S such that the goal states F in $\mathcal{M}$ are exactly representable: i.e., $F = \bigcup_{B \in F^\sharp} B$ for a suitable $F^\sharp \subseteq Q$. Let $\mathit{pre}^{\pm\pm}_{F^\sharp}$ be the valuation transformers in the game $\mathcal{G}_{\mathcal{M},Q}$ as defined in Def. 2. Then it holds that:*

$$\mathit{pre}^{--}_{F^\sharp} = \alpha^{\mathfrak{l}} \circ \mathit{pre}^{-}_{F} \circ \gamma \quad , \quad \mathit{pre}^{+-}_{F^\sharp} = \alpha^{\mathfrak{u}} \circ \mathit{pre}^{-}_{F} \circ \gamma$$
$$\mathit{pre}^{-+}_{F^\sharp} = \alpha^{\mathfrak{l}} \circ \mathit{pre}^{+}_{F} \circ \gamma \quad , \quad \mathit{pre}^{++}_{F^\sharp} = \alpha^{\mathfrak{u}} \circ \mathit{pre}^{+}_{F} \circ \gamma$$

Proof. We sketch the proof for $\mathit{pre}^{-+}_{F^\sharp} = \alpha^{\mathfrak{l}} \circ \mathit{pre}^{+}_{F} \circ \gamma$, i.e., the claim is that, for all $w^\sharp \in W_Q$ and $v \in V_1$, $\mathit{pre}^{-+}_{F}(w^\sharp)(v) = \left((\alpha^{\mathfrak{l}} \circ \mathit{pre}^{+} \circ \gamma)(w^\sharp)\right)(v)$. The claim is trivially fulfilled if $v \in F^\sharp \cup F^\sharp_0$. Otherwise the transformer of the game is defined as $\mathit{pre}^{-+}_{F^\sharp}(w^\sharp)(v) = \min_{v_2 \in E(v)} \max_{v_p \in v_2} \sum_{v' \in V_1} \delta(v_p)(v') \cdot w^\sharp(v')$. The successors of vertex $v \in V_1$ are given by $E(v) = \{\overline{\mathit{Distr}(s)} \mid s \in v\}$. It is easy to see that $\mathit{pre}^{-+}_{F^\sharp}(w^\sharp)(v) = \min_{s \in v} \max_{\pi^\sharp \in \overline{\mathit{Distr}(s)}} \sum_{v' \in V_1} \pi^\sharp(v') \cdot w^\sharp(v')$. Observe that for a distribution π and a block $v' \in V_1$, we have by definition $\overline{\pi}(v') = \sum_{s \in v'} \pi(s)$ and thus $\sum_{v' \in V_1} \overline{\pi}(v') \cdot w^\sharp(v') = \sum_{s' \in S} \pi(s') \cdot w^\sharp(\overline{s'})$. As a final step, we get the equality $\left((\alpha^{\mathfrak{l}} \circ \mathit{pre}^{+}_{F} \circ \gamma)(w^\sharp)\right)(v) = \min_{s \in v} \max_{\pi \in \mathit{Distr}(s)} \sum_{s' \in S} \pi(s') \cdot w^\sharp(\overline{s'})$, which proves the claim. ■

As corollary of Theorem 2, one obtains that the valuation transformers of the games are a valid abstraction for minimal and maximal reachability. Together with Theorem 1 this proves that game-based abstraction yields lower and upper bounds on probabilistic reachability:

$$\gamma(\inf_{\sigma_1,\sigma_2} p^{\sigma_1,\sigma_2}(F^\sharp)) \leq p^-(F) \leq \gamma(\sup_{\sigma_1}\inf_{\sigma_2} p^{\sigma_1,\sigma_2}(F^\sharp)) \quad (1)$$

$$\gamma(\inf_{\sigma_1}\sup_{\sigma_2} p^{\sigma_1,\sigma_2}(F^\sharp)) \leq p^+(F) \leq \gamma(\sup_{\sigma_1,\sigma_2} p^{\sigma_1,\sigma_2}(F^\sharp)) \quad (2)$$

Theorem 2 establishes that the obtained probability bounds are optimal, i.e. any valid abstraction cannot yield more precise bounds.

One can thus compute best transformers by game-based abstraction, yet computational cost is higher than for abstractions that map to MDPs [18]. In the next section, we introduce abstractions for concurrent programs that alleviate this problem and still yield effective lower and upper bounds.

4 Abstraction Refinement for Concurrent Programs

We discuss concurrent probabilistic programs in Sec. 4.1. In Sec. 4.2, we present a novel abstraction tailored to these programs and introduce the corresponding game construction in Sec. 4.3. Together with the refinement algorithm in Sec. 4.4, we obtain the first abstract-refinement method for infinite-state concurrent probabilistic programs that provides both lower and upper bounds.

4.1 Concurrent Probabilistic Programs

As in [2], we consider a variation of the popular PRISM language [15] that additionally supports integer and real variables. We now give the abstract syntax and the semantics of concurrent probabilistic programs. We fix a finite set of program variables X and a finite set of actions $\mathcal{A}$. We denote the expressions over the variables V by $Expr_V$ and Boolean expressions by $BExpr_V$. An *assignment* is a function $E : \mathtt{X} \to Expr_{\mathtt{X}}$.

```
module two_chains
m : [0..3];        // control flow
x : int;           // counter variable
[a] m=0 -> 1.0: (x'=1000) & (m'=1);
[b] m=0 -> 1.0: (x'=2) & (m'=1);
[c] m=1 & x>0 -> 0.3: (x'=x-1) + 0.7:(m'=3);
[d] m=1 & x<=0 -> 1.0: (m'=2);
endmodule
init
 m = 0 & x = 0
endinit
```

Fig. 3. Example program with variables m and x and four commands

A *program* $\mathtt{P} = (\mathtt{X}, \mathtt{I}, \mathtt{C})$ consists of an initial condition $\mathtt{I} \in BExpr_{\mathtt{X}}$ and commands C. A *command* c consists of a unique action a, a guard $\mathtt{g} \in BExpr_{\mathtt{X}}$ and assignments $E_{\mathtt{u}_1}, ..., E_{\mathtt{u}_k}$ weighted with probabilities $p_1, ..., p_k$ where $\sum_{i=1}^k p_i = 1$. We denote by $\mathtt{X}' = E$ the simultaneous update E of variables X. With the i-th update of c, we associate a unique update label $\mathtt{u}_i \in \mathtt{U}$. Updates are separated by a "+": $[a]\ \mathtt{g} \to \mathtt{p}_1 : \mathtt{X}'{=}E_{\mathtt{u}_1}$ + ... + $\mathtt{p}_k : \mathtt{X}'{=}E_{\mathtt{u}_k}$. If the guard is satisfied, the i-th update executes with probability p_i. For a command c, we write $a_{\mathtt{c}}$ for its action, $\mathtt{g}_{\mathtt{c}}$ for its guard and omit subscripts if the command is clear from context.

A *state* over variables X is a type-consistent total function from variables in X to their semantic domains. We denote the set of states by $S(\mathtt{X})$, or S for short, and a single state by s. For an expression $\mathtt{e} \in \mathit{Expr}_{\mathtt{X}}$, we denote by $[\![\mathtt{e}]\!]_s$ its valuation in state s. For a Boolean expression $\mathtt{e} \in \mathit{BExpr}_{\mathtt{X}}$, we have $[\![\mathtt{e}]\!]_s \in \{0,1\}$ and denote by $[\![\mathtt{e}]\!] = \{s \in S \mid [\![\mathtt{e}]\!]_s = 1\}$ the set of states that fulfill $\mathtt{e}$.

The semantics of a program $\mathtt{P} = (\mathtt{X}, \mathtt{I}, \mathtt{C})$ is the MDP $\mathcal{M} = (S, I, \mathcal{A}, R)$ with states $S = S(\mathtt{X})$, initial states $I = [\![\mathtt{I}]\!]$, actions $\mathcal{A} = \{a_{\mathtt{c}} \mid \mathtt{c} \in \mathtt{C}\}$, and transitions induced by the commands. Consider $s \in S$ and $a_{\mathtt{c}} \in \mathcal{A}$. If $s \in [\![\mathtt{g_c}]\!]$, we define $R(s, a_{\mathtt{c}}) = \pi$ such that π fulfills the following dependency where $\{\!|\ldots|\!\}$ delimits a multiset: $\pi(s') = \sum_{i=1}^{k} \{\!| p_i \mid \forall \mathtt{x} \in \mathtt{X} : \ s'(\mathtt{x}) = [\![E_{\mathtt{u}_i}(\mathtt{x})]\!]_s |\!\}$. We use a multiset since two updates may have the same probability and yield the same state.

4.2 Parallel Abstraction

A concurrent probabilistic program consists of the parallel composition of commands. In parallel abstraction, abstract transformers for the program are obtained by the parallel composition of the abstract transformers of the commands.

We first focus on abstraction for maximal probabilistic reachability. Before defining the abstract transformers, we reformulate concrete transformer in terms of transformers $\mathit{pre}_F^+[a]$ for the individual actions. Let $w \in W_S$ be a valuation and $s \in S$ a state. Then $\mathit{pre}[a]_F^+(w)(s)$ equals 1 if s is a goal state, 0 if s cannot reach a goal state or action a is not enabled on s, and, lastly, $\sum_{s' \in S} \pi_{(s,a)}(s') \cdot w(s')$ otherwise. It is obvious that the transformer pre_F^+ for maximal reachability of goal states F is given by:

$$\mathit{pre}_F^+(w)(s) = \max_{a \in \mathcal{A}(s)} \mathit{pre}[a]_F^+(w)(s) \ . \tag{3}$$

We assume that the partition Q is chosen such that the goal states can be represented precisely, i.e. there exists a set of blocks $F^\sharp \subseteq Q$ with $F = \bigcup_{B \in F^\sharp} B$. Further, we assume that, without loss of generality, a block in a partition contains either only absorbing or no absorbing states.

For a block $B \in Q$, we denote by $\mathcal{A}(B)$ the set $\{a \in \mathcal{A} \mid \exists s \in B : \ a \in \mathcal{A}(s)\}$ of actions that are enabled some state in B. By combining abstract transformers of the commands, we get the abstract transformer for the whole program.

Definition 4 (Maximal Parallel Abstraction). *We define the respective abstract transformers for the lower and upper bounds of maximal reachability:*

$$\widetilde{\mathit{pre}}_{F^\sharp}^{\mathtt{l}+}(w^\sharp)(B) := \max_{a \in \mathcal{A}(B)} (\alpha^{\mathtt{l}} \circ (\mathit{pre}[a]_F^+) \circ \gamma)(w^\sharp)(B) \ ,$$

$$\widetilde{\mathit{pre}}_{F^\sharp}^{\mathtt{u}+}(w^\sharp)(B) := \max_{a \in \mathcal{A}(B)} (\alpha^{\mathtt{u}} \circ (\mathit{pre}[a]_F^+) \circ \gamma)(w^\sharp)(B) \ .$$

Similar to maximal reachability, we define transformer $\mathit{pre}[a]_F^- : W_S \to W_S$ for action a as follows. For a valuation $w \in W_S$ and state s, $\mathit{pre}[a]_F^-(w)(s)$ equals 1 if state s is a goal state or the action is not enabled, 0 if the goal states are not reachable from s, and $\sum_{s' \in S} \pi_{(s,a)}(s') \cdot w(s')$ otherwise. As for maximal reachability, the transformer pre_F^- is given by:

$$\mathit{pre}_F^-(w)(s) = \min_{a \in \mathcal{A}(s)} \mathit{pre}[a]_F^-(w)(s) \ . \tag{4}$$

Now we define the abstract transformers for the two bounds in terms of the best transformers of individual commands.

Definition 5 (Minimal Parallel Abstraction). *We define the respective abstract transformers for the lower and upper bounds of minimal reachability:*

$$\widetilde{pre}^{\mathfrak{l}-}_{F^\sharp}(w^\sharp)(B) := \min_{a\in\mathcal{A}(B)} (\alpha^{\mathfrak{l}} \circ (pre[a]^-_F) \circ \gamma)(w^\sharp)(B) ,$$

$$\widetilde{pre}^{\mathfrak{u}-}_{F^\sharp}(w^\sharp)(B) := \min_{a\in\mathcal{A}(B)} (\alpha^{\mathfrak{u}} \circ (pre[a]^-_F) \circ \gamma)(w^\sharp)(B) .$$

The following theorem states that the introduced maximal and minimal abstract transformers are valid abstractions. For $\widetilde{pre}^{\mathfrak{u}+}_{F^\sharp}$ and $\widetilde{pre}^{\mathfrak{l}-}_{F^\sharp}$ one can even show a stronger result: these transformers are exactly the best transformers $\alpha^{\mathfrak{u}} \circ pre^+_F \circ \gamma$ and $\alpha^{\mathfrak{l}} \circ pre^-_F \circ \gamma$ respectively. In general, this does not hold for the other two transformers. Overall we have:

Theorem 3 (Validity of Parallel Abstraction).

1. *$\widetilde{pre}^{\mathfrak{u}+}_{F^\sharp}$ equals the best transformer $\alpha^{\mathfrak{u}} \circ pre^+_F \circ \gamma$,*
2. *$\widetilde{pre}^{\mathfrak{l}+}_{F^\sharp}$ is a valid abstraction of $pre^+_{F^\sharp}$ w.r.t. the Galois connection $(\alpha^{\mathfrak{l}}, \gamma)$, i.e., $\gamma \circ \widetilde{pre}^{\mathfrak{l}+}_{F^\sharp} \leq pre^+_F \circ \gamma$,*
3. *$\widetilde{pre}^{\mathfrak{u}-}_{F^\sharp}$ is a valid abstraction of $pre^-_{F^\sharp}$ w.r.t. the Galois connection $(\alpha^{\mathfrak{u}}, \gamma)$, i.e., $pre^-_F \circ \gamma \leq \gamma \circ \widetilde{pre}^{\mathfrak{u}-}_{F^\sharp}$,*
4. *$\widetilde{pre}^{\mathfrak{l}-}_{F^\sharp}$ equals the best transformer $\alpha^{\mathfrak{l}} \circ pre^-_F \circ \gamma$.*

Proof. Part (1): Let $w^\sharp \in W_Q, B \in Q \setminus F^\sharp$. By definition, we have the equality $(\alpha^{\mathfrak{u}} \circ pre^+_F \circ \gamma)(w^\sharp)(B) = \max_{s\in B} \max_{\pi\in Distr(s)} \sum_{s'\in S} \pi(s') \cdot w^\sharp(\overline{s'})$. Moreover, we have $\widetilde{pre}^{\mathfrak{u}+}_{F^\sharp}(w^\sharp)(B) = \max_{a\in\mathcal{A}(B)}(\alpha^{\mathfrak{u}} \circ (pre[a]^+_F) \circ \gamma)(w^\sharp)(B)$ by Def. 4. This can be rewritten to: $\widetilde{pre}^{\mathfrak{u}+}_{F^\sharp}(w^\sharp)(B) = \max_{s\in B} \max_{a\in\mathcal{A}(s)} \sum_{s'\in S} \pi_{(s,a)}(s') \cdot w^\sharp(\overline{s'})$, which is the same as $\max_{s\in B} \max_{\pi\in Distr(s)} \sum_{s'\in S} \pi(s') \cdot w^\sharp(\overline{s'})$. We are done.

Part (3): we show $(pre^-_F \circ \gamma)(w^\sharp)(B) \leq (\gamma \circ \widetilde{pre}^{\mathfrak{u}-}_{F^\sharp})(w^\sharp)(B)$ for all $w^\sharp \in W_Q$ and $B \in Q$. We consider the Galois connection $(\alpha^{\mathfrak{u}}, \gamma)$ with order $\leq$. By Eq. (4), it holds[2]: $(pre^-_F \circ \gamma)(w^\sharp)(B) = \min_{a\in\mathcal{A}(B)}(pre[a]^-_F \circ \gamma)(w^\sharp)(B)$. Since the best transformer $f := \alpha^{\mathfrak{u}} \circ (pre[a]^-_F) \circ \gamma$ is a valid abstraction of $pre[a]^-_F$, we have $(pre^-_F \circ \gamma)(w^\sharp)(B) \leq \min_{a\in\mathcal{A}(B)}(\gamma \circ f)(w^\sharp)(B)$. To finish the proof we exploit that γ is a morphism [23, Lemma 4.22] w.r.t. $\bigsqcup$:

$$\min_{a\in\mathcal{A}(B)} (\gamma \circ f)(w^\sharp)(B) = \gamma(\min_{a\in\mathcal{A}(B)} (f)(w^\sharp)(B)) = (\gamma \circ \widetilde{pre}^{\mathfrak{u}-}_{F^\sharp})(w^\sharp)(B) .$$ ■

4.3 Parallel-Abstraction Games

In this section we introduce *parallel-abstraction games*, the game construction corresponding to parallel abstraction.

[2] Let $s_B \in S$ such that $B = \overline{s_B}$, obviously, $(pre^-_F \circ \gamma)(w^\sharp)(B) = (pre^-_F)(\gamma(w^\sharp))(s_B)$. Applying Eq. (4), it can be rewritten to $\min_{a\in\mathcal{A}(B)} pre[a]^-_F(\gamma(w^\sharp))(B)$ which is the same as $\min_{a\in\mathcal{A}(B)}(pre[a]^-_F \circ \gamma)(w^\sharp)(B)$.

Definition 6. *Let $\mathcal{M} = (S, I, \mathcal{A}, R)$ be an MDP and Q a partition. The parallel-abstraction game is $\widehat{\mathcal{G}}_{\mathcal{M},Q} = ((V, E), V_{init}, (V_1, V_2, V_p), \delta)$ with $V_1 = Q \cup \{\star\}$, $V_2 = \{(v_1, a) \mid v_1 \in V_1, a \in \mathcal{A}(v_1)\}$, $V_p = \{\overline{\pi_{(s,a)}} \mid s \in S, a \in \mathcal{A}(s)\} \cup \{v_p^\star\}$, $V_{init} = \{B \in Q \mid B \cap I \neq \emptyset\}$, δ is the identity function. Let $v_p^\star(\star) = 1$. The edges E are defined by:*

$$\begin{aligned} E =& \{(v_1, v_2) \mid v_1 \in V_1, v_2 = (v_1, a) \in V_2, a \in \mathcal{A}(v_1)\} \\ &\cup \{(v_2, v_p) \mid v_2 = (v_1, a) \in V_2, \exists s \in v_1 :\ v_p = \overline{\pi_{(s,a)}}\} \\ &\cup \{(v_2, v_p^\star), (v_p^\star, \star) \mid v_2 = (v_1, a) \in V_2, \exists s \in v_1 :\ a \notin \mathcal{A}(s)\} \\ &\cup \{(v_p, v') \mid v_p \in V_p, v_p(v') > 0\}\ . \end{aligned}$$

A player 1 vertex v_1 has a player 2 successor for each $a \in \mathcal{A}(v_1)$. A player 2 vertex (v_1, a) represents the abstraction of the a-transitions. Further, the partition may contain both states on which a particular action a is enabled and states on which it is not, i.e. the abstraction loses information about enabledness. In this case, player 2 vertex (v_1, a) has distribution $v_p^\star$ as a successor.

Example 2. We consider an MDP with states: $S = \{s_0, \ldots, s_7\}$. The state partition is $Q = \{\{s_0, s_1\}, \{s_2\}, \{s_3\}, \{s_4, s_7\}, \{s_5, s_6\}\}$. Figure 4 shows the MDP and the corresponding parallel-abstraction game.

The enabled actions $\mathcal{A}(B_0)$ in $B_0 = \{s_0, s_1\}$ are given by $\mathcal{A}(B_0) = \{a, b\}$. In the corresponding abstract game, blocks are player 1 vertices. For each enabled action, there is one player 2 vertex. For example, for block B_0, there are two player 2 vertices for action a and b respectively. The successors of the player 2 vertex for a reflect that from B_0 there are concrete a-transitions into $\{s_2\}$ and $\{s_3\}$. One successor of the player 2 vertex for b represents the b-distribution out of s_0. Vertex $\star$ reflects that b is not enabled at s_0. ■

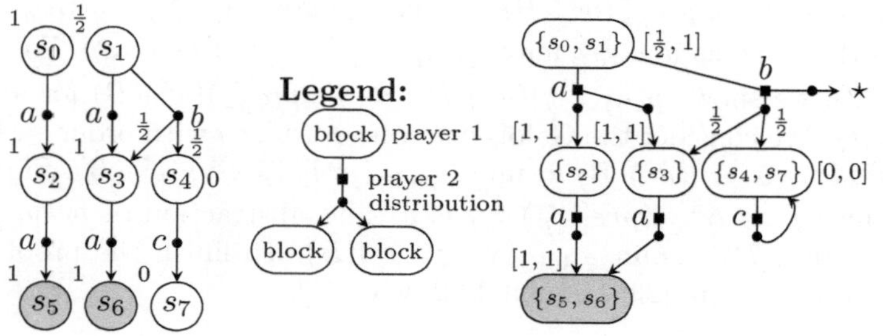

Fig. 4. Illustration of parallel abstraction

Theorem 4 (Parallel-Abstraction Game and Parallel Abstraction). *Let $\mathcal{M}$, Q and $\widehat{\mathcal{G}}_{\mathcal{M},Q}$ as defined in Def. 6. Moreover, let $pre^{\pm\pm}_{V'}$ be the valuation transformers in $\mathcal{G}_{\mathcal{M},Q}$ w.r.t. objective V' as defined in Def. 2. Then we have: $\widetilde{pre}^{l-}_{F^\sharp} = pre^{--}_{F^\sharp \cup \{\star\}}$, $\widetilde{pre}^{u-}_{F^\sharp} = pre^{-+}_{F^\sharp \cup \{\star\}}$, $\widetilde{pre}^{l+}_{F^\sharp} = pre^{+-}_{F^\sharp}$ and $\widetilde{pre}^{u+}_{F^\sharp} = pre^{++}_{F^\sharp}$.*

While the proof proceeds in a similar fashion as Thm. 2, the following example provides some intuition.

Example 3. Figure 4 illustrates the concrete and abstract transformers for minimal reachability. In the MDP the minimal reachability probabilities w.r.t. goal states $\{s_5, s_6\}$ are written next to each state. In the game the probability bounds are annotated at each block as an interval, e.g., $[\frac{1}{2}, 1]$ for $\{s_0, s_1\}$. Now the function of the $\star$-vertex becomes clear. If there was no $\star$-vertex, action b would contribute probability $\frac{1}{2}$ and win against the probability 1 from a, so that for block $\{s_0, s_1\}$ the abstraction would spuriously report $\frac{1}{2}$ as an upper bound. ■

To compute the games for a given set of predicates, we employ SMT-based enumeration along the lines of [17,2] with a few additions. The construction also has the same complexity (number of SMT solver calls). We refer to [2] for details, and focus on background needed to continue our exposition. Let $\mathtt{P} = (\mathtt{X}, \mathtt{I}, \mathtt{C})$ be a program, and let $\mathcal{M}$ be the semantics of P. A predicate φ stands for the set of states satisfying it, i.e., $[\![\varphi]\!] \subseteq S$. A set of predicates $\mathcal{P}$ induces a finite partition of S: two states are in the same block iff they satisfy the same predicates.

Discussion and Comparison. Figure 5 shows a program. Consider predicates $s = 0 \ldots 2, x < 0, x = 0$ and $x > 0$ and the following blocks in the partition: $B_1 = \{s = 0, x > 0\}$, $B_2 = \{s = 1, x < 0\}$, $B_3 = \{s = 1, x = 0\}$, $B_4 = \{s = 1, x = 0\}$ and $B_5 = \{s = 2, x > 0\}$.

```
module main
s   : [0..2];        // control flow
x,y : int;           // integer variables
[a] s=0 -> 1.0:(s'=1)&(x'=y);
[b] s=0 & x>10 -> 0.5:(s'=0)+ 0.5:(s'=2);
endmodule
```

Fig. 5. Example program

Figure 6 shows MDP-based abstraction [2] (6(a)), parallel abstraction (6(b)) and game-based abstraction [16] (6(c)). The MDP-based abstraction contains four distributions. Command a induces three of them, since it assigns y to x, and there are states in B_1 where y is smaller, equal or less than zero respectively. Command b induces one distribution. Parallel abstraction has additionally two player 2 vertices, one for each command, so one can tell which command induces which distributions. Again, the $\star$-vertex reflects that command b is not enabled on all states in B_1. Game-based abstraction introduces six player 2 vertices: these vertices contain abstract distributions from *both* commands.

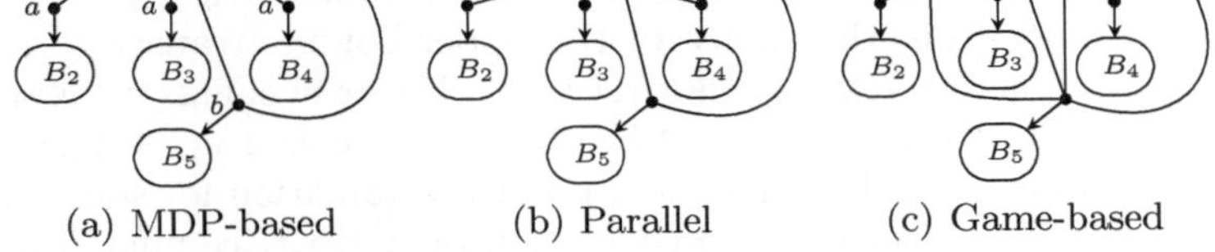

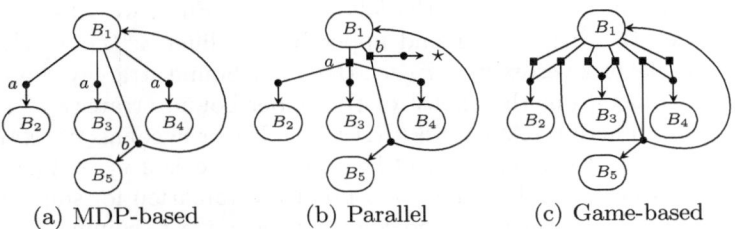

Fig. 6. Example of parallel, MDP-based and game-based abstraction

An advantage of parallel and MDP-based abstraction is that they can be computed by abstracting commands in isolation. Game-based abstraction, on the other hand, requires a different approach in presence of concurrency: certain player 2 vertices result from the combined effect of different commands. As a result, the abstraction needs to track correlations between different commands, which can be expensive [18]. Put differently, the number of player 2 vertices is the sum $\sum_{v_1 \in V_1} |\mathcal{A}(v_1)|$ in parallel abstraction, while, for game-based abstraction [16], this number is $\sum_{v_1 \in V_1} \left|\{\overline{Distr(s)} \mid s \in v_1\}\right|$ and, since each player 2 vertex corresponds to a *subset* of V_p, the worst case lies in the order of $2^{|V_p|}$.

4.4 Refinement

We are interested in (minimal or maximal) reachability probabilities for the initial states of the program. The analysis produces lower and upper bounds $w^{\mathfrak{l}}$ and $w^{\mathfrak{u}}$ respectively for the reachability probabilities w.r.t. to goal states F. Refinement is invoked whenever the bounds for the initial vertices are too imprecise, i.e. $w^{\mathfrak{u}}(v_{init}) - w^{\mathfrak{l}}(v_{init}) > \varepsilon$ for some initial game vertex $v_{init} \in V_{init}$ where ε is the user-specified precision.

The analysis of the game also yields a game strategy for the lower and upper bound respectively. We can use existing techniques [2] to check if abstract paths, ending with a goal block and admissible w.r.t. the strategy, actually correspond to feasible paths in the program. However, in the given framework, we can focus feasibility checks on parts of the game where the bounds are not tight.

The idea is to refine blocks $v_1 \in V_1$ containing states $s \in v_1$ that would achieve more precise bounds if separated from the other states in the block, i.e., more formally, $\left((pre_F \circ \gamma)(w^{\mathfrak{l}})\right)(s) < w^{\mathfrak{u}}(v_1)$ or $w^{\mathfrak{l}}(v_1) < \left((pre_F \circ \gamma)(w^{\mathfrak{l}})\right)(s)$ (where pre_F is the concrete transformer, i.e. pre_F^- for minimal and pre_F^+ for maximal reachability). For example, consider the program in Figure 3 and its abstraction using predicates $\{m = 0, m = 1, m = 2, m = 3, x \geq 1\}$ in Figure 7(a). We want to compute the maximal probability to reach $\{m = 2\}$. Consider block $B = \{m = 1, x \geq 1\}$. All states with $x < 1$ in B (in this case just one state s with $m = 1, x = 1$) can go to the block $\{m = 1, x < 1\}$ via c with probability 0.3. Thus state s fulfills $\left((pre_F \circ \gamma)(w^{\mathfrak{l}})\right)(s) = \left((pre_F \circ \gamma)(w^{\mathfrak{u}})\right)(s) = 0.3$. By introducing the predicate $\{x \geq 2\}$, we obtain the abstraction in Figure 7(b) where block B is split into blocks $\{m = 1, x \geq 2\}$ and $\{m = 1, 1 \leq x < 2\}$ with more precise probability bounds $[0.3, 0.3]$ and $[0, 0.09]$ respectively.

We put these ideas to work in the following way. First, we select a block to be refined such that[3]: (1) lower and upper bound differ $w^{\mathfrak{u}}(v_1) - w^{\mathfrak{l}}(v_1) > 0$ and, (2) for a player 2 vertex $v_2 \in E(v_1)$, the lower-bound strategy chooses some $v \in E(v_2)$ distinct from the choice of the upper-bound strategy $v' \in E(v_2)$. Then we invoke function RefBlock$(v_1, (v, v'))$. If v or v' equals v_p^*, RefBlock returns the guard of command a. Otherwise, there exists $v_1' \in V_1$ such that $v(v_1') \neq v'(v_1')$ where v and v' differ in a predicate valuation for some predicate φ. Then RefBlock returns the precondition of φ w.r.t. command a. In the

[3] This is a relaxation of the criterion that refers to the concrete transformer.

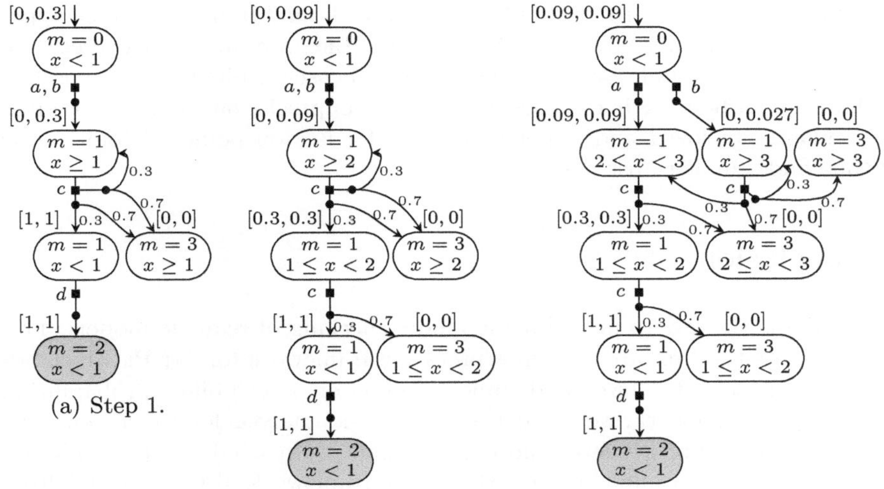

(a) Step 1. (b) Step 2: $x \geq 2$. (c) Step 3: $x \geq 3$.

Fig. 7. Illustration of abstraction refinement

example, we have computed preconditions of predicates $\{x \geq 1\}$ and $\{x \geq 2\}$ w.r.t. command c and update `x'=x-1` which leads to the refinement steps in Figure 7(b) and 7(c). This refinement strategy is inspired by [3]: while they consider sequential programs we consider concurrent programs.

5 Experiments

We have implemented our method in the PASS tool [2], which, until recently, gave only upper bounds for *maximal* probabilistic reachability, and, only in some cases, effective lower bounds from counterexample analysis. The new version PASS 2.0 provides both lower and upper bounds for minimal and maximal probabilistic reachability. Experiments were run on a Pentium 4 with 2.6GHz and 1GB RAM. We considered models of network protocols, including all models from [2] and, examples of probabilistic *C* programs from [3], if they could be translated to PASS models. We first discuss minimal reachability problems (here PASS 1.0 is not applicable): PASS 2.0 computed precise *minimal* reachability probabilities for properties of the `csma` and `wlan` models from [2]. Further, it solved the `zeroconf` and `herman` case study from [3]. Their tool took 1.97s and 33.5s respectively, on a faster machine, compared to 1.3s and 5s for PASS 2.0. In the table below, we compare with PASS 1.0 giving running times (in seconds):

	wlan1		wlan2		csma1		csma2		brp1		brp2		sw1		sw2	
PASS 2.0	43s	✔	115s	✔	10s	✔	5s	✔	27s	✔	1s	✔	18s	✔	2s	✔
PASS 1.0	72s	✗/✔	306s	✗/✔	38s	✗/✔	11s	✗/✔	21s	✔	3s	✔	87s	90%/45%	89s	✔

In the table ✔ means success, i.e. the difference between the two established bounds is less than $\varepsilon = 10^{-6}$. ✗/ ✔ means lower bound 0 and a correct upper bound. 90%/45% means 90% underestimation of the lower and 45% overestimation of the upper bound. PASS 2.0 succeeds in all cases, while PASS 1.0 successfully finds upper bounds, in one case, however, an imprecise one. PASS 2.0 is often faster. Thanks to lower and upper bounds, it focuses on points of imprecision and thus finds smaller abstractions.

6 Conclusion

Abstraction is the key to probabilistic model checking of realistic models. This paper presents the first abstract-interpretation framework for MDPs which admits to compute both lower and upper bounds on reachability probabilities. Based on this framework, we present an automatic analysis for concurrent programs to compute precise lower and upper bounds on reachability probabilities. As future work, we would like to extend our framework also to probabilistic safety, rewards and probabilistic equivalence checking [24,25].

Acknowledgements. This work was supported by the DFG as part of SFB/TR 14 AVACS, by the European Community's FP7 under grant n° 214755, and the NWO-DFG bilateral project ROCKS. We would like to thank the anonymous reviewers, Claire Burguière and Ernst Moritz Hahn for their comments.

References

1. Bianco, A., de Alfaro, L.: Model Checking of Probabilistic and Nondeterministic Systems. In: Thiagarajan, P.S. (ed.) FSTTCS 1995. LNCS, vol. 1026, pp. 499–513. Springer, Heidelberg (1995)
2. Hermanns, H., Wachter, B., Zhang, L.: Probabilistic CEGAR. In: Gupta, A., Malik, S. (eds.) CAV 2008. LNCS, vol. 5123, pp. 162–175. Springer, Heidelberg (2008)
3. Kattenbelt, M., Kwiatkowska, M.Z., Norman, G., Parker, D.: Abstraction Refinement for Probabilistic Software. In: Jones, N.D., Müller-Olm, M. (eds.) VMCAI 2009. LNCS, vol. 5403, pp. 182–197. Springer, Heidelberg (2009)
4. Cousot, P., Cousot, R.: Abstract Interpretation: A Unified Lattice Model for Static Analysis of Programs by Construction or Approximation of Fixpoints. In: POPL, pp. 238–252 (1977)
5. Ball, T., Podelski, A., Rajamani, S.K.: Boolean and Cartesian Abstraction for Model Checking C Programs. In: Margaria, T., Yi, W. (eds.) TACAS 2001. LNCS, vol. 2031, pp. 268–283. Springer, Heidelberg (2001)
6. Cousot, P., Cousot, R., Feret, J., Mauborgne, L., Miné, A., Monniaux, D., Rival, X.: The ASTREÉ Analyzer. In: Sagiv, M. (ed.) ESOP 2005. LNCS, vol. 3444, pp. 21–30. Springer, Heidelberg (2005)
7. Alt, M., Ferdinand, C., Martin, F., Wilhelm, R.: Cache Behavior Prediction by Abstract Interpretation. In: Cousot, R., Schmidt, D.A. (eds.) SAS 1996. LNCS, vol. 1145, pp. 52–66. Springer, Heidelberg (1996)

8. Reps, T.W., Sagiv, S., Yorsh, G.: Symbolic Implementation of the Best Transformer. In: Steffen, B., Levi, G. (eds.) VMCAI 2004. LNCS, vol. 2937, pp. 252–266. Springer, Heidelberg (2004)
9. Cousot, P., Cousot, R.: Systematic Design of Program Transformation Frameworks by Abstract Interpretation. In: POPL 2002, pp. 178–190. ACM, New York (2002)
10. Monniaux, D.: Abstract Interpretation of Programs as Markov Decision Processes. Sci. Comput. Program. 58, 179–205 (2005)
11. Pierro, A.D., Wiklicky, H.: Concurrent Constraint Programming: Towards Probabilistic Abstract Interpretation. In: PPDP, pp. 127–138 (2000)
12. Smith, M.J.A.: Probabilistic Abstract Interpretation of Imperative Programs using Truncated Normal Distributions. ENTCS 220, 43–59 (2008)
13. Coletta, A., Gori, R., Levi, F.: Approximating Probabilistic Behaviors of Biological Systems Using Abstract Interpretation. ENTCS 229, 165–182 (2009)
14. Monniaux, D.: Backwards Abstract Interpretation of Probabilistic Programs. In: Sands, D. (ed.) ESOP 2001. LNCS, vol. 2028, pp. 367–382. Springer, Heidelberg (2001)
15. Hinton, A., Kwiatkowska, M.Z., Norman, G., Parker, D.: PRISM: A Tool for Automatic Verification of Probabilistic Systems. In: Hermanns, H., Palsberg, J. (eds.) TACAS 2006. LNCS, vol. 3920, pp. 441–444. Springer, Heidelberg (2006)
16. Kwiatkowska, M.Z., Norman, G., Parker, D.: Game-based Abstraction for Markov Decision Processes. In: QEST, pp. 157–166 (2006)
17. Wachter, B., Zhang, L., Hermanns, H.: Probabilistic model checking modulo theories. In: QEST, pp. 129–140 (2007)
18. Kattenbelt, M., Kwiatkowska, M.Z., Norman, G., Parker, D.: Game-Based Probabilistic Predicate Abstraction in PRISM. In: QAPL (2008)
19. D'Argenio, P.R., Jeannet, B., Jensen, H.E., Larsen, K.G.: Reachability Analysis of Probabilistic Systems by Successive Refinements. In: de Luca, L., Gilmore, S. (eds.) PROBMIV 2001, PAPM-PROBMIV 2001, and PAPM 2001. LNCS, vol. 2165, pp. 39–56. Springer, Heidelberg (2001)
20. Tarski, A.: A Lattice-Theoretical Fixpoint Theorem and Its Applications. Pacific Journal of Mathematics 5(2), 285–309 (1955)
21. Baier, C.: On Algorithmic Verification Methods for Probabilistic Systems, Habilitationsschrift, Universität Mannheim (1998)
22. Condon, A.: The Complexity of Stochastic Games. Inf. Comput. 96, 203–224 (1992)
23. Nielson, F., Nielson, H.R., Hankin, C.: Principles of Program Analysis. Springer-Verlag New York, Inc., Secaucus (1999)
24. Murawski, A.S., Ouaknine, J.: On Probabilistic Program Equivalence and Refinement. In: Abadi, M., de Alfaro, L. (eds.) CONCUR 2005. LNCS, vol. 3653, pp. 156–170. Springer, Heidelberg (2005)
25. Legay, A., Murawski, A.S., Ouaknine, J., Worrell, J.: On Automated Verification of Probabilistic Programs. In: Ramakrishnan, C.R., Rehof, J. (eds.) TACAS 2008. LNCS, vol. 4963, pp. 173–187. Springer, Heidelberg (2008)

Collections, Cardinalities, and Relations

Kuat Yessenov[1,⋆], Ruzica Piskac[2], and Viktor Kuncak[2,⋆⋆]

[1] MIT Computer Science and Artificial Intelligence Lab, Cambridge, USA
kuat@csail.mit.edu
[2] EPFL School of Computer and Communication Sciences, Lausanne, Switzerland
firstname.lastname@epfl.ch

Abstract. Logics that involve collections (sets, multisets), and cardinality constraints are useful for reasoning about unbounded data structures and concurrent processes. To make such logics more useful in verification this paper extends them with the ability to compute direct and inverse relation and function images. We establish decidability and complexity bounds for the extended logics.

1 Introduction

Deductive verification of software often involves proving the validity of formulas in expressive logics. Verification condition generation produces such formulas directly from annotated source code [3, 5], whereas predicate abstraction techniques [4] generate many formulas during fixpoint computation. Abstract interpretation [6] precomputes parameterized transfer functions; the automation of this process [25] also reduces to proving formula validity.

As the starting point of this paper we consider decidable logics whose variables denote collections of objects, corresponding to, for example, dynamically allocated objects in the heap, or concurrent processes. Our logics include standard set algebra operations such as $\cap, \cup$ and complement. They also include the *cardinality operator*, to compute the number of elements in the collection, and support linear integer arithmetic constraints on the cardinalities. One such logic is QFBAPA (quantifier-free Boolean Algebra with Presburger Arithmetic), which we recently proved to be in NP [16], an improvement over the previous NEXPTIME algorithms based on quantifier elimination [9, 14]. We subsequently generalized this result to quantifier-free constraints on multisets (bags), collections in which an element can occur multiple times [22, 23]. The usefulness of collections and cardinality measures on them has been established through a number of examples from software analysis and verification, including not only decision procedures [16, 14, 29] but also static analyses that operate directly on the set abstraction or the cardinality abstraction [11, 13, 21].

⋆ Work done while Kuat Yessenov was visiting EPFL.

⋆⋆ This research is supported in part by the Swiss National Science Foundation Grant "Precise and Scalable Analyses for Reliable Software".

G. Barthe and M. Hermenegildo (Eds.): VMCAI 2010, LNCS 5944, pp. 380–395, 2010.

To make the logics of collection more useful, in this paper we generalize them in a natural direction: we introduce functions and relations and supports computing images and inverse images of sets under these functions and relations. Our primary motivation is that in verification problems, collections such as sets and multisets are often defined by computing an image of a more concrete data structure, often itself a set (see Section 2). The resulting logics are extensions of both the logics with cardinalities, but also of certain previously studied constraints (none of which include symbolic cardinality bounds): certain Tarskian set constraints [10], certain Description Logics [1], and set-valued field constraints [15]. Our techniques are also related to the technique of bridging functions [19]. What distinguishes our result from previous ones is the (often optimal) complexity that we achieve in the presence of sets, multisets, relations, and symbolic cardinality constraints. Our NEXPTIME fragment includes images of n-ary relations and is thus not expressible in the two-variable logic with counting [20, 24].

Contributions. We summarize the contributions of this paper as follows:

- We describe a new NEXPTIME-complete logic that includes sets, n-ary relations, unary functions, and symbolic cardinality constraints.
- We sketch the extension of the logic above with cardinalities of relations and with n-ary function symbols; we prove 2-NEXPTIME upper bound for its satisfiability.
- We point to a few simple extensions of the above logic that lead to undecidability.
- We consider an extension of QFBAPA [16] with relation image constraints, for a relation between two disjoint sorts of elements results. We show that the sparse model solution phenomenon of QFBAPA continues to apply in the presence of such relations, and use it to prove that the logic remains inside NP.
- We show NEXPTIME completeness (by reduction to [22]) of a logic that allows computing multisets instead of sets as function images, preserving the multiplicity of elements that occur in the range of the function multiple times. This is a natural definition of the notion of multiset comprehension and arises e.g. when using multisets to abstract the content of Java-like linked data structures.

2 Motivating Examples

In this section we list several examples from verification of data structures that have motivated us to consider extending BAPA with functions and relations.

We start with a dynamically allocated data structure (such as a list or a tree) that manipulates a set of linked nodes denoted by the variable `nodes`. The useful content in the data structure is stored in the `data` fields of the elements of `nodes`. The `nodes` set can be either explicitly manipulated through a library data type or built-in type [7], or it can be verified to correspond to a set of reachable objects using techniques such as [27]. The content of the list, stored in

$$\mathsf{nodes} \subseteq \mathsf{alloc} \wedge \mathsf{card\ tmp} = 1 \wedge \mathsf{tmp} \cap \mathsf{alloc} = \emptyset \wedge \mathsf{data[tmp]} = \mathsf{e} \wedge$$
$$\mathsf{content} = \mathsf{data[nodes]} \wedge \mathsf{nodes1} = \mathsf{nodes} \cup \mathsf{tmp} \wedge \mathsf{content1} = \mathsf{data[nodes1]} \rightarrow$$
$$\mathsf{card\ content1} \leq \mathsf{card\ content} + 1$$

Fig. 1. Verification condition for verifying that by inserting an element into a list, the size of the list does not decrease. The variables occurring in the formula have the following types: nodes, alloc, tmp, e, content, content1 :: Set⟨E⟩, data :: E → E.

$$\mathsf{nodes} \subseteq \mathsf{alloc} \wedge \mathsf{card\ tmp} = 1 \wedge \mathsf{tmp} \cap \mathsf{alloc} = \emptyset \wedge \mathsf{data[tmp]} = \mathsf{e} \wedge$$
$$\mathsf{content} = \mathsf{data[nodes]} \wedge \mathsf{nodes1} = \mathsf{nodes} \cup \mathsf{tmp} \wedge \mathsf{content1} = \mathsf{data[nodes1]} \rightarrow$$
$$\mathsf{card\ content1} = \mathsf{card\ content} + 1$$

Fig. 2. Verification condition for verifying that by inserting an element into a list, the size of a list increases by one. The variables occurring in the formula have the following types: nodes, alloc, tmp :: Set⟨E⟩, content, content1, e :: Multiset⟨E⟩, data :: E → E.

the content specification variable, is then an image of nodes under the function data. We consider two cases of specification in our example: 1) content is a *set*, that is, multiple occurrences of elements are ignored and 2) content is a *multiset*, preserving the counts of occurrences of each element in the data structure.

The verification condition generated for the case when the image is a set is given in Figure 1. This formula belongs to the language QFBAPA-Rel defined in Section 3 and a decision procedure presented there checks satisfiability of such formulas. It reduces a formula to a (exponentially larger) quantifier-free BAPA formula [16] by introducing Venn regions [26] and cardinality constraints on them, and eliminating the function symbols such as data. The resulting formula can be decided using the NP algorithm in [16], giving NEXPTIME procedure overall.

A more precise abstraction is obtained if content is viewed as a multiset. Figure 2 shows the verification condition for this case. Section 6 describes a decision procedure for an extension of QFBAPA with function symbols where functions can also return a multiset, not only set. The approach also rewrites sets as a disjoint union of Venn regions. It then constrains the cardinality of the multiset obtained through the image to be equal to the cardinality of the original set. This final formula is a formula in the NP-complete logic for reasoning about multisets and cardinality constraints [23, 22].

Another motivation in software verification comes from regional logic [2], used for proving correctness of programs with shared mutable objects. Regional logic introduces *region variables*, which are finite sets of object references, and uses to express properties about separation and mutation. Following the example presented in [2], consider a finite binary tree and let x be a variable of type *Node*. A node y, $y \neq$ **null**, has three fields: `left`, `right` and `item`. We can express that for $x \neq$ **null**, x has two disjoint subtrees which are closed under `left` and `right` as follows:

$$\begin{aligned} P &\equiv x \neq \mathbf{null} \wedge x.\mathtt{left} \in r_1 \wedge x.\mathtt{right} \in r_2 \wedge r_1 \# r_2 \wedge \mathit{closed} \\ \mathit{closed} &\equiv r_1.\mathtt{left} \subseteq r_1 \wedge r_1.\mathtt{right} \subseteq r_1 \wedge r_2.\mathtt{left} \subseteq r_2 \wedge r_2.\mathtt{right} \subseteq r_2 \end{aligned}$$

Those formulas can be translated into QFBAPA-Rel logic by treating each region as a set and each field as a function defined on a set:

$$\begin{aligned} P_1 &\equiv |X| = 1 \wedge X \neq \emptyset \wedge l(X) \subseteq R_1 \wedge r(X) \subseteq R_2 \wedge R_1 \cap R_2 = \emptyset \wedge closed_1 \\ closed_1 &\equiv l(R_1) \subseteq R_1 \wedge r(R_1) \subseteq R_1 \wedge l(R_2) \subseteq R_2 \wedge r(R_2) \subseteq R_2 \end{aligned}$$

Many of the assertions used in [2] can be easily translated in QFBAPA-Rel. In addition, conditions such as expressing that two regions have the same size can be also expressed in QFBAPA-Rel.

3 QFBAPA-Rel: A Logic of Sets, Cardinalities, Relations, and Unary Functions

This section presents a decision procedure for the language of sets, cardinalities, n-ary relations, and unary total functions. The language we consider is denoted QFBAPA-Rel and is defined by the grammar in Figure 3. It naturally extends quantifier-free fragment of BAPA [16] with unary function symbols (denoted by $f, g, \ldots$) and relations of any arity (denoted by $p, q, r, \ldots$ to distinguish them from functions). The expression $f[B]$ denotes the set $\{y \mid \exists x. x \in B \wedge y = f(x)\}$. Cardinality constraints allow us, in particular, to express whether a function is injective on A (by $|f[A]| = |A|$) or surjective onto A ($f[\mathcal{U}] = A$). For a binary relation r, the expression $r[A]$ is a relational join expression denoting $\{y \mid \exists x. x \in A \wedge (x, y) \in r\}$. Analogously, $r^{-1}[B]$ denotes $\{x \mid \exists y. y \in B \wedge (x, y) \in r\}$. We require functions to be total, whereas relations need not be left-total or right-total. Higher-arity relations have an analogous interpretation with the term $r[B_1, \ldots, B_{i-1}, *, B_{i+1}, \ldots, B_k]$ standing for the set

$$\{x_i \mid \exists x_1 \in B_1, \ldots, x_{i-1} \in B_{i-1}, x_{i+1} \in B_{i+1}, \ldots, x_k \in B_k \wedge (x_1, \ldots, x_k) \in r\}$$

for a relation r of arity k.

The decision problem we are concerned with is the satisfiability problem for QFBAPA-Rel: the question of existence of a finite interpretation α in which formula is true.

An interpretation assigns values to a set, an integer, function and relation variables. If α is an interpretation then $\alpha[x := v]$ is the interpration such that $\alpha[x := v](x) = v$ and $\alpha[x := v](y) = \alpha(y)$ for $x \neq y$.

$$\begin{aligned} F &::= L \mid F_1 \vee F_2 \mid \neg F \\ L &::= B_1 \subseteq B_2 \mid T_1 < T_2 \mid K \,\mathsf{dvd}\, T \\ B &::= x \mid \emptyset \mid \mathcal{U} \mid B_1 \cup B_2 \mid B^c \mid f[B] \mid f^{-1}[B] \mid r[B] \mid r^{-1}[B] \mid \\ &\quad\;\; r[B_1, \ldots, B_{i-1}, *, B_{i+1}, \ldots, B_k] \\ T &::= k \mid K \mid \mathsf{MAXC} \mid T_1 + T_2 \mid \ |B| \\ K &::= \cdots \mid -2 \mid -1 \mid 0 \mid 1 \mid 2 \mid \cdots \end{aligned}$$

Fig. 3. Syntax of QFBAPA-Rel

3.1 Decision Procedure for QFBAPA-Rel

Our decision procedure for QFBAPA-Rel satisfiability is a reduction to the satisfiability of quantifier-free Boolean algebra with Presburger arithmetic (QFBAPA). The first step of the reduction is elimination of function inverses and functional and relational composition from the given formula. Because all functions are total, $B = f^{-1}[A]$ is equivalent to $f[B] \subseteq A \wedge f[B^c] \subseteq A^c$. We allocate a fresh set variable for every functional or relational complex expressions. For example, a formula $f[r[A]] \subseteq h[B \cap C]$ becomes $E \subseteq G \wedge D = r[A] \wedge E = f[D] \wedge F = B \cap C \wedge G = h[F]$. This separates functional and relational terms from the rest of the formula. Using these transformations we obtain (in polynomial time) a conjunction of a QFBAPA formula F_{BAPA} and a conjunction of set constraints F_{IMAGE}.

For every function term f, formula F_{IMAGE} contains constraints of the form $A_i = f[B_i]$ where A_i and B_i are set variables. For every relational term r where r is binary, F_{IMAGE} contains constraints of the form $A_i = r[B_i]$ and $A'_i = r^{-1}[B'_i]$ where A_i, A'_i, B_i, B'_i are set variables. For a relation r of arity k the formula F_{IMAGE} contains constraints of the form $A_i^j = r[B_{i1}^j, \ldots, B_{i(j-1)}^j, *, B_{i(j+1)}^j, \ldots, B_k^j]$ for $1 \leq j \leq k$.

Eliminating function applications. Let $s_1, \ldots, s_m$ be the Boolean algebra terms representing the disjoint Venn regions that are formed by taking intersection $\bigcap_{\alpha_i \in \{0,1\}} b_i^{\alpha_i}$ of all set variables b_i appearing in the entire original formula. For a set x, x^1 denotes x and x^0 denotes x^c. We focus on a single function symbol f and its constraints from F_{IMAGE}, We repeat the following algorithm for every function symbol f that appears in F_{IMAGE}.

Let $\bigwedge_i A_i = f[B_i]$ be the constraints for f. Each term B_i may be written as a disjoint union of cubes $s_{i_1} \cup s_{i_2} \cup \ldots \cup s_{i_k}$ so that $f[B_i] = \bigcup f[s_{i_j}]$. Because the cubes are disjoint, we can define the values of the function on each cube independently. Introduce set variables $t_j = f[s_j]$. Replace each term $f[B_i]$ with the corresponding union $\bigcup t_{i_j}$ of a subset of cube images:

$$A_i = \bigcup_{s_j \subseteq B_i} t_j \tag{1}$$

After this transformation, the set constraints are reduced to QFBAPA by introducing fresh set variables t_i. Moreover, we introduce the following *functional consistency axioms*:

$$\bigwedge |t_i| \leq |s_i| \ \wedge \ (|t_i| = 0 \Leftrightarrow |s_i| = 0) \tag{2}$$

Theorem 1. *The projections of the set of solutions (models) for formulas* (1) $\wedge$ (2) *and the formula* F_{IMAGE} *onto set variables* A_i, B_i *are equal.*

Proof. Given a solution of F_{IMAGE}, define the value of t_j as the value of $f[s_j]$. The result is a model satisfying (1) $\wedge$ (2). Conversely, consider a model α of

(1) $\wedge$ (2); we construct a model α' that agrees with α on A_i, B_i and has the value $\alpha'(f)$ such that $\alpha'(f[s_j] = t_j)$ holds. For different s_j such definitions are independent. For $\alpha(s_j) = \emptyset$ also $\alpha(s_j) = \emptyset$, so condition $\alpha'(f[s_j] = t_j)$ holds. Otherwise, $0 < |\alpha(t_j)| \leq |\alpha(s_j)|$ by (2). Then there is a surjective function $h : s_j \rightarrow t_j$. Pick any such h and define restriction of $\alpha'(f)$ on s_j to be h. ∎

Eliminating binary relations. Previous procedure does not apply in a straightforward way to relations partly because we do not have a way to express directly inverses for relations that are not total. We instead apply the algorithm in Figure 4 for each relation r. The motivation for this algorithm is as follows.

Let $A_i = r[B_i]$ and $A'_i = r^{-1}[B'_i]$ be the constraints from F_{IMAGE} for r. Similarly to the above, let b_j be Venn regions over B_i. Introduce fresh set variables c_j that are constrained by $c_j = r[b_j]$. Because relational join commutes with set union, $A_i = r[B_i]$ is equivalent to $A_i = \bigcup_{b_j \subseteq B_i} c_j$. Repeat this procedure for B'_i using b'_k as Venn regions over B'_i. We obtain constraints of the form $c_j = r[b_j]$ and $c'_k = r^{-1}[b'_k]$.

INPUT: contrains $\bigwedge_i A_i = r[B_i] \wedge \bigwedge_i A'_i = r^{-1}[B'_i]$
OUTPUT: an equisatisfiable QFBAPA formula
1. define Boolean algebra terms b_j for Venn regions over B_i
2. define Boolean algebra terms b'_k for Venn regions over B'_i
3. introduce fresh set variables L_{jk}, R_{jk} for every pair b_j and b'_k
4. introduce constraints $L_{jk} \subseteq b_j \wedge R_{jk} \subseteq b'_k \wedge (L_{jk} = \emptyset \iff R_{jk} = \emptyset)$
5. replace each set constraint $A_i = r[B_i]$ with $A_i = \bigcup_{b_j \subseteq B_i} \bigcup_k R_{jk}$
6. replace each set constraint $A'_i = r^{-1}[B_i]$ with $A'_i = \bigcup_{b'_k \subseteq B_i} \bigcup_j L_{jk}$
7. take conjunction of all set constraints from steps 4,5,6

Fig. 4. Algorithm for eliminating relations from QFBAPA-Rel

Next, introduce new relation variables r_{jk} meant to denote the restriction $\{(x, y) \mid x \in b_j \wedge y \in b'_k \wedge (x, y) \in r\}$ of the relation r to b_j in the domain and b'_k in the codomain. Then r is the disjoint union of r_{jk} over all pairs of j and k. We rewrite the constraints on c_j, c'_k as:

$$\bigwedge_j \left(c_j = \bigcup_k r_{jk}[b_j] \right) \wedge \bigwedge_k \left(c'_k = \bigcup_j r_{jk}^{-1}[b'_k] \right)$$

The behavior of each relation r_{jk} is unrestricted by any other constraints as long as it is a relation from domain b_j to codomain b'_k. That means that the relation r_{jk} is determined for our purposes by its domain and range $r_{jk}[b_j]$ and $r_{jk}^{-1}[b'_k]$. We introduce two set variables to encode these as R_{jk} and L_{jk}, respectively. We rewrite the relation constraints as $c_j = \bigcup_k R_{jk}$ and $c'_k = \bigcup_j L_{jk}$.

The *relational consistency condition* amounts to the following axioms:

$$\bigwedge_{j,k} L_{jk} \subseteq b_j \wedge R_{jk} \subseteq b'_k \wedge (L_{jk} = \emptyset \iff R_{jk} = \emptyset)$$

Because both j and k range over singly exponentially many variables, there are singly exponentially many fresh variables and constraints introduced.

Theorem 2. *The algorithm in Figure 4 produces a QFBAPA formula of singly exponential size with the same set of solutions for* A_i, B_i, A'_i, B'_i.

Proof. Because we only made sound syntactic transformations and introduced variables defined by existing terms, it suffices to show that a model of the generated QFBAPA formula extends to a model of the original formula. Assume we are given an interpretation of the QFBAPA formula, that is values of L_{jk} and R_{jk} and the set variables from the original formula A_i, B_i, A'_i, B'_i. Relation consistency axioms allow us to define total relations r_{jk} by mapping every element from L_{jk} to every element from R_{jk}. An interpretation of r is then the union of all these pairwise non-intersecting relations r_{jk}. To see that we satisfied the set constraints, consider, for example, constraint $A_i = r[B_i]$:

$$r[B_i] = \bigcup_{b_j \subseteq B_i} r[b_j] = \bigcup_{b_j \subseteq B_i} \bigcup_{j',k} r_{j'k}[b_j] = \bigcup_{b_j \subseteq B_i} \bigcup_{k} r_{jk}[b_j] =$$

$$= \bigcup_{b_j \subseteq B_i} \bigcup_{k} r_{jk}[L_{jk}] = \bigcup_{b_j \subseteq B_i} \bigcup_{k} R_{jk} = A_i. \qquad \blacksquare$$

Eliminating higher-arity relations. The algorithm for binary relations extends naturally to higher-arity relations. We sketch the construction in this section. We focus on a single k-arity relation r with set constraints $A^j_i = r[B^j_{i1}, \ldots, B^j_{i(j-1)}, *, B^j_{i(j+1)}, \ldots, B^j_k]$ for $j = 1, \ldots, k$. Similar to above, we introduce Venn regions b^j_l over j-th coordinate set variables B_{ij}. For a k-tuple of Venn regions $\mathbf{v} = (b^1_{l_1}, b^2_{l_2}, \ldots, b^k_{l_k})$, we consider the restriction $r_{\mathbf{v}}$ of the relation r to $b^j_{l_j}$ on every coordinate.

Observe that every set constraint can be replaced with a union of application of the relations $r_{\mathbf{v}}$ to tuples of Venn regions. The key idea is that each such application is uniquely defined by projections of $r_{\mathbf{v}}$ onto every coordinate. That is we introduce k set variables $\{P^i_{\mathbf{v}}\}_{i=1,\ldots,k}$ for every relation $r_{\mathbf{v}}$ such that:

$$\bigwedge_{j=1,\ldots,k} P^j_{\mathbf{v}} \subseteq b^j_{i_j} \wedge \left(\bigwedge_{j=1,\ldots,k} |P^j_{\mathbf{v}}| = 0 \vee \bigwedge_{j=1,\ldots,k} |P^j_{\mathbf{v}}| > 0 \right)$$

Any model to this condition gives rise to a well-defined relation $r_{\mathbf{v}}$ equal to the Cartesian product of the sets $P^1_{\mathbf{v}} \times \ldots \times P^k_{\mathbf{v}}$ (or empty if any of them is empty). This way we can reconstruct the original relation r from the pairwise disjoint interpretations of relations $r_{\mathbf{v}}$.

For instance, the following formula represents a set constraint above (after dropping j super-script):

$$A_i = r[B_{i1}, \ldots, B_{i(j-1)}, *, B_{i(j+1)}, \ldots, B_k] = \bigcup_{\text{cube} b \subseteq B_{il}} r[b_1, \ldots, b_{j-1}, *, b_{j+1}, \ldots, b_k]$$

$$= \bigcup_{b_l \subseteq B_{il}, l \neq j, \mathbf{v}=(b_l)} r_{\mathbf{v}}[b_1, \ldots, b_{j-1}, *, b_{j+1}, \ldots, b_k] = \bigcup_{b_l \subseteq B_{il}, l \neq j, \mathbf{v}=(b_l)} P^j_{\mathbf{v}}$$

The total number of fresh set variables and the size of the resulting formula are still singly exponential in the size of the formula, since we consider Venn regions for each coordinate and take k-tuples of these regions for k linear in size.

3.2 Complexity of QFBAPA-Rel

Combining results of the previous sections, we obtain a reduction from QFBAPA-Rel to QFBAPA. This reduction produces a formula of a singly exponential size by introducing set variables for Venn regions over set variables in the original formula for each function and relation. Because QFBAPA is known to be NP-complete [16], we conclude that QFBAPA-Rel is in NEXPTIME. Moreover, we obtain EXPTIME *BAPA reduction* from QFBAPA-Rel to QFBAPA [28], which means that the method can be used to combine QFBAPA-Rel with other logics, such as the Weak Monadic Second-Order Logic over Trees.

Theorem 3. *QFBAPA-Rel is NEXPTIME-complete, even with no relation symbols and with only one unary function symbol.*

Proof. The algorithm above established the NEXPTIME upper bound, we next prove the matching lower bound. In [10], NEXPTIME lower bound for Tarskian set constraints with constants and binary functions is shown by reduction of a fragment of first order logic. We adapt this proof to QFBAPA-Rel. The proof relies on the result [17] that acceptance of nondeterministic exponential-time bounded Turing machines can be reduced to satisfiability of formulas of the form $\exists z.F_1 \wedge \forall y \exists x.F_2 \wedge \forall y_1 \forall y_2.F_3$ where F_1, F_2, and F_3 have no quantifiers and are monadic (have only unary predicates). Given a formula of this from, we construct an equisatisfiable QFBAPA-Rel formula as a set of constraints, as follows. We identify monadic predicate symbols with set variables, using the same symbols for both. After Skolemizing the formula by introducing a constant symbol a and a monadic function symbol f, and putting F_1, F_2, and F_3 into the conjunctive normal form, there are three types of clauses (as remarked already in [10]); we describe our encoding of each of these clauses.

1. monadic formulas over the constant symbol a (obtained from $\exists z.F_1$)
   We transform the conjunction of all such formula into a set constraint as follows. For each monadic predicate P replace $P(a)$ with P, replace $\vee$ with $\cup$, replace $\neg$ with $\_^c$, and $\wedge$ with $\cap$. Let the result of this replacement be a set algebra expression S; then generate the QFBAPA-Rel formula $S \neq \emptyset$.
2. clauses of the form:

   $$\forall x.P_1(x) \vee P_2(x) \vee \ldots \vee P_m(x) \vee Q_1(f(x)) \vee Q_2(f(x)) \vee \ldots \vee Q_n(f(x))$$

   For each such clause, we generate a constraint:

   $$f\,(P_1^c \cap P_2^c \cap \ldots \cap P_m^c) \subseteq Q_1 \cup Q_2 \cup \ldots \cup Q_n$$

3. clauses of the form:

   $$\forall y_1 \forall y_2.\ P_1(y_1) \vee P_2(y_1) \vee \ldots \vee P_m(y_1) \vee Q_1(y_2) \vee Q_2(y_2) \vee \ldots \vee Q_n(y_2)$$

For each such clause we generate the QFBAPA-Rel formula:

$$(P_1 \cup P_2 \cup \ldots \cup P_m = \mathcal{U}) \vee (Q_1 \cup Q_2 \cup \ldots \cup Q_n = \mathcal{U})$$

(This last constraint differs from the one in [10] and does not require any binary function symbols).

The resulting QFBAPA-Rel formula is equisatisfiable with the original formula, so NEXPTIME lower bound follows from [17]. ■

Decidable Extensions: n-ary Functions, Relation Cardinalities. We have presented QFBAPA-Rel, as a logic with monadic functions and arbitrary relations and shown it to be NEXPTIME-complete. We next sketch how to extend the decidability to include also the functions of higher arity. Generalizing the method for unary functions, we have for e.g. a binary function $f[p_1 \cup p_2, q_1 \cup q_2] = f[p_1, q_1] \cup f[p_1, q_2] \cup f[p_2, q_1] \cup f[p_2, q_2]$. We apply such reasoning to all Venn regions. This creates a singly exponential blowup in formula size. Given Venn regions p, q and image $f[p, q]$, let their cardinalities be k_p, k_q, k_{fpq}, respectively. Then a necessary condition for a function to be definable on $p \times q$ is $k_{fpq} \leq k_p k_q$, which is a non-linear constraint. In general, the satisfiability of QFBAPA-Rel with n-ary function symbols reduces to the satisfiability of a conjunction of 1) such non-linear constraints $x \leq y_1 \ldots y_n$ and 2) linear integer constraints. Such conjunctions are called *prequadratic* in [10] and their satisfiability is shown to be in NEXPTIME. (The quadratic as opposed to higher-degree monomials on right-hand side suffice because replacing $x \leq y_1 y_2 \ldots y_n$ with $x \leq y_1 z_1 \wedge z_1 \leq y_2 \ldots y_n$ preserves the projection of solution set onto $x, y_1, \ldots, y_n$.) The generated prequadtratic formula is singly exponential, which gives an upper bound of 2-NEXPTIME for QFBAPA-Rel extended with functions of arbitrary arity.

A similar construction works for an extension of QFBAPA-Rel with the cardinality operator applied to relations (computing the number of related pairs of elements). In the notation of Section 3.1, we add the prequadratic constraints $|r_{jk}| \leq |L_{jk}|\ |R_{jk}|$ as well as the appropriate linear constraints.

3.3 Undecidable Extensions: Injective Binary Functions, Quantifiers

Injective binary functions. If in addition to introducing binary function symbols we allow stating that they are injective, then instead of prequadratic constraints of the previous section we obtain constraints of the form $x = yz$. Indeed, $|f[p, q]| = |p|\ |q|$ for an injective function f. Together with linear constraints, these constraints can express arbitrary Diophantine equations (polynomial integer equations). The satisfiability in such language is undecidable [18] (Hilbert's 10th problem), and thus adding an injective function symbol to QFBAPA gives an undecidable logic.

Relation cardinality with Cartesian product. We noted that decidability is preserved if we allow computing the cardinality of a relation. However, if we can additionally constrain a relation to be full Cartesian product of two sets, then we again obtain the constraint $|p \times q| = |p|\ |q|$, and the undecidability by [18].

Quantification. Note that BAPA with arbitrary set and integer quantifiers is decidable [14,9]. On the other hand, the logic that allows quantification over sets and one function symbols is also decidable [12, Theorem 8.3]. However, a BAPA extension that allows quantified formulas with unary function symbol images is undecidable. Indeed, define a function f mapping A onto B where each inverse image has k elements: $B = f[A] \wedge \forall e.\ e \subseteq B \wedge |e| = 1 \Rightarrow |f^{-1}[e]| = k$. Then $|B| = k|A|$ and the set of values $(|B|, k, |A|)$ contains precisely the solutions (x, y, z) of the equation $x = yz$. Recall that $f^{-1}[e] = u$ is expressible by $f[u] \subseteq e \wedge f[u^c] \subseteq e^c$, so either direct or inverse function image can be used, or a relation restricted to be functional using a quantified formula, in each case resulting in undecidability by [18].

4 NP-Complete Two-Sorted QFBAPA-Rel Fragment

In this section we identify a fragment of the QFBAPA-Rel logic in Figure 3. Remarkably, this fragment has NP instead of NEXPTIME complexity for the satisfiability problem. Figure 5 shows the syntax of this fragment, QFBAPA-R2, which is an extension of QFBAPA with relation image of one two-sorted binary relation symbol. Compared to full QFBAPA-Rel, there are no function symbols, no inverse images, and there is only one relation symbol, denoted r, which is binary. Moreover, each set contains only elements of sort $\mathcal{A}$, or only elements of a disjoint sort $\mathcal{B}$. There are two disjoint universal sets $\mathcal{U}_\mathcal{A}$ and $\mathcal{U}_\mathcal{B}$ for the corresponding sorts. The boolean operators $\cup, \cap$ and complement apply only to sets of the same sort. We require that the relation r relate sort $\mathcal{A}$ to sort $\mathcal{B}$, that is, the semantic condition $r \subseteq \mathcal{U}_\mathcal{A} \times \mathcal{U}_\mathcal{B}$ holds. An example formula in this fragment is $x = y \rightarrow |r[x]| = |r[y]|$. In this formula x, y have sort $\mathcal{A}$ and the expressions $r[x]$ and $r[y]$ have sort $\mathcal{B}$.

$$
\begin{aligned}
F &::= L \mid F_1 \vee F_2 \mid \neg F \\
L &::= B_1 \subseteq B_2 \mid T_1 < T_2 \mid K\,\mathsf{dvd}\,T \\
B &::= x_B \mid \emptyset \mid \mathcal{U}_\mathcal{B} \mid B_1 \cup B_2 \mid B^c \mid r[A] \\
A &::= x_A \mid \emptyset \mid \mathcal{U}_\mathcal{A} \mid A_1 \cup A_2 \mid A^c \\
T &::= k \mid K \mid \mathsf{MAXC} \mid T_1 + T_2 \mid\ |B|\ \mid\ |A| \\
K &::= \cdots \mid -2 \mid -1 \mid 0 \mid 1 \mid 2 \mid \cdots
\end{aligned}
$$

Fig. 5. Syntax of QFBAPA-R2

Normal form. Consider an arbitrary QFBAPA-R2 formula F. By introducing fresh variables for sets and integers (similarly as in [16]), we can rewrite the formula in (with only linear increase in size) in the form

$$F_C \wedge F_B \wedge F_A \wedge P \tag{3}$$

where:

- F_C is $\bigwedge_{i=1}^n B_i = r[A_i]$ and this is the only part of formula containing r;
- F_B is of form $\bigwedge_i L_i$ where each L_i is of the form $|b| = k$ for some integer variable k and some set algebra expression b of sort $\mathcal{B}$ (it is thus a QFBAPA formula);
- F_A is analogously of form $\bigwedge_i L_i$ where each L_i is of the form $|a| = k$ for some integer variable k and some set algebra expression a of sort $\mathcal{A}$ (it is thus also a QFBAPA formula);
- P is a quantifier-free Presburger arithmetic formula.

In the sequel we assume that QFBAPA-R2 formulas are in normal form. The proof of the following Lemma is straightforward.

Lemma 4 (Models Modulo Venn Regions). *Let p be a Venn region over sets A_i and q a Venn region over sets B_i. If α is a model of the* QFBAPA-R2 *formula F and $\alpha(r) \cap (\alpha(p) \times \alpha(q)) \neq \emptyset$, then α' given as $\alpha[r := w]$ is also a model of the formula F where $w = \alpha(r) \cup (\alpha(p) \times \alpha(q))$.*

By repeated application of the above lemma it follows that it suffices to consider *completed models* α, in which $\alpha(r)$ is a union of products of Venn regions, and is thus given by a bipartite graph, denoted E, between Venn regions of sort $\mathcal{A}$ and Venn regions of sort $\mathcal{B}$.

Sparse models. We are interested in the finite satisfiability problem for QFBAPA-R2 formulas. We show that this problem is in NP. This result is a strict a generalization of the proof that QFBAPA is in NP [16] and similarly proceeds by proving a *sparse model property*: if the formula is satisfiable, it has a model in which only polynomially many Venn regions are non-empty. By Lemma 4, models with sparse Venn regions can also be assumed to have polynomial representations that have polynomial sized bipartite graphs E. By *polynomial* in this section we mean polynomial in the size of formula F, where integer constants are denoted in binary. The following theorem builds on the sparse model property for QFBAPA [16]. QFBAPA models can be represented by introducing an integer variable for each Venn region, and the sparse model property for QFBAPA relies on the integer analogue of Carathéodory theorem [8].

Theorem 5. *If a* QFBAPA-R2 *formula has a model, then it has a sparse model.*

Proof. Let α be a completed model of a formula F in form (3). Using α we simplify F_C as follows. For all sets A_i where $\alpha(A_i) = \emptyset$, replace A_i and B_i with $\emptyset$ and remove such A_i and B_i from consideration. Let K be the number of sets A_i remaining. For the remaining sets A_i, introduce constraint $|A_i| = k'_i$ into F_A and constraint $k'_i > 0$ into P.

Next, apply the sparse model construction of QFBAPA to F_B part, as follows. Consider the result of replacing in F_B each integer variable k with the constant $\alpha(k)$. By [16], consider a sparse solution for the resulting QFBAPA formula that does not introduce any new non-empty Venn regions. That is, consider the Presburger arithmetic formula generated by those Venn regions q over sets B_i for which $\alpha(q) \neq \emptyset$, eliminating the variables corresponding to Venn regions q with $\alpha(q) = \emptyset$. The sparse solution of such Presburger arithmetic formula [16,8] yields a polynomial subset of non-empty Venn regions over B_i for which the integer values of $|b|$ expressions in F_B remain the same. We therefore obtain a set of cubes $C_B = \{q_1, \ldots, q_N\}$ and a model α_1 such that 1) $\alpha_1(q) \neq \emptyset$ iff $q \in C_B$, 2) $\alpha_1(F_B \wedge P)$, and 2) variables other than B_i have same values in α_1 and α.

Next, pick a set C_{A0} of cubes over A_i related to the chosen sparse set of cubes C_B. Let $1 \leq j \leq N$. Let i be any index such that $q_j \subseteq B_i$. Because $\alpha(B_i = r[A_i])$ there exists some pair $(a, b) \in \alpha(r) \cap \alpha(A_i) \times \alpha(q_j)$. Let $a \in p$ where $p \subseteq A_i$ is the cube containing a. Denote such cube p_{ji} and repeat this process for all $1 \leq j \leq N$ and all B_i where $q_j \subseteq B_i$ and let C_{A0} be the resulting set of cubes p_{ji}. The set C_{A0} has at most NK elements, which is polynomially many. In this process we have also identified a bipartite graph $E \subseteq C_{A0} \times C_B$, given by $E = \{(p_{ji}, q_j) \mid 1 \leq j \leq N,\ 1 \leq i \leq K\}$.

Observation about E: If $(p, q) \in E$ and $p \subseteq A_i$, then $q \subseteq B_i$. *Proof:* Let $(p, q) \in E$ and $p \subseteq A_i$. By construction of E, for some witness elements $a \in \alpha(p)$, $b \in \alpha(q)$ we have $(a, b) \in \alpha(r)$. Because $\alpha(B_i = r[A_i])$, we have $b \in \alpha(B_i)$. Because $\alpha(q)$ and $\alpha(B_i)$ intersect, $q \subseteq B_i$, completing the proof of the observation.

We can now apply the sparse model construction of QFBAPA to the F_A part to pick a sparse set of cubes $C_A \supseteq C_{A0}$. Treat again the values of integer variables in F_A as constant, but then also in the resulting non-redundant integer cone generator replace the cardinalities of variables denoting sizes of each selected cube in $p \in C_{A0}$ by the constant $|\alpha(p)|$, thus removing these variables from the integer equation and removing the corresponding elements from the universe $\mathcal{U}_A$. Solve the remaining equations to obtain a sparse solution for the simplified F_A formula, again using the results on sparse solutions of such Presburger arithmetic formulas [16, 8]. We obtain a sparse solution that gives a polynomial number of non-empty cubes C_{A1}. We use the obtained values to define $\alpha_1(p)$ for $p \in C_{A1}$. We let $\alpha_1(p) = \alpha(p)$ for $p \in C_{A0}$. Let $C_A = C_{A0} \cup C_{A1}$. Define $\alpha_1(p) = \emptyset$ for $p \notin C_A$. This yields the sparse interpretation α_1, where only cubes in $C_B \cup C_A$ are non-empty and where $\alpha_1(F_B \wedge F_A \wedge P)$ holds.

Finally, define define $\alpha_1(r)$ as a completed model $\alpha_1 = \bigcup\{p \times q \mid (p, q) \in E\}$ where E is defined (by edges (p_{ji}, q_j)) above. We claim $\alpha_1(F_C)$. Indeed, consider a set A_i. Then A_i is union of certain cubes from C_{A0} and certain cubes from C_{A1}. Because E has no outgoing edges for C_{A1}, we have $\alpha(r[\bigcup C_{A1}]) = \emptyset$. Therefore,

$$\alpha_1(r[A_i]) = \alpha_1(r[\cup\{p \mid p \in C_{A0}, p \subseteq A_i\}]) = \alpha_1(\cup\{q \mid \exists p.p \subseteq A_i \wedge (p, q) \in E\}$$

By the above *Observation about E*, we have that for each q above (belonging to $E[\{p\}]$) the condition $q \subseteq B_i$ holds. Therefore $\alpha_1(r[A_i]) \subseteq \alpha(B_i)$. For the converse set inclusion, let $b \in \alpha_1(B_i)$ be arbitrary and let $q_j \in C_B$ be such that $b \in \alpha_1(q_j)$ and $q_j \subseteq B_i$. Note that $\alpha_1(p_{ji}) \neq \emptyset$, so there exists $a \in \alpha_1(p_{ji})$. Then $(a, b) \in \alpha_1(r)$. Because $p_{ji} \subseteq A_i$, we have $b \in \alpha_1(r[A_i])$. Thus, $\alpha(B_i) \subseteq \alpha_1(r[A_i])$ and the therefore $\alpha_1(r[A_i] = B_i)$. Because i was arbitrary, α_1 is a sparse model for the entire formula. ∎

Theorem 6. *The satisfiability for* QFBAPA-R2 *is NP complete.*

Proof. (Sketch) NP-hardness follows because QFBAPA-R2 subsumes propositional logic. To show NP membership, we use the sparse model property from the previous theorem: we non-deterministically guess a subset of non-empty sets A_i, then guess a polynomial subset C_B of Venn regions over B_i, using the polynomial bounds from [16]. We then guess the subset C_{A0} bounded by $K|C_B|$ and guess C_{A1} conservatively bounded by the same bound as in [16]. Finally, we guess a graph E whose number of edges is bounded by $|C_B|(|C_{A0}|+|C_{A1}|)$. Given such a guess, we can compute a formula that describes all Boolean Algebra expressions and all images of non-empty relations fragments under non-empty Venn regions, and thus describes the existence of a model for this guess of Venn regions and relation between them. As in [16], the entire guessing process can be compiled into a polynomially large quantifier-free formula of Presburger arithmetic with conditional expressions. ∎

We next discuss some extensions of the two-sorted fragment.

NP extensions. Consider any finite number of sorts $s_1, \ldots, s_n$ related by a strict total ordering, and any number of relations of sorts $s_i \times s_{i+1}$ for $0 \leq i < n$. We can then repeat the construction above, starting with relations of sorts $s_{n-1} \times s_n$ and moving towards relations of sort $s_1 \times s_2$. For a fixed number of sorts, we obtain NP complexity. In fact, we can repeatedly apply the sparsity theorem in the case of multiple sorts and multiple relations forming a directed acyclic graph over the sorts.

Limits of membership in NP. Note that if we consider a chain of relations whose sorts form a cycle, through repeated composition we can simulate relations of sort $s \times s$. In this case the above NP construction fails. Moreover, the EXPTIME lower bound follows for such language from the lower bound on the complexity of the ALC Description Logic with general TBox inclusion axioms [1, Theorem 3.27].

5 Logic of Multiset Images of Functions

In this section we illustrate that some of the techniques of the previous section generalize from sets to *multisets*. A multiset M is a function $M : E \rightarrow \mathbb{N}$ mapping the set of elements into the non-negative number of their occurrences. The first NP decision procedure for multisets with the cardinality operator was presented in [23]. In this section we extend the logic of multisets with cardinalities to also include a function image operator that maps a set into a multiset.

We define the function image of a set A to be a multiset $f[A] : E \rightarrow \mathbb{N}$ such that $(f[A])(e) = |\{x.\ x \in A \wedge f(x) = e\}|$. The set of distinct elements occurring in a multiset is obtained using the set operator: $\mathsf{set}(M) = \{x.\ M(x) > 0\}$. This way $\mathsf{set}(f[B])$ is the set corresponding to the standard notion of function image used in previous sections.

Figure 6 shows the logic that embeds the logic of multisets [22, Figure 1], [23], and extends it with the multiset image operator. The logic distinguishes the sorts of sets and multisets, but also includes a casting function $\mathsf{mset}(B)$ which treats

$$
\begin{aligned}
F &::= A \mid F \vee F \mid \neg F \\
A &::= B \subseteq B \mid M \subseteq M \mid T \leq T \mid K \ \mathsf{dvd}\ T \\
B &::= x \mid \emptyset \mid \mathcal{U} \mid B \cup B \mid B \cap B \mid B^c \mid \mathsf{set}(M) \\
M &::= m \mid \emptyset_M \mid M \cap M \mid M \cup M \mid M \uplus M \mid M \setminus M \mid M \setminus\setminus M \mid \mathsf{mset}(B) \mid f[B] \\
T &::= k \mid K \mid \mathsf{MAXC} \mid T_1 + T_2 \mid K \cdot T \mid |B| \mid |M| \\
K &::= \cdots \mid -2 \mid -1 \mid 0 \mid 1 \mid 2 \mid \cdots
\end{aligned}
$$

Fig. 6. MAPA-Fun logic of multisets, cardinality operator, and multiset images of sets

INPUT: formula in the syntax of Figure 6
OUTPUT: multiset formula in the syntax of Figure 1 in [22]

1. Flatten expressions containing the operator **set**:
   $C[\ldots \mathsf{set}(M) \ldots] \rightsquigarrow (B_F = \mathsf{set}(M) \wedge C[\ldots B_F \ldots])$
   where the occurrence of $\mathsf{set}(M)$ is not already in a top-level conjunct of the form $B = \mathsf{set}(M)$ for some set variable B and B_F is a fresh unused set variable
2. Let S be the set of variables occurring in the formula
   Define the set $S_N = \{s_1, \ldots, s_Q\}$ of Venn regions over elements of S
3. Rewrite each set expression as a disjoint union of the Venn regions from S_N
4. **Eliminate function symbols:**
   $C[\ldots f[s_{i_1} \cup \ldots \cup s_{i_k}] \ldots] \rightsquigarrow C[\ldots (M_{i_1} \uplus \ldots \uplus M_{i_k}) \ldots]$
   where each M_{i_j} is a fresh multiset variable denotes $f[s_{i_j}]$
5. Add the conjuncts which states a necessary condition for $M_{i_j} = f[s_{i_j}]$
   $F \rightsquigarrow F \wedge \bigwedge_{i=1}^{Q} |s_i| = |M_i|$
6. Add the conjuncts which state that s_{i_j} are disjoint sets
   $F \rightsquigarrow F \wedge \forall e. \bigwedge_{i=1}^{Q} (s_i(e) = 0 \vee s_i(e) = 1) \wedge \bigwedge_{i \neq j} (s_i \cap s_j = \emptyset)$

Fig. 7. Algorithm for reducing a MAPA-Fun formula to a MAPA formula

a set as a multiset, and an abstraction function $\mathsf{set}(M)$ which extracts the set of distinct elements that occur in a multiset. Unlike the previous section, we do not have disjointness of domains and ranges of functions, and, in terms of expressive power, we effectively treat sets as a special case of multisets.

Given a formula F in the language described in Figure 6, a decision procedure for F works as follows:

1. Apply the algorithm in Figure 7 to translate F into an equisatisfiable multiset formula F' in the syntax given in Figure 1 in [22]. In this step we eliminate function symbols in a way similar to that described in Section 3. The new formula F' has size singly exponential in the size of F;
2. invoke on the formula F' the decision procedure described in [23]. The decision procedure runs in NP time.

The entire procedure runs in NEXPTIME. The lower bound proof from Section 3.2 applies in this case as well, so we conclude that our logic is NEXPTIME-complete.

The correctness of the reduction is stated in the following theorem.

Theorem 7. *Given a formula F as an input to the algorithm described in Figure 7, let the formula F' be its output. Then formulas F and F' are equisatisfiable and their satisfying assignments have the same projections on the set and multiset variables occurring in F.*

Proof. Given a model for F, we construct a model for F' by interpreting M_i as $f[s_i]$. Conversely, let α be a model for F'. We can define f on each disjoint set s_i independently. Because $|s_i| = |M_i|$ holds in the model, we can enumerate both s_i and M_i into sequences $a_1, \ldots, a_K$ and $b_1, \ldots, b_K$ of same length. This enumeration defines a function assigning a_j to b_j for $1 \leq j \leq K$ such that $f[s_i] = M_i$. ∎

References

1. Baader, F., Calvanese, D., McGuinness, D., Nardi, D., Patel-Schneider, P. (eds.): The Description Logic Handbook: Theory, Implementation and Applications. CUP (2003)
2. Banerjee, A., Naumann, D.A., Rosenberg, S.: Regional logic for local reasoning about global invariants. In: Vitek, J. (ed.) ECOOP 2008. LNCS, vol. 5142, pp. 387–411. Springer, Heidelberg (2008)
3. Barnett, M., Leino, K.R.M.: Weakest-precondition of unstructured programs. In: PASTE, pp. 82–87 (2005)
4. Beyer, D., Henzinger, T.A., Jhala, R., Majumdar, R.: The software model checker BLAST. STTT 9(5-6), 505–525 (2007)
5. Cohen, E., Dahlweid, M., Hillebrand, M., Leinenbach, D., Moskal, M., Santen, T., Schulte, W., Tobies, S.: VCC: A practical system for verifying concurrent c. In: TPHOLs 2009. LNCS, vol. 5674. Springer, Heidelberg (2009)
6. Cousot, P., Cousot, R.: Systematic design of program analysis frameworks. In: POPL (1979)
7. Dewar, R.K.: Programming by refinement, as exemplified by the SETL representation sublanguage. In: ACM TOPLAS (July 1979)
8. Eisenbrand, F., Shmonin, G.: Carathéodory bounds for integer cones. Operations Research Letters 34(5), 564–568 (2006)
9. Feferman, S., Vaught, R.L.: The first order properties of products of algebraic systems. Fundamenta Mathematicae 47, 57–103 (1959)
10. Givan, R., McAllester, D., Witty, C., Kozen, D.: Tarskian set constraints. Inf. Comput. 174(2), 105–131 (2002)
11. Gulwani, S., Lev-Ami, T., Sagiv, M.: A combination framework for tracking partition sizes. In: POPL 2009, pp. 239–251 (2009)
12. Gurevich, Y., Shelah, S.: Spectra of monadic second-order formulas with one unary function. In: LICS, pp. 291–300 (2003)
13. Kuncak, V., Lam, P., Zee, K., Rinard, M.: Modular pluggable analyses for data structure consistency. IEEE Trans. Software Engineering 32(12) (December 2006)
14. Kuncak, V., Nguyen, H.H., Rinard, M.: Deciding Boolean Algebra with Presburger Arithmetic. J. of Automated Reasoning (2006)
15. Kuncak, V., Rinard, M.: Decision procedures for set-valued fields. In: 1st International Workshop on Abstract Interpretation of Object-Oriented Languages (2005)

16. Kuncak, V., Rinard, M.: Towards efficient satisfiability checking for Boolean Algebra with Presburger Arithmetic. In: Pfenning, F. (ed.) CADE 2007. LNCS (LNAI), vol. 4603, pp. 215–230. Springer, Heidelberg (2007)
17. Lewis, H.R.: Complexity results for classes of quantificational formulas. J. Comput. Syst. Sci. 21(3), 317–353 (1980)
18. Matiyasevich, Y.V.: Enumerable sets are Diophantine. Soviet Math. Doklady 11(2), 354–357 (1970)
19. Ohlbach, H.J., Koehler, J.: Modal logics, description logics and arithmetic reasoning. Artificial Intelligence 109, 1–31 (1999)
20. Pacholski, L., Szwast, W., Tendera, L.: Complexity results for first-order two-variable logic with counting. SIAM J. on Computing 29(4), 1083–1117 (2000)
21. Pérez, J.A.N., Rybalchenko, A., Singh, A.: Cardinality abstraction for declarative networking applications. In: Bouajjani, A., Maler, O. (eds.) CAV 2009. LNCS, vol. 5643, pp. 584–598. Springer, Heidelberg (2009)
22. Piskac, R., Kuncak, V.: Decision procedures for multisets with cardinality constraints. In: Logozzo, F., Peled, D.A., Zuck, L.D. (eds.) VMCAI 2008. LNCS, vol. 4905, pp. 218–232. Springer, Heidelberg (2008)
23. Piskac, R., Kuncak, V.: Linear arithmetic with stars. In: Gupta, A., Malik, S. (eds.) CAV 2008. LNCS, vol. 5123, pp. 268–280. Springer, Heidelberg (2008)
24. Pratt-Hartmann, I.: Complexity of the two-variable fragment with counting quantifiers. Journal of Logic, Language and Information 14(3), 369–395 (2005)
25. Reps, T., Sagiv, M., Yorsh, G.: Symbolic implementation of the best transformer. In: Steffen, B., Levi, G. (eds.) VMCAI 2004. LNCS, vol. 2937, pp. 252–266. Springer, Heidelberg (2004)
26. Venn, J.: On the diagrammatic and mechanical representation of propositions and reasonings. Dublin Philosophical Magazine and Journal of Science 9(59), 1–18 (1880)
27. Wies, T., Kuncak, V., Lam, P., Podelski, A., Rinard, M.: Field constraint analysis. In: Emerson, E.A., Namjoshi, K.S. (eds.) VMCAI 2006. LNCS, vol. 3855, pp. 157–173. Springer, Heidelberg (2005)
28. Wies, T., Piskac, R., Kuncak, V.: Combining theories with shared set operations. In: Ghilardi, S., Sebastiani, R. (eds.) FroCoS 2009. LNCS, vol. 5749, pp. 366–382. Springer, Heidelberg (2009)
29. Zee, K., Kuncak, V., Rinard, M.: Full functional verification of linked data structures. In: ACM PLDI (2008)

Author Index